Fundamentals of Estate Planning

Huebner School Series

H. King McGlaughon, Jr., Editor

Huebner School Series

Fundamentals of Estate Planning
Ninth Edition

Constance J. Fontaine

The American College Press/*Bryn Mawr, Pennsylvania*

This publication is designed to provide accurate and authoritative information about the subject covered. While every precaution has been taken in the preparation of this material, the author and The American College® assume no liability for damages resulting from the use of the information contained in this publication. The American College is not engaged in rendering legal, accounting, or other professional advice. If legal or other expert advice is required, the services of an appropriate professional should be sought.

The Larry R. Pike Chair in Insurance and Investments

The Larry R. Pike Chair in Insurance and Investments was recently established by The American College and the Union Central Life Insurance Company to support the advancement of learning and professionalism in these areas. The chair is named for Larry R. Pike, CLU, retired chairman of the board of the Union Central Life Insurance Company, and a past trustee of The American College. Mr. Pike is a highly respected insurance industry leader and a role model who has made significant contributions to the industry and to Union Central.

Union Central is creating a $1.5 million endowment to sponsor this chair through an annual corporate gift and the purchase of life insurance contracts on more than 200 of its field and home office associates who are CLUs, ChFCs, or LUTCFs. Funding for the endowment also will come from individual gifts from field and home office associates of the company.

To my mother

Contents

Acknowledgments

I would like to acknowledge H. King McGlaughon, executive vice president, The American College®, and Walt J. Woerheide, vice president and director of the Richard D. Irwin Graduate School® at the College, for providing the support and encouragement necessary to keep this Series at the highest standards.

I would also like to thank the following individuals for their past work in authoring and/or editing parts of this book:

- Ron Duska, PhD, professor of ethics at The American College, for his contributions to chapter 22
- Ted Kurlowicz, JD, LLM, CLU®, ChFC®, professor of taxation and holder of the Charles E. Drimal professorship at The American College, for his contributions and overall assistance with this book
- Stephan R. Leimberg, JD, CLU, former professor of taxation and estate planning at The American College, for his contributions to this book, especially chapters 4, 8, 11, and 15

The individuals mentioned above contributed significantly to the material contained in this text. The material has since been revised and updated, and I retain full responsibility for any errors.

I would also like to express appreciation to Lynn Hayes for editing the manuscript and to Charlene McNulty for production assistance.

Connie Fontaine

About the Author

Constance J. Fontaine, JD, LLM, CLU, ChFC, is an associate professor of taxation in the Solomon S. Huebner School® and holder of the Larry R. Pike Chair in Insurance and Investments of The American College. Her primary responsibility is course development in the estate and gift tax planning areas and examination development. She earned her BS degree from Beaver College, her JD from Widener University School of Law, and her LLM from Villanova University School of Law.

Fundamentals of Estate Planning

Estate Planning:
An Overview

Learning Objectives

An understanding of the material in this chapter should enable the student to

---

1-1. Explain what is meant by estate planning and the purpose that it serves.

1-2. Briefly summarize the historical development of estate planning.

1-3. Describe the impediments to a well-planned estate.

1-4. Describe the basic steps in the estate planning process.

1-5. Explain the interaction of the estate planning team and the specific functions of different team members.

1-6. Explain the relationship between giving estate planning advice and the unauthorized practice of law.

Chapter Outline

The estate planner must combine the talents of an artist with those of an artisan. To develop the necessary rapport with a client, the planner must deal lightly but deftly with the sometimes fragile threads woven into the tapestry of the client's life. As an artisan, the estate planner must have a solid understanding of the tools of the field, including knowledge of property and tax law as well as financial planning. The art lies in the ability to put clients in touch with their true feelings, dreams, and aspirations as well as to assist them in the crystallization of their estate plans. Estate planning is inherently complex because of the technicalities of the applicable law and the foresight required to develop a program that best suits the client's immediate as well as anticipated needs and desires.

PURPOSE

Before beginning the study of estate planning fundamentals, it is important for the student to understand that estate and gift taxation is part of a transfer tax system that is separate from the income tax system (although there are transfer tax aspects that interact with income tax aspects). The generation-skipping transfer tax (GSTT) and qualified domestic trust (QDOT) taxation are additional forms of transfer taxation.

Tax Systems

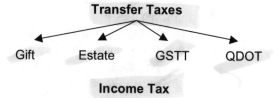

Transfer Taxes

Gift   Estate   GSTT   QDOT

Income Tax

estate planning

There is a common misconception that an estate is only the property that one leaves at death. In reality, it is much more than that. In its broadest sense, the term *estate planning* encompasses the accumulation, conservation, and distribution of an estate. The overall purpose of the estate planning process is to develop a plan that will enhance and maintain the financial security of clients and their families. Estate planning has come to include lifetime financial planning that may lead to increases in a client's estate as well as the conservation of existing assets. Estate planning should provide financial security during retirement years and facilitate the intended and orderly disposition of property at death.

Estate Planning

- accumulation
- conservation
- distribution

HISTORY

Before exploring the art of estate planning, it is important to understand the historical meaning of the term *estate* as well as its meaning today. Under old English common law (discussed in more detail below), estate referred primarily to an interest in land and the buildings or other permanent improvements on the land. Estate described the proprietary rights of the estate owner projected over time. Different types of estate ownership were classified on the basis of (1) the rights an owner could exercise over the property and

life estate

(2) the duration of the owner's interest. A *life estate*, for example, is a property interest for the life of the estate owner with certain limitations on the life tenant's use of the property. It is, therefore, a lesser interest than an *estate in*

estate in fee simple absolute

fee simple absolute, which is an interest that belongs absolutely to the estate owner, the heirs, and assigns forever without condition or limitation. Over the course of time, an estate has come to mean more than an interest in land. It encompasses all the property or property rights that a person owns, even those from which a lifetime benefit will never be received, such as life insurance proceeds or survivor annuities. Modern estate planning focuses on all property-ownership rights (real, personal, tangible, and intangible), attempting to make appropriate arrangements for them during the estate owner's life and to provide for their orderly transfer at death.

The need for an orderly disposition of property at the death of the owner of that property has existed since humans began to accumulate and value possessions. Various cultures have resolved this need in different ways. In some cultures, all possessions belonged to families or tribes, so the death of an individual did not affect their ownership. Other cultures that did recognize individual property provided for a system of inheritance to persons related to the deceased through the mother, father, or both. It was a system not totally dissimilar to today's laws of intestate succession, which provide a rigid scheme for inheritance of a deceased person's property by the heirs. The degree of relationship required to inherit as well as the method of tracing that relationship may have varied considerably from the criteria utilized for intestate succession today. Even in the early days of civilization, a rigid system of inheritance did not meet the needs of every family and it does not do so today. One child may have been favored by the estate owner over others or may have required special assistance because of physical or mental frailties or prowess. In short, no one knows as much about the interrelationships and needs of a family as do the members of that family. Various cultures have recognized that fact for thousands of years by allowing adult family members to provide for postdeath property transfers designed to meet individual or family needs.

As early as the Fourth Egyptian Dynasty (2900–2750 BC), there appeared a testamentary disposition by an official to endow his tomb. In 2548 BC, an instrument was written on papyrus and witnessed by two scribes in which an Egyptian provided for certain property to be settled on his wife and appointed a guardian for his minor children. The Code of Hammurabi (1750 BC) does not mention wills directly but suggests that the culture had a scheme of intestate succession that the individual could alter, if the individual so desired. The provision referred to is the right of an estate owner to favor the eldest son by *sealed deed*. If the sealed deed was executed, the eldest son would have had an absolute right to receive the property described within, sharing equally in the remaining property with his brothers. In the absence of a sealed deed, all male children presumably inherited equally. Total disinheritance of a son was allowed only by judicial proceeding during the lifetime of the father.

Both the Greek and Roman civilizations allowed a testamentary disposition of property pursuant to the wishes of the deceased party. In fact, prior to 40 BC, Roman citizens could totally disinherit children or other relatives. Because part of the state's interest in the orderly disposition of property at death has always been the support of the deceased's dependents to prevent them from becoming burdens of the state, the Romans developed a system of forced heirship for a portion of the deceased's property. This system continues to this day in civil-law jurisdictions (those jurisdictions tracing their judicial system to the ancient Romans and the Napoleonic Code rather than to English common law). Louisiana is the only true civil-law state in the United States and has a forced heirship provision that affects not only Louisiana residents but also Louisiana property owned by nonresidents. Other states, however, may also have some form of forced heirship provisions.

Although our modern statutes retain some traces of ancient Roman law, the most prevalent influence is the English common law that developed after the invasion of William the Conqueror in 1066 AD. In that feudal society, the only property of consequence that a person could potentially pass at death was interest in land. All land in feudal England belonged ultimately to the king. Vast interests in land were granted by the king to the great nobles in return for various payments and services. The nobles, in turn, granted interests in smaller portions of land to lesser members of the nobility in exchange for services. It is readily apparent that an inherent conflict of interest existed between the tenant in possession of the land, the presumptive heirs, and the immediate overlord. In bargaining for the land grant, the tenant wished to give up as few payments or services as possible and the overlord wished to receive maximum benefits. The overlord wanted the land returned to him at the death of a tenant so that he could make a new and possibly more advantageous bargain with another tenant. On the other hand, the tenant in possession wished to be able to dispose of the land to his or her own heirs who, in turn, desired the certainty of knowing they would not be dispossessed. Conflicts were eventually resolved primarily in favor of the tenant in possession of the land by allowing the lifetime transfer by the tenant, thereby defeating both the claims of the presumptive heirs and the overlord (Statute of Quia Emptores, 1290 AD). A testamentary right of disposition over property, however, did not exist until the Statute of Wills in 1540 gave all those except married women, infants, idiots, and the insane the right to dispose of most of their property by written instrument.

The English common law (both the statutes and the case law that construed them) became the foundation for American law in most legal areas including the area of estates. Likewise, the English *use* (by which legal title to property was conveyed to a person in whom the owner had confidence with the instruction that the property be used for the benefit of the original owner's family or other designated persons) became the basis for the modern law of trusts.

The federal government began taxing estates as long ago as 1797. For the following 100 years, the tax went through repeal and reenactment, and it was held, albeit indirectly, unconstitutional in *Pollock v. Farmers' Loan & Trust Co.*, 157 U.S. 429, 3 AFTR 2557 (1895). In 1898, the federal estate tax was imposed once again under the War Revenue Act.

Two other historical occurrences are also important in estate planning. The first occurred in the late 19th century when various state legislatures in this country began to enact state inheritance tax laws based on the value of property distributed to a decedent's beneficiaries. The second occurrence was the federal government's taxation of gratuitous transfers of property (property passing at death [1915] and lifetime gifts [1932]).

Historical Notes

- Code of Hammurabi
- Statute of Wills
- state inheritance taxation
- federal transfer taxation
  - at death (1915)
  - lifetime gifts (1932)

As the legal complexities surrounding transfers of property at death became complicated further by federal and state estate, gift, or inheritance taxes, more people became concerned about protecting their property from erosion by taxes. Consequently, the process of estate planning evolved. In essence, estate planning today is the art of accumulating, conserving, and possibly transferring portions of one's property during lifetime and disposing of property at death in a manner that minimizes taxes, probate costs, and other related expenses but is consistent with one's lifetime goals.

IMPEDIMENTS TO A WELL-PLANNED ESTATE

Failure to Plan

Most people do not realize that even if they have not created an estate plan and executed the appropriate documents to implement their plans, a plan has been created and imposed on them by the state in which they reside. Everyone, no matter how poor, has an estate plan. Each state has drafted its own statutory scheme for the disposition of its citizens' property at death in the event that the resident dies either without a valid will or having made an incomplete disposition of property.

intestate-succession statutes

Each state legislature has drafted a statutory plan that clearly lays out the way in which the property one owns at death will be distributed if the decedent dies without a valid will. These statutes are called *intestate-succession statutes*, or statutes of descent and distribution. In each of these statutes, the state has set out a standardized line of succession that controls who will succeed to ownership of the deceased person's property. These intestate succession statutes are based on spousal relationships and degrees of consanguinity (blood relationship) to the decedent rather than on the distribution of property according to the intentions and desires of the deceased individual. Note that adopted children are generally treated as biological children of a decedent for intestate succession purposes. Without a will, one may not leave property to charity. Neither may a friend who is not related inherit any property from the deceased. If no relatives exist, the property reverts to the state. The property is said to *escheat* to the state. A decedent who dies *intestate* (without a will)

**escheat
intestate**

appears to have had little concern for property, family, friends, or any other potential beneficiary such as a charity.

The same limitations apply to today's statutes of intestate succession that applied to the intestate distribution vehicles of earlier cultures already noted. They are highly standardized and rigid. As a result, they take no account of any special circumstances within families or any special relationships with nonrelated parties. Furthermore, lack of planning can destroy family relationships unintentionally, thereby causing bitterness and hardship for innocent family members. Because of those facts, distribution by intestate succession is only used when decedents have failed to advise the state in a legally acceptable manner through a will or similar document what they intend to do with their accumulated property at death.

will

The most basic legal instrument of all estate plans is a *will*. A will is a legal instrument whereby a person makes disposition of his or her property to take effect after death. Once a valid will has been executed, the statutes of intestate succession are largely displaced by the provisions of the will. While the intestate succession statutes may be largely displaced by a will or other personal disposition by the decedent, they may not be totally displaced. Because the state is concerned with the support of a spouse and minor children so these individuals will not become a financial burden to the state, all states either have common-law rules or have enacted statutory provisions that protect a portion of the decedent's property for a surviving spouse under laws that are labeled variously as dower, curtesy, and homestead rights, or other statutory provisions, such as a spouse's right of election. These provisions may be operative only if the spouse and children have not been provided for by the will, or they may be absolute rights regardless of the will's provisions, such as forced heirship. The specific provisions of such laws vary from state to state, but they are a form of intestate succession. Individuals should understand what form these provisions take in their states and whether or not they can be displaced by the provisions in a will. The surviving spouse's rights can often be enforced only by an election to take against the provisions in a valid will.

Outdated Plan

While a valid will is a good beginning point for an estate plan, the will must be reviewed periodically to assure that a property owner's most recent intentions are honored at death. The birth of new children or grandchildren, the unexpected illness or disability of family members, and changes in the estate owner's objectives are common reasons for revising an estate plan, will, or trust. Major tax law changes may affect the goals of an existing plan or the tax clauses contained in a will or trust. An owner may perceive beneficiaries and their needs differently over time. Guardianship for minor children or arrangements for special needs beneficiaries may need to be altered.

codicil
Will provisions may be altered by an amendment (called a *codicil*) or completely rewritten by the property owner at any time. The modern technology of word processors and computers makes rewriting an entire will even for minor changes a relatively simple task. If family circumstances or laws have changed dramatically since the will was written, the will's provisions may be seriously out of touch with the property owner's current wishes, but the existing will is the one that will be followed until and unless it is replaced with a later valid will. This situation can produce some disturbing results.

Example:	Jane and her cousin Martin were close friends 10 years ago. Jane named Martin as a substantial beneficiary under her will. Later, Martin fell into Jane's disfavor, and for years they seldom spoke. Despite the change in Jane and Martin's relationship, the property set out in Jane's will 10 years ago will pass to Martin at Jane's death unless Jane reviews and revises her will to reflect the change in her feelings toward Martin.

Wills and trusts should be reviewed periodically to make certain that objectives are met.

Overlooked Provisions

The following provisions are sometimes overlooked or forgotten in an estate plan, will, or trust: guardianship, simultaneous death, residuary estate, tax apportionment, and contingent beneficiaries.

The issue of guardians should be addressed by an estate owner with minor children or special needs family members. Frequently, a guardian is named for the minor's personal care while another or others supervise and invest the minor's property. Usually guardians are named in the wills of parents and individuals having the responsibility of other family members. Clearly, arrangements should be discussed with potential guardians prior to naming them in the will.

The possibility of simultaneous deaths should also be considered in an estate plan. An owner should devise backup asset arrangements in case spouses and/or beneficiaries die in a common disaster. (Simultaneous death is discussed further in chapter 15.)

A residuary clause is an important will provision. Even though the estate owner believes all property is provided for and is arranged to pass according to his or her wishes, a residuary clause provides for the transfer of unexpected, unknown, or forgotten assets as well as of assets acquired in the future.

Tax apportionment issues are sometimes neglected in an estate plan. Planners should make certain that clients carefully consider tax payment options and the sources from which tax payments are to be made. In other words, a determination should be made concerning which assets and beneficiaries bear the burden of death taxes.

For example, if an individual directs under the will that all estate taxes are to be paid from the residuary estate, he or she should recognize that the residuary beneficiaries may not receive what the testator originally intended. Generally speaking, most state statutes direct the payment of taxes to be

equitable apportionment

equitably apportioned. *Equitable apportionment* means that each bequest bears the tax it generates. For instance, if a beneficiary receives 15 percent of the taxable estate, the beneficiary is responsible for 15 percent of the death taxes. State law, however, yields to a specific direction in a will or trust document regarding the apportionment of taxes. A carefully drafted tax apportionment clause is tailored to meet the estate owner's intentions.

An estate owner should have provisions in place for contingent beneficiaries in case the primary beneficiaries are no longer living at the time of the owner's death or incapacity or in case the primary beneficiaries disclaim assets passing to them.

Improper Tax Planning

The potential estate and gift tax relief that changes in the federal estate and gift tax laws appear to provide may make many more individuals think that they no longer have a need for a carefully planned estate. However, the truth is that only by utilizing the new tax laws to maximum advantage through professional advice can property owners carry out their postdeath intentions and prevent the unnecessary erosion of their estates due to taxes. For example, the unlimited marital deduction that allows an individual to pass an entire estate free of federal gift and estate taxes to a spouse appears to offer relief from taxation. In reality, use of the unlimited marital deduction (covered in later chapters) may be enormously expensive at the death of the second spouse, since property will pass unprotected by the marital deduction (assuming the surviving spouse does not remarry). Thus, the combined taxes on two estates may be greater than if the unlimited marital deduction had not been used in the estate of the first spouse to die. In short, the need for estate planning has never depended, and does not now depend, solely on whether there is a federal estate tax payable in one particular estate.

While there are important tax planning options that can be utilized in estate planning, tax relief should not be the primary objective of estate planning. The best estate plan is one that accurately reflects the client's wishes, needs, and objectives in a manner that reduces the potential tax liability to the lowest level consistent with the client's aims. This means that various tax options must be balanced against rigidity, loss of control over assets, tax liability, and so on; they must also be explained to clients so they can understand both the limitations and the benefits of these options and choose those that reflect their desires and intentions. An estate plan that reduces the estate tax liability to zero is a poor plan if the cost is the perversion of the client's wishes.

Improper Ownership of Assets

Many times the estate tax liability and even the ultimate ownership of an asset is predetermined by the form of ownership in which it is held prior to the owner's death. An example of an asset that is frequently improperly owned or positioned is life insurance. If the insured retains any incident of ownership in life insurance, the proceeds are subject to estate taxation. This unnecessary estate tax drain can be eliminated and more net dollars can be made available to the estate or its beneficiaries by removing all incidents of ownership from the insured and giving them to a spouse or trust. However, the unlimited marital deduction may now make it more desirable for the decedent to retain ownership of life insurance. Proper ownership of assets, including life insurance, must be analyzed on a case-by-case basis.

Another form of property ownership that can be problematic in estate planning is joint ownership with right of survivorship. This includes ownership as joint tenants with right of survivorship (ownership by the deceased and any other person including the surviving spouse) or as tenants by the entireties (a form of joint ownership restricted to married couples). The postdeath succession of property that is owned in either of these forms is not controlled by the provisions in a valid will. Ownership is transferred automatically by operation of law to the surviving joint tenant or tenant by the entireties. If all or most property is owned in this form, this situation can be the cause of an improperly balanced estate in which the surviving spouse may inherit too much of the property relative to the children, possibly resulting in an excessive estate tax liability at the second death.

Failure to Plan for Disability or Last Illness

The cost of a protracted period of disability or a prolonged last illness may so erode an otherwise adequate estate that the estate owner leaves nothing to the beneficiaries at death, except a crushing amount of debt. The ownership of adequate medical expense and disability income insurance protection is an important consideration in planning any estate. Disability income protection, in particular, is often ignored or misunderstood by clients, despite the fact that statistically there is a greater likelihood of a significant period of disability before retirement age than there is of an early death.

Failure to Consider Inflation

Another impediment to effective estate planning that should not be underestimated is the rate of inflation experienced over the past few years. At the very least, continuing inflation necessitates periodic reviews of existing estate plans to keep abreast of projected estate tax liabilities, as these can be affected by inflation through *tax bracket creep*. It is also necessary to review asset valuations, projected income from assets held, and amounts of life insurance in terms of constant dollars to assure that the estate owner's family would continue to be adequately protected. An inflated economic climate will have a direct impact on all estates as the value of the dollar is eroded. Failure to take inflation into consideration when projecting the adequacy of an estate 10, 20, or 30 years into the future will probably result in the impossibility of carrying out the estate owner's desires.

tax bracket creep

Lack of Liquidity

Lack of liquidity may be a major problem in an otherwise well-planned estate. Three factors are particularly important in assessing liquidity needs in estate planning: (1) the amount and terms of debt of the estate owner, (2) the projected estate tax liability, and (3) the type of assets that make up the estate.

At the time of an estate owner's death, the amount and terms of debt for which a decedent is personally responsible may dramatically reduce either the actual assets or the net income stream that would be available to the beneficiaries. The same is true of the estate tax liability.

The types of assets owned at the time of death also affect the cash available to the beneficiaries for their income needs. For example, when a closely held business is the primary estate asset and is the source of income to the decedent and family through the decedent's salary and bonuses, there is frequently a family cash shortage when salary and bonuses cease. This results in financial stress to a family that is trying to deal with the death of a family member. It is most important that the possibility of such a situation be considered prior to its occurrence, and that both the estate owner and the family make appropriate decisions to avoid these problems. If adequate planning has been done, salary continuation plans are a possible way to soften the financial shock of a breadwinner's death, and additional liquidity may also be available from retirement plans and life insurance proceeds.

If the business is to be sold, it is imperative that the arrangements for the sale be reduced during the lifetime of the shareholder to legally enforceable agreements that are equitable to all parties, including both the persons who will continue the business and the decedent-shareholder's family.

If no such advance planning is done, the estate may be forced to sell assets hurriedly to pay its bills or taxes, and assets may have to be sold under disadvantageous market conditions at greatly reduced prices.

Psychological Impediments

Dealing with One's Own Mortality

Many people avoid making an estate plan because it encompasses planning for the transfer of assets after their death. It is almost as if by failing to participate in estate planning, these individuals avoid confronting the fact that death will happen to them. They perpetuate their denial of death.

Implementation of an estate plan includes provision for the disposition of assets after death and requires an individual to acknowledge the reality of his or her mortality. Very few people can deal comfortably with this. There are many sophisticated and successful professionals who are very comfortable in the high-pressure atmosphere of finance and international business but who are so distressed when attempting to deal with the inevitability of death that they never implement a cohesive estate plan. In this case, it is the family of the estate owner who ultimately suffer when their standard of living is impaired at the decedent's death or when they try to impose some semblance of order on an estate that is in disarray.

Estate planners must make every reasonable effort to work with clients who are avoiding a confrontation with the inevitability of death. They should avoid getting involved in an intense psychological encounter for which they are not trained; therefore, they must be sensitive in handling the difficulties

---

Obstacles to Effective Estate Planning

- failure to plan for death
  - not executing or updating a will
  - not taking the time to think about who gets what and when
  - believing the state succession statutes will cause property to pass the way the estate owner would want it to
- outdated plan
  - birth and death of family members
  - tax law changes
- overlooked provisions
  - guardianship
  - simultaneous death
  - tax apportionment
- improper tax planning
- improper ownership of assets
- failure to plan for disability or illness
- failure to consider inflation
- lack of liquidity
- psychological factors
  - dealing with mortality
  - procrastination

presented by clients in this situation. It may be possible to assist a client past this obstacle by suggesting that estate planning is purely precautionary, and prudence requires that one be prepared for any eventuality. It is also important to educate such a person to the consequences of failing to do estate planning, including the very real possibility that an unplanned estate may cause the dissolution of the achievements of a lifetime of effort devoted to accumulating and preserving wealth.

Procrastination

While procrastination may be another indication that clients are delaying a confrontation with their own mortality, a more common reason for this delay is the feeling that planning for the distribution of an estate is a task so large that it is impossible to achieve. The client can become overwhelmed and simply do nothing. In this circumstance, it is often sufficient for the estate planner to accept a significant part of the responsibility for completing the estate plan and to divide that portion of the task that must be done by the client into manageable chores.

ESTATE PLANNING PROCESS

The estate planning process has a number of identifiable stages. First, data must be obtained. Then the existing estate plan must be evaluated for potential impairments. After that, a plan is designed that is approved by the client. After the client reviews the plan, it must be implemented. This stage includes the execution of any necessary legal documents and transfers for arrangements of property. Last, it is important for the client to be made aware that there should be a periodic review of the plan, particularly at times of change in life or tax laws.

The Estate Planning Process

- Step 1   data-gathering interview (personal information)
- Step 2   evaluation of an existing plan
- Step 3   use of a financial fact finder (financial data)
  – client interview
- Step 4   development and implementation of an estate plan
  – preparation
  – client review and approval
  – execution of documents
  – transfer of property
- Step 5   periodic review

Data-Gathering Interview

The initial stage in creating an estate plan is to gather all relevant facts from the estate owner and to compile them in a systematic manner. These facts should include full disclosure regarding all property ownership (both assets and liabilities), including expected gifts or inheritances. Any known problems connected with particular property, such as the problems surrounding a closely held business interest, should be noted. Detailed information must also be obtained regarding the family structure, the names of all persons in the family who have some connection with the estate owner, and the relationships and attitudes of family members toward each other. For example, it is important to elicit the attitude of the estate owner toward a spouse and younger generations. Information must be obtained regarding philosophy about assets as well as feelings about work, money, risk, philanthropy, and financial security.

Some questions and areas of exploration that will help the estate planner discover the client's personal attitudes are the following: Does the estate owner have strong feelings about charitable giving or particular charitable organizations? Many individuals who have accumulated a substantial estate do have special feelings for some of the institutions that have aided them in achieving their goals and arriving at positions of financial, professional, or business success. What are the estate owner's obligations to a former spouse or to children of a first marriage? In estate planning today, one cannot ignore the subject of divorce. When an estate owner comes to see you with his or her spouse, it is possible that this may not be the first spouse. Also, there might be an elderly parent or a handicapped person in the family for whom the estate owner has some concern. Does the estate owner have a legal or moral obligation to support such a person? The estate owner should also be questioned regarding gifts that have been made during his or her lifetime as well as gifts that the estate owner anticipates making to various persons in the future.

Evaluation of an Existing Plan

Information should be obtained regarding the provisions of the estate owner's current estate plan, if any. Does the client presently have a valid will? Has the client created trusts that may or may not serve his or her needs? These documents and other legal documents should be brought to the interview to assist the estate planner in both evaluating the client's current plan and in making recommendations for improvement.

Use of a Financial Fact Finder

To develop or revise an estate plan for a client the planner needs to have a record containing all the relevant facts and information about the client.

The use of a financial fact finder is a simple, thorough, and accurate way to record the client's information for present and future reference. Fact finders are forms designed to gather data systematically for financial and estate planning. Planners may also create their own fact finders and design them to suit their particular professional needs. Using the information provided in the fact finder, estate planners are able to make decisions by exercising their professional judgment based on their relationships with clients and their assessment of the clients' problems.

It is crucial in gathering facts and information to obtain both objective and subjective information. No questionnaire or fact finder has any value if the personal objectives of the estate owner are not extracted during the interview. Estate planning involves property but more than that, it is planning for human beings. As such, it should be highly personalized. Good estate planners will make sure that they have elicited from clients all their goals and intentions regarding their property as well as their feelings about all family and nonfamily members whom they may want to protect or benefit in some way.

There are pros and cons regarding the submission of a fact finder to a client before an interview. While mailing the questionnaire in advance saves time during the initial interview, the amount of information requested may intimidate or overwhelm a client. In addition, there are many things the estate planner cannot determine from numbers and names on a piece of paper. It is only in a direct, personal interchange that a climate of trust can be established that will enable the estate owner to be comfortable in fully revealing personal information, beliefs, concerns, and attitudes to the estate planner. A good estate planning practitioner is usually able to establish rapport with, and gain the confidence of, a client fairly quickly.

Client Interview

In eliciting or reviewing facts in the initial data-gathering interview, problems that would impede the estate plan should be noted, defined, and explored with the client. As part of the data-gathering process, the estate planner also has a duty to explain to the client various potential options that are available under the current law. The client's responses to these various options provide significant guidance to the estate planner in determining the type of plan that is most suitable for meeting the client's needs and objectives. This involves explaining the law to the client and making certain it is understood. The plan is the client's plan, as is the ultimate decision regarding the arrangement of assets and transfers to beneficiaries. Many clients are intimidated by the professional person, are unfamiliar with the professional's language or terminology, and do not quite know how to ask questions that would help them understand and feel comfortable with the estate plan. It is very important to make certain that clients know what they are doing and why. This can be accomplished by giving the client an analysis of problem areas the planner has identified as well as areas where there may be a choice among alternative solutions. The analysis is helpful to the client only if it is explained in understandable terms.

Development and Implementation of an Estate Plan

The next stage is the actual development of an estate plan. This includes the preparation and presentation of the plan to the client for review and final approval.

The third stage is the implementation of that plan. This entails executing the necessary legal documents and making arrangements for any current transfer of ownership as well as providing for liquidity needs. In choosing between alternative planning options, the estate planner utilizes to the greatest extent possible those vehicles consistent with the client's wishes that provide the most benefits in the areas of estate, gift, and income tax.

Periodic Review

After the appropriate documents are reviewed and executed, the estate owner should be advised that a periodic review of those documents is essential as a final, and ongoing, stage of estate planning. Changes in the tax laws occur at an unprecedented rate, as can changes in financial and interpersonal situations. Through the process of periodic review, the estate owner can assure that such changes are reflected in his or her original estate plan.

When an estate plan is fully implemented and a review procedure is adopted, estate owners should have the satisfaction of knowing that they have taken an active role in the direction of their lives' plans, and they should have greater peace of mind in the knowledge that they have provided for the financial security of themselves and their families.

Advantages of a Well-Planned Estate

- property distribution according to the decedent's wishes
- tax-saving options
- appropriate ownership of assets
- disability and last illness preparedness
- liquidity needs assessment
- personal peace of mind

ESTATE PLANNING TEAM

Individuals from more than one professional discipline are qualified to assist clients in estate planning. The greatest benefit and the best results for a client can be obtained from an approach that enlists the assistance of a variety of advisers in total financial planning, including estate planning. If, however, the client is interested in either estate or death planning only, the estate planner should perform those tasks. It is hoped that the client can be interested in more complete planning through a successful relationship, but the estate planner should not insist that the client either plan comprehensively or not plan at all.

The estate planning team has traditionally consisted of an attorney, an insurance specialist, a bank trust officer, an accountant, and an investment counselor (see figure 1-1). A newer member of the team is the financial planner. It is frequently the financial planner or the insurance specialist who makes the first contact with the client, sensitizes the client to the need for estate planning, and motivates the client to become involved in the process. This is because both the life underwriter and the financial planner can advertise their services and otherwise solicit business. Attorneys and accountants may engage in advertising only in a limited and regulated manner.

FIGURE 1-1
The Estate Planning Team

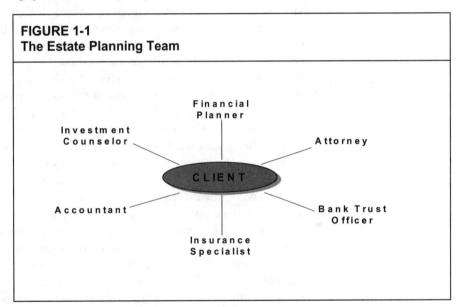

Financial planning is a discipline of relatively recent origin. The financial planner may be an independent businessperson or may be affiliated with a large investment, insurance, accounting, or other institution. The most qualified financial planners are those who have earned a CFP® or a ChFC® designation. The financial planner may provide services solely for a fee, or, if permitted by state law, the fees for planning may be offset, in whole or in part, by commissions on the sale of financial products. Financial planning is a process for arriving at comprehensive solutions to a client's personal, business, and financial problems and concerns. The term covers a wide range of financial services and products. It is the ability of financial planners to cooperate with other members of various disciplines to develop an overall plan for the client that is one of their most significant contributions to client service and to the estate planning team.

The next member of the estate planning team, the accountant, is the adviser most likely to have annual contact with the client through preparation of the client's tax returns. This gives the accountant the opportunity to be familiar with the size, amount, and nature of the client's estate. The accountant may be the person who provides valuations for assets in the estate. Valuation might be particularly crucial if one recommendation in the estate plan is a buy-sell agreement to provide for a transfer of a business interest upon death or disability. The accountant may also be of help in preparing a final estate tax return. Accountants who possess a CPA are typically the best choice for team members.

The trust officer is the next member of the team. This may be the person to whom the client has initially turned for information and estate planning services if professional management is desired in the administration of an inter vivos or testamentary trust. A good trust officer will be familiar with the field of estate planning and the various estate planning tools that can be used. As executors or trustees, trust officers have primary responsibility for settling the estate, investing estate assets during the administration period, and making distributions—as necessary—to the estate or trust beneficiaries. The bank trust department may also be responsible for filing estate and fiduciary income tax returns.

The insurance specialist plays an important role on the estate planning team because he or she can provide products that give the estate the necessary cash to pay the estate tax and other liabilities as well as to fund the income needs of the surviving family. Life insurance may be the primary asset of some estates and, consequently, the major source for family income after an estate owner dies. Life insurance agents who have become CLUs are knowledgeable in the fields of insurance as well as estate planning and taxation and can provide an invaluable service as an informed member of the team.

The next member of the team is the attorney. The attorney is a crucial member because planning cannot be accomplished nor can a plan be executed without using an attorney's knowledge of the law. Typically, the attorney is the professional who drafts all of the legal documents that are necessary to implement the plan. These documents virtually always include wills and may include trusts, buy-sell agreements, or other documents if a more sophisticated estate plan is elected. The attorney is responsible for assuring that the intentions of the client are expressed in legally enforceable documents that serve as the basis for carrying out the client's postmortem plan.

The creation of an estate plan is a highly rewarding experience for the estate planning practitioner regardless of the discipline from which he or she comes. Although there may be a different emphasis in various estate plans stemming from the knowledge and background of the practitioner, the primary objective of a good planner should be to effectuate and implement both the desires and objectives of the individual for whom the plan is created. The client is the director of the plan. The professionals are the producers. An estate plan reflects the personality of the client. It may evidence the client's cares and concerns for other human beings as well as for himself or herself. On the contrary, the plan may reflect or focus on the client's own self-interest, grievances, and grudges. Much is revealed about the client's character, philosophy of life, and attitudes by the types of planning options he or she selects and the reasons for which they are selected.

Estate planning has become vastly more complicated and challenging as a field of practice. In order to be an effective estate planner, one must be familiar with applicable local and federal law. One must also have a working knowledge of subject matter pertaining to property, probate, wills and trusts, federal and state taxation, corporations, partnerships, business, insurance, and divorce. An estate planner must be able to explain relevant portions of these subjects in plain language to a client. If the client is spoken down to or expected to deal with technical jargon, the client will not feel confident and may well abandon the project. A client has an absolute right to fully understand all the options and make his or her own decisions.

UNAUTHORIZED PRACTICE OF LAW

Because much of the knowledge necessary for estate planning deals with legal concepts, there is often concern over whether one is or is not practicing law without a license. Indeed, the line between unauthorized practice and other advice is sometimes a fine one.

What is the unauthorized practice of law? There is no definitive answer to that question. The American Bar Association's Model Rules of Professional Conduct takes the position that the definition of the practice of law is established by the law of the different jurisdictions. This seems to imply that what constitutes the unauthorized practice could vary from jurisdiction to jurisdiction. The Model Code's predecessor, the ABA's Code of Professional Responsibility, took the position that "[i]t is neither necessary nor desirable to attempt the formulation of a single, specific definition of what constitutes the practice of law. Functionally, the practice of law relates to the rendition of services for others that call for the professional judgment of a lawyer. The essence of the professional judgment of the lawyer is his educated ability to relate the general body and philosophy of law to a specific legal problem of a client. . . ."

Neither expertise in a particular subject matter area nor knowledgeability of the law is sufficient to allow anyone other than a lawyer to give legal advice. Giving such advice is clearly reserved to those who are licensed to practice law.

Even with the Bar Association's ambiguous definition of the unauthorized practice of law, there are activities that are universally recognized as the practice of law; therefore, they are to be engaged in only by lawyers. The drafting of legal documents is one such activity. Lawyers themselves, however, can also be engaged in the unauthorized practice of law. If an attorney practices in a jurisdiction in which he or she does not have a license to practice law, it is unauthorized practice. This situation can easily and unintentionally occur when estate planning involves an entire family, members of which reside in several jurisdictions, or for clients who plan to move or retire to another state. To further complicate matters, the definition of the practice of law is established on a state-by-state basis; therefore, what constitutes the unauthorized practice of law may differ from state to state. An attorney must examine the relevant state law definition.

The area of giving advice is even more problematic. For example, when does giving advice about the taxation of a particular trust arrangement that is properly within the province of the CPA or trust officer become *legal advice* and thereby solely within the province of the attorney? This is the crucial question in this difficult area. Some general guidelines are available, however, to assist the nonlawyer. If the advice is generally informational (that is, if the general principles of a proposal or technique are outlined for the client's information), there should not be a problem. Even if the advice is specifically related to the client's situation, there is no unauthorized practice violation if the advice is given on a settled area of law that is a matter of common knowledge in the estate planning field.

Because this problem is so difficult to resolve and penalties can be severe, the early and continuous involvement of an attorney in the estate planning process is perhaps the best way to deal with the unauthorized practice issue.

Unauthorized Practice of Law

- attorney—legal advice/drafting documents
- bank trust officer—trust tax advice
- accountant—tax advice/estate planning
- insurance professional—advice on estate planning/estate liquidity
- investment specialist—estate liquidity/taxation of investments

Note: There is no precise definition of what constitutes the unauthorized practice of law.

CHAPTER REVIEW

Answers to the review questions and the self-test questions start on page 717.

Key Terms

estate planning

life estate

estate in fee simple absolute

intestate-succession statutes

escheat

intestate

will

codicil

equitable apportionment

tax bracket creep

Review Questions

1-1.   Identify the different kinds of taxes within the transfer tax system.

1-2.   What is the meaning of the term *estate planning* in its broadest sense?

1-3.   Briefly describe the historical development of estate planning.

1-4.   All state intestacy statutes share common characteristics as to the distribution of a decedent's property.
   a.   What principles do the intestacy statutes follow in the statutory distribution of a decedent's property?
   b.   Which individuals and organizations typically cannot inherit through intestate succession?

1-5.   To what extent does a valid will displace the statutes of intestate succession?

1-6.   Why is it important for a will to be revised periodically?

1-7.   What provisions in a will or trust are sometimes overlooked?

1-8.   Explain why tax planning objectives should be subordinate to the primary objectives of estate planning.

1-9.   Why is the form of property ownership an important consideration in estate planning?

1-10.   Why are medical expense insurance and disability insurance important concerns in estate planning?

1-11.   How is inflation an impediment to effective estate planning?

1-12.   Identify the factors that are important in assessing an estate's liquidity needs.

1-13.   Why is estate liquidity analysis particularly important for a closely held business owner?

1-14. Explain how psychological impediments may be a barrier to proper estate planning.

1-15. Describe the stages in the estate planning process.

1-16. Identify the various types of professionals on the estate planning team, and explain how their respective functions complement each other.

1-17. What guidelines are available to the estate planner in determining whether an activity may constitute the unauthorized practice of law?

Self-Test Questions

T   F   1-1. Estate planning is concerned only with the conservation of existing assets.

T   F   1-2. Until the mid-19th century, society had no provisions for the orderly disposition of property at death.

T   F   1-3. The most prevalent influence on current laws relating to estate planning in the United States has been English common law.

T   F   1-4. Intestate succession laws generally provide for the distribution of property in accordance with a decedent's wishes.

T   F   1-5. If a person dies intestate and leaves no relatives, the decedent's property will revert to the state.

T   F   1-6. A legally competent person may amend his or her will at any time.

T   F   1-7. The best estate plan is always the one that minimizes taxes.

T   F   1-8. The disposition of a decedent's assets may be predetermined by the form of ownership of each asset.

T   F   1-9. Inflation makes it necessary to periodically review existing estate plans.

T   F   1-10. The types of assets that constitute an estate are an important factor in assessing the estate's liquidity.

T   F   1-11. Lack of liquidity may force an estate to sell assets under disadvantageous conditions.

T   F   1-12. A client's failure to deal with the inevitability of death may be an obstacle to the implementation of a proper estate plan.

T   F   1-13. A common reason for procrastination with respect to estate planning is the feeling that the task is too large to accomplish.

T   F   1-14. Fact-finding for estate planning is concerned only with obtaining information about property ownership.

T   F   1-15. To be useful, fact-finding for estate planning purposes must determine the personal objectives of the estate owner.

T   F   1-16.   It is best in the estate planning process to keep the client uninformed of what is taking place until the final estate plan is completed and presented to the client.

T   F   1-17.   A client's accountant is the most likely member of the estate planning team to have contact with the client on an annual basis.

T   F   1-18.   An attorney is generally not needed as a member of the estate planning team.

T   F   1-19.   It is often difficult to distinguish between advice and the unauthorized practice of law.

T   F   1-20.   Giving information to a client concerning tax laws is considered the unauthorized practice of law.

Ethics for the Estate Planner

Ron Duska[*]

Learning Objectives

An understanding of the material in this chapter should enable the student to

---

2-1. Explain the estate planner's need for professionalism and the four characteristics of a professional.

2-2. Explain the nature and need for an estate planning team.

2-3. Explain the difference between an ethical temptation and an ethical dilemma.

2-4. Identify the four questions to consider in making a decision when faced with a dilemma.

2-5. Understand the ethical complexity of the compensation issue.

2-6. Identify the common areas where ethical issues arise.

2-7. Understand what confidentiality requires.

2-8. Identify ways to avoid or mitigate the force of conflicts of interest.

2-9. Appreciate the need for competency.

2-10. Understand why following the letter of the law in compliance is not enough to be ethical.

2-11. Understand the importance of communication and cooperation.

Chapter Outline

---

[*] Ronald F. Duska, PhD, is professor of ethics at The American College.

INTRODUCTION

The discipline of ethics deals with the actions necessary for an individual to live up to his or her personal and professional responsibilities. Included among such responsibilities is the keeping of commitments and the fair, respectful treatment of others. Generally, the best way in which to determine one's responsibilities is to consider the objective or purpose one is trying to fulfill. It is that objective or purpose that will, in turn, determine the actions necessary for its realization.

The function of the estate planner, as explained in chapter one, is to develop a plan for a client's financial holdings "that will enhance and maintain the financial security of clients and their families. It includes lifetime financial planning that may lead to increases in a client's estate, as well as the conservation of existing assets. It should provide financial security during retirement years and facilitate the intended and orderly disposition of property at death."

This means the ultimate objective of the estate planner is to preserve and enhance the client's estate. Because the provision of such a service requires competence, a certain expertise, and a primary concern for the good of the client, estate planning exhibits all of the characteristics of a profession. Inherent in estate planning, therefore, are all of the ethical responsibilities that accrue to professionals.

THE NEED FOR PROFESSIONALISM IN ESTATE PLANNING

Some of the products and financial instruments necessary for a sound estate plan can be sold over the counter at the bank or on the Internet. In some cases, this may be the best way to sell simple financial instruments and elements of an estate plan. But the needs of many people are not always simple. Often, people do not understand the complexities, scope, and consequences of the available financial instruments well enough to purchase wisely and in their own best interests. They lack the expertise, the time, or the desire to wade through the complexities of the various financial instruments. If they try to advise themselves, there is the risk that they become like the man who, because he defended himself, had a fool for a client. Many people, therefore, need competent, objective, independent advisers when planning their estate in order to achieve their personal goal. Hence, the need for the professional adviser.

The importance of professionalism has a long history in the financial services industry. In 1915, in an address delivered before the annual meetings of Baltimore Life and New York Life Underwriters, Solomon S. Huebner, the founder of The American College, laid out his lifetime dream—to turn the life insurance salesperson into a professional. This dream motivated him to establish The American College in 1927. Just as Huebner elevated life insurance sales to the level of a profession, it is time now to raise estate planning to that same level.

Huebner used physicians, lawyers, teachers, and others as models of what professionals should be and crafted a fine, precise statement of what it takes to be a professional, as valid today as it was in 1915. He cited four characteristics of the professional:

- The professional is involved in a "vocation useful and noble enough to inspire love and enthusiasm on the part of the practitioner."
- The professional's vocation in its practice requires an expert's knowledge.
- "In applying that knowledge, the practitioner should abandon the strictly selfish commercial view and ever keep in mind the advantage of the client."
- The practitioner should possess "a spirit of loyalty to fellow practitioners, of helpfulness to the common cause they all profess, and should not allow any unprofessional acts to bring shame upon the entire profession."

That estate planning meets characteristics one and 2 is obvious. It is evident that estate planners are useful. It is a noble vocation that can help individuals gain financial security and alleviate a client's financial anxiety. With respect to the second criterion, estate planning is a complicated profession. It requires study to become competent. The expert must continually stay current on the latest developments in the field and thoroughly understand the ramifications of those changes with respect to his or her clients.

Possibly the most interesting characteristic of the professional, according to Huebner, is the third because it lays out an ethical prescription. It requires the professional "to abandon the strictly selfish commercial view and ever keep in mind the advantage of the client."

By "the strictly selfish commercial view," Huebner was referring to the attitude of those for whom the *only* concern of business is the making money or increasing profit. This view is current today among some advocates of the free market system who insist that the primary and *only* responsibility of business is to increase profit.

"The strictly selfish commercial view" encourages the pursuit of self-interest with no limits—a pursuit that inevitably leads to the selfishness to which Huebner referred. The English language uses two different words—*self-interest* and *selfishness*—to distinguish between behavior that is perfectly acceptable (self-interested behavior) and that which is ethically inappropriate (selfish behavior). If we pursue our self-interest at the expense of another and, thereby, do them harm or treat them unfairly, we are selfish and acting unethically. To have an ethical world, there are times when people need to sacrifice their own interests because the pursuit of those interests would be unjust or harmful to others. Those are the times when it is necessary to abandon the "strictly selfish commercial view."

This means the estate planner as a professional has two obligations: product knowledge and protection of the client's best interests by avoiding the temptation to take advantage of him or her. Such a mandate is embodied within the ethical pledge that all new Chartered Life Underwriter (CLU) and Chartered Financial Consultant (ChFC) designees of The American College must take. The pledge reads: "In all my professional relationships, I pledge myself to the following rule of ethical conduct: I shall, in light of all conditions surrounding those I serve, which I shall make every conscientious effort to ascertain and understand, render that service which, in the same circumstances, I would apply to myself." The pledge is, of course, a version of that moral precept we know as The Golden Rule: "Do unto others as you would have them do unto you." Variations of this are found in every major civilization and religion since the beginning of recorded history.

The fourth component of the professional according to Huebner—the practitioner should possess "a spirit of loyalty to fellow practitioners, of helpfulness to the common cause they all profess, and [they] should not allow any unprofessional acts to bring shame upon the entire profession"—carries with it another ethical obligation of professionals, and that is to police their own membership. This is handled in most professions by a certifying body that uses a code of ethics on a set of standards for behavior and develops disciplinary boards to govern unprofessional behavior. (See chapter 3 of The American College's HS 300 textbook, 2005 edition, *Financial Planning Process and Environment,* for The American College's Code of Ethics and the Certified Financial Planner Code of Ethics and Professional Responsibility.) For example, there is the American Bar Association (attorneys), the American

Medical Association (doctors), and the American Institute of Certified Public Accountants (accounting professionals).

THE ESTATE PLANNING TEAM OF PROFESSIONALS

Because estate planning quite often requires the cooperation of a number of people from different professions, and each profession has its own code, policing the profession of estate planning becomes somewhat complicated. Estate planning for the preservation and enhancement of an estate can often involve a team of professionals, such as attorneys, accountants, bankers, insurance agents, and financial planners. Each of these professions has a code of ethics. Because they are based on ethical principles, each of the codes requires basically the same thing: competence, confidentiality, integrity, honesty, and fairness.

John Burson and Lana McCormick discussed the concept of the estate planning team in a 1995 article that appeared in *Trusts and Estates*:

> In this era of information-glut, it would take encyclopedic capabilities for one specialist to be fully informed, up-to-date and available to evaluate and respond to the myriad factors and nuances that come down from government and business to affect the financial future of each client.[1]

Burson and McCormick point out that team interaction occurs throughout modern business, and it certainly belongs in estate planning. Few individuals have the talent and expertise to operate alone in estate planning. They logically suggest that "the client is the team captain whose financial needs and interests determine which professional team member will carry the ball at any given time . . . they become part of a seamless interaction in which the attorney is involved with all legal and probate matters; the CPA covers the tax aspects; the insurance agent provides the liquidity required to settle the estate; and the trust officer preserves and builds the estate during the client's life and administers after death."[2]

It is essential for the professional estate planner to not only put the client's needs first, but he or she must look to the long-term ramifications of the plans he or she develops. The expertise required generally derives from a well-functioning team. In some rare cases, one person may be able to do the job. But, if the planner who is not qualified to do all of the jobs necessary persists in doing them, he or she will do the client a disservice. This person, therefore, acts unethically because such incompetent service is not in the best interest of the client. The planner who truly places a priority on the client's needs must know when other areas of expertise are necessary and how to form the appropriate team of experts.

Recognizing the importance of team building, The National Association of Estate Planners recently established the Accredited Estate Planner (AEP) designation "to develop and maintain a certification program to recognize professionals who . . . are committed to the team concept of estate planning."[3] One of several qualifications for becoming an AEP is to provide documentation that the candidate is an attorney, a CPA, a CLU, or a trust officer. Here again, we see the importance of the team concept.

ETHICAL SITUATIONS: TEMPTATIONS AND DILEMMAS

While it is important to build a proper team, the estate planner's activity should be guided by one fundamental ethical principle: Look to the best interest of the client. However, in the pursuit of the client's best interest, the planner may encounter two different types of ethical situations: temptations and dilemmas.

Ethical Temptations

ethical temptation

The first kind of ethical situation is one where there is a temptation to be overcome or guarded against. An *ethical temptation* is a situation in which there is a conflict between the planner's interests and those of the client.

When the professional planner is tempted to serve him or herself through the exploitation of the client's trust, there should be only one decision—a true professional sacrifices his or her own interest for that of the client.

Example 1:	*Temptation:* Peter Planner is tempted to recommend to his client a product Peter is selling that will pay a high commission, even though it is not the optimum product for this particular client.
	Ethical Decision: Peter Planner forgets himself and recommends the best product for his client.
Example 2:	*Temptation:* Peter Planner's client requires an attorney. For every referral Peter makes to his friend, Robert Atlaw, Esq., Peter receives a referral fee. Peter is tempted to refer his client to his friend, even though another attorney would better suit the client.
	Ethical Decision: Peter Planner forgets himself and recommends the best attorney for this client.

In the previous examples, the planner was tempted to put his own interests ahead of those of his clients. This is the selfishness described earlier. It is obvious that the actions Peter Planner had considered are unethical. Fortunately, Peter Planner remembered that a professional is ethically obligated to the client and acted in a professional and ethical manner by putting his client's interests ahead of his own. When there is a conflict between the interests of the professional planner and the client, it is the client's interests that should win—every time.

Ethical Dilemmas

In addition to temptations, there is a second area of ethics that can be even more problematic—conflicting interests (other than a conflict between a planner's interest and that of a client) or conflicting obligations. This can result in an ethical (or moral) dilemma.

ethical dilemma An *ethical dilemma* is a situation in which there are good reasons for acting in a certain way and good reasons for not acting in that way. It is a "damned if you do and damned if you don't" type of situation. When a person is faced with such a conflict, the situation has been compared to being "caught between the horns of dilemma." In illustration, conjure a picture of a raging bull. Whether you turn to the right or to the left, you will be gored by its horns. Your only escape is to position yourself between the horns (of dilemma). Dilemmas are either/or situations. They are situations in which there are only two alternatives. One way of handling such a situation is to ascertain whether or not it is a true dilemma. If you can find a third or fourth alternative by which you can perhaps escape getting "gored" and slide between the horns, it is not a true dilemma; you will then have other options.

It is precisely this search for third, fourth, or even more solutions that elicits what some call moral imagination. Quite often when one discusses a case in which they seem to be faced with an inescapable dilemma with other professionals, someone will suggest a practice or technique he or she has developed to help them escape a similar dilemma. Such discussions can yield a veritable treasure trove of best ethical practices.

Consider the following situation:

Harry and Sally have been married for 20 years. They come to you to make financial plans for the future. Your work with them includes arrangements for liquidating the estate. A day after your meeting, Harry calls to tell you he wants to make some changes. It seems he has a mistress about whom Sally knows nothing, and he wants provisions made for this woman in the event of his death. He states that Sally does not pay too much attention to financial details and she need not know about this change.

In such a situation what should you, as a planner do? What are your responsibilities? What are the responsibilities with respect to confidentiality? Should you keep Harry's confidence and not tell Sally? After all, Sally is your client too. If the best interests of your clients are in conflict, how should you, the planner, handle it? Should you refuse to do what Harry asks? Should you excuse yourself from being adviser to one of them? If so, which one? Should you excuse yourself from being adviser to both of them? Why or why not? How do you do any of that without violating confidentiality?

Obviously, this is a difficult situation to resolve. A general solution, such as "Treat them both fairly," does not help, because it does not spell out what counts as fair treatment in this situation. Another solution, such as "Do the right thing," does not identify the right thing. The maxim, "Look out for the best interest of your client," does not help either, because to help one client is to hurt the other. What do you do? You are facing an ethical dilemma.

Consider another situation:

> Charlie is a client in his 80s who recently lost his wife. Charlie seems to be suffering some sort of dementia. Previously, Charlie had been a meticulous dresser and neat to a fault. Because he was an accountant, his neatness spilled over into financial matters and he kept meticulous records of his worth. On a particular day, he entered his agent's office, looking disheveled and distracted, and demanded that his children be terminated as beneficiaries of his estate. He now has no idea what he is worth, and his books are in disarray. He demands that his entire estate, except enough money to live on, be put in an irrevocable trust in the name of the local SPCA that has a "wonderful woman" in charge. She is to be made trustee. It just so happens that the wonderful women's son is some sort of financial planner whom Charlie claims invested Charlie's money so that it has tripled its worth in a short period of time. The agent is extremely suspicious of the entire situation. In addition, Charlie's children are also the agent's clients.

conflicts of obligations

What are an agent's responsibilities in this situation? A situation like this is replete with problems that involve confidentiality and conflicting interests that lead to what have been traditionally called *conflicts of obligations*. The code of conduct of The Society for Financial Service Professionals requires that "a member shall provide advice and service that are in the client's best interest." But, it is highly unlikely that what Charlie is proposing is in his own best interest. Not only that, what is being proposed is clearly not in Charlie's children's best interests, and they are also the planner's clients. Can, or should, the planner inform them of what is going on so they can try to protect their father from what appears to be an unscrupulous mother and son? Should the planner do what Charlie asks and wash his or her hands of the whole matter? Or, does the planner have an obligation to check further on the status of Charlie and his relationship with the woman at the SPCA and her son? How does the planner do any of that without violating confidentiality? What really constitutes "best interest"—what the client wants, or what truly benefits him? There are many difficulties in this case.

How should such ethical dilemmas be handled?

Perhaps cases like these should be handled by King Solomon in all of his wisdom. However, because he is not available, the individual estate planner needs to do the best he or she can. It is clear in our examples that the planners need to look out for the best interest of Harry and Sally in the one **confidentiality** case, and of Charlie in the other. But the planner's *confidentiality* duty to Harry (to keep his confidence) conflicts with his duty to Sally (to look for her best interest). Which duty takes precedence? In Charlie's case, it may be that the only way to look out for his interests is to share the information with Charlie's children, thereby breaking confidentiality. Such situations are classic examples of ethical (moral) dilemmas.

Types of Ethical Situations

- ethical temptations
- ethical (moral) dilemmas

Earlier in this century, W.D. Ross, a noted ethicist, pointed out the fact that we often face conflicts of duties. He began by claiming, and rightly so, that certain duties or obligations are unquestionable, such as the duty to keep confidence and to look out for the best interest of clients. Ross called these **prima facie duties** clear and unquestionable responsibilities *prima facie duties*. (Literally, *prima facie* means "at first glance.") It is clear we have such a duty and should perform it. It is only when there is another clear duty in conflict that we have a problem. For example, the planner has a duty to keep Harry's information confidential, but he also has a duty to do something that will prevent harm to Sally. These conflicts might seem unresolvable. Still, as indicated, quite often when we reflect long and hard enough, we may come to see that one duty should override another. Ross recommended that we reason through our conflicts and attempt to ascertain our "actual duties."[4]

With respect to Harry and Sally, we might reason in the following way:

> We have a duty of confidentiality to Harry. But, if Sally is also our client, are we better off telling Harry that if he does not level with Sally, we will have to withdraw as his agent? If he forces us to do that, the truth will probably come out eventually.

The example with Charlie raises another issue. We have a duty to look out for Charlie's best interest. But what exactly counts as his best interest? Usually we equate a best interest with preferences. But as anyone knows who ever desired something that was not good for them—such as high-cholesterol foods for those with blocked arteries—we do not always prefer what is in our own best interest. Hence, as an estate planner, we have a conflict between our duty to do what our client, Charlie, asks and our duty to prevent harm from happening to Charlie, if we can.

In the United States, we are inclined to treat clients as autonomous individuals as if they are the ones best able to decide for themselves what they want. However, as a phenomenon like dementia becomes more common, we may find ourselves in a more parental type of role with our clients. In such cases, to what extent, are we obliged to be our client's keeper? Where doing what's in the client's best interest may be the exact opposite of what the client wants. What is to be done? Probably the best course of action is to warn the client of his or her defective perception of what is in his or her self-interest. Encourage the client to a better course of action, and thereafter to resign if the client persists in financially unwise behavior.

When trying to find alternative ways out of a dilemma, there are key questions that can be used to evaluate practices that are best ethically.

Resolving Dilemmas—Key Questions

- Are the proposed solutions fair? (Does everyone get what is owed to him or her?)
- Do the practices meet the agent's responsibilities and obligations? (What does the agent owe, and to whom?) (In Charlie's case, the obligations to his children are not to them as clients but to them as potential guardians of Charlie. To tell them so they could enhance their estate would be wrong. To tell them so they can look after Charlie is a good reason for breaking promises.)
- Are the practices honest? Lying to clients is not justified. (If taking care of Harry's wishes means the agent must deceive Sally, that cannot be required. One must look out for the best interest of the client(s), but only if that does not involve unethical or illegal behavior. The law of agency puts such a constraint on fiduciary responsibilities.) According to the law of agency, the agent has a duty to act solely for the benefit of, and in accordance with, the directions of the client. The agent is a fiduciary of the client and, as such, occupies a special position of trust that imposes on the agent a duty of loyalty to the client.[5]
- Do the actions harm any stakeholders? (Almost no practice is without some harm. The trick is to find the least harmful practices.)

Of course, the best way to escape ethical conflicts is to avoid them in the first place. Make the limits of what you will and will not do clear at the outset. Be certain your clients know you will not lie or do anything illegal. You will not falsify claims or application forms. You will not try to cheat the IRS for the client's sake. Your initial candor will help to avoid some ethical problems. When there are multiple clients and there is the possibility of conflicting interests, it might be helpful for you to abide by something like the following paraphrase of Rule 1.7 of the Model Rules of Professional conduct for attorneys:

> An agent may not represent clients when it appears they have adverse interests unless the lawyer reasonably believes he or she can provide appropriate legal advice without adversely affecting the interests of both parties, and each client consents to representation by the same adviser following consultations and full disclosure of the conflict or potential conflict.[6]

Prospective clients should be advised that conflicts might arise. They should know how you are prepared to handle a conflict including, where necessary, the breaking of confidences. As in most things, an ounce of prevention in the beginning is worth a pound of cure later on.

COMMON ETHICAL ISSUES FOR THE ESTATE PLANNER

Let us examine some common areas in which ethical issues might arise for the estate planner.

In discussing ethics issues that arise for all members of the estate planning team, the Ethics Committee of the Philadelphia Estate Planning Council focused on identifying the general area of concern common to all estate planners. The committee identified team members, explored the roles of the various professionals involved, and presented actual examples of what members of a team do and how they interact for the good of the client. It examined the respective and sometimes overlapping services provided to clients in order to highlight the areas of mutual ethical concern. They then reviewed the relevant respective codes of ethics put forth by the various governing bodies of the different professional disciplines involved in estate planning. From this discussion, the committee developed an ethics matrix.[7] The matrix serves to reinforce the notion that professional associations do care about the relevant ethical behavior of their members. Not only do they care, but they also have identified the behavior and regulate it.

As noted, the matrix was developed by examining the relevant excerpts of the respective codes of ethics for the various professions. The passages cited from the codes of ethics were those that related to the general areas deemed of common concern to estate planning professionals. The areas were arranged into a grid. When finalized, the grid involved the common issues of compensation, confidentiality, conflicts of interest, competence and compliance. We will discuss each of these issues plus two more: communication and cooperation.

Compensation

compensation

In financial services, in general, and estate planning, in particular, the issue of *compensation* can raise a host of problems. Obviously, a planner needs to be compensated for work done. But when the compensation is based on a commission on products sold, a problem can arise. The planner might be tempted to sell a lucrative product that may not be the best product for the client as would be a less expensive product (as we saw earlier with Peter Planner's temptation). To avoid such temptations, should the planner work only on a fee-for-service basis? What sort of commission structure should be set up? Should the planner take fees for referrals? Should the planner split commissions with other members of the team? What system should be set up to guarantee fair compensation with a minimum of temptation?

Andrew Wilusz reported on the Ethics Committee of the Philadelphia Estate Planning Council findings about compensation:

Compensation is an area replete with complicated challenges to our professional ethical behavior. (The committee) . . . examined various methods of billing, such as fixed fees versus hourly versus contingent, or incentive versus salary, or fee-based versus commissioned, or individual versus packaged billing. Is one way of billing more ethical than another? Each method has the potential for abuse. It was generally acknowledged that some billing methods present a greater potential for the appearance of impropriety. Contingent fees and commissions more readily lend themselves to questions of *conflicts of interest* because the practitioner's personal interest could be construed to be given an importance similar to the client's best interest. In our discussion, it was generally agreed that while unethical behavior did not necessarily stem from any choice of billing methods, specific billing practices present a rash of troubling issues that often move beyond the question of compensation. Packaged billing was a case in point.

conflicts of interest

Packaged billing is where one estate planning group or practitioner arranges to have all of a client's estate planning needs handled centrally. The professional organizing the services for the client acts as a general contractor, getting quotes for the various parts of the assignment, engaging and paying the subcontractors, and sending the client a single bill. The committee used as an example a large investment firm that subcontracts out the accounting, the legal, and the business valuation. The first few minutes of the discussion focused on the economic feasibility for estate planning practitioners to offer "packaged" services. It was reasoned that the convenience to the client would be outweighed by an assumed inflated price the general contractor would charge the client. Other, noncompensation issues emerged, such as the question of to whom the subcontracted professionals' loyalty was owed. That is to say, as a subcontracted valuation expert, for example, would my client be the general contractor of the actual client? From this question, another potential problem surfaced involving the general contractor putting pressure on subcontractors to do things in a way that corroborates the general contractor's plan for the client, when, under different circumstances, it would not be done. The general contractor could recommend an estate planning vehicle that a subcontracted practitioner sees as not being the best choice for the client. If the general contractor insists on the planned course of action, despite the subcontractor's expressed concerns, should the subcontractor go and discuss it with the client?[8]

Further problems governing compensation can involve the acceptance of commissions and/or referral fees. For planners who are lawyers, there are specific problems. Paul C. Heintz points out:

> The American Bar Association's Model Rules of Professional Conduct do not specifically prohibit the lawyer's acceptance of rebates, discounts, referral fees and commissions from non-lawyers. However, a lawyer's acceptance of such payments, when combined with the fee received from a client, could result in a fee deemed to be unreasonable pursuant to Rule 1.5. It is also probable that the lawyer's objectivity while representing the client would be materially affected by the prospect of receiving such payments, thus giving rise to a conflict of interest implicating Rule .17(b). Finally, the lawyer may be deemed to have a pecuniary interest adverse to the client or to have received compensation from a person other than the client that interferes with the lawyer's independence of professional judgment implicating Rules 1.8(a) and 1.8(f). These concerns would exist even if the client were to consent to the financial arrangement which consent the lawyer would be required to obtain if he or she were ever to consider accepting and retaining such payments. Although not within the scope of this column, the lawyer should also be certain the sharing of the compensation by the non-lawyer is lawful.
>
> The Commentaries on the Model Rules of Professional Conduct, developed by The American College of Trust and Estate Counsel,

make it clear that ACTEC believes Rules 1.5 and 1.7 prohibit a lawyer from accepting a rebate, discount, commission or referral fee from a non-lawyer. The ACTEC Commentaries say "even with full disclosure to and consent by the client, such an arrangement involves too great a risk of over-reaching by the lawyer and the potential for actual or apparent abuse. The client is generally entitled to the benefit of any economies that are achieved by the lawyer in connection with the representation." The Commentaries further provide that "The receipt by the lawyer of such a payment involves a conflict of interest with respect to the client. It is improper for a lawyer, who is subject to the strict obligations of a fiduciary, to benefit personally from such a representation.[9]

And, if lawyers on the estate planning team have problems, so do accountants. Ron Klein asked whether CPAs should accept commissions from third parties for the performance of professional services for the clients. He pointed out that few issues seem more debatable—or more timely— within the accountancy profession. A commission-based practice can be a lucrative tool to provide additional and improved client services. But it can also open a Pandora's Box of legal and perceptual questions that many would prefer remain closed.

Traditional CPAs that oppose commissions fear the practice poses a threat to their professional reputation. CPAs, they argue, have earned the public's trust as independent advisors. This trust can easily be violated because the CPA places, or is perceived to place, the opportunity to obtain a profitable commission ahead of the clients' best interests.

Other CPAs support a commission-based practice. To compete in today's one-stop-shopping world, many firms are offering a broader array of services. Proponents maintain that clients are willing to accept commission-based practices in exchange for these services, provided their accountant's objectivity and ethics are not compromised.[10]

A myriad of ethical issues can arise over the issue of compensation.

Confidentiality

Confidentiality is a commonsense ethical issue worthy of reflection because of its significance. A client seeking a plan to best suit his or her needs must provide the adviser with full and accurate information about both their financial position and their personal relationships. To do this, the client must feel confident that the information will be protected. Building the right client-adviser relationship through patience and diplomacy is an art that requires both sensitivity to the client's need and the ability to earn trust. Once a plan is completed, the client should then be in control. The authority to release any information concerning that plan should only come from the client. However, we saw in our earlier two examples, conflicts arising over the limits of confidentiality are ever present and must be handled with great care.

A particular area of confidentiality that is often violated can occur within the social circles of advisors, attorneys, accountants, or others—the telling of war stories. It is a natural inclination to want to share the more interesting of our cases.

Example:	Lee Gall, an attorney in Smalltown, USA, attends a party for his friend, Ira Shure, an accountant, who has just received a promotion. Among the crowd are their friends Peter Planner, a financial planner, and Sue Emall, an attorney. As they stand together at the buffet table, Lee says: "I have a case I think you'll find interesting, but I can't say what it is for reasons of confidentiality, you know." He then discusses a situation so specific that most of the others in the conversation, as well as many within hearing range, know exactly about whom he is talking.
	This is a breach of confidentiality and of his client; it is unprofessional behavior.

In today's busy society, the all-too-prevalent use of cell phones also offers many opportunities for confidentiality to be inadvertently breached, because names and private information can easily be overheard. The professional must be aware of the negative possibilities inherent in such a situation.

Conflicts of Interest

One of the most frequently discussed ethical problems is how to avoid conflicts of interest. Every client is entitled to develop an estate plan that uniquely reflects his or her intentions. The client's interest should be paramount. Conflicts with the interests of the clients, other people, or the planner should be avoided.

In an appendix to *Tools and Techniques of Estate Planning*, a list of questions about courses of action that should be taken to avoid such conflicts highlights the breadth of the conflict issue. The following questions from that list effectively communicate the complexity of the conflicts of interest issue[11]:

(1) Did the planner inform the parties he is representing of their respective rights and the pros and cons of the proposed action (or inaction) on each party?

(2) Did the planner draft an instrument giving him or a member of his family any interest in the client's estate (assuming he is not a member of the client's family)?

(3) Has the planner used the special knowledge he has to the detriment of the client in any way?

(4) Does the planner represent two parties who have or are likely to have conflicting interests? (This problem is known as *simultaneous representation*.) If so, is the planner satisfied that he can perform adequately and did he make full disclosure to, and obtain consent from, the parties?

(5) Has the planner, in any way, allowed the pursuit of financial gain or any other personal benefit to interfere with the exercise of sound professional judgment and skills?

(6) Has the planner made full disclosure of any obvious conflicts of interest in writing to the client?

(7) Has the planner drawn an instrument that exonerates him from liability that may be incurred in another role (such as the attorney who may also server as executor)?

Simultaneous representation (item 4 above) more and more frequently presents a problem when a husband and wife are both clients. Marital tensions and divorces happen. Interests that were once shared can now conflict. In *Ethical Issues for Estate Planners*, G. Bradley Rainer employs two illustrations to this point. They involve situations such as the contemplation of divorce or separation by one spouse when the other spouse may not even be aware of such plans. Another common situation involves the possible conflicts in situations in which one or both spouses have children from a previous marriage.[12]

Conflicts obviously are not limited to these examples, and many potential conflict issues are difficult to ascertain before they arise. The point is that the planner must diligently seek to determine if a potential conflict might emerge, and to take the necessary steps to avoid them where possible, and to resolve them when they cannot be avoided.

Section 17 of the Model Rules of Professional Conduct gives attorneys an important guideline that would be well for all members of a financial planning team to adopt. This section states that an attorney cannot represent clients when it is clear they have adverse interests, unless the lawyer reasonably believes he or she can do so without adversely affecting the interests of both parties and *each* client consents to representation by the same adviser following consultation.

In essence, it is better to avoid conflicts or even the appearance of conflicts, where possible, and to solve them judiciously when they arise—always with the foremost concern for the client's welfare.

competence

Competence

Perhaps one of the more difficult ethical issues to deal with is the recognition of one's own competency level. A lawyer is competent in one area, an accountant in another, an insurance agent in still another. By recognizing limits on one's competency, it could mean sharing compensation with another or others, or requiring clients to pay more for higher-quality services. Planners might be tempted to "practice law without a license." Lawyers might be tempted to recommend certain financial instruments they are not qualified to recommend. Tax accountants could be tempted to become financial advisers.

It is possible, of course, to be knowledgeable in several disciplines. Because a person is an accountant does not preclude him or her from knowing tax law, and the fact that an individual is a lawyer does not preclude him or her from recommending insurance. However, when a person gives tax advice, he or she had better be an expert in taxation. Whether they are practicing law or accountancy is not the issue. They are giving tax advice. They should have a competence in that area.

Client Competency

Under the issue of competency is another different ethical issue—the determination of the client's competency. Consider Charlie's case, as reviewed earlier. An ethical adviser should feel a sense of responsibility to determine if the client has the reasoning capability necessary to understand what is being recommended and the ability to grasp the ramifications of the plan's execution. Similarly, the adviser should make every effort to be certain the client understands laws and circumstances change and, in such an event, it may be necessary to revise the plan. Such change is frequently costly, time consuming, and generally burdensome, but it may be necessary if the plan is to produce the desired results. The adviser should periodically review the plan with an eye to the need for updating it. While not always popular with the client, the estate planner worthy of being called a professional should follow through and make certain the client understands to the best of his or her ability to comprehend.

Compliance

compliance

Compliance simply means to obey the law. Most of the time it is certainly ethically required that one obey the law.

Compliance is necessary when the internal controls or mores that provide for an orderly and just society have lost their effect. When ethical expectations are not met, society calls upon legal remedies, which unlike appeals to morality, can impose sanctions and penalize undesirable behavior in the here and now. However, because laws impose sanctions, they use fear as a motivator: "Obey me or pay the price." Therefore, although laws and regulations are necessary, they can be resented for the compliance they require because they restrict liberty and appeal to fear.

While the goal of compliance is to help improve ethical behavior, simply concerning ourselves with being in compliance and satisfying the letter of the law will not improve ethical behavior by itself. Being in compliance with the law is not the equivalent of being ethical. To equate following the law with being ethical is a mistaken view. Because compliance is targeted at meeting basic legal requirements, it emphasizes the letter of the law, rather than addressing the reasons for the law and the spirit of the law.

Simply meeting the demands of compliance does not always make it ethically. For example, consider how upsetting it was when, in response to an ad, you went to the store only to find the product was not the bargain you thought it was because you had not read the small print in the ad. Undoubtedly, the salesperson then pointed out that the small print at the bottom of the ad did, indeed, spell it all out. Of course, you still felt used and deceived. Thus, we can see that while the small print in the ad met the legal requirements and put the company in compliance, it manipulated the customer and failed to live up to the spirit of the laws against false advertising. The fact that some advertising agencies seem to take pride in seeing how far they can go while staying within the letter of the law does not make their behavior ethically laudable. It may make it clever, but thieves can be clever.

The spirit of any law for truth in advertising rests on the moral belief that a prospective customer is like you and me. That customer has a right to know what he or she is purchasing (informed consent) and should be able to make that choice freely without being manipulated. Small print violates that spirit. If the small print is there merely so a company can be in compliance, then being in compliance violates the spirit of the law. Thus, by aiming only at being in compliance we might end up being unethical.

Communication

communication

Communication is necessary at all levels. Planners must communicate with clients and with each other. All communication is time consuming if done properly. In addition to the time involved, *communication* requires honest disclosure and understanding on both the part of the planner and the client or clients. This means it also requires integrity and adequate disclosure.

Problems can arise in this area. For example, consider the situation in which a group of attorneys is asked to sign a confidentiality agreement not to divulge the specifics of a package of planning riders that was formulated for one client to other clients. A similar situation is that of accountants who do not divulge tax schemes to some of their clients because they were developed for other clients. How does such behavior square with the ethical mandate, to look out for the best interest of your client? It does not. Yet it has become a more prevalent practice. The ideal market requires full information and informed consent. Hence, it could easily be argued that a planner needs to communicate all of the latest and best information to his clients. But trust schemes are marketable commodities. What are the limits on selling them?

Cooperation

cooperation

The final ethical issue is that of *cooperation* between members of a planning team, along with the related problem of multi-disciplinary products. As discussed earlier, the codes of ethics of different professions are based on ethical principles and are, therefore, quite similar. However, there may be conflicting obligations among the different professions. An insurance agent has an obligation to the company to disclose the illness of a client, while an attorney has no such obligation. An accountant has an overriding obligation to the general public that can put the accountant at odds with an attorney who has the obligation to be an advocate for a client. At any rate, it should be clear that the members of a team have a responsibility to consult with one another for the best interest of the client, even if that means taking the time to do so.

The current debate over the ethics of multi-disciplinary estate planning practices raises all of these issues. Those who see one-stop shopping as a desirable thing, like to think of one-stop financial planning as a good thing. Why not have a firm where all of one's financial planning needs can be met by one complete staff all under one roof? Numerous accounting firms already do this. Why send the client out for a lawyer to do his work, or to a life insurance agent to get life insurance? Why not have all of this together in a multi-disciplinary firm?

But such an arrangement has its own set of problems. Does the advantage of one-stop shopping overcome the disadvantages of the loss of independence and objectivity? Does it overcome the difficulties of conflicting codes? If a person is part of a multi-disciplinary firm, must he or she use the firm's

---

Common Areas Where Ethical Issues Arise

- compensation
- confidentiality
- conflicts of interest
- competence
- compliance
- communication
- cooperation

lawyer when they know there is a better lawyer available? If an accountant's recommendation goes against the insurance experts costing the firm a large commission, will the accountant remain independent enough to recommend against? Finally, to whom does the member of the team owe loyalty—the team or the client?

All of these and more are problems that can arise in the new multidisciplinary arrangements governing financial planning firms. Are multidisciplinary firms a good idea? There are arguments on both sides.

In spite of the many issues that face the business of financial planning today, what is not at issue is the fact that every professional estate planner owes his or her first responsibility to the client.

CHAPTER REVIEW

Answers to the review questions and the self-test questions start on page 717.

Key Terms

ethical temptation
ethical dilemma
conflicts of obligations
confidentiality
prima facie duties
compensation

conflicts of interest
competence
compliance
communication
cooperation

Review Questions

2-1. Why is professionalism necessary to raise the ethical level of the estate planner's behavior?

2-2. What are the characteristics of a professional?

2-3. Why is an estate planning team usually necessary?

2-4. What is the difference between an ethical temptation and an ethical dilemma?

2-5. What questions should one ask when faced with an ethical dilemma?

2-6. What is the difference between a conflict of duty (obligation) and a conflict of interest?

2-7. Why might compensation structures create conflicting interests?

2-8. What are the common areas where ethical issues might arise in estate planning? Explain how the areas of compensation, confidentiality, conflict of interest, competency, compliance, communication, and cooperation are important in estate planning.

Self-Test Questions

T   F   2-1.   An estate planner, who is a professional, has more obligations to a client than a salesperson.

T   F   2-2.   The professional estate planner has two obligations—product knowledge and protection of the client's best interest.

T   F   2-3.   The only concern of business is to maximize profit.

T   F   2-4.   Most clever estate planners can operate on their own without benefit of an estate planning team.

T   F   2-5.   In a temptation situation, it is usually not difficult to determine what is wrong.

T   F   2-6.   An ethical dilemma is a situation where the client's interest conflicts with that of the planner.

T   F   2-7.   Ethical issues are black and white, so there are always easy answers to conflicts.

T   F   2-8.   Self-interest and selfish are synonymous.

T   F   2-9.   Contingent fees and commissions lend themselves to conflicts of interest more readily than fees for services.

T   F   2-10.   There are few or no problems with "packaged billing" or referral fees.

T   F   2-11.   Fairness, honesty, and responsibility are the only areas one needs to address when trying to resolve a dilemma.

T   F   2-12.   It is okay to talk about a specific client's affairs as long as one does not mention any names.

T   F   2-13.   Confidentiality will not conflict with communication in an estate planning team.

T   F   2-14.   The client should always win in a conflict between the client's and planner's interests.

T   F   2-15.   A conflict between one client's interest and that of another client constitutes a conflict of duty or obligation.

T   F   2-16.   It is all right for a tax accountant to become a financial advisor because being a CPA gives them sufficient competency.

T   F   2-17.   If it is legal, it is ethical.

T   F   2-18.   Simultaneous representation poses no ethical problems as long as the planner fully discloses it.

NOTES

1. John H. Burson and Lana S. McCormick, "Accreditation and the Team Approach in Estate Planning," *Trusts and Estates* (April 1995): 89.
2. Ibid., 89.
3. Ibid., 90.
4. W. D. Ross, *The Right and the Good,* chapter 2 (Oxford: Clarendon Press, 1930).
5. Edward E. Graves and Burke A. Christensen, *McGill's Legal Aspects of Life Insurance*, 3d ed. (The American College, 2002), 338–339.
6. John R. Price, "New Guidance on Ethics for Estate Planners," *Estate Planning.* Jan/Feb 1995 as referred to in Fontaine and Cooper, 1997.
7. September, 1998 issue of *Trusts & Estates Magazine*, "Estate Planning Codes of Ethics and Conduct" by G. Bradley Rainer, 46–49.
8. Andrew Wilusz, "Professionals Should Beware of Relevant Ethical Behavior," *Trusts & Estates*, May 1999, 20.
9. Paul C. Heintz, "The Ethical Question Behind Referral Fees," *Trusts & Estates*, July 1999, 28–29.
10. Ron Klein, "The Commission Commitment: Is it Right for You?" The CPA Journal, Sept. 1999, 14–15.
11. Stephan Leimberg, et al, *Tools and Techniques of Estate Planning*, 12th ed. (Cincinnati: The National Underwriter, 1992), 628.
12. G. Bradley Rainer, "Conflicts of Interest for Estate Lawyers," Ethical Issues for Estate Lawyers (Harrisburg, PA: Pennsylvania Bar Institute), 1.

3

Ownership of Property

Learning Objectives

An understanding of the material in this chapter should enable the student to

---

3-1.   Differentiate between the characteristics of real and personal property and also between the two types of personal property.

3-2.   Differentiate between the various types of ownership interests in property.

3-3.   Explain why the situs of property and the domicile of a property owner are important in estate planning.

3-4.   Explain the different ways in which property can be owned concurrently as well as the advantages and disadvantages of each form.

Chapter Outline

property

Before financial services professionals can fully develop an estate plan, they must familiarize themselves with the property of clients. This includes information about the extent of the client's ownership interests as well as the form in which various assets are held. The term *property,* as used here, encompasses anything capable of being owned. It includes actual outright ownership of material objects as well as a right to possess, enjoy, use, consume, or transfer something. The limited ability to direct who will enjoy or possess some object may also be considered a property right.

One may own property or something of value whether there is present possession or merely the right to come into possession at some designated time in the future. One can own the entire property or a limited portion of it in conjunction with others.

Property can be owned absolutely with no restrictions. It can also be owned subject to a variety of conditions or limitations—such as time duration or use restrictions—whether future or present.

Within the parameters imposed by law, one's imagination sets the bounds of the intricacies of ownership rights. The more common types of property ownership are discussed herein.

REAL PROPERTY

real property

All property falls within two broad categories—it is either real or personal (see figure 3-1).

Real property is land and anything on the land that has been permanently attached or affixed to it. Land refers to the ground and everything attached or growing on it, or otherwise intended to be regarded as going with the ground, such as trees, shrubs, and growing crops.

Real property includes buildings and fixtures that are permanently attached to and go with the land. However, it does not include such things as a mobile home if it is left in a readily moveable condition. For example, a mobile home with unremoved wheels will generally be regarded as personal property. In short, real property is all property other than personal property.

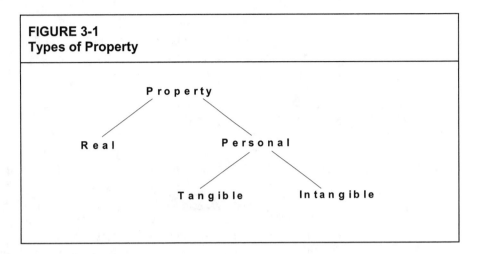

FIGURE 3-1
Types of Property

PERSONAL PROPERTY

All property other than land or any interest in land is personal property. Personal property is further characterized as either tangible or intangible.

Tangible Personal Property

tangible personal property

Tangible personal property is easy to identify. Stated simply, tangible personal property is anything that can be touched, seen, and felt. The property actually represents itself and is the actual object. For example, a chair has the look, feel, substance, and function of a chair. Tangible personal property has intrinsic value.

Property Categories

Real Property	Personal Property
• land	• tangible
• permanent	– furniture
attachments	– jewelry
to land	– cars
– trees	• intangible
– buildings	– bonds
– crops	– leases
	– stock certificates

Intangible Personal Property

intangible personal property

Other forms of personal property are known as intangibles. *Intangible personal property* has no intrinsic value in itself. The real value of intangibles is in excess of the value of the physical object that represents the property. The representation can be touched and felt, but it is not the thing itself. Some examples are stock certificates, leases, mortgages, bonds, and other such representations of property ownership.

MAJOR TYPES OF OWNERSHIP INTERESTS

estate

As explained earlier, at common law, the term estate historically referred to all manner of interests in real property only. An *estate* is defined in the *Restatement of Property* as an interest in land that "is or may become possessory" or "ownership measured in terms of duration." Today, estates in property refer to personal property as well as real property. It is possible to have absolute ownership of property without any limitations. It is also possible to own or have the right to use or possess something for a specified time, such as "use of my vacation house for 10 years." One can also receive an interest in property that will take effect only after a period of time, such as after 10 years, or after the person presently in possession dies. An individual who owns property subject to time limitations possesses an ownership right that is not perpetual or infinite. While these rights are subject to limitations, the property owner may enforce them to the extent of this individual's ownership rights. Although restricted, these rights can be presently valued by taking the limitations into consideration. For example, it is possible to use actuarial tables to place a present value on the absolute right to receive a property interest at a specified future time or when the present owner's interest ends.

Fee Simple Estates

fee simple estate

The largest, most complete interest in real estate that one can own is referred to as a *fee simple estate* or *estate in fee simple absolute*. It is an interest that belongs absolutely to an individual. It is potentially infinite in time. Most individually owned property falls into this category. Someone who owns land, a farm, or a house outright possesses a fee simple estate in that property. The owner has the absolute right to keep it during lifetime and pass it on to his or her heirs (or anyone else) at the owner's death. If the owner wishes, he or she can sell the property or give it away during lifetime.

Most property ownership falls into the category of the fee simple estate. Generally, people who own their residences possess a fee simple interest in the real estate.

Although the fee simple absolute form of ownership provides the most complete interest in property to the owner, it is incorrect to assume that no restrictions exist as to the property rights. Virtually all property interests in modern society are subject to restrictions. For example, zoning laws limit the use of property to specific functions. Also, a property owner cannot use the property for illegal purposes or to create a public nuisance. Finally, all property is subject to being taken by the government, with just compensation to the owner, by the constitutional powers of eminent domain.

Split-Ownership Interests

Life Estates

life estate

A more limited, but common, form of property ownership is a *life estate* in the property. A life estate can be measured by the life tenant's life or by the term of someone else's life, if another person's life has been designated as the measuring life. A life estate gives the owner the absolute right to possess, enjoy, or derive income from the property for the span of the measuring life, at which time the interest terminates.

Example 1:	Under his father's will, Alan Abel has been given the exclusive use and possession of his father's residence for Alan's lifetime. When Alan dies, the residence will be transferred to the beneficiary named under his father's will. Alan can live in the house until he dies, allow others to live in it, or rent it. He can also sell his interest. But his interest (or his buyer's interest) in the property will end at his death. The duration of this type of possessory interest is limited by the life of the life tenant (Alan).
Example 2:	Alan's father's will could have given Alan the exclusive use, possession, and enjoyment of the property for the life of Alan's brother, Bob. This type of transfer would still be a life estate in the property but it would be measured by the life of a person other than Alan, the life tenant. Alan's interest in the property would end when the individual who was the measuring life (Bob) died.

In contrast to an owner in fee simple, the owner of a life estate for his or her own life has no interest in the property to transfer at death. However, if the life estate is for the life of another (not the life tenant), the estate continues until the end of the measuring life and that interest can be transferred.

Although the holder of a life estate has the current rights to income from the property, the life tenant has certain duties to the remainderperson. The life tenant is bound not to waste the property. Examples of waste include

(1) failure to pay property taxes, (2) failure to insure the property against foreseeable losses, and (3) destruction of the property's income-providing source. The waste of the property creates a legal right of action by the remainderpersons against the life tenant.

Estate for Term of Years

estate for a term of years

Another type of estate that may or may not outlast a life estate is one created for a definite, limited period of time. An interest in property established for a specific duration is called an *estate for a term of years*. The period of time involved may be as short as one month or last for many years. It may extend beyond the lifetime of the tenant. The important thing to remember is that it is a right to possess and enjoy property as an owner for a definite period of time.

Example:	Suppose that Alan (in the prior two examples) instead of receiving a life estate was given exclusive rights to the residence for 10 years, after which the property would go to Bob. Thus, Alan would possess an estate for a specified time period or a term of years, instead of a life estate.

If the tenant dies before the end of the term of years, the right to possess the property for the remainder of the term will be determined by the tenant's will or the laws of intestacy. However, the tenant in possession of an estate for a term of years does not have the right to transfer the property at the end of the term of his or her property interest. This is because someone else has retained or has been granted an interest in the property that will commence when the estate for years expires. Perhaps the most common modern example of an estate for a term of years is a leasehold; however, leaseholds may contain certain restrictions (for example, on assignability) that were not part of these estates at common law.

Property Ownership Interests—Present Interests

- fee simple estate
  - largest, most complete ownership
- split ownership
  - life estate
    - duration measured by a life
  - estate for a term of years
    - specific duration period

OTHER TYPES OF PROPERTY INTERESTS

Other types of property interests that can have significance for estate planners are future interests in property. The term *future interest* may be misleading because a future interest is a present right to possess or enjoy property in the future. Some examples of future interests are remainder interests and reversionary interests.

Remainder Interests

remainder interest

A *remainder interest* in property is a present right to future enjoyment as distinguished from a present interest in property that gives an absolute, immediate right to use and enjoy the property. The remainder interest must take effect immediately upon the expiration of another estate. Remainder interests may be vested, which means that the right to receive the property in the future is presently fixed and absolute. In contrast, the remainder interest may be a contingent one, which means that it may or may not come into effect at some future date, depending on the occurrence or nonoccurrence of a condition. If a remainder interest is vested and the remainderperson (the person who possesses a remainder interest) dies before the remainder has become effective, that person has an ownership right belonging to either his or her estate or a named beneficiary. As we shall see later, those limitations may affect whether that property will be included in the interim holder's estate at death. One must take remainders into consideration when valuing an estate, particularly because possession of a vested remainder may evoke unanticipated and undesirable federal estate tax consequences.

As has been previously noted, a remainder interest is a present interest, although it comes into possession or enjoyment only in the future. It may ripen or take effect at a designated future time or on the occurrence of an event, such as the death of the present life tenant.

Example: Don is given property for his life. After that, it passes to Tom absolutely. Don possesses a life estate and Tom is the remainderperson. Tom's right to the use and possession of the property begins when Don's interest expires. In this situation, Tom has a present absolute right to take possession of the property at Don's death.

Vested or Contingent Remainders

To further complicate this type of ownership right, remainders may be either vested or contingent. A vested interest in property is an absolute and presently fixed right to possess and enjoy the property either now or in the future. Postponement of actual possession to a future time does not prevent the interest from being presently vested. When an individual's remainder interest is vested, he or she owns a present legally enforceable right to possess and enjoy that property when the interest comes into being. Note that it is a presently determined right although enjoyment may not occur until a future date. A vested absolute right to receive the entire property at some future time after the present interest ceases is known as an *indefeasibly vested remainder*. Should the remainderperson die before that time, the vested remainder interest he or she possessed at death becomes enforceable by the estate or heirs at the moment the present interest ceases.

On the other hand, a contingent property right is a more uncertain one. It may never become a possessory interest. A contingency is usually dependent on the occurrence or nonoccurrence of an event or condition. Only time will tell if the necessary contingencies occur that determine whether the right to possess and enjoy the property will actually be obtained. If the contingency does not occur, the anticipated property right dependent on the happening would not become a possessory one. On the other hand, if all conditions are met, the interest would vest and become absolute.

indefeasibly vested remainder

Example: Suppose Tom (in the prior example) will receive his interest in property only by surviving Don, who has a life estate. But if Tom dies before Don, the property will go to Ed at Don's death. Tom is a remainderperson but, in this case, he is a contingent rather than a vested remainderperson. The contingency is whether Tom will survive beyond Don's interest in the property. Ed's interest is also a contingent remainder because he will inherit the property only if Tom predeceases Don.

Reversionary Interests

reversionary interest

Another kind of interest in property is called a *reversionary* or *reversion interest*. This type of interest occurs when the owner of an estate transfers a lesser estate to another. A reversionary interest gives the owner (grantor) the right to have all or part of the property that he or she originally owned returned to the owner or the owner's estate.

The fact that the grantor retained a reversionary interest by transferring less than the total estate does not mean that the grantor retained a present right to possess and enjoy the property concurrently with the present estate owner. In fact, a reversion is only a present *retained* right to future enjoyment. Reversions are always vested.

Example:	James owns Blackacre in fee simple absolute. He conveys Blackacre to Ellen for her life. Ellen has a life estate in Blackacre. But because James conveyed less than his total interest, he retained a reversionary interest in Blackacre. Because of the reversionary interest, at Ellen's death Blackacre reverts to James, if he is living, or to his estate.

The method for determining whether a reversionary interest has been retained can be ascertained by applying the following formula: If the estate transferred is less than the estate owned, then a reversionary interest exists.

Both remainder and reversionary interests are fraught with income and estate tax consequences that may create tax traps for the unwary. Essentially these are incomplete transfers that may cause the property transferred or the income generated to be taxed to the original grantor or the grantor's estate as if the grantor were still an owner in possession. It is essential to have property transfers structured so the desired tax consequences are achieved.

Property Ownership Interests—Future Interests

- remainder interest
  - vested/contingent
  - future enjoyment
- reversionary interest
  - future return to grantor

Legal and Equitable Ownership

It is possible to have different types of rights in the same property held by different parties. One may be the legal owner without the right to the beneficial enjoyment from the property, and vice versa.

The legal owner is the one who holds legal title to the property. As a rule, the legal owner is the absolute owner and has all the rights and obligations connected with property ownership. The person with legal title is generally the one in possession. He or she has the full rights of use, enjoyment, and control over the property. Technically, an absolute owner holds both legal and equitable title.

There are certain circumstances, however, in which legal and equitable ownership are split between different parties. A common example of this division of title occurs when property is held in trust. By definition, under our trust laws, legal and equitable title are separated between parties. The

---

Legal vs. Equitable (Beneficial) Ownership

Legal Title	Equitable Title
fiduciary (trustee/ guardian of property)	beneficiary
– has possession of property – has right to invest/manage property	– is entitled to property benefits

---

trustee is the party who holds legal title. According to the terms of the trust, the trustee must invest and manage the property under the fiduciary standards established by state law. However, the income generated by the trustee's efforts is then distributed to or held for the benefit of others (the beneficiaries) who hold equitable title.

The person with equitable title to property is the one who is entitled to all of the benefits from the property. This refers to such benefits as the right to use, possess, or enjoy the property, as well as the right to have income from the property.

Equitable ownership and beneficial ownership mean the same thing and are sometimes used interchangeably. The equitable owner of a trust is the beneficiary of a trust for whose benefit the property is being managed. As long as the trust continues, the trustee will hold legal title (with all the attendant fiduciary responsibilities), and the beneficiaries will be the equitable or beneficial owners only. Upon termination of the trust and final distribution of the trust property to the ultimate beneficiaries, both titles are united in the beneficiaries who become absolute owners.

SITUS

situs

    Situs refers to the place where property is located or kept. Because each state has an interest in the welfare of its residents as well as in the protection of property located within its borders, all transfers of real and personal property are subject to state law. Under both state statute and local ordinances, state and local governmental authorities regulate and tax all real

---

Situs—Location of Property

- real estate (taxable *only* by state of location)
- tangible personal property (taxable *generally* by state of location)
- intangible personal property (may be taxable by any state having a reasonable connection to the property)

---

estate within their jurisdiction. The state has this power over real property within its borders, irrespective of where the property owner actually lives. The situs or location of real property is particularly important to the estate planner because all real property, as well as tangible personal property, is subject to the laws and taxing powers of the jurisdiction in which it is located.

DOMICILE

domicile

Another important factor to consider when developing an estate plan is the domicile of an individual. *Domicile* is the place that individuals consider to be their permanent residence and to which they intend to return if they have temporarily left. Individuals may have personal residences in more than one state. While it was once thought that people could have only one domicile, the U.S. Supreme Court has decided otherwise as shown later in this chapter under the heading "Multiple Taxation." Generally, a husband and wife are presumed to have the same domicile.

Domicile—Property Owner's Primary Residence

- tangible personal property (taxable *generally* by state of owner's domicile)
- intangible personal property (*possibly* also taxable by state of owner's domicile)

When a person dies, the estate is usually probated, distributed, and taxed under the laws of the state in which he or she is domiciled. One's domicile becomes significant because there is great variation among state death tax laws. Simply put, inheritance and estate tax laws imposed by different states are not uniform. A state has an interest in claiming that an individual is domiciled within its borders in order to collect tax revenue.

Depending on the nature of a person's property, it may be taxed (1) by the state of domicile, (2) by the state of location, or (3) by both. Specific types of property are discussed below.

Real Estate

Real estate is taxed solely by the state where the property is located. This results from the principle that one state does not have jurisdiction to take action on real property located in another state. Courts have consistently followed this principle and prevented states from taxing real property located in other states. Another example of this principle is that succession of real property is also determined by the laws of the situs state.

> *Example:*   Ted was domiciled in state X at the time of death but owned real property in state Y. Ted's will is invalid under the laws of state X but valid under the laws of Y. The real property in Y passes under the provisions of Ted's will, but Ted's other property passes under the intestate succession laws of X.

Tangible Personal Property

While it is simple to determine the situs of real estate, tangible personal property may be another matter because it is transportable. Generally, tangible personal property is taxed by the state where the property is kept. Depending on the local law, it may be taxed also by the state of domicile. The situs of tangible personal property is the place where its use is fixed for a reasonable time for ordinary and customary use purposes. Under the theory that all property belonging to a domiciliary is taxable by the state of domicile, that state may also attempt to tax tangible personal property of a decedent located elsewhere.

Intangible Personal Property

In some instances, local jurisdictions also have an interest in the taxation of the intangible personal property of their residents as well as nonresidents. Intangibles are generally taxed by the state of domicile, regardless of their location or connection with another state. It makes no difference where intangibles are kept. Any state with a reasonable connection or nexus to the property may impose a tax on its value.

> *Example:*   If an individual is a resident of Pennsylvania but owns stock in a corporation in Delaware, the state of the corporate domicile (in this case, Delaware) can impose a tax on the transfer of shares of a nonresident stockholder, if its laws so provide. Some states, such as Pennsylvania, exempt intangible personal property of nonresidents from taxation when the property is transferred at death. However, many states (such as Pennsylvania) will tax the intangibles of a resident although the property is situated outside the state.

Establishing Domicile

There are a number of things an individual can do to establish domicile in a particular state.

Some examples that indicate intent to establish domicile are voter registration, automobile registration, driver's license, location of bank accounts and safe-deposit boxes, situs of principal residence, passport, reference to domicile in will, address listed with the Social Security Administration, and payment of property as well as income taxes. In some states, a special form may be filed as a declaration of domicile to establish primary residence. The place where financial and legal advisers are located will assist in determining the state of domicile.

While an individual ideally should sever ties with a former state of domicile, many individuals (particularly those who spend winter months in a warmer climate) may retain residences and other connections in their former states. If so, care should be taken to reside in the state of intended domicile for more than one-half of the year or at least for more time than in any other state. An individual may also establish memberships in social clubs and religious organizations in a particular state to indicate intent of domicile.

Multiple Taxation

Because each state has its own revenue laws and public policy, state death taxation is locally determined. There is no simple way to predict the likelihood of double taxation of property passing at death. It is conceivable that more than one state will attempt to tax the same property. In a well-known Supreme Court case, *In re Dorrance Estate*, the Supreme Court held that it was legal for more than one state to have an interest in the property of an individual.

The statutes of the states involved should be carefully researched when an individual owns property in more than one state, which would subject the property to taxation under that state's jurisdiction. If the courts of two different states have each made a lawful finding of domicile, there is no constitutional barrier to taxation by both states.

Individuals who split their residences between two states should take a definitive position as to the state where they wish their property to be taxed at death. Knowledge of state death tax laws is critical for proper premortem planning. In some instances, the only death taxes due will be state taxes because the federal estate tax deductions and the increased applicable credit amount will eliminate estate taxation at the federal level for all but larger estates.

CONCURRENT OWNERSHIP

Property can be owned entirely by one individual, thereby making that individual the sole owner. A person may also own a portion of the property. Partial interests either may be segregated and delineated or may consist of an undivided interest in the entire property.

> **Example:**   A person can own an undivided one-third interest in real estate. Likewise, a person can own 50 percent of the stock of corporation X. In both cases, the value of the interest owned is measured as a percentage of the whole.

There are several ways to own property in conjunction with other individuals. Following is a discussion of the more common types of co-ownership:

In most common-law states, there are generally three possible ways to own property in conjunction with others. They are (1) tenancies in common, (2) joint tenancies with right of survivorship, and (3) tenancies by the entirety. Each of these categories has distinguishing features. The rights of the co-owners vary depending on the form of co-ownership that exists. Each form of concurrent ownership is governed by local law. In addition, there may be federal, estate, gift, or income tax consequences flowing from the transfer of a co-owner's interest either during lifetime or at death.

Understanding and properly structuring ownership of property interests is critical to the establishment of a carefully designed estate plan for an individual client. At best, there is both mystery and misunderstanding regarding the rights as well as limitations of various forms of co-ownership.

Tenancies in Common

tenancy in common

Property owned concurrently by two or more persons who may be, but are not necessarily, related is generally called a *tenancy in common*. There may be any number of owners who hold property as tenants in common. Each tenant's share is an undivided part of the entire property. However, each tenant need not own an equal share with the other cotenants—ownership interests may or may not be equally divided. Each tenant's share may be based on an allocation that was agreed on by the cotenants. A common method for division of shares may be the percentage contribution that each tenant in common made to the purchase price of the property.

Unless restricted by contract or agreement with the other co-owners, each tenant is free to sell or dispose of his or her interest in the property to whomever the tenant wishes. The tenant does not require the consent or even the knowledge of the other cotenants. In other words, each cotenant is free to be divested of his or her property interest by sale, gift, or will. If the cotenant holds an interest in a tenancy in common and dies without a will, that individual's interest will be distributed to his or her heirs under the intestate laws of the state in which the cotenant resides. In legal parlance, interest of a tenant in common as described above is said to be freely alienable (capable of being transferred), descendible (capable of being passed by descent or inherited), and devisable (capable of being bequeathed).

Concurrent Ownership—Tenancy in Common

- Ownership is by two or more related or unrelated parties.
- Ownership interests may be unequal.
- Property can be real or personal.
- Each ownership portion is an undivided part of the whole property.
- The owner has the freedom to sell, dispose, exchange, gift, or will his or her interest.

A cotenant is generally treated as a separate owner of his or her share of the property for income tax purposes. Each cotenant is entitled to his or her share of any income generated by the property. If the cotenant's interest is sold, gain or loss will be realized as though the cotenant had owned the property individually. A tenant in common will have a certain basis in the property depending on his or her proportionate interest in and contribution to the property.

To the extent that one tenant has received a greater proportionate interest than his or her contribution to the tenancy, a gift has been made from the cotenant who contributed a greater proportionate amount to the cotenancy at its creation. A gift may also occur if the property is sold and a cotenant receives a greater share of the proceeds than his or her contribution represents.

Generally, all tenants are obligated to pay expenses for maintaining or operating the property in proportion to their respective interests. In addition, state law may provide that the cotenant not in possession may be entitled to receive a proportionate amount of rent from the cotenant in possession of the property.

One of the most important characteristics of the tenancy in common is that there are no survivorship rights. Each tenant's interest in the property may be left to the tenant's heirs, and at death, the tenant's gross estate will include the fair market value of his or her proportionate interest.

When a cotenant sells or otherwise disposes of his or her interest in a tenancy in common, the new owner will become a tenant in common with the remaining cotenants. At the time of sale, the cotenant will realize gain or loss on his or her share that will be treated as if it was separate property. If a property is indivisible, a tenant in common may cause the entire property to be sold by a partition sale under local law. In that case, the sale proceeds will be distributed in accordance with the respective interests owned by each cotenant. Use of a forced sale to partition the property at auction will probably not generate a price equal to the true market value of the property potentially obtainable in a private sale.

A tenancy in common may also be created by operation of law when a joint tenancy is severed by agreement of the parties, by divorce of the joint tenants, or by the sale of a joint tenant's interest.

Joint Tenancies with Right of Survivorship

joint tenancy with right of survivorship

Individuals are often intrigued by ownership as *joint tenants with right of survivorship* because they have heard that joint tenancies are nonprobate property. There is a common belief that no tax consequences stem from such jointly held property. Some people think that the elimination of probate fees, including executors' commissions and lawyers' fees, outweighs other considerations. In truth, there are some positive aspects of joint ownership with survivorship rights, especially convenience. In addition, some married couples may derive a sense of unity and partnership from owning some or all of their property in this form of joint ownership. However, as will be seen, joint ownership with survivorship rights also involves giving up some rights in the property and forgoing much flexibility in estate planning.

qualified joint interests

nonqualified joint interests

Joint tenancy with right of survivorship is similar to tenancies in common in that there may be two or more joint tenants. Joint tenants may or may not be related to each other. Spousal joint tenancies with right of survivorship and tenancies by the entireties are referred to as *qualified joint interests* under the Code. However, if a third party (nonspouse) is a joint tenant, all of the joint interests are *nonqualified joint interests*. Each joint tenant is considered to be an owner of the entire property subject to the rights of the other joint owners. Therefore, all joint tenants with right of survivorship must have equal rights and obligations with respect to the property. Unlike tenancies in common there cannot be disproportionate ownership: that is, one joint tenant with right of survivorship cannot have a two-thirds interest while another has a one-third interest.

During lifetime, each joint tenant may sell his or her interest in the property without the other joint tenants joining in the conveyance, but such a transaction will sever the joint tenancy with right of survivorship. One joint tenant may also sell his or her interest in the property to the other joint owners. On severance, the form of ownership may change to another form of joint ownership—generally tenants in common—or the property itself may be divided among the joint tenants. If the property is equitably divisible, a joint owner may receive his or her share of the property free of the other joint owners by physically partitioning the property. However, if the property is not equitably divisible, it must be sold and the proceeds divided.

The primary difference between tenancies in common and jointly held property with right of survivorship is that jointly held property passes to the surviving joint tenants at the death of one of the joint owners. When there are more than two joint tenants, the property ultimately passes to the last surviving joint tenant, who, as sole surviving owner, has all rights in the property. The last surviving joint tenant is free to hold or dispose of it in whatever way desirable. If the last surviving joint tenant owns it at death, the full value will be included in his or her gross estate. Jointly held property is not transferred by will. It passes to the surviving joint tenants by operation of law outside of the will. That is what is meant by the phrase *right of survivorship*. Beneficiaries of a deceased joint tenant other than the surviving joint tenant(s) have no rights in the property. An advantage of a joint tenancy with right of survivorship is that the property passes free of probate in many states. If so, the expenses connected with probate, such as executor's commissions or attorney's fees, may be eliminated. Jointly held property will be includible in the gross estate of the deceased joint tenant for federal estate tax purposes to the extent of that tenant's contribution to or interest for state death tax purposes as well, whereas there are those states that exempt a joint tenant's interest from state death taxes where the joint tenants were married.

Concurrent Ownership—Joint Tenancy with Right of Survivorship

- Ownership is by two or more related or unrelated parties.
- Property can be real or personal.
- Ownership interests must be equal.
- At death, interest passes to surviving tenant(s).
- Ownership can be severed.

Sometimes it is difficult to determine whether a co-ownership of property is a tenancy in common or a joint tenancy with right of survivorship. Local law generally favors tenancies in common over joint tenancies with right of survivorship. Any ambiguity in the form of ownership will be construed as a tenancy in common rather than as a joint tenancy. A jointly owned tenancy should include in the title the phrase *with right of survivorship* to make the intent clear. When a married couple is divorced, their jointly held property will generally be converted to a tenancy in common, unless they decide, by agreement, to hold the property as joint tenants with right of survivorship on a nonrelated basis.

When a joint tenancy is created and one of the joint tenants contributes more than his or her share of personal funds to acquire the jointly held property, that joint tenant makes a gift to the other joint tenant. Also, if one of the joint owners pays more than his or her share of either mortgage payments or the cost of maintenance and operation of the property, that joint owner is making a gift to the other joint tenants. This is true only if the contributing joint tenant cannot regain the property without the other joint tenant participating in the transfer. If the contributing joint tenant has full right of unilateral withdrawal, such as from a joint bank account, no gift is made at the creation of such a joint tenancy. It is only when the donee-joint tenant withdraws the jointly held property that a gift is made.

Example: If Ms. Jones deposits money in a joint savings account that she opens in both her name and her son's name, she has not made a gift until her son withdraws some of the money for his own use. The donee-joint tenant must receive some benefit from the property before a completed gift is made.

Bank Accounts

Each state has its own laws with regard to the legal relationship between joint tenants with right of survivorship who own bank accounts, savings bonds, or securities. If a joint bank account is created, each joint owner owns a proportionate part of the account balance and is entitled to receive his or her proportionate amount of the interest income, on which he or she is taxed (unless it is tax-exempt income). Of course, if the account is owned by spouses who file a joint return, there are not any income-splitting advantages. With other types of accounts, the interest should be reportable by each joint tenant in proportion to the amount the joint tenant contributed to the account. Banks usually report the income as taxable to the joint tenant whose Social Security number is on the account. The most common joint tenancy bank account is often called a revocable account. There is no gift if a person uses personal funds to open a joint bank account. A gift is considered made only when the other joint owner (the donee) makes withdrawals. However, there are also joint tenant bank accounts that vest immediately. The accounts provide the joint tenants with equal interests at the time the account is established.

Government Savings Bonds

When a Series EE (or E) or Series HH (or H) government savings bond is held in joint ownership, there is no gift when the bond is purchased because the joint owner who contributed the funds can cash in the bond at any time and get his or her money back. As with joint bank accounts, a gift occurs when the donee-joint tenant redeems the bond and retains a greater share of the proceeds than he or she had contributed to the purchase price. At that time, a gift is made from the contributing joint tenant to the donee-joint tenant equal to the redemption value of the bond reduced by the percentage contribution to the purchase price that the donee-joint tenant made.

Safe-Deposit Boxes

When a safe-deposit box is held in joint ownership, both joint tenants have access to the contents of the box. This does not mean that the contents of the box would be considered owned in equal shares by each joint tenant.

The contents of the box remain the property of the joint tenant who deposited them. Joint tenants of a safe-deposit box must comply with the joint-ownership requirements of local law with regard to the ownership of the box contents. Depending on the nature of the contents, there should be a written document specifying that a legal transfer from the sole owner to the other joint lessee of the box has occurred if they intend to own the contents equally as joint owners. If true joint ownership with right of survivorship is created, the income and gift tax consequences will depend on the type of property that has been thus transferred in writing.

Securities

Basically the above types of joint ownership (bank accounts and government savings bonds) are revocable creations that do not invoke gift tax ramifications at the inception of the joint tenancy. However, the treatment for joint ownership of securities is different, because there is a formal agreement between the joint owners of securities and the broker.

If the securities are registered in the names of the co-owners as joint tenants with right of survivorship and not as tenants in common, a gift occurs from the contributing joint tenant to the donee-joint tenant when the securities are transferred to the account or purchased for the account. However, the result is not the same if the account has been registered in street name. The term *street name* describes securities held in the name of a broker or another party rather than in the name of the owner(s). There is an IRS ruling that holds that no gift occurs on the creation of a joint street name account when one of the joint tenants has furnished more than one-half of the consideration. A gift occurs when the other party withdraws from the account more than his or her proportionate contribution to the account, because securities registered in individuals' names as joint tenants require the signature of both to sell the securities. However, the signatures of both are not required when the account is in street name.

As to income tax consequences, if securities are registered in joint names, each joint tenant is entitled to a proportionate share of the interest income under local law. Again, if the joint tenants are husband and wife, it is likely that they will file a joint return that would make allocation of income irrelevant.

To summarize, the financial services professional should keep in mind that joint tenancies may have gift tax ramifications depending on the nature of the property held as joint tenants with right of survivorship, when there has been a disproportionate contribution to the property by one of the joint owners. No gift will occur if the contributing tenant can, at any time, withdraw the property contributed and regain sole possession of it, because the transfer is incomplete as long as the contributing joint tenant retains dominion and control over the property. A gift will occur when the noncontributing or donee-joint tenant withdraws from the joint tenancy a greater proportion than the amount contributed. At that time, the gift becomes irrevocable and complete. However, in the case of joint tenancies that require both signatures to sell or transfer property, a gift will be made at the time the property is transferred to a joint tenancy. If the joint tenants are husband and wife, there is no gift tax liability, although one spouse may have contributed more than one-half of the property to the joint tenancy. This is so because the Economic Recovery Tax Act (ERTA) of 1981 defines a married couples as a single economic unit. Although a gift has been made from one spouse to another, the unlimited gift tax marital deduction applies so that there will be no tax to pay. Furthermore, no gift tax return is required for transfers from one spouse to a joint-ownership arrangement with the other spouse.

Tenancies by the Entirety

**tenancy by the
entirety**

A *tenancy by the entirety* is similar to a joint tenancy with right of survivorship although it is more restrictive. It is limited to co-ownership of property held by a husband and wife. By definition, a tenancy by the entirety exists only during marriage and will be terminated upon divorce of the spouses. Local law will determine some of the features of a tenancy by the entirety. For example, in most states each tenant is entitled to one-half of the income from the property. However, in those states still governed by common law, the husband may be entitled to all the net income from the property. At the present time, almost half the states and Washington DC have some type of tenancy by the entirety property interest.

The primary difference between a tenancy by the entirety and jointly held property with right of survivorship is that neither spouse may unilaterally terminate the tenancy by conveying his or her interest to a third party during lifetime. In contrast to the types of ownership previously described, a tenancy by the entirety cannot be severed by selling either party's undivided interest without the consent of the other tenant. Husband and wife must join in a sale or other conveyance to third parties.

Because there are variations under local law with regard to each of these forms of co-ownership, the financial services professional must review the local law before advising clients regarding the rights and obligations of each form of co-ownership. Generally, it will be presumed that the form of ownership is a tenancy in common if co-owners are not married. However, if they are a married couple, a tenancy by the entirety may be presumed. Some jurisdictions insist that the words *right of survivorship* are necessary in order to construe the co-ownership as a joint tenancy or tenancy by the entirety. In many states today, tenancies by the entirety are limited to co-ownership of real estate by a husband and wife. Some states have completely abolished the tenancy by the entirety form of ownership.

Concurrent Ownership—Tenancy by the Entirety

- Ownership can be only by married couples.
- Property can be real or personal property.
- At death, interest passes to the surviving spouse.
- Ownership cannot be severed without consent of both spouses.

Advantages and Disadvantages of Joint Tenancies and Tenancies by the Entirety

There are both advantages and disadvantages to joint tenancies with right of survivorship and tenancies by the entirety beyond tax considerations. Advantages of these forms of joint ownership include the following:

- Under most state laws, property owned as tenants by the entirety generally cannot be reached by creditors of one of the tenants. Such property can be reached only by joint creditors. (Note, however, that in a recent U.S. Supreme Court case, a federal tax lien against one tenant by the entirety was held to attach to the entirety property [*United States v. Craft*, 122 S. Ct. 1414, 2002]).

- These forms of ownership are convenient for certain types of assets, such as bank accounts, because either tenant has access to the account.

- Joint tenancies and tenancies by the entirety may give one or both of the tenants a feeling of security. This is especially true when the owners are spouses and one spouse has contributed most of the funds.

- When one tenant dies, the property passes directly to the surviving joint tenant. There are no probate delays. There may be little or no administrative and transfer cost. The property will remain fully accessible to the surviving owner.

- In many states, these forms of property ownership between spouses pass free of state death taxes.

- Because such property passes by operation of law and not under will, it is a private arrangement and not open for public scrutiny.

While these forms of ownership may be both convenient and psychologically comforting, they may not constitute the best estate plan for all persons and may severely impair an appropriate estate plan when used improperly. As an individual's estate increases, a review and analysis of such property should be made to determine if it is the best form of ownership for the individual's needs.

There are also disadvantages inherent in these jointly held property arrangements. Some of the disadvantages of these forms of joint ownership include the following:

- Under most state laws, property owned as joint tenants with right of survivorship can be reached by creditors of an individual joint tenant.
- There are potential gift taxes at the creation of some of these property ownership interests. (*Note:* transfers may qualify for the unlimited marital gift tax deduction.)
- There may be additional federal estate taxation. The entire value of property held jointly with right of survivorship, except for spousal joint tenancies created after December 31, 1976, may be in the estate of the first joint owner to die. The entire property will then be owned by the surviving tenant and will be fully subject to estate taxation again at the survivor's death. (*Note:* transfers may qualify for the unlimited estate tax marital deduction.)
- The surviving tenant will gain full control over the property and may ultimately dispose of it in any way desired. The decedent's will, trust, or other dispositive documents will have no effect on the disposition of the jointly held property.
- The decedent's estate may be faced with a liquidity problem. Property passing directly to the surviving tenant may not be made available to the decedent's estate for the payment of taxes, debts, or expenses.

It has been stressed that there are both tax and nontax reasons for the creation of different forms of property ownership when held by more than one individual concurrently. There is no one answer with regard to arrangements of property. Generally, a combination of different ownership arrangements will provide the best results in good estate planning. One important factor to examine is the size of the relative estates of potential co-owners of property.

Joint Tenancies with Right of Survivorship and Tenancies by the Entirety

General Advantages	General Disadvantages
• limited access by creditors of one tenant by the entirety	• access by creditors of one joint tenant with right of survivorship
• convenience	
• feeling of security	• gift tax potential
• avoidance of probate delay	• additional estate tax potential
• reduction in administrative and transfer costs	• full control by survivor
• possible avoidance of state death taxes	• insufficient liquidity potential
• privacy	

COMMUNITY PROPERTY

Another form of co-ownership limited to interests held between husband and wife that has particular significance today because of our mobile society is community property. Only 9 of the 50 states are community-property states. The laws of the particular community-property state in which a married couple resides must be examined to determine accurately the specific effect on a married couple's property ownership. Each state has developed its own special variations that make it difficult to generalize about community-property laws for all nine states.

The nine community-property states and the nature and tax treatment of community property are discussed in detail in chapter 4.

CHAPTER REVIEW

Answers to the review questions and the self-test questions start on page 717.

Key Terms

property	reversionary interest
real property	situs
tangible personal property	domicile
intangible personal property	tenancy in common
estate	joint tenancy with right of
fee simple estate	survivorship
life estate	qualified joint interests
estate for a term of years	nonqualified joint interests
remainder interest	tenancy by the entirety
indefeasibly vested remainder	

Review Questions

3-1. Explain what is meant by the real value of intangible personal property.

3-2. There are many types of estates and interests in real property. In each of the following instances, state briefly the type of estate or interest in real property that is created:
   a. Alex grants land to Ben and his heirs forever.
   b. Alex grants land to Ben for life and, upon Ben's death, to Chris and his heirs forever.
   c. Alex gives Ben the right to use his land for 10 years.

3-3. Assume John gives Sally the absolute right to use his beach house for her life. Upon Sally's death, all rights in the beach house will be returned to John or his estate. What type of property interests do John and Sally each have?

3-4. Explain how a person can hold legal title to property but not possess an equitable interest in the property. Give an example of this type of ownership.

3-5. Differentiate between domicile and situs, indicating the steps an individual can take to establish domicile.

3-6. Gloria Gershwin was domiciled in Alabama. She also owned real property in Florida, tangible personal property in New Hampshire, and intangible personal property in Texas. Which states have an interest in taxing these various properties at her death?

3-7. What rights does a co-owner of property held as tenants in common have with respect to
   a. selling one's interest to a third party
   b. giving it away to a third party
   c. leaving it to beneficiaries at death

3-8. At the death of a cotenant in a tenancy in common, what is the relationship of the cotenant's heirs and the surviving cotenant?

3-9. How does jointly owned property with rights of survivorship differ from a tenancy by the entirety with regard to
   a. a sale of the property during lifetime
   b. a gift to a third person
   c. a transfer on the death of one of the tenants

3-10. Explain the ramifications of having each of the following types of property owned jointly with right of survivorship:
   a. bank accounts
   b. government savings bonds
   c. securities

3-11. What are the advantages and disadvantages of owning property jointly with right of survivorship?

Self-Test Questions

T F 3-1. Real property consists of land and anything that has been permanently attached to it.

T F 3-2. All property that is not real property is categorized as personal property.

T F 3-3. A fee simple estate may not be left to a property owner's heirs.

T F 3-4. The owner of a life estate in property has no interest remaining at death to leave to heirs.

T F 3-5. An estate for a term of years is an interest in property for a specified period of time.

T F 3-6. A leasehold interest is an example of an estate for a term of years.

T   F   3-7.   A future interest in property is always contingent.

T   F   3-8.   A reversionary interest exists upon the disposition of property only if no rights in the property have been retained.

T   F   3-9.   A person who has legal ownership of property also automatically has equitable ownership of the property.

T   F   3-10.   The situs of property is generally considered to be the domicile of the property owner.

T   F   3-11.   An estate is generally probated and distributed according to the laws of the decedent's state of domicile.

T   F   3-12.   Tangible and intangible property differ to some degree with respect to the jurisdiction in which such property will be subject to state death taxes.

T   F   3-13.   When a tenancy in common exists, neither cotenant may sell his or her interest in the property without the other cotenant's permission.

T   F   3-14.   Joint tenancies with right of survivorship cannot be severed during the lifetime of either joint tenant.

T   F   3-15.   For federal gift tax purposes, when a person uses his or her own funds to open a joint bank account with someone else, that person has made a completed gift to the other party at the time the funds are deposited in the account.

T   F   3-16.   When property is placed in a safe deposit box that is jointly rented, the ownership of the property within is unaffected by the form of rental of the deposit box.

T   F   3-17.   A tenancy by the entirety is a form of co-ownership in which each tenant may pass the property to anyone he or she chooses when he or she dies.

T   F   3-18.   A tenancy by the entirety held by a husband and wife is not severable by an individual tenant in most states.

T   F   3-19.   One characteristic of property held jointly with right of survivorship or by the entirety is that it passes to the survivor by operation of law, rather than under a will.

T   F   3-20.   Community-property laws are uniformly applied in community-property states.

4

Community Property

Learning Objectives

An understanding of the material in this chapter should enable the student to

---

4-1. Identify the community-property states.

4-2. Describe the nature of community property.

4-3. Explain the general presumption as to marital property.

4-4. Explain how transfer taxes are imposed on marital property.

4-5. Explain why changing domicile between common-law and community-property states can pose estate planning problems.

Chapter Outline

HISTORICAL ORIGINS

The community-property system currently in use in nine states is based on Spanish and French civil law pertaining to marital property rights.

Brought to America by Spanish and French colonists, the ancient concept was grounded in a precept of equality. Because a marriage is a community consisting of two marital partners who, through their joint labors, industry, and efforts, contribute to the prosperity of the marriage, both spouses possess an equal right to the property and its benefits.

The planner must be aware that, while the community-property states share some common features and definitions, there is no one uniform community-property system. Although the fundamental aspects of community property law are similar in the different states, many differences have evolved because of refinements by state legislatures. The estate planner should guard against the expectation that specific aspects of one community-property state carry over to another community-system state.

Arizona, California, Idaho, Louisiana, Nevada, New Mexico, Texas, and Washington are the traditional eight community-property states. Wisconsin is recognized as the ninth community-property state since its version of the Uniform Marital Property Act (UMPA), incorporating many community-property concepts, became effective in January 1986. Instead of the term *community property,* Wisconsin and Texas use the term *marital property.* While Louisiana still closely follows the civil law, the other states have adopted some traditional American common-law principles to meet changes in societal and economic needs. In addition to the above mentioned nine community-property states, Alaska has statutory provisions allowing Alaskan residents to elect community-property status to the extent provided in a community-property agreement or a community-property trust. In 1998,

Community-Property States

★ **Arizona**
★ **California**
★ **Idaho**
★ **Louisiana**
★ **Nevada**
★ **New Mexico**
★ **Texas**
★ **Washington**
★ **Wisconsin (UMPA)**
★ **Alaska (elective)**

Alaska passed a statute permitting nonresidents of Alaska to transfer property into a trust, referred to as a community-property trust. If the trust has one or more Alaskan trustees, any portion or all of the trust property is treated for tax purposes as community property. Generally, these trusts are created so that some or all of the trust property receives a step-up in basis (discussed in a later chapter) at the death of the first spouse.

NATURE OF COMMUNITY PROPERTY

separate property

The community-property principle recognizes the existence of community ownership of property by husband and wife. In essence each spouse is deemed to own a one-half interest in property acquired during the marriage regardless of which spouse actually acquired, earned, gained, or is otherwise responsible for ownership of the property. This is not to say that all property belonging to a married couple is necessarily community property. A husband and wife can own property separately in their own individual rights. For instance, property owned by either spouse prior to the marriage continues to be the spouse's separately owned property during the marriage (unless affirmative steps are taken by the owner spouse to change the ownership status of the separate property). Property inherited by or gifted to an individual spouse during marriage also retains separate property characterization. Wisconsin uses the terminology of the UMPA and refers to separate property as individual property.[1] For purposes of this chapter, the general terms *community property* and *separate property* are used.

Community Property

Property interests acquired during marriage are presumed to be owned equally by spouses in community-property states.

PRESUMPTIONS AS TO MARITAL PROPERTY

Generally speaking, the underlying community-property presumption is that property owned by a husband and a wife belongs to both of them in equal shares, except for that property that can be proven to belong to a spouse separately. Concerning certain issues such as termination of a marriage by death or divorce, the rights of creditors, tort liability, and tax treatment, the community-property system generally presumes that all property owned during a marriage is community property. This presumption is not conclusive, however, if the separate status of property can be proven or if there are other relevant facts that rebut the presumption. In other words, the separate property of a spouse must be specifically designated as separate property to retain its noncommunity character. The fact that property is titled in an individual spouse's name or was acquired with one spouse's separate funds may not in itself be sufficient evidence to rebut the community presumption. The facts and circumstances surrounding the use of the property and the conduct of the parties toward the property may be more evidentiary than the title or the source of funds for its initial purchase. Common-law states (that is, non-community-property states) rely directly on deeds and certificates of title to determine ownership.

transmutation

In addition, practically all the community-property states grant spouses the power to determine or change the character of their property as community or separate. For instance, Texas previously only allowed community property to be transmuted to separate property. Recently, however, Texas law permits separate property to be transmuted to community property.[2] Therefore, spouses may change community property to separate property and vice versa. The legal term for voluntarily changing the nature of property is *transmutation* (in Wisconsin, *classification* or *reclassification*). Depending on the type of property and particular circumstances, transmutation may result from contract (bilaterally) or gifts (unilaterally). There are two important transmutation restrictions, however. First, federal law obligations cannot be circumvented by transmuting property; and, second, a transmutation that is effective between spouses may not be effective against third parties like creditors.

The best way to overcome the general presumption favoring community property is for married partners who reside in or move in and out of community-property states to keep complete, organized, and accurate records of their personal financial matters. Another way to secure property ownership is for couples to file an inventory of assets at the time of marriage to serve as an official record of separate identity. Note that in some community-property states, especially California, the general presumption is less difficult to rebut when the marriage is of relatively short duration. In some states it is possible for individuals to waive their rights in community property in a prenuptial agreement. Although the general community presumption in and of itself is quite straightforward, different circumstances readily lend themselves to more involved issues.

Example: Mary and Anthony became engaged and planned to marry the following spring. They made purchases for their new home and their future together. Although Mary wanted to furnish their home with antiques, Anthony felt that antiques were too expensive and impractical. Before the wedding Mary, the wealthier of the two, decided to purchase the antiques with her own separate funds, and she arranged for delivery to take place after the wedding. In this case, arguments could be made both that the furniture is separate property and that it is community property. Was the furniture acquired before or after the marriage? Although in this scenario the presumption of community property could easily be rebutted, Mary may have intended the property to be community marital property. If the antiques were partially paid for with Mary's separate funds prior to the marriage and the balance paid with community funds after the wed-ding, are the antiques still Mary's separate property? If the antiques appreciate in value and are later sold at a gain, are the profits community property or separate property?

Separate Property

- property acquired prior to marriage
- property acquired by gift
- property acquired by inheritance, bequest, devise
- property acquired in a court award
- property transmuted into separate property

While earnings from the labor of a husband and a wife are nearly always community property, community-property states are almost evenly divided in how they treat "rents, issues, or profits" of separate property realized during marriage. Idaho, Louisiana, Texas, and Wisconsin generally treat the rents, issues, and profits generated by separate property acquired during a marriage as community property but hold that natural increases in the size or value, that is, appreciation, of separate property due to market changes and inflation continue to be separate property. Therefore, if the separate property of community spouses is sold, the gain on the sale continues to be separate property. If the gain is used to acquire other property, the newly acquired property is separate property. In the remaining states, rents, issues, and profits of separate property retain a separate-property identity, but increases in value resulting from community labor and effort belong to the community. In all community-property jurisdictions, however, income and earnings generated by separate property prior to marriage remain separate, and income and earnings produced by community property constitute community property. It is not difficult to imagine the problems that can arise with regard to the benefits flowing from community property. The spouse claiming the separate nature of property has the burden to overcome the community presumption with adequate proof. Evidence of separate ownership is difficult to provide if adequate records are not kept, particularly when there has been commingling of separate and community funds and other assets over the years. Tracing the property's separate identity may be virtually impossible in such cases.

CLASSIFICATION RULES

The general classification rule is known as the *time-of-acquisition rule* or the *inception-of-title rule*. This rule provides that the character of an asset, separate or community, is established at the time the asset is acquired, and once established, the character is not altered by later events. So, if prior to a marriage one of the parties acquires property, it is and remains the acquiring spouse's separate property. If during the marriage the property is improved using community funds, the property is still the acquiring spouse's asset, but the nonacquiring spouse may have a right to reimbursement for one-half of the community funds spent on the improvements.

Example 1:	At the time of H and W's marriage, H owned several acres of unimproved land valued at $15,000. Using community funds, H and W built a home for $175,000 and later improved the residence by adding several bedrooms, bathrooms, and an in-ground pool with bathhouse for $50,000. The value of the home is $350,000 at the time H and W divorce. Although the land remains H's separate property, W has a community claim for reimbursement of her half of the community funds expended to improve H's separate property. In the alternative, H has a claim for the value of the land.
Example 2:	Using the facts of the previous example, assume the $50,000 of home improvements came from W's separate funds, which W inherited at her uncle's death. W has to affirmatively prove that the $50,000 was her separate property in order to overcome the community presumption.

A claim to reimbursement, however, may fail when there is evidence of one spouse's intention to make a gift of a community interest to improve the other spouse's separate property.

To establish that property acquired during a marriage is one spouse's separate property, the claiming spouse may show that the asset was acquired in one of the following ways:

- by gift or inheritance
- by purchase with separate property or by separate credit
- by recovery for personal injuries

In keeping with the lack of uniformity among the community-property states, states vary in applying the time-of-acquisition rule. For instance, Louisiana law provides that the character of personal property is established when title passes but that the title for real estate is determined at the time the property is actually conveyed.

JOINT TENANCY

As discussed in chapter 3, property may be held concurrently by two or more individuals with a right of survivorship. The concept of joint tenancy with right of survivorship is embraced by all common-law states. At the time of one spouse's death, the jointly held property passes automatically, by operation of law, to the surviving spouse. Administrative delay is avoided and, because the property does not go through the probate process, probate costs are reduced. The majority of married partners in common-law states own their family residences as joint tenants with right of survivorship or, similarly, as tenants by the entireties.

None of the community-property states recognize the tenancy-by-the-entireties form of ownership, and joint tenancy with right of survivorship is restricted. Some community-property states, however, statutorily create a right of survivorship in the family homestead so that a surviving spouse is not left homeless.

Generally, a survivorship component is not present with community property. This is not to say that married couples in community states cannot hold property as joint tenants with right of survivorship. About half the states permit a survivorship provision with community ownership of property. Four community-property states—Arizona, Idaho, Nevada, and Washington—have laws permitting residents to own property titled as community property with right of survivorship. In these states, this form of titling overrides a community spouse's disposition of the particular property by will. The property, because it passes by operation of law, is not subject to probate. Generally, community property is probate property except in some community states. In these states, if the decedent-spouse's community share passes to the surviving spouse, it does not pass through probate. In other community states, it is strictly an either-or ownership; couples have the choice of owning property in the community sense, jointly with right of survivorship, or as tenants in common.

Married partners who have acquired property during marriage in a community state and do not want it to be community property have to take affirmative steps to override the community identity with their chosen form of ownership. In most of the community states it is the form of property expressed in the title document that controls. If one of the spouses claims that ownership is other than what is stated in the deed, bank account, certificate, or title, that individual has the burden of proving the alleged form of ownership. For joint ownership to supersede the community presumption, a number of the states require an express reference in the title that the particular property is held as joint tenants with right of survivorship. When community property is titled or retitled in joint tenancy with right of survivorship, a transmutation of the community property into separate property results.

PROPERTY CHARACTER

The character of property is determined by the character of the property used to acquire it initially. For instance, if solely separate property is used to acquire other property during marriage, the newly acquired property is also separate property, and when entirely community property is exchanged for other property, the new property retains a community character (absent an agreement of the spouses to treat the property otherwise).

Example:	John spends his separate funds to make a down payment on a cottage in the mountains to be used as a family vacation home. It is titled in the names of both John and his wife, Jane, since the intention is for the cottage to be community property. It is likely the cottage will be characterized as a community asset, based on the parties' intent.

commingling

Although the rule that property has the same character of the property with which it was acquired seems straightforward, it is not that simple. The characterization of property may become very complex when there has been a commingling of marital property. *Commingling* occurs when properties of different characters are mixed, blended, and jumbled up. In these situations, the community presumption typically prevails over the parties' conflicting claims. Even if the character of the property can be traced, other issues may arise: Do the spouses share the commingled property in percentages proportionate to their separate contributions, or is the commingled property the separate property of one spouse with the other spouse then having the legal right of a creditor for reimbursement of contributions made? Furthermore, some states restrict tracing in certain circumstances.

Example:	Shortly after their marriage, Dave and Betsy open bank accounts in both their names. Each places separate funds in the accounts and over time makes additional deposits using community funds. In the course of the marriage there are withdrawals, purchases, sales, and exchanges of assets with commingled bank funds. If Dave and Betsy should later decide to divorce, they are likely to disagree as to what constitutes community and separate property.

Commingling

Life Insurance

The principles governing the classification of life insurance policies are somewhat different in the community-property states. The treatment of life insurance is an important consideration for estate planners and policy owners because of the impact it may have on a decedent's estate taxes and because it is an asset that is often overlooked by a migrating couple. Fortunately, all of the information needed to classify an insurance policy is written in the policy. To determine and separate policy ownership interests in community-property states, three basic doctrines are used.

The proration or apportionment doctrine concept is favored in California and Washington to establish policy ownership interests. This method views the separate and community components of policy proceeds proportionately to the separate and community funds applied to the premiums paid. In other words, the proration theory looks to the source of the payment of the policy premiums.[3]

The inception-of-the-title doctrine has been adopted in Texas, Louisiana, and New Mexico in many life insurance cases. This approach looks to the character of the funds used to purchase the policy, whether the purchase occurs before or after the marriage. The original funds used to purchase the policy establish its character. If community funds are used for other premium payments, the surviving spouse has a right to reimbursement for his or her share of community funds used for the payments but does not share in the growth in the policy's value.

The third doctrine classifies life insurance ownership according to the nature of the funds used for the final or last premium payment and has been relied upon in Arizona and Idaho in some group life insurance cases.[4] This approach views all but the final payment as voluntary installment payments and the final premium payment as completing the purchase of the policy. Whole life insurance cases, at least in Arizona, follow a reimbursement theory.[5]

Simply stated, each of the doctrines described above seeks to trace the source of the money applied to the premium payments to determine the character of the policy and the proceeds, and each approach may give rise to some inequities.

Business

If a business is started during the marriage with community property and labor, allocation disputes upon termination of the community are normally easier to resolve than if a premarital business is started with separate property and increases in value after marriage are due at least partially to community capital and labor. An increase in business value during marriage because of improved market conditions does not in and of itself change the original separate character of the business.

Example: Prior to marriage Martha started an interior decorating business. The business owned realty valued at $75,000 at the time of Martha's marriage. At the time of Martha's divorce, which occurred 8 years later, the realty had increased in value to $130,000, due solely to favorable market conditions. The $55,000 increase in value is Martha's separate property.

However, when income is generated by separate property acquired during marriage, approximately half the states consider that the rents, issues, and profits belong to the community, while the remaining states hold that these retain their separate character. Increases in business value attributable to the labor efforts of either or both spouses are frequently held to belong to the community. The issue of labor contributions may be at least somewhat resolved if one or both spouses withdraw a salary from the business. On the whole, the courts appear to be more restrictive in applying commingling concepts to businesses than to bank accounts.

Debts, Obligations, and Liabilities

Although it may seem logical to assume that community principles apply similarly to assets and liabilities, this is not the case. The states are in much greater accord in the treatment of community assets than of community liabilities. The widest differences among the nine sets of community-property statutes and case law occur in the treatment of liabilities. (The term *liabilities* is typically used in a broad sense to encompass debts, expenses, and obligations.)

There are some areas of relative agreement: (1) a spouse's separate property is usually subject to the claims of the spouse's creditors for the spouse's separate debts; (2) generally, one spouse's separate property cannot be reached by the creditors of the other spouse's separately created debts; and (3) the separate property of both spouses may be available if both partners contracted for the liability.

Differences are more likely to arise when creditors of separately created debt seek to collect from community assets or from one spouse's half of community assets or regarding the following questions:

- the degree to which community assets are available to satisfy premarital debt
- the order in which assets become available to satisfy liabilities
- the exclusion of specific community assets from the claims of creditors
- the availability of community and/or separate property for liabilities created by one spouse for the benefit of the community
- the use of community property of a later marriage to satisfy alimony and support obligations generated by a spouse's previous marriage and children
- the use of community assets to satisfy one spouse's tort claims

Complexities, problems, and inconsistencies involving community liabilities abound.

COMMUNITY PROPERTY AND TRANSFER TAXES

Federal estate tax law[6] requires a decedent's gross estate to include the value of all property in which the decedent had an interest at the date of death. Property rights, however, are determined under state law. In certain situations this means that federal estate and gift tax provisions are applied to a decedent's property in accordance with state property law provisions. Although it is not explicitly stated in the Internal Revenue Code, case law has traditionally recognized that a decedent-spouse's gross estate includes only the decedent's half interest in community property, even if the community property is titled solely in the decedent's name. On the other hand, in a common-law state, if all the marital property were titled in the decedent-spouse's name alone, the spouse's gross estate would include the value of the entire property. If, however, spouses in a common-law state hold property titled as joint tenants or as tenants by the entireties, only half the property value is included in the decedent-spouse's gross estate.

Example:	Harvey and Joan, a married couple, have always lived in a community-property state. At the time of Harvey's recent death, they owned $3,800,000 of community property, all of which was titled solely in Harvey's name. Harvey's gross estate will include $1,900,000 of community assets. However, if Harvey and Joan lived in a common-law state, the full $3,800,000 would be included in Harvey's gross estate.

Thus, a decedent-spouse in a community-property state will, in most instances, have a smaller gross estate than the same decedent-spouse in a noncommunity-property jurisdiction. Of course, after the Economic Recovery Tax Act (ERTA) and the unlimited marital gift and estate tax deduction became effective in 1982, the transfer tax discrepancies between community and common-law states became moot.

Example 1: Harvey and Joan have always lived in a community-property state. Harvey dies owning $3,800,000 of community property.

Harvey's gross estate	$1,900,000
Allowable marital deduction	(1,900,000)
Harvey's taxable estate	0

Example 2: Harvey and Joan have lived all of their lives in a common-law state. Harvey dies owning $3,800,000 of noncommunity property.

Harvey's gross estate	$3,800,000
Allowable marital deduction	(3,800,000)
Harvey's taxable estate	0

Example 3: Harvey and Joan have lived all of their lives in a community-property state. Harvey dies when there is $3,800,000 of community property. Harvey leaves his community property share to his son.

Harvey's gross estate	$1,900,000
Allowable marital deduction	(0)
Harvey's taxable estate	1,900,000

Although the unlimited marital estate and gift tax deduction serves to equalize the transfer tax results between community- and noncommunity-property states when the surviving spouse is the beneficiary of the decedent

testator

spouse's estate (as in the preceding examples), if someone other than the surviving spouse is the recipient of the decedent's property, transfer tax differences between community and noncommunity jurisdictions are more likely.

Sometimes in community-property states a *testator* (a person who has a valid will at his or her death) attempts to devise or control community assets with a will. For instance, a testator may bequeath community property to third parties, or the testator may provide that a trust be funded at his or her death with community assets, giving the surviving spouse an income interest for life and passing the principal to remainderpersons at the survivor's death. To provide relief when a decedent-spouse has taken control of community assets rightfully belonging to the surviving spouse, community-property

widow's election

states have a device called a *widow's election*. This allows the surviving marital partner to choose whether to take half the property outright or to take the benefits provided under the decedent's will. If the surviving spouse decides to abide by the terms of the decedent's will, and under the will the decedent made a testamentary transfer of community assets to a third party other than the surviving spouse, the surviving spouse may be deemed to have made a gift of his or her share of the community property received by the beneficiary under the decedent's will.

CLIENTS ON THE MOVE

Mobility is a common aspect of modern life in the United States. Whether for employment or for personal or other reasons, a significant number of Americans move from one state to another each year. Unfortunately, mobility is often overlooked by planners. Clearly, changing domicile between common-law and community-property states and even between community states can pose some complicated estate planning problems. Often questions are not raised about the legal implications of family moves until there is a death or divorce. Once a marriage dissolves, a determination of the parties' individual legal rights regarding their assets may be formidable or, worse, impossible unless adequate records have been kept over the years.

Moving from a community-property state to a common-law state does not change the character of marital property acquired in the community jurisdiction unless the parties take steps to expressly change the property to a character other than its community identity. The Uniform Disposition of Community Property Rights at Death Act has been enacted by a number of common-law states. This act provides for the recognition of community property as retaining its community-property identity at death when spouses move from a community-property state to a common-law state and when community-property funds are used for the purchase of real property in a common-law state.[7] As is the case with many uniform acts, however, the

Uniform Disposition of Community Property Rights at Death Act has not been enacted by the adopting states uniformly. Therefore, the act varies within the adopting jurisdictions. Estate planners of migrant couples also need to be aware of the likelihood that judges and lawyers practicing in one system are probably not familiar with the legal issues of the other system.

Clearly, addressing all the legalities of the community-property systems is beyond the scope of this chapter. However, regardless of the state in which an estate planner practices or a married couple presently resides, a planner should understand that there are two different legal systems affecting marital property. The planner must be aware of the many implications of client mobility and must recognize that wills, trusts, disclaimers, antenuptial agreements, buy-sell plans, and so forth, that are drafted in one jurisdiction have to be reviewed to make sure they are effective in the current jurisdiction.

CHAPTER REVIEW

Answers to the review questions and the self-test questions start on page 717.

Key Terms

separate property	testator
transmutation	widow's election
commingling	

Review Questions

4-1. Identify the community-property states.

4-2. Distinguish between separate property and community property in a community-property state.

4-3. Describe the best way for overcoming the general presumption favoring community property.

4-4. Explain the three basic doctrines used to determine and separate life insurance policy ownership interests in community-property states.

4-5. What kinds of property are characterized as separate property?

4-6. Explain why the transfer tax results between community- and noncommunity-property states would be similar when the surviving spouse is the beneficiary of the decedent spouse's estate.

4-7. Why should the estate planner in a common-law state have a working understanding of community-property laws?

Self-Test Questions

T   F   4-1. Community property is a form of property ownership in which various people who are neighbors own a share of real estate in the community.

T   F   4-2. Substantial differences exist among the property laws of the community-property states.

T   F   4-3. Property acquired by either spouse before marriage in a community-property state remains separate property.

T   F   4-4. Property inherited during the marriage by an individual spouse in a community-property state is considered to be separate property.

T   F   4-5. All community-property states recognize the tenancy-by-the-entireties form of ownership.

T   F   4-6. The character of community property is determined by the character of property used to acquire it initially.

T   F   4-7. A widow in a community-property state has no recourse if her decedent husband bequeaths community-property to a third party without her knowledge.

T   F   4-8. Moving from a community-property state to a common-law state does not change the character of marital property acquired in the community jurisdiction unless the parties take steps to expressly change the property to a character other than its community identity.

T   F   4-9. Decedents in community-property states who leave all their assets to their spouses usually owe more estate taxes than decedents in common-law states who leave all their property to their spouses.

T   F   4-10. In community-property states, all property the spouses own (as community or separate property) is subject to claims by creditors of either spouse.

NOTES

1. Wis. Stat. 1985–86, § 766.31.
2. Tex. Fam.Code Secs. 4.201-4.206 (2003).
3. *Coffey's Estate*, 81 P.2d 283 (1980).
4. *Gaethje v. Gaethje*, 442, P.2d 870 (1968); *Travelers Insurance Co. v. Johnson*, 544, P.2d (1975).
5. *Everson v. Everson*, 537 P.2d 624 (1975); *Honnas v. Honnas*, 648 P.2d 1045 (1982).
6. IRC Sec. 2033.
7. Unif. Disp. of Comm. Prop. Rts. at Death Act Sec. 2 (1995).

5

Trusts, Trustees and Other Fiduciaries, and Powers of Appointment

---

Learning Objectives

An understanding of the material in this chapter should enable the student to

---

5-1. Describe the sources of fiduciary powers and the principles that govern the conduct of fiduciaries.

5-2. Explain what qualities are important for a fiduciary.

5-3. Explain the various purposes that trusts serve.

5-4. Describe the characteristics common to all trusts and the types of provisions contained in most trusts.

5-5. Describe the basic types of trusts and their nontax characteristics.

5-6. Explain how powers of appointment may be used to provide flexibility in dispositive planning.

Chapter Outline

Perhaps the best-known and most widely used estate planning device is the trust. Trusts, like people, come in all shapes and sizes. That is, there are many types of trusts and they perform a variety of functions. The purpose for which a trust is created usually influences the type used. Trusts can be designed to accomplish one or many goals. Within the parameters established by state law, the uses of trusts are limited only by the imagination of the creator. The trust device enables an individual to accomplish goals with respect to family and property that would be difficult, if not impossible, to attain otherwise.

There are many types of trusts in existence today, and not all were created by natural persons. In addition to trusts created by individuals, there are corporate trusts, employee benefit trusts, government trusts, and others. Trusts can be created for personal, business, social, or charitable purposes. Basically, any group or organization (whether a business, charitable, or social group) that can legally own property can create a trust. Only living persons, however, can create a testamentary trust (a trust under a will), because wills are made solely by natural persons. This discussion is limited to those trusts created by individuals for personal use. The rule against perpetuities and the subject of powers of appointment are also examined. Testamentary trusts and pour-over trusts are covered in the chapter 8.

No study of trusts would be comprehensible without an understanding of the role of trustees and other fiduciaries. Therefore, this chapter begins with a discussion of the role of trustees and other fiduciaries as well as their appointment, duties, powers, and limitations. Some guidelines to consider in the selection of the most suitable fiduciaries are also presented.

WHAT IS A FIDUCIARY?

Under the common-law system predominant in English-speaking countries, a form of property ownership has evolved in which legal title to property is held by one person or entity separate from the beneficial or equitable ownership interest held by another person or entity. When this arrangement exists, the individual or institution that holds bare legal title has the duty to manage the property for the benefit of the equitable (beneficial) owner. The equitable owner (or beneficiary) is entitled to possess and enjoy the property as well as to receive income generated by the property. The person or institution that holds and manages property for the benefit of another is called a fiduciary.

fiduciary

Fiduciary is a broad term that applies to several types of relationships. By definition, a *fiduciary* is an individual or institution charged with the duty to act exclusively for the benefit of another party as to matters within the scope of the relationship between them. The relationship created between the one who manages the property and the other party (beneficiary) who receives the income as well as other benefits of ownership is called a fiduciary relationship.

All fiduciaries, whether individuals or institutions, are required to manage the property in their care according to strict fiduciary principles and standards established by state law. In accepting the responsibility for management of

Fiduciary Arrangements

- trustee
  - duties exist until trust terminates according to trust terms (may last for many years)
- guardian
  - duties exist until legal disability or minority of ward ends
- personal representative of estate (executor/administrator)
  - duties exist until estate is settled and property is distributed (usually 1–3 years)

another's property, a fiduciary holds a special position of trust in relation to the beneficiaries. Because fiduciaries are entrusted with legal responsibility for the property of others, it is important to understand the role of fiduciaries as well as the scope of their duties and powers. The types of fiduciaries discussed in this chapter are trustees, guardians, and personal representatives of estates (executors and administrators).

Fiduciary relationships are created in different ways depending upon the type of fiduciary relationship involved. Differences and similarities among trustees, guardians, and personal representatives of estates exist as to the source of their powers, the duration of their position, and the nature and extent of their duties and responsibilities.

A person named to a fiduciary position does not have an obligation to accept the appointment. However, once the person accepts the position, he or she is under a legal duty to fulfill all the obligations inherent in the relationship until he or she is relieved of the fiduciary duties or resigns.

Sources of Powers

Fiduciaries receive their power from different sources. When an individual dies, the state has a particular interest in the orderly transfer of the decedent's property to the beneficiaries as well as in seeing that the estate is settled and closed within a reasonably short time, usually no more than one to 2 years. It is in the best interest of the state that beneficiaries be self-sustaining during the administration of an estate and that the decedent's property is transferred as expeditiously as possible. Laws have been enacted that prescribe the procedures for settling estates and managing property during the period of estate administration or guardianship. Likewise, the state has an interest in the protection of the property of minors and incompetents.

Because of the state's concerns noted above, the personal representatives of estates (executors or administrators) and guardians of persons and/or properties all derive their powers from the statutory law. All these types of fiduciaries are appointed by the courts and must make an accounting to the court, either at regular intervals or in order to be discharged from their duties, or both. Upon satisfactory completion of their responsibilities, these fiduciaries may apply to the appropriate court to be discharged from their duties. The court that oversees these fiduciary relationships may be called a probate court, surrogate court, or orphans' court, depending upon the designation used by a particular jurisdiction.

On the other hand, trusts are not usually regulated by the court. Generally, trusts are private arrangements established by a trust settlor (grantor) who appoints another person or entity to manage the individual's property for the benefit of others (possibly including the settlor). The trustee's powers, therefore, are generally derived from the trust instrument.

Duration of Fiduciary Powers and Duties

The average estate exists for a relatively short period, usually only one or 2 years and, in any event, not beyond the time that administration is completed and the decedent's property is transferred to the intended beneficiaries. An executor's (or administrator's) powers and duties generally terminate when the estate assets are distributed to the beneficiaries and the estate is closed. A trust, on the other hand, can last for many years. It is not unusual for a trust to be in existence for 20 or 30 years, or longer. The trustee's duties and powers do not terminate until the termination of the trust. After a guardian is appointed, the guardianship lasts until the legal disability of the ward, be it the ward's minority or incompetency, terminates.

Both guardians and personal representatives are empowered to function as soon as they are appointed by the court. However, trustees do not assume their duties until property is actually transferred to the trust.

Accountability of Various Fiduciaries

A personal representative of an estate or a guardian will file an accounting with the court when his or her task is completed. If everything is in order, the estate is closed or the guardianship terminated and the personal representative or guardian discharged. By contrast, a trustee is not required to make an accounting to the court. A trustee may, however, be required to account regularly to the beneficiaries. As noted earlier, the trustee is appointed by a grantor (creator of the trust) and receives powers and limitations under the terms of the trust instrument itself.

DUTIES OF A FIDUCIARY

Loyalty

The most fundamental duty owed by a fiduciary to the beneficiaries is the duty of undivided loyalty with regard to all matters within the scope of the relationship. A fiduciary can be held accountable to the beneficiaries if he or she does not conform with those standards.

A fundamental doctrine or statement of fiduciary principles has evolved that governs the conduct of all fiduciaries under the common law (now generally codified by state legislatures). Recognized authorities on the law of trusts and trustees are generally in agreement regarding the basic principles under common law that all fiduciary relationships share. They are as follows:

- The fiduciary has a duty to act for the benefit of the other party as to matters within the scope of the relationship.

- Fiduciary responsibilities are not to be delegated to others if they can be performed by the fiduciary.
- If the fiduciary enters into a personal transaction with the other party to the relationship, the fiduciary has a duty to make full disclosure of all facts known to him or her that may affect the transaction. If the transaction is unfair to the other party, the other party has the right to have it set aside. Generally speaking, a fiduciary is held to a higher standard of conduct than that standard acceptable in the business community.

The Restatement of the Law of Trusts[1] contains a list of the following fiduciary principles: Trustees must be loyal to the beneficiaries; traditionally they must not delegate their responsibilities to others if they can be performed by the trustees themselves; they must keep and render accounts of the trust or estate; they must furnish information to the beneficiaries (make full disclosure); and they must administer the trusts or estates with reasonable care, skill, and diligence in the fiduciary performance of their duties. Trustees must also keep control of the property; preserve the property; enforce claims and defend actions against the property; keep the property separate and segregated from their own property and from the property of others; make the property productive; pay income to beneficiaries; and deal impartially with beneficiaries if more than one exists. Trustees have a duty to communicate with other trustees, if any, as well as to act in concert with them. The trust instrument may require the unanimous consent of all trustees (if more than one) or may stipulate that a majority vote of trustees is sufficient. The instrument may also state that a beneficiary-trustee may not take part in decisions involving his or her beneficial share.

A fiduciary generally is said to be held to the standard of a person of ordinary prudence, care, and skill. A trustee must exercise that same degree of care and skill that a person of ordinary prudence would exercise in dealing with his or her own property. There is a different interpretation of this standard of conduct for the lay fiduciary than there is for the professional fiduciary. If trustees are professionals, they are held to higher standards than lay persons, and they are generally held to the prudent-person standard with regard to investment and management of trust property. The professional fiduciary or the corporate trustee is held to a still higher standard because he or she is considered an expert.

Duty Not to Self-Deal

The fiduciary also has a duty, the duty of loyalty, not to self-deal or profit at the expense of the beneficiaries. The duty of loyalty is violated if the trustee sells trust assets to himself or herself as an individual, even if they are acquired at fair market value. However, if the trustee makes full disclosure of all the pertinent facts to all beneficiaries and they are competent to approve the transaction, it might be acceptable. Alternatively, if the appropriate court is made aware of the transaction and orders or approves the sale, the trustee is exculpated from liability for self-dealing. Certainly, a trustee should never sell trust assets to himself or herself at a bargain price, because the beneficiaries could hold the trustee accountable for the difference. The trustee should not permit self-interest to interfere with the duty of loyalty to the beneficiaries. Any sale of trust property to the trustee is voidable (reversible) by the beneficiaries, unless they are fully advised of all pertinent facts and consent.

Some questions arise regarding the duty against self-dealing when the transaction is profitable for the beneficiary. What if a trustee sold personal securities to the trust at fair market value or even at a better price than the marketplace offered? It might be to the financial advantage of the trust or estate to purchase these assets. If the securities are obtained by the trust at a good price and are a proper investment for trust assets, should a trustee be allowed to transact such a sale?

Clearly, unless the trustee obtains the consent and approval of all beneficiaries who are of legal age and competent, the trustee's property should not be sold to the trust, and the trustee should not purchase trust property for himself or herself. If any of the beneficiaries are minors or legally incompetent, they do not have the capacity to consent to a sale; thus, it is not binding on them. If the sale is improper, a trustee can be held personally responsible to the beneficiaries for any loss incurred.

On the other hand, if these same securities were acquired from a stranger and then plummeted in value because the stock market declined, the trustee would have no obligation to restore the loss to the beneficiaries, provided the trustee had acted diligently and with reasonable care when purchasing the securities for the trust. Although there are times when it is to the bona fide financial advantage of everyone concerned for the fiduciary to personally acquire trust property or sell property to the trust, it should not be attempted if there is any appearance of self-dealing or personal profit to be gained by the trustee through the transaction.

Duty to Preserve Property and to Make It Productive

A fiduciary is also under a statutory duty to protect and preserve property as well as to make it productive. The fiduciary has a duty to keep trust property invested so it produces income for the beneficiaries. Otherwise, the fiduciary may be personally surcharged for leaving money idle. In one case, an executor left cash in a checking account for almost 2 years at no interest and was personally surcharged and made to pay to the beneficiaries the amount of interest this money would have earned if invested at current rates.

Duty of Impartiality toward Beneficiaries

A trustee also has a duty to deal impartially with beneficiaries, which can be a difficult task if the income beneficiaries and remainderpersons are different. Investing in capital assets with high current yields but little chance of appreciation could increase the income beneficiary's share at the expense of the remainderperson. This is sometimes a difficult matter to resolve. Certainly, the trustee must try to act as impartially and objectively as possible regarding the interests of the various beneficiaries.

Other duties of trustees generally pertain to investing and managing the property prudently, taking care of trust administration expenses, paying all necessary taxes, keeping records and accounting to the beneficiaries when required to do so, and making payments of income and principal as required under the terms of the trust instrument. The trustee must follow all directions given in the trust instrument (except those that would be either illegal if fulfilled or impossible to fulfill), dealing impartially with beneficiaries and exercising discretion when applicable, according to instructions.

Special Responsibilities of Corporate Trustees

The corporate fiduciary must be particularly careful not to profit or benefit from the relationship. Therefore, when a bank serves as trustee, the deposit of the trust funds into its own bank departments would be equivalent to making an unsecured loan from the trust to itself. There is conflicting authority regarding the deposit by a bank of fiduciary funds into its own banking department. This issue is covered by statute in some states. In other states, the issue has been resolved by the courts.

The Restatement of Trusts provides that a bank depositing trust funds into its own bank department commits a breach of trust, unless it is authorized to do so under the terms of the trust. National banks are not permitted to deposit trust funds in their bank departments, unless collateral security equal to the amount of the deposit is delivered to their trust department. In recent years, with FDIC insurance increasing up to $100,000, this issue is not so significant as previously. As a general rule, a bank fiduciary is not disloyal to the beneficiaries of trusts if the bank is managing the trust funds in a prudent and reasonable way.

What about a corporate trustee who manages two trusts and sells the stock of one trust to the other? There is a conflict of loyalty if the assets from one trust are sold to the other, even at a fair price. Neither should a corporate

---

Fiduciary Duties

- Be loyal to the beneficiary.
- Act for the benefit of the beneficiary.
- Do not delegate responsibilities that the fiduciary is able to perform (Uniform Prudent Investor Act allows delegation).
- Disclose facts affecting any transaction.
- Preserve investment assets for the beneficiary.
- Make assets productive.
- Do not self-deal.
- Be impartial toward income beneficiaries and remainderpersons.

---

fiduciary sell property belonging to the estate or trust to any director, officer, employer, or affiliate of the institution by which he or she is employed. National banks are prohibited by regulation from participating in such transactions, except under certain circumstances that do not actually weaken this restriction.

Today most banks and trust companies do have authority to establish and operate common or collective investment funds for their trust accounts. This means that the assets of many small trusts, guardianships, and estates may be pooled, invested, and managed as a single fund, which is particularly important where small trusts are concerned. It permits the corporate trustee to make sound investments at reduced costs and gives the trust the advantage of expert advice as well as diversification that might not be possible if the trust were invested and managed separately. These commingled or collected investments have come to be known as *common trust funds*. They are allowed by the federal government without becoming taxable entities themselves. A bank or trust company may establish a common trust fund that is not subject to income taxes, provided that the trust is operated in accordance with the regulations promulgated by the Federal Reserve System and that such a fund is allowable under state law. Common trust funds have been proven to provide good investment services for small trusts and guardianships at reduced administration expenses.

common trust funds

FIDUCIARY POWERS

Some common powers of fiduciaries include the power to retain or sell investments, mortgage property, borrow money, and mortgage or pledge property as collateral. There may be a power to register property in the name of a nominee. Other general powers include the power to compromise claims;

employ attorneys, investment advisers, accountants, or other agents; and distribute property in cash or kind or both, and in divided interests at such values that an executor or trustee deems appropriate. Corporate trustees usually desire a power in the trust instrument allowing them to invest and reinvest in common trust funds, irrespective of any local law requiring diversification.

Other powers include leasing property and giving options to buy. Making loans from the trust to third parties is not often allowed under state law, even if secured, unless the instrument specifically authorizes them. Trust instruments may require the unanimous action of trustees, or alternatively, the majority vote to act on a specific matter. The trust instrument can also insulate trust or estate assets from the reach of the beneficiaries' creditors. It may also contain a clause that frees the trustee from all statutory restrictions in investments. A donor or testator generally has wide latitude in the powers given to the trustee or executor.

Investment Powers

In the absence of investment provisions in the trust instrument, the source of investment restrictions on the trustee is the common law, the statutes, and the courts. Typically, states follow the common-law *prudent-person rule*, or a statutory legal list of qualified investments is prescribed.

prudent-person rule

Prudent-Person Rule

A useful legal description of the prudent-person rule is as follows:

> In making investments of trust funds, the trustee is under a duty to the beneficiary (a) in the absence of provisions in the terms of the trust or a statute otherwise providing, to make such investments and only such investments as a prudent person would make of his own property having primarily in view the preservation of the estate and the amount and regularity of the income to be derived; (b) in the absence of provisions in the terms of the trust, to conform to statutes, if any, governing investments by trustees; (c) to conform to the terms of the trust (except under certain specified conditions).

The statement of the prudent-person rule in the model statute is as follows:[2]

> In acquiring, investing, reinvesting, exchanging, retaining, selling, and managing property for the benefit of another, a fiduciary shall exercise the judgment and care under the circumstances then prevailing, which men of prudence, discretion, and intelligence exercise

in the management of their own affairs, not in regard to speculation but in regard to the permanent disposition of their funds, considering the probable income as well as the probable safety of their capital.

Uniform Prudent Investor Act. In 1994, the Uniform Prudent Investor Act was introduced. This act has been adopted in some form by the majority of states. The Uniform Prudent Investor Act provides a new set of rules to guide trustees when investing trust assets.

Under the old standards of the prudent-person or prudent-investor rules, trustees were judged on individual investment performance, which was to be accomplished with due care and prudence in their selection of investments. Under this standard, it was essentially inappropriate to delegate investment responsibilities. Currently, under the Uniform Prudent Investor Act, trustees are encouraged to delegate to professionals when necessary. Furthermore, income and investment diversity are emphasized, and trustees are judged on overall investment portfolios.

One ramification of the Uniform Act is that existing trusts may need to be amended in order to conform to its standards.

Legal-List States

legal-list state

Legal-list states prescribe the investments that fiduciaries must make, unless the terms of the instrument or relationship permit otherwise. Legal-list states are either mandatory or permissive. A legal-list state is said to be mandatory if there is a prescribed list of investments in which the fiduciary must invest. Any investment that the fiduciary makes outside the list is considered a breach of trust, thus making the fiduciary liable to the beneficiaries for any loss suffered. In other words, any investment not specifically named in the list is considered a nonlegal investment. Other legal-list states are said to be permissive. Those states print a list with prescribed investments or classes of investments in which the fiduciary may invest. If the fiduciary invests in a property named in the list, there is no breach of duty to the trust. However, the fiduciary may invest in property not stated on the list and take the chance of a beneficiary objecting to the investment. If any objection is made, it is the fiduciary's burden to show that the investment was proper.

Waiving Statutory Limitations

In addition to the standard of investment delineated under the law, there are authorizations and limitations for investments that are stated in the trust instrument. Most trust instruments expressly provide the powers of the trustee with regard to investments. If directed otherwise by the trust instrument, a trustee may invest outside the scope of the standards set by state statute or common law. Some trusts give the trustee broad discretion, not only with regard to the type of investments the trustee makes but also with the manner as well as type of distribution that is made to the beneficiaries. One of the advantages of creating a trust is the flexibility that it can provide. But in order to obtain maximum flexibility, care should be taken that broad powers are given to the trustee to manage the trust according to the intentions of the grantor.

State Investment Powers

- prudent-person rule
- mandatory legal list
    - Trustee investments are limited to a state-prescribed list.
    - Nonlist investment is a breach of trust.
    - The trustee is liable to beneficiaries.
- permissive legal list
    - The trustee may invest in nonlist investments.
    - The burden is on the trustee to show proper investment.
    - There is no breach of trust for listed investments.
- Uniform Prudent Investor Act

Breach of Fiduciary Duties

As already noted, the trustee is subject to statutory duties to protect and preserve trust property as well as to make that property productive. The trustee has a responsibility to keep the property invested and may be held liable for breach of that duty; for example, for leaving money idle. All fiduciaries are answerable to the beneficiaries for whom they act if they commit any breach of their responsibilities or duties as trustees, executors, or guardians. Occasionally, trustees entrusted with large or small sums of money have been tempted to divert it to their personal use.

Example: A trustee borrowed trust assets for his personal use. He converted these funds and never repaid the trust. When this was later discovered, the beneficiaries had a right of action against him both civilly and criminally.

The foregoing was a clear case of a breach of duty. More frequently, the breach is not as evident.

Example:	A trustee keeps funds in bank savings accounts secured by the Federal Deposit Insurance Corporation. These accounts are earning only a relatively low percentage of interest annually.

Because other liquid investments yield a higher return, is the trustee in the second example breaching fiduciary duty to keep the money invested properly? The trustee walks a fine line in this area. All decisions made by the trustee are fraught with some degree of potential liability. In addition, impartiality among different classes of beneficiaries as well as among beneficiaries of the same class must always be maintained. Can the trustee invest in assets that will increase the income to the income beneficiaries at the expense of safety of principal? The answer is no. Sometimes the investment that produces the highest yield is also acquired at the greatest risk. But if there are two investments approximately equal in safety, the trustee has a duty to invest in the one that produces the higher yield.

Conflict between Trustee and Beneficiary

Not only must there be impartiality among different classes of beneficiaries, there must also be no conflicts of interest between the trustee and the beneficiary. The trustee cannot profit at the expense of the trust. For example, a corporate trustee may retain its own shares of stock in an account when its shares were held as an original investment by the grantor of the trust.

However, in dealing with its own stock, a corporate trustee must exhibit undivided loyalty to the trust. When a trust first comes into existence, there may be shares of the corporate trustee's own stock that were investments originally owned by the settlor and are then transferred to the trust. In that case, a corporate trustee in a prudent-person state may retain its own shares of stock in the trust account. However, if the trust did not already contain the corporate trustee's own stock, a corporate trustee has a duty not to purchase this stock unless the trust instrument authorizes or instructs it to do so. If the trustee is operating in a legal-list state, he or she might have to sell the corporate trustee's stock transferred to the trust within a reasonable time if the stock does not qualify as a legal investment in that state. Of course, the trustee does have a duty to sell the stock at a fair price. Statutory authority generally does not encourage retention of original investments that might create a divided loyalty. The only time a trustee can retain stock owned by the creator of the trust, regardless of whether these stocks have been prudent investments or are qualified under the legal list of a state, is when the trust instrument specifically authorizes or directs the trustee to retain those investments.

The trustee has an obligation to look first to the trust instrument and then to the state's statute for guidance as to the trustee's responsibility. If the trust instrument contains a provision authorizing the trustee to retain original investments without liability to the trustee (except for loss or depreciation resulting from improper retention), the trustee may be permitted to do so without liability. However, in all cases regarding new investments, the trustee's duty is to invest trust assets in such a way that the intent of the trust is carried out and the interest of the beneficiary will be best served.

SELECTION OF A FIDUCIARY

What qualities are valuable in a fiduciary? In addition to the quality of loyalty, which is essential, a fiduciary should be honest, should have a high degree of integrity, and should be responsible and have an interest in the welfare of the beneficiaries. It is also important for a fiduciary to have experience in the management of property and the investment of assets. The fiduciary should be willing to serve and be available to make the appropriate investments as well as to devote sufficient time to the management of the trust. The fiduciary should also be available to communicate with the beneficiaries, should stay in contact with them as necessary, and should also be understanding to the beneficiaries and sympathetic to their needs.

Trustees

One of the most difficult decisions that grantors must make is the selection of appropriate trustees. Sometimes grantors name themselves trustees. In other situations, grantors name their spouses, siblings, trusted employees, or business associates as trustees. The problem that such a nomination presents is that if the grantor or a related or subordinate trustee is named, many (if not most or all) of the usual discretionary powers that create the flexibility in a trust must be forgone to achieve favorable tax consequences. On the other hand, much of the important flexibility inherent in a trust is lost if the grantor chooses not to forgo favorable tax benefits and to obtain them by providing substantial objective standards.

Flexibility is extremely important. Typically a grantor is primarily interested in the financial welfare of the life tenant (usually a spouse or other close relative) and is only secondarily interested in the security of the remainderpersons. Quite often a remainderperson is named in a trust merely to avoid the estate tax that would occur at the life tenant's death. However, trust law favors preservation of capital for the remainderpersons—even at the expense of the life tenant. For this reason, a trustee typically is hesitant to act in a way that might seem to unduly favor the income beneficiary. Without discretionary powers, the trustee is unable to serve the life tenant's best interests.

Would a related or subordinate trustee be deterred from liberally exercising discretionary powers in spite of the existence of substantial objective standards? In other words, would the trustee go along with the suggestions of the grantor and the beneficiaries, even at the risk of assuming liabilities for the remainderpersons? Is the use of a related or subordinate trustee a way to achieve flexibility, while at the same time protecting the tax favorability of a trust?

There are at least five factors that ought to be considered in selecting trustees as well as in deciding between a corporate (and therefore independent) trustee and an individual (often related and/or subordinate) trustee.

- For tax reasons, if a beneficiary is also named as a trustee, that individual may not participate in any discretionary decision that may be personally beneficial. The income tax law treats an individual who can spray the income among a class of which he or she is a member as being in constructive receipt of all such income, no matter how it is actually distributed. Likewise, if an individual, as trustee, can decide how corpus (principal) is to be distributed among a class of beneficiaries of which that individual is a member, that power over the corpus may cause the entire trust property to be part of the trustee's estate because the power to allocate corpus is considered the equivalent of a general power of appointment. Furthermore, if either of these powers is exercised in favor of others, the trustee-beneficiary may be treated as if he or she has made a transfer subject to the gift tax.

- Individuals can die or become incapacitated. Certainly, substantial physical changes are possible (and even likely) over the long period that most trusts run. If an individual trustee is about the same age as a mature grantor, it is likely that the benefits of having an individual trustee would be at best temporary.

- If an individual who is also a family member is selected as trustee, that person is often placed in an uncomfortable and perhaps untenable position. The possibility for a conflict of interest is great. Family discord and bitterness may arise when the trustee must refuse the request of one or more of the beneficiaries for what may be perfectly valid reasons. Most grantors probably prefer not to place a son or daughter in the middle of such a family dispute.

- Regardless of the size of the trust fund, individual trustees are not audited and consistently checked to the same degree as corporate fiduciaries. Temptations and pressures make individual trustees even more vulnerable to breaches of trust through arbitrary action, ignorance of obligations, or defalcations of agents. Unfortunately, lawsuits are generally meaningless, even where *temporary borrowing* of trust funds by individual trustees is discovered. Since their personal fortunes are usually not adequate to compensate the beneficiaries, judgments against them are worthless. Conversely, if an employee of a corporate trustee makes an error or is guilty of embezzlement, the bank almost always has the financial ability to replace the loss.

- The incredible complexity of a rapidly changing tax law coupled with the investment, management, and other responsibilities of a trustee make that position a highly specialized and formidable task.

These five reasons all indicate that the use of an independent corporate trustee (often together with one or more individuals) is indicated where the grantor desires favorable tax treatment as well as flexibility with regard to investment, management, and beneficiary need.

Selecting Trustees

- individual/related/subordinate trustee
  - beneficiary trustee—discretionary powers over trust income or corpus may cause tax ownership
    - death or incompetence potential
  - family member trustee—possible conflicts of interest and family discord
    - little regulatory supervision—opportunities for breach of trust
    - tax law complexities/changes—difficult to stay current
- corporate/independent trustee (bank)
  - holds legal title only—no personal tax ownership
  - fiduciary relationship not affected by employee death or incapacity
  - conflicts of interest avoided
  - regular auditing
  - expectancy of tax expertise

Executors

executor

The only legal requirements in choosing an *executor* are that this person be a mentally competent adult who has not been convicted of a felony. This individual may have to furnish a bond. As already noted, this latter requirement can be waived by will. However, a court-appointed administrator or an out-of-state executor is required to post a bond. In view of this requirement, it is prudent, if possible, to name at least one coexecutor who resides in the state where the will is to be probated.

Choosing the right executor, however, requires some additional, careful consideration. In order to choose the best executor, one must look for qualities in an individual or institution that will best carry out the task with which an executor is charged. At first blush, one may consider an individual who is closest to the family. Yet that individual may have no expertise either in managing assets or in dealing with the court system. Because an executor assumes his or her role at a time when a family may be under great stress after the decedent's death, it is wise to choose someone who is competent in managing property as well as honest and loyal; an executor must also be sensitive to the needs of the beneficiaries. Like other fiduciaries, the executor must adhere to fiduciary principles and exercise reasonable care, skill, diligence, and prudence in performing his or her duties.

When considering whom to name as an executor, one might ask some of the following questions:

- Does the prospective executor have the necessary business, financial, and administrative ability to assemble, conserve, and transfer the assets of an estate?
- Does the individual have the time and effort necessary to carry out an executor's duties, and will he or she be willing to devote energy to estate matters? Particularly when a business is a major estate asset, the executor may find that many more hours must be put in than anticipated when he or she accepted the responsibility.
- Does the individual have knowledge of the testator's business, personal affairs, and family relationships?
- Is the individual likely to have a conflict of interest with other beneficiaries?

If one is writing a will, it is wise to designate a successor executor in the event the original executor is unavailable, unwilling, or unable to serve in that capacity when called upon. Another decision that must be made is whether to name an individual, a corporate fiduciary, or both as coexecutors. A corporate fiduciary has expertise and experience in handling estate or trust property. Presumably, it is objective and impartial in carrying out its responsibilities. A corporate institution affords a measure of continuity and financial responsibility. There is no danger of a corporate trustee or executor dying or becoming incompetent. However, a corporate fiduciary may not have the same concern or personal interest in the beneficiaries. A corporate fiduciary also may not be as accessible to communicate with the beneficiaries on personal matters of concern to them. On the other hand, an individual executor might find the duties burdensome and unfamiliar. Without using professional services, an individual executor may also be incompetent. If all tasks are performed by the executor alone, including the filing of necessary tax returns, the best tax or financial results may not be achieved for the beneficiaries. The corporate executor always charges a fee that is printed on an established fee schedule and may be changed from time to time. An individual may also be allowed an executor fee for services; however, that fee might be voluntarily waived or reduced to a lesser amount if the executor is also a beneficiary under the will.

Perhaps the best of both worlds is to name a corporate executor (who takes primary responsibility for the investment and management of assets as well as the preparation of probate forms and tax returns) and an individual executor (who may be consulted on matters of distribution and who will attend to the personal needs of the beneficiaries). A combination of corporate and individual coexecutors offers checks and balances, thus ultimately providing greater service to beneficiaries.

Another consideration is the size of an estate. A small, liquid estate does not require the same attention or expertise as a complex, large estate. In small estates, an individual executor might be a perfectly acceptable choice.

Guardians

guardian

A *guardian* is someone appointed by the court who is charged with the responsibility of caring for another. The individual who requires a guardian is either a minor or a person who is mentally or physically incompetent to care for his or her personal needs or property. The individual for whom the guardian is appointed is known as a ward. A guardian, unlike a trustee, does not necessarily in some states have legal title to the property administered for the incompetent individual. Guardians are appointed by the court and must be discharged by the court when the term of the guardianship ends. The guardian's source of authority is the statutory and judicial law of the state in which he or she serves. This differs from the trustee, whose authority comes from both state law and from the trust instrument specifying the trustee's powers. Guardianship lasts only for the period of minority or incompetency. In actuality, a guardianship may last for the lifetime of the ward. In contrast, a trustee may serve succeeding generations of beneficiaries. Like an executor, a guardian may be required to post a bond. Once the court is satisfied that the guardian is competent to serve, the court issues letters of guardianship as evidence of the guardian's authority to take responsibility for the ward's property as well as to care for the ward personally. A guardian's duties may be as varied as those of a parent.

There are several types of guardianships. The most common are the guardian of the person and the guardian of the property. When a guardianship pertains to the care and management of the ward's property, it is purely a business relationship for which the guardian receives a fee for services. A guardian of the person usually is given funds from the guardian of the property to take care of the minor or incompetent. The guardian of the person might live with the incompetent and provide food, clothing, shelter, and education for the minor. Another type of guardian, called a *guardian ad litem*, is appointed by the court for a particular purpose, generally to defend a specific law suit or legal proceeding in which the minor is a party. This type of special guardian is discharged by the court when the legal issue is resolved.

guardian ad litem

A parent may name a guardian of his or her minor children in a will. Unless there is good reason to override this choice, the court usually honors it and appoints that person, called a ***testamentary guardian***. The natural guardians of a child are the parents. However, courts in many states may not name the natural parent as guardian of the property of a minor. If the minor is old enough, a guardian may also be elected by the minor child. In some states, a minor over age 14 or 15 may choose his or her own guardian, who will be appointed unless there are reasons not to do so. Occasionally, a person assumes a guardianship of a minor or incompetent without seeking or obtaining court approval. This type of guardian is called a *guardian de son tort* (of his or her own wrong). Because this type of guardian assumes these responsibilities, he or she is held fully responsible for all acts performed as a guardian.

testamentary guardian

guardian de son tort

Because a guardian is a fiduciary, he or she is held to the same standards as trustees or executors. One should not accept a position as guardian unless one intends to devote the attention required by the scope of the relationship.

REMOVAL OF TRUSTEES

Authorities differ on whether to give trust beneficiaries the power to remove a corporate trustee and substitute a new one. There are valid arguments for giving the beneficiaries or other individuals such powers, as well as excellent reasons why such powers should not be given.

Among the reasons that powers should be provided to remove the trustee and substitute a new one are the following:

- The trust department personnel may change, and a beneficiary may not be able to get along with the new bank contact.
- It may be desirable to shift the situs of a trust from one jurisdiction to another because of changes in trust or local tax law.
- The residence of the beneficiary may change. If the beneficiaries have moved a substantial distance, it may be inconvenient and inefficient to have a trustee in one state manage the property of a beneficiary in another state. Personal interest may be lost due to lack of contact between the trust officer handling the account and the beneficiary.

Serious tax hazards exist if the beneficiary who has the power to remove a trustee can appoint himself or herself as successor. This might subject the property and the trust to inclusion in that beneficiary's estate. If the power to remove the trustee is desired, it generally should be specified that another corporate trustee must be designated as successor. For example, the adult income beneficiaries could be given the power to remove the corporate trustee and designate its successor provided "such successor must be another corporate trustee with paid-in capital and retained earnings of at least $_____." (Insert dollar amount, for example, $100,000,000.)

Removal of Trustees

- beneficiary and trustee conflict
- changes in state trust law
- changes in state tax law
- inconvenience—beneficiary has moved

ORIGIN OF TRUSTS

The use of trusts originated in England during feudal times. At that time, there were many burdens associated with the legal ownership of property. By separating legal title from the benefits and use of property, a way was found to remove the burdens from the life tenant. In early times, the words use and trust were applied synonymously and interchangeably, although there were some differences between them. Both terms were first introduced into England shortly after the Norman Conquest in 1066. The fiduciary relationship represented by the trust form of ownership was formalized in 1536 when the Statute of Uses was adopted in England.

In essence, the trust represents a split ownership of property. Legal title is held by one party while equitable ownership rests in another. Originally trusts were used principally

- to avoid the burdens of holding legal title to property, including being subject to rights of creditors as well as rights of dower and courtesy
- to allow religious houses to obtain profits from land, although they were prohibited under the law from owning land
- to provide greater freedom in conveying land during lifetime

In early times, trusts were unknown in countries that followed Roman or civil law. With time, however, substitutes for the trust form of ownership evolved. In recent years, the trust form of ownership has been adopted by statute in some civil-law countries.

FUNDAMENTALS OF TRUSTS

trust

What is this unique and versatile estate planning vehicle called a trust? By definition, a *trust* is a legal relationship in which one acts in a fiduciary capacity with respect to the property of another. Fiduciary capacity requires that a person (the fiduciary) receive and hold title to property that is held for the benefit of another person (a beneficiary), to whom the fiduciary owes the highest duty of good faith. When a fiduciary relationship exists, there is a legally enforceable obligation imposed on the person who holds legal title to the property to keep or use it as well as to deal with the property objectively and solely for the benefit of another. The holder of the legal title is called a

trustee

trustee. The party for whom the property is managed is the equitable title holder and is known as the beneficiary. The trust is thus a fiduciary relationship concerned with certain persons and property to which various rights and duties are attached.

Purposes of Trusts

The purposes for which trusts are created are as varied as their creators. One of the primary reasons for setting up a trust is to obtain competent and professional management as well as investment of trust property. Another purpose is to protect the property for the beneficiaries, thereby providing them with income and asset security.

A trust may supply a missing element or skill in the abilities of the settlor (grantor) or the beneficiaries. For example, the beneficiary may not have the necessary character, knowledge, skill, judgment, or business acumen to properly manage and invest the trust property. If a grantor is concerned that one or more of these characteristics are missing in the heirs, this individual may find that the creation of a trust is an ideal way to provide a substitute for the missing elements.

Ultimately, the grantor wants to be assured that after his or her death, there is some way of achieving a measure of security and protection for the family as well as preserving the property that the grantor had worked so hard to accumulate during lifetime. Creating a trust may be an ideal solution that can relieve the grantor's concerns with the knowledge that care will be taken of his or her beneficiaries.

Another reason to use a trust is to protect the interests of children of an earlier marriage. Also, trust assets may be beyond the reach of a spouse's right of election at the grantor's death. The use of a living trust helps the grantor to leave property to whomever he or she wishes. Today, marital problems are common. There may be multiple parents and multiple children of more than one marriage with whom to contend. Use of trusts can enable the grantor to arrange his or her property so it is channeled to the intended beneficiaries and protected from others.

A trust may also be established for the benefit of the grantor or for the grantor's spouse. If it is a living trust, it can free the grantor to do other things. There will be continuous management of the grantor's property during a trip or disability. A trust can protect one's assets from the reach of creditors if one is involved in a new business venture, particularly a risky one. A living trust also gives the grantor the opportunity to see the trust in operation while alive to make sure that it is being managed appropriately.

Although not directly stated, the trust can give the creator an opportunity to continue to manage after death. By specifying in the trust instrument the conditions and timing of distributions of income, principal, or both, the grantor can control the availability of assets for the beneficiaries after death. If the trust is an inter vivos trust that is in operation before the testator's death, the continuous management of the testator's assets forms a bridge between life and death.

A trust offers an excellent method of handling and consolidating accumulations of wealth. If it is an irrevocable trust and the trust instrument provides for accumulation of income, the trust will function as a separate taxpayer, possibly at a lower tax bracket than the grantor. If there are multiple beneficiaries or multiple trusts, income tax savings may possibly be obtained through allocation of income among the beneficiaries and the trust. For example, the trustee may be given discretionary powers with regard to sprinkling income and/or principal among one or more beneficiaries according to their needs. Or the trust instrument may be more restrictive by providing that income or principal is to be used to provide only such things as medical care, education, the purchase of a primary residence, or entry into a new business.

Trusts can also afford opportunities to save estate taxes. Any appreciation in the value of property transferred to an irrevocable trust escapes taxation in the grantor's estate provided that he or she does not retain certain powers. Should the property appreciate greatly in value after being transferred to the trust, considerable estate tax savings result. Trusts can be structured so that the beneficiaries have broad access to both income and principal, and yet the trust principal is not included in their estates for estate tax purposes. As noted earlier, the judicious use of trusts and their beneficiaries as multiple taxpayers also provides an opportunity to have trust income divided among more than one beneficiary in potentially lower tax brackets.

In addition, if a corporate trustee is used and the trust assets are invested in common trust funds, an individual with a relatively modest estate of $50,000 to $300,000 benefits from the advantages of diversification and regular investment advice that otherwise would not be affordable.

In summary, trusts can be set up to provide management services, income and estate tax savings, and other benefits. However, the greatest benefit of many trusts is the flexibility they afford that enables beneficiaries to have the use of both trust income and principal to achieve the grantor's objectives.

Elements of Trusts

There are five elements common to all trusts:

- the creator
- the trustee
- the property
- the beneficiaries
- the terms of the trust (generally contained in a written document)

Creator

grantor

The creator of the trust is the one who intentionally causes the trust to come into existence and is also variously known as the *grantor,* settlor, trustor, or testator (in the case of a testamentary trust). The creator of the trust is the individual who transfers his or her property to another, the trustee, who agrees to hold and manage the property for the benefit of yet another party, the beneficiary. Unless the grantor retains certain powers over the trust or serves as a cotrustee, his or her role in relation to the trust ceases once the transfers have been completed and the trust becomes operative. Of course, the grantor may continue to be involved with the trust as a beneficiary or trustee. (See figure 5-1.) Unless the grantor falls afoul of the grantor-trust rules (which are discussed later in this book and which can make trust income taxable to the grantor), the grantor's continuing relationship, if any, to the trust is generally nominal.

Terms for an Individual Creating a Trust

- trustor
- settlor
- grantor
- creator

Trustee

It was stated earlier that a trust is a fiduciary arrangement with respect to property. The fiduciary relationship exists between the trustee and the beneficiary, not between the grantor and the trustee. Also, after a trust is established, no fiduciary relationship exists between the grantor and the trust beneficiaries.

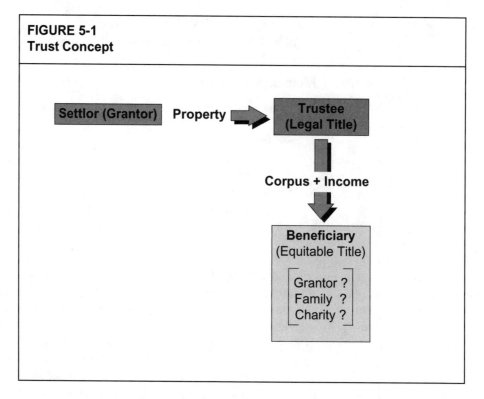

FIGURE 5-1
Trust Concept

A trustee may be a living person or persons. The trustee may also be a corporate institution, such as a bank, or a combination of one or more individuals and a financial institution legally empowered to act in a fiduciary capacity. While every trust requires a trustee, the trust will not fail if the original trustee resigns, becomes incapacitated, or declines to serve. If no provision is made for designation of a successor trustee, the court of the jurisdiction where the trust is administered (the situs of the trust) may be petitioned to appoint a new trustee. If an interim period exists between appointment of trustees, the trust remains temporarily inactive.

Despite the fact that a successor trustee can be appointed by a court of competent jurisdiction, the trust document should always designate at least one successor trustee. In the event that both the original trustee and the successor are individuals, it is a prudent idea to provide a corporate trustee as an ultimate successor if neither of the individual trustees can or will serve. This avoids the necessity for legal proceedings and costs.

It should be noted that a trust will be held invalid if the sole trustee is also the sole beneficiary under the common-law doctrine of merger. When legal and equitable (beneficial) title are merged in one individual, he or she is considered the outright owner and the trust ceases to exist. However, a trustee may also be a beneficiary provided that there are either cotrustees or other beneficiaries of the same trust.

Trust Property

The next essential element in the trust is the trust property. This is also called the trust corpus, res, or principal. Almost anything capable of legal ownership (real, personal, or even an enforceable contract right, such as is evidenced by the ownership of a life insurance policy) may be transferred to and held in a trust. This does not mean, however, that all property is suitable to be placed in a trust.

Beneficiaries

beneficiary

The fourth necessary element is the *beneficiary*. This is the person for whom the trust is created. Beneficiaries hold equitable or beneficial title to the property. The beneficiaries have legally enforceable rights that they may defend and protect in the event that the trust is managed improperly.

In addition to primary beneficiaries, contingent beneficiaries also may be named and provided for in a contingent beneficiaries clause. The trust may also provide separately for beneficiaries who are to receive only income and for remainderpersons to whom the trust principal will be released when the trust terminates (or at an earlier time when distributions of principal are permitted). Note that beneficiaries must be legal persons (that is, persons or institutions who can enforce their rights in a court). This can be illustrated by the fact that, in nearly all states, trusts for the benefit of pets cannot be set up in the United States, although England allows them.

This is not to say that trusts cannot be set up to benefit an individual who is legally incompetent. In such a situation, a guardian is appointed to enforce the incapacitated person's rights.

Trust Terms

trust terms

Trust Term Provisions. The last element necessary for a trust is the *trust terms*. Usually, the trust terms are embodied in a written instrument called the trust instrument, deed of trust, or indenture of trust. The trust terms or powers are derived from those in the trust instrument as well as from the law of the jurisdiction in which the trust is situated and under which it is governed.

The trust terms include a set of powers, usually administrative, that may establish the scope of both the responsibilities and duties of the respective parties. The trust terms may also place limitations and restrictions upon the trustee's powers. The grantor may designate the types of investments permitted by the trustee, or the grantor may give the trustee broad discretion in making investments, limited only by the standard for investments by a fiduciary set forth by the local jurisdiction under which the trust is governed. Clearly, in constructing the trust, the grantor has the original power to give the trustee exclusive, discretionary, or limited powers regarding investing and managing the trust property as well as distributing property to the beneficiaries.

The trustee is guided in the investment and management of trust property as well as in the administration of his or her duties by the above-mentioned sources—the terms of the trust instrument itself and governing state law. To the extent the trust instrument contains explicit directions and mandatory responsibilities, the trustee has an obligation to fulfill these acts with undivided loyalty for the beneficiary. The trustee must act in accordance with the grantor's directions but only as long as there is no impermissible conflict with state law. It may happen that the trust is silent with respect to certain administrative powers and duties. In that case, state law controls.

The trust may contain a spendthrift provision, which provides a restriction against attachment by creditors of trust assets, whether they are creditors of the beneficiary or the grantor. In this way, the trust protects beneficiaries from their own indiscretion and poor judgment. A trust may also contain a savings clause with respect to the rule against perpetuities or state law that limits the duration of trusts. In effect, the provision may provide that, notwithstanding any other provision to the contrary, the trust terminates within the time allowed under the rule against perpetuities or comparable law. This is discussed in more detail later.

Other standard provisions of a trust may provide instructions for appointment of a successor trustee in the event that the existing trustee resigns, is incapacitated, or fails to serve. Grounds for removal of a trustee and instructions for the replacement of a trustee may be found in the trust instrument. The trust may also contain a provision pertaining to the trustee's fee. Generally, a corporate trustee requests that a provision be inserted in the trust stating that the institution be compensated in accordance with its standard schedule of fees in effect at any particular time.

Trust Elements

- creator (grantor/settlor/trustor)
- trustee (legal title)
- property (corpus/principal)
- beneficiaries (beneficial title)
- provisions/terms

Legal Limitations on Trust Duration

rule against
perpetuities

Rule against Perpetuities. There are two limitations pertaining to the duration of trusts that affect the validity of the trust as well as the exercise of any power of appointment created by the trust or will. These limitations were enacted to prevent property from being held in trust indefinitely. The object of the law is that property should be alienable and should eventually take its place within the stream of commerce. (Alienation is the right to sell, give away, or dispose of property at will.) A perpetuity is any limitation or condition that takes away or suspends a person's power to alienate property for an extensive or infinite time period. Historically, the rule against perpetuities is a common-law rule providing that no interest in property is valid unless the interest must vest no later than 21 years plus 9 months (in the case of a posthumous child, the period of gestation) after some life or lives in being when the interest was created.

The date on which the interest is considered to be created is different for revocable and irrevocable trusts. If the trust is irrevocable when created, the date of creation of the trust starts the period within which the interest must vest. If the trust is revocable, the time period begins if and when the trust becomes irrevocable. If the interest is created by will, the date of the testator's death is the initial measuring point for a will or a testamentary trust, since the instrument does not become effective or irrevocable until then. The common-law rule against perpetuities has been enacted into law by statute in many states. Some state legislatures have also shortened the time period for vesting.

In 1986, the National Conference of Commissioners on Uniform State Laws approved The Uniform Statutory Rule against Perpetuities. The Uniform Act was amended in 1990 and is now being adopted by different states. The Act takes a wait-and-see approach to vesting. It allows a 90-year period (as opposed to 21 years and 9 months from lives in being) from the date an interest is created for the interest to vest. Only if an interest does not in fact vest within the 90 years does the disposition become invalid. Consequently, the Uniform Act applies solely to interests that under the common-law rule would be invalid only because of uncertainty as to whether the interests *would* vest within the common-law time period. Under the new act, interests are not considered invalid unless vesting does not actually occur within the 90-year period. Currently, an increasing number of states are statutorily adopting or are considering amendments to the traditional common-law rule against perpetuities.

For states in which the traditional common-law rule applies, the proposed distribution plan should be analyzed to determine that no interest will vest so remotely that the rule against perpetuities would be violated before a trust is drafted. In this analysis, it is crucial to remember the different dates of creation.

Example: A direction in a trust specifies that it shall be held for the life of the grantor's wife and that on her death an equal share for each of the grantor's children shall be set aside and continued in trust for the child's life. At the death of the last of the grantor's children, the corpus is to be distributed to their children (the grantor's grandchildren) per stirpes. If the trust is a testamentary trust, there is no violation of the rule against perpetuities because the corpus beneficiaries (the grantor's grandchildren) will be ascertainable and the interest will vest within a life or lives in being (the grantor's children) at the time the interest is created (the death of the grantor).

However, if the trust is an irrevocable inter vivos trust, it will violate the rule against perpetuities. This results because the interest comes into being at the time the trust is created, and it is possible that the last child of the grantor will not have been born at that time. (For purposes of the rule against perpetuities, the grantor and the grantor's spouse are presumed to be able to have children until they die.) Because distribution of the corpus is not to take place until the death of the last of the grantor's children, there is a chance that the interests will not vest within the prescribed period.

Note that under the traditional rule against perpetuities there is a violation of the rule if even a *possibility* exists when the interest is created that the interest will not vest absolutely within the required time. This means that in many states, the operation of this rule does not wait to see what actually happens, but rather invalidates the interest prospectively. Drafters of trust instruments should be careful to see that shares for any individual not in being at the creation of the trust are made payable to such persons outright or held only during the lives of persons who are living when the trust is created.

A common testamentary scheme is to skip the tax on the primary beneficiary's death and to make a distribution of principal at that time. For example, an older brother may give his younger brother a life estate in property. At the younger brother's death, any of the brother's children surviving him will receive the corpus. If a child is deceased, that child's issue would take his or her parent's share. In this arrangement, there are no problems with the rule against perpetuities, because all interests will vest indefeasibly at the expiration of a life in being at the creation of the interest. In other words, when the interest is created at the death of the older brother (the effective date of his testamentary disposition), all the interests must vest at the expiration of a life in being at the time the interest was created (the younger brother's). This result can be ascertained because at the death of the measuring life in being (the younger brother's) all of his children will be ascertainable and the trust corpus under the terms of the example would belong to them absolutely if they are living. In the event a child of the younger brother is deceased, the deceased child's portion belongs absolutely to his or her issue.

The common-law rule against perpetuities is extremely complex in application. Consequently, most wills and trusts contain a perpetuities-savings clause to eliminate possible perpetuities problems. For testamentary trusts, the following is a typical savings clause:

> Notwithstanding the directions given my trustee above as to the distribution of income and principal, every trust established by this Will shall terminate, if it is not already terminated, 21 years after the death of the last survivor of my wife, my children, and any lineal descendant of mine alive *on the date of my death*. At the termination of such trust or trusts, my trustee shall immediately transfer, convey, and pay over the principal of each of the trusts to the lineal descendants then living of the child of mine on whose account the trust was established, per stirpes. If there are no such individuals living, to my lineal descendants then living, per stirpes, and if none, to The American Heart Association.

If the trust is an inter vivos trust, the italicized phrase (above) should be replaced with a phrase such as "on the date of the creation of this trust."

rule against
accumulations

Rule against Accumulations. There is another historic common-law rule, called the rule against accumulations, that states the period during which income may accumulate. It was enacted using the same principle as the rule against perpetuities, and, in most cases, the permissible period during which the interest must vest is the same as under the rule against perpetuities. There are a few states that have shortened the period for accumulations. Certain states permit accumulations today only for charitable purposes or during a child's minority.

Trust Situs

Because a trust can be established anywhere, the grantor has some flexibility in establishing a situs for the trust. It need not be the grantor's domicile. A trust can generally be established subject to the laws of another state by stating that fact in the instrument. There may be tax or other advantages to setting up a trust outside of the grantor's domicile.

Flexibility through Trustee Discretion

Most modern trusts allow trustees broad latitude and discretion in their investment and management decisions. Trustees may also be given absolute discretion regarding distributions of income or principal to named beneficiaries. The trustee may have the power to distribute income or principal unequally among the beneficiaries, depending on their individual needs. Or there may be specific guidelines provided for allowing special expenditures for such things as undergraduate or postgraduate education, purchase of a principal residence, or investment in a new business. The more flexibility the trustee has, the better he or she may be able to serve and provide for the true needs of the beneficiaries as they arise, just as the grantor would have done if the grantor had retained control of his or her own property. Flexibility is especially important since within the general framework established by the grantor, the trustee generally is required to continue to carry out the grantor's objectives with regard to his or her property and loved ones long after the grantor is incapacitated or dead. In fact, a trust may continue to exist through several generations of beneficiaries. As will be seen later, however, there may be additional generation-skipping taxes with which to contend if the trust benefits more than one generation of income beneficiaries.

TYPES OF TRUSTS

The use of trusts for estate, gift, and income tax planning is discussed at length later. At this time, we will discuss some of the various types of trust arrangements commonly used today. The purpose of this discussion is to help the students become familiar with some basic types of trusts and their nontax characteristics.

Living Trusts

Revocable Trusts

living trust
revocable living trust

A *living* (inter vivos) *trust* is created and operates before the death of the settlor. A *revocable living trust* is a trust created when the grantor transfers the trust property to the trustee but reserves the power to alter or terminate the arrangement and reclaim the trust property. (See figure 5-2.) As we will learn later, a transfer to a truly revocable trust does not change the federal estate, gift, and income tax picture of the grantor. Essentially, the transfer is treated as

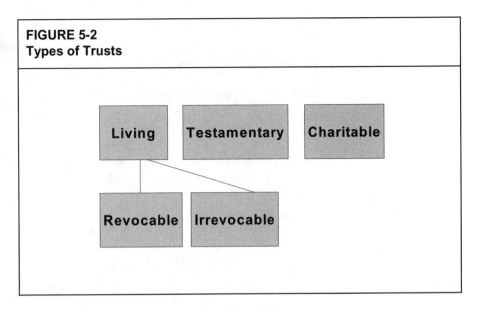

FIGURE 5-2
Types of Trusts

an incomplete gift. Obviously, there must be nontax reasons to create the revocable living trust. The advantages of this arrangement include the following:

- The grantor may not have the ability or time to manage the property to the maximum benefit of the beneficiaries.
- The grantor may be able to enjoy the psychological benefits of gifting property in trust for the trust beneficiaries while retaining the ability to reclaim the property.
- The grantor has the ability to observe the operation of the trust under the current trustee. This also gives the trustee the opportunity to become familiar with the grantor's dispositive intentions before the trust becomes irrevocable.
- The revocable trust becomes irrevocable at the death of the grantor and passes by operation of law to the beneficiary. This avoids the probate costs and provides for a transfer with less publicity.
- Ancillary jurisdiction for out-of-state property can be avoided if the grantor's out-of-state intangibles are transferred to revocable trusts in the grantor's state of domicile.
- A grantor who is a sole proprietor of, or partner in, an ongoing business may transfer the business to a revocable trust to avoid termination of the business at the grantor's death.

Irrevocable Trusts

irrevocable trust   A living trust may also be established as an *irrevocable trust* by the grantor. In this case, the property is transferred to the trust permanently, and the grantor cannot terminate the trust and reclaim the property before the trust terminates by its terms. As we will discuss later, a truly irrevocable trust is treated as a completed gift for gift, estate, and income tax purposes. Irrevocable trusts provide tax advantages, such as estate reduction and income shifting. Unfortunately, transfers to an irrevocable trust are completed gifts and may result in gift tax liability to the grantor.

Many grantors are reluctant to permanently lose possession and control over the trust property. Only extremely wealthy individuals with superfluous assets will typically feel comfortable with a permanent transfer of substantial assets to an irrevocable trust. However, besides the tax advantages mentioned above, there are several nontax objectives that are satisfied by the living irrevocable trust transfer.

Among these objectives are the following:

- The grantor can establish the trust to manage property for a needy dependent. The trustee in this arrangement can provide a valuable service to the grantor. That is, the beneficiary has to deal with the trustee rather than the grantor for the needed funds. This can prevent a continuing undesirable conflict between the grantor and the dependent.
- The trustee may provide investment and accumulation skills not held by the grantor for the management of the trust property.
- The trust property avoids probate at the death of the grantor.
- The trust property provides for the beneficiaries and is not subject to claims of the grantor's creditors.
- The trust may be designed to shelter assets of the grantor from spousal election rights at the grantor's death. Therefore, the grantor can be assured that children from a former marriage will be provided for at the grantor's death.

The terms of the trust should explicitly state whether the trust is irrevocable. If revocable, the trust terms should indicate when it may be revoked and by whom. State law determines this provision if the trust document is silent as to the revocability. Some states presume revocability, while others presume irrevocability. Because this provision has a significant impact on both federal and state taxation of the trust, it is always recommended that the trust provisions be clearly stated.

Testamentary Trusts

testamentary trust

A *testamentary trust* is created under the will of a testator. As such, it is never irrevocable until the death or the permanent legal incapacity of the testator. Testamentary trusts are discussed at length in the next chapter.

Charitable Trusts

charitable trust

Charitable trusts have a long history of development under the common law of England and are valid under the laws of all states of the United States. In a later chapter, we will discuss the estate planning uses for specific types of charitable trusts. However, it is probably true that most gifts in trusts to charity are motivated by benevolent rather than tax-saving objectives.

Characteristics of Charitable Trusts

Charitable trusts have several elements in common with regular trusts. There is the normal requirement that the trust creator have an intention to create the trust and transfer the property to the trust. The legal title to the trust property is held by the trustee, who administers the trust according to the trust terms.

The charitable trust is a type of public trust and has some special characteristics not existing in a truly private trust. First, the trust must be for a specific charitable purpose. Generally, the objective of the charitable trust is to improve society in some manner. Charitable purposes include governmental improvement, advancement of religion, educational or scientific advancement, relief of poverty, and other purposes of community advancement. For tax purposes, the Internal Revenue Code is more specific as to the definition of a charitable purpose.

The terms of a charitable trust must not provide a benefit for a definite individual among the class of potential beneficiaries. However, the charitable trust must have a definite class of beneficiaries. For example, a charitable trust could be created to fund estate planning research at The American College. However, it is not permissible to create a charitable trust to fund a travel budget for your favorite estate planning professor.

cy pres

A charitable trust, as opposed to a private trust, may be created for an unlimited duration. We discussed the rule of perpetuities earlier, which provides that a trust cannot have an indefinite life. This rule does not apply to a charitable trust and there is generally no legal time limit on the length of the trust. The trust continues until it terminates by its terms or fails for some other reason. In fact, it is not necessary for a charitable trust to fail even when its intended purpose becomes impossible. A doctrine of law known as *cy pres* was developed in the law to prevent the failure of trusts that cannot be applied to their original charitable purpose. A court may enforce a trust that has a general charitable intent. When applying *cy pres,* the court attempts to find another charitable purpose similar to the initial charitable intention of the trust settlor. *Cy pres* may be applied when the initial charitable trust does not provide enough property to meet its purpose or when the trust purpose has already been accomplished or becomes impossible and additional funds remain in the trust.

A private trust is enforced in the courts by the intended beneficiary. This is one reason for the requirement that a private trust have specific beneficiaries. Because a charitable trust cannot have specific beneficiaries, there is no logical individual to enforce the terms. In general, the attorney general of the state is empowered to enforce charitable trusts.

POWERS OF APPOINTMENT

Basic Terminology

donee of the power

A power of appointment is an interest held in property by an individual known as the *donee* (or holder) *of the power*. The property interest is a right given to another to designate the disposition of property subject to the power. The act of designating the property by the donee is known as the *exercise* of the power. The possible recipients of the property after the exercise of the power depend on the terms of the power of appointment. Failure to exercise a

lapse

power is known as *lapse* of the power. A power of appointment is created when the owner of the property, known as the donor of the power, creates the power in a donee to designate the donor's property that is subject to the power. The recipients of the property after the donee exercises the power are

appointee

known as the *appointees*. Note that for *gift tax purposes* the term *donee* refers to the recipient of the gift property. For *power of appointment purposes*, however, the term *donee* refers to the recipient of the power. It is the *appointees* who receive the property itself. Depending on the type of power of appointment, a donee may also be an appointee.

Example: Tom Tuttle placed an apartment building he owns in trust under the following terms. The income from the trust is to be provided for Tom's wife, Tina, for life, and Tina is given the power to appoint the property at her death to any of Tom and Tina's children then living. In this case, Tom is the donor of the power and Tina is the donee. Any of their children living at Tina's death are possible appointees. If Tina designates in her will which of the children is to receive the property, the power will be exercised at her death. If Tina fails to make this provision, the power will lapse and the property will fall under these circumstances to Tom's heirs at law.

Types of Powers of Appointment

general power

A power of appointment that gives the donee a right at any time to designate the property to parties that include the donee or the donee's estate or creditors is known as a *general power* of appointment. The donee of a *general power* essentially has all rights to the property at the time the power becomes exercisable. We will learn later that the donee who possesses a general power at the time of death has the property subject to the power included in his or her gross estate.

General Power of Appointment

There is an unlimited right to appoint property to
–   yourself
–   your creditors
–   your estate
–   your estate creditors

---

special (limited) power

A *special (limited) power* of appointment is a power of appointment that restricts the donee's right to designate the property to a specific class of appointees. The power held by Tina Tuttle in the previous example is a special power because she may appoint the apartment building only to any of the children living at the time of her death. With a special power of appointment, the donee of the power cannot be a direct appointee of the property.

Special Power of Appointment

Property may <u>not</u> be appointed to
–   yourself
–   your creditors
–   your estate
–   your estate creditors

The time that a power may be exercised may also be restricted by the donor. That is, the donee may be permitted to designate the property to an appointee at any time, or there may be only a specific time when the power can be exercised. One type of power that is important for estate planning is a testamentary power. This type of power is exercisable only at the death of the donee through the provisions of the donee's will. The power held by Tina Tuttle in the prior example is a testamentary special power of appointment.

Purposes of Powers of Appointment

There are some estate and gift tax consequences to planning powers of appointment. A discussion of these is reserved for future chapters. However, the power of appointment is an obviously flexible and useful dispositive device for nontax reasons. The primary reason for using a power of appointment is to delegate a dispositive decision and/or postpone the time at which the dispositive decision is made. The various types of powers, and the restrictions that can be imposed on the powers, create a flexible transfer mechanism. The donor of the power can retain some control over the property and the dispositive decision while delegating the actual decision to another. For example, the donor chooses the property made subject to the power. The donor can choose when the property will be transferred and restrict its ultimate receipt to a limited class.

The donor may have important reasons for delegating the dispositive powers to another. First, this removes the dispositive decision and any discontent resulting from the decision from the original owner of the property. For example, benevolent grandparents may want to transfer property to their grandchildren. By creating a power to be held by the grandchildren's parents, the grandparents place the decision in the hands of the parents, who best know the needs, worthiness, or goals of the grandchildren.

Furthermore, the donor may wish to postpone the time the transfer of property is to be made. For example, parents may not want to transfer property to their children until the children reach majority. To prepare for the contingency that the donor will not survive the period of postponement of the transfer, it is necessary to delegate the decision to another. Often a parent donates the power to the other parent to make the property transfer. Many powers are created by will for this purpose. By both delaying and delegating the ultimate transfer, the donor can take a wait-and-see approach for transferring property. By using this technique, the donee of the power is able to exercise the power at the time the donor actually desires to transfer the property. The donee of the power can make the appropriate designation in light of the circumstances existing at that time.

Note to Students: See Appendix A for a summary of the advantages and disadvantages of different trusts covered in this chapter and throughout the text.

CHAPTER REVIEW

Answers to the review questions and the self-test questions start on page 717.

Key Terms

fiduciary	prudent-person rule
common trust funds	legal-list state

executor
guardian
guardian ad litem
testamentary guardian
guardian de son tort
trust
trustee
grantor
beneficiary
trust terms
rule against perpetuities
rule against accumulations

living trust
revocable living trust
irrevocable trust
testamentary trust
charitable trust
cy pres
donee of the power
lapse
appointee
general power
special (limited) power

Review Questions

5-1.   Explain what is meant by a fiduciary relationship.

5-2.   Identify the sources of powers of the following:
   a.   trustees
   b.   executors
   c.   administrators
   d.   guardians

5-3.   Describe (a) the duration of the powers and duties and (b) the accountability of trustees, personal representatives of estates, and guardians.

5-4.   What are the principal duties common to all fiduciary relationships?

5-5.   Explain what is meant by the statement that "a trustee has a duty to deal impartially as among the beneficiaries."

5-6.   Explain the difference between states that follow the prudent-person rule and legal-list states, and differentiate further between permissive and mandatory legal-list states.

5-7.   Describe two examples of a breach of fiduciary duties and the remedy that is available to the beneficiaries when a breach has been committed.

5-8.   What factors should be considered in selecting a trustee?

5-9.   What characteristics are important for an executor to possess?

5-10.   Describe the different types of guardians, and explain how they differ from trustees.

5-11.   Identify the elements common to all trusts.

5-12.   Explain whether each of the following trust arrangements is valid:

    a.   A trust is created for the benefit of the settlor's son. The settlor is the sole trustee of the trust.

    b.   A trust is created in which the settlor is the sole trustee. The settlor and his son are the beneficiaries during the settlor's lifetime, and the son is the sole beneficiary after the settlor's death.

    c.   A trust is created for the sole benefit of the settlor. The settlor is also the sole trustee.

5-13.   Describe the legal limitation imposed to prevent a property interest from being left either in trust or in the form of successive life estates forever.

5-14.   Explain why the grantor of a trust might provide the trustee with broad discretion in administration of the trust.

5-15.   Describe the possible nontax advantages for the establishment of revocable living trusts.

5-16.   What differences exist between the creation and the effective dates of living and testamentary trusts?

5-17.   Why might a grantor transfer property to an irrevocable trust?

5-18.   Briefly describe the process of creation and exercise of a power of appointment.

5-19.   Who are the potential recipients of property held by a trustee under a general power of appointment?

5-20.   Mary Planner and her husband, Tom, have three children, aged 5, 3, and 1. Mary transfers property to a trust for the benefit of her children with Tom as trustee. Mary hopes the trust will be used for the children's college educations. Describe how a limited power of appointment, donated to Tom, may be used to meet this goal.

Self-Test Questions

T   F   5-1.   Fiduciaries hold a special position of trust in relationship to the beneficiaries whose property they manage.

T   F   5-2.   A trustee receives powers from the probate court and is regulated in the management and investment activities by the court.

T   F   5-3.   The Uniform Prudent Investor Act of 1994 strictly prohibits the delegation of investment powers by a fiduciary.

T   F   5-4.   Because executors have the limited task of transferring property for the estate, it is not necessary that they have particular skills or knowledge regarding a testator's affairs.

T   F   5-5.   A major purpose of establishing a trust may be to supply an element of character or skill missing in the grantor or the beneficiaries.

T   F   5-6.   When the grantor establishes a trust, it is always for the benefit of other persons for whose welfare the grantor may be responsible.

T   F   5-7.   A spendthrift clause may be designed to protect the corpus of the trust from the creditors of a beneficiary.

T   F   5-8.   The rule against perpetuities has been abolished in most states, and modern trusts may be established for unlimited duration.

T   F   5-9.   State law generally limits the time that a trust is permitted to accumulate income.

T   F   5-10.   The situs of a trust is always the same as the grantor's domicile because the law of the grantor's state of domicile governs the grantor's property.

T   F   5-11.   Through the use of a living trust, the grantor has the opportunity to observe the management and investment skills of the trustee during the grantor's lifetime.

T   F   5-12.   A revocable trust is not permitted to hold an unincorporated business interest.

T   F   5-13.   An irrevocable trust is often used for tax planning purposes as an income-shifting device.

T   F   5-14.   A disadvantage of a living irrevocable trust is that it will pass through probate.

T   F   5-15.   A statement in the trust instrument as to the revocability or irrevocability of a trust is not necessary or desirable as state law prevails.

T   F   5-16.   A testamentary trust may be irrevocably established during the grantor's life.

T   F   5-17.   The terms of charitable trusts should not provide a benefit for a specific individual.

T   F   5-18.   The individual who creates a power of appointment in another (that is, the donor of the power) is the person who exercises the power in favor of the donee at some time in the future.

T   F   5-19.   A general power of appointment allows the donee to transfer the property to anyone, including the donee and the creditors of the donee.

T   F   5-20.   A donor may delay the right to exercise a power of appointment until the donee's death.

NOTES

1. The Restatements are a series of treatises setting out general legal principles.
2. Model statutes are attempts by legal scholars to produce uniform laws and standards that will be adopted in all states.

6

Lifetime Transfers by Gift—
An Overview

Stephan R. Leimberg and Constance J. Fontaine[*]

Learning Objectives

An understanding of the material in this chapter should enable the student to

---

6-1. Identify the nontax advantages of lifetime gifts.

6-2. Explain what constitutes a gift, and identify the types of gifts.

6-3. Describe the types of gratuitous transfers that are not gifts.

6-4. Explain the requirements for a completed gift.

6-5. Explain how property may be valued for gift tax purposes.

Chapter Outline

---

[*] Stephan R. Leimberg, JD, CLU, was professor of estate planning and taxation at The American College. Constance J. Fontaine, JD, LLM, CLU, ChFC, is associate professor of taxation at The American College and holds the Larry R. Pike chair in Insurance **and** Investments. This chapter has been updated due to tax law changes, and portions of it have been substantially revised by the author.

The subject of lifetime transfers by gift is presented in two chapters to enable the student to better understand all aspects and elements of gratuitous lifetime transfers before studying the system of gift and estate taxation in chapter 7. This first chapter discusses the reasons (other than tax advantages) for making gifts, what constitutes a gift, the various types of gifts, how to distinguish between gifts and other gratuitous transfers that are not gifts, gifts that are exempt, requirements for a completed gift, and valuation of gifts for gift tax purposes. Chapter 7 reviews federal gift taxation and its relationship to the federal income and estate tax systems.

NONTAX ADVANTAGES OF LIFETIME GIFTS

Individuals give property away during their lifetimes for many reasons. Although a detailed discussion of the nontax motivations for lifetime giving is beyond the scope of this chapter, some of the reasons include the following:

- privacy that would be impossible to obtain through a testamentary gift
- potential reduction of probate and administrative costs
- protection from the claims of creditors
- vicarious enjoyment of seeing the donee use and enjoy the gift
- opportunity for the donor to see how well—or how poorly—the donee manages business or other property
- provision for the donee's education, support, and financial well-being

TECHNICAL DEFINITION OF A GIFT

Elements of a Gift

gift

Under common law, a *gift* is defined simply as a voluntary transfer without any consideration. But for tax law purposes neither the Code nor the Regulations specifically define what is meant by the term gift.

However, the regulations dealing with the valuation of gifts provide that in cases where property is transferred for less than adequate and full consideration in money or money's worth, the

Value of property transferred – Consideration received = Gift

Note that this definition focuses on whether the property was transferred for adequate and full consideration in money or the equivalent of money, rather than whether the transferor intended to make a gift. This is because Congress did not want to force the IRS to prove something as intangible and subjective as the transferor's state of mind. In fact, the regulations state that donative intent is not an essential element of the transfer for *gift tax* purposes. However, donative intent is required for a gift to be tax exempt for *income tax* purposes. As discussed later, the IRS may show the lack of donative intent to establish that a transfer was in the ordinary course of business and not, in fact, a gift. For gift tax purposes, the key factors are (1) the objective facts of the transfer (adequacy of consideration) and (2) the circumstances surrounding the transfer, not the subjective state of mind of the transferor. The donative intent may become important in the investigation of the circumstances of the transfer.

The courts examine certain factors to determine if a taxable gift was made:

donor
donee

- Was the *donor* (maker of the gift) competent to make a gift?
- Was the *donee* (person to whom the gift is made) capable of accepting the gift?
- Was there a clear and unmistakable intention on the part of the donor to absolutely, irrevocably, and currently be divested of dominion and control over the gift property?

Assuming that these three objective criteria are met, three other elements must be present. There must be

- an irrevocable transfer of the present legal title to the donee so that the donor no longer has dominion and control over the property in question

- a delivery to the donee of the gift (or the most effective way to command dominion and control of the gift)
- acceptance of the gift by the donee

All these requirements must be met before a gift is subject to tax. The essence of these tests can be distilled into the following factors (state law is examined to determine the presence or absence of these elements):

- a transfer of property for less-than-adequate consideration by a donor competent to make a gift
- delivery of the gift property by a donor, which absolutely, irrevocably, and presently divests the donor of dominion and control over the gift property
- acceptance of the gift property by a donee

Adequate and Full Consideration in Money or Money's Worth Defined

Sufficiency-of-Consideration Test

Because the measure of a gift is the difference between the value of the property transferred and the consideration received by the transferor, a $100,000 building that is transferred from a mother to her daughter for $100,000 in cash clearly does not constitute a gift. However, the mere fact that consideration has been given does not pull a transaction out of the gift tax realm. To be exempt from tax, the consideration received by the transferor must be equal in value to the property transferred. This is known as the sufficiency-of-consideration test. If the daughter in the example above pays $60,000, the excess value of the building—$40,000—is within the scope of the gift tax. To escape the gift tax there must be adequate and full consideration equal in value to that of the property transferred.

Effect of Moral, Past, or Nonbeneficial Consideration

Consideration is not in money or money's worth when the consideration is moral consideration, past consideration, or consideration in the form of a detriment to the transferee that does not benefit the transferor. The classic example is a man who transferred $100,000 to a widow when she promised to marry him. (Upon remarriage she would forfeit a $100,000 interest in a trust established for her by her deceased husband; the $100,000 from her fiancé was to compensate her for the loss.) The Supreme Court held that the widow's promise to marry her fiancé was not sufficient consideration because it was incapable of being valued in money or money's worth. Nor was her forfeiture of $100,000 in the trust sufficient consideration, because the benefit of that value did not go to the transferor, her fiancé, although the widow did in fact give up something of value.

Consideration in Marital Rights and Support Rights Situations

Two issues often arise in connection with the consideration question: (1) Does the relinquishment of marital rights constitute consideration in money or money's worth? (2) Does the relinquishment of support rights constitute consideration in money or money's worth?

The Code is specific in the case of certain property settlements. IRC Sec. 2516 provides that transfers of property or property interests made under the terms of a written agreement between spouses in settlement of marital or property rights are deemed to be for an adequate and full consideration. Such transfers are, therefore, exempt from the gift tax—whether or not the agreement is approved by or incorporated into a divorce decree—if the divorce and the agreement occur within a specific 3-year period in relation to each other. For example, if a husband agrees to give his wife $100,000 as a lump-sum settlement in exchange for her release of all marital rights that she has in his estate, the $100,000 transfer is not subject to the gift tax if the requirements stated above are met.

A spouse's relinquishment of the right to support constitutes consideration that can be measured in money or money's worth. Likewise, a transfer in satisfaction of the right to support of the transferor's minor children is made for money's worth. (But most transfers to or for the benefit of adult children are generally treated as gifts, unless state law requires the transferor to support that child for some reason.)

Transfers Pursuant to Compromises or Court Orders

Consideration is an important factor when a transfer is made pursuant to compromises of bona fide disputes or court orders. Such transfers are not considered taxable gifts because they are deemed to be made for adequate and full consideration. For example, if a mother and daughter are in litigation and the daughter is claiming a large sum of money, a compromise payment by the mother to the daughter is not a gift. However, in an intrafamily situation in which the court is not convinced that there is a bona fide arm's-length adversary proceeding, the gift tax will be imposed. For example, in a case where a widow settled with a son who threatened to break his father's will, the gift tax was levied.

Likewise, the gift tax can be applied even in the case of a transfer made pursuant to (or approved by) a court decree if there is not an adversary proceeding. For example, when an incompetent's property was transferred by the incompetent's guardian to another, the transfer has been held to be a gift even though it was approved or mandated by a court decree, assuming the incompetent had no legal duty to transfer the property. (Note, however, that if one who was declared incompetent in appropriate legal proceedings attempts to personally give away property—that is, without the guardian's consent—a gift may not result if the local law requires legal capacity as an essential element of a valid gift.)

Is the Transfer a Taxable Gift?

The factors used to make this determination include whether the

- donor and donee were respectively competent to make and accept the gift
- donor <u>fully</u> gave up all ownership and control of the property
- property was transferred for less than its value in money or money's worth
- property value exceeded the federal annual exclusion amount*
- delivery of the gift is made to the donee

* covered in depth later in this textbook

Types of Gifts

Direct Gifts

Cash or tangible personal property is the subject of most transfers affected by the gift tax law. Delivery of the property itself generally effectuates the gift. Real property is typically given by the delivery of an executed deed. If a person purchases a U.S. savings bond but has the bond registered in someone else's name and delivers the bond to that person, a gift has been made. (If the bonds are titled jointly between the purchaser and another, no gift occurs until the other person cashes in the bond or has the bond reissued in his or her name only.)

Income that will be earned in the future can constitute a gift presently subject to tax. For example, an author can give a right to future royalties to a daughter or son. Such a gift is valued according to its present value; that is, the gift is not considered to be a series of year-by-year gifts valued as the income is paid, but rather a single gift valued on the date the right to future income is assigned. Current valuation is made even if, for some reason, the payments are reduced substantially or they cease. In other words, no adjustment is required—or allowed—if the actual income paid to the donee is more or less than the valuation.

Forgiving a debt constitutes a gift in nonbusiness situations. For example, if a father lends his son $100,000 and later cancels the note, the forgiveness constitutes a $100,000 gift.

Some forgiveness of indebtedness, however, constitutes income to the benefited party. If a creditor tears up a debtor's note in return for services rendered by the debtor, the result is the same as if the creditor compensates the debtor for the services rendered and the debtor then uses the cash to satisfy the debt. The debtor realizes income and does not receive a gift.

Payments in excess of obligations can be gifts. Clearly a person does not make a gift when he or she pays the bills. Therefore, when a person pays bills or purchases food or clothing for a spouse or minor children, that person is not making gifts. Courts have allowed considerable latitude in this area. But if a father gives his minor daughter a $50,000 ring, the IRS may claim the transfer goes beyond his obligation of support. Payments made on behalf of adult children are often considered gifts. For example, if a mother pays her adult son's living expenses and mortgage payments or gives an adult child a monthly allowance, the transfer is a gift subject to tax.

In another situation the taxpayer, pursuant to an agreement incorporated in a divorce decree, created two trusts for the support of his minor children. He put a substantial amount of money in the trusts, which provided that after the children reached age 21 they were to receive the corpus. The court measured the economic value of the father's support obligation and held that the excess of the trust corpus over that value was a taxable gift. Only the portion of the transfer required to support the children during their minority was not subject to the gift tax.

Indirect Gifts

Indirect gifts, such as the payment of another's expenses, are subject to the gift tax. For instance, if a father makes payments on an adult son's car or pays premiums on a life insurance policy his wife owns on his life, such payments are gifts.

The shifting of property rights alone can trigger gift tax consequences. In one case, an employee gave up his vested rights to employer contributions in a profit-sharing plan. He was deemed to have made a gift to the remaining participants in the plan. Similarly, an employee who has a vested right to an annuity is making a gift if the choice is made to take—irrevocably—a lesser annuity coupled with an agreement that payments are continued to the designated beneficiary. No gift occurs until the time that the employee's selection of the survivor annuity becomes irrevocable.

Third-party transfers may be the medium for a taxable gift. For example, if a father gives his son $100,000 in consideration of his son's promise to provide a lifetime income to the father's sister, the father has made an indirect gift to his sister. Furthermore, if the cost of providing a lifetime annuity for the sister is less than $100,000, the father also has made a gift to his son.

The creation of a family partnership may involve an indirect gift. The mere creation or existence of a family partnership (which is often useful in shifting and spreading income among family members and in reducing estate taxes) does not, per se, mean a gift has been made. But if the value of a family member's services is nil or minimal and earnings are primarily due to assets other than those contributed by the partners in question, the creation of the partnership (or another partner's contribution of assets) may constitute a gift.

At the other extreme, if new partners contribute valuable services in exchange for their share of the partnership's earnings and the business does not own a significant amount of capital assets, the formation of a family partnership does not constitute a gift.

Transfers by and to corporations are often forms of indirect gifts. Technically, the gift tax is not imposed upon corporations, but transfers by or to a corporation are often considered to be made by or to corporate shareholders. The regulations state that if a corporation makes a transfer to an individual for inadequate consideration, the difference between the value of the money or other property transferred and the consideration paid is a gift to the transferee from the corporation's stockholders. For example, a gratuitous transfer of property by a family-owned corporation to the father of the shareholders of a corporation could be treated as a gift from the children to their father.

Generally, a transfer to a corporation for inadequate consideration is a gift from the transferor to the corporation's other shareholders. A gift to a corporation (that is, shareholders) is usually treated as a future-interest gift because shareholders do not have present and immediate access to the gift. For example, a transfer by a mother to a corporation that she and her children own is treated as a gift from the mother to the children. (The amount of such a gift is computed after subtracting the percentage of the gift equal to the percentage of the transferor's ownership.)

A double danger lies in corporate gifts. The IRS may argue that (1) in reality the corporation made a distribution taxable as a dividend to its stockholders and (2) the shareholders in turn made a gift to the recipient of the transfer. Because any distribution from a corporation to a shareholder generally constitutes a dividend to the extent of corporate earnings and profits, the IRS could claim that a transfer was first a constructive dividend to the shareholders and then a constructive gift by them to the donee. For example, if a family-owned corporation sold property with a fair market value of $450,000 for $350,000 to the son of its shareholders, the transaction could be considered a $100,000 constructive dividend to the shareholder-parents, followed by a $100,000 constructive gift by them to their son.

There are exceptions to the general rule that transfers to or from corporations are contraindicated. A transfer may be deemed to be a charitable contribution from the corporation, not from the shareholders, and a contribution to a corporation for inadequate consideration may be deemed to be a contribution to capital rather than a gift. For example, a corporation may make a contribution to the Boy Scouts of America and take a deduction of up to 10 percent of its taxable income (with certain adjustments) (IRC Sec. 170(b)(2)). Furthermore, if there is a legitimate business motive, the transfer may not be a gift even if adequate consideration is lacking. Generally, gift tax problems arise only when the corporation is family owned and closely held.

Life insurance—or life insurance premiums—can be the subject of an indirect gift in three types of situations: (1) the purchase of a policy for another person's benefit, (2) the assignment of an existing policy, and (3) payment of premiums. (The first two situations are discussed directly below. Premium payments are discussed later.)

The insured has made a gift measurable by the cost of the policy if the insured purchases a policy on his or her life and

- names a beneficiary or beneficiaries other than his or her estate
- does not retain the right to regain the policy or the proceeds or revest the economic benefits of the policy (that is, retains no reversionary interest in himself or herself or the estate)
- does not retain the power to change the beneficiaries or their proportionate interests (that is, makes the beneficiary designation irrevocable)

All three of these requirements must be met, however, before the insured is deemed to have made a taxable gift.

If an insured makes an absolute assignment of a policy or, in some other way, relinquishes all rights and powers in a previously issued policy, a gift is made. It is measurable by its replacement cost (which, in the case of a whole life policy, is equal to the interpolated terminal reserve plus the unearned premium at the date of the gift).

This can lead to an insidious tax trap. Assume a wife owns a policy on the life of her husband. She names her children as revocable beneficiaries. At her husband's death, the IRS could argue that the wife has made a constructive gift to the children equal to the entire amount of the death proceeds. It is as if the wife received the proceeds to which she was entitled and then gave that money to her children.

An extension of this reasoning, which was actually (and successfully) applied by the IRS, is a case in which the owner of policies on the life of her husband placed the policies in trust for the benefit of her children. Because she reserved the right to revoke the trust at any time before her husband died, she did not make a completed gift—until his death. It was not until his death that she relinquished all her powers over the policy. When her husband died the trust became irrevocable, and the gift, therefore, became complete. The value of the gift was the full value of the death proceeds rather than the replacement value of the policy when it was placed in trust.

GRATUITOUS TRANSFERS THAT ARE NOT GIFTS

A number of common situations do not incur the gift tax because they do not involve gifts in the tax sense. These situations fall into three basic categories: (1) property or an interest in property that has not been transferred, (2) certain transfers in the ordinary course of business, and (3) sham gifts.

Requirement That Property or Interest in Property Be Transferred

Gratuitous Services Rendered

The gift tax is imposed only on the transfer of *property* or an *interest in property*. Although the term *property* is given the broadest possible meaning, it does not include services that are rendered gratuitously. Regardless of how valuable the services are that one person renders for the benefit of another person, those services do not constitute the transfer of property rights and, therefore, do not fall within the scope of the gift tax (Rev. Rul. 56–472, 1956–2 C.B. 21).

Difficult questions often arise in this area. For example, if an executor performs the multiplicity of services required in the course of administering a large and complex estate, the services are clearly of economic benefit to the estate's beneficiaries. Yet, because services are just that, they do not constitute a transfer of property rights. If the executor formally waives the fee (within 6 months of appointment as executor) or fails to claim the fees or commissions by the time of filing and indicates through action (or inaction) that he or she intends to serve without charge, no property is transferred. Conversely, once fees are taken (or if the fees are deducted on an estate, inheritance, or income tax return), the executor has received taxable income. If the executor then chooses not to (or neglects to) actually receive that money and it goes to the estate's beneficiaries, an indirect (and possibly taxable) gift is made to those individuals.

disclaimer

Disclaimers (Renunciations)

Generally, a potential donee is deemed to have accepted a valuable gift unless it is expressly refused. But, in some cases, an intended donee may decide (for whatever reason) that he or she does not want or does not need the gift. If the donee disclaims the right to the gift (that is, refuses to take it), it will usually go to someone else as the result of that renunciation.

By disclaiming, the intended transferee is in effect making a transfer to the new recipient that is subject to the gift tax—unless the disclaimer meets the IRC disclaimer requirements.

qualified disclaimer

A disclaimer that does meet those requirements is called a *qualified disclaimer* and is treated for gift tax purposes as if the property interest passes directly from the original transferor to the person who receives it because of the disclaimer. In other words, the disclaimant is treated as if no transfer of property or an interest in property was made to the person to whom the interest passes because of the disclaimer. The property is treated as though it passed directly from the original donor to the eventual recipient. This makes the qualified disclaimer an important estate planning tool.

There are a number of requirements for a qualified disclaimer of gifted property under federal law:

- The refusal must be in writing.
- The writing must be received by the transferor, or the transferor's legal representative, or the holder of the legal title to the property no later than 9 months after the later of (1) the date on which the transfer creating the interest is made (date of death) or (2) the date the person disclaiming becomes 21.
- The person disclaiming must not have accepted the interest or any of its benefits.
- Because of the refusal, someone other than the person disclaiming must receive the property interest. The person making the disclaimer cannot in any way influence the selection of who will be the recipient of the disclaimed property.

Note that state law requirements for disclaimers may vary from federal law so that what constitutes a qualified disclaimer under federal law may not be valid for state law disclaimer purposes.

The Promise to Make a Gift

Although income that will be earned in the future can be the subject of a gift, the Tax Court holds that the promise to make a gift in the future is not taxable—even if the promise is enforceable. This is because a mere promise to make a transfer in the future is not itself a transfer. The IRS agrees—as long as the gift cannot be valued. But if the promise is enforceable under state law, the IRS will attempt to subject it to the gift tax when it becomes capable of valuation.

Transfers in Ordinary Course of Business

Compensation for Personal Services

Situations often arise in business settings that purport to be gifts from corporate employers to individuals. The IRS often claims that such transfers are, in fact, compensation for personal services rather than gifts and argues that the property transfer constitutes income to the transferee rather than a gift by the transferor. In these cases, the focus is on the effect to the transferee; did the transferee receive taxable income or a tax-free gift?

A payment may be taken out of the normal gift tax rules (and thus be considered taxable income to the recipient) by the regulations, which state that "the gift tax is not applicable to . . . ordinary business transactions." An *ordinary business transaction,* defined as a sale, exchange, or other transfer of property (a transaction that is bona fide, at arm's length, and free from donative intent) made in the ordinary course of business, is considered as if made for an adequate and full consideration in money or money's worth.

ordinary business transaction

A situation is considered an ordinary business transaction and is not classified as a tax-free gift to the recipient if it is "free from donative intent." This means that donative intent becomes quite important. The taxpayer-recipient, of course, likes to have the transaction considered an income-tax-free gift, while the IRS reaps larger revenues if the transfer is considered compensation and is, therefore, taxable income. A payment is considered a tax-free gift to the recipient (the donor must still pay any gift taxes) rather than taxable income, if the donor's dominant reason for making the transfer is detached and disinterested generosity rather than consideration for past, present, or future services (an example being an employer who makes flood relief payments to employees because of a feeling of affection, charity, or similar impulses). It is not a gift if the primary impetus for the payment is (1) the constraining force of any legal or moral duty or (2) an anticipated economic benefit.

Among the factors typically studied in examining the donor's intent are

- the length and value of the employee's services
- the manner in which the employer determined the amount of the reputed gift
- the way the employer treated the payment in the corporate books and on tax returns; that is, whether the payment is deducted as a business expense. (The corporation's characterization of payment is often persuasive when the corporation makes a payment or series of payments to the widow or widower of a deceased employee. The employer generally prefers to have such payments taxed as compensation to the employee's survivors so the corporation can deduct payments as compensation for the employee's past services.)

In one case, a business friend gave a car to the recipient after the recipient had furnished him with the names of potential customers. The car was not a gift but was intended as payment for past services as well as an inducement for the taxpayer to supply additional names in the future. In another case, however, an employer made a payment of $20,000 to a retiring executive when he resigned. After examining the employer's esteem and kindness as well as the appreciation of the retiring officer, the court stated that the transfer was a gift and not taxable income. In a similar case, another court came to the same conclusion when it found payments were made "from generosity or charity rather than from the incentive of anticipated economic benefit."

This type of issue—whether the transfer is a gift or compensation—is settled on a case-by-case basis after an analysis of the circumstances evidencing motive or intent. Generally, the intrafamily transfer is considered a gift even if the recipient rendered past services, while transfers to persons outside the family are usually considered compensation.

Bad Bargains

bad bargain

A *bad bargain* is another ordinary-course-of-business situation. A sale, exchange, or other property transfer made in the ordinary course of business is treated as if it was made in return for adequate and full consideration in money or money's worth. This assumes the transaction is bona fide, at arm's length, and not donative in intent.

There are a number of court-decided examples of bad bargains that have not resulted in gift tax treatment. In one case, certain senior executive shareholders sold stock to junior executives at less than fair market value, as part of a plan to give the younger executives a larger stake in business profits. The court noted that the transfers were for less-than-adequate consideration but stated that "the pertinent inquiry for gift tax purposes is whether the transaction is a genuine business transaction, as distinguished, for example, from the marital or family type of transaction." Bad bargains (transfers for less-than-adequate money's worth) are made every day in the business world for one reason or another, but no one would think for a minute that any gift is involved, even in the broadest sense of the term *gift*.

Another example of a no-gift situation is a group of business people conveying real estate to an unrelated business corporation with the expectation of doing business with that corporation in the future.

But the ordinary-course-of-business exception has its limits; there is no protection from the gift tax law if the transferor's motive is to pass on the family fortune to the following generation. In one case, a father transferred property to his children at a price below the fair market value. In return he received non-interest-bearing notes rather than cash and continued to make certain payments on the children's behalf with respect to the property. The court ruled that these actions showed that, in reality, he was not dealing with his children at arm's length. That same result could occur if the father employs the son at a wage of $50,000 a year, but the son renders services worth only $20,000 a year. The IRS could claim that the $30,000 difference constitutes a gift.

What Is __Not__ a Taxable Gift

- transfer in which transferor receives consideration equal to transferred property's value
- transfers made due to court orders
- transfers made due to dispute compromises
- promises to make a gift
- gratuitous services
- qualified disclaimed property
- transfers in ordinary course of business
- transfers within the annual exclusion amount*
- certain transfers between spouses pursuant to divorce
- transfers to providers of educational or medical services
- transfers to political organizations
- incomplete gifts

* covered elsewhere in this textbook

Sham Gifts

It is often advantageous—for income or estate tax purposes—to characterize a transaction as a gift. The taxpayer's goal is to shift the burden of income taxes from a high- to a relatively low-bracket taxpayer and yet keep the income within the same family unit. But if the transfer has no real economic significance other than the hoped-for tax savings, it is disregarded for tax purposes. That is, if the transaction does not have meaning—apart from its tax sense—it is not considered a gift by the IRS or by the courts and, therefore, does not shift the incidence of taxation.

For example, a well-known golfer contracted with a motion picture company to make a series of films depicting his form and golf style. In return, the golfer was to receive a lump sum of $120,000 plus a 50 percent royalty on the earnings from the picture. But before any pictures were made he sold his father the right to his services for $1. The father, in turn, transferred the rights in the contract to a trust for his son's three children. The court held that the entire series of transactions had no tax effect and that the income was completely taxable to the golfer.

Assignment-of-income questions are among the most common and confusing in tax law because they often involve inconsistent property, gift, and income tax results. For example, a mother could agree to give her son one-half of every dollar she earned in the following year. The agreement might be effective for property law purposes, and the son could have an enforceable legal right to one-half of his mother's income. Gift tax law might also recognize the transfer of a property right, and the present value of a mother's future income could be subject to the gift tax. Yet for income tax purposes, the mother remains liable for taxes on the entire earnings.

A general agent for a life insurance company assigned renewal commissions to his wife. Although the wife had a property law right to the commissions and the present worth of the renewals the wife would receive was treated as a gift, the general agent was subject to income tax on the commissions as they were paid. In a similar case, a doctor transferred the right to accounts receivable from his practice to a trust for his daughter. Again, the court held that as the trustee received payments from the doctor's patients, those sums were taxable to the doctor even though he had made an irrevocable and taxable gift.

Gifts of income from property meet a similar fate. For example, if a woman assigns the right to next year's rent from a building to her daughter or next year's dividends from specified stock to her grandson, the transfers are effective for property law purposes and generate gift taxes, but the income is taxable to the donor for income tax purposes.

Gifts of the income-producing property, however, produce a more satisfactory result for donors; if the tree (property), the source of the income generated, is given away, the fruit (income) it bears is taxable to the tree's new owner. Thus, if the donor in the examples above had given both the building and the stock, gifts equal to the value of those properties would have been made, and the income produced by those assets would be taxed to her daughter and grandson, respectively. Likewise, if stock that cost the donor $1,000 is transferred to a donee when it is worth $2,500 and is later sold by the donee for $3,500, the donee takes the donor's cost ($1,000) as basis (with adjustments for any gift taxes paid) and pays taxes on the gain ($2,500).

EXEMPT GIFTS

A few types of gratuitous transfers are statutorily exempted from the gift tax. A qualified disclaimer, described above, is a good example (IRC Sec. 2518(a)). Certain transfers of property between spouses upon divorce (IRC Sec. 2516) are other examples.

Tuition paid to an educational institution for the education or training of an individual is exempt from the gift tax, regardless of the amount paid or the relationship of the parties (IRC Sec. 2503(e)). It is not required that the donor and donee be related for the gift to be exempt. This means parents, grandparents, or even friends can pay private school or college tuition for an individual without fear of incurring a gift tax.

Still another exempt transfer is the payment of medical care. A donor can pay for the medical care of a donee without making a gift. This allows children or other relatives—or friends—to pay the medical expenses of needy individuals (or anyone else) without worrying about incurring a gift tax (IRC Sec. 2503(e)).

Also, transfers of money or other property to a political organization (as defined in IRC Sec. 527(e)(1)) are exempt from the gift tax if the transfer is for the use of the political organization (IRC Sec. 2501(a)(5)). But contributions to individuals do not come within the exemption.

Exempt Gifts

- qualified disclaimer
- educational tuition
- medical care
- political organization contributions

REQUIREMENTS FOR A COMPLETED GIFT

completed transfer

A completed transfer is necessary before the gift tax can be applied. The phrase *completed transfer* implies that the subject of the gift is beyond the donor's recall; that is, the donor has irrevocably parted with dominion and control over the gift. There is no completed gift if the donor has the power to change the disposition of the gift and thus alter the identity of the donee(s) or the amount of the gift. Technically stated, if the donor can revoke the gift (either alone or in conjunction with a party who does not have a substantial amount to lose by the revocation), it is not a completed gift.

Parting with dominion and control is a good test of completeness, but in a number of cases it is difficult to ascertain just when that event occurs. Some of the more common problem areas are (1) incomplete delivery situations, (2) cancellation of notes, and (3) incomplete transfers to trusts.

Incomplete Delivery

There is incomplete delivery when certain technical details are omitted or a stage in the transfer process is left uncompleted. For example, no gift is made at the moment the donor gives the donee a personal check or note. The transfer of a personal check is not complete and taxable until it is paid (or certified or accepted) by the drawee, or until it is negotiated for value to a third person. For instance, depending on the particular circumstances, if a check is mailed in December, received in late December, but not cashed until January of the following year, it may be treated for gift tax purposes as though no gift is made until that later year. This is because the maker of a check typically is under no legal obligation to honor the check until it is cashed (presented for payment or negotiated to a third person for value). Likewise, a gift of a negotiable note is not complete until it is paid.

An individual on his or her deathbed will sometimes make a gift in anticipation of imminent death from a specific illness, indicating that he or she wishes the donee to have the gifted property at the donor's death. Such a gift is called a *gift causa mortis*. It is a gift conditional upon the donor's dying as he or she anticipates. What happens if the donor recovers? Assuming the facts indicate that the gift was indeed a gift causa mortis (that is, the transfer was made in anticipation of death from a specific illness and the gift was contingent on the occurrence of the donor's death), neither the original conveyance nor the return of the property to the donor is subject to the gift tax if the transferor recovers and the transferee returns the property. A gift causa mortis is a conditional gift that becomes complete only at the donor's death and is, therefore, incomplete as long as the donor is alive.

gift causa mortis

A gift of stock is completed on the date that properly endorsed stock certificates are delivered to the donee or the donee's agent by the donor. If the donor instead delivers the stock to his or her agent or broker, or to the issuing corporation or its transfer agent, for the purpose of having the stock certificates transferred into the name of the donee, the gift is complete on the date the stock is transferred to the donee on the books of the corporation (Treas. Reg. 25.2511–2(h)).

Transfer of U.S. government bonds is governed by federal law rather than state law. Even if state law requirements for a valid gift are met, for tax purposes no completed gift is made until the registration is changed in accordance with federal regulations. For example, if a grandmother purchases a U.S. savings bond registered as payable to her and her two grandchildren as co-owners, no gift is made to the grandchildren until one of them surrenders the bond for cash.

The creation of a revocable joint bank account (checking or savings) constitutes a common example of an incomplete transfer. Typically, the person making a deposit can withdraw all the funds or any portion of them. Therefore, the donor retains a power to revoke the gift, and it is not complete. When the donee makes a withdrawal of funds from the account (and thereby eliminates the donor's dominion and control), a gift of the funds occurs.

A similar situation exists in the case of a joint brokerage account. The creation and contribution to a joint brokerage account held in street name is not a gift until the joint owner makes a withdrawal for personal benefit. At that time, the donee acquires indefeasible rights, and the donor parts irrevocably with the funds. Conversely, if a person calls a broker and says, "Buy 100 shares of Texas Oil and Gas and title them in joint names—mine and my spouse's—with rights of survivorship," the purchase constitutes a gift to the spouse. The spouse acquires rights that he or she did not have to a portion of the stock. (No gift tax is due in this case owing to the unlimited gift tax marital deduction described in a later chapter.)

Totten trust

Totten trusts (bank accounts in which the donor who is the named "trustee" makes a deposit for the donee—"Joanne Q. Donor in trust for James P. Donee"—and retains possession of the savings book) are typical revocable transfers. Because the donor retains the right of withdrawal until death (when the balance passes to the beneficiary), no gift occurs at the creation of the account, and the named donee is not generally entitled to the property until the donor's death. This type of nonprobate arrangement is also called a *pay-on-death (POD) account*. Generally, a Totten trust or pay-on-death account may be in the form of a checking account, savings account, money market account, or certificate of deposit.

pay-on-death (POD) account

Some property cannot be delivered conveniently to the intended donee; farm property is a good example. When it would be difficult or impossible to make physical delivery of the gift, a gift is usually considered completed when the delivery is as complete as possible. In one case, a father owned cattle he wished to give to his minor children. The court held that the gift was complete when he branded the livestock with each child's initials, even though he kept the cattle with others he owned. The court held that the father was acting as the natural guardian of the children and had done everything necessary to make a completed gift.

Real estate is transferred through the execution of a deed in favor of the donee. But if the donor retains the deed, does not record it, makes no attempt to inform the donee of the transfer, and continues to treat the property as his or her own, no transfer occurs.

Cancellation of Notes

In many cases, a transfer of property is made and then the transferor takes back notes from the donee. The transaction is not characterized as a sale until the transferee pays off the notes. But if the transferor forgives the notes, the forgiveness is a gift.

Cancellation of notes is a frequently used technique for two reasons. First, it provides a simple means of giving to a number of donees certain property that is not readily divisible. Second, by forgiving the notes over a period of years, the donor can maximize the use of the federal gift tax annual exclusion and applicable credit amount discussed in a later chapter. A good example is a donor who deeds real estate to her sons and takes back notes payable serially on an annual basis. Each son is required to pay his mother $11,000 per year. But when the notes come due, the donor marks the notes "canceled by." The gift occurs in the year each note is canceled—as long as there is no preestablished plan for the donor to forgive notes on a systematic basis in future years.

Incomplete Gifts in Trust

Donors sometimes transfer property to a trust but retain the right to revoke the transfer. When property is transferred to such a revocable trust, that transfer is not a completed gift. Only when the donor relinquishes all retained control over the transferred property (that is, when the trust becomes irrevocable) is a completed gift made.

Tax liability is measured by the value at the moment the gift becomes complete rather than at the time of the transfer. This can have harsh tax consequences. For example, if the donor retains the power to alter the interests of the trust beneficiaries, even if no powers can be exercised for the donor's own benefit, the transfer is not complete. For instance, assume that a father transfers stock to a trust for his two children and three grandchildren. The income of the trust is payable to the donor's children for as long as they live, and then the remainder is payable to his grandchildren or their estates. If the donor retains the power to vary the amount of income his children receive or to reach into corpus to enhance their security, the gift is incomplete. But the gift becomes complete when the donor relinquishes control. If that happens when the stock has substantially increased in value, as is often the case, the gift tax payable by the donor also substantially increases.

Incomplete Transfers for Gift Tax Purposes

- checks (incomplete until paid/certified/accepted)
- anticipation of imminent death (causa mortis)
- stock (incomplete until endorsed and delivered to donee or titled in donee's name on corporate books)
- U.S. government bonds (incomplete until federal registration requirements are met or bonds are surrendered by donee for cash)
- joint bank accounts (incomplete until donee withdraws funds)
- deeds (incomplete until delivered to donee/recorded in donee's name)
- forgiveness/cancellation of debt (incomplete until debt on property is canceled)
- incomplete gifts (incomplete as long as donor/grantor retains rights in transferred property

---

VALUATION OF PROPERTY FOR GIFT TAX PURPOSES

Valuation is the first step in the computation of the gift tax. Only after the property is valued can the applicable annual exclusion and various deductions be applied in arriving at the amount of the taxable gift and the ultimate gift tax.

The amount of the gift is the fair market value of the property on the date the gift becomes complete. For gift tax purposes, value is defined as "the price at which the property would change hands between a willing buyer and a willing seller, neither being under any compulsion to buy or to sell, and both having reasonable knowledge of relevant facts."

What Is Fair Market Value?

Fair market value is the amount a willing buyer and a willing seller would accept and pay with neither being obliged to buy or to sell.

Although the provisions of the gift tax law on valuation parallel the estate tax law in many respects, there is one major difference—property transferred during lifetime is valued for gift tax purposes on the date the gift is made. No alternate valuation date is allowed.

There are certain valuation problems unique to the gift tax law. These include problems associated with (1) indebtedness with respect to transferred property, (2) restrictions on the use or disposition of property, (3) transfers of large blocks of stock, (4) valuation of mutual fund shares, and (5) valuation of life insurance and annuity contracts.

Gift Tax Property Valuation Problem Areas

- encumbrance of debt or obligation
  - fair market value diminished by debt amount (unless donor has personal liability for debt)
- restrictions in use or disposition
  - fair market value diminished by limitations
- transfers of large blocks of stock
  - valuation discount may apply
- mutual fund shares
  - public redemption price per share valuation
- life insurance
  - replacement value of similar policy

Indebtedness with Respect to Transferred Property

Generally, when the subject of a gift is encumbered or otherwise subject to an obligation, only the net value of the gift—the value of the property less the amount of the obligation—is subject to the gift tax. Under this rule, which assumes the donor is *not* personally liable for the debt, the amount of the gift is the donor's equity in the property.

However, if the donor is personally liable for the indebtedness—which is secured by a mortgage on the gift property—a different result occurs. In this case, the amount of the gift may be the entire value of the property, unreduced by the debt. The reason for the difference is that if a solvent donor makes a gift subject to a debt and the creditor proceeds against the pledged property, the donee is, in effect, paying the donor's personal debt. In some cases, this makes the donee a creditor of the donor. If the donee can then collect from the donor the amount paid to the donor's creditor, the donee has received the entire value of the gift rather than merely the equity.

For example, assume a donor transfers a $100,000 building subject to a $40,000 mortgage on which the donor is personally liable. If the donor's creditors collect the $40,000 by proceeding against the pledged building and the donee is subrogated to that creditor's rights against the donor-debtor (that is, the donee now stands in the shoes of the creditor), the donee can collect an additional $40,000 from the donor.

A third possibility is that the donor-debtor is personally liable for the indebtedness secured by a mortgage on the gifted property, but the donee has no right to step into the creditor's shoes and recover the debt from the donor. In this case, the amount of the gift is merely the amount of the donor's equity in the property. In this example, that amount would be $60,000 ($100,000 fair market value minus $40,000 of indebtedness).

If the donee has no right to proceed against the donor and recover the debt, the actual facts determine the result. If the donor in fact pays off the liability after transferring the mortgaged property to the donee, the donor makes an additional gift. But if the donee pays off the liability (or if the mortgagee forecloses), the gift is only the donor's equity.

net gift

One of the obligations that can be imposed upon a donee is a requirement that the donee pay the gift tax. The donor has the primary liability to pay the gift tax, and the donee is only secondarily liable. The donor can—expressly or by implication—require the donee to pay the donor's gift tax liability. If the donee is required to pay the gift tax imposed on the transfer (or if the tax is payable out of the transferred property), the gift is referred to as a *net gift*. With a net gift, the value of the donated property is reduced by the amount of the gift tax. Net gifts are discussed more in a later chapter.

Obviously, the two figures—net amount transferred and tax payable on the transfer—are interdependent. Fortunately, there is a revenue ruling formula for making the computation when such interdependent variables are involved.

It is important to note that, for income tax purposes, there are cases that state the donor must recognize gain if the donee pays the tax or if payment is made from the gifted property. Gain is realized by the donor for income tax purposes to the extent the gift tax paid by the donee exceeds the donor's basis for the property.

Restrictions on Use or Disposition of Property

Value is affected by restrictions placed on the donee's use or ability to dispose of the property received. The general rule is that most restrictive agreements do not fix the value of such property but often have a persuasive effect on price.

For example, a donor gives stock to his daughter subject to an agreement between the corporation and its shareholders. Under that agreement, the corporation is entitled to purchase those shares at their book value, $30 per share, upon the retirement or death of the stockholder. Does the existence of such an agreement fix the value of the shares at book value? After all, no buyer would pay more than $30 a share while the restriction is operative. But if the stock has *use values* other than sale values (for example, if it pays dividends of $10 a year), it may have a fair market value in excess of $30 a share.

On one hand, the corporation's option right to purchase the stock at $30 a share limits the fair market value; on the other hand, use values, such as the right to receive dividends, increase the fair market value. How much the use values increase the fair market value is largely dependent on how much time is likely to pass before the corporation has an opportunity to exercise its option and also on the probability that the corporation will exercise its option at that time.

In the example above, a court would probably state that the existence of a restrictive agreement would not fix the purchase price, because the circumstances requiring purchase (retirement or death) do not exist at the date of the gift. But the existence of the agreement itself is likely to have a depressing effect on the market value of the stock and result in a discounted gift tax value.

Transfers of Large Blocks of Stock

blockage discount

A principle that applies to the valuation of both lifetime gifts and testamentary transfers is the so-called *blockage discount*. This blockage rule may allow the taxpayer the benefit of a discount below the actual listed market value of transferred stock. The rule applies if the taxable transfer consists of a block of stock large enough to depress the market value of each share if the entire block is sold at once. The discount is allowed for the hypothetical reduction in value of the shares, assuming a sale of the entire block over a reasonable period of time. However, the transferor may diminish or remove the advantage of the blockage discount if the block of stock to be transferred is divided among several donees or the transfer is spread over a number of tax years.

Valuation of Mutual Fund Shares

Mutual fund shares are generally valued at their public redemption price per share.

Valuation of Life Insurance and Annuity Contracts

When a life insurance policy is the subject of a gift, the value is the policy's replacement value: the cost of similar or comparable policies issued by the same company.

If the policy is transferred immediately (within the first year) after its purchase, the gift is equal in value to the gross premium paid to the insurer.

If the policy is paid up at the time it is assigned (or is a single-premium policy), the amount of the gift is the amount of premium the issuing company would charge for the same type of single-premium policy of equal face amount on the insured's life, based on the insured's age at the transfer date. (The impaired health of the insured is not considered by the regulations, but the IRS might argue that the adverse health of the insured at the time of the gift affects valuation.)

If the policy is in a premium-paying stage at the time it is transferred, the value of the gift is generally equal to (1) the interpolated terminal reserve plus (2) unearned premiums on the date of the gift.

Inclusion Value of Policies Owned on Life of Another

Policy	Value
• new	• gross premium paid
• paid-up or single premium	• replacement cost
• premium-paying whole life	• unearned portion of last premium plus interpolated terminal reserve
• term	• unused premium

Except in the early years of most contracts, the interpolated terminal reserve is roughly equivalent to the policy's cash value. In special conditions—such as when the interpolated terminal reserve does not approximate the policy's true value (for example, if the insured donor is terminally ill and has only one or 2 months to live)—the value of a premium-paying policy may be more than the sum of the interpolated terminal reserve plus unearned premiums as of the date of the gift. (Unearned premiums are defined as the proportionate part of the last premium paid that is attributable to the remainder of the period for which the premium was paid.)

Example: Todd transferred a whole life insurance policy to his son Otto on January 1, 2004. The policy terminal reserve was $18,000 on July 1, 2003, and $21,000 on July 1, 2004. If Todd paid the full $1,400 annual premium on July 1, 2004, the value of the policy for gift

> tax purposes is $20,200. The interpolated reserve was
> $19,500 on January 1, 2004, because this is the mid-
> point of the year during which the reserve increases by
> $3,000. Half the premium ($700) is unearned at the
> time of the gift. Therefore, the policy value was
> $20,200 ($19,500 + $700) on January 1, 2004.

Premiums paid by (or on behalf of) the donor after the transfer are also gifts. Therefore, when an owner of a life insurance policy irrevocably assigns that policy to another person or a trust, each premium the owner pays subsequent to the transfer is considered a gift to the new policyowner (or the beneficial owner or owners of the trust's assets).

Usually the premium payer and the donor are the same. However, the IRS has stated that if an employee assigns his or her group life insurance policy to an irrevocable trust established for the employee's family, a cash premium paid by the employer is deemed to be a gift in the amount of the premium. The deemed gift is from the employee to the beneficiaries of the trust. But a rather poorly considered and not widely accepted ruling has held that the assignment of the group term coverage itself is not a taxable gift because the coverage has no ascertainable value.

CHAPTER REVIEW

Answers to the review questions and the self-test questions start on page 717.

Key Terms

gift	completed transfer
donor	gift *causa mortis*
donee	Totten trust
disclaimer	pay-on-death (POD) account
qualified disclaimer	net gift
ordinary business transaction	blockage discount
bad bargain	

Review Questions

6-1.   What are the nontax advantages of making lifetime gifts?

6-2.   Describe the factors that must be present for a transfer to be considered a taxable gift for gift tax purposes.

6-3.   Steven agrees to give his wife, Ellen, $100,000 as a lump-sum settlement upon their divorce. In turn, she agrees to give up all the marital rights she may have had in his estate. What requirements must be met for Steven's transfer to escape gift tax liability?

6-4. Mr. John Powers lends his adult son, Eric, $15,000 with interest at the rate of 10 percent. Mr. Powers cancels the note his son gave him. Explain the gift tax implications, if any, involved in this transaction.

6-5. George pays the rent for his 24-year-old daughter who is an aspiring actress living in New York. Has George made a gift?

6-6. Marty gives Mary, his daughter, $15,000 with the requirement that she must transfer an automobile she owns to her brother, Mark. The car is worth $11,000. Has a gift been made? To whom? Explain. (Ignore the annual exclusion.)

6-7. Steve is the sole proprietor of a small firm with a net worth of $300,000. He makes his 12-year-old daughter, Lara, a one-third partner.
   a. Has a gift been made in this transaction?
   b. Has a gift been made to Lara if she is an adult and performs bookkeeping services for the firm without a salary?

6-8. Alan and his wife, Sally, are the only stockholders in the AB Corporation, a real estate development company that owns various small parcels of undeveloped real estate. Alan is thinking of having the AB Corporation transfer certain individual parcels of real estate to his children for a price that is well below their true market value. What tax problems do you see in this proposed plan? Explain.

6-9. Joan Bolton owns a policy on the life of her husband, Jim. She names her children as beneficiaries because she has a large estate. Explain the potential problems of this arrangement.

6-10. Mr. Caruthers, a retired executive, takes over and manages the business owned by his son during his son's illness. The son would have had to pay $10,000 for a comparable replacement, but his father makes no charge for the services. Has a gift been made? Explain.

6-11. Describe the requirements necessary to have a qualified disclaimer of gifted property.

6-12. List the factors you would examine to determine whether property transferred to an employee is a gift or compensation for personal services.

6-13. A general agent for Wildlife of Arkansas assigns all his renewal commissions to his daughter. Explain the
   a. gift tax effect of the transaction
   b. income tax effect of the transaction

6-14. Identify the types of gifts that are exempt from the gift tax.

6-15.   Explain whether the following transactions are completed gifts:

    a.   Ed Smith gave his son a check in October of last year. As of February of this year, the son had not yet cashed it.

    b.   Jim Johnson, who thought he was dying of a rare disease, transferred title to his $200,000 home in Ocean City, Maryland, to his sister. Miraculously, Jim survived, and his sister deeded the house back to him after his complete recovery.

    c.   Jenny Moore purchased a $10,000 U.S. savings bond and had the bond titled in Jenny's name as well as the names of her three adult grand-children as co-owners. She has just told them of the gift.

    d.   The tennis pro, Harry Hathaway, placed his summer earnings in a joint bank account with his brother, Stewart. Stewart withdrew $8,000 of the $10,000 Harry had placed in the account.

6-16.   Gloria Gordon established an irrevocable trust for her son, Brian, and her daughter, Jamie. Gloria placed $100,000 of common stock into the trust.

    a.   Explain the gift tax effect of the transfer of stock to the trust if Gloria retained the power to alter the amount of income and principal for each of her children.

    b.   Describe the potential result if Gloria relinquished the right to allocate income to her beneficiaries at some future date.

6-17.   Drew Mazino owns land worth $60,000 with a mortgage of $20,000 against it. Drew is not personally liable for the debt. Drew gives the property to his daughter.

    a.   Compute the amount of the gift.

    b.   Describe how your answer would change if Drew were personally liable for the debt in a state where the donee is subrogated to the rights of Drew's creditors.

    c.   Would your answer to 6-17b differ if the donee had no right to proceed against Drew to recover the debt?

6-18.   Describe the effect of *blockage* on gift taxation.

6-19.   Ben Huggins is going to transfer the ownership of three policies on his life to his four adult children. Explain how the following types of policies are valued for gift tax purposes:

    a.   a 20-pay life policy in its 21st year (a whole life policy that becomes paid up after 20 years of premium payments)

    b.   a 10-year-old whole life policy on which Ben pays premiums annually

    c.   a newly purchased policy

6-20.   Alec transferred a whole life insurance policy to his son on July 1, 2004. The policy terminal reserve was $25,000 on January 1, 2003, and $28,000 on January 1, 2004. If Alec paid the full $2,500 annual premium on January 1, 2004, what is the value of the policy at the time of the gift?

Self-Test Questions

T   F   6-1.   One advantage of lifetime gifts is the potential reduction of probate costs.

T   F   6-2.   A gift may be subject to tax even though the donee is incapable of accepting the gift.

T   F   6-3.   If property is transferred for adequate and full consideration, no gift has occurred.

T   F   6-4.   Transfers between spouses in settlement of their marital or property rights are not considered gifts under the Internal Revenue Code if the spouses enter into a final decree of divorce within a specified 3-year period.

T   F   6-5.   Forgiveness of a debt between family members does not constitute a gift.

T   F   6-6.   Payment of living expenses for another person for whom one had no support obligation would be considered a gift to that person.

T   F   6-7.   In contrast to direct gifts, indirect gifts are exempt from gift tax.

T   F   6-8.   Gratuitous transfers made by a closely held corporation to a third party may be considered a gift from the shareholder(s).

T   F   6-9.   Payment of life insurance premiums for another person is not considered a gift.

T   F   6-10. A gift is made if an insured makes an absolute assignment of a life insurance policy.

T   F   6-11. The contribution of one's services can be considered a taxable gift if the services are rendered to an individual rather than a charity.

T   F   6-12. A valid disclaimer of a gift may be either oral or written to be exempt from gift taxes.

T   F   6-13. The gift tax is not generally applicable to ordinary business transactions.

T   F   6-14. If Mary gives her son the right to receive future income from her rental property, the son will be subject to income taxation on the rental income.

T   F   6-15. A gift is completed when the donor has irrevocably parted with dominion and control of the property interest that is the subject of the gift.

T   F   6-16. If Sam cashes a personal check in January that was given to him the previous October by his father, the father may elect either January or October as the date the gift was completed.

T   F   6-17. A Totten trust or pay-on-death account is an arrangement in which a donor makes a completed gift to a donee during lifetime, but the donee must wait until the donor's death to take possession of the asset.

T   F   6-18. A gift to a trust is considered complete even if the donor retains the right to revoke the gift.

T   F   6-19. For gift tax purposes, property is valued on the date the gift is completed.

T   F   6-20. If a donor requires a donee to pay the tax on gifted property, the value of the gift is reduced by any gift tax imposed.

T   F   6-21. Under the blockage rule, a block of stock is valued at its full listed market value.

T   F   6-22. The gift of a life insurance policy is valued differently depending upon whether the policy is newly issued, paid up, or in a premium-paying stage.

T   F   6-23. When a donor makes a taxable gift to a donee and the donor pays gift tax, the gift is referred to as a net gift.

Lifetime Transfers by Gift— An Overview of Federal Gift Taxation

Stephan R. Leimberg, Ted Kurlowicz, and Constance J. Fontaine*

Learning Objectives

An understanding of the material in this chapter should enable the student to

---

7-1. Describe the purpose, nature, and scope of the federal gift tax.

7-2. Describe several tax-related advantages of making lifetime gifts.

7-3. Describe the allowable reductions that can be used in determining taxable gifts.

7-4. Explain the procedure for computing the federal gift tax.

7-5. Explain the requirements for reporting gifts and paying the tax.

7-6. Explain the relationship of the federal gift system to the income tax system and to the estate tax system.

7-7. Explain how the basis of gifted property is determined.

7-8. Identify the various strategies and factors that must be examined in selecting property for gifts.

---

* Stephan R. Leimberg, JD, CLU, formerly was professor of taxation and estate planning at The American College. Ted Kurlowicz, JD, LLM, CLU, ChFC, AEP, is professor of taxation and holder of the Charles E. Drimal estate planning professorship at The American College. Constance J. Fontaine, JD, LLM, CLU, ChFC, is associate professor of taxation at The American College and holds the Larry R. Pike chair in Insurance and Investments.

Chapter Outline

PURPOSE, NATURE, AND SCOPE OF GIFT TAX LAW

Purpose

If individuals could give away their entire estates during lifetime without the imposition of any tax, rational people would arrange their affairs so that at death nothing would be subject to the federal estate tax. Likewise, if individuals could give income-producing securities or other property to members of their families, freely and without tax cost, the burden of income taxes could be shifted back and forth to lower brackets, and income taxes would be saved.

Originally, the federal gift tax was designed to equalize the transfer tax treatment between taxpayers who make inter vivos (lifetime) transfers and those who transfer their assets at death. Prior to the Economic Growth and Tax Relief Reconciliation Act of 2001 (EGTRRA 2001), the nature of the federal estate and gift tax system combined both tax systems and a common set of rates was applicable to both inter vivos and after-death transfers. Although the gift and estate tax system still share many commonalities, beginning in 2002 as a result of EGTRRA 2001, there are distinctions.

Nature

The gift tax is an excise tax. An excise tax may be any of various taxes, duties, or fees upon certain privileges like the privilege to transfer property. It is not levied directly on the gift itself or on the right to receive the property, but rather on the right of an individual to transfer money or other property to another for less than full and adequate consideration. (The tax is imposed only on transfers by individuals, but certain transfers involving corporations are treated as indirect transfers by corporate stockholders.)

The gift tax is based on the value of the property transferred. It is computed on a progressive schedule based on cumulative lifetime gifts. In other words, the tax rates are applied to total lifetime taxable gifts (all gifts less the exclusions and deductions) rather than only to taxable gifts made in the current calendar year.

Scope

The Treasury regulations summarize the comprehensive scope of the gift tax law by stating that "all transactions whereby property or interests are gratuitously passed or conferred upon another, regardless of the means or device employed, constitute gifts subject to tax." Almost any transfer or shifting of property or an interest in property can subject the donor (the person transferring the property or shifting the interest) to potential gift tax liability to the extent that the transfer is not supported by adequate and full consideration in money or money's worth—that is, to the extent that the transfer is gratuitous. Direct and indirect gifts, gifts made outright, and gifts in trust (of both real and personal property) can be subject to gift tax. The gift tax is imposed on the shifting of property rights, regardless of whether the property is tangible or intangible. It can be applied even if the property transferred (such as a municipal bond) is exempt from federal income or other taxes.

This broad definition of gifts includes transfers of life insurance, partnership interests, royalty rights, and gifts, checks, or notes of third parties. Forgiving a note or canceling a debt may also constitute a gift.

Almost any party can be the donee (recipient) of a gift subject to tax. The donee can be an individual, partnership, corporation, foundation, trust, or other "person." (A gift to a corporation is typically considered a gift to the other shareholders in proportion to their proprietary interests. Similarly, a gift to a trust is usually considered to be a gift to the beneficiary or beneficiaries in proportion to their interests.)

In fact, a gift can be subject to the tax (assuming the gift is complete) even if the identity of the donee is not known at the date of the transfer and cannot be ascertained.

TAX ADVANTAGES OF LIFETIME GIFTS

estate and
gift tax systems

The unification of the *estate and gift tax systems* in 1976 was an attempt to impose the same tax burden on transfers made during life as on those made at death. The disparity of treatment between lifetime and testamentary gifts is minimized through the adoption of a single unified estate and gift tax rate schedule. Both lifetime and testamentary gifts subject to the same rate schedule and are taxed cumulatively, so that gifts made during a lifetime increase the rate at which gifts made at death will be taxed. Although EGTRRA 2001 deunified the estate and gift tax systems, in a few respects, some significant benefits of inter vivos gifts are the following:

- First, an individual can give up to $11,000 (after 2001) gift tax free every year to each of an unlimited number of donees. This means that a father desiring to make an $11,000 gift to each of his four children and four grandchildren could give a total of $88,000 each year without gift tax liability. (This $11,000 annual gift tax exclusion is described in greater detail later.) Because an individual's spouse can also make such gifts, up to $22,000 per year of money or other property—multiplied by an unlimited number of donees—can be transferred gift tax free. In the example above, the donor and spouse together could give up to $176,000 annually on a gift-tax-free basis. In fact, one spouse can make the entire gift if the other spouse consents; the transaction can then be treated as if both spouses made gifts. This is known as *gift splitting*. (Provisions are covered in detail later.)

- A second tax incentive for making an inter vivos gift, as opposed to a testamentary gift, is that if a gift is made more than 3 years prior to a decedent's death, the amount of any gift tax paid on the transfer is not brought back into the computation of the gross estate. In the case of a sizable gift, avoidance of the gross-up rule can result in meaningful tax savings. The gross-up rule means that all gift tax payable on taxable gifts made within 3 years of the donor's death is included in calculating the value of the gross estate, even if the gift itself is not added back. For example, if an individual makes a $2 million *taxable* gift and has not previously used his or her $1 million applicable credit for gift tax, the gift tax payable or paid on the value of the gift in excess of the gift tax applicable exclusion amount will not be brought back into the estate tax computation if the gift was made more than 3 years before the donor died.

- Third, when a gift is made during lifetime, any appreciation accruing between the time of the gift and the date of the donor's death escapes estate taxation. This may result in a considerable estate tax (as well as probate and inheritance tax) savings. If a father gives his daughter stock worth $100,000 and it appreciates to $600,000 by the date of the father's death 5 years later, only the $100,000 value of the stock at the time of the gift enters into the estate tax computation as an *adjusted taxable gift*. The $500,000 of appreciation does not enter into the computation as an adjusted taxable gift and, thus, does not increase the decedent's marginal estate tax bracket. An excellent example of both advantages is a gift of life insurance made more than 3 years prior to the insured's death. A substantial death benefit could be removed from a donor's estate at the cost of only the gift tax, if any, on the value of the policy at the time of the transfer. In the case of a whole life policy, this is usually roughly equivalent to the policy cash value plus unearned premiums at the date of the gift. If the insured lives for more than 3 years after the transfer and the premiums are present-interest gifts of the annual gift tax exclusion amount per year or less, there is no estate tax inclusion, and none of the *appreciation* (the difference between the death benefit payable and the adjusted taxable gift, if any, at the time the policy was transferred) is included in the insured's estate.

appreciation

- Fourth, there are often strong income tax incentives for making an inter vivos gift. This advantage derives from moving taxable income from a high-bracket donor to a lower-bracket donee. Of course, this advantage is limited by the tax rules related to unearned income of children under age 14.
- Fifth, gifts of the proper type of assets may enable a decedent's estate to meet the mathematical tests for an IRC Sec. 303 stock redemption, an IRC Sec. 6166 installment payout of taxes, and the IRC Sec. 2032A special-use valuation of farms and certain other business real property.
- Sixth, no gift taxes have to be paid until the transferor makes cumulative *taxable* gifts in excess of the applicable exclusion amount (credit exemption equivalent amount) in the year of the gift. The (then called) unified credit equivalent amount for 1984 was $325,000. It increased to $400,000 in 1985, to $500,000 in 1986, and to $600,000 from 1987 through 1997. In 1998, the (now called) applicable exclusion amount was $625,000; in 1999 it was $650,000; in 2000 and 2001 it was $675,000; in 2002 the *gift tax* exclusion was $1 million and remains at

---

The Advantages of Gifting

- $11,000 federal gift tax annual exclusion (after 2001) ($22,000 if gift splitting)
- gross up rule—gift *tax* paid at least 3 years before donor's death avoids *gross* estate
- appreciation in property not subject to *estate* tax
- income tax savings—transfer of property from high-income-tax-bracket donor to lower-bracket donee
- achievement of other favorable tax treatment
    - IRC Sec. 303 stock redemption
    - IRC Sec. 6166 estate tax installment payouts
    - IRC Sec. 2032A special-use valuation
- applicable credit amount leverage

---

that amount thereafter. The top gift tax rates for gifts exceeding $1 million will be the same as the top estate tax rates until 2010 when the top gift tax rate will be the highest individual income tax rate of 35 percent. Therefore, the top gift tax rate from 2002 through 2010 will be as shown in table 7-1.

TABLE 7-1
Gift Tax Rate: 2002–2010

Year	Exclusion	Top Rate
2002	$1,000,000	50%
2003	$1,000,000	49
2004	$1,000,000	48
2005	$1,000,000	47
2006	$1,000,000	46
2007–2009	$1,000,000	45
2010	$1,000,000	35

ALLOWABLE REDUCTIONS FOR GIFT TAX

Gift tax rates are applied to a net figure—*taxable gifts*. Before the tax on a transfer is computed, certain reductions are allowed. These reductions may include the following:

- gift splitting
- an annual exclusion
- a marital deduction
- a charitable deduction

Gift Splitting

gift splitting

The tax law permits a married donor—with the consent of the nondonor spouse—to elect to treat a gift to a third party as though each spouse has made one-half of the gift. The election must be made on the applicable gift tax return of the donor spouse.

Gift splitting is an artificial mechanism; even if one spouse makes the entire gift, for tax computation purposes the single transfer is treated as though each spouse made only one-half of the gift. This means that the rate of tax that each will pay is calculated separately by reference to each spouse's prior gifts.

Furthermore, if a nondonor spouse agrees to gift splitting, it has a direct effect on the future gift tax and estate tax that the nondonor spouse may eventually have to pay if the gift exceeds the annual exclusion. Even though the nondonor spouse did not *actually* make one-half of the gift, to the extent it exceeds the annual gift tax exclusion it becomes an *adjusted taxable gift* to be added (1) to all other gifts deemed to have been made for purposes of calculating the future gift tax bracket and (2) to the taxable estate at the nondonor spouse's death.[*]

Gift splitting applies only to gifts that are made by a married donor to a third party and only with respect to noncommunity property. It was introduced into the tax law to equate the tax treatment of common-law taxpayers with that of community property residents. When one spouse earns a dollar in a community-property state, 50 cents is automatically and immediately deemed to be owned by the other spouse. Therefore, if the couple gives that dollar to their daughter, each spouse is treated as giving only 50 cents.

Gift splitting places the resident of a common-law state in the same position. For example, if a married individual in a common-law state gives her son a gift worth $22,000 and the requisite gift-splitting election is made, this individual is considered to have given only $11,000 (after 2001) for purposes of the gift tax computation. Her spouse is treated as if he has given the other $11,000—even if none of the gift was his property.

If the spouses elect to split gifts to third parties, all gifts made by either spouse during that reporting period must be split.

The privilege of gift splitting applies only to gifts made while the couple is married. Therefore, gifts made by the couple before they were married may not be split, even if they were married later during the same calendar year. Likewise, gifts made after the spouses are legally divorced or after one spouse dies may not be split. But gifts made before one spouse dies may be split even

---

[*] This occurs unless the gift has already been included as an adjusted taxable gift in computing the estate tax of the donor spouse.

if that spouse dies before signing the appropriate consent or election; the deceased spouse's executor can make the appropriate election or consent.

Annual Exclusion

Purpose of the Exclusion

A *de minimis* rule is instituted primarily to avoid and lessen administrative record keeping. The $11,000 annual gift tax exclusion (as indexed for inflation after 1998—Taxpayer Relief Act of 1997) is a classic example of such a rule. It was instituted to eliminate the need for a taxpayer to keep an account of or report numerous small gifts. Congress intended that the amount of the annual exclusion be set large enough so that no reporting is required in the case of wedding gifts or other occasional gifts of relatively small amounts.

Effect of Gift Splitting Coupled with the Exclusion

Generally, the annual exclusion allows the donor to make up to $11,000 worth of gifts (other than future-interest gifts, defined below) tax free to any number of persons each year. Because an exclusion of up to $11,000 is allowed per donee per year, the total maximum excludible amount is determined by multiplying the number of persons to whom gifts are made by $11,000. For example, if an unmarried man makes cash gifts this year of $2,000, $8,000, and $16,000 to his brother, father, and son, respectively, the $2,000 and the $8,000 gifts are fully excludible; $11,000 of the $16,000 gift to his son is excludible.

If the same individual is married and his spouse consents to split the gift, each spouse is deemed to have made one-half of the gift. This means both spouses can maximize the use of their annual exclusions. Assuming the nondonor spouse makes no gifts, table 7-2 shows that none of the $26,000 is subject to tax.

TABLE 7-2
Effect of Gift Splitting with Annual Exclusion

Donee	Amount of Gift to Donee	Treated as if Donor Gave	Exclusion	Subject to Tax	Treated as if Nondonor Spouse Gave	Exclusion	Subject to Tax
Brother	$ 2,000	$1,000	$ 1,000	0	$ 1,000	$ 1,000	0
Father	8,000	4,000	4,000	0	4,000	4,000	0
Son	16,000	8,000	8,000	0	8,000	8,000	0
Totals	$26,000	$13,000	$13,000	0	$13,000	$13,000	0

Present-Interest versus Future-Interest Gifts

present-interest gift

An annual exclusion is allowed only for *present-interest gifts* and is denied to *gifts of future interest*. A present interest is one in which the donee's use, possession, or enjoyment begins at the time the gift is made. Stated technically, a present interest is an immediate, unfettered, and ascertainable right of the donee to use, possess, or enjoy the gift.

future-interest gift

A *future-interest gift* refers to any interest or estate in which the donee's possession or enjoyment will not commence until some period of time after the gift is made. Technically, "future interest is a legal term, and includes reversions, remainders, and other interests or estates, whether vested or contingent, and whether or not supported by a particular interest or estate, which are limited to commence in use, possession, or enjoyment at some future date or time." (Treas. Reg. Sec. 2503-3(a).)

Present and Future Interest

- present interest—immediate, unrestricted, and ascertainable right to use, possess, or enjoy the gift
- future interest—commencement of donee's possession or enjoyment commences at some period in time after the gift is made

---

Clearly, the outright and unrestricted gift of property to a donee (even a minor) that passes legal and equitable title qualifies as a present-interest gift.

A single gift can be split into two parts: One is a present interest that qualifies for the annual exclusion; the other is a future interest that does not.

Example: A widowed donor creates a trust this year and places income-producing property in the trust. The income is payable annually to the donor's son for life, and at the son's death the remainder is payable to the donor's grandson. The gift to the son of the right to receive income annually for life is a present-interest gift because he has an unrestricted right to its immediate use, possession, or enjoyment. If the son is 30 years old at the time of the gift and $100,000 is placed into the trust, the present value of that gift is $91,617 ($100,000 times .91617, which is the present value of an income stream payable for the life of a 30-year-old based on a principal amount of $100,000. The factor for the life interest [.91617] is based on a hypothetical interest rate of 6.6 percent and current mortality. The valuation of life estates, term interests, and remainder interests is based on an interest rate adjusted monthly as mandated in IRC Sec. 7520. The valuation methodology is further discussed in chapter 10.) Because the annual exclusion is available for the gift of a life income interest, $11,000 of the $91,617 gift is excludible.

If the donor in the above example is married and the appropriate election and consent are filed, each spouse can claim a $11,000 exclusion even though only the donor places property in the trust. No exclusion is allowed with respect to the ultimate gift of the corpus to the grandson, because his possession or enjoyment may not commence until sometime in the future.

If the donor provides that her son is to receive income for 10 years and then the principal is to pass to her grandson, and the donor places only $1,000 in the trust, the exclusion for the gift of the income interest is $472.25 ($1,000 times .47225, the value of a 10-year term interest at a hypothetical interest rate of 6.6 percent). Gift splitting with a spouse does not increase the amount of the exclusion, and each spouse is allowed a $236.12 exclusion. Again, no exclusion is allowed for the gift of the future interest (remainder) that passes to the grandson at the end of 10 years, even though he has an interest that cannot be forfeited. This is because he does not have the right to immediate possession or enjoyment; any delay in the absolute and immediate right of use, possession, or enjoyment of the property or the income therefrom is fatal to the gift tax annual exclusion.

Note that if the trustee in either situation above is given the power or discretion to accumulate the income, rather than distribute it, the donor's son would not receive the unfettered and immediate use of the income, and it would be impossible to ascertain the present value of the income interest. For example, assume the trustee is directed to pay the net income to the son for as long as the son lives but is authorized to withhold payments of income during any period the trustee deems advisable and add such payments to corpus. In this case, even the income interest is a gift of a future interest, and no annual exclusion is allowed.

When the trust agreement requires the trustee to accumulate income for a time (or until the occurrence of a specified event), the income interest is also a future interest.

Gifts of Life Insurance. An outright, no-strings-attached gift of life insurance qualifies for the annual exclusion. Life insurance (and annuity policies) is subject to the same basic test as any other type of property in ascertaining whether the interest created is a present or future interest, even though the ultimate obligation under a life insurance policy—payment of the death benefit—is discharged in the future. It is not necessary that a policy have cash value at the time of the gift for the transfer to be a present interest. But the annual exclusion is lost if the donor prevents the donee from surrendering the policy or borrowing its cash value or limits the donee's right to policy cash values in any way.

Gifts of Life Insurance to Trusts. If the grantor transfers a life insurance policy to a trust, the present-interest rules instead of the future-interest rules discussed above apply. That is, the annual exclusion is available only if the donee beneficiaries receive a present interest. Simply transferring life insurance to a trust does not typically create a present-interest gift. The life insurance trust usually pays no income, or the income is used to provide premium payments and is not currently available to donees. Qualifying as a present interest would be a significant hurdle for the life insurance trust if there were no exceptions to the general rule. Remember that, typically, the initial cost of the life insurance policy transferred to the trust and the annual premiums that must be contributed to the trust by the grantor each year are under $11,000. Therefore, if the annual exclusion applies, most irrevocable life insurance trusts will not incur gift tax liability. Fortunately it is possible to design an irrevocable life insurance trust that qualifies as a present-interest gift for annual-exclusion purposes.

Crummey powers

Crummey Powers. The present-interest requirement for annual-exclusion purposes indicates that a gift in trust has to currently provide the donees with an unfettered right to use, possess, and benefit from the trust. The benefit could be a current disposition of income or corpus, or the beneficiaries could be provided with current withdrawal rights or powers. Tax rules provide that if each trust beneficiary has, at a minimum, the so-called *Crummey* (demand) *powers,* the transfer to the trust qualifies as a present-interest gift for the beneficiaries. Because there is an interrelationship between Crummey powers and the exception for lapses of general powers of appointment, to avoid having the beneficiary treated as having a general power of appointment, the demand powers held by the beneficiary should allow the beneficiary the noncumulative right to demand the lesser of (1) the annual addition to the trust or (2) the greater of $5,000 or 5 percent of the trust corpus at the time the power is exercised. When there is more than one beneficiary, the Crummey powers should be given ratably to each. Because there is no chance that the beneficiaries can request an amount greater than the grantor's annual addition to corpus, the insurance policy will not be stripped by the beneficiaries. In actual practice, the beneficiaries cooperate since they realize that the long-term benefit of the trust is more important than the current demand rights. For the irrevocable life insurance trust with Crummey powers to qualify as a present-interest gift, the trustee must notify each beneficiary of the right to exercise the powers. This right must exist for a reasonable period of time each year (such as

30 days). If each beneficiary's demand power is limited to the amounts specified above, the annual lapse of this power is not treated as a taxable gift to other trust beneficiaries by the lapsing beneficiaries.

Identity of Donees

The number and amount (or availability) of annual exclusions depend on the identity of the donee(s), the type of asset involved, and the restrictions, if any, placed on the asset. When a gift is made in trust, the beneficiaries of the trust (and not the trust itself) are considered the donees. For instance, if there are three life-income beneficiaries, up to three annual exclusions could be obtained. Conversely, if five trusts are established for the same beneficiary, only one exclusion is allowed. (Technically, the actuarial value of each gift in trust to that beneficiary is totaled and added to direct gifts the donor made to that beneficiary to ascertain whether and to what extent an annual exclusion remains and is allowable for the present transfer.)

Transfers to two or more persons as joint tenants with right of survivorship, tenants by the entirety, tenants in common, or tenants in partnership are considered multiple gifts. Each tenant is deemed to receive an amount equal to the actuarial value of his or her interest in the tenancy. If, for example, one person has a one-half interest in a tenancy in common, a cash gift of $6,000 to the tenancy is treated as a $3,000 gift to that person. This is added to other gifts made directly to the donee by the same donor to determine how much of the exclusion is allowed. (However, note that a tenancy by the entirety, where neither spouse can sever an interest without the other's consent, is considered a future-interest gift and does not qualify for the annual exclusion.) In all probability, gifts to partnerships should follow the same rules as other tenancies: A gift to a partnership (that is, a tenancy in partnership) should be treated as if made to each partner in proportion to his or her partnership interest.

Gifts to Minors

Outright gifts to minors pose no particular qualification problem concerning the annual exclusion. The IRS states in a revenue ruling that "an unqualified and unrestricted gift to a minor, with or without the appointment of a guardian, is a gift of a present interest." But there are, of course, practical problems involved, especially with larger gifts. Although minors can buy, sell, and deal with some limited types of property, such as U.S. savings bonds, gifts of other types of property create difficulties. For example, some states do not give minors the legal capacity to purchase their own property, care for it, or sell or transfer it. Some states forbid the registration of securities in a minor's name, and a broker may be reluctant to deal in securities titled in a minor's name. In many states, a minor has the legal ability to disaffirm a sale of stock sold at a low price that later rises in value. Furthermore, a buyer receives no assurance of permanent title when a minor signs a real estate deed. Legal guardianship of the minor is not a viable answer in many situations. Because guardianship laws are rigid, a guardian must generally post bond, and periodic and expensive court accounting is often required. Most important, a parent may not want to give a minor control over a large amount of cash or other property.

To minimize these and other practical problems involved with most large gifts to minors, such transfers are generally made in trust or under some type of guardianship or custodian arrangement. An incredible amount of litigation developed over whether such gifts qualified for the annual exclusion. Sec. 2503 of the Internal Revenue Code provides clear and precise methods of qualifying gifts to minors for the annual exclusion. There are three basic means of qualifying *cared-for gifts* to minors under Sec. 2503:

- a Sec. 2503(b) trust
- a Sec. 2503(c) trust
- the Uniform Transfers (Gifts) to Minors Act

Sec. 2503(b) trust

Sec. 2503(b) Trust. To obtain an annual exclusion for gifts to a trust, an individual can establish a trust that *requires* income to be distributed at least annually to (or for use of) the minor beneficiary. Income is the actual accounting income of the trust as determined by the trust agreement and state law. The trust agreement states how income is to be used and gives the trustee no discretion as to its use. The minor receives possession of the trust principal whenever the trust agreement specifies. A distribution does not have to be made by age 21; corpus may be held for as long as the beneficiary lives—or for any shorter period of time. In fact, the principal can actually bypass the income beneficiary and go directly to the individuals whom the grantor—or even the named beneficiary—specifies. The trust agreement can also control the dispositive scheme if the minor dies before receiving trust corpus. Trust assets do not have to be paid to the minor's estate or appointees.

In reality, the mandatory payment of income to (or in behalf of) beneficiaries seems onerous—especially while the beneficiary is a minor. But such income can be deposited in a custodial account and used for the minor's benefit or left to accumulate in a custodial account until the minor reaches majority (at which time the unexpended amount is turned over to the beneficiary).

Although the entire amount of property placed in a 2503(b) trust is considered to be a gift, for exclusion purposes it is split into two parts: income and principal. The value of the income—measured by multiplying the amount of the gift by a factor that considers both the duration over which the income interest will be paid and the discounted worth of $1 payable over the appropriate number of years—is eligible for the annual exclusion. The balance of the gift (principal) does not qualify for the annual exclusion.

For example, assume a donor places $10,000 into a Sec. 2503(b) trust that is required to pay her 10-year-old daughter all income until she reaches age 25. The present value of the income the daughter receives over those 15 years is $7,793.66. If the income is payable for her entire life, the present value jumps to $9,894.90.

It is important to note that, according to at least one revenue ruling, the annual exclusion is denied for a 2503(b) trust that permits the principal to be invested in non-income-producing securities, real estate, or life insurance policies.

Sec. 2503(c) trust

Sec. 2503(c) Trust. The *Sec. 2503(b) trust* described above has the advantage of not requiring distribution of principal when the minor reaches age 21, but it does require a current (annual) distribution of income. The Sec. 2503(c) trust, on the other hand, requires that income and principal be distributed when the minor reaches age 21 but does not require the trustee to distribute income currently.

Certain requirements make it possible for a donor to obtain the annual exclusion by a gift to a minor under Sec. 2503(c): the trust must provide that (1) income and principal are expended by or on behalf of the beneficiary, and (2) to the extent not so expended, income and principal pass to the beneficiary at age 21, or (3) if the beneficiary dies prior to that time, income and principal go to the beneficiary's estate or appointees under a general power of appointment. (The annual exclusion is not lost merely because local law prevents a minor from exercising a general power of appointment.)

A substantial amount of flexibility can be built into the 2503(c) trust. Income that has been accumulated, as well as any principal in the trust, can be paid to the donee when the donee reaches age 21. This may be indicated if the sums involved are not substantial. But the donor may want the trust to continue to age 25 or some other age. It is possible to provide continued management of the trust assets and, at the same time, to avoid forfeiting the annual exclusion by giving the donee, at age 21, a right for a limited period of time to require immediate distribution by giving written notice to the trustee. If the beneficiary fails to give written notice, the trust can continue automatically for whatever period the donor provided when the donor established the trust. Alternatively, some states have lowered the age of majority from 21 to 18, or some in-between age. A trust can provide that the distribution can be made between the age of majority and age 21 without jeopardizing the Sec. 2503(c) exclusion. (The rule is that 21 is the maximum rather than the minimum age at which the trust assets must be made available.)

A 2503(c) trust has a number of advantages over the type of custodianship found in the Uniform Gifts to Minors Act (UGMA) or Uniform Transfers to Minors Act (UTMA) arrangements described below, as shown in table 7-3.

TABLE 7-3
Gifts to Minors

Factor	Trust	UGMA or UTMA
Type of Property	Donor can make gifts of almost any type of property.	Type of property must be permitted by appropriate statute. Gift of real estate may not be permitted.
Dispositive Provisions	Donor can provide for disposition of trust assets if donee dies without having made disposition.	Disposition must follow statutory guidelines.
Investment Powers	Trustee may be given broad, virtually unlimited investment powers.	Custodian limited to investment powers specified by statute.
Time of Distribution of Assets	Trust can continue automatically even after beneficiary reaches age 21. Trustee can make distribution between state law age of majority and age 21.	Custodial assets must be paid to beneficiary upon reaching majority. (Note: Some states have extended the distribution age requirement past age 21.)
Format	Multiple beneficiaries and unequal distributions permitted.	Only one minor for each account.
Income Taxation	Irrevocable trust is a separate tax-paying entity.	Custodial account is not a separate tax-paying entity; minor is the taxpayer.
Special Provisions	Spendthrift and simultaneous death clauses permissible.	No spendthrift clause allowed; simultaneous death not relevant.
Other	Irrevocable trust property avoids inclusion in decedent trustee-grantor's estate.	Death of donor custodian causes inclusion of custodial property in custodian-donor's estate.

UTMA/UGMA

Uniform Transfers (Gifts) to Minors Act (UTMA/UGMA). The *Uniform Transfers (Gifts) to Minors Act* (or comparable laws, such as the Model Gifts to Minors Act) provides an alternative to the Sec. 2503(c) trust. The Uniform Transfers to Minors and Uniform Gifts to Minors Acts are a simple way to make fiduciary gifts to minors. These custodial arrangements are frequently utilized for smaller gifts not only because of their simplicity but also because they offer the benefits of management, income and estate tax shifting, and the investment characteristics of a trust with little or none of the document drafting costs. There is no court supervision of UGMA and UTMA accounts.

All states and the District of Columbia have enacted laws that simplify making gifts to minors and permit adults to make gifts of property to minors with the property registered in the name of a custodian. The custodian, who may be the donor, holds the property for the minor. The initial forms of UGMA statutes included restrictive limits on the categories of investments permitted for a UGMA transfer. UGMA accounts are permitted to hold cash, life insurance, securities, and annuities, but not real property. UTMA accounts, on the other hand, can hold, in addition to UGMA property interests, any type of transferable property interests such as intellectual property, real property, patents, partnership interests, and so forth. Under both the UGMA and UTMA, custodial property is distributed at age 21 unless the jurisdiction has modified the age of majority. Some states allow a donor to select ages up to age 25.

Most states, however, amended their statutes to include broader investment powers. Today, practically all states have adopted the Uniform Transfers to Minors Act (UTMA). The UTMA statutes generally permit any type of property transfer.

For example, in Pennsylvania the UTMA gift may be made as follows:

- if the subject of the gift is a security in registered form, by registering it in the name of the transferor, other adult person, or trust company, followed in substance by the words "as custodian for <u>(name of minor)</u> under the Pennsylvania Uniform Transfers to Minors Act"

- if the subject of the gift is a security not in registered form, by delivering it to an adult other than the transferor or to a trust company, accompanied by a statement of gift in the following form or substance, signed by the donor and the person designated as custodian: I, <u>(name of transferor or name and representative capacity if a fiduciary)</u>, hereby transfer to <u>(name of custodian)</u>, as custodian for (name of minor) under the Pennsylvania Uniform Transfers to Minors Act, the following: (Insert a description of the custodial property sufficient to identify it.) Dated:_____

  _____
  (Signature)
  <u>(name of custodian)</u> acknowledges receipt of the property described above as custodian for the minor named above under the Pennsylvania Uniform Transfers to Minors Act. Dated:_____

  _____
  (Signature of custodian)

- if the subject of the gift is money, by paying or delivering it to a broker or financial institution for credit to an account in the name of the transferor, an adult other than the transferor, or a trust company followed in substance by the words "as custodian for (name of minor) under the Pennsylvania Uniform Transfers to Minors Act"

- if the subject of the gift is a life or endowment insurance policy or annuity contract, by causing the ownership of such policy or contract to be recorded on a form satisfactory to the insurance company or fraternal benefit society, in the name of the transferor, an adult other than the transferor, or a trust company, followed in substance by the words, "as custodian for (name of minor) under the Pennsylvania Uniform Transfers to Minors Act," and having the policy or contract delivered to the person in whose name it is thus registered as custodian

---

Ways to Transfer Cared-for Gifts to Minors

Sec. 2503(b) trust

- The present value of income for the term of the trust qualifies for the annual exclusion.
- Trust income must be distributed for the minor's benefit at least annually.
- Trust corpus may be held after the age of majority or for the benefit of others.

Sec. 2503(c) trust

- Trust income can be accumulated.
- Income and principal must be distributed at majority.
- Income and principal must be distributed to a deceased minor's estate.

Uniform Transfers/Gifts to Minors Act (UTMA/UGMA)

- A custodial account is created.
- Property is registered in custodian's name for the benefit of the minor.
- Requirements are set by state law.
- UGMA restricts types of property the account holds.
- Income and principal must be distributed at majority (or later in some states).

How Type of Asset Affects the Exclusion

The type of asset given and the restrictions placed on that asset may prevent the donor from obtaining the annual exclusion.

Clearly, an outright gift of non-income-producing property qualifies for the gift tax exclusion. Does the same property qualify if placed in a trust? The IRS uses three arguments to disallow annual exclusions: (1) the right to income (which is the only current right given to a life beneficiary) from a gift of non-income-producing property is a future interest because its worth is contingent on the trustee's converting it to income-producing property; (2) it is impossible to ascertain the value of an income interest in property that is not income producing at the time of the gift; and (3) if a gift tax exclusion *is* allowable, the exclusion must be limited to the actual income produced by the property (or expected to be produced) multiplied by the number of years over which the income beneficiary is expected to receive the income—discounted to its present value according to tables in government regulations.

Non-dividend-paying stock held in trust is a good example of property that may not qualify for the gift tax exclusion. In a number of cases, the IRS has been successful in disallowing an exclusion for gifts in trust that consisted of stock in closely held corporations paying no dividends. Gifts in trust of life insurance policies pose the same problem: a mother assigns policies on her life to a trust created to provide financial protection for her daughter. The trust provisions do not provide the daughter with Crummey withdrawal powers. At the mother's death, the policy proceeds will be reinvested and the daughter will receive the net income of the trust for life. Is the mother allowed the exclusion for the present value of her daughter's income interest? The regulations say no, since the daughter will not receive income payments until her mother dies.

Summary of Rules for Ascertaining the Amount and Availability of the Gift Tax Annual Exclusion

The rules regarding the annual exclusion can be summarized as follows:

- A gift in trust is a gift to a trust's beneficiaries and not to the trust for determining the number of annual exclusions to which a donor is entitled.
- The value of an income interest in a trust qualifies for the exclusion if the trustee is required to distribute trust income at least annually— even if the value of the remainder interest does not qualify.
- The gift of an interest that is contingent upon survivorship is a gift of a future interest. (If a gift in trust is made with income going to the grantor's son for life and then to the grantor's daughter for life, the gift to the son will qualify but the daughter's interest will not.)
- A gift is one of a future interest if enjoyment depends on the trustee's discretion. (The nature of the interest must be present as of the date of the gift and is not, for example, determined by what the trustee may subsequently do or not do in the exercise of a discretionary power.)
- A gift must have an ascertainable value to qualify for the exclusion. (The exclusion is denied if the donor or anyone else can divert the income from the beneficiary.)

Exclusion of Transfers for Educational and Medical Expenses

For public policy reasons, Congress provided another exclusion for specific qualified transfers. A gratuitous transfer is excluded from taxable gifts if made on behalf of an individual (1) for tuition to an educational institution for the education or training of the individual or (2) to a provider of medical services for medical care received by the individual. This exclusion is not limited in amount and is independent of the annual exclusion. However, it is important to note that the payments must be made directly to the provider of services to qualify for the exclusion. Payments made directly to an individual as reimbursement for educational or medical expenses incurred are taxable gifts unless such gifts are eligible for an annual exclusion.

Gift Tax Marital Deduction

gift tax marital deduction

An individual who transfers property to a spouse is allowed an unlimited deduction (subject to certain conditions) known as the *gift tax marital deduction*. The purpose of the gift tax marital deduction is to enable spouses to be treated as an economic unit.

Requirements to Qualify for Gift Tax Marital Deduction

For a gift to qualify for the gift tax marital deduction, the following conditions must be satisfied:

- The recipient of the gift must be the spouse of the donor at the time the gift is made.
- The recipient spouse must be a U.S. citizen.
- The property transferred to the donee spouse must not be a terminable interest that disqualifies the gift for the marital deduction.

Most of the qualifications above are self-explanatory. The terminable-interest rule for marital-deduction gifts is similar to the rule employed for estate tax purposes. The effect of these rules is that generally no marital deduction is allowed if the donee spouse's interest in the transferred property terminates after a lapse of time or on the occurrence or nonoccurrence of a specified contingency, at which time the donee spouse's interest passes to another person who receives his or her interest in the property from the donor spouse and who did not pay the donor full and adequate consideration for that interest.

The exception is for a gift of *qualifying terminable interest in property* (QTIP) assets. (In the past, a gift or bequest of a terminable interest in property—one that could end at a spouse's death, for example, and would therefore escape taxation—was not eligible for the gift or estate tax marital deduction.)

Current law provides that if a donor spouse gives a donee spouse a *qualifying income interest for life*, it qualifies for the gift (or estate) tax marital deduction. To qualify for QTIP treatment, the following requirements must be met:

- The spouse must be entitled to all the income from the property (and it must be payable annually or more frequently).
- No person can have a power to appoint any part of the property to any person other than the spouse.
- The property must be taxable at the donee spouse's death. (In the case of a bequest, the first decedent's executor makes an irrevocable election that the property remaining at the surviving spouse's death is taxable in the survivor's estate.)

Terminable Interest Rule

- *disallows* gift tax marital deduction when the donee-spouse's interest in the gifted property will end
  - after a specified period of time or
  - on the happening or nonhappening of a specified contingency

  Exception: qualifying terminable interest property (QTIP)

- *allows terminable* interest to qualify for marital deduction if
  - spouse is entitled to income from property
  - power to appoint property is limited to spouse
  - unconsumed property is included in spouse's estate

Lifetime Gifts to an Alien Spouse

alien spouse

The marital deduction is denied for gifts to a spouse who is not a U.S. citizen. Presumably the purpose of this limitation is to prevent the avoidance of the federal estate and gift tax system by permitting deductible transfers to an *alien spouse*, who could, conceivably, avoid the transfer tax system entirely by leaving the country with the gifted assets.

super-annual exclusion

However, a special provision was enacted to permit significant non-taxable transfers to an alien spouse as an exception to the rule. Transfers to an alien spouse qualify for a basic *super-annual exclusion* amount of $100,000 ($117,000 in 2005 as indexed for inflation) each year if

- the gift otherwise qualifies as an annual-exclusion gift
- the gift meets the requirements for a gift tax marital deduction (except for the requirement that the donee is a U.S. citizen)

gift tax charitable deduction

Gift Tax Charitable Deduction

A donor making a transfer of property to a qualified charity may receive a charitable deduction equal to the value of the gift (to the extent not already covered by the annual exclusion). The net effect of the charitable deduction—together with the annual exclusion—is to avoid gift tax liability on gifts to qualified charities. There is no limit on the amount that can pass gift tax free to a qualified charity.

The gift tax deduction is allowed for all gifts made during the calendar year by U.S. citizens or residents if the gift is to a *qualified* charity. A qualified charity is defined as

- the United States, a state, territory, any political subdivision, or the District of Columbia, if the gift is to be used exclusively for public purposes
- certain religious, scientific, or charitable organizations
- certain fraternal societies, orders, or associations
- certain veterans' associations, organizations, or societies

Technically, the charitable deduction is limited and is allowable only to the extent that the gift is included in the total amount of gifts that are made during the year. The phrase *total amount of gifts* refers to gifts in excess of the annual exclusion.

Example: This year a single client makes total gifts of $45,000: $20,000 to his daughter and $25,000 to The American College. After taking annual exclusions, the client's gross gifts are $9,000 (the gift of $20,000 to the daughter, less an $11,000 exclusion) and $14,000 (the $25,000 gift to The American College, less the $11,000 annual exclusion). Therefore, the client's charitable deduction is limited to $14,000.

The reason for the rule that the annual exclusion is taken first is obviously to prevent the allowance of a charitable deduction equal to the total amount of the gift, which, in turn, when added to the allowable annual exclusion, would result in an extra annual gift tax exclusion.

In certain cases, a donor transfers a remainder interest to a qualified charity. A noncharitable beneficiary is given all or part of the income interest in the transferred property, and the charity receives the remainder at the termination of the income interest. When a charitable remainder is given to a qualified charity, a gift tax deduction is allowable for the present interest value of the remainder interest only if at least one of the following four conditions is satisfied:

- The property that was transferred was either a personal residence or a farm.
- The transfer was made to a charitable remainder annuity trust.
- The transfer was made to a charitable remainder unitrust.
- The transfer was made to a pooled-income fund.

The terms *charitable remainder annuity trust*, *charitable remainder unitrust*, and *pooled-income fund* are defined in essentially the same manner as they are for estate and income tax purposes. These terms are further discussed in chapter 16.

Net Gifts

Sometimes a donor gratuitously transfers property to a donee that is subject to some form of obligation. In some cases, a donee voluntarily agrees to pay the gift tax on the value of the donor's gift. In other instances, the donor makes the gift with the understanding that the donee must pay the gift tax. The gross value of the gift is reduced by the amount of the gift tax paid by the donee, and the gift tax is then calculated on the remaining (net) amount of the gift. Net gifts may also have income tax ramifications to the extent the donee's payment of gift tax is greater than the donor's basis in the property.

The donee's gift tax liability is calculated according to this formula:

$$\text{Tentative tax} \div (1 + \text{donor's gift tax rate})$$

Note: Students will not be expected to know how to calculate a net gift. It is the concept of a net gift that is important for students. The following example of a net gift software calculation is for illustrative purposes only.

Example :   In 2005, Susan, a widow about to move into a small condominium, told her nephew Reginald that she would give him her mansion valued at $1.5 million if he would pay the gift taxes on the gift. Reginald agreed. Susan had no prior taxable gifts.

	Net Gift	No Net Gift
Taxable gift (after tax)	$1,353,147	$1,500,000
Tentative tax base	$1,353,147	$1,500,000
Tentative tax	$492,653	$555,800
Tentative tax on prior gifts	$0	$0
Gross gift tax	$492,653	$555,800
Allowable unified credit	$345,800	$345,800
Net federal gift tax	$146,853	$210,000
Net amount received by donee	$1,353,147	$1,500,000

The reduction in gift tax as a result of the net gift in this example is $63,147. This is the result of the tax cost of a lower value gift.

CALCULATING GIFT TAX PAYABLE

Computing the gift tax payable begins with ascertaining the amount of taxable gifts in the current reporting calendar year. To find the amount of taxable gifts, all gifts are valued first. If appropriate, the gift is then split, and annual exclusions as well as the marital and charitable deductions are applied. Note that the gift and estate tax credit and the issue of whether gift tax actually has to be paid are irrelevant for the limited purpose of computing taxable gifts.

An example and the accompanying computation format illustrate the process.

Example: Assume a single donor makes certain outright gifts in the last month of this year: $60,000 to his son, $2,500 to his daughter, $4,000 to his grandson, and $5,000 to The American College (a total of $71,500).

Computing Taxable Gifts

Step 1	*List* total gifts for year		<u>$71,500</u>
Step 2	*Subtract* one-half of gift deemed to be made by donor's spouse (split gifts)	<u>0</u>	
	Gifts deemed to be made by donor		<u>71,500</u>
Step 3	*Subtract* annual exclusion(s)	(22,500)	
	Gifts after subtracting exclusion(s)		49,000
Step 4	*Subtract* marital deduction	0	
Step 5	*Subtract* charitable deduction	0	
	Taxable gifts		<u>$49,000</u>

Although there were four donees, the annual exclusion is $22,500 and does not total four times $11,000, or $44,000. This is because the annual exclusion is the lower of (1) the annual exclusion and (2) the actual net value of the property transferred. In this example, the annual exclusion for the $2,500, $4,000, and $5,000 gifts is limited to the actual value of each gift.

A slight change in the facts in the example above illustrates the computation when the donor is married and his spouse consents to splitting their gifts to third parties. In this case, only one-half of the gifts made by the donor is taxable to the donor (one-half of the gifts made by the donor's spouse to third parties is also included in computing the donor's total gifts). A separate (but essentially identical) computation is made for the donor's spouse. That computation would show (a) the other half of the husband's gifts to third parties plus (b) one-half of the wife's actual gifts to third parties (since all gifts must be split if any gifts are split).

Computing Taxable Gifts

Step 1	*List* total gifts for year		$71,500
Step 2	*Subtract* one-half of gift deemed to be made by donor's spouse (split gifts)	(35,750)	
	Gifts deemed to be made by donor		35,750
Step 3	*Subtract* annual exclusion(s)	(16,750)	
	Gifts after subtracting exclusion(s)		19,000
Step 4	*Subtract* marital deduction	0	
Step 5	*Subtract* charitable deduction	0	
	Taxable gifts		$19,000

(The calculation on the wife's return parallels this return.)

Note that in this example the annual exclusions are computed *after* the split, and each donor's exclusions are

gift to son	$11,000
gift to daughter	1,250
gift to grandson	2,000
gift to The American College	2,500
	$16,750

If the married donor in this example also makes an outright spousal gift of $120,000, the computation is as follows:

Computing Taxable Gifts

Step 1	*List* total gifts for year		$191,500
Step 2	*Subtract* one-half of gift deemed to be made by donor's spouse (split gifts)	(35,750)	
	Gifts deemed to be made by donor		155,750
Step 3	*Subtract* annual exclusion(s)	(27,750)	
	Gifts after subtracting exclusion(s)		128,000
Step 4	*Subtract* marital deduction	109,000	
Step 5	*Subtract* charitable deduction	0	
	Taxable gifts		$ 19,000

When the total value of taxable gifts for the reporting period is found, the actual tax payable is computed using the following method:

Computing Gift Tax Payable

Step 1	Compute gift tax on all *taxable* gifts regardless of when made (use rate schedule)	$_____
Step 2	Compute gift tax on all *taxable* gifts made prior to the present gift(s) (use rate schedule)	$_____
Step 3	Subtract step 2 result from step 1 result	$_____
Step 4	Enter gift tax credit remaining	$_____
Step 5	Subtract step 4 result from step 3 result to obtain *gift tax payable*	$_____

For instance, a widow gives $200,000 to her daughter and $25,000 to The American College in the last month of this year. Both transfers are present-interest gifts. If she has made no previous taxable gifts in prior years, the computation is as follows:

Computing Taxable Gifts

Step 1	*List* total gifts for year		$225,000
Step 2	*Subtract* one-half of gift deemed to be made by donor's spouse (split gifts)	0	
	Gifts deemed to be made by donor		225,000
Step 3	*Subtract* annual exclusion(s)	(22,000)	
	Gifts after subtracting exclusion(s)		203,000
Step 4	*Subtract* marital deduction	0	
Step 5	*Subtract* charitable deduction	(14,000)	
	Taxable gifts		$189,000

To find the gift tax payable on this amount, the procedure is as follows:

Computing Gift Tax Payable

Step 1	Compute gift tax on all *taxable* gifts regardless of when made	$ 51,280
Step 2	Compute gift tax on all *taxable* gifts made prior to the present gift(s)	0
Step 3	Subtract step 2 result from step 1 result	$ 51,280
Step 4	Enter gift tax credit remaining	$ 345,800
Step 5	Subtract step 4 result from step 3 result to obtain *gift tax payable*	$ 0

The step 1 entry—$51,280—is found by using the rate schedule for estate and gift taxes, which shows that the tax on $150,000 is $38,800 and that there is a 32 percent tax on the remaining $39,000, which comes to $12,480. ($38,800 + $12,480 = $51,280.)

Note that the rate table is used regardless of when the gifts were made.

If the donor in the example above made $100,000 of additional taxable gifts in prior years, the computation is as follows:

Computing Gift Tax Payable

Step 1	Compute gift tax on all *taxable* gifts regardless of when made	$ 84,060
Step 2	Compute gift tax on all *taxable* gifts made prior to the present gift(s)	23,800
Step 3	Subtract step 2 result from step 1 result	$ 60,260
Step 4	Enter gift tax credit remaining	$ 322,000
Step 5	Subtract step 4 result from step 3 result to obtain *gift tax payable*	$ 0

This illustrates the cumulative nature of the gift tax (the $100,000 prior taxable gifts pushed the present $189,000 of taxable gifts into a higher bracket) and the progressive rate structure. The tax on $289,000 is $84,060, and the tax on $100,000 of prior taxable gifts is $23,800. The difference, $60,260, is the tax on the current gifts.

Credits

The Tax Reform Act of 1976 unified the gift and estate tax systems and created a credit against gifts made either during lifetime or at death. The gift tax credit, which provides a dollar-for-dollar reduction of the tax otherwise payable, was $96,300 in 1984, $121,800 in 1985, $155,800 in 1986, and $192,800 in 1987 until 1998. Under the Taxpayer Relief Act of 1997, the term "unified credit" became "applicable credit amount" and the term "unified credit equivalent" became "applicable exclusion amount." The applicable credit amount was increased to $202,050 in 1998; to $211,300 in 1999; to $220,550 in 2000 and 2001. Under EGTRRA 2001, the applicable credit amount for gifts is $345,800 after 2001.

REPORTING GIFTS AND PAYING TAX

Future-Interest Gifts

A gift tax return (Form 709) is required for a gift of a future interest regardless of the amount of the gift. For example, if a grantor transfers $100,000 to an irrevocable trust payable to the grantor's spouse for life and then to the grantor's son, a gift tax return is required regardless of the value of the son's remainder interest. The term *future interest* is defined in the same manner as for annual exclusion purposes: a gift in which the donee does not have the unrestricted right to the immediate use, possession, or enjoyment of the property or the income from the property.

Present-Interest Gifts

Because of the annual exclusion no gift tax return is due until present-interest gifts made to one individual exceed $11,000. At that point, a return must be filed on an annual basis when a gift to one person in one year exceeds $11,000, even if no gift tax is due (such as when gift-splitting provisions eliminate the tax). For example, if a married woman gives $11,001 to her son, the transfer is tax free. However, a gift tax return is required, because the gift exceeds the annual-exclusion limit and because the gift is split. A return must be filed when a couple elects to split gifts.

A gift tax return must be filed and the gift tax, if any is due, must be paid by April 15 of the year following the year in which the taxable gifts were made. If an extension is granted for filing the income tax return, the time limit for filing the gift tax return is automatically extended also.

Gifts to a spouse that qualify for the marital deduction do not require the filing of a gift tax return. However, a 709 gift tax return must be filed when one spouse makes a marital deduction gift to a donee spouse and elects to have the transfer treated as qualifying terminable interest property (QTIP).

Gifts to Charities

Currently, gift tax returns are not required for charitable contributions made to domestic (U.S.) charities (Taxpayer Relief Act of 1997) of a donor's entire interest in the property transferred and the donor has not transferred any of the interest to a noncharitable donee. In the case of a noncharitable donee, the charitable transfer must be reported at the same time the noncharitable gift is noted on a gift tax return.

If a split-interest gift is made to a charity (when there are charitable and noncharitable donees of the same gift), the donor cannot claim a charitable

---

Qualified Charities

- U.S. states, territories, any political subdivision, District of Columbia
- certain religious, scientific, or charitable organizations
- certain fraternal societies, orders, or associations
- certain veterans' associations, organizations, or societies

---

deduction for the entire value of the transfer. In this case, the donor must file and report the transfer subject to the filing requirements discussed above. For example, if an individual establishes a charitable remainder trust with the income payable to the individual's daughter for life and the remainder payable to a charity at her death, a gift tax return must be filed.

Liability for Payment

The donor of the gift is primarily liable for the gift tax (Sec. 2502(c)). However, if the donor for any reason fails to pay the tax when it falls due, the donee becomes liable to the extent of the value of the gift (Sec. 6324(b)). This liability begins as soon as the donor fails to pay the tax when due.

Generally, the tax must be paid at the time the return is filed. However, reasonable extensions of time for payment of the tax can be granted by the IRS—but only on a showing of *undue hardship*. This means more than inconvenience. It must appear that the party liable to pay the tax will suffer a *substantial financial loss* unless an extension is granted. (A forced sale of property at a sacrifice price is an example of a substantial financial loss.)

RELATIONSHIP OF GIFT TAX SYSTEM TO INCOME TAX SYSTEM

When the gift tax law was written, one of its principal purposes was to complement the income tax law by discouraging taxpayers from making gifts to reduce their taxable income. It is true that to some extent the gift tax does supplement the income tax system and there is some overlap. However, it is important to note that the tax treatment accorded a given transaction when the two taxes are applied will not necessarily be consistent.

A lack of consistency between the gift and income tax systems forces the practitioner to examine three different issues:

- Is the transfer one on which the gift tax will be imposed?
- Will the transfer constitute a taxable exchange subject to the income tax?
- If the transfer was made in trust, will the income from the transferred property be taxable to the donor, or will the incidence of taxation be shifted to the recipient of the property (the trust or its beneficiaries)?

In summary, the treatment of a transaction for gift tax purposes is not necessarily consistent with the income tax consequences. Therefore, it is important not to place undue reliance on the provisions and interpretations of the income tax law when determining probable results or potential interpretations of the gift tax system (or vice versa).

DETERMINATION OF BASIS OF GIFTED PROPERTY

carryover of donor's basis

When property is transferred from a donor to a donee and the donee later disposes of it through a sale or other taxable disposition, gain or loss depends on the donee's basis. In return, the donee's basis is carried over from the donor. *Carryover of donor's basis* means the *donor's* basis for the gift property immediately prior to the gift becomes the *donee's* basis for that property.

For example, if an individual pays $10 a share for stock and transfers it when it is worth $20, and the donee sells it when it is worth $30, the donee's basis for that property is the donor's $10 cost. The gain, therefore, is the difference between the amount realized by the donee, $30, and the donee's adjusted basis, $10.

An addition to basis is allowed for a portion of any gift tax paid on the transfer from the donor to the donee. The addition to basis is for that portion of the tax attributable to the appreciation in the gift property (the excess of the property's gift tax value over the donor's adjusted basis determined immediately before the gift). This increase in basis may be added to the donee's carryover basis for the property.

Stated as a formula, the basis of gifted property is the donor's basis increased as follows:

$$\frac{\text{Net apprecation in value of gift}}{\text{Amount of gift}} \quad \text{x} \quad \text{Gift tax paid}$$

This means that the basis carried over from the donor is increased only by the gift tax on the net appreciation in the value of the gift. For example, ignoring the annual exclusion, an individual bought stock worth $40,000 and gave it to his daughter when it was worth $100,000. If the donor paid $23,800 in gift taxes at the time of the gift, the daughter's basis is as follows:

Donor's basis $40,000

plus

Gift tax on *net appreciation in value* (here, the difference between the $100,000 value of the gift at the time of transfer and the donor's cost, $40,000)

$$\frac{\$60,000}{\$100,000} \quad \text{x} \quad \$23,800 \ = \ \$14,280$$

equals

Daughter's basis $54,280

RELATIONSHIP OF GIFT TAX SYSTEM TO ESTATE TAX SYSTEM

There are many correlations between the gift and estate tax systems. However, although gift tax law and estate tax law do share many commonalties, there are, clearly, differences between the two tax systems. When a gift is made, certain issues must be considered. In spite of the lifetime transfer, will the transferred property be included among the other assets in the donor's gross estate on the donor's death? Will the property a donor transfers during his or her lifetime be subjected first to a gift tax and later included in the donor's gross estate? For example, if the donor transfers property but retains a life interest, both gift and estate taxes will be payable. Although any gift tax paid (after the applicable credit amount is exhausted) may be subtracted in arriving at the estate tax liability, because of the *time value* of money—the donor's loss of the use of the money paid in gift taxes—the net result is less favorable than a mere washout (in essence it is a prepayment of the death tax).

GIFT-SELECTION FACTORS

Gift tax strategy must be part of a well-planned and carefully coordinated estate planning effort. This, in turn, requires careful consideration as to the type of property to gift. With any gifting plan, the selection of assets for gifting depends on the donor's particular goals and circumstances. There are a number of strategies and factors that must be examined in selecting the types of property that are appropriate for gifts. Some of the general considerations in planning gift tax property are as follows:

- Is the property likely to appreciate in value? Other things being equal, planners generally try to pick property that will appreciate substantially in value after the time of the transfer. Removal of the appreciation in the property (as well as the income generated by the transferred property) from the donor's estate should save a meaningful amount of estate taxes. These transfers will remove the anticipated future appreciation from the donor's estate at a time when the property value for gift tax is lower than the later estate tax value. Real estate, certain securities, artwork, collectibles, and life insurance are common examples of assets likely to appreciate. Life insurance, for example, is property with a low present value but a high appreciation potential. If held until the date the insured dies, its appreciation in value is guaranteed. Furthermore, because there are no carryover-basis problems, the proceeds are exempt from income tax. However, if the death of the donor is imminent, gifts of donor-owned life insurance are not recommended. The 3-year rule under

IRC Sec. 2035 will cause inclusion of the policy proceeds in the decedent-donor's estate if the policy is gifted within 3 years of death. Even if a donor's property item has already appreciated by the time the donor considers gifting it, the asset may still be a good transfer choice. This could be the case if the property is expected to be sold and the donee is in a lower income tax bracket than the donor.

- Is the donee in a lower income tax bracket than the donor? Income splitting between the donor and the donee may be obtained by transferring high-income-producing property to a family member in a lower bracket. Naturally, high-income-producing property is best for this purpose. Generally, though, high-income-producing property should not be gifted to children under the age of 14 because of the kiddie tax rules. High-dividend participating preferred stock in a closely held business or stock in a successful S corporation is a good example of high-income-producing property. (Note: S corporation stock should not be gifted if the transfer will terminate S status.) Conversely, if the donor is in a lower bracket than the donee (for instance, if the parent who is retired makes a gift to a financially successful middle-aged child), the use of low-yield, growth-type property may be indicated.

- Is the property subject to indebtedness? A gift of property subject to indebtedness that is greater than its cost to the donor may result in a taxable gain. A gift of such property causes the donor to realize capital gain on the excess of the debt over basis.

- Does the property have a sale price lower than the donor's basis in the property? If so, the donor should consider selling the property to take advantage of the loss deduction for income tax purposes and either gift the sale proceeds or select other gift property.

Example: The gift of a building that cost the donor $10,000, appreciated to $100,000, and was mortgaged to $70,000 results in an income tax gain to the donor on the difference between the debt outstanding at the time of the transfer and the donor's basis (assume $70,000 and the donor's basis of $10,000). In this example, the gain is $60,000. It is realized at the time the gift becomes complete.

- Is the donor likely to need or want to use the property in the future? If there is a reasonable possibility the donor may want the property, such as a residence, at some later time, other gift property should be selected.

- Is the property necessary for qualification of favorable tax benefits under Secs. 303 (special provision for capital gains for redemptions), 6166 (installment payment of estate taxes), and 2032A (special-use valuation)? To qualify under these Internal Revenue sections, a decedent's estate must include specified percentages of certain businesses or farm property. Therefore, if a donor is considering making gifts of business interests or closely held stock, the donor needs to consider whether or not the transfer(s) will disqualify the donor's estate from obtaining the favorable tax treatment allowed to farms and small businesses under Code Secs. 303 (redemption of stock for death taxes), 6166 (installment payments of estate tax), and 2032A (current-use valuation).

- Is the gift property's basis above, below, or approximately the same as the property's fair market value? As stated above, income tax law forbids the recognition of a capital loss if the subject matter of the gift has a basis above the property's present fair market value. Neither the donor nor the donee can recognize a capital loss with respect to such property. Furthermore, if the gift property's basis is above present fair market value, there is no gift tax addition to basis because that addition depends on appreciation at the time of the transfer. Since there is no appreciation, no gift tax addition is allowed. Factored into any gratuitous transfer arrangement, whether it is an occasional transfer or a structured gifting plan, is that the donor and donee must be mindful of the general rule that the donor's basis in gifted property carries over to the donee.

Conversely, if the donor's basis for income tax purposes is very low relative to the fair market value of the property, it might be advantageous to retain the property until death because of the *stepped-up-basis-at-death rules*. (This is especially true if inclusion of the property will generate little or no estate tax because it will pass to a surviving spouse and qualify for a marital deduction, or if the asset owner is sheltered by the applicable credit amount.) The result of the stepped-up-basis provision is that a portion of the future capital gain is avoided in the event the property is later sold by the estate or heir. But if the property should be sold, it may pay to transfer it to a low-bracket family member by gift; that individual could then sell it and realize a lower capital-gains tax.

Another possibility is that the donor's basis is approximately the same as or only slightly below fair market value. Again, the rules providing for a gift tax addition to basis are of little help, since the addition to basis is limited to the gift tax allocable to appreciation in the property at the time of the gift.

There are also numerous nontax subjective issues that donors making sizable gifts should address:

Factors in Gift Selection

- property's likelihood of appreciating in value
- unlikelihood of donor's needing the property in the future
- property's not being subject to indebtedness (greater than basis)
- the income tax brackets of the donor and donee
- carryover of basis to donee
- possible estate disqualification from other favorable tax treatment Code sections

---

- Is the gift likely to cause the donor any financial concerns or reduce the donor's customary standard of living?
- Does the donor have expectations or concerns with respect to the donee's ability to manage or invest the gift?
- Is the donor concerned about equalizing the value or nature of gifts to donees such as children or grandchildren?
- Is conflict likely among donees if more than one potential donee wants the same property subject to gifting?
- Is the donor concerned about the stability of the donees' marriages or the potential for future divorce?
- Is the donor worried about the donees having creditors' claims?

Note to Students: See Appendix A for a summary of the advantages and disadvantages of different trusts covered in this chapter and throughout the text.

CHAPTER REVIEW

Answers to the review questions and the self-test questions start on page 717.

Key Terms

estate and gift tax systems	Sec. 2503(c) trust
appreciation	UTMA/UGMA
gift splitting	gift tax marital deduction
present-interest gift	alien spouse
future-interest gift	super-annual exclusion
Crummey powers	gift tax charitable deduction
Sec. 2503(b) trust	carryover of donor's basis

Review Questions

7-1.   What is the nature of the gift tax, and what is its objective?

7-2.   What is the effect of the estate and gift tax system?

7-3.   What are the tax-related incentives for making lifetime gifts?

7-4.   Larry and Louise Longfellow are considering giving $15,000 to each of their three children this year.
  a.   Can Louise make the entire gift from her own funds and still split the gift with Larry?
  b.   How much is each spouse deemed to be giving after the split?
  c.   Explain whether the consent for the split gift can be made after Larry's death.

7-5.   Explain the purpose of the annual gift tax exclusion.

7-6.   Cecelia and Henry Hunt have seven children. Henry would like to give each child as much money as possible this year without exceeding the annual exclusion limits. Assume Cecelia will join in the gifts. Compute the maximum total amount Henry can give the children this year within the limits he has established.

7-7.   Will the following transfers qualify for the annual exclusion? Explain.
  a.   Bill Nagle gives his son, Bill, Jr., an outright gift of $15,000 this year.
  b.   Bill transfers $11,000 in cash to a trustee. Income from the trust is to be paid to Bill's daughter annually, and the remainder is to go to Bill's son upon the daughter's death.
  c.   Same facts as in 7–7b above, but the trustee is given the discretion to accumulate rather than to distribute income.
  d.   Bill transfers $11,000 in cash to a trust, but the trustee is required to accumulate all trust income until Bill, Jr. is 21, at which time the entire principal is to be distributed to him.

7-8.   Mrs. Martin is considering the gratuitous transfer of an apartment house valued at $50,000 to her daughter, Nancy, in trust for Nancy's lifetime, with remainder to Nancy's children. The trustee has discretion to distribute income. Explain whether this gift qualifies as one of a present interest, future interest, or both, if trust income is distributable to Nancy at the discretion of the trustee only.

7-9.   For what reasons might a donor consider making large and/or recurring gifts to minors in a form other than as outright gifts?

7-10. Explain if and when the following types of property may qualify for the annual exclusion:
  a.   an outright gift of life insurance
  b.   life insurance transferred to a trust with no Crummey demand powers

    c.   premium payments on life insurance owned by a trust where the beneficiary has Crummey demand powers

    d.   gifts in trust of closely held non-dividend-paying stock

7-11. Distinguish between an IRC Sec. 2503(b) trust and a Sec. 2503(c) trust regarding

    a.   distribution of income

    b.   discretion of trustee in accumulating income

    c.   time by which trust principal is required to be distributed

    d.   payment of trust assets if minor dies

7-12. Compare an IRC Sec. 2503(c) trust to the Uniform Gifts to Minors Act regarding

    a.   type of property that can be used

    b.   allowable dispositive provisions for gift assets

    c.   investment flexibility that can be given to the trustee

    d.   time by which assets must be distributed

7-13. Josephine Carmeron gave her husband, Thomas, $210,000. How is this gift treated for gift tax purposes?

7-14. Mr. Fisher is married and has made gifts of his own property this year. Neither Mr. Fisher nor his wife has made any prior gifts. Mrs. Fisher joined in making all gifts to the following third parties: $25,000 in cash to their son; $52,000 (market value) of common stock, which cost $35,000, to Mr. Fisher's brother; $23,000 (market value) of common stock, which cost $5,000, to the XYZ Hospital—a nonprofit public charitable institution; and a gift to Mrs. Fisher of $50,000 (market value) of corporate bonds, which cost $60,000.

    a.   What would be the total taxable gifts, if any, made by Mr. Fisher this year after taking into account all available exclusions and deductions? Explain each step in your answer.

    b.   What would be the total taxable gifts, if any, made by Mrs. Fisher this year? Explain each step in your answer.

7-15. Assume that Paul Gaffney, an unmarried donor, gave $60,000 to his friend, Ellen, and $25,000 to the American Red Cross this year.

    a.   Compute the gift tax payable, assuming Paul had made no prior gifts. Use the tax rate schedule found near the end of chapter 18 for computing the estate and gift tax.

    b.   Compute the gift tax payable, assuming instead that Paul had made $100,000 of taxable gifts in 1990.

7-16. Explain if and when a gift tax return would be required in the following situations:

    a.   Marvin Jackson gives his niece a $2,000 charm bracelet for her birthday.

    b.   Jessie Rotelli gives her husband a Mercedes-Benz valued at $60,000.

      c. Pat Cressito places $15,000 in trust for her niece. The trustee has the discretion to accumulate income until Pat's niece is 21. After that, all principal and income will be distributed to the niece.

7-17. Compute the donee's basis for income tax purposes in the following situation: Lee Rostler bought stock for $50,000. He gave it to his son when it was worth $150,000. Lee paid $38,800 in gift taxes on the transfer. Assume Lee had already used his applicable credit amount for gift tax purposes and his annual exclusion amount for the year of the gift to his son.

7-18. You have been discussing the use of a gift-giving program with a client. Explain to her in general terms what characteristics the ideal subject of a gift would have.

Self-Test Questions

T   F   7-1. Gift taxation was enacted to discourage individuals from transferring their property during their lifetime to avoid an estate tax.

T   F   7-2. The gift tax is imposed on the person who gives the property.

T   F   7-3. A gift tax is not imposed on transferred property that is exempt from federal income taxation, such as a municipal bond.

T   F   7-4. After 2001, an individual can make present-interest gifts of up to $11,000 every year gift tax free to an unlimited number of donees.

T   F   7-5. One advantage of gifting property is that the postgift appreciation in value will be excluded from estate taxation.

T   F   7-6. Gift splitting means that an individual donor will split the gift among several donees, rather than giving it to just one donee.

T   F   7-7. If a taxable gift by a spouse to a third party is to be treated as a split gift, both spouses must consent on the gift tax return of the donor-spouse.

T   F   7-8. The gift of a life insurance policy will always qualify for the annual gift tax exclusion, whether the policy is transferred outright or to a trust.

T   F   7-9. When a gift is made in trust, the trust is considered the donee.

T   F   7-10. Substantial gifts to minors are generally more likely to be made in trust rather than under the Uniform Transfers to Minors Act.

T   F   7-11. The Uniform Gifts to Minors Act allows gifts of all types of property to minors to qualify for the annual gift tax exclusion.

T   F   7-12. Only a few states have adopted the Uniform Transfers to Minors Act.

T   F   7-13. If certain requirements are met, an individual may give unlimited property to a spouse who is a U.S. citizen without incurring any gift tax and without filing a gift tax return.

T   F   7-14. It is possible to give a spouse a qualifying terminable interest in property and have the gift qualify for the marital deduction.

T   F   7-15. When a gift is made to a qualified charity, there is a gift tax charitable deduction equal to the fair market value of the gift reduced by the annual exclusion.

T   F   7-16. Every individual has two transfer tax credits—one is applied against gift tax and the other against estate tax.

T   F   7-17. A future-interest gift requires that a gift tax return be filed regardless of the value of the gift.

T   F   7-18. Assuming there are no future-interest gifts, no gift tax return is currently required until a present-interest gift to one individual in a calendar year exceeds $11,000.

T   F   7-19. The treatment of a transaction for income tax purposes is always consistent with its gift tax consequences.

T   F   7-20. The donee generally receives a basis in gifted property equal to the fair market value of the property at the time of the transfer.

8

Transfers at Death

Learning Objectives

An understanding of the material in this chapter should enable the student to

---

8-1. Describe the advantages of a will, and explain the requirements for a valid will.

8-2. Describe the two common modes of distribution under wills, and explain what types of provisions are found in wills.

8-3. Describe the types of wills and explain how a will may be amended or revoked.

8-4. Explain the spouse's right of election against a will, and describe the grounds for contesting a will.

8-5. Describe the use of testamentary trusts and pour-over trusts in wills.

8-6. Explain how property can be transferred at death by contract.

8-7. Explain how property can be transferred at death by operation of law.

Chapter Outline

Property is transferred at death by one of several methods. It can pass under the terms of a validly drawn will. Property may also be transferred or assigned by contract designations in, for example, life insurance policies and antenuptial and postnuptial agreements. Finally, property may pass by operation of law. Jointly owned property with right of survivorship falls into this category, as does property passing by intestate succession.

TRANSFERS BY WILL

will

A *will* is a personal declaration of one's intentions regarding the disposition of property at death. It describes matters to be taken care of after death. It becomes legally enforceable at death and is not operative until that time. Prior to one's death, a will may be amended, revoked, or destroyed by the maker at any time.

Fiduciaries of Estates

- executor/executrix
- personal representative
- personal administrator

executor/executrix

Much can be accomplished by writing a will. A properly drawn will can assure the orderly and sound distribution of an estate. It is a way to control disposition of one's property, especially when all property is held in an individual name. Because all property not transferred by contract or operation of law must be transferred through probate, the will becomes the complete estate plan for all probate property. Writing a will allows the decedent to name a personal representative of his or her choice, who is called an *executor/executrix*. The decedent may direct that the executor be allowed to serve without posting a security bond if one is otherwise required by statute. The decedent also has the flexibility through the will to name a successor executor should the named executor be unable or unwilling to serve. Those matters can be attended to privately without court intervention.

Wills

- testate—dying *with* a valid will
- intestate—dying without a valid will

A carefully drawn will contains positive directions and instructions to the executor. An executor is someone chosen by the decedent who is responsible for administering the estate. The executor should be an individual or corporate fiduciary who is competent to perform the required duties and whom the testator can trust. The testator can give the executor broad powers and discretion with respect to the management and distribution of the estate. It is as if the executor steps into the shoes of the decedent during the estate administration period. The executor is charged with the following duties:

- gathering the assets of the estate
- probating the will
- filing tax returns
- paying taxes and other debts of the estate
- providing interim support for the beneficiaries
- settling business interests of the decedent
- collecting benefits and income due to the estate
- filing an accounting with the probate court (also referred to as orphans' court or surrogate's court in some states)
- distributing property to intended beneficiaries
- closing the estate

Advantages of a Will

It is only by will that an executor of choice can be named. The will also may provide that an executor shall serve without posting a bond or other security in order to perform his or her duties. Under a will, a decedent may transfer real estate, stock, or business interests as he or she wishes. The decedent can direct disposition of tangible personal property separately from the residue (the part of the estate that remains after all other gifts have been made). The decedent can also assure the maximum marital deduction desired for property passing to a spouse. The estate's share of the tax burden can be specified. In the absence of an instruction regarding payment of taxes, state statutes will generally allocate the expenses of the estate, including federal estate taxes, to the residuary share of the estate—that is, the residuary beneficiaries—in proportion to their respective inheritances. This means that the beneficiaries bear the tax burden proportionately. For example, both federal and state law could empower an executor to collect federal estate taxes from the named beneficiaries of life insurance policies included in a decedent's gross estate. Alternatively, by inserting a tax apportionment clause in the will, the decedent has the power to direct the source of tax money. A direction could also be given that taxes are to be paid from the residue of the estate to relieve the marital share or specific bequests of the tax burden.

A guardian may also be designated to care for minor children or other legally incompetent dependents. A will may contain trust provisions to protect the interests of beneficiaries from their creditors. Trusts under a will can be created to control the management and timing of the distribution of income and principal from the estate. Executors and trustees can be given broad powers to invest and manage property.

Wills give testators the ability to leave their property as they choose, not as the state dictates. Testators have the ability to name charitable beneficiaries in their wills. They can make gifts to anyone they choose, regardless of the relationship. In writing wills, testators may also disinherit someone who would otherwise take under the intestacy laws.

Testators can designate orders of survival of themselves and their spouses in the event of a common disaster. This prevents the loss of the marital deduction and avoids potential additional taxation. Of course, it must be assumed that a will has been validly drawn and executed to obtain the above advantages.

Advantages of a Valid Will

- choice of executor
- waiver of executor requirement to post bond
- distribution of property to chosen beneficiaries
- transfer of property to charity
- take maximum advantage of marital deduction
- direct source of property to pay death taxes
- designation of guardian for minor children

Requirements of a Typical Will

While most wills are professionally drafted and executed under the guidance of an attorney, other types of wills may be acceptable as valid under state law if they conform to certain formalities and statutory requirements. Other kinds of wills are *holographic* and *nuncupative* wills, and the requirements for them are discussed later in this chapter. A primary requirement of all written wills is that the instrument be signed at the end. All writing after the testator's signature or mark, other than the acknowledgment of witnesses or a self-proving provision, is not recognized as part of the body of the will. In addition to the testator's signature, a will should be dated. Many states require witnessing the signing of the will by two or three competent witnesses. To prevent the possible voiding of an inheritance, a beneficiary with a financial interest should not be a witness to the signing of a will. Most, but not all, states require a will to be witnessed at the time of execution. However, all states require some attestation by witnesses when the will is admitted to probate. The attesting witnesses must swear that they are familiar with the signature of the testator and that the signature at the end of the document is the true signature of the testator.

General Will Requirements

- signature of testator at end of document
- date
- witnesses
- testamentary/legal capacity of testator at time will is executed (not at death)
  - age of state majority
  - mental competence

---

self-proving provision

Many states have passed laws that permit self-proving provisions at the end of wills. A *self-proving provision* eliminates the need to locate attesting witnesses at the time of probate. At the time of execution, the witnesses sign a notarized acknowledgment that they saw the testator sign the will and that the testator was of sound mind as well as competent to execute a will at that time.

testamentary capacity

Testamentary Capacity

State laws strictly prescribe the conditions necessary for a valid will. The maker or testator (another name for the maker) must have the legal capacity to make a will. Legal capacity pertains to age and mental competence. In some states, the person making a will must have reached the age of majority. In other states, the age may be considerably younger. The testator must be of sound mind, which means that he or she understands what is being done. In other words, the testator knows that he or she is writing a will. The testator must have both recognition and knowledge of the property that he or she possesses and intends to dispose of by a will. The testator must recognize relatives and friends who are the natural objects of his or her love and affection. Lastly, the testator must understand how and to whom the property is being distributed. All of these combined attributes, called *testamentary capacity*, are measured as of the time the will is written. The document is considered valid if the testator understood what he or she was doing when it was written, even if the testator is mentally incompetent at the time of death.

Modes of Distribution under Wills

There are two common forms of distribution for the property of a decedent. Distributions may be made *per stirpes,* which means "by roots or stock," or *per capita,* which means "by the heads." This distinction becomes particularly important when an individual bequeaths property to children and one or more of those children dies survived by children.

per stirpes distribution

Per stirpes distribution provides that members of a designated class, including deceased members, inherit as members of the class. Representatives (heirs) of a deceased member take the decedent's share by representation of the deceased ancestor, not as individuals. *Per capita distribution* provides that members of a class, including heirs of deceased members, share in the inheritance as individuals.

per capita distribution

Example:	Suppose Adam had four children, three of whom are alive and one of whom is deceased but survived by four children at the time of Adam's death. If distribution is to be made per stirpes, the estate is divided equally into four parts. Each of the three living children receives a one-quarter interest and the four surviving children of the deceased child equally share that deceased child's one-fourth interest.
	On the other hand, if distribution is to be made on a strict per capita basis, each lineal descendant, regardless of the degree of relationship to the decedent, inherits the property. Thus, the estate is divided equally among the three living children and the four children of the deceased child. This results in each of Adam's children and grandchildren taking one-seventh of the property.

The interpretation of the terms per stirpes and per capita differs under the various state laws. In the absence of a specification in the will, the applicable method is determined by local law. The majority of states adopt per stirpes distribution in the absence of the testator's clear intent to distribute per capita. To avoid confusion and to guarantee that the intent of the testator is fulfilled, the preferred method is to provide for the desired distribution in the will.

Will Distribution Methods

- per stirpes (by the roots/class)
- per capita (by the heads/persons)

Contents of Wills

A will is a legal declaration of a person's intended disposition of property. The beginning usually includes a statement by the testator regarding the testator's intention of domicile. The statement usually reads: "I, John Jones of Marion County, Indiana, declare this to be my last will, hereby revoking all former wills and codicils." Thus, John Jones has declared himself to be a resident of the state of Indiana. The statement implies that he wishes his property to be governed by Indiana law. This statement is particularly important if the testator owns residential real estate in more than one state. A will should contain clear, positive directions. It is not the best place to make wishes. If the testator hopes, but does not wish, to direct absolutely that some of his or her wishes will be followed, it might be better to have a separate written document or letter expressing those desires. A will is usually looked to for guidance as if the testator were present directing the disposition of the property.

Under common law, a husband was responsible for his wife's debts. Therefore, a wife's will usually contained a provision directing the executor to pay all debts as well as expenses of her last illness and funeral from her estate. This permits these expenses to be borne by the estate rather than the surviving husband. On the other hand, a husband was always held responsible for his own debts. Therefore, a similar provision in his will was unnecessary. A final distribution of his estate could not be made without payment to his creditors. Today, many states hold women responsible for their own obligations and debts. In such states, the debt provision is not necessary in the wife's will to relieve her surviving spouse of the responsibility for her sole debts. But such a provision may still be necessary to preserve estate tax deductions for these expenses for the wife's estate (Rev. Rul. 76-369, 1976-2, C.B. 281).

A will may contain directions regarding burial or cremation, perpetual care of a gravesite, and payment for a tombstone or memorial plaque. If there are specific bequests, they are usually made early in the will. These bequests may be made to individuals or charities in specific amounts or of specific objects. When a testator wants some possessions to pass to specific persons but realizes that his or her current wishes may change, the use of precatory language in the will may solve matters. *Precatory language* is a written expression of the testator's wishes regarding specific matters. Precatory language in a will usually states that the testator has preferences and wishes concerning his or her

precatory language

bequest

personal effects. The will may even mention a separate list or letter that identifies particular items and desired distributions. Although the separate writing is not part of the will, it is kept with the will. The testator is then able to alter the list or letter as necessary. Although the executor is not bound to carry out the specific preferences, the separate writing provides guidance. State law should always be reviewed prior to using precatory language. Property passing to others under a will may be referred to as a *bequest*.

Bequests may be made in one of four ways:

- bequests of specific property
- bequests of cash
- bequests of cash to be paid from a special source
- bequests that are paid out of the residue or from what remains after all other legacies and expenses have been paid

Example: An unmarried individual with several friends may make many specific bequests of cherished objects, cash, and intangible personal property. The testator may then direct that the residue of the estate be given to several charities after payment of all expenses and taxes. In other words, the charities will get what is left rather than receiving specific gifts. A will may also be written the other way, with a specific gift to a charity made before the residue is distributed.

Also found in the early part of the will is a paragraph directing the disposition of the decedent's tangible personal property, including the transfer of automobiles and automobile insurance. An executor is usually given broad discretion either to dispose of tangible personal property that is not usable or to allocate such property among the beneficiaries at the executor's sole discretion if agreement cannot be reached among them.

It may happen that the decedent does not have sufficient assets to make all the bequests provided for in the will. The state statute provides the order in which bequests are to be abated or satisfied if there are insufficient assets for all of them. In addition, if the decedent disposed of a particular piece of

ademption

property that was the subject of a specific bequest, the issue of *ademption* arises. The legatees of that bequest get nothing unless the will contains a provision to substitute other property.

After taking care of specific bequests and tangible personal property, the residue of the estate is distributed. This provision may or may not include the disposition of specific real estate or of a business interest that may be treated separately. If the residue of the estate is made payable to a trust, the direction is contained in the residuary clause.

In a will, the testator designates an executor, a successor executor, or coexecutors. A will usually contains clauses that give the executor specific and general powers, such as the power to pay the taxes and debts of the decedent as well as the taxes and debts of the estate, the power to collect life insurance proceeds payable to the estate, and all other powers that an executor must have over the property to make the appropriate transfers and distributions. As noted elsewhere, it is usual for the will to contain a clause stating that the executor may serve without bond.

A will may also contain a clause stating that the testator either exercises or declines to exercise a power of appointment, if such a power of appointment has been granted to him or her. Carefully drafted powers of appointment often require that they be specifically exercised or waived within the donee's will. However, if a testator is the holder of a power of appointment, his or her wishes in regard to this power should be expressly set out in the will. This prevents an inadvertent exercise of the power if it is imperfectly drafted.

Another useful type of provision is one directing that the executor hold any assets for the benefit of minors or incompetents or transfer these assets to the individuals responsible for caring for such disabled persons.

There is no question that having a valid will has many advantages in comparison to intestacy. However, a will rarely provides all the guidance the decedent's executor and surviving relatives may need. Typically, there are many questions to be resolved that are not addressed in the will. To help solve this problem a testator can also leave additional written instructions to help answer anticipated questions.

One area that is sometimes in doubt involves funeral arrangements. It is not uncommon for surviving loved ones to differ as to what the deceased wanted in terms of burial. Did the decedent want a memorial service, cremation or burial, open casket or closed casket?

These are just some of the questions that routinely arise. If the decedent had the foresight to prepare a separate document stating the desired funeral arrangements, there would be no doubt or decision-making for grieving relatives. The instructions could include the names of the individuals(s) the decedent would like to speak at a service, the clothing the decedent wishes to be buried in, the amount of money to be spent, the name of the funeral home, type of religious service, and so forth.

It is also useful for the instructions to include the names and phone numbers of the decedent's lawyer, doctors, accountant, broker, insurance agent, veterinarian, plumber, electrician, and lawn care service, as well as insurance and pension plan information. A written inventory of assets, location of assets, value of each asset, length of time owned, and instructions regarding the assets (such as directions about investments or family business) is certain to help the executor and family.

For instance, a decedent may have owned some furniture or artwork that only he or she knew was quite valuable. The article may be gifted, thrown away, or sold for far below its true value by an unknowledgeable family member or executor. An inventory and instructions relieve the burden on the survivors to guess what the decedent would have wanted and help to preserve family harmony during an often stressful time.

Types of Wills

Holographic Wills

holographic will

Approximately one-third of the states allow a will that is totally handwritten by the testator to be accepted for probate. This type of will is called a *holographic will*. It must be signed at the end but need not be witnessed. Some states require that a holographic will be dated by the testator, and at least one state requires that it be found among the valuable papers of the testator to be accepted as a valid will.

Nuncupative Wills

nuncupative will

Nuncupative wills are oral wills made by the testator, in the presence of witnesses, during a final illness shortly before death when it is impossible to write a will. Where such wills are permitted, the witnesses must submit an affidavit declaring the testator's final wishes. Some states allow nuncupative wills.

Joint and Mutual Wills

joint will
mutual will

Joint wills and *mutual wills* are sometimes called love wills. Two related persons may decide to execute a single joint will if they have a common scheme for the disposition of their property. Most often, a joint will is written by a husband and a wife. Both parties sign the one document. As a practical matter, joint wills may create a problem upon probate. The original will for both parties is admitted to probate at the death of the first party to die. Consequently, if the surviving party does not write a later will, it is cumbersome and possibly costly to search for the original will that was filed with the probate court and made part of the probate record of the first decedent. A question may also arise as to whether the living individual is, in some way, contractually bound when the original will is filed.

A joint will should be distinguished from a mutual will. Mutual wills exist when two or more parties agree to have their property distributed in a particular fashion upon their death. They execute separate wills that have reciprocal provisions. Mutual wills may also be signed jointly, which makes them be both mutual and joint wills. In a mutual will, the parties have bound themselves, morally if not legally, to deal with their property according to a prearranged plan. After the death of one of the parties, it is questionable whether the second party is bound to the preexisting plan or is free to change the will. In many situations, the courts have held that a binding contract existed between the parties that becomes irrevocable upon the death of the first party to a mutual will arrangement. Both joint and mutual types of will arrangements are cumbersome. They should not be entered into without objective advice regarding the ramifications. Many disputes among beneficiaries of contrary documents arise from writing such agreements. An example of an agreement to write a mutual will may be part of a property settlement agreement pursuant to a divorce.

Example:	Both parties may agree that no one but the offspring of their marriage will inherit any of their property. As part of the agreement, each party executes a reciprocal will leaving all their property to the children born of their marriage. There is some question of whether the parties can legally be contractually bound not to revise or revoke their wills. Such an agreement is contrary to the law of wills and the general principles providing that a will is a unilateral declaration that can be voluntarily altered, amended, or revoked at any time during the testator's life.

Amending or Revoking a Will

Wills are a unilateral declaration of intention and may be amended or revoked at any time. They are legally enforceable only if they meet the qualifications for validity and are still in effect at the time of death. Sometimes a will requires minor changes that may be made by writing a **codicil** codicil. A *codicil* is a modification of the will. One or more paragraphs may be revoked or amended, leaving the rest of the will intact. A codicil must be signed with the same requirements and formality as the original will.

A will may be revoked in its entirety in one of several ways. Most commonly, a more recent will is written declaring that all prior wills are revoked. Revocation can also occur by making a codicil that specifically invalidates the will. Not all subsequent wills or codicils have the effect of revoking a former will. To effect total revocation, a new will must state that it is intended to revoke the former document. In the absence of such a declaration, it is a matter for construction and interpretation by the courts as to whether the new will revokes the earlier one or merely modifies it. A modification may be accepted if there is a partial inconsistency. Making a later, valid will that is totally inconsistent with an earlier one can also constitute a revocation of the former will.

Alternatively, a will can be revoked by the maker if he or she intentionally destroys it or mutilates it by tearing. However, inadvertent or unintentional destruction of an original will would not cause a revocation if there is some way of proving its existence and validity. A copy that is certified as the last will is usually accepted as such if it can be shown conclusively that the original was inadvertently destroyed.

In some states, wills may also be totally or partially revoked by an act that causes invalidation under state law. If a divorce occurs that is not contemplated in the will, in some states the entire will is revoked. In other states, only the provisions of the will that pertain to the former spouse are revoked by operation of law.

Revocation of a Will

- subsequent will expressly revoking prior wills
- codicil expressly revoking prior wills
- subsequent will totally inconsistent with prior will
- intentional destruction or mutilation of prior will
- certain acts (divorce, marriage, after-born or after-adopted children)

When a testator marries subsequent to the writing of a will, the will may be revoked entirely unless it specifically contemplates the marriage, or the new spouse is entitled to the equivalent of an intestate share. Similarly, after-born or after-adopted children not contemplated in the will may cause the will to be revoked, or these children may be entitled to an intestate share unless the property in question passes to a surviving spouse or the omission of the after-born or after-adopted child is intentional.

Furthermore, a murderer of the testator cannot inherit under the will. States do not allow these individuals to profit from such an act.

Spouse's Right of Election against a Will

spousal right of election against the will

A spouse who is legally married to the testator at the time of death cannot be totally disinherited under most state laws. Even though a will can disinherit a spouse totally, the spouse can generally assert a statutory right to claim a certain share of the estate (for example, a surviving spouse may have a right to 30 percent of the estate). In many states, property subject to the *spousal right of election against the will* includes not only property owned by the testator at death, but also certain property that the testator gave away during lifetime—as long as he or she retained the right to the income or other use of the property until death. In some states, life insurance paid to a named beneficiary avoids the right of election. The exercise of a right of election can also be avoided by a valid, properly drafted antenuptial agreement.

Right of Election against the Will

Election right of a spouse to receive a specific portion or percentage of decedent-spouse's estate in spite of will

---

Testamentary Trusts

testamentary trust

A *testamentary trust* is one created within a will as a part of the will. It becomes both effective and irrevocable at the time of death. Because a testamentary trust is contained in the body of the will, it becomes a matter of public record when the will is probated. Thus, it is open to public scrutiny. By definition, a testamentary trust generally becomes part of the probate estate. The trust is created under the will when the testator uses language indicating an intent to have some of the property held in trust. Frequently, a trust under a will is a contingent trust. An example of such a provision is the testator who bequeaths all the property outright to a surviving spouse. However, in the event that the spouse predeceases the testator, he or she gives the property to the minor children in trust until they reach majority or other suitable age for distribution. The testamentary trust must contain the same elements as a living trust discussed in chapter 5. There must be an intention to create the trust and trust property, as well as a method to determine beneficiaries.

A testamentary trust may be a trust that provides a lifetime income to the surviving spouse with the remainder passing to other beneficiaries at the spouse's death. If a testator creates this type of trust, the trustee manages and invests property to provide income for the income beneficiary (surviving spouse). At the death of the income beneficiary, the trust principal is distributed to the remainderperson in accordance with the terms of the trust. As with living trusts, the trustee holds legal title to the property with the beneficiaries holding equitable title. The testator may direct that principal be distributed either on the happening of an event, such as the death of an income beneficiary, or upon a remainder beneficiary reaching a stated age. A testator may also direct that the remainder beneficiary or beneficiaries receive partial distributions of principal at specific ages. It is also possible to accumulate income until the beneficiary attains a certain age, at which time it is distributed. The testamentary trust may contain a power-of-appointment provision giving the donee of the power (for example, the surviving spouse) the ability to apportion assets among proposed remainderpersons at some future time when distribution is to be made. This power provides flexibility in making sure that assets are distributed according to need as opposed to a fixed-share division determined when the trust is executed. As long as this power is limited so that the person who holds the power can only appoint to the remainderperson, it does not cause the testamentary trust to be included in the power holder's estate for estate tax purposes.

Because the testamentary trust is created under a will and becomes part of the probate estate, there are no savings in estate taxes or income taxes during the testator's lifetime. Moreover, there is no protection from probate costs. A testamentary trust is frequently used when the testator does not wish to part with property during lifetime but recognizes the need for a disposition in trust for the benefit of one or more family members after his or her death. While there is no estate tax saving in the testator's estate, by creating a life estate for the first generation of beneficiaries, the property can be available to provide income and possible distributions of principal as needs arise during the beneficiaries' lives without passing through their estates at their death. Testamentary trusts can have built-in flexibility with discretion in the trustee to sprinkle income and possibly principal among various beneficiaries in different income and estate tax brackets whose needs may differ.

Tax savings may also be accomplished with the establishment of separate trusts. Trusts can be divided into separate shares when the youngest or oldest remainder beneficiary attains a specific age, thereby creating additional tax-paying entities. The trustee may also be given discretionary powers to accumulate or pay out income, again taking into consideration the relative tax brackets of the beneficiaries as compared with the trust as well as their needs in any taxable year. Furthermore, the trustee may be given authority to purchase life insurance on the life of a life income beneficiary that provides security for that beneficiary's family at the beneficiary's death. For example, a life income beneficiary who receives $50,000 of income per year from a trust is a good illustration. At that individual's death, a substantial change in his or her family's living conditions may result when the income from the trust ends. The life insurance proceeds can be used to replace that income. Payment of life insurance premiums on the life of a beneficiary is not taxable income to the beneficiary. Compared with the beneficiary's purchasing his or her own life insurance with after-tax dollars, more tax savings can result if the trust is in a lower income tax bracket than the beneficiary.

To summarize, a testamentary trust functions similarly to any other kind of trust after the testator's death. Because it is part of a will, the testamentary trust is revocable until death, at which time it becomes irrevocable. The trust can provide security and professional management for beneficiaries after the testator is gone. It also gives the testator some control even after death with regard to the intermediate and final distribution of property. While no estate taxes are saved at the testator's death, the trust may provide for life income beneficiaries so that assets escape taxation at the death of the income beneficiaries. Because the trust is irrevocable once it is operative, it can provide tax savings through income splitting and accumulation of income.

The testator may provide for any one or more of a variety of methods for the distribution of principal from a testamentary trust. For instance, the trust terms may provide that the principal is to be distributed at the discretion of the trust beneficiary. The discretion amounts to giving the trust beneficiary complete control over the trust principal. Another possibility is to provide for trust principal to be distributed at the sole discretion of the trustee. This arrangement gives the beneficiary no control over when principal may be received. A variation of this arrangement is to provide that trust principal be distributed at the discretion of a designated third party, other than the trustee or the trust beneficiary. Under either of these last two methods, trust principal can be distributed at any time but requires the approval of someone other than the trust beneficiary. The testator may specify when trust principal is to be distributed. For example, the trust may provide that determined percentages of trust principal are to be distributed as one or more beneficiaries attain a specific age. Alternatively, there may be directions for a certain percentage of trust principal to be distributed each year or every second, third, or fourth year. A third possibility is to provide for no distributions of trust principal until termination of the trust itself. Here, postponement of distribution of trust principal is limited only by the rule against perpetuities. There are numerous choices available to the testator other than those previously mentioned. Generally, a testator has complete flexibility to determine the method of the distribution of trust principal, subject only to limitations on accumulations for an unreasonably long period of time.

pour-over trust

Pour-Over Trusts

Pouring over refers to a dispositive device that has come into use in recent years. It simply means that property is transferred or poured over from an estate or trust into a preexisting estate or trust. It may occur in one of several ways. An individual may create a living trust executed prior to a will that provides that, at the individual's death, the residue of his or her estate is payable to a preexisting trust to be administered with the other trust assets. Pour overs can also take place the opposite way. A preexisting living trust may be poured into the estate and administered and distributed under the terms of the will as part of the residuary estate. By either means, the pour-over device can be used to consolidate the grantor's assets, thereby simplifying administration. Another benefit is that administration costs are reduced.

If the pouring over is from a will into a living trust, a legal question arises concerning the preexistence of the trust. For example, a will cannot be made stating that assets are to be poured over into a trust that is not executed until the following year because the named trust was not in existence at the time the will was written. To have legal effect, pouring over must be done into existing instruments. Therefore, the trust must be executed prior to a will if that is the type of pour-over arrangement in question. Also, a question arises if the preexisting trust is amended or terminated after the will is executed. Because the amendment was not within the contemplation of the testator when the testator's will was written, does the pour-over device also refer to the amendment to the trust agreement? This problem has been resolved by statute in many states by authorizing the pouring over into an amended trust agreement, if the original trust agreement was in existence at the time the will was executed. The financial services professional should consult the statutes of the jurisdiction(s) in which a client resides to determine whether an amended trust will have validity for pouring over under a preexisting will. Otherwise, a new will should be drafted after the amendments to the trust are made. There is an act called the Uniform Testamentary Additions to Trust Act that has been adopted by a number of states. In those states that have adopted the act, amendments to a living trust enacted subsequent to the execution of a will from which assets will pour over to the trust are deemed valid.

Contesting a Will

Disappointed heirs, entirely or partially overlooked in the will, may attempt to have the will set aside through legal channels. After a will is admitted to probate, any interested parties may file an action to contest the will's validity. An interested party is one who stands to benefit if the will is overturned. There are six grounds on which a will may be contested. One or more of them may be alleged in an attempt to have the will invalidated.

- The first ground is improper execution. In other words, some ingredient essential to the valid execution of a will is missing, such as the fact that the requisite number of witnesses did not sign the declaration.
- It may be claimed that the testator was not legally competent to make a will at the time of execution.
- A third ground commonly alleged is that the testator was under duress or unduly influenced by another to make the will as he or she did. This has sinister implications. The accusation is that the testator was not functioning as a free agent in expressing personal intentions but was following the advice of another party (usually someone with a financial interest in the outcome).
- The fourth ground for contesting a will is fraud. Someone defrauded the decedent into making a particular will by outright lies or otherwise misleading him or her.
- The will is alleged to be a forgery. That means it is not the true will of the testator, and the testator did not sign it.
- A will may be contested on the ground that the one admitted to probate had been revoked by an act of the testator before death.

will contest

Some of the warning signs that indicate an increased likelihood for a *will contest* include the following:

- a will that is created, arranged, and/or paid for by a primary beneficiary
- a will that has bequests that are very different from prior wills
- a will that disinherits one or more natural heirs
- a will disposing of great wealth
- a will created and signed by a testator without the benefit of an attorney
- a will with unusual dispositions
- a will by a physically or mentally weak person
- a will passing significant property to other than lineal heirs who are representative of the estate

A will may also be wholly or partially revoked by operation of law. In other words, the provisions of the will are not legally enforceable in that the directions or bequests would not be legal if made.

Note that contesting a will is very different from a spouse's election to take against the will. Contesting a will is aimed at destroying the entire will's validity while the statutory election only gives a spouse a certain share of the estate while leaving the will otherwise intact.

TRANSFERS BY CONTRACT

Property may also be transferred at death by contract. The most usual situation involves life insurance contracts. In addition, antenuptial and postnuptial agreements are becoming more common.

Life Insurance and Other Contracts

Life insurance proceeds payable to a named beneficiary pass outside the will to the beneficiary, be it an individual or a trust. Policy proceeds are always distributed according to the beneficiary designation on the policy. Directions for distribution in the will have no effect, unless no designated beneficiary is named or the policy is made payable to the estate. Likewise, death benefits from retirement plans pass to named beneficiaries outside the will unless they are made payable to the estate or the executor in his or her capacity as personal representative of the estate.

Antenuptial and Postnuptial Agreements

antenuptial (prenuptial) agreement

It is not uncommon today for persons to make prenuptial or antenuptial agreements with their intended spouse. An *antenuptial* or *prenuptial* (the terms are synonymous) *agreement* is a legally binding agreement between two parties in anticipation of marriage. The agreement provides for limitations on transfers of property between them in relinquishment of their marital rights to each other's property. These agreements can be very useful when it is not a first marriage for one or both spouses. Either spouse may wish to protect property accumulated before the present marriage for children of a prior marriage. An alternate way of preserving property for children is through the use of trusts. However, antenuptial agreements may serve a variety of purposes. The agreement may provide for certain transfers from one party to the other before the marriage as an inducement to enter the legal relationship. Antenuptial agreements may also substitute for statutory elections and other inheritance rights of a spouse at death. The agreement may provide that when one spouse dies, the other spouse will receive a fixed sum in full satisfaction of his or her rights to share in the deceased spouse's estate. The spouse who accepts the terms of an antenuptial agreement will receive that property on the death of the decedent in lieu of a statutory share that is the right of a surviving spouse. As stated earlier, the antenuptial agreement has the full force and effect of an arm's-length contract. Unless duress, fraud, and similar wrongs were involved, false information was supplied, or information was hidden regarding the extent of assets and size of the estate of either party when the agreement was reached, a court of law generally upholds its terms. Aside from trusts, antenuptial agreements can provide full protection of one's estate for one's intended beneficiaries.

Postnuptial agreements may be entered into between spouses in settlement of marital rights and property usually pursuant to a divorce. Typically, in such an agreement, each spouse gives up all rights in the other spouse's estate. These agreements may or may not provide for postdeath support benefits. To the extent that payments cease upon the death of either spouse, the other spouse gives up all rights as a creditor of the estate. However, if the benefits of a postnuptial or property settlement agreement survive death, the other party has rights against the decedent's estate as a creditor.

Transfers at Death by Contract

- life insurance proceeds
- retirement plan death benefits
- antenuptial and postnuptial agreements

TRANSFERS BY OPERATION OF LAW

operation of law

Property not passing by will or contract may pass by what is called *operation of law*. An example of property passing by operation of law is the transfer of jointly held property to the surviving joint tenant. In addition,

---

Transfers of Property at Death

- by will
- by contract
- by operation of law

---

certain property may pass to survivors under laws pertaining to family allowances and homestead allowances. Another type of transfer in this category is intestate succession.

Joint Tenants with Right of Survivorship

Property held jointly with right of survivorship (including tenancies by the entirety) automatically passes to the surviving joint tenant. In addition, a bank account held in trust for a named individual passes automatically to the beneficiary. This type of account is called a *Totten trust* or a pay-on-death account. The term is somewhat of a misnomer because it is not a legal trust. Totten trusts and pay-on-death accounts are payable-on-death arrangements. The decedent retains the right to control the assets in the account until death, at which time it passes automatically to the named beneficiary outside the will. The survivorship form of ownership takes precedence over provisions in a will.

Family Allowance

One of the first distributions from a decedent's estate permitted by many states is called a *family allowance*. It is a small, specified amount set aside for the interim support of a surviving spouse and minor children during the period of estate administration. The family allowance is property the family may keep. It is not considered part of the distributable estate and is usually exempt from state death taxation.

Homestead Allowance

Another amount set aside in many states is the homestead allowance or rights. Basically the homestead allowance is an exemption that keeps a specified amount of real property and, in some states, personal property of the decedent out of the reach of creditors.

Intestacy

All property not passing by contract, will, or by operation of law passes under the laws of intestate succession (called *laws of descent and distribution* in some states). Intestate means "without making a will." A person who dies without a will or with a will that has been revoked, annulled, or in some other way declared invalid is said to die intestate. A decedent can also die partially intestate. Partial intestacy occurs when a testator has a valid will but the document does not dispose of all of the testator's property. There are intestate laws of each jurisdiction that prescribe the way an intestate's (the word as used frequently signifies the decedent) property is to be distributed. The law of the state where the person is domiciled controls the distribution of all the person's property located within the state. The intestate distribution of real property, or tangible personal property, of the decedent located outside of the state of domicile is determined by the laws of the state where the property is located.

No distinction is usually made between real and personal property with respect to distribution under the laws of intestate descent. To provide for all property not otherwise transferred, each state has established laws of intestate succession. There is a prescribed order for disposition to the heirs of the deceased person. Intestate succession refers to the specified order of distribution by the state of the property of persons who die without leaving a valid will.

Example:	Henry dies, leaving $900,000 worth of property. He does not have a will; $300,000 passes to Henry's wife. The remaining $600,000 is divided equally among his three adult children despite the fact that he was very close to his sister and planned to leave her a significant amount of assets at his death.

There are variations among the states with respect to the descent and distribution of an intestate's property. Usually, the person given primary consideration is the surviving spouse. That is not to say that the surviving spouse takes all. Generally, a surviving spouse receives from one-third to one-half of the decedent's estate if there are living children or parents of the decedent. One scheme of intestate succession provides that a share first be set aside for the surviving spouse. An example is a provision for the first XXX dollars plus one-half of the estate to go to the surviving spouse. The remaining one-half is then divided equally among all children of the decedent. If there is no surviving spouse, surviving children may inherit the entire estate in equal shares. Next in line of lineal heirs are parents of the decedent. If a spouse survives but there are no children, the parents generally share the probate estate with the surviving spouse. Brothers and sisters usually come next in line, and so on. The order is a rigid one.

State intestacy statutes do not provide for inheritances for friends, business associates, or charities. Nor do they always make adequate provision for surviving spouses. Relatives of an individual who died intestate are frequently shocked, angered, and financially hurt by the controls put on the decedent's assets by the court. No amount of persuasion can alter the

---

Transfers at Death by Operation of Law

- joint tenants with right of survivorship
- family allowance
- homestead allowance
- intestacy

---

statutory scheme or convince the court that the decedent intended the property to pass to other persons.

If there are no living relatives, the property *escheats* to the state. Escheat means that property reverts to the state for lack of any individual competent to inherit the property. In other words, there are no heirs or next of kin who exist to whom the property can pass by way of intestate succession. The state is the ultimate owner and taker of the estate and usually designates some state institution to receive the property.

Note to Students: See Appendix A for a summary of the advantages and disadvantages of different trusts covered in this chapter and throughout the text.

CHAPTER REVIEW

Answers to the review questions and the self-test questions start on page 717.

Key Terms

will	joint will
executor/executrix	mutual will
self-proving provision	codicil
testamentary capacity	spousal right of election against the
per stirpes distribution	will
per capita distribution	testamentary trust
precatory language	pour-over trust
bequest	will contest
ademption	antenuptial (prenuptial) agreement
holographic will	operation of law
nuncupative will	

Review Questions

8-1.   What are the advantages of having a will?

8-2.   What are the requirements for a valid will?

8-3.   What are the elements of testamentary capacity with respect to a valid will?

8-4.   What are the typical provisions that a person can make in a will?

8-5.   Explain how a person may revoke or amend his or her will.

8-6.   Distinguish between
     a.   a wife electing to take against her husband's will
     b.   a wife contesting her husband's will

8-7.   What are the grounds for contesting a will?

8-8.   What property disposition planning purposes can a testamentary trust accomplish?

8-9.   Describe the various methods of distributing principal from a testamentary trust.

8-10.   When would life insurance proceeds be distributed under the provisions of a will?

8-11.   Under what circumstances is a person considered to have died intestate?

Self-Test Questions

T   F   8-1.   A will is inoperative until a decedent's death.

T   F   8-2.   A primary requirement of a typical will is that the document be signed at the end.

T   F   8-3.   A decedent must have testamentary capacity at the time of death for the decedent's will to be upheld as valid.

T   F   8-4.   Per stirpes distribution provides for all beneficiaries under a will to take as individuals by their own right.

T   F   8-5.   A will should contain clear, positive directions concerning a testator's intentions.

T   F   8-6.   If property subject to a specific bequest under a will is no longer owned by the decedent at the time of death, the legatee of the bequest must be paid in cash.

T   F   8-7.   A holographic will is oral and made in the presence of witnesses.

T   F   8-8.   A codicil is a modification of a will.

T   F   8-9.   A will cannot be revoked during the testator's lifetime except by court order.

T   F   8-10.   In most states, it is impossible for a decedent to totally disinherit a nonconsenting surviving spouse.

T   F   8-11.   A testamentary trust is a trust created under a will that becomes effective and irrevocable at the death of the testator.

T   F   8-12.   A major advantage of a testamentary trust is that it avoids probate.

T   F   8-13.   Pour-over trusts have legal effect only when they are written after a will is created.

T   F   8-14.   A will may be set aside only if the testator was not of sound mind at its creation.

T   F   8-15.   Under a typical postnuptial agreement, each spouse gives up all rights to the other spouse's estate.

T   F   8-16.   A typical intestate-succession scheme allows a widow to receive all the decedent's property whether or not there are minor children.

T   F   8-17.   If a person dies intestate and has no living relatives, the decedent's property escheats to the state.

Administration of the Estate

Learning Objectives

An understanding of the material in this chapter should enable the student to

---

9-1.   Explain the process of probating the will.

9-2.   Describe the appointment of an executor or an administrator.

9-3.   Explain what is involved in assembling estate property.

9-4.   Explain what is involved in managing the estate.

9-5.   Explain the executor's responsibility for paying debts and taxes and keeping estate records.

9-6.   Describe the final estate settlement step of distribution.

Chapter Outline

Death does not always forewarn. It sometimes strikes suddenly and when it is least expected. The business affairs and personal obligations of an individual may be in order or, alternatively, when one's life is cut short, there may be many entanglements to unravel. After death, a process begins called estate administration. The purpose of estate administration is the resolution of all outstanding responsibilities, obligations, and rights of the decedent as well as the transfer of all property to intended beneficiaries. Before the final transfers can be accomplished, the decedent's unfinished business and personal obligations must be resolved. These include payment of debts and taxes, transfers of any business interests, and collection of all amounts owed to the decedent while living as well as amounts that would be payable to beneficiaries or the estate because of the individual's death, such as life insurance proceeds, veterans' or employee death benefits, and so forth. The funeral director must be paid as well as the medical and hospital bills resulting from the last illness. In addition, cash must be made available for the immediate living needs of the family and others for whom the decedent had some financial responsibility.

Basically, whether the decedent died testate (with a will) or intestate (without a will), the estate settlement process is similar. There are several stages in the settlement process:

- initial responsibilities
- probating the will
- appointing an executor or administrator
- assembling property
- managing the estate
- paying debts and taxes
- distributing the estate

INITIAL RESPONSIBILITIES

Even before a personal representative is appointed, there are matters that require attention. They may involve arranging the funeral, notifying relatives and close friends, and making arrangements for distant relatives to come to the funeral. Action may be necessary to temporarily protect and preserve estate assets. If the decedent was a professional person, someone must temporarily assume these professional duties. If the decedent was the owner of a closely held business or farm, responsibility for business activity may have to be delegated so that the business or farm may remain in operation. Once the funeral is over, a determination must be made as to the existence of a will.

PROBATING THE WILL

probate

The probate process begins when the original will is deposited with the probate court of the county where the decedent resided. By definition, *probate* is the act or process of proving a will. To probate the will means to prove to the court that the instrument presented is the last valid will of the deceased person. The proof must be made before a duly authorized person that the document presented as the last will and testament of a deceased person is, in fact, the document it purports to be. The term *probate* has come to refer to all matters over which probate courts have jurisdiction, including settlement of decedents' estates, appointment and supervision of guardianships, and will contests. The jurisdiction of the probate, surrogate, or orphans' court extends to the probate assets of the decedent. Probate assets are the property that passes under and is subject to the terms of the will or, if no will exists, the property subject to administration by the court due to intestacy.

When a will is admitted to probate, the signature of the testator (the individual leaving a will in force at death) must be verified. This is done by calling the subscribing witnesses (witnesses who were present at the signing of the will). If there were no witnesses to the signing or the subscribing witnesses cannot be found, attesting witnesses must be summoned to verify the decedent's signature. These are persons who can attest to the fact that the signature on the will is the decedent's true signature and that they are familiar with the signature of the decedent as they have seen it written on various occasions. Fortunately, self-proving wills are now widely accepted. Self-proving wills contain a notarized acknowledgment by the witnesses that they saw the testator, being of sound mind, voluntarily sign the will. A self-proving will can be admitted to probate without calling witnesses to the signing. The self-proving will saves the executor the time, expense, and inconvenience of locating subscribing witnesses.

Once the will is validated, the executor or administrator is sworn in and formally appointed. Letters testamentary or letters of administration (as they are called if an administrator is appointed) are then issued.

Probate and Nonprobate Assets

A decedent's estate consists of all property owned outright, in conjunction with others, or in which the decedent possessed certain rights at the time of death. This property is characterized as either real estate or tangible and intangible personal property. Intangibles are such items as stock certificates, corporate or government bonds, bank accounts, bank certificates, mutual fund shares, or money market trust assets.

Other intangible assets and rights (such as Social Security benefits, veterans' benefits, proceeds of life insurance, benefits under private or government pension plans, benefits under state workers' compensation acts, and survivors' interests in joint and survivor annuity contracts) may represent the bulk of the estate assets. These amounts may be payable to a decedent's survivors by operation of law or under the terms of a contract. If these assets are payable to named beneficiaries, they pass directly to the beneficiary and not under the will. They are not subject to probate. Therefore, they are nonprobate assets unless they are made payable to the estate. If payable to the estate, they become probate property subject to estate administration.

While they pass outside the will, nonprobate assets may still be taxable for either or both federal and state estate and inheritance tax purposes. An example of a nonprobate asset that may be taxable for state inheritance purposes is a bank account owned by the decedent but held in trust for a named individual, that is, a Totten trust. The proceeds of such an account are transferred to the named beneficiary by operation of law. However, because this account was owned by the decedent alone but in trust for another (as opposed to joint ownership with rights of survivorship, which is exempt from *state* death taxes in some states), the account may be taxable under state law for estate or inheritance tax purposes. The administrator has a duty to include this property in the inventory submitted to the court and to pay any death taxes resulting from inclusion of such property in the estate.

It should be remembered that the probate process is not automatic. Someone (either the executor named in the will or another interested party) must present the will for probate if letters testamentary are to be granted to the executor.

Advantages and Disadvantages of Probate

There are both advantages and disadvantages to probate. The primary advantages of probate include the following:

- The will is validated.
- The executor's actions are supervised.
- A dispute-resolution forum is provided for estate issues, including the guardianship of minors and conservatorship of incapacitated parties.
- The inventory and valuation of the decedent's assets and liabilities are carried out.
- Proof of legal title to real property is established.
- A time frame is set for creditors' claims to be presented prior to the distribution of assets to the estate beneficiaries.
- Philanthropic bequests receive public recognition.

The primary disadvantages of probate include the following:

- There is a lack of privacy in that the decedent's will, beneficiary information, and the claims of creditors are a matter of public record.
- Property distribution may be time-consuming, depending on the complexity of the estate, will disputes, and the jurisdiction.
- There is inflexibility because probate must be carried out according to state statute.
- Costs result from court supervision according to state statute.
- Executor commissions and attorney fees are generated.
- Property owned in nondomicilary states or countries may be subject to ancillary probate.

Methods to Avoid Probate

If, after weighing the pros and cons of probate, an individual wants to avoid probate for some or all property, there are several possible avoidance methods or will substitutes, some of which are discussed below.

Joint Tenancy

Property that is titled as joint tenants with right of survivorship or property that is titled as tenants by the entireties is not subject to probate at the death of the first joint tenant.

Property Passing by Contract at Death

Property passing to a beneficiary (other than the decedent's estate) under the terms of a contract is also considered nonprobate property. These assets may include, for example, the proceeds of life insurance, Social Security benefits, pension plan proceeds, IRAs, and survivors' interests in annuities. Generally, property passing to beneficiaries by small estate administration also avoids the probate process.

Government Savings Bonds

When an individual purchases Series EE and Series H U.S. savings bonds and designates someone else to be paid at the purchaser's death, the proceeds are not included in probate.

Totten Trusts and Payable-on-Death Accounts

Certain types of accounts established at financial institutions become payable to the named beneficiary at the death of the individual who established the account. The depositor has sole control and access to the account during lifetime.

Deeds

deed

Deeds are another will substitution device. To be a completed transfer the *deed* must be irrevocably delivered to the transferee or to an escrow agent. If the deed is transferred to an escrow agent, the agent holds the deed for an established period of time or until the transferor's death, at which time it is delivered to the eventual intended recipient. When an escrow agent holds a deed for future delivery, any income tax liability with regard to the property subject to the deed remains the responsibility of the transferor. Recordation of the deed is not necessary until delivery is made to the transferee-owner.

Living Trusts

Another probate-avoidance method is the living (revocable) trust. Property that is transferred to a trust during an individual's lifetime is distributed according to the terms of the trust. Because the trustee rather than the grantor owns and manages the trust assets, at the time of the grantor's death, the probate court has no authority (except in limited circumstances) over the property.

The living trust is often a favored probate-avoidance technique because there are many other benefits to holding property in this way. The decedent continues to control the property after the death through the trust terms; trust assets receive a full-basis step up at the decedent's death; transfers to the trust are not subject to public knowledge; the grantor is able to observe the operation of the trust during lifetime; and out-of-state property held by a trust can avoid ancillary probate.

Small Estate Administration

Most states exempt an estate from probate if the decedent's total estate or real property does not exceed a specific dollar amount.

Methods to Avoid Probate

- Title property in joint tenancy with right of survivorship or tenancy by the entirety.
- Pass property by contract (such as life insurance, IRAs, pension plan benefits, and so on).
- Create Totten trusts and payable-on-death accounts, which are nonprobate.
- Transfer property by deed.
- Establish living trusts (property in a living trust is nonprobate).

---

ancillary probate

Ancillary Probate

If the decedent owned property in other states, the executor has a duty to locate the property and make all necessary transfers, either by taking possession of the property or by selling it on behalf of the estate. Typically, an estate administration proceeding has to be conducted in each state in which a nondomiciled decedent owned real property. The court in the county where the property is situated appoints an ancillary administrator to oversee the transfer of these assets. Multiple proceedings result in added expense and inconvenience. If the owner transfers the properties to a trust during lifetime, however, the additional expenses and inconvenience of ancillary probate can be avoided. Ancillary administration of assets is avoided because the trustee holds title to the property and it is administered according to the terms of the trust.

APPOINTMENT OF EXECUTOR OR ADMINISTRATOR

If the decedent had a will, an executor was probably named to whom authority was given for settlement of the estate. An executor is also known as the personal representative of an estate. Broadly speaking, a personal representative is the individual or institution charged with responsibility for management of the estate, including gathering all assets, collecting all amounts owed the decedent, paying debts, expenses, and taxes, and distributing assets to the beneficiaries. The position requires a high degree of responsibility and involves many duties. Although named in the will, an executor must petition the probate court for formal appointment to be recognized by all persons dealing with the estate as the estate's personal representative.

If a valid will is not found, a petition must be filed in the probate court of the county where the decedent resided to have an administrator appointed. Procedures for appointment of an executor or an administrator are prescribed by state statute and vary according to local law.

If the decedent did not name an executor, state law prescribes the order of persons entitled to be appointed as administrator. This order is based on degree of relationship to the decedent. To qualify for the position of executor, one must be legally competent and have reached legal age—18 years in most states.

If a corporation is chosen, it must be one authorized to act as a fiduciary in that state. In some states, courts will not appoint an individual who is a nonresident. A court is usually influenced by the wishes and recommendations of the family. As to the choice of a competent administrator, sometimes a family member who is eligible to be an administrator may not feel qualified to serve. The appointment may be renounced in favor of other persons or an institution better suited for the position. Also, the court may exercise its discretion in the appointment of an appropriate administrator so that, in its judgment, the estate will be settled properly. It is not bound to follow the order prescribed by state statute.

Posting Bond

posting a bond

Individuals may state in their wills that named executors may serve without *posting a bond* as security. The courts will honor this direction provided that an executor is competent to serve.

Some states, however, require bond to be posted despite the testator's waiver of bond. If an individual administrator is appointed by the court, a bond with surety (secured by cash or other collateral) is required to protect the estate's beneficiaries and creditors. In most states, if an institution is named as administrator, a bond may still be required but usually without surety.

The amount of the bond varies depending on the approximate size of the estate and the fee schedule prescribed by state statute. Generally, bonds are posted in amounts up to twice the value of the probate estate. Because the exact size of the estate is unknown at this early stage, it may be necessary to post an additional bond at a later date when the full value of the estate has been determined.

Letters Testamentary

letters testamentary

After the bond is obtained, *letters testamentary* or letters of administration are issued by the court. These letters are certifications by the court that the named personal representative was granted authority to act on behalf of the estate during the administration period until he or she is discharged by the court, at which time the estate may be closed.

Advertising

The personal representative has an obligation to publicize the existence of the estate, thereby notifying all interested parties (including creditors and debtors of the decedent) that this personal representative has authority to act as the estate's representative for all purposes. This is done by advertising in a local newspaper of general circulation and in a legal periodical in the county in which the estate is being probated.

Advertising provides notice to all creditors and debtors that the decedent has died and that creditors and debtors may settle their accounts with the decedent's personal representative. Advertising starts the statute of limitations running. If creditors do not notify the executor of their claim within a fixed period set by local law (generally 3 to 6 months but certainly within one year of the advertisement), they will be barred from collecting any amounts owed to them by the decedent.

ASSEMBLING ESTATE PROPERTY

One of the first tasks of the personal representative is to assemble the property belonging to the estate. All estate assets must be gathered, safeguarded, and managed during this interim period of estate administration. This task ranges from a relatively simple one to an extremely complex, time-consuming, and expensive project. Executors should make every reasonable effort to collect all accounts receivable due to decedents from their business or profession. They may find themselves involved in the sale or continued operation of a decedent's business.

Complications may arise if the decedent owned property or partial interests in property in conjunction with others, such as interests in limited partnerships. These may be based in states other than the state of domicile (where the will is usually probated), or abroad. The decedent may also have possessed assets or business interests in foreign countries. The decedent may have been the beneficiary of one or more trusts or the custodian of the assets of another. The estate may be entitled to death benefits under an employment contract. The decedent may have possessed or retained remainder interests in property. There are many involved property rights.

The executor is the one with the responsibility to take possession of and make all appropriate transfers of a decedent's property. In addition to assembling the assets, the executor has a duty to make certain that valuables are safeguarded and insured, if necessary, during the administration period. This might involve the use of safe-deposit boxes and storage vaults.

The executor may find that it is necessary to possess the instincts of a sleuth and the patience of a saint if the estate was left in a disorganized condition. Whether a simple or complex matter, it is the personal representative who has the legal responsibility to gather all estate property, wherever situated, making the transfers necessary to do so.

Safe-Deposit Boxes

One of the first places to look for information and valuable papers is the decedent's safe-deposit box. Once an individual passes away, a safe-deposit box titled in the decedent's own name is closed, except for limited purposes.

Usually a representative of the bank is present when the box is opened for the first time after death. The will may be found in a safe-deposit box, which is not necessarily a good location for a will as one of the first things to find out is who has been named executor.

A will itself has no intrinsic value. If possible, for simplicity's sake, it should be kept among the valuable papers of the decedent or with the decedent's attorney rather than in a safe-deposit box. The personal representative should make a diligent search for more than one safe-deposit box to assure that all safe-deposit boxes in the name of the decedent have been located. In some states, the safe-deposit box cannot be opened except in the presence of a representative of the state taxing authority in addition to a representative of the bank. If the box contains possessions belonging to someone other than the decedent, the personal representative should not surrender this property without obtaining a receipt from the person taking possession of the property.

Proceeds of Life Insurance and Qualified Plans

Life insurance policies should be located and a claim made for all life insurance benefits. The insurance company will provide the executor with Form 712, to be filed with the federal estate tax return. There are optional modes of payment of life insurance proceeds. These various settlement options should be discussed with the beneficiaries. An appropriate settlement option should be chosen, unless the insurance is made payable to the estate or to a trust, in which case the insurance is usually paid in a lump sum. If the decedent had a right to receive death benefits from pension or profit-sharing plans, these proceeds should be applied for. Here, again, there may be a choice of payment plan. The mode of payment may have significant income tax consequences and should be reviewed carefully.

Surviving spouses may also apply for the lump-sum Social Security death benefits and any Veterans' Administration survivor benefits to which they are entitled.

MANAGING THE ESTATE

Once the estate is assembled, the executor is obligated to properly manage the assets of the estate. This includes managing cash, securities, and business interests; valuing assets; and obtaining necessary legal and accounting services.

Estate Accounts

Any cash belonging to the decedent should be deposited in an estate checking account as soon as assets are released to the estate. Checks should be ordered for payment of the estate's debts. Although funds necessary to pay bills should be kept in a checking account, the executor has an obligation to keep other reasonable sums of money producing interest income during the estate administration period. Therefore, a savings account or money market trust account in the name of the estate should also be opened as well. If the decedent had a personal brokerage account, it should be closed and the securities or cash should be transferred to an estate account, unless the decedent's will specifically directed the executor to keep that account open for a specific time or purpose.

Valuation of Assets

Besides locating and taking possession of the decedent's property, the executor must determine the value of all estate assets as of the date of death. These values fix the value of assets in the estate for both estate and inheritance tax purposes. All banks in which the decedent had accounts must be contacted to obtain the date-of-death values, including all accrued interest for the short taxable year ending with the decedent's death. Real property and unique personal property of any special value (such as art objects or coins) may require appraisal by an independent appraiser. Copies of the decedent's income tax returns and canceled checks for the past 3 years should be obtained. They provide a record of the time of financial transactions as well as their cost. It will also be necessary to learn of any valuable rights the decedent may have owned, such as patent rights, royalties, or contract rights, and to determine the fair market value of these rights on the date of death. If the decedent was a professional or a sole proprietor, the value of the decedent's business or profession must be appraised for estate tax purposes.

After all assets have been located and appraised, an inventory listing all the assets and their values is filed with the probate court.

Legal and Accounting Work

If the executor is inexperienced in financial, business, and tax matters, or if the estate is complicated, administrative duties may be delegated to others. For example, the executor may hire an attorney specializing in estate matters as well as an appraiser to obtain reasonable values for the estate property. The decedent's accountant may be consulted about the decedent's tax and business matters. An attorney specializing in estate planning may be called in by the executor to perform all legal work and assist with some of the financial matters as well. This is often the same attorney who drafted the will. Today, many banks, although not named as a fiduciary under the will, are willing to offer estate settlement services on a fee-for-service basis. The trust department of a bank handles these matters routinely. A bank's trust department has the capacity to perform all administrative tasks for the estate, including the preparation of all tax returns.

Management or Sale of Business

In addition to the foregoing responsibilities, an administrator or executor may have to sell assets of the estate by personal sale or auction to raise the necessary cash to pay the debts, taxes, and administration expenses of the estate. This may involve sale of a personal residence or all or part of a business interest. The executor must decide whether the business interest or professional practice of the decedent must be sold or whether it can be maintained to provide a source of income for the family. The executor may become intimately involved in making decisions regarding the business until such time as it may be liquidated, sold, or transferred to the heirs. The executor is responsible for the interim management and investment of all assets of the estate.

PAYMENT OF DEBTS AND TAXES

It is the executor's responsibility to pay all bills and debts of the decedent and to keep records of all costs of administering the estate. The administrator or executor is also responsible for payment of any court costs, attorney fees, administrator or executor fees as well as fees for appraisals of property, and probate costs. Executors may also have some out-of-pocket expenses for which they may reimburse themselves.

Order of Payment of Claims

The executor has to establish the validity of all claims against the estate. A creditor must present a claim within a statutory time period. As stated previously, this time varies from state to state and may be as much as one year, but in recent years the time period has been shortened by many states to 9 or 6 months. There is a prescribed order of priority for payment of claims. If there are insufficient assets to pay all the claims in full, then the primary classes are paid in full first, with lower priority claims remaining unpaid entirely. Within a class of claims, each debt must be paid pro rata. While each state establishes its own order of preference for payment of debts, the following is a typical order: (1) debts that have a special lien on property not exceeding the value of the property; (2) funeral expenses; (3) taxes; (4) debts owed to the United States government and to the state; (5) judgments of any court of competent jurisdiction to the extent that they are a lien against the property of the decedent at death; (6) wages due to any domestic servant or mechanical or agricultural laborer for the year immediately prior to the decedent's death; (7) medical expenses and services provided during the year preceding the death; and (8) all other debts and claims.

Filing of Tax Returns and Payment of Taxes

Records of any federal gift tax returns must be obtained; gift tax returns for any taxable gifts made in the year of death must also be filed. If the gross estate plus adjusted taxable gifts exceeds a statutory amount equal to the applicable exclusion amount (exemption equivalent of the applicable credit amount), the executor must file a federal estate tax return within 9 months after the decedent's death. Also, any elections or disclaimers must be made by the time the estate tax return is filed, including extensions.

In addition to payment of federal estate taxes, the estate may be liable for taxes on real property, personal property, and possibly intangible personal property located in the state. There will also be federal and state income taxes to be paid, both for the short taxable year prior to the decedent's death and the remaining period of that tax year after death. This may include filing a joint return with the surviving spouse for the year of death. State inheritance or estate taxes must be paid if any tax is due. If there is a discount for early payment of state inheritance tax, the executor must decide when to pay the inheritance tax and weigh the advantages or disadvantages of paying it early. Sometimes early payment is impossible because there are no liquid assets in the estate that can be used for this purpose. For example, the major asset of an estate may be real estate. Prior to the sale of such property, the estate will not have cash to pay many of its obligations. In that case, early payment of inheritance taxes is not possible and the discount is, of necessity, lost. If a trust has been established, some taxes may be payable by the trust.

A determination must be made as to who the taxpayer is and how the taxes will be allocated among the estate, any trust, or the beneficiaries of each. Frequently, a will contains a tax clause that directs the way taxes are to be apportioned. If there is no tax clause in the will, taxes are allocated according to the state statutory scheme.

There are still other decisions that an executor should make with regard to payment of taxes. A choice must be made whether to have all assets valued on the date of death or the alternate valuation date, which is 6 months from the date of death. For decedents dying after July 18, 1984, the alternate valuation date can be used only if both the value of the gross estate and the amount of federal estate tax will decrease by using the alternate valuation date (IRC Sec. 2032(c)). An example of an estate that could still use the alternate valuation date is one that has substantial amounts of stocks and bonds whose prices have dropped significantly within the 6-month period between the date of death and the alternate valuation date. In that case, the executor may select the alternate valuation date to reduce taxes. Also, if more than 35 percent of the adjusted gross estate consists of a closely held business or farm, the executor should consider the advisability of electing a 15-year payment of the estate tax attributable to the value of that closely held business or farm included in the estate. An extension of time to pay the tax may also be requested based on reasonable cause.

There is also a provision in the Internal Revenue Code for special valuation of a farm or business real estate. Any election to specially value these properties at their current-use value rather than at their highest and best use must be made when the federal estate return is filed. If the estate contains qualified terminable interest property, the executor must also decide whether to elect to qualify this property for the marital deduction. There may be some credits or deductions that can be taken for taxes previously paid on the estate of a person whose property was inherited by the decedent within 10 years of the decedent's death. Also, the executor may be given discretion in the will to take deductions either in the federal estate tax return or in the decedent's income tax return to achieve the lowest tax liability. All of the above decisions fall within the scope of the executor's discretion and responsibilities.

DISTRIBUTING THE ESTATE

As the estate administration process draws to a close, the executor will prepare an accounting for the court and the beneficiaries. This procedure varies from state to state. An accounting is filed in the county where the will was probated. It may be a formal proceeding with notice to interested parties, or it may be an informal proceeding. At this time, any interested parties have the right to object to the accounting and to have any matters at issue resolved by the judge with whom the accounting is filed.

If there is no objection to the accounting, the executor or administrator then proceeds to make final distribution of the estate assets. When the executor makes distributions, it is important that releases and receipts be obtained from the beneficiaries to relieve the executor from further liability to each beneficiary because of the property transferred to him or her. When that has been accomplished, the administrator or executor may be discharged by the court, at which time the estate can be closed. If any property is found after that, it may be necessary to reopen the estate on a limited basis to have this property probated.

Disclaimers

The possibility may arise that a beneficiary does not wish to accept either a bequest under the decedent's will or an intestate share of the estate that he or she is entitled to receive. A reason may be that the beneficiary's own estate is substantial. The beneficiary may not want to further burden his or her own estate with additional estate taxes. Alternatively, it may be a way of releasing an inheritance so that it will go to other beneficiaries in greater need than himself or herself. If a beneficiary does not wish to accept an inheritance, it is possible to refuse this legacy by making a qualified disclaimer. If the requirements of a qualified disclaimer are met, the property will be treated as if it had never passed to that individual. As stated in chapter 4, there are four requirements under the Internal Revenue Code to qualify a disclaimer for federal estate tax or gift tax purposes: (1) there must be an unqualified refusal by the beneficiary to accept the bequest or the gift; (2) this refusal must be written and received by the donor, the donor's legal representative, or the legal titleholder of the property within 9 months of the decedent's death or 9 months from the date of the gift or, if later, within 9 months after the beneficiary becomes 21 years of age; (3) the beneficiary must not have accepted the interest or any of its benefits; (4) the interest must then pass to someone other than the person making the disclaimer or to the spouse of the decedent without the beneficiary's direction.

The law provides that a disclaimer complying with the requirements of the federal tax statute is considered to qualify for federal estate and gift tax purposes, regardless of qualification under local law. The law provides some uniformity in the application of the federal disclaimer statute, although state law may still hold the disclaimer ineffective to pass title directly to the later beneficiary without gift tax considerations.

All or part of an interest in property may be disclaimed. However, the disclaimed part must represent an undivided portion of the interest. The beneficiary of an estate has 9 months following the decedent's death in which to make this disclaimer. It must be received by the executor or administrator of the estate in writing. If a federal estate tax return is filed, a copy of the disclaimer must be filed with the return. It is also possible to disclaim a power of appointment over property if one meets the same four requirements stated above.

Note to Students: See Appendix A for a summary of the advantages and disadvantages of different trusts covered in this chapter and throughout the text.

CHAPTER REVIEW

Answers to the review questions and the self-test questions start on page 717.

Key Terms

probate
deed
ancillary probate

posting a bond
letters testamentary

Review Questions

9-1.   What property in a decedent's estate is subject to probate?

9-2.   What are the advantages and disadvantages of probate?

9-3. What are the responsibilities of an executor?

9-4. What is the problem associated with having a will located in a safe-deposit box?

9-5. What functions must an executor or administrator perform in managing an estate?

9-6. Describe the general priority for paying claims if an estate has insufficient assets to pay all claims in full.

9-7. Describe the responsibilities of an executor or administrator with respect to filing tax returns and paying taxes.

9-8. For what reasons might a beneficiary disclaim an inheritance?

Self-Test Questions

T F 9-1. The steps in the estate settlement process differ significantly according to whether the decedent died intestate or with a will.

T F 9-2. Probate is the act or process of proving a will.

T F 9-3. Ancillary probate refers to probate in the state where the decedent had his or her principal residence.

T F 9-4. The administrator is the person named in the decedent's will to settle the estate at the decedent's death.

T F 9-5. Individuals may state in their wills that an executor may serve without posting a bond as security.

T F 9-6. The executor has a duty to make certain that valuables are safeguarded and insured, if necessary, during the administration period.

T F 9-7. The executor has the duty to determine the value of all estate assets.

T F 9-8. If a will does not contain a tax apportionment clause, the executor has discretion in directing how taxes are to be apportioned.

T F 9-9. If any estate property is found after the estate is formally closed, the executor is entitled to keep the property.

T F 9-10. A disclaimant may disclaim a part of an interest in property instead of having to disclaim the entire interest.

Valuation of Assets for Federal Estate and Gift Tax Purposes

Stephan R. Leimberg, Ted Kurlowicz, and Constance J. Fontaine*

Learning Objectives

An understanding of the material in this chapter should enable the student to

---

10-1.   Explain why it is important to value assets for estate planning purposes and why the lowest value that can be placed on an asset may not always be the best value.

10-2.   Explain when an asset has to be valued for estate tax purposes and the general rules that need to be followed in the valuation process.

10-3.   Identify problems that may occur in the valuation process.

10-4.   Describe how real property is valued, and explain the special-use method of valuation.

10-5.   Explain how certain types of assets are valued.

10-6.   Identify the general methods used to value closely held businesses.

10-7.   Explain how various types of lifetime transfers with retained interests are valued.

Chapter Outline

* Stephan R. Leimberg, JD, CLU, formerly was a former professor of estate planning and taxation at The American College. Ted Kurlowicz, JD, LLM, CLU, ChFC, AEP, is professor of taxation and holder of the Charles E. Drimal professorship at The American College. Constance J. Fontaine, JD, LLM, CLU, ChFC, is associate professor of taxation at The American College and holds the Larry R. Pike chair in Insurance and Investments.

IMPORTANCE OF VALUING ASSETS

One of the most complex and uncertain aspects of the estate planning process is the valuation of property for federal estate and gift tax purposes. Frequently, the taxpayer's representative values property at one amount; the IRS attempts a second figure; and, if the issue cannot be settled between the taxpayer and the IRS, the courts generally settle on some middle ground. Thus, value is a variable upon which reasonable minds can and will differ. Value is not determined merely by flipping a coin. There are techniques to substantiate values. These devices include careful and thorough appraisals by qualified experts, documentation of sales of similar property recently sold, and well-drawn, arm's-length restrictive agreements, such as buy-sell arrangements.

The estate planning professional must be keenly aware of the problems and costs associated with the lack of predeath valuation planning. There are a number of reasons why valuation is of particular importance in the estate planning process.

First, it is impossible to determine potential liquidity needs that an executor may experience unless values are placed on the various assets owned by the client. A hypothetical *probate* of the estate is impossible until values are assigned to various assets. Qualification for stock redemptions under Sec. 303 or installment payments of taxes attributable to business interests under Sec. 6166 depend on the value of the decedent's stock relative to the value of the decedent's other assets. If the appropriate test(s) cannot be met, neither technique for paying estate taxes is available. For planning purposes, this means that both the value of a client's stock and the worth of other assets must be "guesstimated" with reasonable accuracy.

In addition, many estate owners are thinking about establishing gift programs or have already done so. Because of the income and estate tax advantages still inherent in gifts, gratuitous transfers of property may be meaningful when they are subject to minimal gift tax costs. Furthermore, inter vivos gifts to charity can yield large, immediate income tax deductions. But to properly consider the various ramifications and potential advantages involved in a lifetime transfer, a knowledge of valuation is essential.

The third reason that valuing assets is an important technique for the estate planner relates to the funding of buy-sell agreements. For example, if a client is one of several owners of a business, quite often a buy-sell agreement is advisable. The first step in arranging such an agreement is to arrive at a fair market value for the business. Obviously, it is impossible to assure each costockholder (or partner) that beneficiaries will receive an equitable price on death or disability unless the current worth of each person's business interest is ascertained.

WHY THE LOWEST VALUE IS NOT ALWAYS THE BEST

Because both federal estate and gift taxes are based on the value of property interest transferred, at first glance it makes sense to attempt to value property at the lowest reasonable figure. Yet achieving the lowest possible valuation for an asset is not always the most appropriate objective.

One example where a higher valuation might be advantageous is the formula for a buy-sell agreement. Especially from the point of view of the decedent's survivors, where alternative liquidity funding is impractical, it may be better to set a formula in a buy-sell agreement that puts a higher value on the stock in a closely held business (and thereby provide more cash for the decedent's survivors) than to establish a formula that provides a lower estate tax value (yielding a lower price for the decedent's business interest).

When closely held stock is valued high relative to other estate assets, the disadvantage of the additional tax payable due to the higher valuation may be more than offset by the advantages of qualifying for a Sec. 303 stock redemption or a Sec. 6166 election to pay federal estate taxes attributable to a business interest in installments. In a number of situations, a corporation may purchase key person life insurance to deliberately increase the relative value of the decedent-shareholder's stock and thereby make it more likely to qualify for one of the above liquidity devices.

DATE ASSETS ARE VALUED

Generally, federal estate taxes are based either on the fair market value of the transferred property as of the date the decedent died or, if applicable, on

alternate valuation date

the value of the property 6 months after the date of the decedent's death (*alternate valuation date*). Once the date-of-death valuation or the alternate valuation date is selected, that date applies to all assets in the estate, subject to the exceptions noted below.

If the alternate valuation date is selected and property is distributed, sold, exchanged, or otherwise disposed of within the 6-month period after the decedent's death, that property is valued as of the date of distribution, sale, exchange, or other disposition, not as of the 6-month date.

Certain types of property diminish in value as time goes on. Any property interest or estate whose value is affected by the mere passing of time, such as an annuity, is valued as of the date the decedent died, even if the alternate valuation date applies to other estate assets.

Federal Estate Tax—Asset Valuation Dates

- date of death (earliest date)
- date of sale, exchange, distribution, disposition
- alternate valuation date (6 months after death)

GENERAL VALUATION RULES

There is very little in the Internal Revenue Code about how to value items for federal estate tax purposes. Although the value of the gross estate is mentioned in the Code, the word *value* is not defined. The estate and gift tax regulations provide that value is meant to be *fair market value*, which is defined as

fair market value

> the price at which the property would change hands between a willing buyer and a willing seller, neither being under any compulsion to buy or to sell and both having reasonable knowledge of relevant facts

By this definition, the value that may be placed on property can vary substantially, depending on who is valuing the item and what factors are used. The regulations state that it is not necessary to have either an established market for an item or a willing buyer and seller as mentioned above. In the absence of an actual sale, the value of an asset is based on a hypothetical sale.

Generally, the following external factors are examined in deciding the extent to which sales price is indicative of value:

- the frequency of sales (Courts tend to disregard isolated or sporadic sales.)
- the relationship between the seller and the buyer (Sales between parents and children or employers and employees are seldom given great weight in light of their almost inherently unequal bargaining position.)
- options to purchase or sell (Offers, as opposed to options, present little evidence of value.)

Once all these value-affecting factors are considered, each factor must be given a relative weight.

SPECIFIC PROBLEMS IN VALUATION

Some items present minimal valuation problems. If there is an established market for identical property, value is basically a question of fact. But evidential proof—and often opinion—is necessary when the following occurs:

- There are different markets for the same property, such as in the case of a property with both wholesale and retail markets.
- The appraisal of worth must be made on the basis of comparison with somewhat similar property. (Which comparable property should be selected? How comparable is it?) In such a case, what is derived is at best an opinion based on fact.
- The property in question is unique, such as a patent or copyright, in which case the data must be analyzed (Is the examiner capable of making an adequate analysis?), and an opinion must be formulated as to how much the potential anticipated benefits are worth.

In practice, valuation problems are frequently viewed by the IRS and the courts as problems of negotiation and compromise. An appraiser's objective is to derive a fair and sound value that, if litigated, would likely be sustained in court.

VALUATION OF SPECIFIC PROPERTY

It is beyond the scope of this chapter to examine the valuation process for all types of property. However, the valuation of real property as well as stocks of closely held corporations provides a good example of the essential gift and estate tax valuation process.

Valuation of Real Property

Land is unique. Therefore, the value of any real property (land or property affixed to land) on a given date may be subject to widely differing opinions. If there is no market for such property, a controlling factor is the greater of (1) the highest price available and (2) the *salvage* value, which is the disposal value of the property at the end of its useful life. When there is a market for real property, the basic factors that affect valuation are

- the size, shape, and location of the property
- the nature and condition of the property, its physical qualities and defects, and the adequacy or inadequacy of its improvements
- the actual and potential use of the property and how the trends of development and economic conditions (such as population growth) affect it
- the suitability of the property for its actual or intended use
- zoning restrictions
- the age, size, and condition of the buildings (degree of deterioration and obsolescence)
- the market value of other properties in the area in which the property is located
- environmental factors such as the presence of or nearness to hazardous materials and wetlands laws' restrictions
- the value of net income received from the property (Rentals are often capitalized at a rate of between 6 and 12 percent and then adjusted for depreciation; the same principle can be applied to gross rents after adjustment for operating cost.)
- prices at which comparable property in the same area was sold at a time near the applicable valuation date—providing the sale was an arm's-length transaction for the best price available
- the cost to duplicate the property after taking depreciation into account
- the value accepted by state probate courts for purposes of state death taxes, if based on appraisals made by qualified real estate experts
- unusual facts

In the event of a sale of real property within a reasonable period of time after the decedent's death in such a manner as to ensure the highest possible price, the amount received is usually accepted as its value. Unaccepted offers to purchase the property are also considered. What about a sale at auction? Usually this price is accepted only if it appears there was no other method to obtain a higher price.

Land does not have to produce income or have an active market to attain substantial value. When land is in or adjacent to a settled community, owners frequently hold such land in anticipation of realizing its true value from future sales. For example, a home at the edge of an expanding shopping center might be worth far more to the shopping center developer than it would be to a potential home buyer.

Special-Use (Current-Use) Valuation for Certain Real Property*

The test of fair market value described above is the *highest and best price* that would be agreed upon between a willing buyer and a willing seller. This has often caused farm or business real estate to be valued at the price at which it might have been valued if it was going to be used for residential or industrial development rather than at the price it is worth according to its current use. For special-use valuation purposes, a "farm" includes stock, dairy, fruit, fur-bearing animals, truck farms and dairy farms, nurseries, ranches, woodlands, orchards, plantations, greenhouses, and other horticultural or agricultural commodity structures. An executor (if certain conditions are met) can elect to use a *special-use (current-use) valuation* approach. That is, the real estate is valued taking into consideration how it is currently being utilized instead of how it *might* be used if placed in its most profitable use.

special-use valuation

The special-use valuation provided by this method cannot be used to reduce a decedent's gross estate by more than $750,000 ($870,000 in 2005), as indexed for inflation—TRA '97.

Example:	At the time Stuart Sims died in 2004, his estate included qualifying real property that had a highest and best-use value of $24 million. The special-use value of the property is $1.5 million. Because the difference between the highest and best-use value and the special-use value is $900,000 ($2,400,000 − $1,500,000), Stuart's estate is allowed a maximum reduction of $870,000 in 2005.

Requirements for Special-Use Valuation. The following conditions must be satisfied before current-use valuation is allowed for estate tax purposes:

- The decedent must have been a U.S. citizen or resident.
- The farm or other closely held business must constitute at least 50 percent of the decedent's gross estate (after certain adjustments for mortgages and liens).

---

* IRC Sec. 2032A

- At least 25 percent of the adjusted gross estate must be qualified real property.
- The real property in question must pass to a *qualified heir* (essentially, a lineal descendant of the decedent's grandfather).
- Either the decedent or a family member must have owned the real property—and used it as a farm or in a closely held business—for at least 5 of the 8 years immediately prior to the date the decedent died.
- Either the decedent or a member of the decedent's family must have materially participated in the operation of the farm or business for at least 5 out of the 8 years immediately prior to the decedent's death.
- The property must continue in its special use by qualified heirs for 10 years after the decedent's death.

A special tax lien is placed on all real property valued according to current use until the conditions for special-use valuation are met. If the special-use valuation requirements are not fulfilled, the lien remains on the property until a recapture tax is paid. The heirs remain personally liable to pay that tax.

Furthermore, a written agreement must be filed with the estate tax return. It must be signed by everyone who has an interest in the real property qualifying for special valuation. Each of these individuals must consent to the imposition of the recapture tax described below.

Interestingly, if the qualified heir dies during the 10-year recapture period, the recapture requirements die, too.

Special-Use Methods Available. There are a number of methods allowed for valuing real estate of closely held businesses or farms. One way the farm method might work can be illustrated in the following example.

farm-method formula of valuation

Example: Farmer Jones owns 300 acres of farmland in Swedesboro, New Jersey. Nearby farmland of about the same acreage produces an average annual gross rental of $72,000. Average annual state and local real estate taxes are $4,000. Assume the interest rate for loans from the Federal Land Bank is 8 percent.

The average annual computations are made on the basis of the 5 most recent calendar years before the farmer's death.

Under the *farm-method formula of valuation*, valuation of the farmer's land is computed as shown below:

$$(\$72,000 - \$4,000) \div .08 = \$850,000$$

This formula for valuing farmland is not used if there is no comparable land from which the average rentals can be determined. In that case, an executor might elect to value the farmland in the same manner that closely held business real property is valued (through a capitalization method, comparable sales prices, or any other factor that fairly values the farm or other closely held business).

Recapture of the Special-Use Tax Benefit. As previously stated, if the property is disposed of to nonfamily members within 10 years after the death of the decedent, there is an additional estate tax or *recapture* tax imposed on the qualified heir. If the heir or a member of the heir's family fails to participate materially in the business operation for 10 years after the decedent's death, it is treated as a cessation of the qualified use, causing recapture.

recapture

Recapture of the difference in tax between the current-use and highest-and-best-use methods of valuation occurs when the real estate is sold, disposed of, or no longer used for the same qualified use within the 10-year period. Also the eligible qualified heir must be engaged in the active management of the farm or business during the recapture period. If during this period the heir is under age 21, disabled, a full-time student, or the surviving spouse, a fiduciary may qualify in providing active management for the heir. Leasing arrangements may be entered into when the decedent or heirs are unable to or do not wish to meet the qualified use restrictions themselves.

If recapture occurs and results in additional estate taxes, the real estate receives a new basis stepped up to what the basis would be if special-use valuation had not been elected. Otherwise, the basis upon a subsequent sale of the property by the qualified heir(s) is the current-use valuation. However, the increased basis obtained if recapture occurs does not include retroactive changes in depreciation, other deductions, or credits reflecting the increased basis.

Exceptions to the recapture rules are loss of the property through involuntary conversion or exchange of the real estate in a like-kind exchange. No recapture is triggered generally under these circumstances. There are also special rules for woodlands and a limited right of judicial review.

Planning point: Qualified heirs and advisers must weigh the estate tax savings against the restrictions on the qualifying property's use and disposition for the 10-year period after the decedent's death versus the potential for higher capital gains tax resulting from a sale of the qualifying property after the decedent's death.

Valuation of Household and Personal Effects

willing buyer-willing seller rule

The general rule for valuing household property and personal effects, such as watches, rings, and so forth, can be called the *willing buyer-willing seller rule.* A room-by-room itemization is typical, especially when household goods include articles of artistic or intrinsic value, such as jewelry, furs, silverware, paintings, engravings, antiques, books, statuary, oriental rugs, and coin or stamp collections.

In non-community-property states, *household goods* and the like personally acquired by and used by husband and wife during marriage are generally presumed to be the property of the husband. Therefore, in the absence of sufficient evidence to rebut this presumption, household goods and personal effects are includible in the husband's estate.

Valuation of Listed Stocks

Where a stock has an established market and quotations are available to value the stock as of the date in question, the fair market value (FMV) per share on the applicable valuation date governs for both gift and estate tax purposes.

The FMV is based on selling prices when there is a market for the stock or bond. This is the mean between the highest and lowest quoted selling price on the valuation date. If there were no sales on the valuation date, but there were sales on dates within a reasonable period both before and after the valuation date, the FMV is determined by taking a weighted average of the means between the highest and lowest sales on the nearest date before and the nearest date after the valuation. The average is then weighted inversely by the respective number of trading days between the selling date and the valuation date.

When a large block of stock cannot be marketed in an orderly manner, the block might depress the market because it cannot be converted to cash as readily as a few shares could be. Therefore, selling prices and bid-and-asked prices may not reflect fair market value. Sometimes it may be necessary to value this type of stock as if it was closely held and not actively traded. If this can be established, a reasonable modification of the normal basis for determining FMV can be made. In some cases a *blockage discount* is determined by the effect that block would have had on the market if it was sold over a reasonable period of time and in a prudent manner. A similar situation occurs when sales at or near the date of death are either few or of a sporadic nature and may not indicate a fair market value.

The converse of the blockage situation above occurs when the block of stock to be valued represents a controlling interest (either actual or effective) in an ongoing business. Here the price of normally traded shares may have little relation to the true value of the controlling lot. The large block can have the effect of increasing value because of its element of control.

Valuation of Corporate Bonds

Valuation of bonds is similar to valuation of listed common stock. The means of the selling prices on or near the applicable valuation date (or—if there were no sales—the means of bona fide asked prices weighted inversely to the number of trading days from the valuation date) determine the fair market value of the bonds.

In the absence of sales or bid-and-asked prices, the value must be determined by

- ascertaining the soundness of the security
- comparing the interest on the bond in question to yields on similar bonds
- examining the date of maturity
- comparing prices for listed bonds of corporations engaged in similar types of business
- checking the extent to which the bond is secured
- weighing all other relevant factors, including the opinion of experts, the goodwill of the business, the industry's economic outlook, and the company's position in the industry as well as its management

Valuation of U.S. Government Bonds

Series EE (or E) bonds are valued at their redemption price (market value) as of the date of death, since they are neither negotiable nor transferable and the only definitely ascertainable value is the amount at which the Treasury will redeem them.

Certain U.S. Treasury bonds (so-called *flower bonds*) owned by a decedent at the date of death and forming part of the gross estate may be redeemed at par value if used to pay federal estate taxes. These bonds are valued at the higher of the market price and par value.

Even if such bonds are not used to pay estate taxes, the courts have often held that when the bonds could be used for the payment of estate taxes, they are valued at the higher of market and par value. When the bonds could not be applied to pay the estate tax, their value is market (the mean quoted selling price value).

Valuation of Life Insurance

Proceeds of life insurance on the life of the decedent receivable by or for the benefit of the decedent's estate are taxed in the decedent-insured's estate. In addition, when the decedent held incidents of ownership, such ownership invokes taxation. The amount includible is the amount receivable by the beneficiary. This includes dividends and premium refunds. In determining how much is includible, no distinction is made between an ordinary life policy, a term policy, group insurance, or an accidental death benefit.

If a settlement option is elected, the amount that is payable as a lump sum is the amount includible. If the policy did not provide for a lump-sum payment, the amount includible is the commuted amount used by the insurance company to compute the settlement option payments.

The value of an unmatured policy owned by a decedent on the life of another is included in the policyowner's gross estate (when the policyowner predeceases the insured) according to the following:

- If a new life insurance policy is involved, the gross premium paid is the value.
- If the policy is a paid-up or a single-premium policy, its value is its replacement cost—that is, the single premium that company would have charged for a comparable contract of equal face value on the life of a person who was the insured's age (at the time the decedent-policyholder died).
- If the policy is a premium-paying whole life policy, the value is found by adding any unearned portion of the last premium to the interpolated terminal reserve.
- If the policy is a term policy, the value is the unused premium.

Valuation of Stock of Closely Held Corporations

The valuation of closely held corporate stock is often one of the most difficult and time-consuming problems faced by the executor of a decedent's estate. By definition, closely held stock is incapable of valuation solely by recourse to an established market (that is, closely held stock is seldom traded). In fact, the criteria used to define closely held stock include (1) a limited number of stockholders, (2) restrictions imposed upon a shareholder's ability to transfer the stock, (3) the absence of an exchange listing or regular quotation in the over-the-counter market, and (4) an irregular and limited history of sales or exchanges.

There is no formula provided by the Internal Revenue Code or the regulations that is applicable to every closely held stock valuation situation. However, there are guidelines that should be considered in every valuation case. The key IRS ruling on point, Rev. Rul. 59–60, suggests that the following factors be considered:

- the nature of the business and the entire history of the enterprise
- the economic outlook in general as well as the condition and outlook of the specific industry
- the book value of the stock and the financial condition of the business (The Tax Court considers this factor in almost every case.)
- the company's earning capacity (For many businesses—especially those that do depend heavily on capital to produce profits—this will be the most important valuation factor.)
- the company's dividend-paying capacity

goodwill

- the existence of *goodwill* (Goodwill can be defined as the economic advantage or benefit that is acquired by a business *beyond* the mere value of the capital invested in it because of the patronage it receives from constant or habitual customers, its local position, its reputation for skill or punctuality, other accidental circumstances or necessities, or public partialities or prejudices. In short, goodwill is a broad term implying that a company has a purchase value exceeding the worth of its tangible assets. Note: A business may have goodwill value even if no amount for goodwill is shown on its accounting statements.)
- prior stock sales and size of the block of stock to be valued
- fair market value of stock of comparable corporations engaged in the same or similar type of business where the stock is actively traded in an established market

Rev. Rul. 59–60 reaffirms that no fixed formula of valuation can be devised that is applicable to all situations and that, ultimately, the fair market value of closely held stock must be determined on an individual basis.

When faced with a gift or estate tax valuation question, courts sift through innumerable elements—besides the eight basic factors mentioned in Rev. Rul. 59–60. Some of the valuation factors used by the courts (but given varying weight depending on the circumstances) are

- the values accepted by the IRS when other estates held the same stock
- the price for the stock in the decedent's will
- the values as determined by expert witnesses
- the relationships between prices, earnings, and book values
- the degree of control of the business represented by the block of stock to be valued
- the value of the services of the key individual who has died

Valuation Methods Used by the IRS

Although the Internal Revenue Service incorporates many factors into most valuations of closely held businesses, the two methods consistently used as starting points are (1) adjusted book value and (2) capitalization of adjusted earnings.

book value

Adjusted Book Value. *Book value* (stated assets less liabilities, divided by the number of outstanding shares) is particularly applicable in the following instances:

- when the business in question is primarily an asset-holding company, such as an investment company

- when the company is in the real estate development business and assets, rather than earnings, are the key to valuation
- when the company is a one-person corporation, which is generally worth only its liquidation value
- if the corporation is being liquidated at the valuation date or it is likely that it will be liquidated in the near future (It is important also to consider the impact of sacrifice sales and capital-gains taxation, since the true value of a liquidating corporation is the amount that is actually available to the shareholders after the liquidation.)
- when the industry is highly competitive but the business is only marginally profitable (Adjusted book value is particularly useful in these cases, because past earnings are probably an unreliable tool in the measurement of potential future profits.)

adjusted-book-value method

The *adjusted-book-value method* involves adjusting the asset components of a business to an approximate fair market value for each such component. An adjustment is necessary, since most accounting statements carry assets at some figure other than fair market value. Adjustments are necessary to reflect the difference between true market value and book figures when

- assets are valued at cost (Most accounting statements carry land, for example, on the balance sheet of a company at an amount far less than what it is worth on the open market. The result is a book value bearing little or no relationship to present worth.)
- assets have been depreciated at a rate in excess of their true decline in value (For instance, equipment may have been purchased for $500,000 and depreciated to $200,000. Although it is carried on the firm's books at $200,000, the asset may really be worth a lot more or a lot less than its cost, or the $200,000 used on the balance sheet.)
- mention of items such as potential future lawsuits or unfavorable long- term leases has been omitted or not clearly noted in the footnotes or body of the firm's balance sheets
- assets have been completely written off even though they possess substantial value, resulting in a book value far below reality
- assets such as franchises and goodwill are shown on accounting statements at nominal cost or not shown at all
- there are difficulties in collecting accounts receivable
- a firm's inventory includes items that have become obsolete or are not readily marketable

There are still other factors that indicate the need for adjustment of pure book value. For instance, a downward adjustment from pure book value is indicated when the business's liquidity position is poor (the business has low current assets relative to its current liabilities), the firm is experiencing a shortage of adequate working capital, or it is burdened with sizable long-term debt. If large selling expenses and capital-gains taxes are likely in the event of liquidation, downward adjustments from book value are indicated.

Another factor that is difficult to ascertain but quite important is the need, if any, to adjust book value because of retained earnings. The book value of a business might appear to be high because of the retention of earnings over a number of years. This might be deceptive, since the company's current earnings may be low and the outlook for increased earnings in the future may be poor. Since valuation is an attempt to ascertain what a hypothetical willing buyer would pay, such a situation indicates the need to reduce book value.

After these adjustments to book value are made, the adjusted book value is then divided by the number of shares outstanding to determine the per-share value of the stock.

capitalization-of-adjusted-earnings method

Capitalization of Adjusted Earnings. The second of the two basic starting-point methods is the *capitalization-of-adjusted-earnings method*. Here the IRS multiplies adjusted earnings by a factor appropriate for the specific industry at the predetermined valuation date. The capitalization rate varies inversely with the degree of risk and the rate of return, as illustrated in table 10–1.

With the capitalization-of-earnings method, a closely held business is valued according to a projected amount of sustainable earnings, which is then "capitalized" by a rate of return that has been adjusted for risk. In simple terms, a money-making machine generating $_____ amount of earnings is being valued for a potential buyer. The fundamental steps of the capitalization method of valuation are as follows:

- Select a capitalization rate appropriate for the business.
- Project sustainable earnings for the business.
- Multiply the capitalization rate by the projected sustainable income to determine the business's operating value.
- Add the amount of operating value and the value of the business's nonoperating assets.

The investment return on capital invested in a well-established business with minimal risk is relatively low. Another way of stating this same principle is that it takes a long time to recover the capital invested in such a business. However, the low-risk factor coupled with a yield in excess of the amount possible from alternative investments encourages potential buyers to offer relatively high prices. Conversely, an individual investing in a business with a higher risk factor demands a higher rate of return, wants to receive capital back more quickly, and therefore is willing

TABLE 10-1
Capitalization-of-Adjusted-Earnings Method

Risk	Categories	Rate of Return	Capitalization Rate
Low to medium	Old, established businesses with large capital assets and established goodwill (Few businesses are in this category.)	8%	12
Medium to high	Established businesses of competitive character needing highly competitive management (such as factories manufacturing products under patents and trademarks)	10% to 15%	7 to 10
High	Businesses requiring skill in management but no special or rare type of knowledge; earnings constantly present under highly competitive conditions; large capital not required to enter field	18% and above	6
High	Small businesses—highly competitive—requiring small capital	18% and above	5
High	Businesses depending on special skills of one person or a small group of individuals; highly competitive; small capital required; high mortality	18% and above	2 to 4
High	Personal businesses involving minute amount of capital and depending on the skill of one person	18% and above	1 to 2

to pay less for the business. A comparison of two companies might be helpful in illustrating this point. Assume that both companies earn $100,000 a year after taxes.

Company A: The Goforit Company is relatively small and is in a highly competitive industry. It is likely that a buyer would desire a return of 20 percent per year on his or her money (in other words, for this level of risk, the buyer wants to recover capital fairly quickly) to warrant the risk of purchasing this company. So the less paid for the business, the faster the recovery of capital. A buyer who thought he or she could receive 20 percent per year on his or her money would be willing to pay no more than, for example, five times the annual after-tax earnings: $500,000 ($100,000 x 5). This is essentially the procedure the IRS uses to value the firm; it multiplies after-tax earnings by an appropriate capitalization rate.

Company B: Assume the Solid Company is an older corporation with a proven record of profits; it has a strong management team, high profit potential, and a substantial average annual earnings growth rate. The same investor might be willing to settle for a much lower rate of return given this level of risk. In other words, an investor would value the business at a higher amount because of its safety-of-principal factor—say, a total of $800,000 (8 years' after-tax earnings).

It is important to note that table 10–1 is only a guideline. The return a potential buyer would demand varies from time to time depending on (1) the specified level of risk and (2) the earning rates of comparable alternative investments. There are no correct capitalization rates; there are different rates used at different times and under different circumstances by the IRS and the courts.

Another factor that must be considered even before applying the capitalization rate to the after-tax earnings is that in many cases the earnings themselves must be adjusted. A realistic appraisal of the earning power of a company can sometimes be obtained only through first adjusting earnings by

- adding back bonuses paid to stockholders or their families
- adding back salaries that were excessive, or reducing earnings when salaries paid were inordinately low
- adding back excessive rents paid to stockholders, or subtracting nominal and unrealistically low rents paid to stockholders
- eliminating nonrecurring income items
- adjusting for excess depreciation
- adjusting earnings to take into consideration nonrecurring expenses, a major change in accounting procedures, widely fluctuating or cyclical profits, abnormally inflated or deflated earnings, or strong upward to downward earning trends. (Sometimes the IRS averages earnings over a 3- to 5-year period and then weights the average so that an upward earnings trend is given greater weight.)

The total capitalization result is then divided by the number of shares outstanding to ascertain the per-share value.

The reasonableness of the final result obtained by capitalization can be checked by a method once officially used (and still unofficially used) by many IRS agents. This is known as the ARM (Appeals and Review Memorandum) 34 method. Basically, under ARM 34 a five-step process is used:

(1) Figure a reasonable rate of return on the tangible assets of the business.
(2) Subtract that return from the annual earnings figure used. The difference is the portion of earnings generated by intangibles.

(3) Capitalize profits generated by those intangibles to determine their value.

(4) Add the results of the above computation to the net worth of tangibles. The total is the value of the corporation.

(5) Divide the total value of the corporation by the number of shares outstanding for the per-share value of the corporation.

Effect of Minority or Controlling Interest

When the shares that are being valued represent a minority interest in a business, a reduction in value is often allowed. This minority-interest discount arises because, by definition, minority shares have no power to force dividends, compel liquidation, or control corporate policy. This makes the stock less appealing and narrows the potential market to the remaining (and usually controlling) shareholders. It therefore reduces the price at which each share might be purchased. Discounts of from 10 to 30 percent are often allowed.

Valuation of Specific Property

- publicly traded stock/corporate bonds (date of death/alternate valuation date fair market value [FMV] per share on established market/exchange)
- U.S. government bonds (date of death redemption price)
- closely held corporation stock
  - adjusted-book-value method
  - capitalization-of-adjusted-earnings method

The opposite result occurs when the shares in question represent a controlling interest. In this case, the IRS generally seeks to substantiate a higher value. In other words, the size of the block of stock itself is a relevant factor. Although it is true that a minority interest in an unlisted corporation's stock is more difficult to sell than a similar block of listed stock, by the same token the controlling interest of a corporation represents an added element of value. It, therefore, justifies a higher valuation for a specific block of stock. More than 50 percent of the voting shares constitutes a controlling interest, while less than 50 percent constitutes a minority interest.

Note that if a father leaves two shares to his son who already has 49 shares (assume that only 100 shares are outstanding), the two shares represent in value more than a mere 1/50 of the value of the outstanding stock. Together with the interest that the son already owns, those two shares represent control of the corporation.

Use of Restrictive Agreements

Although a closely held corporation has a limited market by definition, most shareholders restrict the marketability of coshareholders' stock even further through purchase options or mandatory buy-sell agreements. If the terms of such an agreement definitely fix the value of the shares in question, it is not necessary to examine either book value or earnings. The price fixed in the restrictive agreement generally serves as the fair market value of the shares if the agreement was formed by *unrelated parties*. However, to peg the value of *family* corporation stock for federal estate tax purposes, the following three requirements must be met:

(1) *the bona fide business arrangement rule.* The agreement must be part of a bona fide business arrangement.
(2) *the device rule.* The agreement must not be a device to transfer the property to members of decedent's family for less than full and adequate consideration in money or money's worth.
(3) *the comparability rule.* The terms of the agreement must be comparable to similar arrangements entered into by persons in an arm's-length transaction.

Treasury regulations indicate that tests are presumed satisfied if the parties are not family members (or natural objects of the bounty) of the transferor. For these purposes the terms *family members (or natural objects of the transferor's bounty)* pertain to the transferor's spouse, the transferor's or spouse's lineal descendants, and the spouses of the lineal descendants.

The valuation of a closely held business interest continues to be a critical component in any estate planning. The ability to establish the value of a business interest serves to quantify the liquidity needs of the estate and make planning predictable. If buy-sell restrictions and price provisions are not recognized for gift, estate, or generation-skipping tax purposes, many estates will find themselves embroiled in expensive and time-consuming valuation disputes with the IRS and faced with potentially major liquidity shortfalls. Thus, planning must be aimed either at meeting the requirements so that provisions and prices in agreements are given validity in establishing the value of the closely held business interest or at obtaining greater life insurance to fund the additional liquidity needs. The regulations indicate that all three requirement tests must be satisfied independently.

Bona Fide Business Purpose Test. The desire to retain control of the business within the current closely held group (the family) and provide for the successful transition after the departure of an owner has generally been found to be a bona fide business purpose. The terms of the agreement should clearly state this purpose.

Device Test. Planners must now carefully document facts that indicate the arrangement was not a device to pass the property to members of the decedent's family (the natural object of the decedent's bounty) at a bargain price. Presumably, this means the agreement should provide a fair price when executed and be expected to provide a fair market value price at any time in the future. Proving this is both expensive and time consuming since appraisal reports and expert testimony will probably be required if a dispute arises.

Comparability Test. The requirement of comparability is also likely to prove difficult to satisfy. In order to fix estate tax value, it must be shown that the arrangement is one that could have been obtained in an arm's-length transaction. Would the decedent have entered into such an arrangement with an unrelated third person? This requirement of comparability applies not only to price but also to all the other terms of the contract between the parties.

Factors to be taken into account for comparability include (a) the expected term of the agreement, (b) the present value of the property, (c) the expected value of the property at the time of exercise, and (d) the consideration, if any, offered for the option.

The four different types of restrictive agreements that have been successful in pegging the value of stock for federal estate tax purposes are the following:

- reciprocal options among stockholders, during life and death. Under an option a specified person is given the right to purchase the stock at a designated price for a fixed period of time. Here, the buyer controls the event.
- options granted to one stockholder only (but the price must be fair and arrived at by arm's-length bargaining). Intrafamily arrangements in this category are suspect.
- options granted to the corporation
- mandatory buy-sell (cross-purchase and stock-redemption) agreements under which the estate of a deceased stockholder must sell and the corporation (or other stockholders) must buy at a predetermined price or according to a predetermined formula. The obligation to sell at the agreed-upon price, however, must be binding not only upon the decedent's executor at the decedent's death but also upon the stockholder himself or herself during lifetime. The price at death does not control if a shareholder is free during lifetime to realize a higher price. Likewise, restrictions that are binding only during the decedent's lifetime but not at death are equally ineffective. In a mandatory buy-sell agreement neither party controls the event.

A mere right of first refusal, which requires that any shares offered for sale must first be offered to the corporation (or other shareholders) at the proposed transfer price, does not conclusively peg the value of the stock. However, a first-offer commitment may have the effect of depressing the value of the stock.

While restrictions on the transfer of closely held shares are never conclusive regarding value for gift tax purposes, they are a factor to be considered in arriving at valuation.

VALUATION OF LIFETIME TRANSFERS WITH RETAINED INTERESTS

The Estate Freeze

estate freeze

An estate freeze is an estate planning technique designed to meet several goals. The primary goal is estate tax reduction. An *estate freeze* can be defined as any method designed to restrict to its current value an individual's eventual taxable estate. Following an estate freeze transaction, the appreciation in property subject to the freeze accrues to someone other than the original owner (presumably his or her heirs). However, an individual considering an estate freeze generally has a second goal—to retain enough wealth to provide for his or her needs until death. Under prior transfer tax law, elaborate schemes were employed to provide the transferor with an effective estate freeze through the transfer of appreciation rights in property to the next generation heirs, while at the same time leaving the transferor with enough strings attached to the property to provide a substantial current income stream. Thus, an estate freeze can be distinguished from an outright gift by the fact that the transferor does not transfer all interests in the property during his or her lifetime.

Under previous tax law, the freeze was often accomplished mainly through techniques that took advantage of valuation manipulations. Because some portion of the freeze property was actually transferred, the gift tax value of the transfer had to be determined. Valuation of transfers with retained interests was normally accomplished for gift, estate, and generation-skipping purposes through the subtraction method of valuation. The subtraction method of valuation determines the value of the transferred interest as the difference between (a) the value of the entire property interest and (b) the value of all interests in the property that continue to be held by the donor and are *not* transferred.

Stated simply:

> The value of the whole less the value of what is kept equals the
> gift tax value of what is given away.

Because substantial transfer-tax revenue was lost if the freeze transaction was effective, the Treasury always maintained a jaundiced view of estate freezes. The post-transfer appreciation of the property in a successful freeze escaped both estate and gift taxes. This tax savings is, of course, a goal of lifetime gifting. The concern of both Congress and the IRS was that the typical estate freeze transaction differs from an outright gift of property because the transferor has not disposed of all interests in the property when the freeze is completed.

Valuation of Retained Preferred Stock and Partnership Interests

Congress in the Revenue Reconciliation Act of 1990 established gift tax Secs. 2701–2704 in IRC Chapter 14 Special Valuation Rules to deal with the perceived valuation abuses.

Sec. 2701 focuses on the valuation of assets at the time of transfer for the purposes of determining a gift tax. The general rule under Sec. 2701 provides a harsh result for the freeze. For the purposes of determining (a) whether the transfer of an interest in a *controlled* corporation or partnership to, or for the benefit of (such as through a trust), a *member of the family* of the transferor is a gift and (b) what the gift tax value of such gifts is, the value of certain *retained rights* with respect to an *applicable retained interest* held by the transferor or an *applicable family member* immediately after the transfer is generally deemed to be zero. In other words, no valuation credit is given for the value of rights that are retained. The subtraction method of valuation cannot be used (or if it is used, a value of zero is given to what is retained by the transferor), and the gift tax value of the stock transferred is equal to the value of the transferor's entire interest prior to such transfer.

Example: A, the sole owner of ACO, Inc., owns 100 shares of common stock valued at $100,000. ACO recapitalizes and issues $90,000 (valued under traditional valuation rules) of 10 percent noncumulative preferred stock to A in exchange for 90 shares of common stock. A then gifts 10 shares of ACO common stock to A's child. A believes the gift of common stock is entirely sheltered by the gift tax annual exclusion. However, Sec. 2701 applies, since A transfers an interest in a controlled corporation to a family member and retains rights (the preferred stock) after such transfer. The value of the gift is, in fact, $100,000, since A's retained preferred stock must be given a zero value under Sec. 2701.

The following definitions are necessary at this time:

- **member of the family.** For these purposes, *member of the family* means only the transferor's spouse, the lineal descendants of the transferor or transferor's spouse, and a spouse of any such descendant. Thus, the statute is applicable only if a transfer is made to the transferor's spouse or to junior generation issue (and spouses) of the transferor. This makes sense, since the estate freeze implies a transfer of the growth interests to future generations for discounted transfer tax cost.

- **applicable family member.** *Applicable family member* means only the transferor's spouse, an ancestor of the transferor or transferor's spouse, and the spouse of any such ancestor. Thus, the retained interest must be held by the transferor, his or her spouse, or senior generation family members (and spouses) for the statute to apply. Again, this is logical, since the freeze involves the retention of frozen rights by the generation whose estate tax concerns are more immediate.

- **applicable retained rights.** Retained rights for Sec. 2701 purposes include certain distribution (dividend) rights but only if the transferor and all applicable family members control the corporation or partnership. In determining whether sufficient interest is held within the family, the transferor and any applicable family member are deemed to hold any interest held by a brother, sister, or lineal descendant. Retained rights also include "extraordinary payment rights" such as a liquidation, put, call, or conversion rights. These applicable retained rights are valued at zero, unless they are qualified payment rights (described later), for the purposes of determining the gift tax value of a transferred interest.

- **retained rights not treated as "applicable retained rights."** The harsh rule provided to applicable retained rights does not apply to any right that must be exercised at a specific time and at a specific amount. It also does not generally apply to a right to convert into a fixed number (or a fixed percentage) of shares of the same class of stock in a corporation as the transferred stock (or which would be of the same class but for nonlapsing differences in voting power). In other words, if a retained interest carries rights that are not valued at zero under Sec. 2701, the value of these rights is their fair market value determined under traditional valuation methodology.

- **controlled entity.** An entity is controlled if, immediately before the transfer, the transferor, applicable members, and any lineal descendants of the parent of the transferor (or parents of the transferor's spouse) hold at least 50 percent (by vote or value) of the stock of a corporation or at least 50 percent of the capital or profits interests in a partnership.

The bottom line is that many traditional rights on preferred stock retained by the transferor-client are given no effect to support or further reduce the gift tax value placed on what was given away or sold to a family member. So the general rule of Sec. 2701 is that an estate freeze involving the intrafamily transfer of corporate stock or partnership interests results in an immediate gift tax based on the entire value of the business held by the senior family member. The transferor gets no credit for the value of the senior business interest retained upon a gift (or sale) of a junior interest to a family member.

The Sec. 2701 rules do not apply to the following retained interests, which can be accorded full fair market value for gift tax purposes:

- **marketable transferred interests.** Sec. 2701 does not apply if there are readily available market quotations on an established securities market for the value of the transferred interest.
- **marketable retained interests.** Similarly, these rules do not apply to any applicable retained interest if there are readily available market quotations on an established securities market for the value of the applicable retained interest.
- **interests of the same class.** Sec. 2701 does not apply if the retained interest is of the same class of equity as the transferred interest. For this purpose, nonvoting common stock is treated as the same class as voting common.
- **proportionate transfers.** Sec. 2701 does not apply to a transfer by an individual of equity interests if the transfer results in a proportionate reduction of each class of equity interest held by the transferor.

Qualified Payments Exception

Although the general rule is that applicable retained rights are valued at zero (which under the subtraction method means that the value of what was given away or sold is assigned a value equal to the entire worth of the business), retained rights to *qualified payments* are valued under general valuation principles.

Qualified payments are dividends payable on a periodic basis under cumulative preferred stock (or comparable payment under a partnership interest) to the extent that such dividend (or comparable partnership payment) is determined at a fixed rate. A payment is treated as having a fixed rate if it is in fact fixed once and for all or if it is determined at a rate that bears a fixed relationship to a specified market interest rate.

Example:	Parent (P) holds all the outstanding stock of X Corporation. Assume the fair market value of X is $1.5 million. X is recapitalized so that P holds 1,000 shares of $1,000 par value preferred stock bearing an annual cumulative dividend of $100 per share (the aggregate fair market value of which is assumed to be

$1 million) and 1,000 shares of voting common stock. P transfers the common stock to P's child. Sec. 2701 applies to the transfer because P has transferred an equity interest (the common stock) to a member of P's family and immediately thereafter holds an applicable retained interest (the preferred stock with its distribution and other rights). P's right to receive annual cumulative dividends is a qualified payment right and is valued for purposes of Sec. 2701 at its fair market value of $1,000,000. The amount of P's gift, determined using the subtraction method of valuation is $500,000 ($1,500,000 minus $1,000,000).

The Minimum-Value Rule

Congress wanted to be sure that at least some minimum value was assigned to an equity interest transferred to a family member in an estate freeze. Even if there are actual or deemed qualified payments (or other rights valued under traditional methods), the Code now specifies a minimum valuation for any *junior* equity interest transferred by gift or sale to a family member. Examples of junior equity interests include common stock or partnership interests with rights to capital and profits junior to other partnership interests.

For example, if a father gives common stock to his son while retaining cumulative preferred stock, the minimum-value rule requires that the total common stock of the corporation may not be valued at less than 10 percent of the sum of the total value of all stock interests in the corporation *plus* the total indebtedness of the corporation to the transferor or an applicable family member. What this means is that the gift tax value of common stock that is gifted to a family member must be at least 10 percent of the total value of stock that is held by the transferor. A similar minimum-value rule applies in the partnership context.

Additional Gift Taxes

These new rules also prevent parents from shifting growth to the next generation by failing to make distributions on the retained preferred interest. Any payments that are not made accrue to the transferred growth interest. If the qualified payments are not in fact made at the times and in the amounts used in valuing the retained right to the qualified payments, the transferor's taxable gifts (or the transferor's estate if appropriate) may be increased to reflect the value of the preferred stock based on the actual distributions made.

Valuation of Transfers in Trust with Retained Interests

Before 2702, estate freezes were often created using trusts to hold the property. A classic example was the grantor-retained income trust (GRIT).

Example:	A 63-year-old mother contributed $100,000 to a trust that would provide income to herself for the shorter of 10 years and her life and then pay the remainder to her daughter. The mother made two transfers: first, an income interest for the shorter of 10 years and the life of a 63-year-old (which she retains the value of) and, second, a gift of the remainder interest following the retained income interest. The total transfer-tax cost (under prior law) would be the value of the remainder at the time the trust was created. Thus, the subtraction method of valuation resulted in a gift equal to the total value of the property less the value of the retained income interest. The appreciation on the property while held by the trust completely escapes transfer taxes, which is, of course, the purpose of the freeze.

Prior Law

In general, prior to the creation of Sec. 2702, transfers to trusts with retained interests by the transferor or family member were valued using actuarial tables described under the general valuation rules of Sec. 7520 (described below). These mathematical tables show the worth of a stream of dollars at various discount rate assumptions using the government's life expectancy tables. Typically, the value of a remainder interest was determined (under the now-familiar subtraction valuation concept) as the difference between (a) the value of entire amount contributed to the trust and (b) the actuarial value of the retained interest (as determined under the Sec. 7520 tables). The actual income generated by the trust's assets might have been significantly more or less than the table values, but actual income was not considered in the gift tax valuation of contributions made to a trust.

IRC Sec. 2702

Under the IRC Sec. 2702 rules, for the purpose of determining (a) whether a transfer in trust to or for the benefit of a member of the family of the transferor is a gift and (b) the value of the gift, the value of any interest in the trust retained by the transferor or any applicable family member is generally treated as zero. In other words, if you make a transfer to a trust benefiting a member of your family, you are deemed to have retained none of the cash or other assets and are treated as if you had given away the entire amount you transferred to the trust. In the preceding example, the mother would be treated as having gifted the full $100,000 and would not be able to deduct the value of her retained income rights for the 10 years of trust income.

Again there are exceptions. Some retained interests in trust are given "subtraction" value effect for determining the gift tax value of transfers in trust.

Qualified Interests. A retained *qualified interest* in the trust by the transferor or applicable family member is valued at its full Sec. 7520 table value. A qualified interest is either

- a right to receive fixed amounts payable at least annually (a GRAT, or grantor-retained annuity trust interest), or
- a right to receive amounts payable at least annually that are a fixed percentage of the trust's assets determined annually (a GRUT, or grantor-retained unitrust interest), or
- any noncontingent remainder interest if all other interests in the trust are GRATs or GRUTs.

A GRAT is an irrevocable trust in which the grantor retains a right to receive fixed payments (just like a fixed annuity) payable at least annually for his or her life (or the joint lives of the grantor and one or more life tenants) or for a term of years (actuarially identical to a charitable remainder annuity trust). At the end of the term or life interest, the remaining trust corpus is paid to designated beneficiaries. The annuity interest is valued under Sec. 7520 rules and the gift value of the remainder is determined by subtracting the value of the annuity interest from the total value of the principal placed in trust.

A grantor-retained unitrust, or GRUT, is an irrevocable trust in which the grantor retains the right to receive payable, at least annually, that are a fixed percentage of the trust's assets as revalued annually (just like a variable annuity). The GRUT is actuarially identical to a charitable remainder unitrust. The term of the trust may be based on the life of the annuitant (or joint lives of two or more annuitants) or a specified term of years. At the end of the term of the trust, all remaining trust assets pass to the designated remainderpersons. The gift tax value of the GRUT may be subtracted from the value of the property transferred to the trust to determine the gift tax value of the remainder interest.

Thus, a grantor-retained income trust (GRIT), which provides the actual trust income, and other retained interests are valued at zero and are generally ineffective for estate planning purposes unless other exceptions (discussed below) apply.

Personal Residences and Tangible Personal Property. Regular (Sec. 7520) valuation rules also apply in cases where

- the property is a property to be used as the personal residence of the person holding a term interest in the trust, or
- the exercise or nonexercise of the holder of a *term interest* in tangible property does not affect the valuation of the remainder interests in such property.

GRITs are effective for estate planning if the property is used as the personal residence of the person holding the term interest. In this situation the remainder interest is valued in the regular manner, even if the remainder interest is held by a family member. Second, where the exercise or nonexercise of rights by the holder of a term interest in tangible property (such as artwork) does not affect the valuation of the remainder interest in such property, the term interest is not valued at zero for gift tax purposes, even if the remainder interests are held by family members.

If the trust corpus consists of the property described in this exception, retained interests—not limited to GRATs or GRUTs—are valued under normal valuation rules. Thus the subtraction method of valuation results in a reduced gift tax cost of transferring the remainder interest. (The use of GRATs, GRUTs, and qualified personal residence trusts is discussed in chapter 22.)

Valuation of Partial Nonconcurrent Property Interests

It is sometimes necessary to value partial interests in property such as annuities, term interests, and life estates, since these property rights are often transferred to heirs and become subject to either estate or gift taxes. In addition, certain charitable transfer techniques, such as charitable remainder and lead trusts, must be valued to determine the estate, gift, and/or income tax deductions. Congress revamped the tax valuation methodology for such partial interests and added to the complexity of the process in an effort to stamp out perceived abuses in the old methods.

Sec. 7520 of the Internal Revenue Code now mandates that the current mortality rates and the current interest rate (revised monthly) must be used to determine the actuarial present value of annuity, term, remainder, and life interests in property. The new mortality rates are based on 1990 census data and gender-neutral tables.[1] The interest rate used to discount the partial interests to present value is 120 percent of the applicable federal midterm rate (AFMR) for the month in which the valuation is made.[2] The actual factor used to determine the value of a partial nonconcurrent interest involves several calculations and varies month to month according to changes in the AFMR.

The nature of the calculation for determining such valuations requires a significant degree of mathematics acumen and creates a high possibility for error. As a result, most practitioners rely on software for making such calculations. An additional problem with using these rules is the monthly variation in the interest rate. The tax value of such partial interests must be determined at a specific point in time. For example, gift tax calculations must be made at the time of the transfer. Thus the gift tax imposed on the inter vivos transfer of a partial nonconcurrent interest is based on the value of the interest using the applicable rate for the month in which a completed transfer is made. The same rule holds true when determining the income or gift tax deduction for a charitable remainder or lead interest donation. The applicable rate for the month in which the decedent dies is used to value the testamentary transfer of such partial interests. Therefore, the tax benefits or detriments of the transfer of remainder, term, annuity, or life interests in property depend on the month of the transfer.

Example:	Suppose Donor (D) creates a charitable remainder trust by placing $1 million of marketable securities in the trust. D gifts the current interest to her son (S), aged 50, for his life with the remainder interest to The American College. Suppose that at the time the trust is executed and irrevocably funded, the applicable Sec. 7520 rate is 6.6 percent. The tax valuations are as follows:

Remainder factor	.22391
Income and gift tax deduction	$223,910
Life interest factor at age 50	.77609
Taxable amount of gift to S	$776,090

Note to Students: See Appendix A for a summary of the advantages and disadvantages of different trusts covered in this chapter and throughout the text.

CHAPTER REVIEW

Answers to the review questions and the self-test questions start on page 717.

Key Terms

alternate valuation date	goodwill
fair market value	book value
special-use valuation	adjusted-book-value method
farm-method formula of valuation	capitalization-of-adjusted-earnings
recapture	method
willing buyer-willing seller rule	estate freeze

Review Questions

10-1. Why is it important to establish a reasonably accurate valuation of assets for estate tax purposes?

10-2. Explain why the lowest possible valuation for an asset may not be the price an executor would place on property for federal estate tax purposes.

10-3. What are the general rules for valuing property?

10-4. What are some of the problems that may occur in the valuation process?

10-5. George Smith died this year, and his estate consists primarily of a 1,000-acre family farm. Farms of this size rent for $84,000 annually in the area near the Smith farm. Local real estate taxes are $8,000 and the average federal land bank loan interest rate is 8 percent. Under the farm-method valuation formula, what is the special-use valuation of the Smith farm?

10-6. In general terms, describe the events that could cause a recapture of the special-use valuation tax benefit.

10-7. Explain how the following assets are valued for estate or gift tax purposes:
    a. household and personal effects
    b. listed stocks
    c. corporate bonds
    d. U.S. government bonds
    e. life insurance

10-8. Explain why it is difficult to evaluate stock in closely held corporations.

10-9. In what situations is the use of the adjusted-book-value method applicable for valuing closely held businesses?

10-10. Why does the book value of business assets often differ from their fair market value?

10-11. What adjustments to earnings must often be made to appraise a company's earning power realistically?

10-12. Distinguish between the effect of a minority interest and that of a controlling interest on the valuation of closely held stock.

10-13. Under what conditions will the price established under a buy-sell agreement for the stock of a deceased stockholder normally fix the value of the decedent's stock for federal estate tax purposes?

10-14. Explain how the subtraction method of valuation is used to value transfers with retained interests.

10-15. Explain the significance of the minimum-value rule in the context of an estate freeze.

Self-Test Questions

T   F   10-1.   It is impossible to determine potential liquidity needs that an executor may experience at an estate owner's death unless values are placed on the estate owner's assets.

T   F   10-2.   For estate tax purposes, it is always best to establish a low value in a buy-sell agreement.

T   F   10-3.   An executor may have a choice between valuing most assets for federal estate tax purposes at the date of death or on the alternate valuation date, which is 6 months after the date of death.

T   F   10-4.   When a property owned by a decedent is unique and difficult to value, the IRS is required to accept the executor's valuation amount.

T   F   10-5.   When there is no market for a decedent's real property, it may be valued according to its salvage value.

T   F   10-6.   The maximum amount by which the gross estate can be reduced when special-use valuation was elected by the executor is $250,000.

T   F   10-7.   Special-use valuation allows an executor to elect to value farm or business real estate for federal estate tax purposes based on actual current use, as opposed to the fair market value of the property if it was sold for development purposes.

T   F   10-8.   Special-use valuation is available to the estate of any and all decedents as long as the property is located in the United States.

T   F   10-9.   In approximately 50 percent of the estates electing special-use valuation, the IRS allows a nonfamily member to be a qualified heir.

T   F   10-10.   There are a number of methods allowed for valuing real estate of closely held businesses or farms.

T   F   10-11.   Once special-use valuation has been elected and the IRS has allowed it, taxes are not subject to recapture.

T   F   10-12.   When a large block of listed common stock cannot be marketed in an orderly manner, selling prices and bid-and-asked prices may not reflect fair market value.

T   F   10-13.   The valuation of corporate bonds is similar to the valuation of common stock.

T   F   10-14.   U.S. government bonds, such as Series E bonds, are valued at the price the decedent paid at purchase.

T   F   10-15.   Because closely held stock cannot be easily valued, the IRS will accept the value imposed by the executor because he or she is most familiar with the value of the business.

T   F   10-16.   Goodwill plays a definite role in the valuation of a closely held business.

T   F   10-17.   If buy-sell restrictions and pricing terms are not recognized for gift, estate, or generation-skipping tax purposes, expensive and time-consuming valuation disputes with the IRS could result.

NOTES

1. The actuarial tables are presented in the *Actuarial Tables Alpha and Actuarial Tables Beta* available by writing the Superintendent of Documents, United States Government Printing Office, Washington, DC 20404.

2. The applicable federal rates are published monthly in the *Internal Revenue Bulletin* and are reprinted in numerous loose-leaf services on tax and financial planning. The actual rate used for Sec. 7520 purposes is 120 percent of the AFMR rounded to the nearest two-tenths of 10/1/200210/1/20021 percent. For example, 6.56 percent is 6.6 percent for the purposes of valuing remainder, term, annuity, or life interests.

Buy-Sell Agreements

Learning Objectives

An understanding of the material in this chapter should enable the student to

11-1. Describe the purposes served by buy-sell agreements, and identify their advantages.

11-2. Identify the common provisions found in most types of buy-sell agreements.

11-3. Describe the various types of buy-sell agreements used in business entities, and explain how life insurance can be used to fund each type.

11-4. Describe how each type of price-setting mechanism used in buy-sell agreements works.

Chapter Outline

buy-sell agreement

Buy-sell agreements are the most common planning method used for the disposition and continuation of small business interests. The goal of any business continuation arrangement is the acquisition of a decedent business owner's interest by one or more business survivors or by the entity itself. Another purpose of a buy-sell agreement is to provide cash to the decedent's heirs for the sale of the business interest. Because an owner's death is typically disruptive, failure of the business often results. When a business owner dies, his or her executor's fiduciary role is to collect, preserve, and distribute the decedent's assets. The business interest presents numerous difficulties for the executor unless the decedent had a business continuation plan prior to his or her death.

A properly designed buy-sell agreement assures that the estate will be able to sell its interest in the business for a reasonable price. The business purchasers, usually the surviving co-owners, will then obtain the decedent's business interest according to the terms of the agreement and avoid the difficulties associated with probate. If no business continuation plan is in place, the executor may be compelled to sell the decedent's business interest to pay the estate's settlement costs and death transfer taxes within 9 months (or less) after death. These circumstances may result in a forced sale of the business for less than fair market value. Without a buy-sell contract the survivors face significant uncertainty: Will the executor or heirs sell the decedent's interest to outsiders? Will the other owners' interests be greatly devalued?

ADVANTAGES OF A BUY-SELL AGREEMENT

The benefits of a buy-sell agreement can be summarized as follows:

- It guarantees a market for the business interest.
- It provides liquidity for the payment of death taxes and other estate settlement needs.
- It makes the estate planning process more reliable for the owners because it helps to peg the estate tax value of the decedent's business interest.
- It provides for the continuation of the business in the hands of the surviving owners and/or employees.
- It makes the business more attractive to creditors since a plan to continue the business is in place.

FORMAT OF BUY-SELL AGREEMENTS IN GENERAL

Most properly drafted buy-sell agreements have several common provisions, regardless of the specific type of agreement. Common terms of a typical buy-sell agreement include the following:

- *parties involved.* All buy-sell agreements should contain a provision clearly identifying the parties to the agreement.

- *purpose.* All agreements should have a statement indicating the agreement's purpose. This provision serves to document the intent of the parties should a later dispute occur.
- *commitments.* The agreement should state the obligations of all parties to it (for example, that the decedent-business owner's estate will sell the decedent's interests to the surviving owners according to the terms of the agreement).
- *business interest description.* The document should contain a description of the business interests subject to the agreement.
- *transfer restrictions during lifetime.* Most buy-sell agreements should include a clause, which is referred to as a first-offer or right-of-first-refusal provision, that prevents the parties to the agreement from disposing of the business interest to outsiders while the parties are living.
- *purchase price.* The agreement should specify a fixed purchase price or a method for determining a price at which the business interest is to be bought and sold.
- *funding.* The document should specify how the purchase price is to be funded. In most instances life insurance is used for funding. It is uniquely suited for funding buy-sell agreements, since the very event that creates the need for cash provides the cash. If life insurance is selected as the funding method, the agreement should indicate the type of policies being used, who are the owners and beneficiaries of the policies, and who is responsible for paying their premiums.
- *transfer details.* The agreement should describe the actual specifics of the business transfer. For instance, when and where the settlement is to occur are important aspects of the agreement.
- *modification/termination.* There should be provisions for modification or termination of the buy-sell agreement if the parties later determine that the form of the current agreement no longer achieves the parties' objectives.

All parties to a buy-sell agreement should obtain competent legal counsel in creating the agreement.

BUSINESS CONTINUATION AGREEMENTS

Sole Proprietorships

A sole proprietorship is a business that has only one individual owner. It is distinct from other forms of business ownership in many ways. Most important, this type of business is not treated as a business entity separate unto itself. There is no legal distinction between the business's and the owner's personal assets. This means that when the sole proprietor dies or loses legal capacity to operate the business, the sole proprietorship must terminate. Planning for this contingency is vital if the proprietor's family expects to get full value for the business.

Often a buy-sell agreement is used to ensure a definite sale and purchase when the time comes. The agreement binds the proprietor's estate to sell and the purchaser(s) to buy the business interest.

Determining a Purchaser

In some cases there may be an obvious successor to the sole proprietorship, such as an adult child or other family member who is willing and capable to take over. Sometimes the potential purchaser is a key employee or group of employees. Employees may be willing to enter into a buy-sell agreement to protect their own future employment. If there are no key employees or natural successors to the sole proprietor, it is often recommended that the sole proprietor hire an employee who has the potential to take over the business and provide a training program for that employee.

Characteristics of Proprietorship Buy-Sell Agreements

- one owner
- potential purchaser(s)
  - key employee
  - group of employees

Life Insurance Arrangements for Sole Proprietorships. The life insurance arrangements for a sole proprietorship buy-sell agreement are relatively simple. The purchasing party is obligated to provide sale proceeds to the decedent-proprietor's estate. The applicant, owner, and premium payer of the life insurance on the proprietor's life should be the purchasing party. The coverage on the proprietor's life should be sufficient to make the required payments to the estate. In addition, the insurance funding the agreement should be reviewed periodically. It may be necessary for the future purchaser to obtain additional coverage later because of increases in the value of the proprietorship.

Partnerships

By operation of law, a general partnership terminates at the death of the partner unless the partnership agreement provides for continuation. If there has been no lifetime planning, a decedent partner's business interest will have to be liquidated by the surviving partner(s). The surviving partners are required to provide a fair liquidation price to a decedent partner's estate. However, it is often difficult for the surviving partners to make these payments without imposing a tremendous burden on the future partnership income.

The goal of the surviving partners is to continue the partnership business without interruption. Obviously, they would like to keep liquidation payments to a minimum. Therefore, the surviving partners' goals are incongruent with those of the decedent partner's estate. Unless there is a prearranged plan, a dispute between the heirs and the remaining partners is likely.

The solution is a binding partnership buy-sell agreement. Since a partnership has more than one business owner, the buy-sell agreement must address the possibility that any of the partners will be the next to die. Consequently, the partnership agreement should contain mutual promises between the partners that provide for different purchasers and sellers depending on the circumstances. Each partner binds his or her estate to sell if he or she is the first to die. Each partner also agrees to purchase the partnership interest held by the decedent-partner's estate if he or she is among the surviving partners.

Types of Partnership Buy-Sell Agreements

entity-purchase agreement

Entity-Purchase Agreement. Under the *entity-purchase agreement*, it is the partnership entity that becomes the purchaser in the buy-sell agreement. Technically, the partnership liquidates the interest held by the decedent-partner's estate. In other words, the partnership makes payments to the estate that liquidate the interest held by the estate. Under an entity buy-sell agreement both the partners and partnership are parties to the contract that provides for continuation of the partnership business by the surviving partners.

cross-purchase buy-sell agreement

Cross-Purchase Agreement. With a *cross-purchase buy-sell agreement*, the individual partners are the sellers and purchasers. The partners make mutual promises to be a buyer or seller depending on the circumstances. Each partner agrees to purchase a share of any decedent partner's interest and to bind his or her estate to sell its partnership interest to the surviving partners.

The choice between the entity and cross-purchase approach is complex. Factors such as the number of partners, the differences in income tax treatment, the cost basis of the different partners, and the financial considerations of the partnership will dictate the appropriate choice.

Types of Partnership Buy-Sell Agreements

- entity-purchase agreement
  - partnership makes payments to estate to liquidate decedent-partner's interest
- cross-purchase agreement
  - surviving partners purchase decedent-partner's interest

Insurance Arrangements for Partnership Buy-Sells

entity (liquidation) agreement

Entity (Liquidation) Agreement. The entity buy-sell approach provides that the partnership will liquidate the interest of a decedent-partner at death. If life insurance is used to fund the agreement, the partnership is the applicant, owner, and beneficiary of the policies on the lives of each partner who is a party to the agreement. Ideally, the partnership strives to maintain face amounts of coverage equal to its obligations under the agreement. Generally, the partnership should adopt the entity approach if it is in a better financial position to make the premium payments than the individuals themselves or if there are a large number of partners entering into the agreement.

Cross-Purchase Agreement. The cross-purchase agreement provides that the surviving partners are obligated to buy a prearranged share of a decedent-partner's interest from the decedent's estate. The agreement is usually funded by life insurance policies owned by the individual partners. Each partner should purchase life insurance policies on the lives of the other partners whose deaths obligate the policyowner to purchase the decedent's partnership interest. Thus, the individual partners become owners, beneficiaries, and premium payers for life insurance policies covering the lives of the other partners. Assuming "N" represents the number of business owners, the formula used for determining the number of policies needed is $N \times (N - 1)$. Therefore, four partners would require 12 life insurance policies. When a partner dies, the surviving partners receive the policy proceeds that are transferred to the decedent's estate in exchange for the partnership interest. Ideally, each partner acquires a policy with a death benefit equal to his or her share of the purchase price of a decedent-partner's interest.

Closely Held Corporations

A corporation is a legal entity separate from its shareholders. It provides limited liability to its shareholders and is treated as a separate taxpayer with tax rates and rules quite different from those applicable to individual taxpayers. In a closely held corporation, the key individuals usually include the shareholders. Because of this situation, the death, retirement, or disability of these key individuals threatens the future of the corporation. Therefore, it is reasonable for the corporation and its shareholders to adopt a buy-sell agreement.

Types of Corporate Buy-Sell Agreements

stock-redemption buy-sell agreement

Entity (Stock-Redemption) Purchase Agreement. With a *stock-redemption buy-sell agreement*, the corporation is the purchaser of the stock at the death of a shareholder. Each shareholder-party to the agreement binds his or her estate to transfer the stock to the corporation in exchange for the required purchase price. The corporation redeems a decedent-shareholder's stock in exchange for a redemption distribution. The corporation either retires the stock or holds it as treasury stock. From the surviving shareholders' standpoint, the practical effect of a stock redemption is that the percentage ownership held by each surviving shareholder increases proportionately when a decedent-shareholder's stock is redeemed.

The tax treatment of a stock redemption is extremely complex and beyond the scope of this book. Traditionally, a stock redemption is treated as a distribution of cash or property from the corporation to a shareholder and constitutes a taxable dividend to the redeemed shareholder. Under certain exceptions, a redemption may be treated as a sale or exchange subject to capital gains. It is essential to qualify the stock redemption as a sale or exchange to avoid harsh tax consequences to the redeemed shareholder's estate. Generally speaking, a stock-redemption plan does not qualify for the favorable sale-or-exchange tax treatment if family members of the decedent own stock in the corporation and plan to be the decedent's successors in the corporation. Other tax issues associated with a stock-redemption agreement concern income tax cost-basis problems for the surviving shareholders.

Corporate Cross-Purchase Agreement. The corporate cross-purchase agreement is similar to the partnership agreement. Each shareholder agrees to purchase a specified percentage of the decedent-shareholder's stock at the time of death. Although the corporation is not a direct party to the agreement, the stock certificates it issues should be endorsed with a statement that the stock is subject to the terms of the buy-sell agreement.

If only a few corporate shareholders are involved, there are two primary tax advantages to a cross-purchase agreement:

- The sale of stock by a decedent-shareholder's estate is treated as a sale or exchange, allowing the estate favorable capital-gains treatment.
- Because the surviving shareholders are direct purchasers, each receives an income tax cost basis in his or her stock equal to the amount of the purchase price paid.

Types of Closely Held Corporation Buy-Sell Agreements

- entity (stock-redemption) purchase agreement
  - corporation purchases decedent-shareholder's interest
- corporate cross-purchase agreement
  - surviving shareholder(s) purchase(s) decedent-partner's interest

---

Insurance Arrangements for Corporate Buy-Sells

Stock-Redemption Agreements. If life insurance is chosen as the funding mechanism for a stock-redemption buy-sell agreement, the corporation should be the applicant, owner, and beneficiary of the policies. The corporation acquires life insurance on the life of each shareholder who is a party to the agreement. The receipt of policy proceeds at a shareholder's death provides the cash necessary to redeem the decedent-shareholder's stock. The stock-redemption buy-sell agreement should be updated periodically to prevent the face amounts of insurance coverage from becoming inadequate for redemptions as the corporation increases in value.

Example:	Barney, Ben, and Bart form a closely held corporation, LMN, Inc., and each receives 100 shares of stock. The three shareholders enter into a stock-redemption (entity-purchase) buy-sell agreement so the surviving shareholders can continue the business in coequal ownership if one dies prematurely.
	Suppose Ben dies first. Ben's death obligates LMN, Inc., to purchase his stock at a prearranged price. Corporate funds are then transferred to Ben's estate in return for his 100 shares of stock. This stock is retired by the corporation, with the result that Barney and Bart now own 100 shares each of the 200 shares of stock outstanding in LMN. (See figure 11-1.)

Cross-Purchase Agreements. If life insurance is used to fund a cross-purchase agreement, each shareholder should purchase adequate life insurance on the life of the other shareholders. Each individual shareholder then becomes owner, beneficiary, and premium payer for the life insurance policies covering the lives of the other shareholders. As with the partnership cross-purchase agreement, the formula for determining the number of policies needed is $N \times (N - 1)$. If there are three parties to the contract, six insurance policies are necessary.

At a shareholder's death, the surviving shareholders receive the death benefits from the policies and transfer the proceeds to the decedent-shareholder's estate in exchange for the appropriate amount of his or her stock. Because individual shareholders must be relied upon to maintain the funding for the agreement, there is often the concern that some parties will not live up to the terms of the contract. To ensure that the cross-purchase agreement is carried out, a trustee is often used as an overseer to hold the policies and consummate the purchase and sale of stock at a shareholder's death.

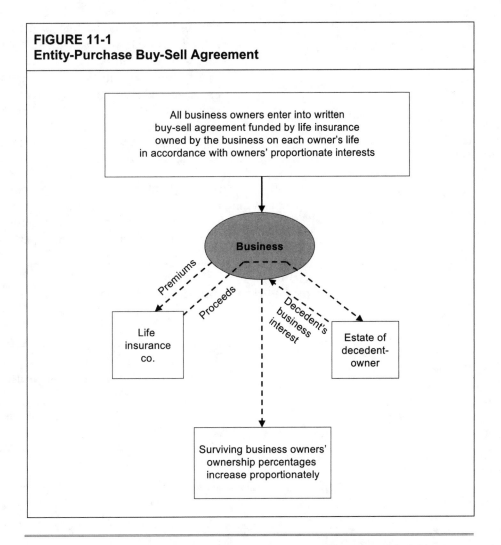

FIGURE 11-1
Entity-Purchase Buy-Sell Agreement

All business owners enter into written buy-sell agreement funded by life insurance owned by the business on each owner's life in accordance with owners' proportionate interests

Business

Premiums

Proceeds

Decedent's business interest

Life insurance co.

Estate of decedent-owner

Surviving business owners' ownership percentages increase proportionately

Example: Mannie, Mo, and Mac form a closely held corporation, XYZ, Inc., and receive 100 shares of stock each at the time of incorporation. The three shareholders also enter into a cross-purchase buy-sell agreement at this time. The premise of the agreement is for the surviving shareholders to continue the business in equal ownership. In the contract Mannie, Mo, and Mac execute the buy-sell agreement to bind their estates to sell their shares of stock to the surviving shareholders. Each shareholder agrees to purchase one-half of the shares of stock held by the estate of a deceased shareholder.

Suppose Mannie is the first to die. When the agreement is carried out, Mo and Mac each purchase 50 shares of stock in XYZ, Inc., from Mannie's estate. Mannie's estate will then have liquid funds to meet expenses and distribution requirements. Mo and Mac will continue to operate XYZ after the buyout. Each will hold 150 shares of stock out of the 300 shares outstanding in XYZ. (See figure 11-2.)

Clearly, the tax and nontax implications of buy-sell agreements are complex and unique to each business arrangement. The specifics of any buy-sell contract should be hammered out only after careful deliberation by all the parties to the contract and with the advice of experts in this area.

FIGURE 11-2
Cross-Purchase Buy-Sell Agreement

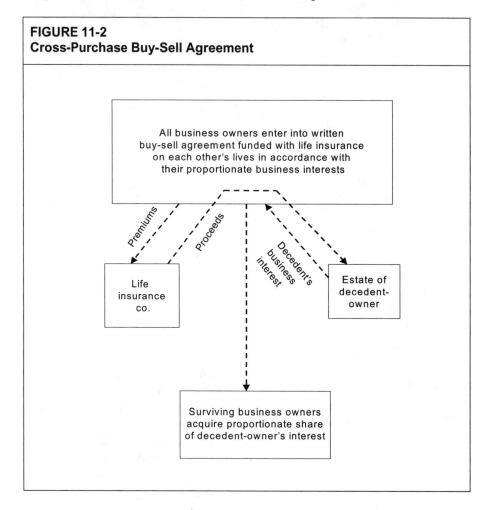

Funding Buy-Sell Agreements with Life Insurance

- entity purchase/stock redemption
  - entity is applicant, owner, premium payer, and beneficiary of the policies on lives of business owners (partners/shareholders)
- cross-purchase
  - each business owner is applicant, owner, premium payer, and beneficiary of policies on the other business owner's lives

SETTING A PRICE IN A BUY-SELL AGREEMENT

In general, the first decision that must be made in developing a buy-sell agreement is the establishment of a price. The problem is difficult because so many factors (such as the time of death, the condition of the business on the date of the buy-out, and the influence of economic conditions) pose a multitude of variables that are not only unknown and unknowable but also interdependent. In spite of these problems, it is necessary to arrive at a price-of-valuation formula. Obviously, there is no *right* method and every method has its problems.

There are essentially four methods that business individuals use as a price-setting mechanism in a buy-sell agreement:

- fixed price
- formula-determined price
- appraisal-determined price
- combination of the above mechanisms

Fixed Price

Setting a price and stating it in the agreement has the advantage of being simple and clear. If Steve, Robert, and Lee are all parties to the agreement, each person knows exactly what his family would receive upon his death as well as what he would receive in the event of disability. For example, if they use a fixed price of $900,000 and each individual owns a one-third interest, each person's interest would be worth one-third of $900,000, or $300,000.

There are drawbacks to a fixed-price mechanism. The main disadvantage is that the agreement will likely fail the tests to peg the value of stock in a family corporation. Because a fixed price does not adequately reflect fluctuations in market value, it is likely that the IRS will find the agreement to be either (1) a device to pass the stock to family for less than full consideration or (2) inconsistent with the terms of an agreement reached at arm's length. Even if the parties are unrelated, the fixed-price provision generally provides an inaccurate result.

Can the drawback of the fixed-price mechanism be alleviated by a requirement that the parties revalue the business each year and that the value as of the last revaluation control? In theory, the solution seems sound. However, as a practical matter, the parties to a buy-sell agreement seldom actually make their intended annual revaluation. If the value of the business increases substantially from the time the fixed price is set, the survivors of the deceased business owner will receive an amount that does not accurately reflect the true value of the business. Likewise, if one of the business owners becomes ill, he or she will want to readjust the price upward to provide more cash for the family in return for the business owner's business interest. But the interest of the healthy business owners is diametrically opposed to that of the sick colleague. The result is that the equal bargaining position contemplated by the agreement no longer exists.

It may make sense to set a fixed price (using one or more of the valuation methods discussed above that are used by the IRS and the courts) and then provide in the contract for yearly revaluations plus an additional provision that if no revaluation has been made within X months of the date of death, then the price shall be the average of the valuations rendered by two qualified appraisers (or some similar technique).

Formula Pricing Mechanism

The main disadvantage of a fixed-price mechanism for valuing a business interest is definitional (that is, the price is fixed by agreement while the value of the business interest may fluctuate widely). What is indicated is a pricing mechanism based on a formula. The formula itself may take a number of factors into consideration. For example, the formula may be an adaptation of an ARM 34 or some other method that considers various, easily ascertained, objective factors.

The most common formula approach uses some type of capitalization-of-earnings method. Often the parties take other value-affecting factors into consideration by the multiple used. For example, one business may be valued at 10 times average earnings for the past 5 years, while another might be valued at 3 times average earnings for the past 8 years. Obviously, the greater the risk and the lower the stability of a business, the lower the earnings multiple is. Industry studies by statistical analysis companies can be used to discover the multiple for any given type of industry. Adjustments for specific facts or abnormalities with regard to a particular business may have to be made. Many of these adjustments are discussed above. The multiple itself may vary from time to time as economic conditions change. In some cases, the formula gives more weight to the earnings of those years immediately preceding the decedent-business owner's death than to the earnings of prior years. If family members are parties, it is imperative that the formula chosen be consistent with similar arm's-length agreements.

Appraisal

Many authorities feel that the fairest means of ascertaining the value of a business is to state in the buy-sell agreement that two appraisers should be employed. One appraiser is hired by the surviving shareholders, while the other represents the decedent's interest. The two appraisers would come to an agreement on an appropriate valuation, or in the absence of agreement, a third appraiser would be appointed by the first two to make a final binding determination of value.

The parties can give the appraisers carte blanche in their appraisal process, or they can instruct them to take into consideration certain factors and ignore others. For example, the buy-sell agreement can specify that the appraisers are to ignore goodwill or value it in a certain way.

The Uniform Standards of Professional Appraisal Practice (USPAP) contain the rules of valuation followed by many appraisers.

Combination Mechanism

A fixed-price mechanism coupled with an appraisal and a formula method, which begins with a fixed price as a floor and enhances that amount if earnings or book values reach a certain level, are other ways to solve the difficult and perplexing problem of providing variable but realistic prices for a business owner's interest.

CHAPTER REVIEW

Answers to the review questions and the self-test questions start on page 717.

Key Terms

buy-sell agreement
entity purchase agreement
cross-purchase buy-sell agreement

entity (liquidation) agreement
stock-redemption buy-sell
  agreement

Review Questions

11-1.   What are the advantages to entering into a buy-sell agreement?

11-2.   Identify some of the provisions that all buy-sell agreements typically contain.

11-3. Explain why life insurance is the preferred method for funding buy-sell agreements.

11-4. Why might a business continuation agreement be necessary for a sole proprietorship?

11-5. Describe the two basic types of buy-sell agreements for
   a.   partnerships
   b.   corporations

11-6. Describe four methods for specifying or determining the purchase price in a buy-sell agreement.

Self-Test Questions

T   F   11-1. Although a buy-sell agreement can provide many benefits to co-owners of a business, it does not keep the business from going through probate.

T   F   11-2. One advantage of a buy-sell agreement is that it makes a business more creditor friendly because it provides for a business continuation arrangement.

T   F   11-3. Most buy-sell agreements should include a first-offer or right-of-first-refusal provision.

T   F   11-4. Although life insurance is becoming more popular as a funding source for buy-sell agreements, it is still used to fund a minority of buy-sell agreements.

T   F   11-5. Under a fully insured proprietorship buy-sell agreement, the applicant, owner, and premium payer of the life insurance on the proprietor's life should be the purchasing employee.

T   F   11-6. Under a fully insured corporate cross-purchase agreement, the corporation acquires life insurance on the life of each shareholder who is a party to the agreement.

T   F   11-7. In general, the first decision that must be made in developing a buy-sell agreement is the establishment of a price.

T   F   11-8. The main advantage of using a fixed price in a buy-sell agreement for a family corporation is that it pegs the value of the stock for federal estate tax purposes.

12

Federal Estate Taxation: The Gross Estate—Part I

Learning Objectives

An understanding of the material in this chapter should enable the student to

12-1.   Distinguish between the federal estate tax and other death taxes.

12-2.   Describe the general rule for inclusion of property in the gross estate of a decedent.

12-3.   Describe the federal estate tax treatment of dower or curtesy interests.

12-4.   Explain the various types of property that are includible in the gross estate if transferred or disposed of within 3 years of death.

12-5.   Explain how transfers of property with retained interests and powers may be treated for federal estate tax purposes.

Chapter Outline

INTRODUCTION

If a meaningful estate plan is to be written, a clear understanding of the size of the client's gross estate is essential. The concept of the *federal gross estate*, as it is called, is crucial because its size and the types of assets it includes directly determine what planning techniques the financial planner should employ.

This clear understanding of the federal gross estate begins with the Internal Revenue Code. The Internal Revenue Code divides the manner in which a gross estate is to be constructed into two broad categories: (1) what the estate owner *actually* owned at the date of death and (2) what the estate owner is *deemed* to have owned at the date of death. The first of these categories is simple, the second quite complex.

The concept of the *actual estate* is logical. The doctrine requires all property interests the decedent owned at the date of death to be included in the gross estate. This inclusion results in estate taxation. The legal requirement that such property be included as part of the gross estate is logical: If a decedent *owned* the property at the date of death, he or she should be taxed on that ownership interest for federal estate tax purposes.

There is a second, more complex tier to our twofold system of federal estate taxation. We have labeled this second element the *constructive estate*. There are several provisions in the estate tax portion of the Internal Revenue Code that result in the pulling back of former property interests into the decedent's gross estate so that the fair market value of those interests, either at the date of death or on the alternate valuation date, become taxable as part of the estate. A statutory framework does exist that may result in a significant amount of federal estate tax being imposed upon the constructive estate.

A two-tiered system of inclusion exists because the IRS convinced Congress that there are many actual and potential situations when estate owners, bent on estate tax avoidance, transfer property interests so that the value of that property will not *actually* be owned by the estate owners at the date of death. If the statutory framework were such that only interests *actually* owned by decedents could be subjected to federal estate taxation, a transfer of property interests would successfully defeat the tax. But often, the IRS concluded, estate owners want the best of both worlds, that is, to transfer property interests to others so that as a matter of property law they no longer own the property, but as a matter of practicality they continue to enjoy the property as if they still owned it.

One primary objective of estate planning traditionally has been to obtain the maximum savings in federal and local death taxes as well as other transfer costs. Most clients want to transfer their property to family members and other beneficiaries at a minimum cost with the least shrinkage to the estate. For many persons with small and medium-sized estates, the applicable credit amount shelters the estate from tax.

In addition, there is now an unlimited maximum marital deduction that allows married individuals to pass their entire estate to their surviving spouses free of federal estate tax. In spite of these benefits, under current law the federal estate tax must be taken into consideration in planning an estate for the following reasons:

- The applicable credit amount shelters only up to $3 million per married couple from tax in the years 2004 and 2005.
- The marital deduction is available only at the first death of a married couple (presuming the survivor does not remarry).
- Inflation may cause even modest estates to exceed the applicable credit amount.
- The size of the federal deficit might cause Congress in the future to look for increased revenue from the estate and gift tax system.

As a cautionary word, the financial planner must determine the unique objectives of a client in the estate planning process. Overall objectives must be planned. The effect of taxes on the estate is only one consideration in preparing an estate plan. While no plan should be implemented without an analysis of the tax consequences, federal estate taxes should not be the controlling factor, regardless of the size of the estate. The field of tax law, based on tax statutes as well as regulations and further supported by interpretations through case law and revenue rulings, is a dynamic and constantly shifting area. This chapter and subsequent chapters on the federal estate tax laws are limited to a review of general principles in the field that are sufficient to enable the financial planner both to understand and to explain the impact of federal estate taxation to a client. These chapters, however, provide only an introduction to a complex, continually changing area of tax law.

THE FEDERAL ESTATE TAX

The federal estate tax is imposed on the transferor or the transferor's estate and is based on the privilege to transfer property. Congress recognized that a tax limited to property transferred at death would have been an open invitation to tax-avoidance schemes to dispose of property during lifetime. Therefore, under the Tax Reform Act of 1976, a unified estate and gift tax system was enacted to prevent lifetime dispositions from escaping taxation or being taxed at lower rates. The 1976 act provided a unified, cumulative system for taxation of certain transfers by gift during lifetime and transfers at death at the same tax rates. Since January 1, 1977, adjusted taxable gifts (as they are called) are taken into consideration and added to the taxable estate in computing any federal estate tax due at death.

The Economic Growth and Tax Relief Reconciliation Act (EGTRRA) of 2001, however, enacted some provisions that resulted in discrepancies with the 1976 Act unified system.

Beginning January 1, 2002, the gift tax exclusion increases to $1,000,000 and remains at $1,000,000 even though the estate tax exclusion is slated to increase to $1.5 million in 2004 and 2005; $2 million in 2006, 2007, and 2008; $3.5 million in 2009; and is then repealed for 2010. Although the gift tax is not repealed and the exclusion is to remain at $1 million through 2010, the gift tax rate decreases each year in conjunction with the top estate tax rate.

For 2010, the top gift and income tax rate is 35 percent.

Under certain sections of the federal estate tax law, Congress also addressed situations where the donor transferred property to another during lifetime but continued to retain powers, controls, or interests over the transferred property for his or her lifetime. Congress perceived these incomplete lifetime dispositions as the equivalent of testamentary transfers at death, since the donor still had some control over or enjoyment from the property during lifetime or power over the property at death. These types of rights or powers, if held by a decedent at death, may cause the property to be included in the decedent's gross estate.

federal estate tax

All property, either owned directly by the decedent at the time of death or subject to the decedent's control in a manner sufficient to cause that property to be included in the gross estate under one of the federal estate tax rules, is included in the estate for federal estate tax purposes. The *federal estate tax* applies to the entire estate and is imposed on the estate itself, which is primarily liable for payment of the tax. The way in which property is transferred is irrelevant in this regard. In other words, the property may be transferred by will, intestacy, contract, or operation of law. To the extent that there are assets in the estate, the estate is responsible for the tax liability. However, if the estate does not contain sufficient assets to pay the tax liability, beneficiaries of the estate may be charged with the tax liability to the extent of the value of property they inherit.

Estate Taxation of Residents, Citizens, and Nonresident Aliens

gross estate

All property owned by citizens or residents of the United States at the time of their death is subject to the federal estate tax, regardless of where the property is located. The *gross estate* includes all property owned by a citizen or resident of the United States at death valued at its fair market value on the date of death or alternate valuation date (6 months after death). The tax is a progressive tax similar to the federal income tax. It is based on a graduated rate schedule that increases with the size of the estate.

The federal estate tax is applied differently to those who are considered nonresident noncitizens (nonresident aliens). As for nonresident noncitizens, only the value of their property located in the United States and owned by them at the time of their death is subject to federal estate tax. Note that the property owned by noncitizens may also be subject to foreign death taxes, as may foreign property held by U.S. citizens. The federal taxation of such individuals and their property often depends on the terms of the estate tax treaty (if any) between the United States and the applicable foreign nation.

IRC SEC. 2031: BASIC INCLUDIBILITY

Our system of federal taxation is controlled by statute. Because the federal estate tax is no exception, our starting point in studying the concept of the gross estate is to look to the specific Internal Revenue Code section defining the gross estate. Sec. 2031 provides, in very vague fashion, that the gross estate shall include "the value of all property, real or personal, tangible or intangible, to the extent provided by Secs. 2033 through 2046." Obviously, Sec. 2031 is an empty provision, devoid of much substance, because it merely cites other Internal Revenue Code sections for justification of inclusion of assets. Unless a particular property interest is covered by Secs. 2033–2046 there is no gross estate inclusion. Sec. 2031 may be thought of as a road map, telling us where else to look in the Internal Revenue Code to determine whether property has to be included as part of a decedent's gross estate.

Because of the vague nature of Sec. 2031, it is important to treat the subsequent provisions of the estate tax sections in detail.

THE CATCHALL PROVISION (IRC SEC. 2033)

Section 2033 of the Internal Revenue Code states the general rule that the gross estate includes the value of all property interests, real or personal, tangible or intangible, of an individual on the date of death to the extent of his or her interest in the property. Sec. 2033 is designed as nothing more than a catchall provision. Subsequent Code provisions provide the fine-tuning.

In order to include a property or a property interest under this section, the decedent's interest must rise to the level of an *interest in property*. This is broader than merely stating that property *owned* by the decedent at the time of death is to be included. It requires the inclusion of property interests to the extent of any interest in such property.

Once we know that property in which the decedent possessed an *interest* will be required to be included as part of the decedent's gross estate, the question arises, what is an *interest*? The answer lies in *state* law.

Types of Property Interests Includible under Sec. 2033

State law creates legal interests and rights. This Code section has been interpreted to mean that federal taxation is to be applied based on locally determined rights and interests. Accordingly, if under state law a decedent is considered to own property or possess an interest in such property, then Sec. 2033 will apply to that particular property and the value of it will be pulled into the federal gross estate.

For situations in which there is a factual or legal question about a decedent's property interest, the federal court rules on such questions, but it is required to apply principles of state property law.

The regulations are not particularly helpful in this regard as they say only that the property interest must be one that was a beneficial interest (Treas. Reg. Sec. 20.2033–1(a)). That is to say that for purposes of IRC Sec. 2033, a mere legal interest—such as holding title purely as a fiduciary—is not an interest that rises to the level of a property interest in which the decedent had a beneficial interest. Therefore, the interest is not includible in the decedent's gross estate.

Property and property interests that are includible under Sec. 2033 are those that are "owned" by the decedent. While this ownership concept may provide a convenient shorthand way of describing the property interests includible in a decedent's gross estate under this Code section, it is not always precise. Some other limitations exist that may cause property or property interests owned by a decedent to be excluded from this particular section. However, the same property or property interests may be specifically included in the gross estate under other sections of the federal estate tax law.

For example, the right to borrow money against the cash value of an insurance policy may not be a property interest sufficient to include the policy proceeds in the decedent's gross estate under Sec. 2033, but the proceeds are included because of another section that specifically requires their inclusion. (Those types of interests in property that are specifically includible in the decedent's gross estate are discussed later in this and the following chapter.)

Limitations on Property Interests Includible under Sec. 2033

The federal estate tax is levied on the right to transfer property at death. Therefore, if the decedent had no right to transfer property or a property interest to another at death, either by will or under the intestacy laws, the value of those property interests is not includible in the gross estate under this section no matter how great the decedent's interests were during lifetime. An example of an interest in which the decedent possessed no right to pass the property at death is a life estate created by another. Any interest in property that was given to the decedent by another, the transfer of which the decedent cannot control and that ceases at the decedent's death, is not included in his or her gross estate. Only inheritable interests (interests that can be transmitted to another by the decedent at death) are subject to the tax.

There are three factors to be applied to all property in determining whether it is includible in the decedent's gross estate under Sec. 2033. First, what types of property are includible under state or federal law? Second, was the decedent's interest in the property large enough to warrant its inclusion in the estate? Third, did the decedent possess this interest at the time of death and to what extent?

Specific Types of Property Includible under Sec. 2033

Under Sec. 2033, the decedent's estate includes any interest in real estate whether the property comes into the possession of the personal representative or passes directly to the heirs. The decedent's estate also includes cash or money equivalents, whether kept in a bank, savings or checking account, certificates of deposit, money market funds, or a safe-deposit box. The gross estate includes any stocks, bonds (including tax-exempt bonds), notes, and mortgages owned by the decedent, as well as the value of any outstanding loans the decedent made to others. His or her estate also includes the value of income tax refunds not yet paid, patents, and copyrights.

Property subject to indebtedness is also includible in the decedent's gross estate. If the decedent is personally liable for the indebtedness, the full value of the property is included in the gross estate and the estate is allowed a deduction for the amount of the debt. If the decedent is not personally liable for the indebtedness (for example, a nonrecourse note), only the value of the decedent's equity in the property is included in the gross estate and no deduction is allowed for the debt.

Under Sec. 2033 the gross estate also includes any amount to which the decedent was entitled before he or she died. For example, a claim for damages for pain and suffering as a result of someone else's negligent act is includible in the decedent's estate because it could have been recovered by him or her before death. On the other hand, the proceeds of a wrongful death claim, although brought by the decedent's personal representative on behalf of his or her heirs, are not included in the gross estate because the decedent had no right of action or interest in the proceeds at any time before death. It is not relevant that the decedent's death was instrumental in someone else's acquiring an interest in the property. The relevant test is whether there was anything the decedent had a right to own or receive while alive that passes to another by reason of the decedent's death.

If the decedent were entitled to a refund because of an income tax overpayment, this income tax refund is an asset includible in the gross estate under Sec. 2033. The same is true if the decedent and the decedent's spouse had filed a joint return. In the case of a joint return in which an income tax refund is due, the amount includible in the decedent's gross estate is the amount by which his or her contribution toward payment of the income tax exceeds the decedent's income tax liability. Any medical insurance reimbursements due to the decedent at the time of death are also includible in the gross estate.

Also, outstanding dividends declared and payable to the stockholders of record on or before the date of the decedent's death are included in the decedent's gross estate (Treas. Reg. § 20.2033–1(b)). Thus, if a shareholder dies after the record date but before the dividend is paid, the dividend is the shareholder's property and is included in the decedent-shareholder's estate. The critical date is the ownership on the record date of the dividend. If the decedent dies after the dividend is declared but before the record date, he or she did not own the right to the dividend at death. Therefore, the value is not included in the decedent's gross estate. Of course, if the dividend is declared after the date of death, it is not included in the gross estate because the decedent's right to receive the dividend did not accrue while the decedent was alive.

Sec. 2033 has sufficient scope to include in a decedent's gross estate not only tangible and intangible assets actually owned by the decedent at death but also assets that were due the decedent but not yet received by him or her.

income in respect of a decedent (IRD)

Income items that have already been earned by a decedent but not collected as of the date of death are *income in respect of a decedent (IRD)*. Even though such items are taxed for federal income tax purposes, the items may also be required to be included as part of the gross estate. They may, therefore, be subject to federal estate tax as well.

Examples of income in respect of a decedent include the following:

- fees earned by a decedent but not yet paid and collected as of the time of death
- royalties earned by the decedent but not yet paid
- rents accrued up to the date of the decedent's death on property owned by the decedent
- bonuses, unpaid salary, and the like previously earned by the decedent but not yet paid

- dividends on shares of stock owned by a decedent at the time of death but payable subsequent to death

Although such items trigger both income tax and estate tax liability, Sec. 691(c) of the Internal Revenue Code does allow an income tax deduction for that amount of estate tax to the party who receives and reports the income for federal income tax purposes.

Example:	Becky is the beneficiary of her Uncle's Pete's IRA. In 2005, Uncle Pete died with a taxable estate of $4 million and an IRA with a value of $1.8 million. The federal estate tax in 2005 is $1,720,800 due to the inclusion of the IRA in the estate. Without inclusion of the IRA in the gross estate, the estate tax is $874,800. The tax difference with and without inclusion of Uncle Pete's IRA is $846,000. Therefore, $846,000 (the additional amount of estate tax liability resulting from inclusion of the IRA in the decedent's estate) can be claimed as a deduction on Becky's income tax return. (See table 12-1).

Also included in the decedent's estate is miscellaneous property, such as interests in partnerships and unincorporated businesses. These interests are listed in the estate tax return on a separate schedule from stock that a decedent

TABLE 12-1
Difference in Estate Tax between Inclusion and Exclusion of IRA

Estate Tax with IRA Inclusion		Estate Tax without IRA Inclusion	
Year of death	2005	Year of death	2005
Adjusted gross estate	$4,000,000	Adjusted gross estate	$2,200,000
Taxable estate	$4,000,000	Taxable estate	$2,200,000
Adjusted taxable gifts	$ 0	Adjusted taxable gifts	$ 0
Tentative tax base	$4,000,000	Tentative tax base	$2,200,000
Tentative tax	$1,720,800	Tentative tax	$ 874,800
Gift tax paid	$ 0	Gift Tax paid	$ 0
Gross federal estate tax	$1,720,800	Gross federal estate tax	$ 874,800
Allowable applicable credit amount	$ 555,800	Allowable applicable credit amount	$ 555,800
Net federal estate tax	$1,165,000	Net federal estate tax	$ 319,000

might own in either a publicly held or a closely held corporation. All the decedent's tangible personal property—including furniture, jewelry, and household items—is includible in the gross estate. Frequently, however, household items and wedding gifts are considered to be the wife's property if acquired at or near the time of the marriage. In such cases, the value of these items is not included in the decedent husband's gross estate; however, documentation may be necessary to successfully support the exclusion of such items.

Under Sec. 2033 the decedent's estate also includes any vested rights to receive property in the future. These future interests in property include reversionary interests as well as remainder interests and are includible at their values on the date of death as computed actuarially according to IRS tables.

> *Example:*   If Stephen creates a trust for the benefit of his divorced wife, Betty, and gives Betty income for life with the property to revert to Stephen or his estate upon her death, his reversionary interest is an includible asset. Because the property reverts to Stephen if he survives her or to his estate should he predecease her, his estate and heirs have an absolute right to receive the trust property at some future time. Therefore, a value for this reversionary interest will be determined at Stephen's death.

Includible future rights also include fixed ascertainable rights to receive income from the property as well as remainder interests in the corpus either at some future time or upon the happening of some future event. These future interests are also includible. Examples include postdeath partnership profits. Entitlement to future income (such as renewal commissions) is another example of property rights owned outright by the decedent that must be included in the gross estate. Property representing future income will, of course, be income taxable to the estate or beneficiaries when it is actually received. As already noted, to the extent that estate tax was attributable to the inclusion of these items in the estate, a special income tax deduction for the amount of estate tax allocated to these items is allowed to the property recipient in the year the item is includible in income.

Sec. 2033 includes in the decedent's gross estate the value of his or her share of property held in conjunction with others. Thus, if the decedent owns property as a tenant in common with others, the decedent's tenancy share is includible in the gross estate. If disproportionate shares as tenants in common are not specified, the interests are presumed to be equal. For example, if there are three tenants, they are each presumed to own a one-third interest. The value of the decedent's share of community property is included in the estate.

As stated before, if the decedent's interests are limited to lifetime enjoyment and there is no property interest to pass at death (for example, a life estate given to the decedent by another), the value of that right is not included in the gross estate. This results because the decedent never possessed rights in the property that could be transferred at death and the estate tax is levied on transfers of property. However, an interest in property is includible in the gross estate although it is limited, contingent, or remote, provided that it does not end with the decedent's death. Of course, the contingency or remoteness of the interest affects its valuation.

Sec. 2033 may also apply to inclusion of life insurance. If a decedent owns a life insurance policy on his or her own life at the date of death, the face amount of that policy is required to be included in the gross estate pursuant to Sec. 2042(2). Sec. 2042(2) establishes a standard regarding *incidents of ownership* whereby the owner of a life policy is required to include the proceeds in the gross estate in the event that he or she possessed any incidents of ownership.

incidents of ownership

Sec. 2033 Inclusion

- real property
- cash/money equivalents
- stocks/bonds
- notes
- mortgages
- outstanding loans by decedent to others
- income tax refunds due
- patents/copyrights
- damages owed decedent
- dividends declared and payable
- income in respect of decedent (IRD)
- partnership/unincorporated business interests
- tangible personal property
- vested future rights
- decedent's share of property held with others

If, however, the decedent at the time of death owns a life insurance policy on the life of another person, such as the decedent's spouse, child, or business associate, Sec. 2042 has no application because the decedent possesses no incidents of ownership over a policy on his or her own life. But such a life insurance policy is *property* for Sec. 2033 purposes, and as such, the value of the decedent's interest is included as part of the decedent's gross estate. In other words, when one spouse dies, the cash value of the life insurance policy owned by that spouse on the life of the other will be drawn into the gross estate. Because of this, it is felt that "cross-ownership" of life insurance policies between husband and wife is not always a prudent choice.

As already emphasized, the estate tax imposed under Sec. 2033 is predicated upon the extent of the decedent's ownership interest at death. This can raise difficult questions as to whether any property transferred by the decedent was void or voidable as well as whether the decedent disposed of any interest before death by a gift or sale. Transfers, sales, loans, partnership, or business ventures—especially those involving spouses and intrafamily arrangements where legal formalities have not been meticulously observed—present particularly difficult problems that must be resolved on an individual basis.

Qualified Family-Owned Business Deduction (Now Repealed)

The IRS Restructuring and Reform Act of 1998 created Code Sec. 2057. This section allowed for a $1.3 million deduction for qualified family-owned business interests (QFOBIs).

EGTRRA 2001 repealed the Sec. 2057 qualified family-owned business interest estate tax deduction beginning in 2004. Therefore, for decedents dying after 2003, EGTRRA 2001 under Sec. 2057(j) provides that the estate tax deduction for QFOBIs will not apply. Hence, the estate tax applicable exclusion amount will not need to be coordinated with this deduction beginning in 2004.

DOWER OR CURTESY INTERESTS (IRC SEC. 2034)

Sec. 2034 of the Code concerns the inclusion requirements of dower and curtesy interests, which are property rights created under state law to protect a widow's or widower's claim of right in the decedent-spouse's property. A dower right is property set aside for a widow under state law if it has been established that the decedent had an interest in the property. Curtesy pertains to the rights of a widower in his deceased wife's property. Many states have abolished *dower* and *curtesy*, replacing them with statutory rights of surviving spouses.

dower
curtesy

Sec. 2034 Dower/Curtesy Interests

- dower right—property set aside for widow under state law if decedent-husband had an interest in the property
- curtesy right—property set aside for widower under state law if decedent-wife had an interest in the property

(These interests have been abolished in most states and replaced by statutory rights to elect against the decedent-spouse's will.)

This Code section clarifies the fact that the amount of a property interest includible in a decedent's gross estate is not diminished by the fact that the property is subject to a dower or curtesy interest or a statutory interest created in lieu of dower or curtesy. Note, however, that if the property subject to dower or curtesy is transferred to the surviving spouse, the dower or curtesy interest may qualify for the marital deduction and thereby reduce the taxable estate.

INCLUSION OF CERTAIN GIFTS, TRANSFERS, AND GIFT TAXES (IRC SEC. 2035)

As a general rule, gifts made within 3 years of death are not included in the gross estates of decedents dying after December 31, 1981, except for certain limited purposes. The following are some exceptions to the general rule:

- transfers with retained interests for life
- transfers taking effect at death
- transfers in which the decedent reserves the right to alter, amend, revoke, or terminate the transfer or the power to affect the beneficial interest in the transferred property
- transfers of life insurance policies by the insured
- gift taxes paid

Note that Sec. 2035 does not cause inclusion of the transfers noted above if the decedent retains the interest until the time of death. Sec. 2035 deals only with a disposition of the interest by the decedent during the 3 years preceding death. A disposition may be a gift of or the exercise or release of a right or power. Except for gifts of life insurance and gift taxes paid, the initial transfer of property need not be made within the 3-year period preceding the decedent's death, for it is the date of the disposition of *the retained interest* that is determinative.

Transfers with Retained Interests for Life

The first exception to the general rule that lifetime gifts are not includible in the gross estate pertains to property transferred by the decedent during lifetime in which the decedent retained certain rights or powers for his or her lifetime. It is the giving up, releasing, or exercising of these retained rights or powers within 3 years of death that causes the property to which the retained rights applied to be includible in the decedent's gross estate under this Code Section. Therefore, includible in the decedent's gross estate are those lifetime transfers in which the decedent reserved (1) the right to receive or determine who receives income from the property or (2) the right to designate who is entitled to possession or enjoyment of the property (including himself or herself) either (a) for life, or (b) for a period that did not actually end before death, or (c) for a period that cannot be determined without reference to the decedent's death. If the decedent gave up the retained rights pertaining to the property more than 3 years before death, such property is not includible in the gross estate. Transfers of retained rights by the decedent within 3 years of death that cause inclusion under Sec. 2035 include the use, possession, income, or other enjoyment of the transferred property for himself or herself, or the right to name other persons who may possess or enjoy the transferred property or income from the property. It makes no difference whether the decedent either retains this right alone or can exercise the right only with another. Furthermore, it is insignificant as to whether or not the person with whom the decedent has to act possesses an adverse interest in the property (meaning that the other person is a beneficiary or potential beneficiary of the property).

Example:	Ten years ago, Tom Smith transferred, for no consideration, ownership in his farm to his three daughters. He retained the right to live on the property rent free. Two years ago, Tom moved to another state and relinquished any and all rights over the farm property, including the right to live there. He died a few months after moving. The fair market value of the farm property at the date of death (or alternate valuation date) will be drawn into his gross estate because he gave up the retained right over the asset within 3 years of the date of his death.

More of the specific rules and some examples of transfers under this exception are included later in a full discussion of IRC Sec. 2036.

Transfers Effective at Death

Other rights that cause the property to be includible in the gross estate are transfers that become effective at death. These are transfers to others that can be obtained only by surviving the decedent provided that the decedent retained a reversionary interest in the property and the reversionary interest exceeds 5 percent of the value of the property at the date of death. This type of transfer is includible in the decedent's estate under Sec. 2035 if he or she either exercised the power or transferred it within the 3 years prior to death. If the decedent retained the power until death, the transferred property is includible in the estate under IRC Sec. 2037.

Example:	Lois Forbes transferred a portfolio of marketable securities to her sister, Joan, several years ago. Under the terms of the transfer, if Joan predeceases Lois, the portfolio of securities is to be returned to Lois. Actuarial tables reflect the fact that this reversionary interest exceeds 5 percent of the value of the property. Two years ago, Lois modified the arrangement by relinquishing the right to receive the marketable securities back if Joan dies before her and instead arranged for the property to pass to Lois's brother, Ronald, if Joan dies before Lois. If Lois dies within 3 years of relinquishing the right to receive the marketable securities back, the fair market value of the securities portfolio on the date of Lois's death (or on the alternate valuation date) will be required to be included in Lois's gross estate under Sec. 2035.

Transfers in which Decedent Reserves Certain Rights

If a decedent disposes of any of the retained rights to alter, amend, revoke, or terminate the transfer, or to affect the beneficial interest in the transferred property within the 3 years preceding death, the value of the property is includible in the decedent's gross estate under Sec. 2035. If the interests are retained until his or her death, the value of the transferred property is includible under IRC Sec. 2038.

Example:	Bob created a trust into which he transferred $110,000 worth of marketable securities. The trust was irrevocable, but Bob had the power to amend the instrument, including the right to add beneficiaries and the right to change what existing beneficiaries were to receive. The trust had originally been created 7 years ago. Bob amended the document so he could no longer make any changes, alterations, or revisions to the trust 2 years ago and died 4 months later. The fair market value of the corpus of the trust on the date of death or the alternate valuation date would be included in Bob's gross estate under Sec. 2035 because he relinquished a Sec. 2038 power within 3 years of his death. Had no such relinquishment been made, Sec. 2038 would have applied to pull the property in the trust into Bob's gross estate.

Gifts of Life Insurance within 3 Years of Death

The next type of inclusion under Sec. 2035 pertains to gratuitous transfers of life insurance made by the insured within 3 years of death. Gifts of life insurance policies made within 3 years of death are includible in the gross estate whether or not a gift tax return was required to be filed. Life insurance is an unusual product because its value as a gift for gift tax purposes may easily fall below the level of the annual exclusion amount necessary to file a gift tax return or to make a taxable gift. Yet the value of the proceeds is undoubtedly much more substantial than any gift tax value. Therefore, gratuitous transfers of life insurance made within 3 years of death are included in the gross estate at the full value of the proceeds.

Gift Taxes on Gifts within 3 Years of Death

The *gross estate* of a decedent includes any gift taxes paid by either the decedent or the decedent's estate on any gift made by the decedent or the decedent's spouse within 3 years of the decedent's death. This provision prevents a reduction in the size of a decedent's gross estate because of dollars that were previously spent to satisfy the federal gift tax obligation. The amount of tax subject to this rule is the tax paid on gifts made after 1976 and within 3 years ending on the date of the donor's death.

gross-up rule

This *gross-up rule* also includes any taxes attributable to the decedent's consent to split a gift made by the decedent's spouse within 3 years of the decedent's death. The decedent's share of the gift tax on a gift split with a spouse is the amount of tax attributable to the decedent's share of the gift. Gift taxes paid by the spouse of the decedent on gifts split with the decedent are not includible in the gross estate of the decedent under this rule. The effect of this rule is to discourage deathbed gifts that would otherwise remove the amount of gift taxes paid from the donor's estate.

Example:	Suppose the decedent made a taxable gift of $1 million to an individual on which a gift tax of $345,800 was payable, and the donor died 2 years later. The $1 million is excluded from his or her gross estate. (As discussed in another chapter, it is brought back as an adjusted taxable gift in computing the estate tax liability.) However, the amount of gift tax, $345,800, is includible in the decedent's gross estate under the gross-up rule of Sec. 2035.

Exceptions to the 3-Year Rule

Note that current law provides that no transfer made within 3 years of death need be included in the gross estate if no gift tax return was required to be filed. This refers to present-interest gifts worth less than the annual gift tax exclusion. In 2002, the annual exclusion increased from $10,000 to $11,000 of gifted present-interest property per donee per year. Therefore, no gifts worth less than the amount of the annual exclusion are included in the gross estate, since no gift tax return need be filed. The value of these transfers is includible only for the limited purposes of determining qualification for certain tax benefits.

Also, since ERTA, the value of all property effectively transferred within 3 years of death is includible in the gross estate for the limited purpose of determining whether the estate qualifies for

- deferral of estate tax under Sec. 6166
- redemption of stock to pay administrative and funeral expenses and estate taxes under Sec. 303
- special-use valuation under Sec. 2032A
- determining the amount of property subject to federal estate tax liens

This exception has been added to the law to prevent a decedent from making deathbed transfers solely to facilitate qualification for the foregoing favorable tax benefits under Secs. 303 (special provision for capital gains for redemptions), 6166 (installment payment of estate taxes), or 2032A (special-use valuation). Otherwise, a decedent could easily gift nonbusiness or nonfarm property, thus increasing the relative percentage value of the closely held business or farm in the estate so that the estate may qualify for special tax treatment.

Example: Mr. Murray is gravely ill. From his deathbed, he arranges to transfer the stock in his closely held business to his son, John. Mr. Murray dies 2 weeks later. For estate tax purposes, the fair market value of the transferred stock does *not* return to the *gross* estate because the Sec. 2035 3-year rule does not apply in this situation. However, to determine whether the estate qualifies for the installment payout provisions of Sec. 6166, the value of the stock will be considered to be part of the gross estate.

The same exception to the rule applies to gratuitous transfers made to a spouse within 3 years of death. Although no gift tax return is required to be filed because of the unlimited gift tax marital deduction, the law provides that the value of gifts between spouses made within 3 years of one spouse's death is includible in the gross estate for the limited purpose of determining the qualification for the above-mentioned tax benefits.

TRANSFERS WITH RETENTION OF LIFE INTEREST (IRC SEC. 2036)

A decedent's gross estate includes the value of all property transferred gratuitously by the decedent during lifetime in which he or she retained or reserved (1) the right to use, possess, or enjoy the property or the right to receive the income from the property; or, alternatively, (2) the right, either alone or in conjunction with any other person, to designate the persons who should possess or enjoy the property or the income from the property. In order for the property to be included in a decedent's gross estate under this Code section, the rights must be retained or reserved for

- the decedent's life, or
- for a period not ascertainable without reference to the decedent's death, or
- for any period that does not, in fact, end before the decedent's death

Thus, whereas *Sec. 2035* speaks to the transfer of retained rights (held in previously transferred property) within 3 years of death, *Sec. 2036* speaks to retained rights (in previously transferred property) that the decedent held for life, or for a time period not determinable without reference to the decedent's death, or for a time period that did not end before the decedent's death.

Retention or reservation by the decedent of any of these rights or interests in the property causes the entire value of the property transferred to be includible in the decedent's gross estate under this Code section. The value, however, is reduced by the value of any income interest that (1) is not subject to the decedent's interest and power and (2) is actually being enjoyed by another person at the time of the decedent's death. Therefore, if the decedent retained income from only part of the property transferred, the amount includible in the gross estate corresponds proportionately to the value of the entire property.

Example: Sheila Gordon transfers 1,000 shares of AT&T stock to her daughter but retains the right to receive income from one-half of the shares. The value of 500 shares at the time of Sheila's death is includible in her gross estate, since she reserved the right to receive the income from 500 shares for her life.

Retention of Rights for Benefit of Transferor

A transfer with retained interests is taxable in the gross estate when the transferor retains either the possession of, enjoyment of, or the right to the income from the transferred property for the indicated periods. It is not necessary that the transferor retain all rights.

Retention of Rights for Decedent's Lifetime

Example: If Michael makes a gift to Rachael of a Renoir painting, but reserves the right to keep the painting in his home for his lifetime, the value of the painting is includible in his estate.

The retained life estate need not be legally enforceable as long as the donor has retained a substantial economic benefit.

Example: If Michael conveys his personal residence to Rachael but reserves the right (either expressly or by implication) to occupy the premises rent free during his lifetime, the value of the property at the time of his death is includible in his gross estate.

Thus, in the above example, Michael actually did transfer the residence to Rachael by deed. She was the legal titleholder. However, there was an implied understanding that he was entitled to continue living there until his death, although he could not have legally enforced that understanding. The retained interest or powers that result in the inclusion of property in a decedent's gross estate need not be expressly provided for in the instrument of transfer, but may be inferred from the conduct of the parties.

Furthermore, a decedent will be considered to have retained the right to income to the extent that the income is to be used to discharge the decedent's legal obligations, such as the support of dependent children.

Another type of situation where property may be includible in the estate of the decedent is the following example.

> *Example:*   A decedent, Katherine, is the life income beneficiary of
> a testamentary trust created by someone else. She did
> not retain a life estate, because she had never possessed
> the original trust property. However, she was allowed
> to transfer additional property to the trust under the
> terms of the trust. During her lifetime, she added
> $100,000 to the existing trust principal of $200,000. At
> her death, all trust property passed to her heirs. Assum-
> ing that no other property was contributed to the trust,
> the proportionate share of the principal she contributed
> from which she received income for life is treated as a
> retained interest and is includible in her estate when
> she dies. Thus, if the trust was required to distribute all
> income currently, and the value of the principal
> passing at Katherine's death was $300,000, $100,000
> (representing her contribution to the trust, from which
> she retained income for life) is includible in her estate.

In one Tax Court case, a decedent transferred bonds to a trust for the
benefit of her grandchildren. She did not retain any interest in the bonds.
However, she detached the interest coupons and kept them as her own at the
time of the creation of the trust. The value of the bonds was included in her
gross estate because she indirectly kept control over and retained the income
from the trust property.

reciprocal trusts

Reciprocal Trusts. Another type of plan that is legally unenforceable but
from which there is a course of conduct implying agreement to provide
income for life involves the use of *reciprocal trusts*. If irrevocable reciprocal
trusts are created (such as those created by a husband and wife for each other
as life beneficiaries), the property of each trust is includible in the life
beneficiary's estate if the arrangement leaves both grantors in approximately
the same economic circumstances in which they would have been had they
created trusts naming themselves as life income beneficiaries.

The reciprocal-trust doctrine can best be introduced by the following
example.

> *Example:*   Adam creates a trust for the benefit of Bette, and
> simultaneously Bette creates a trust of equal value for
> the benefit of Adam. The trust Adam has created has
> a corpus of $400,000 and provides that any income
> generated by the trust corpus is to be paid to Bette for

Bette's life with a remainder interest to Bette's children. The trust Bette has created also has a corpus of $400,000 and provides that any income generated by that trust corpus is to be paid to Adam for Adam's life with a remainder interest to Adam's children.

In this example, neither Adam nor Bette has technically retained a life interest. But, as a practical matter, both Adam and Bette are in the same situation, as though nothing had ever been transferred into any trust.

Because such an arrangement was perceived to be an unfair loophole in Sec. 2036, the courts have developed what has come to be referred to as the reciprocal-trust doctrine. The trusts created by Adam and Bette are disregarded for tax purposes. Each grantor is treated as having created a trust under which he or she retains a life interest for himself or herself. Under the reciprocal-trust doctrine, the trusts are "uncrossed," and the court will deem each beneficiary to be the grantor of the trust that was created for the beneficiary's benefit for purposes of estate tax liability (*U.S. v. Estate of Grace,* 395 U.S. 316). This approach results in inclusion of the corpus in the gross estate. Therefore, in the example above, the $400,000 corpus in the trust created by Adam will be included in Bette's gross estate, and the $400,000 corpus in the trust created by Bette will be included in Adam's gross estate.

There are, however, some planning methods that may prevent IRS challenges based on the reciprocal trust doctrine in some instances: (1) varying the terms of the two trusts so that they are not substantially identical, (2) funding each trust with different assets, and (3) creating the trusts at different times, possibly even a few years apart.

Right to Vote Stock in a Closely Held Corporation. Another danger for the unwary planner may occur when an individual transfers stock of a controlled corporation but retains the right to vote the shares (either directly or indirectly). This retention of voting rights is considered a retention of the enjoyment of the transferred property. The value of the transferred stock will be included in the gross estate of the decedent. A *controlled corporation* is one in which the decedent directly or indirectly owned or had the right, either alone or with any other person, to vote stock having at least 20 percent of the total combined voting power of all classes of stock. This rule pertains to persons who have irrevocably transferred stock for less than full consideration after June 22, 1976. If the stock is not in a controlled corporation, it is not includible in the decedent's gross estate although the decedent did hold the power to vote the transferred shares.

In one case, an individual transferred 19 shares of a closely held corporation's stock to a trust and gave the trustee sole authority to vote the shares. However, it was agreed at the time of the transfer that the trustee

controlled corporation

would consult with the grantor with respect to voting and that the trustee would vote only with the grantor's consent. It was held that the grantor-decedent indirectly retained the right to vote the transferred shares, although they were transferred to an irrevocable trust. The full value of the shares at the time of death was includible in the grantor's gross estate.

Retention or Reservation by Decedent of Property for a Period Not Determinable without Reference to Decedent's Death

This test involves a situation where the retained interest is tied to the time of the decedent's death. If the facts and circumstances are such that the lifetime test discussed above is not met, but this second test is met, Sec. 2036 will still apply.

This concept can be illustrated by the example that follows.

Example: Mr. Harris transfers property to a trust with the provision that he receive quarterly installments of income. However, there is a condition that no part of the income accruing during the quarter in which he dies is to be paid to him or to his estate. Because the trust is set up in this way—that the transferor is not to receive income up until the time of his death—the lifetime test is not met. Clearly, this appears to be an attempt to thwart the rule regarding retained interests. Because the last payment cannot be ascertained without reference to his death, however, the value of the trust property is includible in his estate.

Retention or Reservation by Decedent for a Period That Does Not, in Fact, End before Decedent's Death

This third test makes Sec. 2036 applicable when the transferor has retained an interest for a period of time not phrased in terms of his or her life or death, but only in the event that this time period does not end prior to the death of the transferor. Because of this third test, there does not have to be any reference to the decedent's life or death in the transfer agreement.

This concept can be illustrated by the following example.

Example: Samantha Connors transfers Blackacre to her son, Henry, reserving the right to the income from the property for 10 years. Samantha dies in the eighth year. Based on these facts, the entire value of Blackacre is includible in Samantha's estate because she reserved an income interest not for her lifetime but for a period that did not, in fact, end before her death.

Right to Designate Who Shall Possess or Enjoy the Property

Even though a decedent did not retain the right to enjoy or possess the property, Sec. 2036 requires that the gross estate also include the value of all property over which the decedent retained the right to designate (alone or with any other person) who may enjoy or possess the property as well as the right to vary beneficial interests. Thus, if a grantor creates an irrevocable trust for beneficiaries other than himself or herself but is named as trustee and has the power to accumulate or distribute income, the value of the trust property is included in the grantor's gross estate. The reason for inclusion is that the grantor had power to withhold income from the beneficiaries, thereby denying them possession and enjoyment of that income. This power to accumulate income is a retention of the right to designate who may enjoy the property. Retention of certain administrative and management powers over the trust also may cause the value of the trust property to be included in the grantor-trustee's estate.

In another case, the grantor created an irrevocable trust giving the trustee power to vary beneficial interests. She reserved in herself the right to fill vacancies for the position of trustee. There was no prohibition against the grantor appointing herself as trustee. The court held that in reserving this right the grantor retained an interest sufficient to cause the trust property to be includible in her estate.

As a general rule, property placed in an irrevocable trust is not included in the grantor's gross estate if the grantor merely retained the right to appoint a successor-trustee other than himself or herself upon resignation of the original trustee. In *Estate of Wall*[1] the Tax Court reasoned that because independent commercial trustees are under a fiduciary obligation to beneficiaries, the retained power to substitute an independent corporate trustee was not sufficient to cause inclusion of the trust property in the decedent's gross estate under Secs. 2036 or 2038. In 1995, as a result of the *Wall* case and other cases, the IRS issued Revenue Ruling 95–58,[2] which provides that a grantor's power to remove a trustee and appoint a corporate trustee or a person other than the grantor who is not related or subordinate to the grantor is not, in and of itself, equivalent to the grantor's retention of control over the trust. In essence, Rev. Rul. 95–58 means that a grantor's mere right to remove and replace a trustee with an independent trustee will not cause inclusion of the trust in the grantor's gross estate under Secs. 2036 or 2038.

Also, the Internal Revenue Service has attempted to include trust property in situations where the grantor-trustee retained only certain administrative and managerial powers over the trust but not the power to accumulate or distribute income. Most courts have held that the existence of these "boilerplate" powers does not give a decedent the right to designate persons who shall possess or enjoy the transferred property such that it is includible in the gross estate.

A frequently used estate planning device involves the irrevocable assignment of life insurance policies to a trust by the insured during the insured's lifetime. Proceeds of life insurance are not taxable in the insured's gross estate if the insured was totally divested of all incidents of ownership in the policy more than 3 years prior to death and the proceeds are not payable to the estate. Under current law, the result is not changed even if the insured continues to pay premiums on the policy assigned. However, suppose rather than continuing to pay the premiums directly, the insured funds the trust with income-producing property. Any income is to be applied first to the payment of premiums. The regulations under this section of the Internal Revenue Code provide that, if the income from property transferred by the decedent is required to be applied by the transferee for the decedent's pecuniary benefit, the decedent is considered to have retained the right to income or enjoyment of the transferred property. Whether payment of premiums by the trustee with trust income is a *pecuniary benefit* that requires the value of the property to be included in the decedent's gross estate depends on the irrevocability of the assignment.

If policies of life insurance are irrevocably assigned and the decedent is divested of all incidents of ownership in favor of the trust, the value of property transferred by the decedent to fund that trust should not be included in the decedent's estate merely because the income from the property was used to pay premiums. It is the trust and the beneficiaries who have benefited from the premium payments, not the decedent. Alternatively, if the decedent retained any incidents of ownership in the policies, the payment of premiums from the trust income can certainly be regarded as having been for the decedent's pecuniary or economic benefit. Therefore the value of the policies is includible in the decedent's gross estate.

If an individual transfers property to an insurance company in exchange for a commercial annuity, this section has no application upon the transferor's death. The transfer is free and clear. It was made for full and adequate consideration in money or money's worth, and the insurance company is obligated to pay the annuity without regard to the income or principal of the property transferred. Whether this section has application in the case of a private annuity depends upon the transfer and the circumstances surrounding it. It has been held that a transfer of property by the decedent to an individual in return for a promise to make periodic payments to the decedent during lifetime is not an includible transfer, provided that the transferee is under an absolute obligation to make the payments and the amount of the payments is not determined by reference to the actual or estimated income from the property transferred.

Example:	Alex transfers property to Bruce in consideration of Bruce's promise to support Alex for the rest of Alex's life. If Bruce is free to use the property transferred in any manner that Bruce wishes and if Bruce discharges the obligation to support Alex irrespective of the amount of income from the transferred property, there is no inclusion. An opposite result was reached when a decedent transferred property to her children in return for their promise to pay her a stipulated amount of income for her life. At the time of the transfer, the estimated annual income from the property was equal to the amount of the annuity, but the income averaged less than the amount of the annuity after the transfer. Her children made no attempt to make up the difference. The Tax Court held that the value of the property was includible in the decedent's gross estate.

Amount Includible in Gross Estate

Under Sec. 2036 pertaining to retained interests for life, the amount that is includible in the decedent's gross estate is not the value of the interest retained or controlled by him or her but the value of the entire property transferred, valued on the date of death. The lifetime transfer is treated as if the decedent had retained the entire property and not just the right to income or beneficial enjoyment for life. It should be remembered that if retained rights are subject to a definite external standard, the property subject to the rights is not includible.

TRANSFERS THAT TAKE EFFECT AT DEATH (IRC SEC. 2037)

Sec. 2037 is the includibility section of the Code that pulls transfers of reversionary interests taking effect at death into the decedent's gross estate. The decedent's gross estate includes the value of property transferred by him or her for less than full and adequate consideration if the possession or enjoyment of the transferred property can be obtained only by the beneficiary surviving the decedent *and* the decedent retained a reversionary interest (an ability to have the property returned to him or her) that was worth more than 5 percent of the value of the transferred property immediately before death.

Under the first condition, any beneficiary must survive the decedent in order to obtain possession or enjoyment of the property through ownership. In other words, the possession or enjoyment of the transferred property is conditional on surviving the decedent-transferee.

Example 1: Sam Smith transfers property irrevocably in trust for the benefit of his wife, Barbara. Barbara is to receive income for life. The remainder is to go back to Sam, if living, at her death. If he is not living, the property goes to their children, Michael and Rachael. If Sam predeceases his wife, the interest to Michael and Rachael is includible in Sam's gross estate, because it is contingent upon Sam's death. In this case, Sam possesses a reversionary interest (assumed to be worth more than 5 percent of the value of the property transferred). The entire value of the transferred property subject to the reversion, less the actuarial value of the outstanding income interest possessed by his wife, is included.

Example 2: A decedent, Harvey, transferred property to a trust that was to pay income to his daughter for life. At his daughter's death, the trust terminates and the property passes to his daughter's surviving child or, if there is no surviving child, to the decedent or to his estate. Each beneficiary can possess or enjoy the property without surviving the decedent. Therefore, the property is not includible in the decedent's gross estate as a transfer taking effect at death no matter how great the value of the decedent's reversionary interest.

A reversionary interest includes the possibility that the transferred property either may return to the decedent or the decedent's estate or may be subject to the decedent's power of disposition. It does not apply to the reservation of a life estate or to the possibility of receiving income solely from the transferred property only after the death of another individual. The term *reversionary interest* also does not include the possibility that the decedent may receive an interest in the transferred property by inheriting the property through the estate of another person.

Example: A transferor is not considered to retain a reversion in an outright gift to a spouse merely because of the possibility that the spouse will give the property back to the transferor or that the transferor will inherit the property back from his or her spouse by will. If some alternate event (such as the expiration of a term of years or the exercise of a power of appointment) triggers a transferee's possession or enjoyment of the property, such property generally is not included in the decedent's gross estate under this section. This is because the transferee could possibly obtain possession and enjoyment of the property while the transferor was still alive.

Caution should be exercised in the creation of irrevocable transfers to make certain that no interest or power with respect to income is retained. Although it appears that no reversionary interests exist, there may be an oversight if the grantor unintentionally neglects to provide for all contingencies. Under local law, the result might be that the property reverts to the decedent or the decedent's estate if no designated beneficiary survives him or her (implied reversion). Included under this provision is the common situation of using a short-term trust to provide temporarily for the support of another individual.

Example:	A father creates an irrevocable trust for the benefit of his son. The son receives income for 11 years, after which time the trust corpus is returned to the father, if living, otherwise to the father's issue. Should the father die before the expiration of the trust term, his reversionary interest in the property calculated actuarially is includible in his estate.

The reversionary-interest requirement is met not only if the decedent or the decedent's estate might have reacquired the transferred property but also if there exists, immediately prior to death, a possibility that the property would be disposed of by the decedent.

Example:	Anne transfers property in trust for Barbara during Anne's lifetime, with remainder to Carol, but if Carol dies without issue, Carol's estate is limited to a life interest and the property passes to the individual(s) designated to inherit under Anne's will. Carol's interest is contingent upon surviving Anne. The property is includible in Anne's estate, although it might not become known until well after Anne's death whether said power of disposition actually comes into effect.

For the value of the property subject to the reversionary interest to be includible in the decedent's estate, it must be worth more than 5 percent of the value of the property transferred as of the moment preceding the decedent's death. Furthermore, for the property to be included in the decedent's gross estate under this section, all of the conditions that are described in this section must be met.

REVOCABLE TRANSFERS (IRC SEC. 2038)

Sec. 2038 presents one more method to draw transferred property back into the gross estate. If property transferred gratuitously by the decedent during lifetime is subject to any change through the exercise of a power to alter, amend, revoke, or terminate, or to affect beneficial enjoyment either by the decedent alone or in conjunction with any other person, and these powers exist at the decedent's death, the value of the property subject to the power is includible in the decedent's gross estate under Sec. 2038. This is true if the power is exercisable by the decedent alone or in conjunction with anyone (including beneficiaries who would have an adverse interest). The language is all-encompassing and causes taxation in the decedent's estate. Thus, if a grantor-trustee has the power to distribute principal to an income beneficiary prior to the date the beneficiary is entitled to receive principal, the value of the property subject to the power is includible in the grantor-trustee's estate. It does not matter that the prohibited power is not exercisable in favor of the decedent or is exercisable only in conjunction with persons having adverse interests; nor does it matter in what capacity the power is exercisable. Neither is it essential that the decedent did not retain the power but acquired it from another source (IRC Sec. 2038(a)(1)). The critical factor is that the decedent possessed the power at the time of death.

Examples of the types of powers addressed by this section of the Internal Revenue Code include the power (1) to change the beneficiaries, (2) to hasten the time that the beneficiary can receive the property, or (3) to increase or decrease the amount of property allocated to any beneficiary.

As stated before, the decedent—either alone or with others—must have possessed one of the prohibited powers at the time of death to cause inclusion under this section. If, however, there was a condition beyond the decedent's control that limited the use of the power and that condition did not occur before the decedent died, the property is not included in the decedent's gross estate as a transfer subject to the power to revoke.

It makes no difference in what capacity the decedent could have exercised this power. For example, if the decedent transferred property to a trust naming himself or herself trustee and then gave the trustee the power to revoke the trust, the property is included in the decedent's estate. Similarly, if the decedent appointed another person as trustee but retained the power to appoint a successor-trustee upon the resignation of the original trustee (including naming himself or herself as trustee), the property is also included in the estate. Reservation of a power to remove a trustee at will and appoint another trustee causes a similar result. However, if any rights to revoke, alter, amend, or terminate the trust or change trustees are given to another person and the decedent reserves no rights whatsoever with regard to these powers, the value of the property in the trust is not included in the decedent's gross estate.

While the property is included in the decedent's gross estate whether he or she had the power to change or terminate the property interest by himself or herself or only together with others, regardless of their capacity or interests, there are two exceptions to this rule: (1) if the decedent's power can be exercised only with the consent of *all* parties having an interest (either vested or contingent) in the transferred property and (2) if this power adds nothing to the rights of the parties under local law, the property is not included in the decedent's estate. Note that this exception applies only if all parties must consent to the exercise of a power to change or end the property interest.

The following powers have been determined to be powers to alter, amend, revoke, or terminate that cause the property subject to the power to be included in the decedent's gross estate. Note that only the part of the transferred property that is subject to the decedent's power as described above is included in the gross estate under this provision of the Code. Powers to alter, amend, revoke, or terminate include (1) power to revoke or terminate a trust to which the property is transferred, whether this power results in a return of corpus to the grantor or acceleration of enjoyment by the beneficiaries; (2) power to control and manage the trust property, except where this power is limited to administrative or mechanical details only, such as designation of funds as income or principal, investment policy, issuance of voting proxies, or other matters that do not alter the rights or interests of the beneficiaries; (3) power to change beneficiaries or to vary the amounts distributable; (4) power to appoint by will or change shares of beneficiaries by will; (5) power to revoke, which exists by virtue of state law; (6) power to invade a trust created by another for whose benefit the decedent created a similar trust (reciprocal trusts); and (7) power to replace without cause the trustee with another.

Sec. 2038 Inclusion Powers

- Change beneficiaries for income or corpus.
- Increase/decrease a beneficiary's share.
- Terminate the trust.
- Revoke the trust.
- Manage/control trust property.
- Replace the trustee with self/spouse.

The following powers have been determined *not* to constitute powers sufficient to cause taxation in the decedent's estate under Sec. 2038:

- power in others than the grantor to revoke the transfer or return part of it to the grantor (but such transfers may be taxed under another section discussed earlier as transfers intended to take effect at death)
- certain powers contingent on the happening of a particular event
- powers as to mechanics or details only, such as powers to direct issuance of voting proxies, to help determine investment policies, and to direct investment and reinvestment of funds
- power to add to corpus
- power over trusts created by others with funds not derived from the decedent and not supported by similar trusts created by others. An example of this last power is the power in the decedent as trustee over another's trust in which the decedent has no beneficial interest.

Sec. 2038 Noninclusion Powers

- Add to trust corpus.
- Help determine investment policies.
- Direct the issuance of voting proxies.

An example of retained powers under Sec. 2038 is shown in the following situation.

Example: The decedent, Mr. Jones, creates a trust that provides income to Mark for life with the remainder going to Sandra or her heirs. The decedent retains the power to invade principal for the benefit of Sandra during Mark's lifetime. The entire property is included in the decedent's gross estate under this Code provision. The decedent, by exercise of his power to invade, can affect the time when Sandra receives enjoyment of the property as well as the amount of income Mark receives. If, however, the decedent retains only the power to accumulate income and add it to corpus, the only interest the decedent can affect is that of Mark, the income beneficiary. Therefore, it is only the value of Mark's income interest that will be included in the decedent's gross estate under this provision.

Remember that this provision sometimes overlaps and can operate in conjunction with the provision discussed earlier where the decedent retains powers to possess, enjoy, or receive income for life, or designate who is to receive or possess the property. That section (Sec. 2036) brings the entire value of the property on the date of death into the decedent's gross estate. Sec. 2038 includes only the value of the interest in property subject to the powers to alter, amend, revoke, or terminate.

Example:	Ed Smith transfers property to a trust for the benefit of his 20-year-old son, Sandy. The trust provides that Sandy is entitled to all the income from the trust until he is 40, when he is to receive the corpus. Ed retains the right to terminate the trust at any time, with corpus to be distributed to Sandy upon termination. Ed dies when Sandy is 30. The amount includible in Ed's estate under Sec. 2038 is the amount of the trust corpus less the value of the income interest (over which Ed had no power). The value of the income interest is determined actuarially at the time of Ed's death.

ascertainable standard

There are cases where transferred property otherwise subject to Sec. 2038 escapes gross estate inclusion. Such a situation involves the presence of an *ascertainable standard*. In other words, although the decedent possessed prohibited powers, the property interest subject to the powers is not included in the decedent's gross estate if the power is subject to an ascertainable standard. This refers to an external standard imposed upon the decedent limiting the exercise of the power strictly to provide for the support, maintenance, health, or education of a beneficiary.

Example:	A decedent transfers property in trust to provide income to Ken for life, remainder to Don or his heirs. The decedent retains the power to invade corpus for Ken's benefit but only for his health, maintenance, support, or education. Because the decedent's power to invade corpus is subject to a standard that may be reviewed by the court, the situation is as if the decedent really holds no power at all. Note that if the decedent's power was not governed by an *ascertainable standard*, the fact that he or she could exercise this power only with the consent of the beneficiary whose interest would be adversely affected would not prevent the value of the property subject to this power from being included in the decedent's gross estate.

It is obvious from the discussion above that there are many potential problems to consider in planning gratuitous lifetime transfers of property in order to avoid inclusion of the property in a decedent's gross estate. Careful drafting of trust instruments can allow the decedent to retain some degree of control without triggering estate taxation under one of the Code sections. If the decedent wishes to retain some powers over property transferred during lifetime, he or she would be wise to consult a planner experienced in these areas. With good planning, the decedent can accomplish personal objectives, yet avoid inclusion of transferred property interests in the gross estate.

Note to Students: See Appendix A for a summary of the advantages and disadvantages of different trusts covered in this chapter and throughout the text.

CHAPTER REVIEW

Answers to the review questions and the self-test questions start on page 717.

Key Terms

federal estate tax	curtesy
gross estate	gross-up rule
income in respect of a decedent (IRD)	reciprocal trusts
	controlled corporation
incidents of ownership	ascertainable standard
dower	

Review Questions

12-1. Describe the theories underlying the federal estate tax.

12-2. Who is primarily responsible for payment of the estate tax?

12-3. Mr. Jones transferred $60,000 to a trust that was to last for 11 years. During that time, all income was to be distributed to his two children who were beneficiaries of the trust. At the end of 11 years, the trust was to terminate and all principal was to be returned to Mr. Jones or his estate. The trust was irrevocable. Mr. Jones died 7 years after the trust was created. What, if anything, will be includible in his gross estate?

12-4. Explain whether the following items owned by an individual at the time of his death will be included in his gross estate for federal estate tax purposes and why. At what value, if any, will the property be included?
  a. real estate in Atlantic City valued at $200,000 where the decedent had a right to live rent free for life. This property had been given to the

decedent by his father for his life, after which it was to pass to his son under the terms of his father's will.

b. $160,000 par value of municipal bonds due the year after the decedent's death

c.   10 acres of undeveloped land in Arizona owned by the decedent and his two brothers as tenants in common

d.   IBM stock valued at $30,000 owned by the decedent individually

e.   proceeds of a wrongful death claim brought by the decedent's personal representative after his death in an automobile accident

f. $5,000 in dividends declared and of record but not paid at the time of the decedent's death

g.   a claim for damages arising from a car accident in which the decedent was involved prior to his death

h.   commission income that the decedent had earned for the month prior to his death but that had not yet been paid to him

i.   a Matisse painting hanging in his home

j.   property in a trust established by his brother for the benefit of his brother's son of which the decedent was the sole trustee. The property in the trust is valued at $50,000.

12-5.   Jennifer Johnson, a businesswoman, died 2 years ago with uncollected accounts receivable of $94,000. She was also holder of a note from her brother for $25,000 due last year, and she owned rental real estate. The present tenants had executed a 5-year lease agreeing to pay $7,000 in rent annually for the entire lease term.

a.   Explain which of these items will be includible in her gross estate and at what values.

b.   To whom will the income be taxable when received?

12-6.   Richard Ricardo, CLU®, a life insurance agent, had $128,000 of renewal commissions that were to be payable to him over the next 3 years. After his death, they were payable by contract to his surviving spouse. He died last year.

a.   Explain whether the rights to this future income are includible in Ricardo's estate.

b.   What is the rationale behind the allowance of an income tax deduction to the recipient on future income items that have been subject to tax in a decedent's estate?

12-7.   Sam Mason, the decedent, owned a 600-acre farm outright at his death. Sam and his wife, Sarah, were domiciled in a state that retains dower rights. Explain what effect Sarah's dower rights will have on

a.   the inclusion of the farm in Sam's gross estate for estate tax purposes

b.   the value of the farm in Sam's gross estate for estate tax purposes

12-8. Sandra Taylor dies this year and is survived by her husband and two minor daughters. Explain which of the following items will be included in her gross estate and at what values:

   a. a $100,000 certificate of deposit that Sandra gave to her husband last year

   b. a life insurance policy on her life for $200,000 that she transferred to an irrevocable trust for the benefit of her children last year

   c. a $50,000 amount that she placed in a custodial account for each of her daughters 10 years ago. She is the custodian of the account.

   d. a condominium in Florida that she transferred to her brother 10 years ago but which she retained the right to use for her life

   e. an inter vivos irrevocable trust established by Sandra in which she retained only the power to allocate the income distributions between her two daughters who are the named beneficiaries of both income and corpus

   f. an inter vivos irrevocable trust established by Sandra 10 years ago. Her husband is to receive income for his life after which the corpus would be returned to Sandra if living, and, if not, it would pass to her two daughters.

   g. a revocable trust containing $150,000 of securities that Sandra established for the benefit of her mother. Sandra was to receive income for life and, at her death, the property was to be held in further trust for her mother for life. At her mother's death, the corpus was to be distributed to Sandra's two daughters.

12-9. Bobby Block transferred a life insurance policy to a trust 15 years ago. It was a paid-up policy with a gift tax value of $1 million, and he paid a gift tax in the amount of $345,800. He died this year. How much, if anything, is includible in his gross estate?

12-10. John Jamison transferred $200,000 of tax-exempt bonds to a trust for the benefit of his grandchildren 2 years ago. He died this year. Assume the gift tax paid was approximately $60,000.

   a. What amount, if any, is includible in his gross estate and why?

   b. Would your answer to 12-10a. be different if the transfer were made to his spouse?

12-11. Assume Arthur gave property worth $50,000 to his nephew 10 years ago. He had exhausted his applicable credit amount. He received an annual exclusion amount gift of $10,000 (the exclusion amount 10 years ago) and paid a gift tax of $18,000 on the transferred property. At the time of Arthur's death last year the property had appreciated in value to $130,000. What amount, if any, is includible in Arthur's gross estate?

12-12. A donor gratuitously transferred property worth $250,000 12 years ago. However, the donor retained the right to income from the property for life. Upon the donor's death this year, the property was worth $475,000. What amount, if any, is includible in the decedent's gross estate?

12-13.   Mr. Johnson established a trust for the benefit of his minor children. The trust income was $10,000 annually, $2,500 of which was used to pay for the support and maintenance of the children. The remainder of the income was accumulated in the trust for distribution to the children at age 21. Mr. Johnson died before either of his children reached maturity. What amount, if any, will be includible in his estate?

12-14.   Mitchell Mellen gave his niece, Margaret, his townhouse in New York City. By unwritten understanding, he continued to live in the house until his death 5 years later. Is any of the property includible in his gross estate? If so, under what theory is it includible?

12-15.   Karen created a trust naming her brother, Michael, as life income beneficiary. At his death, the corpus was to go to Michael's children. At the same time, Michael created a trust and named his sister, Karen, as life income beneficiary with the corpus to go to Karen's children at her death. Each trust was funded with $75,000. All income was to be distributed at least annually. Karen died 6 years later. How would these trusts be treated for federal estate tax purposes?

12-16.   Watson Howard gratuitously transferred all of his stock in Safe Aircraft to his daughter. He had owned 35 percent of the total voting stock of Safe Aircraft. Mr. Howard retained no right to income from the trust; however, he kept the right to vote the stock he had transferred. One year before his death, he transferred his voting rights to his daughter. What, if anything, is includible in his gross estate?

12-17.   Alan Anderson owned a ranch in Colorado that he placed in trust for the benefit of his adult daughters, Carla and Toni. Under the terms of the trust, he retained the right to determine each year what percentage of the income would go to each daughter and what amount would be retained in the trust. He could make this decision only in conjunction with the Turner Trust Company, an independent trustee. He died 4 years after the property was placed in trust. At the time of his death, the ranch was worth $700,000. At the time of the transfer, the ranch was valued at $450,000. What amount, if any, is includible in his gross estate?

12-18.   Richard Allison created a trust that provided income to his son, Roger, for life. At Roger's death, the trust principal is to be distributed to Roger's children. However, Mr. Allison retained the right to distribute principal to his grandchildren during Roger's lifetime. Two years before his death, he distributed one-half of the principal to his grandchildren. What amount, if any, is includible in Mr. Allison's estate?

Self-Test Questions

T   F   12-1.   Because so few estates are affected by the federal estate tax after application of the applicable credit amount, estate planning is no longer necessary.

T   F   12-2.   All taxable gifts made by a decedent during his or her lifetime are brought back into the estate tax computation as adjusted taxable gifts.

T   F   12-3.   The federal estate tax is a tax on the right to transfer property at death and is imposed on the estate itself.

T   F   12-4.   If there are no assets left in the estate to pay estate taxes, taxes will be borne by nonprobate property passing to beneficiaries in proportion to the amount that the beneficiary receives.

T   F   12-5.   The federal estate tax is applied uniformly to citizens, residents, nonresidents, and noncitizens of the United States for property they own regardless of location.

T   F   12-6.   Property located outside the United States is exempt from federal estate taxation.

T   F   12-7.   The United States and some foreign nations have formed estate and gift tax treaties that may have an effect on resident aliens and foreign situs property of U.S. citizens.

T   F   12-8.   All property owned outright by the decedent at death is included in the decedent's gross estate.

T   F   12-9.   If the decedent owns property subject to a mortgage for which that individual is personally liable, the full value of the property will be includible in the decedent's gross estate.

T   F   12-10.   Income that the decedent was entitled to receive but had not yet received at the date of death is includible in his or her gross estate as income in respect of a decedent.

T   F   12-11.   If income in respect of a decedent is includible in the gross estate, the estate tax attributable to that income item is deductible by the recipient of the income on the recipient's income tax return.

T   F   12-12.   Gifts of life insurance made within 3 years of death are includible in the decedent's gross estate only if the value of the gift at the time of the transfer exceeded the amount of the annual gift tax exclusion.

T   F   12-13.   Any property that a decedent may have owned but transferred gratuitously after 1976 is not brought back into the gross estate.

T   F   12-14.   A gift tax paid on completed lifetime transfers is excluded from the gross estate.

T   F   12-15.   Completed transfers of property within 3 years of death are included in the gross estate for the limited purpose of determining whether the estate qualifies for deferral of estate tax under Sec. 6166 and for certain other tax purposes.

T   F   12-16.   The value of gifts made to spouses within 3 years of death is included in the gross estate for the purposes of determining eligibility for Sec. 303 and Sec. 6166.

T   F   12-17.   Any property that was given away during lifetime but in which the donor retained an interest for life will cause inclusion in the donor's gross estate.

T   F   12-18.   A decedent's gross estate does not include the value of a residence transferred by him to one of his children 4 years before his death, even though he continues to reside there informally without paying rent until his death.

T   F   12-19.   If the decedent transferred stock in a corporation in which he or she remained a more than 20 percent owner either directly or indirectly during lifetime but retained the right to vote the stock and did not give up these rights within the 3 years preceding death, the fair market value of the stock on the date of the decedent's death is includible in his or her gross estate.

T   F   12-20.   If the grantor retains the right to alter beneficial enjoyment only with the consent of an independent trustee, the value of the property transferred to a trust will not be includible in the grantor's gross estate.

T   F   12-21.   A decedent's gross estate includes all property transferred during his or her lifetime in which the decedent held any reversionary interest at the time of his or her death.

T   F   12-22.   Property transferred by a decedent to an inter vivos irrevocable trust is included in his or her gross estate if the decedent retained the power to accelerate distribution of principal to income beneficiaries.

NOTES

1. *Estate of Helen S. Wall,* 101 T.C. 300 (1993).
2. Revenue Ruling 95-58, IRB 1995–36, 16 (Sept. 5, 1995).

Federal Estate Taxation: The Gross Estate—Part II

Learning Objectives

An understanding of the material in this chapter should enable the student to

---

13-1.   Explain the general rule and exceptions for estate taxation of annuities.

13-2.   Explain the rules for inclusion of jointly held property in the gross estate.

13-3.   Explain the estate taxation of general powers of appointment, and differentiate between general powers and special powers with respect to inclusion in the gross estate.

13-4.   Explain the general rules concerning the inclusion of life insurance in the gross estate, and describe some ways in which life insurance can avoid estate taxation.

Chapter Outline

ANNUITIES (IRC SEC. 2039)

Sec. 2039 of the Internal Revenue Code concerns the federal estate taxation of annuity products. With certain limited exceptions, a decedent's gross estate includes the present value of an annuity or other payment receivable by any beneficiary as a result of having survived the decedent. Included under this section are any agreements, commercial or private annuities, and employee retirement annuities (including all proceeds from qualified plans generally for decedents dying after December 31, 1984). Annuities or payments under certain contracts included in the gross estate are those that were payable to or receivable by the decedent

- for his or her lifetime
- for a period that did not, in fact, end before the decedent's death
- for a period that cannot be ascertained without referring to the decedent's death

A decedent's right to a payment is sufficient. The decedent need not have actually received or be receiving payments by the date of death, nor must the time at which payments would commence have passed by the date of death. However, those annuities that end at the decedent's death and do not provide payments to any beneficiary afterward are not subject to inclusion in the decedent's gross estate. Thus, contracts under an annuity for life that provide payments to the decedent and end at his or her death are not included in the gross estate, because there is nothing that the decedent can transfer or pass on to another at death. In other words, nothing is included in the decedent's gross estate because the decedent possessed no transferable interest.

Definition of Terms

The provisions of Sec. 2039 concerning estate tax inclusion of annuities are complicated. It may be helpful to define some of the terms so the student understands the types of arrangements and rights to payment that may or may not cause their inclusion in the decedent's gross estate. As used under this Internal Revenue Code section, the term *annuity or other payment* refers to one or more payments extending over any period of time. That means there may be several payments or a single lump-sum payment to be made to a beneficiary after the decedent's death. There is no requirement that these payments be equal, unconditional, or periodic. Stated differently, the amount as well as the timing of each payment may vary.

The meaning of the term *contract or agreement* is very broad and includes any arrangement, agreement, understanding, plan, or combination of them arising from the decedent's employment. An includible annuity may be a bona fide contract between the employer and the employee or it may be a plan for salary continuation, such as one that was established unilaterally by the decedent's employer. It may even include an unwritten arrangement for payments to an employee's beneficiary pursuant to a practice consistently followed by the employer.

The statutory term *was payable to the decedent* refers to annuity payments or other payments that the decedent was actually receiving at the time of death, regardless of whether he or she had an enforceable right to have these payments continued. Furthermore, an annuity is considered *receivable* by the decedent although it may be forfeitable on the occurrence or nonoccurrence of a particular event, such as the recipient's remarriage. However, if the annuity agreement contains a provision that certain occurrences or nonoccurrences make it forfeitable, the possibility of forfeitability has an effect on the value of the annuity in the gross estate. In addition, an annuity is included in the gross estate if the decedent, immediately before death, had a right to receive payments in the future. In other words, as long as the decedent had an enforceable right to receive payments at some time, these payments need not have been immediately payable before death. If the decedent was in compliance with the obligations under the contract or agreement up to the time of his or her death, the decedent is considered to have had an enforceable right to receive future payments under a contract.

annuity

As stated earlier, the term *annuity* includes periodic payments for a specific time. There may be a single agreement or a combination of several agreements between the parties. Examples of contracts or agreements for payments that constitute annuities or other payments included in the gross estate are the following:

- a contract under which the decedent was receiving or was entitled to receive an annuity or other payment immediately before death and for the duration of his or her life. The contract provides that payments are to continue after the decedent's death to a beneficiary named by him or her if the beneficiary survives the decedent.
- a contract under which the decedent was receiving payments before death together with another person for their joint lives. Payments would continue to the survivor after the death of either individual. This type of contract is called a *joint and survivor annuity*.

joint and survivor annuity

- a contract or agreement between the decedent and his or her employer under which the decedent was receiving or entitled to receive an annuity or other stipulated payment after retirement for the duration of the decedent's life with payments to a designated beneficiary upon the decedent's death, if such beneficiaries survive the decedent. It makes no difference whether the payments to the survivor were fixed by contract, or subject to any options or elections exercisable by the decedent.
- a contract or agreement between the decedent and the decedent's employer that provided for an annuity or other payments to a designated surviving beneficiary, if the decedent died prior to retirement or before the expiration of a specific time
- a contract or agreement under which the decedent, immediately before death, was receiving or entitled to receive an annuity or other payment for a specified time period, with payments to continue to a named beneficiary if the decedent died prior to the expiration of the specified time period

As stated earlier, the value of an annuity contract is includible in the decedent's gross estate although payments are not to begin until after the death of the purchaser and primary annuitant (generally the same individual). A key is whether the decedent had an enforceable right to receive payments from a plan or combination of plans during lifetime had he or she lived. For example, a right to receive disability income in the event of disability prior to retirement causes a salary continuation plan to the employee's surviving spouse to be includible in the employee's gross estate if the employee dies before retirement. This is true even if the employee was never disabled. In other words, the value of a surviving beneficiary's annuity or other payment is includible in the gross estate only if the contract or agreement (or combination) under which payments are to be made to the survivor also gave the decedent a payment or a right to payment. It is the *right* to the payment that controls inclusion in the gross estate, not whether the decedent actually received any amount under the annuity before death. Also, any combination of arrangements or plans arising out of the decedent's employment may be includible under this section. Such contributions are treated as if they were made by the decedent. Payments are includible whether they are paid to the estate or to a named beneficiary.

Amount Includible

The amount includible in the decedent's gross estate is the value of the payments to the surviving beneficiary that represents the proportionate part of the purchase price of the contract contributed by the decedent. This includes contributions made by the decedent's employer, if they were made by reason of the decedent's employment. However, to the extent that the surviving beneficiary or anyone other than the decedent furnished part of the original purchase price, that portion is not included in the decedent's gross estate.

Example:	Tom Taylor purchased a joint and survivor annuity for himself and his sister, Ann. If he paid the total purchase price, the entire value of Ann's survivorship interest will be included in Tom's gross estate if he predeceases Ann. On the other hand, if Tom contributed 60 percent of the money to purchase the annuity and 40 percent of the contribution came from Ann's separate funds, only 60 percent of the value of the survivor's income interest would be includible in Tom's estate. It should be noted that if the decedent's employer or former employer contributed to the purchase price of the contract, the employer's contribution shall be treated as if it was made by the decedent. Therefore, if Tom's employer purchased an annuity for him as a key employee and contributed the entire purchase price, the employer's contribution will be treated as if it was made by Tom, the decedent. Thus, any survivorship interest will be fully includible in Tom's estate.

Specifically *excluded* from taxation under this Code section are all amounts paid "as insurance under policies on the life of the decedent." This is not to say that proceeds of life insurance will not be included in the decedent's gross estate. Proceeds of life insurance on the decedent's life are includible in the gross estate under another Code section (IRC Sec. 2042) if certain conditions exist. If a single contract contains or has contained both life insurance and annuity elements, the amount that is includible, if any, under this section is based on whether or not there was any insurance element in the contract at the moment of death.

Only those contracts that contain no life insurance elements are includible under Sec. 2039. The amount of insurance a contract contains, if any, may be determined by the relationship of the policy's reserve value to the value of the death benefit at the time of the decedent's death. If the decedent dies before the reserve value equals the death benefit, an insurance element exists under the contract and the contract is considered to be an insurance policy for estate tax purposes. Alternatively, if the decedent dies after the reserve value equals the death benefit, no insurance element exists any longer under the contract, and the agreement is considered to be solely a contract for an annuity. Notwithstanding the above, if a death benefit under a contractual arrangement can never exceed the total premiums paid plus interest, there is no insurance element present (Treas. Reg. Sec. 20.2039–1(d)).

The following situation is adapted from the aforementioned regulations section.

Example:	Under a nonqualified retirement plan, an employer, Marge, purchased a contract from a life insurance company that would provide her employee, Sam, with an annuity of $100 per month for life upon the employee's retirement at age 65. Under the contract, a beneficiary named by the employee would receive a similar annuity for life upon the employee's death after retirement. In addition, the contract provided for a lump-sum payment of $20,000 to the designated beneficiary instead of the annuity described above if the employee died before he reached retirement age. Assume that the reserve value of the contract would be $20,000 when the employee reaches age 65. Thus, if the employee died after reaching retirement age, the death benefit to the beneficiary would be considered an annuity, includible in the employee's gross estate. On the other hand, if the employee dies before reaching age 65, the death benefit would constitute insurance under a policy on the life of the decedent because the reserve value would be less than the death benefit. Therefore, the includibility in the gross estate would be determined under the estate tax section dealing with insurance (IRC Sec. 2042) and not under Sec. 2039.

Valuation

Commercial annuity contracts (those issued by companies regularly engaged in the sale of annuities) are valued differently from others. A commercial contract is valued based on the cost of comparable contracts sold by the issuing company as of the date of the decedent's death. Therefore, referring to an earlier example, if Tom had purchased a commercial annuity for himself and Ann, the value in Tom's estate would be the cost of a single life annuity on Ann's life at the time of his death if he had contributed the entire purchase price (Treas. Reg. Sec. 20.2031-8(a)). If, however, the annuity was payable under a private contract, it would be valued for estate tax purposes according to the actuarial tables found in the federal estate and gift tax regulations (Treas. Reg. Secs. 20.2031–10; 25.2512–9).

Valuation Date

Date-of-Death Value

reduction in value by mere lapse of time

The value of benefits under an annuity contract is determined on the primary annuitant's date of death. Because an annuity is an asset that experiences a *reduction in value by mere lapse of time* (mortgages and notes receivable are examples of other "wasting assets"), the alternate valuation date does not apply to any annuity included in the gross estate (IRC Sec. 2032(a)(3)) even though the estate qualifies for and elects the alternate valuation date for other assets.

Benefits under an annuity contract are always valued on the date of death. Therefore, when the alternate valuation date applies to an estate, the benefits paid out during the 6-month period between the date of death and the alternate valuation date cannot be used to reduce the value of the annuity for estate tax purposes. Also, if the benefits are payable in a lump sum, the amount payable becomes the date-of-death value that is used on the estate tax return. However, as stated earlier, the amount included in the decedent's gross estate is proportionately reduced if the decedent did not pay the full cost of the annuity contract.

Value of Annuity Reduced by Other Than Mere Lapse of Time

A different value may apply, however, if a reduction in value occurs for a reason other than mere lapse of time.

Example:	Suppose a husband had purchased a joint and survivor annuity for himself and his wife. The husband dies, and after his death his wife is entitled to receive payments for the remainder of her life. Unfortunately,

the wife dies 4 months after the husband. In this case, an event other than mere lapse of time occurred during the period between the date of death and the alternate valuation date that reduced the value of the annuity to zero. The only amount includible in the husband's estate is the value, as of his death, of the payments received by his widow during the 4-month postdeath period. It is determined by finding the difference between the value of an annuity for her life determined as of the husband's death and the actual value of the annuity determined as of the date of her death.

Lump-Sum Payments

lump-sum payment

As will be seen later, *lump-sum payments* are included at full value. When payments are made in installments, whether for a fixed period, in a fixed amount, or for the life of the beneficiary, the valuation is made on a commuted basis (the present value of the right to receive future income).

Annuities Receivable from Qualified Employee Retirement Plans

The Deficit Reduction Act of 1984 generally repealed all estate tax exclusion of qualified plan proceeds for decedents dying after December 31, 1984. There are two exceptions:

(1) A nonemployee-spouse's interest in qualified plan proceeds that arise solely as a result of the application of community-property laws is totally excluded from his or her gross estate provided that the nonemployee-spouse predeceases the employee plan participant (IRC Sec. 2039(c)).

(2) If the proceeds of a qualified plan were in pay status on December 31, 1984, and prior to the date of enactment of the Deficit Reduction Act of 1984 (July 18, 1984) the participant had irrevocably elected a beneficiary designation that would have qualified the plan proceeds for estate tax exclusion, the $100,000 exclusion amount is still available (DRA Secs. 525(b)(2); (b)(3)).

JOINTLY HELD PROPERTY WITH RIGHT OF SURVIVORSHIP (IRC SEC. 2040)

Sec. 2040 covers the way jointly titled property is included in a decedent's gross estate.

Joint Tenancies Held by Married Couples (Qualified Joint Interests)

A special rule has been enacted that controls the estate taxation of joint property with right of survivorship held solely by husband and wife (qualified joint interests) as well as property held as tenants by the entirety. Section 2040(b)(1) was created under the Tax Reform Act of 1976 (TRA '76). This section pertains to the one-half inclusion rule for spouses. As a result of TRA '76, after December 31, 1976, the rule is that one-half the value of such property, regardless of which spouse furnished all or part of the consideration, is included in the gross estate of the first spouse to die. This is an automatic rule. The actual contribution of each spouse is irrelevant. For some spousal joint tenancies with right of survivorship created prior to January 1, 1977, however, the percentage-of-contribution rule applies.

Percentage-of-Contribution (or Consideration-Furnished) Rule (Nonqualified Joint Interests)

percentage-of-contribution (consideration-furnished) rule

All property held in joint tenancy with right of survivorship by joint tenants other than a husband and wife alone (nonqualified joint interests) is treated under a different rule. The property is included in a deceased joint tenant's estate according to a *percentage-of-contribution rule*. Property held as joint tenants with right of survivorship by a decedent is included in the decedent's estate to the extent of the decedent's interest (the fractional share of the joint tenancy) at the time of death. However, any part of the decedent's interest in the joint tenancy is not included in the decedent's gross estate if it can be proved that the joint tenancy originally belonged to a surviving joint tenant or was purchased by funds contributed by the surviving joint tenant. The percentage-of-contribution rule pertains to all nonqualified joint interests, including joint tenancies in which spouses and one or more nonspousal parties are joint tenants.

In addition, if it can be shown that the surviving joint tenant's interest in the property was received from the decedent for less than full and adequate consideration, that portion of the joint tenancy is included in the decedent's estate. In this case, the amount included in the decedent's gross estate is the value of the actual gift of property itself or the amount of funds transferred to the donee joint tenant for the purpose of purchasing property to be held in joint tenancy.

Example:	Ted and Carol are siblings who hope to purchase a vacation home at the New Jersey shore. Because Ted is currently short on funds, Carol provides the entire purchase price. Ted dies tragically 3 years after the

purchase of the property, when the vacation home is worth $350,000. The general rule is that Ted's interest in the property, valued at $175,000 at the time of his death, is included in his gross estate. However, Ted's estate is capable of rebutting the general rule by proving that Carol provided all of the original purchase price. If such evidence can be established, no amount of the joint tenancy will be included in Ted's estate at the time of his death.

Thus, if one joint tenant gave income-producing property to another joint tenant and if the posttransfer income was contributed toward the purchase of jointly held property, the amounts attributable to such income are not deemed to have been received from the other joint tenant.

Example: Father (F) made numerous $10,000 gifts of cash to Son (S) over the past years. S invested the gifts and earned $12,000 of interest. This year F and S purchased unimproved land for $36,000 and titled the property in joint tenancy. S used the $12,000 interest toward the purchase price, and F contributed the balance. If F predeceases S, for F's estate tax purposes S will be treated as contributing $12,000 of the land's purchase price and $24,000 will be included in F's gross estate.

Burden of Proof

Under the percentage-of-contribution rule, the burden of proof to demonstrate that the surviving joint tenant made some contribution to the acquisition of the joint tenancy is on the surviving joint tenant or the decedent's estate. If successful, that portion representing the percentage of contribution made by the surviving joint tenant is excluded from the gross estate.

Joint Property Acquired by Gift or Inheritance

Jointly held property that is acquired by gift, bequest, or inheritance is treated in a slightly different way. If the decedent and the decedent's spouse acquired the property by gift or inheritance, one-half of the value is included in the decedent's estate. However, if the decedent acquired the property as joint tenants with right of survivorship as a gift or inheritance with persons other than a spouse, the value representing his or her fractional interest is includible in the estate. To determine the decedent's fractional share, the value of the property is divided by the number of joint tenants with right of survivorship, presuming that each joint tenant owns an undivided interest in the entire property.

> ***Example:***   If a decedent, James, inherited a farm from his father in equal shares with his three sisters and a brother, and he is the first joint tenant to die, one-fifth of the value of the property is included in his gross estate.

Advisability of Marital Joint Tenancies with Right of Survivorship

Advantages

There are still advantages in holding property jointly with right of survivorship by spouses. Jointly held property between spouses is generally nonprobate property. This means that the property is not subject to estate administration. All benefits of ownership remain available to the surviving joint tenant without interruption during the administration period. Because the property does not pass through probate, total administration expenses and attorney fees may be reduced. One-half of the property attributed to the decedent's interest included in the decedent's gross estate is entitled to the full benefit of the unlimited marital deduction. Therefore, there is no estate tax liability because of the property's inclusion. Another benefit of joint ownership is the comfort and feeling of harmony and security that it creates between husband and wife.

Disadvantages

A disadvantage may be that the surviving joint tenant obtains full control over the future disposition of the property. This may defeat a portion of the original estate plan of the first joint tenant to die. Should the survivor remarry, the property becomes subject to a spouse's right of election by the survivor's second spouse.

In addition, only one-half of the property receives a step up in basis at the first joint tenant's death. As mentioned earlier, the savings in estate tax and probate costs may possibly be worth less than the potential savings in capital-gains tax had the property been fully included in the decedent's gross estate and acquired a fully stepped-up basis.

basis   As you may recall from a previous assignment, *basis* is a term used for income tax purposes. There are special rules concerning the basis of property transferred at death. Property that is included in a decedent's gross estate acquires a new basis. The new basis is either an increase to or a decrease from the fair market value of property on the date of death.

The basis of property transferred at death is discussed in more detail in chapter 19.

Characteristics of Joint Tenancies

- nonprobate property
- passage of property by operation of law
- partial basis step up at first death
- uninterrupted ownership for survivor
- full control and ownership for survivor

Alternatives

Alternate solutions involve keeping the property in sole ownership, as illustrated in the example below.

Example: If a decedent-husband held the property in his name alone and left the property outright to his wife as a special bequest in his will, the entire property, although included in the gross estate, is also eligible for the marital deduction. Therefore no estate tax results from inclusion of the property in his estate. In addition, the basis in the hands of the surviving wife becomes the fair market value on the date of the husband's death or alternate valuation date, if applicable. Of course, the property is then probate property, which may generate additional costs to the estate. There also may be a delay in formally transferring the property to the surviving spouse. Furthermore, if the husband retains ownership of the property with the intention of passing it to his surviving spouse using the unlimited marital de-duction and his wife predeceases him, he loses the benefit of the marital deduction for the property passing through his estate. However, when he dies, the entire property receives a stepped-up basis in the hands of his beneficiaries. Remember that even if the husband dies first, at his spouse's death the entire value of the property is taxable for federal estate tax purposes in the second estate. In other words, to the extent that either spouse does not dispose of the property during their lifetimes, it is included at full value in the estate of the second spouse to die. Of course, the next tier of beneficiaries will obtain another step-up in basis to fair market value at the second death.

Other factors to consider when arranging property ownership are the relative sizes of the parties' estates as well as the variation in their ages and health factors. Likewise, the quality of the parties' relationship is significant. Although no-fault divorce laws and equitable distribution statutes now apply to some extent in almost all states, jointly held personal property is freely accessible to either spouse whether together or separated. Possession by the donee may defeat the interest of the donor's spouse temporarily or permanently, to the extent the asset is converted or consumed.

Because of one or more of the above considerations, the estate planner may recommend the termination of a joint tenancy between spouses, thereby transferring the entire interest to one of the spouses. Keep in mind that the unlimited marital deduction for gift tax purposes now makes it possible to transfer property back and forth between spouses without the gift tax ramifications that previously existed. For example, if the decedent's estate includes a closely held business that qualifies for special-use valuation, the deferral of estate tax payments, or a Sec. 303 stock redemption, and the business was in the decedent's own name alone, the value of the business in relation to the decedent's adjusted gross estate would be increased if he or she had transferred some *nonbusiness* joint assets to the decedent's spouse as sole owner. The proportionate increase in the value of the *business* interest in relation to the decedent's estate may enable the estate to qualify for any of these potentially desirable tax benefits by meeting the percentage tests for eligibility. Alternatively, if the property under consideration is solely owned nonbusiness property, placing it in joint names removes one-half of the date-of-death value from the decedent's estate, thereby easing the possibility of qualifying for a Sec. 303 redemption, Sec. 6166 deferral to pay estate tax, or special-use valuation under Sec. 2032A.

The following example illustrates how ownership of property in joint names as opposed to sole ownership affects the ability to qualify for one of the tax benefits mentioned above where qualification is based on a percentage test.

| *Example:* | Mr. Jones is the sole shareholder of a closely held business that has a fair market value of $1 million. His gross estate is valued at $4 million. He desires to leave approximately one-half of his estate to his second wife, with the net balance after payment of taxes and expenses to his two sons from a prior marriage, who |

work with him in the business. Debts and expenses of the estate will probably be about $75,000. Under such a plan, the estate would not qualify for the tax relief provided by either Sec. 6166 (providing for installment payment of estate tax over 14 years) or a Sec. 303 redemption (providing for a redemption of stock to pay estate taxes and funeral and administrative costs). This is because the value of the business interest equals only 25 percent of this adjusted gross estate, not the 35 percent required by Secs. 303 and 6166. Considering the division of property described above, his sons would have difficulty meeting the estate tax liability payable from the residue unless the closely held business had significant amounts of cash.

As an alternative plan, if Mr. Jones desires to maintain the flexibility to qualify for the tax benefits described, he can transfer a sufficient portion of nonbusiness property to joint ownership with his spouse. This transfer, in turn, reduces his adjusted gross estate by an amount that enables the estate to qualify under the 35-percent-of-adjusted-gross-estate test under Sec. 6166 and Sec. 303. Bear in mind that if he does not survive more than 3 years after making the transfer to a joint tenancy with his spouse, the property transferred will be included in his estate for purposes of qualification under Sec. 6166 and Sec. 303. However, the use of joint tenancies for this purpose has interesting potential for estate tax planning possibilities.

POWERS OF APPOINTMENT (IRC SEC. 2041)

power of appointment

Sec. 2041 concerns the way a power of appointment is included in a decedent's gross estate. A *power of appointment* over property is the right of the holder of the power to specify who will become the recipient or owner of the property. Depending on the type of power of appointment, the holder of the power may or may not be able to designate himself or herself as the property owner.

General Powers

A decedent's general power of appointment over property has value for federal estate tax purposes under Code Sec. 2041. The gross estate includes

---

Power of Appointment Terminology

- donor—grantor of power over property
- donee—holder of power
- appointee—recipient of property

---

general power of appointment

the value of all property subject to a *general power of appointment* possessed by the decedent at the time of death. When an individual is given a legal right to appoint (direct the disposition of) property that is not his or hers, that right is called a power of appointment. A general power is a power over property so broad that it approaches actual ownership or control over the property subject to the power. Property subject to such a power will be includible in the estate of a person who holds that power, the so-called donee of the power. If the decedent has been given a power by another person (called the donor of the power) and this power allows the decedent to appoint the property to himself or herself, his or her creditors, the estate, or the estate's creditors, it is considered a general power of appointment. Note that the decedent need not have the power to appoint property to all four categories. The power to appoint to one of the four is sufficient for a power to be a general power of appointment for estate tax purposes (*Estate of Edelman v. Comm'r*, 38 T.C. 972 (1976)). Again, the person who possesses the power and has the right to exercise it is called the donee or holder of the power.

General Power of Appointment

You have an unlimited right to appoint property to

- yourself
- your creditors
- your estate
- your estate creditors

As long as the decedent holds the power, it makes no difference whether the power is exercisable by him or her only during lifetime, only at death, or both during life and at death (*Snyder v. U.S.*, 203 F.Supp. 195 (W.D. Ky. 1962); *Jenkins v. U.S.*, 428 F.2d 538 (5th Cir. 1970)).

Example: The decedent, a surviving spouse, was given income from the property for life with the right to appoint or dispose of the property at death to his or her estate, creditors, or beneficiaries by will. Although the power

FIGURE 13-1
General Power of Appointment

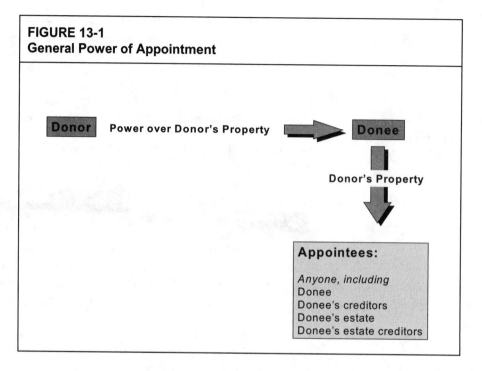

to transfer the property did not include lifetime transfers in this case, the value of the property subject to the power is included in the surviving spouse's estate because there was full power over the disposition of the property at death.

A general power includes the unlimited right of the decedent-donee to use the corpus of a trust for the decedent's own benefit.

Example: If the decedent, Herman, was given the power in a trust to distribute or appoint trust principal to or among any of four beneficiaries not including himself, this would not be a general power of appointment. However, if the trust contained an additional power in the decedent to invade corpus without limitation for his own benefit at any time, the power would be a general power of appointment since he had the power to deplete corpus partially or totally for his own benefit, thereby defeating the rights of the other beneficiaries. It is immaterial for estate tax inclusion whether or not he actually exercised this power in favor of himself.

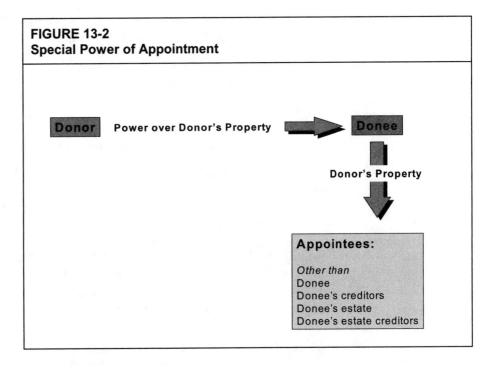

FIGURE 13-2
Special Power of Appointment

Because a general power over property is, by definition, so closely akin to actual ownership, a formal surrender of the power (a release) or failure to use the power (a lapse) may be treated similarly to a transfer of the property itself. Therefore, if the release or lapse is coupled with a lifetime retention of the income produced by the property subject to the power (as is typically the case when a grantor gives the same person a lifetime income interest and a withdrawal power), or if the transfer is conditioned on surviving the decedent or subject to the former holder's power to alter, amend, revoke, or terminate the transfer, the property subject to the power may have to be included in the gross estate.

This type of transfer is includible because it is considered the tax equivalent of a transfer of property actually owned by the decedent.

Special Powers

A general power of appointment is to be distinguished from a limited or **special (limited) power of appointment** special power. A *special (limited) power of appointment* is one in which the donor of the power limits the donee with respect to the persons to whom the donee may appoint the property.

As already noted, a power of appointment does not qualify as a general power unless it is exercisable in favor of at least one of the following: the decedent, the decedent's estate, the decedent's creditors, or the creditors of the estate. If the power is exercisable only in favor of one or more persons

---

Special Power of Appointment

Property may <u>not</u> be appointed to

- yourself
- your creditors
- your estate
- your estate creditors

(or all other persons) not including the decedent, the decedent's creditors, the estate, or the creditors of the estate—or if it is specifically not exercisable in favor of the decedent, the decedent's creditors, the estate, or the creditors of the estate—it does not qualify as a general power.

Property over which the decedent has a special or limited power is not includible in his or her gross estate. However, if the decedent had a power over property that he or she exercised in favor of someone else but the decedent retained an interest in the property for life, the value of the property will be includible in the decedent's gross estate.

Example:	A decedent, Franklin, was given a lifetime general power of appointment by his sister to designate who would receive a lakefront vacation home. The decedent exercised this power in favor of his daughter but retained the right to use the property for his life. The right to use the property for life brings the value of the property subject to the power into his gross estate, although he had previously exercised the power and disposed of the property.

Limitations by Ascertainable Standard

ascertainable standard

If the decedent possesses the power to consume or invade for his or her own benefit but the power is limited by an *ascertainable standard* (such that the property may be used or invaded only for reasons of the decedent's health, education, support, or maintenance), the power of appointment is

---

Ascertainable Standard

- health
- education
- support
- maintenance

---

considered a special and not a general power. Support and maintenance are generally construed in accordance with the standard of living to which the decedent was accustomed.

Example:	If Mr. Smith creates a trust and gives his son, Walter, the right to invade corpus for Walter's health, education, support, or maintenance, Walter has a special power of appointment that will not cause the corpus subject to the power to be included in his gross estate (IRC Sec. 2041(b)(1)(A)).

Powers Exercisable Only with Consent of Others

A power of appointment that otherwise causes the value of property subject to the power to be includible in the estate of the donee of the power may escape inclusion, wholly or partially, if the power can be exercised only with the consent of others.

Powers Exercisable Only with Consent of Donor of Power

A power created after October 21, 1942, that can be exercised only with the consent or joinder of the creator (donor) of the power is not considered a general power of appointment for federal estate tax purposes (IRC Sec. 2041(b) (1)(C)(i)).

Powers Exercisable Only with Consent of Person Having a Substantial Adverse Interest

A power created after October 21, 1942, that can be exercised only with the consent or joinder of a person having a substantial adverse interest is not treated as a general power, and the property subject to the power is not includible in the estate of the donee (IRC Sec. 2041(b)(1)(C)(ii)).

Example:	Assume that Albert grants John and Betty the unrestricted power to appoint property to Betty during Betty's lifetime. In default of the appointment, the property will pass to John at Betty's death. At Betty's death, if the property has not been appointed to her, no portion of the value of the property is includible in her gross estate because she is not deemed to have a general power of appointment because John had a substantial adverse interest.

If the consent of the person without an adverse interest is required, the value of the property subject to the power is fully includible in the donee's estate.

Example:	Assume that Albert grants John and Betty the unrestricted power to appoint property in favor of Betty during Betty's lifetime. In default of appointment, the property passes to Carol on Betty's death. When Betty predeceases John, Betty is deemed to possess a general power of appointment because John does not have a substantial adverse interest in the property subject to the power. In no event could John have been the beneficiary of the property. The entire value of the property subject to the power is included in Betty's gross estate at her death. This is so because Betty and John could have appointed the property to Betty during her lifetime and she was not limited to exercising the power only in conjunction with the creator of the power or someone having an adverse interest in the property.

Note that a trustee whose only powers are administrative ones exercisable in a fiduciary capacity is not a person who has an adverse interest in the property.

If a power created *before* October 21, 1942, is exercisable by the decedent only in conjunction with *any other person*, it is not treated as a general power (IRC Sec. 2042(b)(1)(B)). For general powers created before October 21, 1942, it is irrelevant that the party whose consent was required had no interest, adverse or otherwise, in the property. The mere requirement of the consent of another person is sufficient to defeat inclusion of property subject to such powers in the decedent-donee's estate.

Powers Exercisable Only with Consent of Others in Whose Favor Power Could Be Exercised

If a person is given a power that can be exercised only in conjunction with others in whose favor the power could be exercised, only a fractional part of the property is includible in the donee's estate. The fractional portion is determined by dividing the value of the property by the number of persons in whose favor the power could be exercised (IRC Sec. 2041(b)(1)(C)(iii)).

Example:	Assume that Albert grants John and Betty the unrestricted right to appoint property to either of them (with the consent of the other) during their lifetimes.

In default of an appointment, the property passes to Myrna. At Betty's death, one-half of the value of the property is includible in her gross estate.

Other Limitations on Powers

5-and-5 power

Although the decedent is given what is otherwise a general power of appointment, it is not included in the gross estate if the decedent's power is limited to a noncumulative right to withdraw the greater of $5,000 or 5 percent of the aggregate value of the property each year. This power is sometimes referred to as a *5-and-5 power*. Failure to withdraw the money each year is said to be a lapse constituting a release of the power. If the decedent dies possessing this power, the amount includible in the estate is only the amount that the decedent could have appointed in favor of himself or herself in the year of death. To the extent that the power to appoint the property exceeds the greater of $5,000 or 5 percent of the value of the assets subject to the power, there is a taxable disposition by the decedent's failure to exercise the power of withdrawal. In other words, the decedent is deemed to have made a gift to the remainderperson of the excess property that is not withdrawn each year. The gift tax effect is exactly the same as if the decedent had appointed the property to himself or herself and gifted it to the remainder portion of the trust.

5-and-5 Power

Noncumulative right to withdraw the *greater* of

$5,000

or

5%

of the aggregate value of property annually

Example: A trust established by Mr. Ford was funded with $500,000 worth of securities. His son, Frank, is to receive all income for life with the remainder to Frank's children. Frank was given a noncumulative right to withdraw $40,000 a year from the trust. Because this is a noncumulative right, he releases those funds each year that he does not withdraw all or part of the $40,000. Releasing the excess of the greater of $5,000 or 5 percent of the trust corpus is treated as a taxable transfer (it is a gift to the trust). In this example, 5 percent of the trust corpus equals $25,000. The excess distribution equals $15,000 ($40,000 minus $25,000). It is a taxable transfer with a reserved right to income from the portion remaining in the trust. Because he is the life income beneficiary, a portion of the trust valued at the date of his death will be included in his gross estate. The ratio for inclusion is determined by dividing the excess distribution ($15,000) by the total current value of the trust ($500,000—assumed for the purpose of this example). In this case, 3/100 or 3 percent of the value of the trust corpus at Frank's death will be includible in his gross estate.

If failure to exercise a power of withdrawal occurs in more than one year, the proportionate amount of property over which the power lapses that is treated as a taxable disposition is determined separately for each year. It is the aggregate of all taxable portions for all years (not to exceed 100 percent) that is includible in the decedent's gross estate. Remember that the value of the 5-and-5 power in the year of death is also includible.

Disclaiming a Power

If a decedent refuses to accept a power of appointment in a manner consistent with the requirements of a qualified disclaimer under the federal disclaimer statute (IRC Sec. 2518), the decedent is considered to have disclaimed or renounced the power of appointment. Although the power was a general power, nothing will be included in the decedent's gross estate because that power was never accepted by the decedent. A disclaimer is invalid once the power over the property has been accepted. Also, a qualified disclaimer does not result in a taxable gift if the necessary federal requirements are met.

If the donee of a power does not wish it to be included in his or her gross estate, the donee must release or exercise the power during lifetime. Also, the donee must not exercise the power and retain any rights or power over the property that would cause it to be included under IRC Secs. 2036, 2037, or 2038 (for example, the right to income for life), or the property will still be included in the donee's gross estate unless he or she releases these impermissible retained rights more than 3 years prior to death (IRC Sec. 2041(a)(2)).

Time and Method of Creation of a Power

A power of appointment created by will is considered to be created on the date of the testator's death. A power of appointment created by deed or other instrument during the creator's lifetime is deemed to be created on the day the instrument becomes effective.

The use of the words *general power of appointment* is not essential. Determination of the existence of a power is based on what it purports to accomplish rather than on either the wording used by the creator or local property law connotations. Therefore, a right given to a person with a life estate in a trust to withdraw or consume the trust principal may rightly be considered a general power of appointment over the property.

Effect of Legal Competence to Exercise a Power

Property subject to a general power of appointment is includible in the decedent's estate even though the decedent could not exercise the power because he was legally incompetent or a minor (Rev. Rul. 75-351, 1975-2 C.B.368; Rev. Rul. 55-518, 1955-2 C.B. 384). Numerous U.S. Circuit Court of Appeals decisions support this conclusion, and there no longer appears to be any doubt about this issue. (See *Estate of Gilchrist v. Comm'r*, 630 F.2d 340 (5th Cir. 1980); *Pennsylvania Bank & Trust Co. v. U.S.*, 597 F.2d 382 (3d Cir.), cert. denied, 444 U.S. 930 (1979)).

It has even been held that the possession of a general power at death is sufficient to cause inclusion of the property subject to the power in the decedent's estate even though the decedent was not aware of the existence of the power (*Estate of Freeman v. Comm'r*, 67 T.C. 202 (1976)).

LIFE INSURANCE (IRC SEC. 2042)

Sec. 2042 defines when the proceeds of life insurance are included in the gross estate of the insured for federal estate tax purposes.

Types of Contracts Included

Life insurance as used in this section refers to all types of policies. It includes whole life policies, term insurance, group life insurance, limited-payment life, endowment contracts (prior to being paid up), retired lives reserves insurance, and death benefits paid by fraternal societies operating under the lodge system. In addition, the proceeds of certain other types of insurance policies (such as accident insurance and flight insurance available at air terminals) are considered proceeds of life insurance for estate tax purposes. Likewise, proceeds of war-risk insurance and national service life insurance are included in the gross estate, as well as insurance paid under double indemnity clauses by reason of the accidental death of an insured.

To be considered an insurance contract, there must be an actuarially determined element of risk on which the premium cost of the contract is based. There must be risk sharing between the insured and the insurer so that the insurer stands to sustain a loss if the insured does not live for the intended life expectancy.

Another element inherent in insurance policies is that the original purchaser must have an insurable interest in the policy.

Proceeds of life insurance on the decedent's life are included in the gross estate under this Code section if (1) the decedent possessed any incidents of ownership in the policy, (2) the proceeds are receivable by the estate, or (3) the proceeds are receivable by another for the benefit of the estate.

incidents of ownership

The term *incidents of ownership* refers to a number of rights of the insured or the insured's estate in the economic benefits of the policy. It is not limited to ownership in a technical sense. Rights that are considered incidents of ownership include the following:

- the power to name or change beneficiaries or beneficial interests
- the right to assign the policy
- the right to revoke an assignment
- the right to surrender or cancel the policy
- the right to pledge the policy for a loan
- the right to obtain a loan against the surrender value of the policy
- the power to change the beneficiary when the policy is owned by a closely held corporation of which the decedent is a sole or controlling shareholder. (However, to the extent that proceeds are payable to the corporation or a third party for a valid business purpose, such as payment of a corporate debt, the corporate-owned policy on the life of the sole or controlling shareholder will not be attributed to the shareholder and will not be includible in his or her estate.)
- the right to prevent cancellation of an insurance policy owned by the decedent's employer by purchasing the policy for its cash surrender value
- the power to change the beneficial ownership in a policy or its proceeds, or to change the time or manner of enjoyment of the policy or its proceeds should the policy of life insurance on the insured's life be owned by a trust
- the reservation of rights to deal with the policy even if the policy is physically transferred to another
- the power to require the nominal owner of the policy to exercise an incident of ownership, thereby having control over the actions of the owner of record
- the right to a reversionary interest worth more than 5 percent of the value of the insurance policy immediately before the insured's death. (In other words, there must be more than a 5 percent chance based on the value of the policy immediately before the death of the insured that the right or rights will return to him or her.)

Avoidance of Sec. 2042 Inclusion

- no responsibility for insured's estate expenses
- no incidents of ownership

If the insured possesses any of the above rights, the full proceeds of life insurance will be included in the gross estate even if the insured cannot exercise these rights without the consent of some other person. Inclusion in the estate occurs, regardless of the decedent's ability to exercise the right at death. For example, the decedent might have been in flight or incompetent at the time of death. If the insured retains rights of ownership while acting in a fiduciary capacity, the policy proceeds will be included in the estate if any of the rights of incidents of ownership can be exercised for the insured's personal benefit.

Decedent as Trustee

In general, if the decedent-insured has no beneficial interest in the insurance policies while acting as a trustee, he or she is not considered to have powers equivalent to a testamentary disposition that would bring the proceeds of life insurance into the estate. There is at least one court case that rejected this differentiation and included proceeds in the decedent's estate when a mere incident of ownership was possessed, regardless of the manner in which the decedent acquired it and the capacity in which he or she possessed it (as trustee). In this case, the decedent-insured was the owner and beneficiary of life insurance policies as sole trustee of three trusts created by his brother. As trustee, he had the power to change the time and manner of enjoyment of the policies and proceeds by his power to withdraw dividends, to obtain loans, and to convert the policies from whole life insurance to endowment life insurance (*Rose v. U.S.*, 511 F.2d 259 (5th Cir. 1975)).

In essence, planners should be cognizant that there have been numerous cases involving a decedent's possession of similar rights that have reached contrary outcomes. Without question, a financial services professional should make a client aware that any meaningful rights in the policy held by the client at the time of death may cause the entire proceeds to be includible in the client's gross estate. It is irrelevant how the decedent obtained these ownership attributes or whether exercise of these rights or powers would directly or indirectly benefit him or her. The distinguishing factor that causes inclusion of the policy in the decedent's estate is whether the decedent possessed the right at his or her death and not whether the decedent had the capacity or ability to exercise it.

proceeds payable to or
for the benefit of an
estate

Proceeds Payable to or for the Benefit of an Estate

The full proceeds of life insurance are also included in the decedent's estate if they are "payable for the benefit of the estate." This phrase is operative if the life insurance is receivable by the estate, the executor, or any other person who has the power to act on behalf of the estate. It is immaterial that the policy was purchased and owned by someone other than the decedent and that the owner retained complete control over the policy during the decedent-insured's lifetime (IRC Sec. 2046(1)).

Similarly, the proceeds are included in the decedent's estate if they are made payable to a trust that is required to use the proceeds for the payment of death taxes, claims, and administrative expenses of the decedent or the estate. However, if the trustee is merely given a discretionary power to pay these expenses and is not required to use trust assets to satisfy estate obligations, the proceeds will not be included in the estate except to the extent they are actually used to satisfy estate obligations.

If proceeds were used as collateral security for a loan held by a corporation, they are considered receivable for the benefit of the estate since the corporation is a creditor of the estate. However, the value of the unpaid balance at the date of the decedent's death with interest accrued is deductible from the gross estate as a debt of the estate.

If the proceeds of life insurance made payable to the decedent's estate are community assets in community-property states, only one-half belongs to the decedent. Therefore, only one-half is included in the decedent's gross estate as proceeds receivable by or for the benefit of the estate (Treas. Reg. Sec. 20.2042–1(b) (2) *Estate of Madsen v. Comm'r*, 690 F.2d 164 (9th Cir. 1982)).

Proceeds Used to Pay Estate Taxes

As noted in the preceding example, insurance proceeds are also includible in the decedent's gross estate as insurance receivable by the personal representative when the proceeds are actually used to pay estate taxes. Also, if proceeds are receivable by an individual beneficiary but the beneficiary is legally obliged to pay taxes, debts, and other expenses of the estate, the proceeds are includible in the estate to the extent of the beneficiary's obligation to use the proceeds for these purposes.

Life insurance proceeds paid directly to a divorced spouse are includible in the decedent's gross estate if the decedent was required to name the former spouse as beneficiary of the insurance proceeds on his or her life and if the decedent was required to maintain the policies, unless the former spouse died or remarried. However, the above is an arm's-length, bargained-for agreement; as such, as deduction in the amount of the proceeds is allowed from the gross estate as a debt of the estate.

Group Life Insurance

Group life insurance is treated similarly to other types of life insurance. A group life insurance policy taken out by an employer is included in the decedent employee's estate if the decedent had the right to change beneficiaries, terminate the insurance policy, or prevent cancellation of the contract by purchasing the policy.

However, if the employee's power to terminate the policy is limited to terminating employment, that is not an incident of ownership sufficient to bring the policy proceeds into the employee's gross estate. Also, a right to convert the group policy to an individual policy when the decedent's employment ends is not a right sufficient to bring the policy proceeds into the estate if this right is transferable and the decedent irrevocably assigns the policy as well as the conversion privilege to another. In such a case, the decedent has no control over the assignee's right to the proceeds and no incidents of ownership over the policy.

Inclusion of Life Insurance

- proceeds received by decedent-insured's estate (Sec. 2042)
- decedent-insured's incidents of ownership in policy (Sec. 2042)
- proceeds received by another for the benefit of decedent-insured's estate (Sec. 2042)
- decedent's ownership of policy on life of another (Sec. 2033)
- insured's gift of policy within 3 years of death (Sec. 2035)

Proceeds from the Estate of Another

The terms *incidents of ownership* and *reversionary interest* do not apply to either a life insurance policy or to the proceeds a decedent receives by inheritance through the estate of another person (such as a surviving spouse under a statutory right of election).

Insurance on the Life of Another

Policies of life insurance that the decedent owns on the life of another are not included under this section. However, the value of these policies is included in the decedent's gross estate as property that is owned at death under Sec. 2033, the general inclusion section. If the decedent owns a policy on someone else's life, the amount that is includible in the decedent's estate is determined as follows:

- If the policy is new, the gross premium paid is the value.
- If the policy is a paid-up or a single-premium policy, its value is its replacement cost—that is, the single premium that the issuing company would have charged for a comparable contract of equal face value on the life of a person who was the insured's age (at the time the decedent policyholder died).
- If the policy is a premium-paying whole life policy, the value is found by adding any unearned portion of the last premium to the interpolated terminal reserve.
- If the policy is a term life insurance policy, the value is the unused premium.

Relationship to Marital Deduction

If insurance is payable to the spouse or the spouse's estate in a lump sum or in the form of an annuity only if the spouse survives the decedent by up to 6 months, the proceeds qualify for the marital deduction assuming they have been included in the gross estate. If proceeds are left at the interest option for the life of the surviving spouse, they qualify for the marital deduction if they are payable to the spouse's estate or to persons to whom the spouse appoints the property at death. If the spouse fails to exercise this power of appointment over the proceeds, they may still qualify for the marital deduction if the proceeds are received by named contingent beneficiaries as a result of the spouse's failure to appoint them. Likewise, if proceeds are to be paid in installments for a definite period of time or if there is a refund feature, the proceeds qualify if payments following the death of the surviving spouse are payable to those beneficiaries whom the surviving spouse has designated to receive the remaining payments. Proceeds also qualify for the marital deduction if the spouse receives all the interest for life and proceeds pass to a trust or named beneficiary at the spouse's death under the qualified terminable interest rules. Note that if life insurance is payable to a surviving spouse but is not includible in the decedent's gross estate because he or she retains no incidents of ownership, the marital deduction does not apply.

Transfers of Life Insurance within 3 Years of Death

Any gratuitous transfer of a life insurance policy by an insured made after 1976 and within 3 years of a decedent's death is includible in the decedent's gross estate as a transfer made within 3 years of death. In these circumstances, however, the proceeds are not reportable on the life insurance schedule as proceeds owned at death, but are reportable on the schedule provided for lifetime transfers. Motivation or intention in making the transfer is irrelevant. Although other completed gifts made within 3 years of death are excluded from the gross estate by the Economic Recovery Tax Act of 1981 effective for decedents dying on or after January 1, 1982, there is a specific exception for gratuitous transfers by the insured of life insurance policies on the insured's life within 3 years of death. The full value of life insurance proceeds from policies on the decedent's life transferred by the decedent within 3 years of death is included in the gross estate (IRC Sec. 2035(d)(2)).

All insurance on the decedent's life, whether or not owned by the decedent, is reported on Schedule D of the federal estate return. If proceeds are received in a lump sum, the value reported is the net proceeds received, but if policy proceeds are paid other than in a lump sum, the value listed is the value of proceeds as of the date of the decedent's death. Insurance proceeds on the life of a nonresident noncitizen (nonresident alien) are not taxable for federal estate tax purposes and need not be reported. Along with the schedule on the estate tax return, the personal representative must file a Form 712 Life Insurance Statement for each life insurance policy listed in the schedule that is included in the gross estate. These statements may be obtained from the insurance company that issued the policy.

Life insurance taken out in a business context is not discussed in this chapter. However, the subject is reviewed in a later chapter that discusses the uses of life insurance in estate planning.

Table 13-1 summarizes the estate tax inclusion sections discussed in chapters 12 and 13.

MINI-CASE

Based on the following fact pattern and assuming Mr. Smith died today, predeceasing Mrs. Smith, indicate, with reasons, the assets and their values that would be included in Mr. Smith's gross estate for federal estate tax purposes.

Business Situation

Mr. Smith is president of the GBH Corporation, a manufacturer of chemicals and solvents. Mr. Smith founded the corporation 20 years ago, and it has grown steadily over the years.

The corporation has 900 shares of common stock outstanding, of which Mr. Smith owns 750 shares and Mrs. Smith owns the remaining 150 shares.

Personal Situation

Mr. Smith is 53 years old and his wife is 52. They have two children: a son, Bruce, aged 28, who is a dentist; and a daughter, Claire, aged 22, a music student at a conservatory in Rome. Bruce is married and has three children, aged 4, 3, and 1.

Neither Mr. Smith nor Mrs. Smith expects to receive a substantial inheritance from any family member in the future.

TABLE 13-1 Gross Estate Inclusion Section	
IRC Section Number	**Inclusion Section Description**
2031	Broad, nonspecific provision for inclusion to the extent provided by Secs. 2033 through 2046
2033	General miscellaneous ("catchall") inclusion of any property in which the decedent had an interest: any interest in real estate, cash and cash equivalents, stocks, bonds, notes, mortgages, the value of outstanding loans, the value of tax refunds due to the deceased, tangible personal property, outstanding dividends that have been declared and are payable, income receivable, interests in unincorporated businesses, and/or cash value of life insurance owned by the decedent on the lives of others
2034	Dower/curtesy interests (replaced by statutory law most states)
2035	Certain interests transferred within 3 years of death
2036	Interests in previously transferred property that were retained at death
2037	Reversionary interests in previously transferred property that are obtained by surviving decedent
2038	Interests in previously transferred property that are subject to potential alteration, change, amendment, revocation, termination, or affectation of beneficial enjoyment
2039	Annuities and/or payments under certain contracts if the decedent had the right to the payments during his or her lifetime and payments continue beyond his or her death
2040	Joint tenancies with right of survivorship and/or tenancies by the entireties
2041	Value of property subject to a general power of appointment held by the decedent at the time of his or her death
2042	Proceeds of a life insurance policy if: the decedent had any incidents of ownership in the policy; the proceeds are payable to the estate; or the proceeds are receivable by another for the benefit of the estate

Wills and Other Information

Mr. Smith's will provides that, should Mrs. Smith survive him, his household and other tangible personal property are to go outright to her. The residue of his estate is to be divided as follows: one-half to Mrs. Smith outright and the remaining one-half to be distributed outright in equal shares to Bruce and Claire or to their issue, per stirpes. All debts, administration expenses, and taxes are to be paid from the share of the estate going to Bruce and Claire. Mrs. Smith's will provides that her estate is to be divided equally and distributed outright to Bruce and Claire or to their issue, per stirpes.

Neither Mr. Smith nor Mrs. Smith has made any previous gifts.

Property Other than Life Insurance

Mr. Smith owns the following property in his name:

GBH Corporation stock	$2,250,000
Listed common stock	125,000
Marketable corporate bonds	90,000
Savings accounts	75,000
Household and other tangible personal property	70,000

Mrs. Smith owns the following property in her own name:

GBH Corporation stock	$250,000
Listed common stock	210,000
Checking account	12,000

Mr. Smith and Mrs. Smith own the following property as joint tenants (with the right of survivorship):

Principal residence purchased in 1985. Entire purchase price contributed by Mr. Smith. No gift tax return was filed.	$450,000
Summer residence purchased in 1989. Entire purchase price contributed by Mrs. Smith from her separate income. No gift tax return was filed.	220,000
Investment real estate purchased in 1991. Two-thirds of purchase price contributed by Mr. Smith, one-third by Mrs. Smith. No gift tax return was filed.	300,000

Life Insurance

Mr. Smith owns the following life insurance contracts on his own life:

Type	Age When Purchased	Beneficiary Designation	Settlement Arrangement	Face Amount
Life paid up at age 65	31	Mrs. Smith	Life income with no refund feature	$500,000
Ordinary life	35	Mrs. Smith	10-year fixed-period option with no right of withdrawal and with any remaining installments at Mrs. Smith's death to go to the Smith's children in equal shares	250,000

| Ordinary life | 45 | Mrs. Smith | Fixed-amount option with full right of withdrawal and with any remaining installments at Mrs. Smith's death to go to the Smith's children in equal shares | 150,000 |
| Group life | 38 | Mr. Smith's estate | Lump sum | 100,000 |

Mrs. Smith owns the following life insurance contract on Mr. Smith's life:

Type	Age When Purchased	Beneficiary Designation	Settlement Arrangement	Face Amount
30-payment life	46	Bruce and Claire	Lump sum equally	$200,000

CHAPTER REVIEW

Answers to the mini-case, the review questions, and the self-test questions start on page 717.

Key Terms

annuity

joint and survivor annuity

reduction in value by mere lapse
   of time

lump-sum payment

percentage-of-contribution
   (consideration-furnished) rule

basis

power of appointment

general power of appointment

special (limited) power of
   appointment

ascertainable standard

5-and-5 power

incidents of ownership

proceeds payable to or for the
   benefit of an estate

Review Questions

13-1. When is the value of an annuity included in a decedent's gross estate?

13-2. Differentiate between annuities and amounts paid as life insurance proceeds.

13-3. What are the different types of annuities that are includible in a decedent's gross estate?

13-4. How will the following annuities be taxed under Sec. 2039 for federal estate tax purposes with respect to the decedent, Mr. Leonard?

a.   Mr. Leonard purchases a life annuity for himself to end at his death.

b.   Mr. Leonard purchases a life annuity for his wife 5 years before his death.

c.   Mr. Leonard purchases a joint and survivor annuity for himself and his sister, Zelda, who furnished one-third of the purchase price.

13-5.   What is the general rule for determining the valuation of annuities in the gross estate?

13-6.   As of what date must annuities be valued for federal estate tax purposes?

13-7.   To what extent and under what conditions are benefits from a qualified retirement plan included in a decedent's gross estate?

13-8.   Explain the rule for estate taxation of jointly held property with right of survivorship when the only joint tenants are spouses.

13-9.   Ten years ago, Harry Hargrave and his son, Jimmy, acquired some real estate in Atlantic City for $50,000. Harry contributed 75 percent of the purchase price, and Jimmy contributed the remainder, using money that Harry gave him as a gift to pay for his share. They own the property as joint tenants with right of survivorship. The property was worth $200,000 at the beginning of this year when Harry died.

a.   How much, if anything, is included in Harry's gross estate? Explain the reason for your answer.

b.   Would your answer be different if Jimmy's contribution had been made with his own funds?

c.   What would your answer be if the gift to Jimmy had been made 5 years earlier and Jimmy had used income generated by the gift to purchase his share of the jointly held property?

13-10.   Tom and Mary Taylor acquired their personal residence 20 years ago for $150,000. Tom furnished all the consideration for the property. Assume Mary dies this year when the house is worth $310,000.

a.   How much of the value of the house, if any, is included in her gross estate for federal estate tax purposes?

b.   Two years after Mary's death, Tom sold the property. Assuming that the house was worth $320,000 when he sold it, how much, if any, gain would he have?

13-11.   What are three advantages for a married couple of owning property as joint tenants with right of survivorship?

13-12.   What are two disadvantages for a married couple of owning property as joint tenants with right of survivorship?

13-13.   How will property over which the decedent held a general power of appointment be treated for federal estate tax purposes?

13-14. Graham Green's wife gave him a general power of appointment in her will. Mrs. Green died 9 years ago. Mr. Green exercised the power in favor of his two children. He died last year. The value of property subject to the power in the year he exercised it was $250,000. It had increased to $350,000 by the time of his death. How much, if anything, is includible in his gross estate?

13-15. If, at the time of his death, a person possesses a power of appointment that allows him to appoint property to himself, but that is limited by an ascertainable standard so that the property may be appointed to himself only for his health, education, support, or maintenance, how will the property subject to the power be treated for estate tax purposes?

13-16. a. What is the estate tax effect of a general power of appointment (created after 1942) that can be exercised only with the consent of another person who is not an adverse party?
   b. What if the power can be exercised only in conjunction with another person having a substantial adverse interest in the property?
   c. What is meant by an adverse interest in property?
   d. Describe the effects of the *5-and-5 power* as a limitation on the general rule of estate tax inclusion for powers of appointment.

13-17. What is the effect of an individual's disclaiming a general power of appointment if she accepts the power and then tries to transfer it to another after 3 months?

13-18. Explain the general rule for estate taxation of life insurance proceeds.

13-19. In each of the following situations, indicate whether or not the life insurance proceeds on Edgar's life are includible in his estate at his death.
   a. a $25,000 policy owned by Edgar's wife and payable to Edgar's estate
   b. a $100,000 policy owned by Edgar and payable to Edgar's wife
   c. a $50,000 policy owned by Edgar's wife, Sue, and payable to herself as beneficiary. Sue possesses all ownership rights in the policy with the exception that Edgar may borrow the loan value of the policy without security.
   d. a $100,000 policy on Edgar's life transferred 12 years ago to an irrevocable trust for Edgar's children. The trustee is not authorized to use the proceeds to pay Edgar's estate tax. Edgar dies this year.
   e. a group term policy owned by Edgar and payable in equal shares to his wife and two daughters

13-20. a. If the decedent owns life insurance on another party's life, will any part of the value of these policies be includible in the decedent's gross estate?
   b. If so, how will it be valued?

13-21. How can life insurance proceeds payable on the death of the insured qualify for the marital deduction?

13-22. Garland Grant owned a life insurance policy on his life, with a face amount of $200,000. There were no policy loans outstanding. He made an absolute transfer of the policy to an irrevocable trust 2 years ago. He died this year. The named beneficiaries of the trust were his two nieces and two nephews in equal shares.
  a. Are any or all of the proceeds includible in Mr. Grant's gross estate?
  b. How will the proceeds be treated for estate tax purposes if he transfers the policy to the trust for the benefit of his nieces and nephews and dies 5 years afterward?

Self-Test Questions

T   F   13-1. An annuity is includible in a decedent's gross estate if there is a survivorship feature.

T   F   13-2. The value of a survivor's benefit in an annuity contract is includible in the decedent's gross estate, whether paid to his estate or to a named beneficiary, if the decedent had an enforceable right to receive payments during his lifetime or if his estate had a right to receive future payments after his death.

T   F   13-3. The death benefit payable under a nonqualified retirement plan receivable by a beneficiary of an employee who died after reaching retirement age will be excluded from the employee's gross estate if it is received in the form of an annuity.

T   F   13-4. Annuities includible in the estate may be valued either at the date-of-death value or the alternate valuation date.

T   F   13-5. Death benefits from qualified employer retirement plans are always excluded from the gross estate.

T   F   13-6. The general rule is that the entire value of property held by spouses in tenancies by the entireties created after 1976 is includible in the estate of the first spouse to die, except to the extent that the surviving spouse can prove contribution.

T   F   13-7. One-half of property held by unrelated parties as joint tenants with right of survivorship is includible in the gross estate of the first joint tenant to die, regardless of the respective contributions.

T   F   13-8. If a contribution to a nonspousal joint tenancy comes from a gift previously made to the donee-decedent by the donor-joint tenant, it is still considered a contribution by the donee-joint tenant.

T   F   13-9.   If a property is acquired by gift, bequest, or inheritance by nonspouses as joint tenants with right of survivorship, only the value of the fractional interest of the first tenant to die is includible in that individual's gross estate.

T   F   13-10.   One advantage of a joint tenancy with right of survivorship is that it is nonprobate property, thus resulting in a savings in probate costs.

T   F   13-11.   If a husband and wife own property jointly with right of survivorship or as tenants by the entirety, the surviving spouse will receive a stepped-up basis for the entire value of the property.

T   F   13-12.   A disadvantage of property held jointly with right of survivorship is that the decedent loses control over future disposition of the property because a surviving joint tenant can dispose of the property in any way he or she wishes.

T   F   13-13.   If the decedent was a recipient of a power to appoint property only to and among any of his children in any proportion, the value of the property subject to the power will be includible in his gross estate.

T   F   13-14.   A power of appointment that the donee can exercise only with the consent of an adverse party is treated as a special rather than a general power of appointment.

T   F   13-15.   If a person's power of appointment is limited to a noncumulative right to withdraw for his or her own benefit the greater of $5,000 or 5 percent of the aggregate value of the property each year, it is considered a limitation on a general power of appointment that will remove the value of the property subject to the power from his or her gross estate.

T   F   13-16.   If a person releases a general power of appointment (retaining no other rights over the property subject to the power) and dies 2 years later, the value of the property subject to the power will be included in his or her gross estate.

T   F   13-17.   A person possessing a general power of appointment at death must have been legally competent to exercise the power at the time of death for its value to be included in his or her gross estate.

T   F   13-18.   Proceeds of life insurance will be includible in a decedent's gross estate if at the time of death he or she possessed the right to pledge the policy for a loan and the right to revoke an assignment of the policy.

T   F   13-19.   If a decedent was a cotrustee of a life insurance trust that contained a policy on his or her life, the proceeds will be includible in his or her estate regardless of what rights as trustee only he or she may have had over the policy.

T   F   13-20.   Life insurance proceeds payable to an irrevocable trust that requires the trustee to use the proceeds to pay estate taxes on a settlor-decedent's estate will be includible in the decedent's estate.

Deductions from the Gross Estate

Learning Objectives

An understanding of the material in this chapter should enable the student to

---

14-1.   Describe the deductions allowable from the gross estate.

14-2.   Explain any decisions that need to be made to minimize taxes.

Chapter Outline

THE TAXABLE ESTATE

adjusted gross estate

After the gross estate is determined, the next step in calculating the taxable estate is to determine the *adjusted gross estate.*

Calculation of the Taxable Estate

(1) Determine the gross estate

(2) Determine the adjusted gross estate by deducting the following:[*]

- funeral expenses
- administration expenses attributable to property subject to claims against the estate
- claims against the estate
- unpaid mortgages
- other administration expenses
- losses

The deductions above are described in this chapter. It should be noted that, as an alternative, some of these items may be deducted from other tax returns that must be filed (for example, the decedent's last income tax return or the income tax return for the estate). However, if a certain deduction is taken on the income tax return, that same deduction cannot also be taken on the estate tax return (except as noted later under the heading "Taxes").

This chapter concludes with a discussion of the factors involved in determining where it might be best to take the deductions.

taxable estate

All the foregoing are allowable deductions from the gross estate to arrive at the *adjusted gross estate*. Three additional deductions are then permitted—the marital deduction, the charitable deduction, and the state death tax deduction (after 2004) to arrive at the *taxable estate*. The marital and charitable deductions are treated in the next two chapters. The state death tax deduction is discussed in chapter 17.

Allowable Deductions from Gross Estate

- funeral expenses (reasonable amount)
- administration expenses (court costs, attorney/executor fees)
- claims against estate (decedent's debts; certain taxes, not including federal or state death taxes)
- unpaid mortgages
- other estate administration expenses
- theft/casualty losses

---

[*] Editor's note: The adjusted-gross-estate calculation is not a required calculation on Form 706 (federal estate tax return). However, this calculation is required for a variety of other reasons: for example, to determine if a Sec. 303 redemption is permissible, where a formula marital deduction provision is used (for decedents who never amended the marital provisions since the enactment of the unlimited marital deduction), and where a closely held business is part of the gross estate; and to help ascertain whether installment payments of federal estate taxes are possible under Sec. 6166.

FUNERAL EXPENSES

Certain expenditures, such as funeral expenses limited to a *reasonable* amount, are deductible for estate tax purposes only. Such expenses include costs associated with interment, a burial lot or vault, a grave marker or monument, the perpetual care of the gravesite, and transportation of the body to the place of burial. The traveling costs of relatives are generally not an allowable deduction.

EXPENSES OF ADMINISTERING CERTAIN ESTATE PROPERTY

estate administration expenses

The costs of administering property that is included in the decedent's gross estate are generally deductible from either the estate tax return (Form 706) or the estate's income tax return (Form 1041). Deductible items include expenses incurred in the collection and preservation of probate assets, the payment of estate debts, and the distribution of probate assets to estate beneficiaries. These *estate administration expenses* include court costs, executor's commissions, attorney fees, accounting fees, and miscellaneous costs, such as the expenses incurred on the sale of estate property as well as the excise taxes included in these sales if a sale was necessary to settle the estate. Any expenses that were incurred for the benefit of the heirs individually are not deductible. The key question is whether the expenditure was essential to the proper settlement of the estate. For community-property states, the extent to which administration costs and claims are allowable deductions depends on the particular community state's law. Expenses and debts of community property are 50 percent deductible.

Medical Expenses

Medical expenses relating to the decedent's last illness may be deducted on either the estate tax return or the decedent's last income tax return. However, these expenses are deductible on the decedent's last income tax return only if the estate files a statement waiving the right to an estate tax deduction.

CLAIMS AGAINST ESTATE

All claims against the estate, including any bona fide debts that the decedent was validly obligated to pay while alive plus interest accrued to the date of death, are deductible only from the gross estate. These obligations must be based on a promise or agreement. They are deductible only to the extent that they are based on adequate and full consideration in money or money's worth and represent personal obligations of the decedent existing at the time of death, whether or not they have matured. The interest on the indebtedness is deductible but is limited to the amount accrued to the date of death, although the executor may choose the alternate valuation date. Also, liabilities imposed by law or arising out of torts are deductible. If the decedent made a pledge or subscription that is evidenced by a promissory note or other proof, it may be deductible by the estate only to the extent that the liability contracted for was both bona fide and based on adequate consideration in cash or other property. Alternatively, if the pledge is a bequest and thus an allowable charitable deduction, it is deductible under this section.

Taxes

Certain taxes are deductible on the estate tax return as claims against the estate. These include income taxes, unpaid gift taxes, and real property taxes accrued prior to the date of death as long as the property taxes are enforceable obligations at the time of the decedent's death. Federal income taxes owed to the date of death are deductible only on the federal estate tax return. After 2004, state death taxes are also a permissible deduction on the federal estate tax return, but death taxes paid to a city are not deductible. State, local, or foreign income taxes, as well as property taxes, may be deducted on either the federal estate tax return or the federal estate income tax return. Real estate taxes not accrued before death, as well as local and foreign income taxes on estate income, are deductible on the income tax return of the estate. Any federal income taxes on estate income are not deductible either on the estate tax return or for income tax purposes. There is, however, an exception to the general rule denying a double deduction: taxes, interest, and business expenses accrued at the date of the decedent's death that are attributable to income in respect of a decedent are deductible on both the decedent's final income tax return and also the estate tax return as administration expenses.

MORTGAGE DEBT

A deduction is also allowed from the gross estate for the full unpaid balance of a mortgage or other indebtedness, including interest accrued to the date of death, if the following two conditions are met: (1) the full value of property that is not reduced by the mortgage amount or indebtedness must be included in the value of the gross estate; and (2) the decedent's estate must be liable for the amount of the mortgage or indebtedness.

OTHER ADMINISTRATION EXPENSES

Deductions allowed in this category refer to expenses in administering property not subject to claims. *Property that is not subject to claims* usually refers to the nonprobate estate. Jointly held property and life insurance are typical nonprobate assets. Expenses for administering nonprobate assets included in the gross estate are deductible, provided that the expense is paid before the time for filing the federal estate tax return.

CASUALTY LOSSES

casualty loss
theft loss

Casualty loss and *theft loss* are deductible expenses that are incurred during the estate settlement period but only to the extent that these losses are not compensated by insurance. Casualty and theft losses are deductible if the loss arose from fire, storm, shipwreck, or other casualty or theft. The loss must have occurred during the estate settlement process and before the estate was closed. The loss is reduced to the extent that restitution was made through insurance or other compensation to offset the loss. Such a casualty loss to property permits a deduction from the gross estate for either estate tax or estate income tax purposes. However, the estate may not claim the same deduction on both returns.

DECISIONS TO BE MADE TO MINIMIZE TAXES

Deductions from Either Estate Tax Return or Income Tax Return

As previously mentioned, the executor has discretion regarding the deduction of certain items on the federal estate tax return or on income tax returns. This choice does not apply to all debts and expenses. Some expenses are allowable on the federal estate tax return only. Some expenses may be allowed on either the estate tax return or the income tax return.

The primary reason for concern about where to take a deduction is the minimization of taxes. Before any administration expenses or casualty losses may be deducted for income tax purposes, the executor must file a timely statement waiving the right to claim these expenses on the decedent's federal estate tax return. Unless the estate tax deduction is waived, deductions for administration expenses are not allowed from the income of either the estate or the beneficiary for income tax purposes. The executor may file a waiver for a portion of the deductible items while the rest are allowed for estate tax purposes. Once the waiver is filed, it cannot be revoked. The waiver should be filed with the income tax return in the year that the expenses are taken as deductions for income tax purposes. This statement does not apply to deductible expenses that relate to income in respect of a decedent (IRD).

Splitting Deductions between Returns

Sometimes the best result is obtained by taking certain deductions on the estate tax return and other deductions on the income tax return. The regulations permit splitting deductions between the income and estate tax returns. This allows the executor to deduct some administrative expenses on the estate tax return and other allowable expenses on the estate income tax return.

In situations where distributions are made to beneficiaries, the relative estate and income tax brackets of the beneficiaries must be examined. If the beneficiary is in a low-income tax bracket, tax savings may be achieved by splitting the deduction between the beneficiary's income and the estate's income. Also, proper timing of distributions may allow additional tax savings, particularly if the estate has chosen a fiscal year different from the taxable year of the beneficiary.

When the income tax rate is lower than the relevant estate tax rate (after the applicable credit amount is applied), the "optional" deductions are generally more valuable on the estate tax return. However, many estates are not taxable due to the marital deduction and applicable credit amount. In these cases the deductions may be more useful on the estate's *income* tax return.

The executor often has to wait and see before making the appropriate choice. Quite often the executor will deduct the expenses on both returns and later amend one return by removing the deduction after this choice is finalized.

Executor Fees as Either Bequest or Income

Executors who are also named beneficiaries of the decedent may consider the desirability of waiving their executor fees, since they receive a bequest that is income tax free. If an executor's commission is deductible on the federal estate tax return, it is then received as taxable income whether or not the executor is a beneficiary of the estate. However, if the commission or devise is considered a bequest, it is not deductible by the estate for either estate or income tax purposes. Executors must act promptly to waive any commissions if they find that more tax is saved by receiving the bequest income tax free than is saved by characterizing the executor's commission as a deductible expense of the estate. The critical factor to evaluate is whether greater tax savings results from a deduction on the federal estate tax return when the additional income tax incurred by the executor is taken into consideration.

CHAPTER REVIEW

Answers to the review questions and the self-test questions start on page 717.

Key Terms

adjusted gross estate	casualty loss
taxable estate	theft loss
estate administration expenses	

Review Questions

14-1.   What are the basic categories of deductions allowable from a decedent's gross estate to determine the adjusted gross estate?

14-2.   What taxes are deductible on a decedent's federal estate tax return?

14-3.   Melvin Marvel died leaving an $800,000 apartment complex as well as other items. He was not married and was the sole owner of the apartment complex. The apartment complex has a $300,000 mortgage on it, and the full value of $800,000 is included in his estate. Is the estate entitled to a deduction for the mortgage? Explain.

14-4.   Simon Simple's estate included a yacht valued at $150,000 on the federal estate tax return. During the period of estate administration, it was severely damaged by fire. It cost $80,000 to repair the yacht. The estate received $55,000 under its insurance claim.
   a.   State what amount, if any, the estate may deduct on the decedent's estate tax return.
   b.   Would it be possible to deduct this or some other amount as a casualty loss on the decedent's final income tax return instead?

14-5.   If an executor is also a beneficiary of the estate, when would it be wise for the executor to waive the fee?

Self-Test Questions

T   F   14-1.   Funeral expenses are deductible either on the federal estate tax return or on the decedent's last income tax return.

T   F   14-2.   Executors' commissions are considered to be costs of administering property that are included in a decedent's gross estate and are, therefore, deductible from the gross estate.

T   F   14-3.   Unpaid mortgages on property included in the gross estate for which the decedent was liable are allowable as deductions from the gross estate in arriving at the adjusted gross estate.

T   F   14-4.   Expenses in the administration of nonprobate assets are deductible if incurred on behalf of assets includible in the gross estate.

T   F   14-5.   There are certain deductions that may be taken on either the federal estate tax return or the estate's income tax return.

T   F   14-6.   When an executor who is an heir takes a commission for services, he or she must report the commission as ordinary income.

The Marital Deduction

Stephan R. Leimberg and Constance J. Fontaine*

Learning Objectives

An understanding of the material in this chapter should enable the student to

---

15-1. Describe the purpose behind the creation of an unlimited marital deduction, and explain what is meant by the net value of a qualifying interest passing to a surviving spouse.

15-2. Explain the requirements that must be met before property qualifies for the marital deduction.

15-3. Describe how either an overqualification or an underqualification may affect federal estate tax liability, and explain how formulas can be used to minimize the tax.

15-4. Describe the advantages and disadvantages of different forms of marital bequests, and explain the factors that should be considered in deciding to what extent the marital deduction should be used.

Chapter Outline

---

* Stephan R. Leimberg, JD, CLU, formerly was professor of estate planning and taxation at The American College. Constance J. Fontaine, JD, LLM, CLU, ChFC, is associate professor of taxation at The American College and holds the Larry R. Pike chair in Insurance and Investments.

Property included in a decedent's gross estate for federal estate tax purposes that passes (or has passed) to a surviving spouse may qualify for a deduction from the *adjusted gross estate* in arriving at the *taxable estate*. No deduction is more important to the typical married individual's estate than the estate tax marital deduction. It is often possible, through judicious use of this deduction, to reduce or eliminate the estate tax on the death of the first spouse. But if used improperly, the marital-deduction transfer can result in an overall combined estate tax on the total estates of both spouses that is far greater than if no transfer to a surviving spouse was made.

For these reasons, and because the rules in the Internal Revenue Code for qualifying for the marital deduction are strictly construed, a member of the estate planning team must have a thorough knowledge of the marital-deduction requirements.

BACKGROUND

As previously discussed in chapter 4, married residents of nine states (Arizona, California, Idaho, Louisiana, Nevada, New Mexico, Texas, Washington, and Wisconsin) operate under a community-property system. Therefore, all property acquired (other than by gift, devise, bequest, or inheritance) by husband and wife during marriage while living in one of these states belongs to the *community*; that is, each spouse automatically and from the inception of ownership owns one-half of the property. Upon death, a decedent can dispose of only his or her share of the community property by will. Because of this state property law concept, only one-half of the community property is includible in the estate of whichever spouse dies first.

Example:	Assume Herb and his wife, Roz, live in California. Herb's salary is large enough to allow him to save $50,000 a year. One-half of that, $25,000, is deemed to be Roz's property. Therefore, only one-half of the $50,000 is includible in Herb's estate if he dies first. Likewise, if Roz dies first, $25,000 is includible in her estate even though Herb earned the entire $50,000.

This tax advantage has been reflected in the income and gift taxation of community-property residents as well as in the estate taxation. As a result, residents of common-law states grew indignant, recognizing that their community-property neighbors were taxed more favorably under a state property law system that treated one-half of the earnings of either spouse as automatically belonging to the other.

Some traditionally common-law states (such as Pennsylvania, Michigan, Hawaii, and Nebraska) sought to achieve tax parity by converting to what was, in effect, a community-property system. Great interstate resentment and confusion about the disparities that developed prompted Congress to aim for tax parity by making a federal estate tax marital deduction available to married residents of common-law states.

Therefore, the Internal Revenue Code now allows a deduction for the value of any qualifying property interests includible in the decedent's gross estate that pass from the decedent to the surviving spouse.

AMOUNT OF MARITAL DEDUCTION

Today, a federal estate tax-free interspousal transfer is allowed either during lifetime or at death. In other words, the law now allows a deduction for unlimited assets passing from one spouse to another. Even residents of community-property states can take advantage of this unlimited marital deduction, because community property now qualifies for the marital deduction to the extent that it is includible in the decedent spouse's estate. Conceivably, this means that a decedent-spouse could leave his or her entire $10 million estate to his or her surviving spouse and not pay any federal estate tax. However, the deduction cannot exceed the net value of the *qualifying interests* (defined below) passing to the surviving spouse.

QUALIFICATIONS ON AMOUNT OF MARITAL DEDUCTION

The estate tax marital deduction is allowed on the net value of a qualifying interest passing to a decedent's surviving spouse. Therefore, it is necessary to define the term *net value*.

Net value refers to the gross estate tax value of a property interest—that is, its date-of-death value or, if applicable, its value as of the alternate valuation date, minus any charges against that interest.

Generally speaking, this means that the gross value of a property interest passing to the surviving spouse must be reduced by (1) taxes payable out of the interest, (2) mortgages or liens against the interest, and (3) administration expenses payable out of the interest.

Taxes payable out of the interest include any federal estate tax or state death tax. The word *payable* is important because, in order to reduce the marital deduction, it is not necessary that the taxes actually be paid out of the marital share—only that they be *payable*.

Example:	If Lara's will authorizes her executor to pay death taxes out of Lara's husband's share of her $300,000 estate, the value of the interest passing to the husband is reduced for purposes of computing the marital deduction, even if, in fact, Lara's executor uses other funds to pay the tax.

If the surviving spouse takes an interest subject to a mortgage or a lien, the gross value of the interest is reduced by the amount of that obligation. For instance, if Lara left her husband a $100,000 boat on which she owed $20,000, only $80,000 of qualifying property would pass. However, if Lara's will (or state law) required the debt to be discharged before the title to the boat was transferred to her husband, the gross value of the boat would be used in the marital-deduction computation; the amount of the lien would not reduce the marital deduction.

When administration expenses are chargeable (under a decedent's will or under state law) against the surviving spouse's share of the estate, the amount of those expenses reduces the allowable marital deduction.

These reductions are usually avoided by requiring in the decedent's will that expenses, debts, and taxes be paid out of the share of the estate passing to beneficiaries other than the spouse.

TRANSFERS QUALIFYING FOR MARITAL DEDUCTION

A number of very strictly construed technical requirements must be met before property qualifies for the marital deduction, and there are certain qualifications and limitations that must be considered:

- the citizenship requirement for the surviving spouse
- the requirement that property be included
- the requirement that property must pass or have passed
- the marital-status requirement
- the terminable-interest rule

Citizenship Requirement for Surviving Spouse

The marital deduction is generally allowed only for transfers to a spouse who is, at the date of the decedent's death, a U.S. citizen. The marital deduction can be preserved if the surviving spouse becomes a citizen before the decedent's estate tax return is filed.

Transfers to a Surviving Resident-Alien Spouse

resident alien

While the marital deduction provides an opportunity for a married couple to avoid federal estate taxes at the death of the first spouse, it is not available for property passing to a surviving resident-alien spouse. A *resident alien* is one who resides in the Unites States but is not a U.S. citizen.

This limitation on the use of the marital deduction reflects Congress's concern that if a surviving resident-alien spouse were to receive marital assets at the death of the citizen spouse, the survivor could return to his or her home country with such assets. Because the United States does not have jurisdiction to tax a nonresident alien for property located outside of the country, the assets transferred to the surviving resident-alien spouse could completely escape federal estate and gift taxation. This occurrence would be inconsistent with the underlying concept of the marital deduction—that is, that the wealth accumulated by a married couple will, to the extent it is unconsumed, be subject to transfer tax at the second spouse's death. The marital deduction is intended only to provide a deferral mechanism. If, however, the resident-alien spouse is the first spouse to die and property is transferred in a qualifying manner to the surviving citizen spouse, the marital deduction is allowed. In this case, transfer taxes can be imposed whenever the surviving U.S. citizen spouse transfers property.

Because the general rule is that transfers to a resident-alien spouse will not qualify for the unlimited federal estate or gift tax marital deduction, there is a special concern for marriages that include a resident-alien spouse. As previously mentioned, the transfer taxes facing such marriages often depend on which spouse survives. If the survivor is the resident alien, a substantial first-death estate tax may be payable. Fortunately, there are some exceptions to this harsh rule.

The Surviving Spouse Obtains Citizenship

Transfers to a surviving resident-alien spouse are eligible for the marital deduction if (1) the surviving spouse becomes a U.S. citizen before the decedent spouse's estate tax return is filed and (2) the surviving spouse remains a U.S. resident after the death of the citizen spouse.

Qualified Domestic Trust (QDOT)

qualified domestic trust (QDOT)

If the surviving resident-alien spouse does not obtain U.S. citizenship, a *qualified domestic trust (QDOT)* can be used to transfer assets to a surviving resident-alien spouse while preserving the marital deduction for such transfer.

Congress created an exception for transfers to a qualified domestic trust to alleviate some of the harsh estate tax implications associated with the denial of the marital deduction for transfers to a resident-alien spouse. A QDOT is a unique transfer vehicle for marital-deduction transfers to surviving resident-alien spouses. Unfortunately, the QDOT rules also include a new type of transfer tax. Although the QDOT appears to provide all the usual tax benefits of the marital deduction, it has several disadvantages not applicable to transfers between citizen spouses. It is beyond the scope of this chapter to explore in depth the aspects of the marital deduction and marriages involving resident-alien spouses. The complex nature of this area requires the advice of an experienced estate planner.

Requirement That Property Be Included

A transfer does not qualify for the marital deduction unless the property interest is included in the decedent's gross estate for federal estate tax purposes. For example, no marital deduction is allowed when a wife purchases a life insurance policy on the life of her husband with her own funds and is the owner and beneficiary of such a policy. Because the proceeds of the policy are not includible in the husband's gross estate in the first place, they do not qualify for a marital deduction. However, if for any reason the life insurance proceeds are includible in the decedent's gross estate, they can qualify for the marital deduction if passing to the surviving spouse.

Requirement That Property Must Pass or Have Passed

The *pass-or-have-passed requirement* has two implications:

- An interest owned by the decedent must pass from the decedent to a surviving spouse; that is, the surviving spouse must receive the property by means of a transfer from the decedent, as opposed to a transfer from someone else.
- The surviving spouse must receive the interest as beneficial owner rather than as trustee or agent for someone else.

An interest can be transferred from the decedent to a surviving spouse in a number of ways that qualify for the marital deduction. These include transfers from the decedent

- by will, intestacy, or similar law
- by election against the will. In many states, a decedent cannot disinherit a surviving spouse because the survivor can elect to receive the amount that would have been received had the decedent

died intestate—that is, without a will. The amount received as a result of the election is *property passing*.

- by transfer to a spouse made by the decedent during lifetime and for some reason includible in the estate (for example, a transfer the decedent made when a life estate was retained)

- in the form of life insurance death proceeds. This assumes the decedent retained incidents of ownership in the policy.

- by survivorship (for example, when the surviving spouse was a joint tenant with rights of survivorship). Note that, in this case, the marital deduction is allowed only to the extent the jointly held property is includible in the decedent's estate for federal estate tax purposes. Because only 50 percent of all spouse-owned jointly held property (that is, spousal joint tenancies created after December 31, 1976) is includible, only the value of that portion is counted in computing the actual marital deduction even though the survivor receives title to the entire property.

- by power of appointment. For example, the surviving spouse could have been the appointee of a general power that the decedent, as donee, exercised, or a *taker in default* when the decedent failed to exercise a general power.

If the decedent leaves a bequest to a surviving spouse and the spouse *disclaims* (in other words, states in a timely disclaimer, "I renounce all my rights to the property"), the interest disclaimed is treated as if it never passed to the surviving spouse. Therefore, it does not qualify. But, if the bequest was first accepted by the surviving spouse and then transferred to a child, the property is considered to have passed from the decedent to the surviving spouse. (The spouse may be subject to gift tax on the value of the transfer to the child.)

Example:	Frank named his wife, Mary Jo, primary beneficiary of a $100,000 life insurance policy he owned on his life. He named his daughter, Julia, secondary beneficiary. At Frank's death, Mary Jo could have taken the proceeds in a lump sum. Instead she directed the insurance company to hold the proceeds at interest. In this case, an includible interest (the $100,000 in proceeds) is considered to have passed from the decedent to the surviving spouse. Her disposal of the property after that point does not affect the marital deduction. But if Mary Jo had made a timely disclaimer, she would have been treated as if she had never received the proceeds and, therefore, no marital deduction would have been allowed.

There is another way a disclaimer can affect the marital deduction. Sometimes a decedent's will leaves the entire estate to a son or daughter. If the child makes a timely disclaimer, the result is the same as if no interest had ever passed to the child. If the child's refusal to accept the property causes all or a portion of it to pass to the surviving spouse, it qualifies as property passing from the decedent to a surviving spouse. In other words, if the effect of a disclaimer by a third party is to increase the amount of property passing from the decedent to the surviving spouse, the result may be to increase the marital deduction.

Types of Marital Deduction Transfers

Transferred by
- intestacy
- will
- election against the will
- contract (Sec. 2042 life insurance inclusion)
- survivorship (decedent's joint tenancy interest)
- lifetime spousal transfers (Secs. 2036, 2037, and 2038 retained interests/inclusion)
- successful will contest
- qualified disclaimer

There is another implication to the pass-or-have-passed requirement. Regardless of whether the surviving spouse receives property outright or in trust for his or her benefit, the interest must be as an equitable owner in order to qualify; if the spouse is merely made a trustee for somebody else or is bound by agreement to transfer the property to another person, it is not considered to pass to the surviving spouse. So a bequest in a will providing that "my land in Wildwood is to go to my wife, Lynne, for the benefit of my invalid son, Marvin," does not qualify.

Marital-Status Requirement

Appropriate marital status is an essential element. The decedent must have been (1) married at the date of death and (2) survived by the spouse receiving the property in question.

Obviously, the words *surviving* and *spouse* present difficult questions in two situations: (1) when there has been a divorce or separation and (2) when the decedent's and spouse's order of deaths cannot be established by proof.

The status of the surviving spouse is determined as of the date of a decedent's death. A legal separation or interlocutory (temporary and not yet final) decree of divorce that has not ended the marital relationship by the date of the decedent's death does not change the surviving spouse's status. So a bequest to a spouse when the decedent is legally separated still qualifies for the federal estate tax marital deduction.

However, if, for example, a property interest passes from the decedent to a former wife who is not married to him at the date of his death, even though she may survive him, the interest does not pass to a surviving spouse.

If the decedent transferred property to someone who at the time of the transfer was not a spouse but who was a spouse on the date of death, the transfer is considered made to a surviving spouse. If for any reason that transfer must be included in the decedent's estate, it will qualify for the marital deduction. For instance, if Mary gives IBM stock to Pat but retains the right to the dividends that it produces, the stock is includible in her estate. If Mary has married Pat (either before or after the gift) and they are still married at the time of Mary's death, a marital deduction is allowed with respect to the stock.

The survivorship requirement is generally not difficult to meet in most cases. But problems can occur when deaths result from a common accident and the order of deaths cannot be determined.

At the time an estate is planned, a conflict of interest can develop. On one hand, the marital deduction may be desirable only if it is likely that the surviving spouse will be able to use and enjoy the marital property for a relatively long period of time. If the surviving spouse dies immediately or shortly after receiving the marital share, that property (1) will be subject to a second probate and its consequent costs, (2) may be subject to federal estate taxation, and (3) will be subject to a second round of state inheritance tax in states that have neither a marital deduction nor a credit for previously paid taxes. Furthermore, the original decedent's property may pass to his or her spouse's heirs—a result the decedent may not have desired and would have taken steps to prevent had it been known that his or her spouse would live only a short period of time.

Conversely, there are situations in which the use of the marital deduction makes good planning sense, even if the surviving spouse will probably not enjoy the property for long. One such case is when the original decedent has a large estate and the spouse has a small estate. The present value of the tax dollar saved through the use of the marital deduction at the first death, together with the availability of a second estate tax applicable credit amount, can be a sizable advantage.

Will the marital deduction be allowed if there is no evidence as to the order of deaths? The regulations provide that when it is impossible to ascertain which spouse died first, any presumption, whether established by the decedent in a will, by state law, or otherwise, will be recognized. This means that, to the extent the presumption results in the inclusion of a bequest in the gross estate of the spouse deemed to have survived, a marital deduction is allowed.

This presumption is generally made in a will or life insurance settlement option in the form of a *presumption-of-survivorship clause*. A typical clause might read as follows:

> In the event my wife and I die under such circumstances that there is no sufficient evidence to establish who survived the other, I hereby declare that my wife shall be deemed to have survived me, and this will and all its provisions shall be construed upon that assumption and basis.

The importance of a presumption-of-survivorship clause in a decedent's will or life insurance settlement should not be underestimated. It can be an especially worthwhile tax savings device when the spouse and/or nonmarital beneficiaries are less wealthy than the testator. This is because the clause makes optimal use of the marital deduction and multiple applicable credit amounts possible. Assume that for the current year a husband owns property in his own name worth $2,800,000 and the wife's assets are nominal. The husband leaves his entire estate to his wife. He has made no taxable lifetime gifts. If the wife either actually survives or, because of a presumption clause in a will or life insurance settlement option, is deemed to survive, the difference can be sizable, as the illustrations below show. (Assume funeral and administrative expenses of $40,000 as well as debts and taxes of $30,000.)

If the marital deduction is lost, the difference in cost in this hypothetical example (computed before credits) is $1,131,200, the difference between the tentative tax when no marital deduction is allowable ($1,131,200) and the tentative tax if the marital deduction is obtained ($0).

What happens if there is a common disaster in which both spouses die and no presumption-of-survivorship clause has been inserted in a will or life insurance settlement option? As mentioned above, state laws will govern.

With the Marital Deduction

Gross estate		$2,800,000
Funeral and administration costs	40,000	
Debts and taxes	30,000	
		(70,000)
Adjusted gross estate		2,730,000
Marital deduction		2,730,000
Taxable estate		—
Adjusted taxable gifts		—
Tentative tax base		—
Tentative tax		—

Without the Marital Deduction

Gross estate		$2,800,000
Funeral and administration costs	40,000	
Debts and taxes	30,000	
		(70,000)
Adjusted gross estate		2,730,000
Marital deduction		0
Taxable estate		2,730,000
Adjusted taxable gifts		—
Tentative tax base		2,730,000
Tentative tax		$1,131,200

Practically all states have adopted the Uniform Simultaneous Death Act (USDA). This act provides that if the order of deaths of the spouses cannot be determined and there is no presumption-of-survivorship clause in the will and/or life insurance contract, each decedent's estate will be distributed as though he or she were the survivor. In other words, in the probate of the husband's will, it will be assumed that he survived his wife. In the probate of the wife's will, it is presumed that she survived her husband. This results in a tax tragedy—the loss of the marital deduction, which, in the example above, would be quite costly to their heirs.

In 1991, a new Uniform Simultaneous Death Act (USDA '91) was developed, with several technical amendments added in 1993. The original Uniform Simultaneous Death Act (USDA) was developed in 1940. Its application is limited to situations involving the simultaneous deaths of a testator and beneficiary. The original Act is inapplicable to deaths that occur within short intervals of each other. The primary purpose of USDA '91 is to resolve survivorship dilemmas when the deaths occur within a close interval. It presumes that a testator would prefer assets to pass to a second beneficiary if the primary beneficiary does not survive the testator by 120 hours. The effect of the original act is retained in true simultaneous death cases.

Terminable-Interest Rule

The term *qualifying interest* is frequently used in discussions of the marital deduction; the implication is that some transfers may not qualify for the marital deduction because of the nature of the property interest itself.

Why are some interests deductible and others nondeductible? Obviously, if the transfer does not meet the tests discussed, it is nondeductible. But there **terminable-interest rule** is a further roadblock to deductibility known as the *terminable-interest rule*.

To understand how the terminable-interest rule operates—and when exceptions apply—it is necessary to review briefly tax history and philosophy.

The principal purpose of the marital deduction is to create tax parity after death between residents of common-law and community-property states—assuming, of course, equal estates. Given the same size estates and general dispository schemes, the federal tax consequences should be substantially equal, regardless of the decedent's domicile.

This thrust toward equalization grew out of the fact that in a community-property state, one-half of what one spouse acquired through earnings or as income from community property during the marriage was automatically considered the property of the other spouse. If the wife survived, she owned the property outright. She could give it away (and it would be subject to gift taxes), or she could keep it until death (and it would be subject to estate taxes). Regardless of whether she made a lifetime gift or a testamentary gift, the IRS had its proverbial bite of the tax apple.

The marital deduction was designed to give residents of common-law states the same federal estate tax treatment—but no more. In other words, because the share of a community-property decedent's surviving spouse has to be included in the surviving spouse's gross estate (the one-half portion not taxed at the decedent's death because community-property law deems it to be the surviving spouse's), it is only fair that when the surviving spouse of a decedent in a common-law state dies, the share of the decedent's estate that escapes estate taxation at the decedent's death by virtue of the marital deduction should be taxed at the surviving spouse's death. The marital deduction is, therefore, not a tax-avoidance device; it merely defers taxation until the death of the second spouse.

This is the terminable-interest rule's general theory and goal: to allow the marital deduction only when the nature of the interest passing to the spouse is such that, if retained until death, it will be taxed in the surviving spouse's estate.

Emphasis should be placed on the words *general, theory*, and *goal*. Generally, the *intent* of the law is to deny a deduction for any interest acquired by a surviving spouse that would not be includible in the surviving spouse's estate for federal estate tax purposes if held until death. For example, if a wife in her will gives her husband the right to land in Wildwood for life, with the remainder going to their children at his death, no part of the value of the land would be includible in the husband's estate. To allow a marital deduction for such a devise would favor common-law over community-property residents.

If an interest will be includible in a surviving spouse's estate if it is held until death, does the converse of the general rule make it deductible? The answer is no. There can be situations in which an interest is nondeductible, even though it causes estate tax liability at the surviving spouse's death.

The *includible-in-the-surviving-spouse's-estate* rule should be remembered, therefore, only to review the basic intent of the law. But to understand how the terminable-interest rule is actually applied and when exceptions are operative, it is more helpful to examine the rule—and its exceptions—directly.

Actually, there are two terminable-interest rules. The first provides that property is considered a nondeductible terminable interest if the following conditions exist:

- *It is a terminable interest*, that is, if it is an interest in property that will terminate or fail upon the lapse of time or upon the occurrence or non-occurrence of some contingency. Life estates, annuities, and copyrights are good examples of this rule. Upon the death of a life beneficiary, a life estate or life annuity ends. Likewise, a patent will expire at the end of a given period of time. Other terminable interests include an estate for a term of years, such as "to my wife for 10 years," and a widow's support allowance that—under state law—ends when the widow dies or remarries. If Ed left Joyce property in Wildwood in the following manner, "to my wife, Joyce, during the time until she remarries," her interest would terminate at that event. If Ed had said, "to my wife, Joyce, absolutely but if she does not survive my father, then the property is to go to my sister," again Joyce's interest is terminable. Note that it is not necessary that the contingency or event actually occur—or fail to occur—in order that the interest be considered terminable; all that is required is that the surviving spouse's interest could terminate.
- *Another interest in the same property passed from the decedent to some person other than the surviving spouse or the spouse's estate.* For example, if the decedent gave her husband a life estate and provided that at his death their children would receive the remainder, such remainder interest would be *another interest in the same property*, and it would be passing from the decedent to someone other than the surviving spouse or his estate.
- *The interest passes or has passed to the "other person" for less than adequate and full consideration in money or money's worth.* In the example discussed above, the remainder interest would pass to the children without payment by them in money or money's worth. However, if the children had purchased the remainder interest for its fair market value and the proceeds were given to the decedent's estate, this provision would not be met (and, therefore, the interest would qualify for the marital deduction).
- *Because of its passing, the "other person(s)" or his or her heirs could possess or enjoy any part of the property when the surviving spouse's interest terminated.* Note that if a decedent left property "to my daughter, Pat, for life, then to my wife, Lynne, absolutely," the present value of the wife's interest (that is, the value after subtracting the daughter's life interest) is not disqualified for the marital deduction, since no one can possess or enjoy any part of the property when the wife dies. In fact, the wife's interest is not terminable.

So, generally, a terminable interest—such as a life estate—is disqualified only if it falls within all of the last three categories. Therefore, a transfer "to my wife for life, then to her estate" qualifies for the marital deduction. This lifetime bequest to the surviving spouse qualifies, since the decedent designated his surviving spouse's estate (rather than their children) as the remainderperson; hence, no interest passes to someone other than the surviving spouse or her estate.

Terminable Interests

- to spouse unless remarriage occurs
- to spouse for life, then to children
- to spouse on a condition/event
- to brother, then to spouse

There is a second type of terminable interest that does not qualify for the marital deduction—even though no person other than the surviving spouse acquires an interest in the property. This is a situation in which the decedent in his or her will has directed the executor (or a trustee) to take assets ostensibly available to the surviving spouse and purchase a terminable interest with them. For example, if Al leaves $100,000 to his wife, Leslie, in a specific bequest in his will but directs his executor to use the $100,000 as the purchase price for a straight life annuity (no refund) for her, the $100,000 bequest will not qualify for the marital deduction. Likewise, if Al's executor is directed to use the $100,000 to purchase a patent, copyright, or other terminable interest for Leslie, such a bequest will not qualify.

Marital Deduction Requirements

- The surviving spouse must be a U.S. citizen.
- Marital status must exist.
- The property must be included in the decedent-spouse's gross estate.
- The property must pass to the surviving spouse.
- The transfer must not be a terminable interest.

Exceptions to Terminable-Interest Rules That Qualify for Marital Deduction

There are important exceptions to the terminable-interest rules. Exceptions are listed directly below and are then discussed in the paragraphs that follow.

- An interest will still qualify for the marital deduction (it will not be considered a nondeductible terminable interest solely because it will terminate or fail upon the surviving spouse's death) if the bequest to the surviving spouse was conditional upon his or her surviving for up to 6 months after the decedent's death—as long as the surviving spouse does, in fact, survive for the specified period. (For example, an interest is not disqualified for the marital deduction merely because it states "if my husband fails to survive me by 6 months, this will and all its provisions shall be construed as if he predeceased me.") However, if the specified termination does occur, the marital deduction is lost.
- A bequest of a life estate can qualify for the marital deduction if it is coupled with a general power of appointment. An interest passing to a surviving spouse for life with the remainder payable to his or her estate may also qualify for the marital deduction.
- A life insurance policy payable to the surviving spouse for life can qualify if the spouse has a general power of appointment over the proceeds.
- A qualified terminable-interest property election can also qualify.

Normally, these transfers of property would violate the terminable-interest rules and, therefore, not qualify for the marital deduction. The exceptions to the terminable-interest rules, however, specifically permit these kinds of transfers to a surviving spouse to qualify for the deduction if the requirements of the exceptions are met. All of the exceptions other than the 6-month survival contingency exception involve trust arrangements that qualify for the marital deduction.

Six-Month Survival Contingency. The first exception to the terminable-interest rule provides that an interest passing to a surviving spouse is not considered nondeductible merely because it will terminate or fail upon the surviving spouse's death within a period of not more than 6 months of the decedent's death. (This type of provision is sometimes used to prevent *double probate* and *double state death taxation* when the death of one spouse occurs within a short time of the other spouse's death.)

Example:	Ike leaves his land in Stone Harbor to his wife, Tina. But Ike's will provides that Tina will receive no interest in the land if she does not survive Ike for 6 months. If Tina, in fact, survives the 6-month period, a marital deduction will be allowed in Ike's estate. If Tina does not survive Ike by the required period of time, no deduction will be allowed.

If Ike required Tina to survive him by some period in excess of 6 months (such as survival by one year or survival "until my estate is closed"), the transfer would not qualify because it exceeds or could exceed the 6-month permissible period. If Ike's will provided "my land is to go to Tina, my wife, for life, and the remainder, at her death, is to go to my son, Sophocles, but for my wife to receive her interest, she must survive me by 3 months," the interest would not qualify for the marital deduction even if Tina did survive the 3-month period. This is because the failure of a contingency to occur cannot convert what is otherwise a nonqualifying terminable interest (the life estate to the wife and remainder to the son) into a qualifying interest.

A second part of this exception deals with common-disaster provisions. Assume Ike's will stated, "I leave my entire estate to my wife, Tina, but if she and I die in a common disaster, my estate goes instead to my son, Sophocles." Assume also that state law defines a common disaster as an event in which both spouses die within 30 days from injuries attributable to a common accident. If Tina survived for 2 months and then died, she would have received Ike's estate. Since the terminating contingency—the deaths of both spouses in a common disaster as defined by state law—did not occur, the marital deduction would be allowed in Ike's estate. But if Tina died 3 weeks after the accident, no marital deduction would be allowed because the terminating contingency did, in fact, occur.

Power-of-Appointment Trust. The second exception to the terminable-interest rule is that the interest is not disqualified if it meets the following five conditions:

- The surviving spouse is entitled to all the income from the interest in question.
- The income is payable annually or more frequently. (The marital trust is the receptacle into which probate assets qualifying for the marital deduction are placed. If the marital trust has a specific provision either authorizing investment in non-income-producing assets or allowing the trustee to retain unproductive—that is, non-income-producing—assets, this requirement may not be satisfied. This militates against the purchase of life insurance by the marital trust or leaving closely held stock that has never paid a significant dividend or unproductive land in the trust, unless the surviving spouse has an unqualified right to demand that trust assets be sold and converted into income-producing property.)
- The surviving spouse has the power to appoint the interest to himself or herself or to his or her estate.
- The power must be exercisable by the surviving spouse alone and in all events. It can be a lifetime power or power exercisable by the

surviving spouse only at death—that is, by will—or a power exercisable in either event.

- No person other than the surviving spouse has a power to appoint any part of the interest to anyone other than the surviving spouse.

power-of-appointment trust

This second exception makes the *power-of-appointment trust* the most widely used method of qualifying property in trust for the marital deduction. Essentially, the power-of-appointment trust is, as its name implies, a trust designed to hold assets for the surviving spouse and to qualify for the marital deduction by providing the surviving spouse with a general power of appointment over the corpus (see figure 15-1). The primary purpose of such a trust arrangement is to require the surviving spouse to take affirmative action to direct the corpus at death from the original estate owner's planned disposition.

Generally, the testator's will sets up two trusts: a marital (spouse's) trust (often referred to as the A trust) and a nonmarital (family) trust (B trust). The marital trust is designed to hold assets that qualify for the marital deduction, while the nonmarital trust is intended to provide management for assets that are taxable at the testator's death.

If it is drafted properly, the nonmarital (family) trust provides the spouse with additional income and even limited amounts of principal without causing

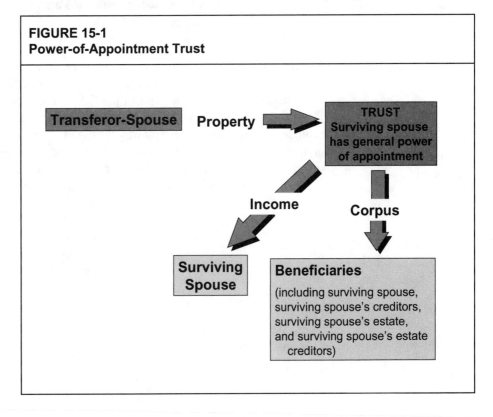

FIGURE 15-1
Power-of-Appointment Trust

bypass trust

credit-exclusion/ equivalent bypass trust (CEBT)

an inclusion of principal in the survivor's gross estate. In a sense, this trust is a *bypass trust*, because it provides security for the spouse but bypasses taxation in the surviving spouse's estate when the spouse dies. Quite often this trust is called a *credit-exclusion/equivalent bypass trust (CEBT)* because—ideally, at least—it should be funded with assets equivalent to the testator's applicable exclusion amount (credit equivalent).

Example:　　Assume Joan McFadden's adjusted gross estate was worth $2,325,000. The formula in her will for determining how assets are to be divided might provide that an amount equal to the applicable exclusion amount (credit equivalent)—$1.5 million (in 2004 and 2005)—go to the CEBT and the balance of her estate to her surviving spouse. The federal estate tax on the $1.5 million that goes into the CEBT would be eliminated by the credit (the $1.5 million of assets generates $555,800 of estate tax, which would be wiped out by the $555,800 credit). The $825,000 passing to her husband (either directly or in trust) would qualify for the unlimited marital deduction and, therefore, escape federal estate tax at Joan's death.

The advantage of *carving out* a credit-exclusion/equivalent bypass trust before determining the marital deduction is that when the spouse dies, at least the applicable exclusion amount in the CEBT escapes taxation in his estate. Through a more effective use of his wife's applicable credit amount (and the avoidance of *stacking* assets into the husband's estate), significant estate tax savings can be realized. (The results are even more dramatic if there is a substantial increase in asset values between the first and second deaths.) For instance, in the example above assume that the surviving spouse had no estate of his own. At his death, examine the following:

	If husband received only $825,000	If husband received $2,325,000
Tentative tax base	$825,000	$2,325,000
Tentative tax	$ 277,550	$933,550
Applicable credit amount (2004/2005)	$555,800	$ 555,800
Tax	$ 0	$ 377,750

The same result is often obtained by establishing an inter vivos trust during the grantor's lifetime, and then *pouring over* probate assets by will into this trust and naming the trust direct beneficiary of death benefits from life insurance proceeds and employee benefit plans. At the grantor's death, the trust is split into two (or more) trusts or two (or more) portions—marital and nonmarital—with the same functions as the testamentary trusts described above.

When the surviving spouse is given a general power of appointment over assets that are in the marital trust, the trust is known as a *power-of-appointment trust*.

The intended result can be accomplished by giving the surviving spouse a power to withdraw the property in the marital trust anytime during life or to direct by will that the property is to become part of the survivor's estate or be used to satisfy creditors at death.

The surviving spouse can be restricted to a power exercisable only by will; the trust will qualify for the marital deduction even if the spouse has no power to withdraw the corpus during lifetime.

estate trust

Estate Trust. In addition to the power-of-appointment trust, the *estate trust* is also a viable method of obtaining a marital deduction. An estate trust is one in which the surviving spouse is given an interest for life, with the remainder payable to his or her estate. In effect, this gives the surviving spouse the equivalent of a general power of appointment by will, since that spouse can *transfer* (or, more correctly, shift) property subject to the power to anyone he or she chooses (see figure 15-2).

The estate trust does not run afoul of the nondeductible terminable-interest rule for another reason: no interest passes to anyone other than the surviving spouse or to the surviving spouse's estate.

An estate trust is a useful alternative to the power-of-appointment trust for a number of reasons.

First, in contrast to the power-of-appointment trust, under which all income must be payable to the surviving spouse annually or more frequently, the trustee of an estate trust can accumulate income within the trust instead of paying it out. If the trust is in a lower income tax bracket than that of the surviving spouse, the power to accumulate can result in income tax savings. The income tax rates for trusts and estates enacted under the Revenue Reconciliation Act of 1993 (RRA '93), however, have generally eliminated this benefit.

Second, because the spouse does not have to receive all of the income annually, a trustee can either invest in nonproductive (non-income-producing) property or retain nonproductive assets, such as non-dividend-paying stock in a family-owned corporation.

These advantages must be weighed, however, against the certainty that any income accumulations (together with the original corpus) will be includible in

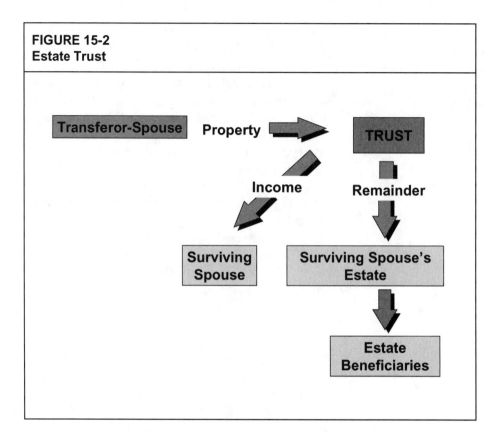

FIGURE 15-2
Estate Trust

the surviving spouse's estate. This, in turn, may result in increased administrative costs, be subject to the claims of creditors, and attract state inheritance taxes. (For example, compare this with the power-of-appointment trust, which, under the laws of a state such as Pennsylvania, is not part of the probate estate and the corpus of which is not taxed for state inheritance tax purposes at the death of the donee of the power.)

Interest in Life Insurance Proceeds. The third exception to the terminable-interest rule parallels the second: an interest in life insurance proceeds (or an endowment or annuity contract) is treated as passing solely to the surviving spouse, if both of the following conditions exist:

- Under the settlement option, the surviving spouse is entitled to all of the interest for life (or the right to installment payments of the proceeds for life).
- The surviving spouse has the right to appoint to himself or herself, or to his or her estate, any proceeds or installment payments remaining.

This exception makes it possible to qualify life insurance proceeds under a settlement option if the surviving spouse is given the equivalent of a general power of appointment, even if there is a gift-over. For example, a settlement option could qualify for the marital deduction if it provided that (1) the surviving spouse is to receive *interest only* for life; (2) there is an unlimited right of withdrawal or the right to a one-sum settlement; and (3) if no withdrawal is made, any proceeds remaining are to be paid to the children born of the marriage of the insured and said spouse.

Qualified Terminable-Interest Property. A fourth exception allows a qualifying terminable-interest property to qualify for the marital deduction. A person can provide that his or her spouse will receive only the income from property and, at the death of the surviving spouse, it must pass to the person or persons specified in the will of the original transferor-spouse. This otherwise nondeductible terminable interest qualifies for the marital deduction—hence the name *qualifying terminable-interest property (QTIP)*—if certain requirements are met. This provision permits a spouse to provide for the surviving spouse through a transfer sheltered by the marital deduction and still retain control over the ultimate disposition of the assets. The QTIP is a way for a spouse to protect the interests of other heirs (perhaps children from a prior marriage) while also providing for the surviving spouse.

qualified terminable interest property (QTIP)

Exceptions to Terminable-Interest Rules

- conditioned on spouse's surviving decedent by 6 months
- life estate in spouse *and* spouse has general power of appointment over property
- power-of-appointment trust
- life estate in spouse *and* property passes to spouse's estate (estate trust)
- life insurance policy payable to spouse for life and spouse has general power of appointment over proceeds
- qualified terminable-interest property (QTIP) election
  - spousal life estate
  - first spouse to die controls remainder

There are four conditions that must be met before QTIP treatment is allowed. (Keep in mind that other property besides property that is placed in trusts can satisfy these requirements and achieve the same favorable results.)

- The decedent-spouse (or donor, in the case of a lifetime gift) must make a transfer of property. The transfer can be in trust or through insurance proceeds or in other forms, such as the death proceeds of a nonqualified deferred-compensation plan.

- The surviving spouse (donee, in the case of a lifetime transfer) must be given the right to all the income. The income must be payable at least annually, and the surviving spouse must be entitled to that income for life.
- No one can be given the right to direct that the property will go to anyone (other than the spouse) as long as that spouse is alive. (It is permissible to give someone other than the surviving spouse the power to appoint QTIP property, if that power can be exercised only after the surviving spouse dies.)
- The first decedent-spouse's executor must make an irrevocable election on the decedent's federal estate tax return. The election provides that, to the extent the QTIP property has not been consumed or given away during the lifetime of the surviving spouse, its date-of-death value (at the surviving spouse's death) will be included in the surviving spouse's estate. In the case of a lifetime gift of QTIP property, the donor spouse must file a similar election on the gift tax return so that the QTIP property will be in the estate of the donee spouse, unless disposed of during the donee spouse's lifetime.

In other words, under this elective provision even *terminable interests* passing to a spouse can qualify for a marital deduction. Property passing to a surviving spouse for life with the remainder going to some other person(s) is eligible for the marital deduction on the condition that the property will be subject to tax at the surviving spouse's death.

QTIP—The Problem of Unproductive Property

At first glance, it appears that the QTIP concept satisfies all needs for all people. However, this is not the case. If all or most of a client's estate consists of unproductive real estate (and/or stock in a closely held corporation that has not paid, and probably never will pay, any significant dividends), will the surviving spouse receive the statutorily required "all income at least annually"? Most authorities think the answer is no.

The surviving spouse must be given an interest that realistically is expected to produce income (or will be usable by the spouse in a manner consistent with its value). Most closely held stock will never pay dividends or realistically be expected to produce an income consistent with its value. Therefore, without planning, the marital deduction could be lost. What can be done to save the marital deduction? If there is no state law giving the surviving spouse the power to require that trust assets be sold and that trust property be made productive in a reasonable period of time, the attorney drafting the marital formula must insert a provision in the will or trust clearly giving the survivor that power. If the surviving spouse can demand that the trustee sell the stock (or other unproductive assets) and use the proceeds to purchase income-producing property, the marital deduction can be saved (even if the power is never actually exercised).

Unfortunately, even if the surviving spouse is given the power to demand that the trustee sell the stock, there are practical problems.

For example, suppose that a client's objective was to pass the stock to his daughter, an employee of the business, at his wife's death. If the wife can force a sale, what assurance does the daughter have that she will be the purchaser? Who would purchase the stock if it is a minority interest? If it is a majority interest, what would happen to the daughter's job if the stock is sold to a third party? Even if the wife is not given the power to require the trustee to sell the stock, can she obtain the corpus of the trust by electing against her husband's will? If the wife doesn't force a sale of trust assets, where will she obtain income sufficient to maintain her current standard of living?

Solutions include the creation of a life-insurance-funded irrevocable trust by the husband. At his death, the trust would provide income to the wife for life and at the wife's death the corpus would pass to their daughter. This would relieve pressure on the wife to force the trustee to sell the stock in the QTIP trust. In fact, the irrevocable trust might provide income but make the surviving spouse's right to that income conditional on not demanding a sale of QTIP assets. If she demands that the trustee sell the QTIP assets, she loses her right to income from the irrevocable trust.

An alternative solution is a funded buy-sell agreement between the father and the daughter. If the daughter has the insurance proceeds at her father's death, she can purchase the stock from his estate. That way cash rather than stock goes into the QTIP trust. Another possibility is a recapitalization coupled with a Sec. 303 stock redemption and/or a cross-purchase agreement with the daughter.

OVERQUALIFICATION AND UNDERQUALIFICATION

overqualification

Overqualification occurs when there is an underutilization of the estate owner's applicable credit amount. The result is that more property than necessary to reduce the estate owner's federal estate tax to zero goes to the surviving spouse. Thus, at the surviving spouse's death, more property than necessary is exposed to tax. This is where proper funding of a CEBT is important. It assures efficient use of both spouses' applicable credit amounts and prevents unnecessary stacking of assets in the surviving spouse's estate.

underqualification

Underqualification means that less property passed to the surviving spouse in a qualifying manner than should have passed tax free. For instance, assume that this year a wife had a $2,425,000 adjusted gross estate but left only $100,000 to her spouse in a qualifying manner. There is a $825,000 underqualification—$1.5 million (2004/2005) goes to the CEBT and no tax is payable; that leaves $925,000 that could qualify for the unlimited marital deduction. In other words, the marital deduction is underutilized by $825,000. (However, keep in mind that for tax and other reasons planners sometimes deliberately pass less than the maximum allowable marital deduction and thus deliberately underqualify.)

Formulas for Minimizing Tax

formula bequest

Obviously, a clause is needed in the will that can provide, by formula, an amount or share of the estate that effectively utilizes the estate owner's applicable credit amount and coordinates it with the unlimited marital deduction. These are appropriately known as *formula bequests*.

Because of the applicable credit amount, it is often desirable to provide that use of the marital deduction be limited to the amount required to reduce the estate owner's federal estate tax to the lowest possible figure after considering the applicable credit amount for the year of death. For example, if, in 2005, a decedent's gross estate is $4 million and he leaves the full $4 million to his wife, there will be no federal estate tax at his death—but there may be a federal estate tax at the death of his wife that is equal to her tentative tax base less the applicable credit amount, depending on the applicable credit amount in the wife's year of death.

If, instead of the unlimited marital share, the decedent gave his spouse an amount exactly sufficient (and no larger) to reduce the federal estate tax due at his death to the lowest possible figure and gave the balance to his children (directly or through a CEBT), then (assuming the decedent dies this year) his children would receive $1.5 million and his wife would receive $2.5 million. Upon his wife's subsequent death, there would probably be no or little federal estate tax liability (especially under EGTRRA 2001 and the phase-in of increased applicable credit/exclusion amounts). In essence, what has been done is to "fund the residue" (the children's portion of the estate) to the extent of the applicable exclusion amount (exemption equivalent) before funding the marital gift.

There are two types of formula bequests:

- the pecuniary (dollar) amount
- the fractional share

pecuniary-amount bequest

The *pecuniary-amount bequest* provides that the survivor will receive a fixed-dollar amount and takes into consideration not only property passing under the will but all property qualifying for the marital deduction. The pecuniary-amount bequest might read as follows:

> If my wife, Allene, survives me, I give, devise, and bequeath to her a sum of money that shall be exactly sufficient to reduce the federal estate tax (after applicable credits) due as a result of my death to the lowest possible amount less the value of all interests in property, if any, that pass or have passed to her under other items of my will or outside my will, but only to the extent that such interests are included in determining my gross estate and allowed as a marital deduction.

fractional-share bequest

The *fractional-share bequest* is an attempt to accomplish the same goal by giving the surviving spouse a fractional share in the residue of the estate—that is, a fractional share of each asset, after specific bequests have been made.

Marital Deduction Formula Bequests

- pecuniary amount
    - fixed-dollar marital deduction amount
- fractional share
    - fractional share of estate residue

How much should the surviving spouse be given under the marital bequest? Should the surviving spouse be given even less than the amount necessary to reduce taxes in the decedent's estate to zero? Should the surviving spouse be given only one-half of the estate? Will the time-use (or psychological) value of tax money saved on the death of the first spouse offset the cost, the (potential) increase in total taxes payable? Perhaps. Much depends on the size of the estates and the use to which tax savings are put at the first death. If the money is used to assure or enhance the lifestyle of the surviving spouse, then it will result in a long-run benefit.

But if the excess of the amount necessary to *equalize the two estates* is invested by the surviving spouse and is eventually taxed at a higher rate when he or she dies, the net result will be fewer assets passing to the next generation. (Until 2010, there may be—mathematically, at least—a tax savings by equalizing the estates, if it is assumed that the second spouse is merely accumulating and not spending the equalization amount.) Any planning and assumptions must take the increasing applicable credit/exclusions amounts provided for in the Economic Growth and Tax Relief Reconciliation Act of 2001 (EGTRRA) into consideration. Generally, EGTRRA 2001 has the effect of diminishing the greater benefits of equalization that could be achieved under prior law.

The actual solution varies according to the circumstances, needs, and desires of the parties involved. The time value of money, as well as the survivor's ability to consume or give away property, must be considered.

FORMS OF MARITAL BEQUESTS: ADVANTAGES AND DISADVANTAGES

There are many means of obtaining the marital deduction. One method is the outright transfer of property to the surviving spouse by will or through life insurance death proceeds. There are advantages to an outright bequest:

- The surviving spouse has the right to use and manage marital assets as he or she desires.
- No trustee fees or court accountings are required.
- Giving the surviving spouse the marital share discourages him or her from electing against the testator's will.
- Assets the surviving spouse receives are available to his or her executor to meet estate liquidity needs.
- The surviving spouse can be given—and can safely retain—non-income-producing assets, such as the non-dividend-paying stock in a family-owned corporation.

But an outright bequest has a number of disadvantages:

- No protection is provided for a spendthrift spouse.
- There is no management with investment expertise.
- The surviving spouse's creditors can attach the bequest both during lifetime and at death.
- The surviving spouse can easily dispose of the bequest however he or she wishes during lifetime—even to the exclusion of his or her children and in favor of a second spouse and children.
- Assets the surviving spouse has not given away or consumed will be included in his or her probate estate.

A second method of providing a marital bequest is to leave property in a power-of-appointment trust. Typically, the power-of-appointment trust gives the spouse a lifetime interest in the trust property, coupled with the right to specify the identity of the remainderperson during lifetime or in his or her will. It usually also provides that if the surviving spouse fails to name the beneficiaries of trust assets, the trust corpus will go to a *taker in default*, a beneficiary named by the grantor of the trust. The trustee (as well as sometimes the surviving spouse) is often given additional powers over trust assets. These might include the right to use trust principal for emergencies or to make gifts to children and grandchildren.

The advantages of a power-of-appointment trust include these:

- As in the case of an outright gift, the surviving spouse may be discouraged from electing against the decedent's will.
- Protection is afforded to some degree against the surviving spouse's possible spendthrift habits.
- Protection is provided against the surviving spouse's creditors and the creditors of the spouse's estate.
- Principal distributions can be varied, depending on the surviving spouse's needs.
- The surviving spouse's right to dispose of the property during lifetime can be limited.
- Probate of the trust corpus can be avoided when the surviving spouse dies.
- Management and financial guidance are provided for the surviving spouse.

But there are disadvantages of a power-of-appointment trust:

- Certain trustee fees and accounting costs are involved.
- Assets in a power-of-appointment trust may not be available to the surviving spouse's executor for the payments of costs and taxes (unless the surviving spouse appoints the assets to his or her estate).
- Non-income-producing property, such as life insurance, cannot safely be obtained or retained in the trust.

The third form of marital bequest under a will is known as an *estate trust*. This type of trust is not required to give the surviving spouse all the income during his or her lifetime, but pays all the accumulated income and the corpus to the surviving spouse's estate when he or she dies. (During lifetime, the surviving spouse can, of course, be given income or principal at the discretion of the trustee, but the surviving spouse personally has no lifetime right to demand either income or principal.)

Advantages of the estate trust include the following:

- Non-income-producing property can be purchased and safely retained by the trustee.
- Protection is provided against the surviving spouse's spendthrift habits, if any.
- Protection is afforded against the surviving spouse's creditors during lifetime.

- The surviving spouse is unable to make lifetime assignments of trust property.
- Assets are available to the surviving spouse's executor.

Disadvantages of the estate trust consist mainly of its inflexibility from the surviving spouse's viewpoint:

- The surviving spouse has no freedom to use and manage trust assets.
- The surviving spouse is restricted in disposing of any property in the trust during lifetime.
- Assets in the trust generate trustee fees and accounting costs.

The fourth form of marital bequest is through the QTIP trust. The QTIP trust gives the spouse a lifetime interest in the property but no general power either during lifetime or at death. At death, assets in the trust pass to the beneficiary or beneficiaries named by the testator.

The advantages of a QTIP trust include the following:

- The grantor can be more certain that the trust assets will eventually be received by the parties the grantor has designated.
- Protection is afforded against the surviving spouse's spendthrift habits, if any.
- Protection is provided against the surviving spouse's creditors and the creditors of the survivor's estate.
- The surviving spouse is given no power to dispose of the trust corpus.
- Probate of the trust corpus is avoided at the surviving spouse's death.

Note that in many states a surviving spouse may be able to *take against* the decedent-spouse's will and thereby defeat some of the objectives and advantages described above.

Disadvantages of the QTIP trust include the following:

- There may be a false sense of security that the first decedent-spouse's objectives will be accomplished.
- Non-income-producing property can be safely used to fund the trust only if the surviving spouse is given the power to demand that trust assets be made productive (income producing).
- The surviving spouse is restricted in the use of trust assets.
- Assets in the trust generate trustee fees and accounting costs.

EXTENT TO WHICH MARITAL DEDUCTION SHOULD BE USED

There are a number of factors that should be carefully considered in deciding how much of a decedent's gross estate should be transferred to the surviving spouse:

Factor	Consideration
Tax savings desired at first death	Maximum utilization of marital deduction is indicated.
Tax savings—both estates	To the extent not consumed or given away through present-interest gifts, marital-deduction assets may compound estate tax problems at second death.
Lack of confidence in spouse's judgment	Marital assets are subject to spouse's dispository desires, either during lifetime or at death.
Fear of spouse's remarriage and aversion to the new spouse's obtaining marital property	Right of new spouse to elect against spouse's will indicates use of less than maximum marital transfer.
Size of surviving spouse's estate	Until size of surviving spouse's estate equals the exemption equivalent of the federal credit, assets should be transferred to him or her. But, if his or her estate is as large as or larger than decedent-spouse's or a sizable inheritance from a third party is likely, the use of sizable marital transfers is contraindicated.
Time value of money	Tax money saved by maximum use of marital deduction can be invested and may offset any additional tax on second death. Investment opportunities available to the surviving spouse must be taken into account.
Availability of marital assets for spouse to give away and consume	Spouse's age, health, number of children and grandchildren, financial needs (including educational and health needs of children), living standard, and even inflation must be considered; generally, the younger the spouse, the greater the financial needs.
Income tax bracket of	If surviving spouse is already in high-

surviving spouse	income tax bracket, additional income from marital assets may be counter-productive.
Liquidity needs of decedent's estate	If decedent's estate is relatively nonliquid, maximum use of marital deduction is indicated.
State death tax laws	Some states do not tax property subject to a power of appointment in donee's estate unless power is exercised by donee. This makes it possible, in some cases, for property in a marital (spouse's) trust to escape state death taxation at donee spouse's death.

Note to Students: See Appendix A for a summary of the advantages and disadvantages of different trusts covered in this chapter and throughout the text.

CHAPTER REVIEW

Answers to the review questions and self-test questions start on page 717.

Key Terms

resident alien
qualified domestic trust (QDOT)
terminable-interest rule
power-of-appointment trust
bypass trust
credit-exclusion/equivalent bypass
    trust (CEBT)
estate trust

qualified terminable-interest
    property (QTIP)
overqualification
underqualification
formula bequest
pecuniary-amount bequest
fractional-share bequest

Review Questions

15-1. Briefly explain the reason Congress enacted the marital deduction for married residents of common-law states.

15-2. What is meant by "net value of a qualifying interest passing to a surviving spouse"?

15-3. What are the requirements to qualify for the marital deduction?

15-4. Explain the circumstances under which a U.S. citizen decedent spouse's transfers to a resident-alien spouse are eligible for the unlimited marital deduction.

15-5. What is the effect of a valid disclaimer on the marital deduction if the disclaimed property passes to the surviving spouse?

15-6. a. What is meant by a presumption-of-survivorship clause?
b. How does a survivorship clause affect the marital deduction?

15-7. What are the general theory and goal of the terminable-interest rule?

15-8. a. Explain the terminable-interest rule as it applies to a nondeductible terminable interest.
b. What are the exceptions to the terminable-interest rule?

15-9. Describe the requirements that must be met by a power-of-appointment trust before the property contained in such a trust will qualify for the federal estate tax marital deduction.

15-10. In what way is an estate trust a useful alternative to the power-of-appointment trust?

15-11. Describe the four conditions that must be met before qualified terminable interest property (QTIP) can qualify for the marital deduction.

15-12. What is the role of the executor in qualifying property as QTIP?

15-13. a. Describe problems that may arise if unproductive property is transferred to a QTIP trust.
b. How can these problems be resolved?

15-14. What important drawback generally is associated with overqualification of estate assets for the marital deduction?

15-15. Assume a decedent's estate consisted of $75,000 in cash or cash equivalents, $250,000 in life insurance payable in a lump sum to his wife, and a residence (purchased after 1976) valued at $320,000 that he owned as tenants by the entirety with his wife. There is no mortgage on the property. He also owned an automobile titled in his own name worth $10,000 and a sole proprietorship worth $1,600,000. His will states that his entire estate is to go to his wife. Assume debts and administrative expenses are $155,000. Assume also that the decedent had two adult children, one of whom was working with him in the business at the time of his death this year.
a. Compute the gross estate.
b. Compute the adjusted gross estate.
c. Compute the marital deduction, listing all assets that qualify.
d. Explain how estate taxes could have been minimized in the combined estates of the decedent and his wife by the use of trusts.

15-16. Describe the two types of formula bequests.

15-17. Under what circumstances might it be advantageous to qualify an estate for less than the maximum unlimited marital deduction? Explain.

15-18. What are the advantages and disadvantages of outright marital bequests?

15-19. a. Compare power-of-appointment trusts with estate trusts.
        b. State the benefits and disadvantages of each.

Self-Test Questions

T   F   15-1. The maximum marital deduction is the greater of $250,000 or one-half of the adjusted gross estate.

T   F   15-2. The estate tax marital deduction is allowed on the full gross estate tax value of the property left to the spouse, regardless of whether taxes, mortgages, or administration expenses are payable out of the marital interest.

T   F   15-3. The marital deduction will be reduced if taxes are payable out of the marital share of the estate.

T   F   15-4. Both the decedent and the surviving spouse must be citizens of the United States for transfers to such survivor to qualify for a marital deduction.

T   F   15-5. Only probate property qualifies for the marital deduction.

T   F   15-6. Although the marital deduction is now unlimited for both estate and gift tax purposes, the property actually must pass or have passed to the surviving spouse in order to qualify for the marital deduction.

T   F   15-7. The marital deduction is not allowed if a married couple is separated but not divorced at the time of the first spouse's death.

T   F   15-8. The goal of the unlimited estate tax marital deduction is to treat the spouses as one unit for transfer-tax purposes and to ultimately subject the property to transfer tax in one estate.

T   F   15-9. An example of a terminable interest is a will provision leaving a life estate to a surviving spouse with the property then passing in equal shares to the decedent's children.

T   F   15-10. If the decedent directs the executor or trustee to purchase terminable-interest property with a money bequest for the benefit of the spouse, the property will not qualify for the marital deduction.

T   F   15-11. A bequest of a life estate can qualify for a marital deduction if it is coupled with a general power of appointment.

T   F   15-12.   When property is placed in a power-of-appointment marital trust, there is an obligation to make the property income producing.

T   F   15-13.   A credit-exclusion/equivalent bypass trust (CEBT) is another name for the marital trust.

T   F   15-14.   One of the requirements of property left in a power-of-appointment trust that will qualify for the marital deduction is that the income from the trust is payable at least annually to the surviving spouse and no one else.

T   F   15-15.   The term QTIP, or qualified terminable interest property, refers to property that pays income at least annually to the surviving spouse, but at the surviving spouse's death, the principal passes to a person or persons other than the surviving spouse's estate.

T   F   15-16.   Most authorities believe that unproductive real estate and/or closely held stock (not paying dividends) will satisfy the *all-income-at-least-annually* requirement for a QTIP.

T   F   15-17.   If the estate of the first spouse to die is underqualified for the marital deduction, there may be less property passing to the surviving spouse's estate tax free.

T   F   15-18.   Because of the unlimited marital deduction, it is no longer necessary to do any estate planning.

16

The Charitable Deduction

Learning Objectives

An understanding of the material in this chapter should enable the student to

16-1. Identify the types of organizations that entitle an estate to a charitable deduction, and explain why such a deduction might be denied as well as how qualified disclaimers and the payment of death taxes are treated.

16-2. Explain the types of charitable bequests, and briefly describe how such bequests are valued.

Chapter Outline

An estate tax charitable deduction is allowed for the full value of property transferred to a qualified charity, but only if the property is included in the donor's gross estate. As there are income tax rules about gifts to qualified charities, so are there specific rules governing charitable gifts of property included in an estate. Furthermore, it is possible for a charitable contribution made during the donor's lifetime to generate both an income tax deduction and an estate tax deduction if the value of the property is includible in the donor's gross estate. The value of a lifetime transfer may be included in the gross estate if the donor retains some interest in the property or powers over the property for life. A gift of a life insurance policy to a qualified charity, made within 3 years of the donor's death and includible in the gross estate, also qualifies for the deduction.

The charitable deduction is presently and has been an unlimited deduction for property passing to a qualified charity as defined in the Code. Qualified charitable organizations include

- corporations operated exclusively for religious, charitable, scientific, literary, or educational purposes, including the encouragement of art and the prevention of cruelty to children or animals
- the United States, any state or political subdivision, or the District of Columbia, provided that contributions are made exclusively for public purposes
- a fraternal society, order, or association, if the contributions are used exclusively for the charitable purposes listed above
- the use of any veterans' organization incorporated by an act of Congress or its departments, local chapters, or posts

DENIAL OF DEDUCTION

A charitable deduction for any of the above bequests is denied if any part of the net earnings of these organizations inures to the benefit of a private stockholder or individual. The deduction is also denied if a substantial part of the charitable organization's activities involves preparation of propaganda or other methods that attempt to influence legislation. Likewise, a deduction is denied if the charity engages in any political campaign in behalf of a candidate for public office or other prohibited transactions. A deduction is also denied if, at the time of the donor-decedent's death, the gift is contingent upon the happening of an event or some act, unless the probability that this contingency will not occur is so remote that it is negligible. In addition, if the charitable beneficiary or a trustee has the power to use the property or funds contributed to the charity in whole or in part for noncharitable purposes or uses, the charitable deduction applies only to that part of the property or money not subject to this power.

DISCLAIMERS

If property is transferred from a decedent's estate to a charitable organization because there has been a qualified disclaimer by a prior beneficiary, a charitable deduction is allowed for amounts that are actually transferred to the charity. For purposes of the charitable estate tax deduction, a complete termination of a power to consume, invade, or appropriate property for the benefit of an individual prior to the exercise of such power is considered to be a qualified disclaimer if the termination occurs before the due date for filing the estate tax return. The requirements for a qualified disclaimer for federal estate tax purposes (basically, an absolute refusal to accept the bequest made prior to the time the estate tax return must be filed) were discussed in chapter 6.

PAYMENT OF DEATH TAXES

If, under the terms of the will or provisions of local law, payment of death taxes or other deductible expenses is to be made from the charitable bequest, the charitable deduction is reduced by those amounts used to pay debts or taxes. In other words, the deduction is limited to the actual amount that passes free and clear to the charity for its charitable purposes. If the will provides that taxes and administration expenses are to be paid from the residue and the charitable bequest is also payable out of the residue, the residuary bequest is diminished by the amount of expenses and taxes paid. This creates a complex circular problem because a reduction of the charitable deduction has the effect of increasing the taxable estate as well as the estate tax. There is an estate tax regulation that addresses this situation where death taxes are paid from a deductible interest. It is called an *interrelated computation* and is beyond the scope of this material.

TYPES OF CHARITABLE BEQUESTS

In addition to outright bequests of entire interests, charitable gifts can be in other forms, including

- partial interests
- charitable remainder trusts
- guaranteed annuity interests
- split gifts
- powers of appointment

Powers of Appointment

A charitable deduction is allowed for property that is included in the decedent's gross estate because the decedent possessed a general power of appointment over the property that passes to a charity by virtue of an exercise, release, or lapse of that power. It is considered to be a deductible bequest by the decedent to a charitable beneficiary.

Partial Interests

split-interest arrangement

There are many instances in which a donor, although wishing a charity to receive certain property eventually, wants a family member to enjoy the property first. This situation, called a *split-interest arrangement*, is governed by IRC Secs. 170, 2522, and 2055. Charitable income, gift, and estate tax deductions are allowed for the value of less than an entire interest passing to a charity if certain complex rules are met. The provisions in the tax law state that gifts of a remainder interest in trust are deductible for federal income, estate, or gift tax purposes only if the trust is a charitable remainder annuity trust, charitable remainder unitrust, or pooled-income fund. The valuation rules mandated by Secs. 664 and 7520 must be used to determine the specific amount of the deduction available. The tables of actuarial factors for calculating the deductions are found in *Actuarial Values Aleph Volume* and *Actuarial Values Beth Volume*, IRS Publications 1457 and 1458. The size of the deduction is based on the length of the noncharitable term or the measuring life of the noncharitable life interest(s), the size of annuity or unitrust payment paid to the noncharitable beneficiary, and the Sec. 7520 rate in effect at the time of the donation. The types of interests that may be bequeathed to a charity and qualify for the charitable deduction are

- a testamentary gift of an undivided portion of the decedent's entire interest in property not held in trust. An undivided portion means a fraction or percentage of each interest or right owned by the decedent in the property. Furthermore, the decedent's interest in a fraction of every part of the whole must persist over the entire term that his or her interest in the property exists.
- a nontrust remainder interest in a personal residence. A charitable deduction is allowed for the transfer by the decedent at death of a remainder interest in his or her personal residence. The residence need not be the decedent's principal residence. It includes any residence used by the decedent for any part of the year (even as a vacation home). The charitable remainder interest pertains to the residence itself as opposed to any proceeds received on the sale of the residence.
- a nontrust remainder interest in a farm transferred by the decedent at death to a qualified charity, or a transfer of a partial interest in property

to a charitable organization exclusively for conservation purposes. Special rules must be adhered to upon the transfer of these partial interests either in real estate or for conservation purposes.

- remainder interests in trust to charitable remainder trusts and pooled-income funds

charitable remainder trust

Charitable Remainder Trusts

If the decedent transfers a remainder interest in property to a charity in trust, it must be made in the form of a charitable remainder annuity trust, unitrust, or pooled-income fund. Otherwise, no estate tax charitable deduction is allowed. These arrangements usually provide for an income interest to a noncharitable beneficiary with the remainder to the charitable organization. The trust instrument must provide that payments of the unitrust or annuity amounts begin as of the date of death if the charitable interest is to qualify for the estate tax charitable deduction. Gifts made in one of these forms are the only way to provide for income to individuals who are noncharitable beneficiaries while making a gift at the same time to a charitable organization that qualifies for an income, estate, or gift tax deduction. A donor transferring property to a CRT during lifetime is entitled to a federal income tax deduction as well as a gift tax deduction. Both the federal income and gift tax deductions are limited to the actuarial value of the remainder interest. If the noncharitable beneficiary is someone other than the donor, the transfer may be subject to gift taxation.

Annuity Trusts

charitable remainder annuity trust

A *charitable remainder annuity trust* is one that provides to a noncharitable income beneficiary a fixed annuity that is worth not less than 5 percent of the initial net fair market value of the property paid in trust. This amount must be paid at least annually to one or more noncharitable beneficiaries who are alive when the trust is created. Upon the death of the last income beneficiary or at the end of a term of years not greater than 20 years, the remainder interest must be held for or paid to a qualified charitable organization. (See figure 16–1.)

Unitrusts

charitable remainder unitrust

A *charitable remainder unitrust* differs from an annuity trust in that a fixed percentage (not less than 5 percent of the net fair market value of the trust assets as annually revalued) is paid at least annually to one or more noncharitable income beneficiaries. Again, as with the annuity trust, the remainder interest will be paid to or held for the benefit of a qualified charitable organization, either at the death of the last income beneficiary or after a term of years not greater than 20 years.

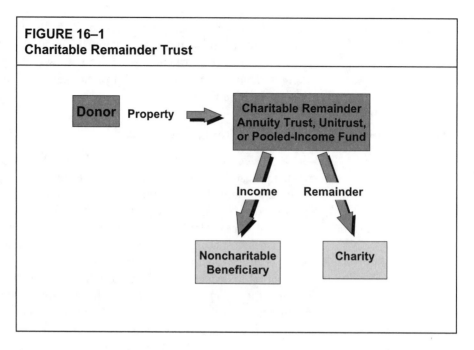

FIGURE 16–1
Charitable Remainder Trust

In essence, the unitrust differs from the annuity trust in that the annual income is more in the form of a variable annuity. Both types of trusts may be created during lifetime or under a person's will. Another distinction made between the two trusts is with regard to payment of income. In the annuity trust, if trust income is insufficient to meet the annual payment, the income beneficiary must be paid out of principal. In the case of the unitrust, however, the trust may provide that if income is insufficient, no payment will be made out of principal. Payments are made from income only. In any year that a trust has more than enough income to meet its present payments, the deficit of earlier years may be paid at that time. (See NIMCRUTs.) Also, no further contributions may be made to an annuity trust after the initial payment, but additional contributions may be made to a unitrust.

The Taxpayer Relief Act of 1997 has imposed two limitations with respect to charitable remainder trusts (CRTs):

- For transfers in trust after June 18, 1997, the percentage of assets required to be distributed at least annually cannot exceed 50 percent of the initial fair market value of the trust assets for charitable annuity trusts (CRATs), or 50 percent of the annual value of the trust assets for charitable unitrusts (CRUTs).
- For transfers in trust after July 28, 1997, the value of the remainder interest of a CRT must be at least 10 percent of the value of the property transferred to the trust. In other words, the value of the

remainder interest must be at least 10 percent of the fair market value of all trust contributions. This limitation may affect the number of individuals who can qualify for CRT planning.

Although both the annuity trust and the unitrust are based on the same provisions in the tax law and exist for the same reasons, there are practical distinctions between the two types of trusts.

If a client is particularly concerned with the assurance of a fixed payout, the charitable remainder annuity trust is the better choice. The payout will not increase if the value of the trust assets increases during a period of inflation, and the payout will not decrease if the value of the trust corpus falls during an economic downturn.

On the other hand, if the client is more interested in an approach in which the payout depends on the annual value of the trust assets, the charitable remainder unitrust is more appropriate.

Net Income Unitrusts (NIMCRUTs)

NIMCRUT

One flexible payout pattern for charitable remainder trusts is called a net income unitrust, or *NIMCRUT*. This type of arrangement is available only for CRUTs. In essence, NIMCRUTs are a regular unitrust except that the NIMCRUT's payout is limited to the lesser of the stated unitrust payout percentage or the net income earned by the CRUT during the year. What constitutes income is determined by a state's principal and income laws as modified by the CRUT document. NIMCRUTs are different from standard CRUTs in that, if the NIMCRUT does not realize enough current income to make the stated unitrust payment, the annual payment is reduced to the amount of the actual income earned. Thus, the NIMCRUT protects the interests of the remainder beneficiary (that is, the charitable beneficiary) against invasion of principal, because the trustee is prohibited from invading principal for the benefit of noncharitable beneficiaries.

Beneficiaries of a standard CRUT receive their annual payments, regardless of the income the CRUT realizes, while beneficiaries of a NIMCRUT might receive smaller payments, depending on trust income. Fortunately, NIMCRUTs have a make-up feature under which noncharitable beneficiaries can receive payments in excess of the stated unitrust percentage in future years to make up arrearages that might have occurred when the NIMCRUT did not have sufficient income to pay the full stated unitrust amount. NIMCRUTs, therefore, can offer good flexibility for CRTs that invest in property that produces little or fluctuating income and/or does not lend itself to be readily converted into cash to make a required payment such as, for example, an undivided parcel of real estate. It is important for planners to be aware than NIMCRUT arrangements are scrutinized by the IRS.

Pooled-Income Funds

pooled-income fund

A *pooled-income fund* is much like a mutual fund maintained by a qualified charity. The fund contains commingled donations from many sources. In effect, a donor's donation purchases units in the fund; the income attributable to these units is paid at least annually to the noncharitable beneficiary(ies). Of course, the remainder interest must be irrevocably earmarked to the charitable organization.

Charitable Remainder Trusts

- charitable remainder annuity trust (CRAT)
  - fixed annuity to noncharitable beneficiary
  - remainder to charity
- charitable remainder unitrust (CRUT)
  - fixed percentage to noncharitable beneficiary
  - remainder to charity
- pooled-income funds
  - commingled donation of many sources
  - income to noncharitable beneficiary
  - remainder to charity

Charitable Lead Trusts

charitable lead trust

These types of gifts work in reverse of the remainder trusts; hence, they are commonly called *charitable lead trusts (CLT)*. (See figure 16–2.) There is a transfer by the decedent of an income interest in property to a charity with the remainder to a noncharitable entity. The time period is not limited to 20 years, as it is with a CRT. Unless this interest is in the form of a guaranteed annuity interest or unitrust interest, the charitable deduction will be disallowed. These guaranteed interests refer to the right to receive a determinable amount at least annually for a specific term or for the life or lives of individuals living at the time of the decedent's death. The guaranteed annuity must be paid by an insurance company or a similar organization regularly engaged in the business of issuing annuity contracts. A guaranteed unitrust interest refers to the right to receive payment of a fixed percentage of the net fair market value of the property that funds the unitrust at least annually. The unitrust interest must be paid by an insurance company or any other similar organization, as mentioned above.

Charitable Lead Trust

- income to charity
- remainder to noncharitable beneficiary

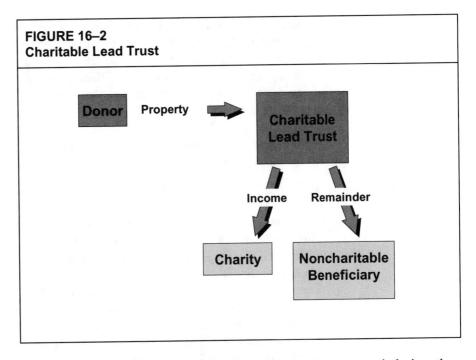

FIGURE 16–2
Charitable Lead Trust

Like charitable remainder trusts, a CLT may be arranged during the donor's lifetime or at death. A CLT may be structured as annuity (CLAT) or as unitrust (CLUT) interests and may vary as to the income, gift, and estate tax consequences. This device is a useful income-tax-savings approach for lifetime transfers because the donor is allowed to take a current income tax deduction (subject to limitations) for the value of the income interest transferred to charity. In essence, if the trust is structured as a grantor trust for income tax purposes, the donor is responsible for paying income tax on the income generated by the trust property and is entitled to a charitable income tax deduction. If the trust corpus (remainder interest) is to revert to the grantor, there is no gift liability upon creation of the trust. In this case, the donor may take an income tax deduction for the present value of the income stream passing to the charity and is liable for income tax on income generated by the trust property in the future. If the trust is a nongrantor trust for income tax purposes, the trust is responsible for income tax on income that exceeds what is paid to the charity. When, at the end of the trust term, the property is to pass to someone other than the donor or donor's spouse, such as the donor's children, the donor has made a taxable gift to the children. This gift is reduced by the value of the lead interest passing to charity. A testamentary CLT may also be used to reduce the estate tax burden on large estates because the estate may receive a charitable estate tax deduction for the value of the lead payments to charity. For example, suppose a wealthy decedent leaves his entire residuary estate to a CLT. The trust provides various charities, selected by the trustees, with, for instance, 8 percent of the initial value of the principal for 25 years. At the termination of the trust, the decedent's family will receive the remaining principal. Due to an assumed favorable Sec. 7520 interest rate in effect at the time of death, the estate tax charitable deduction could be a large percentage of the value of the decedent-transferor's residuary estate.

A charitable lead trust is a popular device when the donor wants to keep the property within the family unit but at the same time wishes to benefit one or more charities.

Split Gifts

For transfers made after 1981, a donor-decedent may create a charitable remainder trust and obtain deductions for both the charitable and noncharitable bequests. If a spouse is the only noncharitable income beneficiary for life, the estate obtains a marital deduction for the income interest to the surviving spouse as well as a charitable deduction for the gift of the remainder interest to the charity. The result is that no transfer tax is imposed on the creation of a charitable remainder annuity or unitrust for either the remainder or income portion, provided that the income interest to a spouse qualifies under the *qualifying terminable interest rules*. Thus, a split gift to a spouse and charity in the form of a charitable remainder annuity or unitrust may pass entirely estate tax free by use of the combined marital and charitable deductions.

In addition to the more recognized charitable remainder trusts and charitable lead trusts, there are numerous charitable contribution devices that can be used in estate planning. General descriptions of the types of charitable arrangements frequently used in estate and gift planning are discussed below.

Charitable Gift Annuities

charitable gift annuity

A *charitable gift annuity* (CGA) is a contract entered into between a donor and a qualified charity. This type of charitable arrangement provides a deferred gift to a qualified charity and annual income payments to the donor for the rest of his or her life. The donor makes a transfer to the charity of cash or appreciated property. In return, the charity agrees to pay an annuity to an annuitant who may be the donor or one or more others chosen by the donor. In essence, the donor is purchasing an annuity from the charity and at the same time making a future-interest gift to the charity. The donation qualifies for a tax deduction because the fair market value of the contributed property is in excess of the present value of the life annuity. Because the charity's promise to pay must be unsecured, the donor bears the risk of the charity's honoring the agreement. The precise income tax implications of charitable gift annuities vary according to the specific contract terms: whether there are one or more annuitants, when the annuity payments to the annuitant(s) commence, and so forth. The charitable gift annuity device is used when the donor wants to make a contribution to charity and at the same time receive or give to another an income stream—that is, make a charitable donation but get some value back from the gifted property. For income tax purposes, each annuity payment is composed of a return of principal, capital gain, and ordinary income. Although tax is avoided on any appreciation of capital gain at the time the property is transferred to the charity, a proportionate amount of the unrealized capital gain is allocated to each payment. If the annuitant lives beyond life expectancy, payments received are treated as ordinary income.

Advantages of a charitable gift annuity include the following:

- The donor receives an immediate income tax deduction.
- If appreciated property is donated, the donor is able to defer gain over the donor's lifetime.
- It is simple in design and administration.
- No trust agreement or trustee's fees are required.
- The donor receives fixed annual payments for life that, among other possibilities, may be used to supplement retirement income.

As mentioned above, for gift tax purposes, the donation qualifies for a gift tax deduction because the fair market value of the contributed property will be in excess of the present value of the life annuity. The charity benefits because it will receive the excess value at the annuitant's death. The annual gift tax exclusion may apply if it is an immediate rather than deferred annuity. A 709 gift tax return should be filed for charitable gift annuities.

Community Foundations

community foundation

Community foundations have been a form of charitable organization for almost a century. They are grant-making entities that benefit the specified community. Generally speaking, a community foundation is a nonprofit grant-making organization that consists of an amalgamation of separate grant-making accounts. Donations to the organization are used to make grants for the benefit and needs of the general community. Community needs are determined through the efforts of foundation committee members, sometimes with the involvement of donors. Knowledgeable management and investment of donations by the foundation serve to maximize benefits provided to the local community. There may be separate funds or trusts within a community foundation. The separate funds may be either restricted or unrestricted. Committee members of the foundation determine how the unrestricted funds are used for community needs; donors are able to determine how restricted funds are spent.

Contributions of property to community foundations are popular when a donor wants to play a charitable and decision-making role in benefiting his or her local community. Donor contributions are used to establish a fund or account. The contributions made may be completely unfettered or may be made with the direction as to the specific use of the fund. Although the focus of community foundations is usually to provide support for local charitable efforts, such as the ballet, art museum, and so forth, it is not uncommon for grants to be made on a nationally recognized basis such as to universities. Making gifts to community foundations is desirable because the organization is an already established charity and does not require the donor to bear the ongoing expenses that are associated with other charitable enterprises like supporting organizations[1] and private foundations. There are no transfer tax consequences for donations to community foundations as a result of the charitable gift and estate tax deductions. Lifetime donations allow for income tax deductions.

Donor-Advised Funds

donor-advised fund

A *donor-advised fund* is another type of charitable and estate planning technique. With this arrangement, a donor makes a donation to a public charity or community foundation and the charity establishes a set-aside or subaccount fund named by the donor. Subject to the sponsoring charity's approval, the donor, or someone designated by the donor, makes recommendations for grants to be made from the fund for the benefit of certain permissible charitable beneficiaries. The donor may make the contributions to the charity anonymously or in his or her name or family name.

Again, there are no transfer tax ramifications due to the charitable gift and estate tax deductions. The donor is entitled to an income tax deduction that varies according to the donor's adjusted gross income and the type of property contributed to the donor-advised fund.

Private Foundations

private foundation

For federal tax purposes, there are two types of charities: public charities and private foundations. A *private foundation* is typically a charitable entity that is created, funded, and run by a donor or the donor's family. It is through the foundation organization that a donor makes contributions to one or more public charities. Private foundations are subject to strict and limiting tax rules and could, additionally, become subject to harsh excise taxes. Despite the rules and taxes associated with private foundations, they are an attractive charitable device because of the flexibility and control they offer to philanthropically inclined donors. Private foundations, also called family foundations, are created by donors who have substantial wealth. They provide an excellent means for combining family and philanthropic purposes because the organization provisions typically require family members to meet regularly to determine charitable expenditures. Original donors look to the family foundation as a way to instill social and philanthropic responsibility in their heirs in generations to come.

Private foundations are also advantageous because highly appreciated property contributed to the entity avoids capital gains taxes. If publicly traded securities are contributed, the full fair market value can be taken. Private foundations allow donors who desire visibility to receive public recognition of their philanthropic endeavors.

The disadvantages of private foundations include potentially costly administration expenses. The main administrative costs result from the creation of the organization and compliance with private foundation rules, maintenance of tax-exempt status, and annual reporting. Excise taxes are imposed on the foundation and its managers if the foundation fails to comply to the letter of the private foundation rules. For income tax purposes, lower annual charitable deduction percentages are allowed as compared to public charities: 20 percent instead of 30 percent of adjusted gross income for donations of capital gain assets, and 30 percent instead of 50 percent of adjusted gross income for cash donations. There are also restrictive rules pertaining to the donor-owners of closely held businesses.

VALUATION

The gift of a partial interest (including a remainder interest to a charity) is valued at the fair market value of the interest on the appropriate valuation date. This may be the date of the gift or the date of death. The fair market value of an annuity, life estate, term of years, remainder, reversion, or unitrust interest is its present value. The present value of remainder interests in charitable remainder annuity trusts, unitrusts, or pooled-income funds is determined under the income tax regulations. The present value of a guaranteed annuity interest is determined under estate tax regulations. The present value of a unitrust interest is found by subtracting the present value of all interests in the transferred property other than the unitrust interest from the fair market value of the transferred property.

MINI-CASE

George Johnson, an executive employee of a Fortune 500 company, died early this year, leaving property in his own name consisting of

Cash in the bank	$125,000
Real estate	$810,000
Municipal bonds	$500,000

In addition, George and his wife owned their home jointly with right of survivorship. The entire purchase price for this property, which was purchased 20 years ago, was $100,000, all paid by George. Its value at the date of his death was $370,000.

George made a gift of stock to his daughter in the year before his death. The stock was worth $51,000 on the date of the gift. The gift tax George paid after subtracting the annual $11,000 gift tax exclusion was $8,200.

George owned three life insurance policies on his life: policy A for $50,000, payable in a lump sum to his wife; policy B for $500,000, payable to his wife with interest for life and full right to withdraw principal at any time, otherwise to her estate; and policy C for $130,000, payable to a qualified nonprofit educational institution.

In addition, his wife is the beneficiary of the death benefit under a qualified noncontributory retirement plan maintained by George's employer. The death benefit payable as an annuity is valued at $450,000 at the time of George's death.

At the time of George's death, his debts amounted to $2,000. Funeral expenses were $2,000, and the cost of the administration of his estate— including executor's and attorney's fees—is estimated at $20,000. Accrued taxes at the time of George's death were $7,000.

George's will leaves one-half of his probate estate outright to his wife and one-half outright to his daughter. All expenses, taxes, and debts are to be paid from the share given to his daughter.

    a.   List the items that will be included in George's gross estate, indicating whether they are probate or nonprobate assets (passing outside the will). Explain why each is included. Calculate his gross estate.

    b.   Determine George's adjusted gross estate before reduction by any marital or charitable deduction.

    c.   Compute the taxable estate, listing those items that qualify for the marital or charitable deduction and their values. Assume no death taxes are imposed by George's state.

Note to Students: See Appendix A for a summary of the advantages and disadvantages of different trusts covered in this chapter and throughout the text.

CHAPTER REVIEW

Answers to the mini-case, the review questions, and the self-test questions start on page 717.

Key Terms

split-interest arrangement	charitable remainder annuity trust
charitable remainder trust	charitable remainder unitrust

NIMCRUT	charitable gift annuity
pooled-income fund	community foundation
charitable lead trust (guaranteed annuity)	donor-advised fund
	private foundation

Review Questions

16-1. Describe the general rule for the charitable deduction and any limitations on the deduction.

16-2. How may a disclaimer be used to pass property to a charity?

16-3. Assuming that all debts, expenses, and taxes are to be paid from the residuary estate, how is the amount of a charitable bequest affected if the charitable gift is to be made from the residue?

16-4. Identify the types of charitable bequests that qualify for the charitable deduction.

16-5. What are the three ways that remainder interests in trusts may be given to charities so they will qualify for the charitable deduction? In all cases, assume that there is also a noncharitable beneficiary.

16-6. What is the rule for qualifying split gifts to charities when the income beneficiary of a charitable unitrust is the surviving spouse?

Self-Test Questions

T   F   16-1. A charitable deduction is allowed for the entire value of a bequest to a qualified charity even though the property is not included in the donor's gross estate.

T   F   16-2. A charitable deduction will be allowed for the full value of property that passes to a qualified charity as a result of a qualified disclaimer made by a prior beneficiary.

T   F   16-3. It is now possible to create a charitable remainder trust in combination with a qualified terminable interest property (QTIP) trust in favor of the surviving spouse and to avoid federal estate tax liability entirely.

NOTE

1. A supporting organization is created when a donor establishes a separate charitable trust or corporation affiliated with a community foundation. The resulting grant-making entity is classified as a supporting organization.

17

State Death Taxes and Estate Planning

Learning Objectives

An understanding of the material in this chapter should enable the student to

17-1. Identify the types of state death taxes.

17-2. Explain how states group beneficiaries who are entitled to receive estate assets into classes.

17-3. Describe the three classifications of property subject to state death taxes.

17-4. Explain how various types of property are affected by state death taxes.

Chapter Outline

Frequently, the subject of state death taxes is overshadowed by the attention given to the federal estate tax. Although the emphasis on federal estate taxation is warranted for estates that have a value of more than the applicable exclusion amount, statistically this tax affects a relatively small percentage of all estates settled. On the other hand, most estates are within reach of the death taxes levied by states. Therefore, state death tax planning is an important component of the overall estate planning process, albeit to varying degrees.

TYPES OF STATE DEATH TAXES

Inheritance Tax

inheritance tax

The *inheritance tax* is a tax imposed on an individual's right to *inherit* property from the estate of a decedent. The amount of inheritance tax is based on two factors: (1) the value of the property received by each beneficiary and (2) the rate of the tax (and the amount of exemption, if any exists), which depends on the beneficiary's degree of blood relationship to the deceased. Generally, the closer the beneficiary's blood relationship is to the decedent, the lower the tax rate is and the greater the exemption is. Since during recent years many states have opted for an estate tax or credit estate tax, fewer than one-third of the states currently impose an inheritance tax.

Estate Tax

A state estate tax is similar in nature to the federal estate tax. It differs from the inheritance tax in that the inheritance tax is imposed upon a beneficiary's right to inherit, while the estate tax is imposed on a decedent's right to *transfer* or *pass* property to beneficiaries.

Credit Estate Tax (Prior to 2005)

Prior to 2005, all states imposed a credit estate tax. This tax was referred to as a *sponge, slack,* or *gap* tax. Additionally, this tax served to supplement a state's inheritance or estate tax. Its objective was to boost the amount of state death taxes up to the maximum amount of paid state death taxes allowed to be credited against the federal estate tax that is payable. A dollar-for-dollar amount was applied against the federal estate tax payable, thereby reducing it. The maximum federal credit for state death taxes prior to 2005 is shown in table 17-1, and it is also given in the instructions to the federal estate tax return Form 706. Thus, for the years 2002 through 2004, if a state's death tax was less than the amount allowed as a credit against the federal estate tax payable, the credit estate tax allowed the state to pick up the difference for the state coffers (regardless of death taxes paid to nondomiciliary states in which the decedent may have held taxable property) instead of that

---

TABLE 17-1
Maximum Allowable Credit for State Death Taxes through 2004*

Column 1 Adjusted taxable estate equal to or more than—	Column 2 Adjusted taxable estate less than—	Column 3 Credit on amount in column 1	Column 4 Percentage rate of credit on excess over amount in column 1
$ 0	$ 40,000	$ 0	None
40,000	90,000	0	0.8
90,000	140,000	400	1.6
140,000	240,000	1,200	2.4
240,000	440,000	3,600	3.2
440,000	640,000	10,000	4.0
640,000	840,000	18,000	4.8
840,000	1,040,000	27,600	5.6
1,040,000	1,540,000	38,800	6.4
1,540,000	2,040,000	70,800	7.2
2,040,000	2,540,000	106,800	8.0
2,540,000	3,040,000	146,800	8.8
3,040,000	3,540,000	190,800	9.6
3,540,000	4,040,000	238,800	10.4
4,040,000	5,040,000	290,800	11.2
5,040,000	6,040,000	402,800	12.0
6,040,000	7,040,000	522,800	12.8
7,040,000	8,040,000	650,800	13.6
8,040,000	9,040,000	786,800	14.4
9,040,000	10,040,000	930,800	15.2
10,040,000		1,082,800	16.2

*Computation of maximum credit for state death taxes (based on federal adjusted taxable estate, which is the federal taxable estate reduced by $60,000 and then reduced by 25 percent each year beginning 2002 through 2004). State death tax payable becomes a deduction after 2004 for federal estate tax purposes.

adjusted taxable
estate

amount going to the federal government. Note that the credit for state death taxes was available only when the property subject to the state tax was included in the decedent's gross estate for federal estate tax purposes and when death taxes were actually paid to the state. The table used to compute the credit for state death taxes makes reference to the term *adjusted taxable estate*. This is the decedent's *taxable estate* less $60,000.[1] (The adjusted taxable estate is not to be confused with the adjusted gross estate.)

Figuring the federal credit for state death taxes became more complicated for decedents with property that is taxable by states other than the decedent's state of domicile. Some states claimed the full credit for resident-decedents' estates in spite of the fact that state taxes may have been payable to other nondomiciliary states. Other states recognized the right of nondomiciliary states to a proportionate percentage of the credit.

Types of State Death Taxes

- inheritance tax
  - tax on right of beneficiary to receive estate property
- state estate tax
  - tax on right of decedent to leave property to beneficiaries
- credit estate tax
  - tax to bring state death tax up to credit amount allowed by federal law

---

Economic Growth and Tax Relief Reconciliation Act of 2001

The Economic Growth and Tax Relief Reconciliation Act (EGTRRA) of 2001 made some significant changes to state death taxation. Under EGTRRA 2001, the state death tax credit was reduced by 25 percent in 2002, 50 percent in 2003, and 75 percent in 2004. Beginning in 2005, the state death tax credit is fully repealed and replaced with a deduction for any amount of state death taxes paid.

Example: A decedent, Anne, a widow, has a gross estate of $5 million and an adjusted gross estate of $4.5 million Because Anne was a widow, there is no marital deduction. Under her will, Anne directed her executor to leave $700,000 to her favorite charity, The Humane Society. Her state has imposed $900,000 in state death taxes. Anne's taxable estate is $2,900,000:

$4,500,000	adjusted gross estate
− 700,000	charitable deduction
− 900,000	state death tax deduction
$2,900,000	taxable estate

Hence, the federal rules have encouraged the states, especially those states with only a federal state death tax credit, to legislate new state death tax laws.

Although many states have varying types of an inheritance tax and/or estate tax, *all* states have at least this tax credit pick-up tax, even those states that claim to have no death tax. The states' rational is, why turn down what the federal government will take out of its own pocket and allow the state to have? Clearly, under the EGTRRA 2001 rules, however, the credit is completely repealed in 2005, and even states that claim to have no death tax will truly be left with *no* state death tax revenue. The loss of revenue has had an understandably negative effect on the state coffers.

decoupling

Consequently, many states have acted to prevent future death tax revenue losses by *decoupling* from the EGTRRA state credit phase-out and federal exclusion increases. Although the decoupling arrangements many states have made vary, the simplest form of decoupling is when a state references the full federal credit that was available prior to the 2001 changes. In other words, those states "froze" the amount of the state death tax credit allowed before EGTRRA for state death tax purposes. Complicating matters more, not only did the state death tax credit change under EGTRRA, but the *exclusion amounts* also changed with the phase-in of increasing exclusion amounts until 2010 when, for one year, the federal estate tax is completely repealed. The final result of these EGTRRA 2001 rules is that some states have enacted legislation that froze the pre-EGTRRA state death tax credit; some states have enacted legislation that froze the applicable exclusion amounts allowed under pre-EGTRRA law, and some states have enacted legislation that adopted both the prior state death tax credit amount and a specific prior federal applicable exclusion amount.

As an example, under prior law, the federal exemption amount was $700,000 for deaths in 2003, rather than the $1 million allowed under EGTRRA in 2003. Prior law capped the $1 million amount after 2005 and beyond, while EGTRRA increases it through 2009. States that decoupled from EGTRRA have enacted legislation mandating certain previous exemption amounts to retain previous and relied-upon death tax revenue. For example, State X retains the $600,000 federal exclusion amount before it imposes a state estate tax, while State Y imposes a state estate tax when a decedent-domiciliary's gross estate exceeds $675,000.

Although EGTRRA 2001 is a federal law, it has a significant impact on state death taxation. It is important for estate planners and advisers to keep current with the laws of states in which clients have a potential for transfer taxation.

BENEFICIARY CLASSES AND BENEFICIARY EXEMPTIONS

In the majority of states, state law groups beneficiaries who are entitled to receive estate assets into classes. The closest blood relatives of the decedent have the lowest state death tax rate and the largest exemption. In a state that provides for two classes, class 1 (or class A) may include the deceased's surviving spouse, children, parents, and grandchildren. Class 2 (or class B) may include aunts, uncles, brothers, sisters, nephews, nieces, and all other beneficiaries. The class 2 individuals are subject to a higher tax rate than the members of class 1. If the particular state also provides exemptions, the beneficiaries in class 2 will have smaller exemptions than those in class 1. A state may also have different exemptions within a class according to how closely the beneficiary is related to the decedent.

Classes

Some states have numerous classes.

Example: For inheritance tax purposes, state X has six possible classes:

Class	Class Member	Exemption
1	Spouse	Full
2	Lineal issue and adopted children	$25,000
3	Lineal ancestors	5,000
4	Siblings and their descendants; sons and daughters-in-law	500
5	Siblings of parents and their descendants	100
6	Others	None

Tax Rates

There are two types of tax rates used by states that have death taxes: (1) flat percentage rates and (2) graduated percentage rates. In states with a flat rate, the value of the whole share passing to a beneficiary is taxed at the same percentage rate. The flat rate may vary, however, according to the beneficiary's degree of blood relationship to the decedent.

Example: Tony, the decedent's son, inherited $100,000 from his father. The state provides for a flat tax rate of 6 percent for class 1 (direct lineal descendants of the deceased). There are no exemptions. Tony's state tax is $6,000. Martha, the decedent's niece, inherited $10,000. State law mandates that all beneficiaries other than direct lineal descendants and ancestors belong to class 2 and are taxed at a flat 15 percent rate. Martha's state tax is $1,500.

In states with graduated tax rates, a beneficiary's inheritance is broken down into sections. The first section is taxed at the lowest percentage rate. Each additional section is taxed at an increasing rate (similar to the federal gift and estate and income tax rate schedules).

Example: Assume the same facts as in the preceding example except that the state uses graduated tax rates. The inheritance tax rates are as follows:

Value of Property from Decedent to Class 1 Beneficiaries

Column (1) From	Column (2) To	Tax on (1)	Rate on Excess
$ 0	$ 50,000	$ 0	0
50,000	150,000	0	3%
150,000	250,000	3,000	4%
250,000	300,000	7,000	5%
etc.			

Value of Property from Decedent to Class 2 Beneficiaries

Column (1) From	Column (2) To	Tax on (1)	Rate of Excess
$ 1,000	$ 6,000	$ 0	7%
6,000	25,000	350	8%
25,000	150,000	2,000	9%
etc.			

Tony's state tax is $1,500 [.03 x $50,000, which is the amount Tony inherited in excess of $50,000 (in column 1)]. Martha's state tax is $670 [.07 x $5,000 ($6,000 minus $1,000) = $350, plus .08 x $4,000 ($10,000 minus $6,000) = $320; or $350 + $320 = $670.]

Two Types of State Death Tax Rates

- flat percentage rates
  - entire value of a beneficiary's share taxed at same rate
- graduated percentage rates
  - progressive rates applied to a beneficiary's share

Exemptions

If a state provides for exemptions within classes, the amount of the exemption usually depends on the closeness of the beneficiary's blood relationship to the deceased. (Some states reduce the exemption amounts for nonresident estates that have taxable property within the state.) Closest relatives receive the biggest exemptions and lowest tax rates. Where exemptions do apply, it is important to determine when the exemption is taken. In some states, the exemption is taken from the entire share of property passing to the beneficiary prior to applying the tax rates. In other states, the exemption amount is deducted from the portion of the beneficiary's share in the bottom tax bracket. Because the lowest tax rate applies to the first or bottom section, only the amount in excess of the exemption gets the most favorable lowest percentage rate. This method is less beneficial to the beneficiary with regard to taxes.

Example: Referring to the example and tax table for class 1, suppose that Tony, as a child of the decedent, is entitled to an exemption of $30,000. If the $30,000 exemption is taken from Tony's total inheritance of $100,000 before any tax rates come into play, for tax percentage rate and tax computation purposes, Tony would start with an inheritance of $70,000. According to the tax rate table in the example, the first $50,000 of property is taxed at a zero rate, so only the remaining $20,000 is subject to the 3 percent tax rate. In this case, Tony would owe $600 (.03 x $20,000) in state death taxes. However, if the state requires the exemption to apply to the first section or block of the tax table, only $20,000 of property is entitled to the zero percent rate and the remaining $50,000 is taxed at the 3 percent rate. In this situation, Tony's state death tax payable would be $1,500 (.03 x $50,000).

CLASSIFICATIONS OF PROPERTY SUBJECT TO STATE DEATH TAXES

As discussed in chapter 3, there are three main classifications of property: real property, tangible personal property, and intangible personal property.

- *Real property* is real estate and property that is permanently attached to the land. Generally, real property is taxable only by the state in which the property is located (has situs).
- *Tangible personal property* is property such as cars, furniture, jewelry, and artwork. In general, tangible personal property is taxable by the state in which the property is usually kept, whether or not the state is the decedent's state of domicile.
- *Intangible personal property* includes stocks, bonds, insurance policies, mortgage liens, notes, debt instruments, and the like. These kinds of property may be taxable by more than one state if the states can establish a sufficient nexus or contact with the property. Therefore, intangible property may be subject to multiple state death taxation. Such taxation can occur in a number of different circumstances:
    - The decedent owned residences in more than one state.
    - It is unclear which of two or more states is the decedent's state of domicile.
    - Intangibles held in trust may be taxable by the deceased grantor's and the trustee's states of domicile.
    - Securities transferred due to the shareholder's death may be taxable by the shareholder's state of domicile and by the issuing company's state of incorporation.

Clearly, intangibles may present some unexpected tax results. Estates that have significant holdings of intangible assets may suffer disastrous

---

State Death Taxation of Types of Property

- real property (land, buildings)
    - taxed by state of location
- tangible personal property (cars, furniture, artwork)
    - taxed by state of location
- intangible personal property (stocks, bonds, notes)
    - multiple state taxation possible
        - decedent's state of domicile
        - states having significant contacts with property
            - state of trust situs
            - state of incorporation

consequences from the imposition of death taxes if several states have a nexus to the property. The right of more than one state to tax intangibles has been upheld in a number of Supreme Court decisions.[2] It is understandable that a decedent-owner's domiciliary state may levy a death tax. Other states' power to tax the property rests on whether the owner can seek state court protection of his or her rights in the property. In other words, if the intangibles had sufficient nexus with another state so as to provide the decedent's rights in the property some protection under the law of that state, the state has the power to tax the property.

PROPERTY SUBJECT TO STATE DEATH TAXES—GENERAL PRINCIPLES

The laws of each state determine the specific types of property that are taxable by the state as transfers taking effect at death. Death tax statutes of many states have some similarities to federal estate tax provisions. Generally speaking, property is taxable if the decedent directly owned the property at death, retained certain rights or powers over the property during lifetime, made lifetime transfers of property in contemplation of death and within a certain period (one to three years) of death, held the property in a revocable trust, or made vesting of the property in another dependent upon surviving the decedent.

Property Jointly Held with Right of Survivorship

As might be expected, the rules regarding property held jointly with right of survivorship vary widely among the states. Some states do not tax jointly held property that passes from a decedent to a surviving spouse. Other states completely exempt all survivorship joint property from state transfer taxation. Still other states tax the full fair market value of the property in the estate if the joint tenant dies absent proof of contribution by the surviving tenant(s). A few states divide the property's value by the number of joint tenants and tax the decedent's fractional share.

Life Insurance

Again, there is a wide variation among the states. If the proceeds are payable to or for the benefit of the decedent-insured's estate or to a personal representative, the proceeds are taxable in most states. A few states, however, exempt a portion or all of such proceeds. In a number of states if the proceeds are payable to named beneficiaries other than the estate or personal representative, they are not taxed. Exemptions from tax may vary according to the beneficiary designation. For instance, if a surviving spouse or children are the named beneficiaries, the proceeds may pass tax free; whereas if the proceeds are payable to any other beneficiary, they are taxable. Some states tax the proceeds if the decedent held certain incidents of ownership. If the decedent did not possess any incidents of ownership and did not name the estate as beneficiary, the proceeds are usually not taxed.

Annuities

As a general rule, if a decedent-annuitant held a period-certain or refund annuity and payments are made to a beneficiary, the payments are taxable. State death taxes often apply to survivor interests in joint and survivor annuities.

Business Situs of Intangible Property

Careful thought should be given before intangible property is used for business-related purposes in a state other than the business's state of domicile (that is, the state of incorporation or main headquarters). If intangibles are given business applications in another state, that state may be able to claim the intangibles are taxable because they have a business situs in the state. For instance, if business property is used to secure a loan in another state, the state may claim the intangible has a business situs within the state and therefore is subject to tax.

Powers of Appointment

There is wide variation in the states' death tax treatment of powers of appointment. If a state does not have statutory law concerning death taxation of powers of appointment, common law may prevail, resulting in taxation at the decedent-donor's death. In other states, the value of the property subject to a power is taxed in the estate of the donee (the individual with the power to appoint the property). In some instances, it is the distinction between the exercise and nonexercise of the power or general power versus limited or special power that determines tax liability. In Pennsylvania, assets under a general power of appointment are exempt from taxation in the power holder's estate.

Retirement Benefits

The majority of states have statutes that closely track federal law regarding death taxation of retirement benefits. Benefits payable to the decedent-employee's estate are generally taxable. Benefits paid to other beneficiaries are exempt from state death tax to the extent of the decedent's contributions. Although the death benefits and survivor benefits of qualified plans and governmental retirement arrangements are usually taxable in states that have inheritance taxes, most states have exemption provisions.

Community Property

A decedent-spouse's one-half interest in community property is subject to death taxation in most of the community-property states.

Nonresident Exemptions

Fortunately, the likelihood of multiple taxation is decreased by the fact that many states either exempt the intangible property of nonresidents or grant a reciprocal exemption for nonresident-decedents. Reciprocity laws typically serve to exempt a nonresident's intangibles from tax if the nonresident's domiciliary state also exempts the intangibles of nonresidents. To avoid duplicate taxation some states have adopted the Uniform Interstate Compromise of Death Taxes Act[3], under which state tax authorities and executors reach agreements in compromise of state taxes owed. Some states provide for arbitration concerning death tax disputes. Most multiple tax dilemmas arise when the decedent's state of domicile is not definitively established, when intangibles were used for business purposes in other states, or when trusts are located in other states.

Time of Payment

When state death taxes become due varies among the states. Many states have adopted the same time frame for filing and paying as the federal government, 9 months from the date of the decedent's death.

It is a common policy for many states to allow a discount for early payment. For instance, in a manner similar to the federal estate tax return, Pennsylvania requires inheritance tax returns to be filed and payment made within 9 months of the decedent's death (assuming no extensions have been granted) but allows a 5 percent discount from the inheritance tax due for payments made within 3 months of the decedent's death. In turn, interest and penalties are charged for late payment. Extensions for filing are granted if there is proof of sufficient cause for the delay.

Responsibility for Payment

Generally, the decedent's personal representative is responsible for paying state death taxes. Unless the decedent directed otherwise through a tax apportionment clause in his or her will, the personal representative deducts the tax proportionately from each beneficiary's interest in the estate prior to distribution.

CHAPTER REVIEW

Answers to the review questions and the self-test questions start on page 717.

Key Terms

inheritance tax	decoupling
adjusted taxable estate	

Review Questions

17-1.   Briefly describe the two current types of state death taxes.

17-2.   A few months after Mrs. Smith's death, her executor determined that her federal taxable estate is $920,000. What is the maximum allowable deduction for state death taxes for Mrs. Smith's estate?

17-3.   What effect do beneficiary classes and exemptions have on state death taxation?

17-4.   Describe the general rules used to determine which state has the right to tax the following types of property:
   a.   real estate
   b.   tangible personal property
   c.   intangible personal property

17-5.   Describe the most common circumstances in which intangible property is subject to double or multiple state death taxation.

Self-Test Questions

T   F   17-1.   At the present time, there are basically two types of state death taxes—state estate taxes and inheritance taxes.

T   F   17-2.   For federal estate tax purposes, after 2004, state death taxes are a deduction for the entire amount of state death taxes paid

T   F   17-3.   Decoupling refers to states that have both an inheritance tax and a state estate tax.

T   F   17-4.   If a decedent's estate does not have to file a federal estate tax return (Form 706), there is no deduction for state death taxes paid.

T   F   17-5.   In many states, beneficiaries of different classes are taxed at different rates.

T   F   17-6.   The closest blood relatives of a decedent typically have the lowest state death tax rate and the largest exemption.

T   F   17-7.   Real estate transferred at a decedent's death is taxed only by the decedent's state of domicile.

T   F   17-8.   Intangible personal property may be subject to death taxation by more than one state.

T   F   17-9.   Life insurance proceeds payable to a named beneficiary other than the estate are specifically exempt from state death taxes in some states.

T   F   17-10. A decedent-spouse's one-half interest in community property is exempt from state death taxation in most of the community property states.

T   F   17-11. Many states have adopted the time frame of 3 months from the date of the decedent's death for filing and paying death taxes.

NOTES

1. Prior to 2005, $60,000 was the amount of a previous estate tax exemption. Although the unified credit replaced the $60,000 exemption, the $60,000 figure was retained for purposes of determining the state death tax credit in IRC Section 2011(b).
2. *Curry et al. v. McCanless*, 307 U.S. 357 (1939); *Utah v. Aldrich*, 316 U.S. 174 (1942); *Graves v. Elliott*, 307 U.S. 383 (1939).
3. Uniform Laws Annotated, vol. 8A (St. Paul: West Publishing Co.).

Computation and Payment of Federal Estate Tax

Learning Objectives

An understanding of the material in this chapter should enable the student to

18-1.   Explain how the tentative tax base is determined, and describe how the estate tax payable before credits is computed.

18-2.   Describe the credits that may be applied in determining the net federal estate tax payable.

18-3.   Explain when a federal estate tax return must be filed, when the tax due must be paid, and when payment of a tax may be delayed.

18-4.   Explain what is meant by a Sec. 303 redemption.

Chapter Outline

As set forth in prior chapters, the taxable estate is found by deducting from the gross estate all allowable estate debts, taxes, and administration expenses. Further reductions that may be applicable are the marital deduction and the charitable deduction. (As previously stated, under EGTRRA 2001, beginning January 1, 2005, a state death tax deduction replaces a state death tax credit.) The result is the *taxable estate.*

In this chapter the remaining steps necessary to compute the federal estate tax are discussed. These include

- the determination of the tentative tax base
- the determination of the estate tax before credits
- the determination of the net federal estate tax payable

A convenient chart for computing the federal estate tax is located near the end of this chapter.

In addition, the chapter discusses who must file an estate tax return, the procedures for filing the estate tax return, and paying the estate tax.

DETERMINATION OF TENTATIVE TAX BASE

Once the taxable estate is determined, the amount of adjusted taxable gifts made after 1976 is added to the taxable estate. The result is the tentative tax base.

adjusted taxable gift

Adjusted taxable gifts are taxable gifts made after 1976 that are not includible in the decedent's gross estate. (The term *taxable* in this context means either that gift tax liability occurred or that the applicable exclusion amount [credit equivalent] applied to the gift.) Consequently, the following are excluded from treatment as adjusted taxable gifts:

- post-1976 gifts within the amount of the annual exclusion ($3,000 after 1976 and prior to January 1, 1982; $10,000 after December 31, 1981 and prior to January 1, 2002; $11,000 after December 31, 2001)
- gifts made to a spouse that qualified for the gift tax marital deduction
- gifts that qualified for the gift tax charitable deduction

- gifts that have already been included in the decedent's gross estate for whatever reason. In this latter category is the value of certain transfers that were included in the decedent's gross estate because the decedent retained certain interests, rights, or powers in the property for life, or because such interests were retained initially and were given away less than 3 years before death.
- educational and medical expense exclusion amounts

Tentative Tax Base

taxable estate

\+

adjusted <u>taxable</u> gifts

(all post-1976 <u>taxable</u> gifts decedent made during lifetime that are <u>not</u> included in gross estate)

\=

tentative tax base

Estate Tax Treatment of Split Gifts

Inclusion or Exclusion of the Gift Value

If the split gift does not exceed the annual exclusion amount ($22,000 [after 2001] per donee), nothing is included in the gross estate or adjusted taxable gifts of the donor-decedent.

If the split gift does exceed the annual exclusion (and is not includible in the gross estate because of retained interests or powers), the excess over the annual exclusion amount becomes an adjusted taxable gift in the estate tax computation of the donor-decedent.

If a donor-decedent made a split gift within 3 years of death and retained certain interests or powers (for example, retained income for life) or transferred certain types of property (such as insurance policies on his or her life), the entire value of the gifted property is brought back into the *gross estate* of the donor-decedent. If subsequent to the death of the donor spouse, the consenting spouse died (within 3 years of a gift with retained interests or powers), the consenting spouse's portion of the gift is not includible in his or her gross estate, since the entire value of the gift had already been included in the donor spouse's gross estate.

Includibility of Gift Tax Paid within 3 Years of Death

With respect to the gift taxes paid on the split gift, only the gift tax paid by the donor spouse is includible in the donor spouse's gross estate. Indeed, the gift tax paid by the consenting spouse will be includible in his or her own gross estate. (On the other hand, if the donor spouse pays the entire gift tax, then the total amount of the gift tax is included in the donor spouse's gross estate and no gift tax is included in the consenting spouse's gross estate.)

Credit for Gift Taxes Paid

When the entire gift is includible in the donor spouse's gross estate, any tax that was actually paid by the consenting spouse is, in fact, allowed as a credit in computing the donor spouse's estate tax; therefore, any credit allowed in the donor spouse's estate is not allowed as a credit for gift tax paid by the consenting spouse.

The foregoing concept involves computations beyond the scope of this chapter and is presented for informational purposes only.

DETERMINATION OF ESTATE TAX BEFORE CREDITS

Under the Tax Reform Act of 1976, a unified estate and gift tax system was created. This means that the same rate schedule was applied to transfers both during a decedent's lifetime and at death. The system used a cumulative approach to all transfers made during lifetime, culminating in the final gratuitous transfer of property at death. Cumulating taxable lifetime gifts with dispositions at death had the net effect of increasing the tax rates applied to the taxable estate by adding adjusted taxable gifts to the value of transfers taking effect at death. Because the estate and gift tax rate schedule is progressive, any individual who made lifetime taxable gifts after 1976 was subject to a higher combined estate tax rate than if the computation did not include lifetime gifts. That was the rationale for adding adjusted taxable gifts to the taxable estate to arrive at the tentative tax base—the amount to which tax rates are applied. In other words, this transfer tax rate schedule (near the end of this chapter) applies to cumulated transfers, and the result is the *tentative tax*.

Once the tentative tax is determined, gift taxes generated by taxable gifts made after 1976 in excess of the applicable credit amount are subtracted from this figure. The determination of the amount of reduction allowable because of taxes attributable to post-1976 taxable gifts is made through the following steps:

(1) Total all post-1976 taxable gifts.
(2) Compute the gift tax payable by applying the rate schedule in effect at the decedent's death (see "Rate Schedule for Computing Estate and Gift Tax: 2002 and Beyond," which is located near the end of

this chapter) to the total taxable gifts. In other words, all the post-1976 taxable gifts are treated as if they were made at one time—the date of the decedent's death.

(3) Reduce the gift tax payable by the applicable credit amount for the year of the decedent's death (for gift tax purposes, the credit amount is, $121,800 for 1985; $192,800 for 1987 through 1997; $202,050 for 1998; $211,300 for 1999; $220,550 for 2000 and 2001; and $345,800 after 2001.

(4) If the gift tax payable exceeds the applicable credit amount, subtract the excess from the tentative tax.

The result is the *estate tax payable before credits*.

DETERMINATION OF NET FEDERAL ESTATE TAX PAYABLE

Once the estate tax is computed, there are four possible credits that may be applied against the tax to arrive at the *net federal estate tax payable*. As with income tax credits, these credits are allowed as a dollar-for-dollar reduction of the estate tax. They are the

- applicable credit amount
- credit for foreign death taxes
- credit for gift tax paid on pre-1977 gifts
- credit for taxes paid on prior transfers

No refund is allowed if the sum of the credits exceeds the estate tax otherwise payable.

Estate Tax Credits

- There are four credits that may be subtracted from the estate-tax-payable-before-credits amount:
    - applicable credit amount
    - credit for foreign death taxes
    - credit for gift tax on pre-1977 gifts
    - credit for tax on prior transfers

---

applicable credit amount

Applicable Credit Amount

Under TRA '76, the unified estate and gift tax credit came into existence for estates of decedents dying after December 31, 1976. The term *unified credit* was adopted because the credit may be used as an offset against gift taxes as well as estate taxes. Actually, the credit must first be used to offset gift taxes on lifetime transfers. Any remaining credit is applied as a credit against the federal estate tax. The unified credit was gradually increased each year until it reached $192,800 in 1987. At that time, a unified credit of $192,800 was equivalent to $600,000 of taxable transfers. Thus, the unified credit was commonly, albeit mistakenly, referred to as a $600,000 credit; stated correctly, the $600,000 amount was a credit equivalent.

After 1997, the unified credit became known as the *applicable credit amount*, and it increased incrementally until EGTRRA 2001. The credit for 2001 was $220,550, and the applicable exclusion amount (credit equivalent) was $675,000.

Applicable Credit Amount

Currently, an estate tax credit of $555,800 is allowed to offset estate taxes on the equivalent of $1.5 million of taxable transfers.

The Economic Growth and Tax Relief Reconciliation Act (EGTRRA) of 2001 made a number of fundamental changes to the federal wealth transfer tax system. The Act set in motion the eventual objective of federal estate and generation-skipping transfer tax repeal while curiously retaining the gift tax. A modified carryover basis replaces the transfer tax in 2010. Interestingly, under EGTRRA 2001, the estate and GST tax repeal is effective for only one year—2010. The repeal provisions are to "sunset" after 2010 unless Congress acts prior to 2011. This means that in 2011 federal wealth transfer taxes will revert to the law that was in effect in 2001.

The applicable exclusion amount (that is, the credit equivalent) is $1 million for 2002 and 2003; $1.5 million in 2004 and 2005; $2 million in 2006, 2007, and 2008; $3.5 million in 2009; and repealed in 2010 (Code Sec. 2010(c), as amended by Sec. 521(a) of EGTRRA.

In addition, the federal transfer tax marginal rates are reduced from 2002 to 2009. In 2002, the maximum federal estate, gift, and GSTT rate is 50 percent; 49 percent in 2003; 48 percent in 2004; 47 percent in 2005; 46 percent in 2006; and 45 percent for 2007, 2008, and 2009. The top marginal rate for gift taxes after the estate and GSTT repeal in 2010 is a flat (no longer progressive) rate of 35 percent.

The applicable credit amount, therefore, has the effect of eliminating the lower brackets allocated to taxable transfers below the applicable exclusion amount. As the gift and estate tax rate schedule near the end of this chapter indicates, the first dollar of estate tax imposed above the credit exclusion amount for 2004 and 2005 is paid at a marginal rate of 41 percent for gift tax purposes and at a marginal rate of 45 percent for estate tax purposes.

state death tax credit

State Death Tax Credit (Repealed)

Subject to statutory limits, before 2005, there was a credit against the federal estate tax for any estate, inheritance, legacy, or succession taxes actually paid to a state if the state death tax was attributable to property included in the gross estate. The Internal Revenue Code prescribed a graduated rate table for determining the maximum state death tax credit allowable (IRC Sec. 2011). (See Appendix B.) The credit for state death taxes was further limited to the federal estate tax liability after reduction by the applicable credit amount. As mentioned in a prior chapter, EGTRRA 2001 reduced the maximum state death tax credit allowed on the federal estate tax return (Form 706) from its entire credit level to 75 percent in 2002, 50 percent in 2003, and 25 percent in 2004. Prior to 2005, the credit was computed by applying the statutory rate table to the *adjusted taxable estate*,

adjusted taxable estate

which is the *taxable estate reduced by $60,000* ($60,000 refers to the amount of the specific estate tax exemption allowed prior to 1977). In 2005 through 2009, an estate may take a deduction on the federal estate tax return for state death taxes actually paid.

Credit for Foreign Death Taxes

There is a credit allowed against the federal estate tax for taxes actually paid by the decedent's estate to any foreign country for any estate, inheritance, legacy, or succession taxes. The purpose of the *credit for foreign*

credit for foreign death taxes

death taxes is to prevent double taxation. It is allowable only to the estate of a decedent who was either (1) a citizen of the United States or (2) a resident of the United States who was not a citizen at the time of death. Nonresident aliens are denied the foreign death tax credit. The credit exists for taxes actually paid by the decedent's estate to any foreign country, U.S. possession, or political subdivision of a foreign state.

Credit is given for death taxes paid on property that is located within the foreign country to which the tax is paid and that is also included in the decedent's gross estate for federal estate tax purposes. In other words, the property taxed by a foreign jurisdiction must also be taxed by the United States under our estate tax system. The United States recognizes that the same property is taxed doubly and allows a credit for taxes paid to the foreign jurisdiction. This credit is limited to the proportionate share of federal estate tax attributable to the property located in and taxed by the foreign country.

The maximum credit allowed is the *lesser* of (1) the amount of foreign death tax imposed on the property situated in the foreign country that was also included in the decedent's gross estate for federal estate tax purposes and (2) the amount of federal estate tax attributable to that same property located and taxed in the foreign country that also is included in the decedent's gross estate for federal estate tax purposes. In comparing the two taxes to determine which is the lesser, the exchange rate for converting foreign currency into U.S. dollars in effect when each foreign tax payment is made is used. No credit is given for interest owed or penalties connected with the payment of foreign death taxes.

If the federal estate tax is attributable to a remainder or reversionary interest in the foreign property and an election is made to postpone payment of that part of the tax, the credit applies to the portion of foreign death taxes that are paid and claimed as a credit before the time for payment expires. The credit must be claimed by the *latest* of the following: (1) 4 years from the time the estate tax return is filed, (2) the expiration of any extension for paying the tax, and (3) 60 days after the Tax Court has reached a decision on a petition for redetermination of a deficiency.

Credit for Gift Tax Paid on Pre-1977 Gifts

Gift tax payable on post-1976 gifts becomes part of the computation for determining estate tax liability under the gift and estate tax system, as explained earlier. Therefore, no separate credit is allowed for taxes attributable to these gifts. However, a credit still exists for federal gift tax paid by a decedent on taxable gifts made before 1977 if the property is included in the gross estate. This concept can be illustrated by the following.

Example:	A grantor, Michael, established a trust for the benefit of his son. The grantor reserved the right to all income from the trust during his life. The gift of the remainder interest was a taxable gift on which gift tax was paid. The grantor died last year and the trust property was includible in his gross estate because of the retained life interest. A credit was allowed (within certain technical limitations) for the gift tax attributable to the gift.

Additional complications arise if there are several pre-1977 gifts to which this credit could be applicable. A discussion of the rules regarding these complications and technical limitations of this credit is beyond the scope of this chapter.

credit for tax on prior transfers

Credit for Tax on Prior Transfers

Circumstances may arise in which a decedent has inherited property from someone who died less than 10 years before the decedent's death or within 2 years following the decedent's death and the property transferred to the decedent was already taxable in the estate of the transferor-decedent. To avoid double taxation on double transfers of property occurring within a reasonably short time period (that is, 10 years before or 2 years after the decedent's death), a credit is allowed against the federal estate tax paid by the present decedent as a result of this inherited property inclusion in the decedent's gross estate. (See table 18–1.)

TABLE 18–1
Credit for Tax on Prior Transfers

Percent Allowable	Period of Time between Transferor's Death and Death of Present Decedent
100 percent	up to 2 years after
100 percent	up to 2 years before
80 percent	2 to 4 years before
60 percent	4 to 6 years before
40 percent	6 to 8 years before
20 percent	8 to 10 years before
0 percent	more than 10 years before

Amount of Credit

If the decedent's death occurs within 2 years before or after the transferor's death, the credit is limited to the lesser of (1) the amount of the federal estate tax attributable to the transferred property in the transferor's estate and (2) the amount of the federal estate tax attributable to the transferred property in the present decedent's estate. If the transferor died within 2 years before or 2 years after the death of the present decedent, the allowable credit for the tax on the prior transfer is determined by the lesser of (1) or (2) above. In other words, the full credit is allowed if both deaths occur within 2 years of each other. However, if the transferor died more than 2 years before the present decedent, the credit is reduced by 20 percent for each 2-year period in excess of 2 years.

Example: If the transferor died 3 years before the present decedent, 80 percent of the credit will be allowable. The allowable percentages are provided in table 18-1.

A formula for determining the credit is contained in the Treasury regulations. The Code further defines how the property transferred to the present decedent from the transferor's estate shall be valued.

Allowance of Credit

Property included in the transferor's gross estate that is eligible for the credit includes any beneficial interest in property received by the present decedent from the transferor. The credit may also be allowed with respect to property received by the present decedent as the result of the exercise or nonexercise of a general power of appointment by the transferor-decedent. Of course, if the present decedent was the surviving spouse of the transferor, the credit will be disallowed to the extent that property included in the transferor's gross estate qualified for the marital deduction. The credit pertains to many types of property interests that the present decedent may have received from the transferor, including annuities, life estates, terms for years, remainders, and other interests. The necessary ingredient is that the present decedent inherited these interests from the transferor and became the beneficial owner of the interest. Determining the credit may be further complicated if property for which the credit on prior transfers was sought is also subject to a generation-skipping tax. (The interaction of the credit and the generation-skipping tax is complex and beyond the scope of this chapter.)

Planning for Estate Tax Repeal

Clearly, the future repeal of the estate and generation-skipping transfer taxes, as current law under EGTRRA 2001 provides, is riddled with uncertainty. However, 2010 is not so distant that the questionable likelihood of the repeal's actual occurrence should prevent planning for it. Often, when Congress takes a source of revenue away, it replaces it with another source even more to the government's benefit. That is what is happening with the repeal. Capital gains taxes will replace the estate (but not gift) and generation-skipping taxes—government revenue in a different form.

Only approximately 2 percent of taxpayers pay estate and generation-skipping transfer taxes. For the year 2010 (and perhaps following years if the repeal is made permanent), the expectation is that income tax on inherited property will be paid by a significantly larger percentage of taxpayers. EGTRRA 2001 provides for a "modified carryover basis" in estate planning. A full step up in basis for transfers of inherited noncash assets to nonspousal beneficiaries is limited to $1.3 million. Spousal transfers are permitted an additional $3 million worth of property to receive the full basis step up. For transfers exceeding these amounts, the basis of inherited property will be equal to the lesser of the decedent's adjusted basis or the fair market value of the property on the date of the decedent's death. The majority of transfers will probably result in the beneficiary's acquiring the property with the decedent's carryover adjusted basis. This is especially likely in light of the fact that many owners of low-basis property retained the property during lifetime to obtain the step up at death.

Liquidity planning, record keeping, and record tracing are two ways to prepare for transfers during and perhaps after 2010. The situation is exacerbated if the decedent's property is highly leveraged real estate with a low tax basis. In that case, the estate has capital gain liability when the estate transfers the property to the beneficiary. Finding records to substantiate basis and adjustments to the real property may prove difficult, if not impossible, when the property was purchased many decades or several generations ago when basis was not a concern because the property was expected eventually to receive one or more basis step ups. Determining which beneficiaries receive stepped-up property or carryover basis property is also a potential source of conflict for executors.

State death tax increases add complexity to estate planning after EGTRRA 2001. As a result of the full repeal of the federal state death tax credit in 2005, many states have decoupled from the federal estate tax law (disassociated from the federal credit repeal, causing decedents' estates to continue to have state death tax liability for the full amount of the credit that existed prior to EGTRRA 2001) or will legislate new death tax laws, (inheritance taxes, for example) to compensate for the loss of state revenue from the credit repeal.

Even knowing that Congress may promulgate future laws that modify or significantly change EGTRRA 2001 estate planning provisions, advisers must rely on current law to assist their clients in planning for the changes that are slated to take place in the future.

FILING AN ESTATE TAX RETURN

The personal representative of the estate of every U.S. citizen or resident must file Form 706—The United States Estate Tax Return—if the value of the gross estate plus adjusted taxable gifts on the date of death exceeds the statutory filing requirement. The gross estate and adjusted taxable gifts must exceed the applicable exclusion amount for filing to be required. In other words, these statutory filing limitations are applied to the value of all property included in the gross estate plus the total amount of taxable gifts made after 1976 that were not included in the decedent's estate. (Note that the value of adjusted taxable gifts is included for this purpose at the date-of-gift value, not the value at the date of death.) The value of these lifetime gifts also plays a part in establishing the rate of estate tax to be applied.

PAYMENT OF ESTATE TAX BY PERSONAL REPRESENTATIVE

A primary duty of the personal representative is to file the federal estate tax return when due and to see that estate taxes are timely paid. The personal representative must also timely file any estate income tax returns when they are due. If the estate is sizable enough to warrant filing a federal estate tax return, the return is due and the tax is payable no later than 9 months after the decedent's death unless an extension is granted (IRC Sec. 6075(a)).

The personal representative is required to gather and retain records as well as supplemental data supporting the amounts stated or claimed on the federal estate tax return. If the estate assets are insufficient to pay all the decedent's taxes, the decedent's federal tax liabilities must be paid first. This includes the decedent's income tax liabilities up to the time of death, the income tax liability of the estate, and the estate tax liability. An executor (or administrator) will be held personally liable for the tax if he or she was aware of a potential tax liability or failed in the responsibility to determine if any such tax obligations existed prior to distribution of the estate's assets and the executor's discharge from responsibility (IRC Sec. 2202). In other words, an executor will be liable if he or she was either aware of or should have been aware of the existence of tax obligations. In addition, if the estate is insolvent, the individual beneficiaries will be responsible for paying any federal estate tax accruing from the inclusion of their inheritances in the decedent's gross estate.

Extension for Filing

Generally, a personal representative may obtain an extension for filing a return if it is either impossible or impractical to complete the return within the 9-month period after the decedent dies. This extension is limited to 6 months, unless the personal representative is abroad (IRC Sec. 6081(a)).

Although a 6-month extension is automatically granted, the personal representative of an estate must file Form 4768 with the Internal Revenue Service for the 6-month extension on or before the original due date of Form 706, along with an estimate of the full amount of tax due. An extension of the time for filing an estate tax return does not prevent interest from accruing on any unpaid taxes beginning on the date the return was originally due (IRC Sec. 6601(b)(1)). Also, an extension of time to file does not automatically extend the time for payment. Penalties of 5 percent per month up to 25 percent will be added to the final tax liability unless reasonable cause is shown (Treas. Reg. Sec. 20.6081–1(a)). Thus, if it is impossible or impractical to file a return by the due date, consideration should be given either to paying the estimated amount of estate tax by the due date for filing or to obtaining an extension for payment of the tax.

Extension for Tax Payment

There are mitigating circumstances that the IRS will accept for granting an extension of time to pay the estate tax. An extension for up to 12 months to pay the estate tax will be granted if the Internal Revenue Service determines there is reasonable cause (IRC Sec. 6161(a)). While no definition of reasonable cause is given in the Code or regulations, the following situations are provided in the regulations as a basis for granting an extension of time to pay the tax:

- Although an estate includes sufficient liquid assets, assets are located in several jurisdictions and cannot be marshaled readily by the executor, despite a diligent effort to do so by the time for filing the return.
- A great part of the estate consists of assets that will provide future payments, such as annuities, copyright royalties, contingent fees, or accounts receivable. Because these assets constitute the major part of the estate, the estate does not contain sufficient cash to pay the estate tax within the due period. Borrowing against these assets would inflict considerable losses upon the estate.
- The estate includes a major asset that cannot be collected without litigation. It is unknown whether this asset will ever be collectible, and the size of the gross estate is not determinable at the time for filing the return.
- Unless the estate borrows at a higher-than-normal rate of interest, it does not have sufficient funds to pay the entire estate tax when due as well as to provide reasonable subsistence for the decedent's spouse and dependent children during the remaining period of estate administration. Also, funds are insufficient to satisfy claims currently due against the estate despite reasonable efforts by the personal representative to convert assets into cash (other than an interest in a closely held business to which Sec. 6166 applies).

While the initial extension for *reasonable cause* pertains to a 12-month period from the time the estate tax return is due, a finding of reasonable cause may allow a deferral of payment of estate taxes for reasonable periods up to 10 years for decedents dying after December 31, 1976 (IRC Sec. 6161(a)(2)).

Extension for Paying Tax on Closely Held Business Interests

There is a special provision that allows the personal representative to elect a deferral for payment of estate tax attributable to the inclusion of a closely held business or farm business in the decedent's gross estate if certain conditions are met (IRC Sec. 6166). The law provides that an executor may elect to defer payment of estate tax attributable to inclusion in the estate of a farm or other closely held business if that business consists of more than 35 percent of the *adjusted gross estate*. If the estate qualifies, such an election is made at the sole discretion of the estate's personal representative. Payments of tax attributable to the business interest may be deferred for 5 years from the due date. Interest only on the unpaid balance is due annually for the initial 4 years (four annual installments of interest only). In the fifth year and thereafter, the tax plus installments of interest on the unpaid balance is payable in equal annual installments over a maximum of 10 more years. Note that the total payment period actually extends over 14 years rather than 15 years because the first installment of tax becomes due simultaneously with the last payment of interest. To determine whether more than 35 percent of the adjusted gross estate is made up of a closely held business or farm, the adjusted gross estate is defined as the gross estate reduced by deductible debts, expenses, claims, and losses, but before reduction by the marital or charitable deductions (IRC Sec. 6166(b)(6)).

Filing and Tax Payment Extensions

- 6-month extension
  - easily granted
  - extension Form 4768 filed on or before 9 months of death
  - interest on estate tax due commences to run 9 months after death
- 12-month extension [Sec. 6161(a)]
  - granted for "reasonable cause"
    - pending estate litigation
- 10-year extension [Sec. 6161(a)(2)]
  - difficult to marshal assets
  - assets providing future payments
  - only higher than normal rate of interest for loan available
- 14-year extension for closely held business or farm interest [Sec. 6166]

For purposes of the 35 percent rule, an interest in a closely held business is defined as (1) an interest in a proprietorship, (2) an interest in a partnership carrying on a trade or business with no more than 45 partners or where 20 percent or more of its assets helped determine the decedent's gross estate, or (3) stock in a corporation with no more than 15 shareholders or where 20 percent of its voting stock is included in the decedent's gross estate (IRC Sec. 6166(b)(6)(1)). Property owned by a corporation, partnership, estate, or trust is regarded as owned proportionately by its shareholders, partners, or beneficiaries. In addition, for purposes of this election, interests in two or more closely held businesses are treated as a single closely held business if 20 percent or more of the total value of each business is included in the decedent's gross estate (IRC Sec. 6166(c)). Also, all stock and partnership interests belonging to a decedent and any family members will be aggregated in order to meet the requirements of stock ownership. The family members whose interests are considered as held by the decedent are the decedent's brothers, sisters, spouse, parents, grandparents, children, and grandchildren.

For purposes of this election, stock in a closely held business must be stock that is not readily tradable. At the time of the decedent's death, this means stock that is not listed on a stock exchange and for which there is no market in over-the-counter trading. When a farm or other business is included in the estate and the executor has elected special-use valuation, the special-use value is treated as the property value to which Sec. 6166 applies.

In some cases, an executor may be uncertain whether the estate will need to defer payment of tax or will qualify for deferred payment of tax. In that event, the executor may file a protective election with the estate tax return. Filing such an election preserves the executor's right to elect estate tax deferral.

Special 2 Percent Interest Rate

The present law contains a special 2 percent rate of interest (compounded daily) attributable to the deferred estate tax on the first $1 million of closely held business or farm property included in the gross estate. The $1 million figure for purposes of calculating the 2 percent portion of deferred estate taxes is indexed for inflation under TRA '97 ($1,170,000 in 2005).

It should be noted, however, that the tax for which the 2 percent rate is available is in addition to the applicable credit amount. The remaining amount accrues interest at 45 percent of the applicable federal rate on underpayments of tax (compounded daily) determined on a calendar-quarter basis.

Note: Students will not be expected to know how to make this Sec. 6166 calculation. The following calculation is for illustrative purposes only.

Example: Suppose the total estate tax due on John Q. Public's estate is $1 million and his closely held business is 50 percent of the adjusted gross estate. Under the rules of Sec. 6166, $500,000 50 percent of the estate tax burden of $1 million can be deferred.

The actual dollar amount of tax to which the 2 percent rate applies is the lesser of $532,200 (in 2004) and the estate tax burden that can be deferred under Sec. 6166, calculated as follows:

(1) Take the amount of the business value that can qualify for the special 2 percent rate (as indexed for inflation). $1,170,000 (2005)

(2) Determine the applicable
exclusion amount in effect. <u>+1,500,000</u> (2005)

(3) Add lines 1 and 2. $2,670,000

(4) Calculate the estate tax
due on the amount in line 3. $1,095,700

(5) Subtract the applicable
credit amount in effect. <u>−$ 555,800</u> (2005)

(6) The result is the maximum $ 539,900
Sec. 6166 amount that
can qualify for the special
2 percent interest rate.

Again, the maximum amount applicable to an estate is the lesser of this maximum amount or the estate tax burden that can be deferred under Sec. 6166. For example, if John Q. Public's estate tax burden was $1 million and the estate was able to defer $500,000 in estate taxes under Sec. 6166, then only $500,000, and not $539,900, would qualify for the special 2 percent rate (in 2005).

It is also interesting to note that interest begins to accrue on the date the tax was required to be paid without regard to any allowable extensions. However, the adjusted gross estate is determined on the date the estate tax return is filed, including any extensions of time for filing (IRC Sec. 6166(b)(6)). This differential allows the estate to deduct the interest payments that accrue up to the date the return is actually filed. Thus, an estate that barely misses qualifying under the 35 percent rule may qualify for tax deferral by delaying filing and accruing interest. The interest deduction accrued from 9 months after the date of death to the date of filing will increase the amount of deductible expenses from the gross estate in arriving at the adjusted gross estate. This will decrease the value of the adjusted gross estate and increase the percentage of the closely held business or farm relative to the adjusted gross estate. Thus, an estate that came close to qualifying but failed to do so under the 35 percent eligibility rule may then qualify for installment payment of tax.

Acceleration

Under certain circumstances, the estate forfeits its right to installment payment of tax. If any of the following actions occurs, all remaining unpaid estate tax becomes due and payable immediately upon notice and demand by the Internal Revenue Service. The events that cause acceleration are as follows:

- late payment or failure to pay any individual installment
- withdrawal of 50 percent or more of the assets (including cash and property) from the business
- distribution, sale, exchange, or disposition of 50 percent or more of the value of the business interest to anyone other than a beneficiary who is entitled to receive the interest under the decedent's will or trust or under state intestacy laws

These withdrawals are cumulative. If the decedent's interest in a closely held business is transferred because of either the death of the original heir or the death of any subsequent transferee receiving the interest as a result of the prior transferor's death, acceleration of taxes will not be triggered if each subsequent transferee is a family member of the transferor. The term *family member* for the purposes of Sec. 6166 acceleration is determined under Sec. 267(c)(4), which includes brothers, sisters, spouse, ancestors, and lineal descendants as family members of the transferor.

Furthermore, acceleration will not be triggered by late installment payments of tax by the executor in the first 6 months. An executor is now given a grace period of 6 months after each installment is due within which to pay the tax without causing acceleration of the unpaid tax. However, late payment causes the estate to lose the benefit of the 2 percent interest rate with respect to that payment. In addition to the higher interest rate, the estate will be required to pay a penalty of 5 percent for each month or part of a month that the payment is overdue.

Because an executor may be held personally liable if other distributions are made from the estate prior to payment of the estate tax, installment payment of the estate tax could leave executors vulnerable over a long period of time. To alleviate this problem, there is a special lien procedure available

---

Sec. 6166 Installment Payment of Estate Tax

- inclusion in decedent's estate of closely held business interest or farm valued at more than *35% of adjusted gross estate*
- deferral of tax payments for 5 years from due date of return
- interest payments only on unpaid balance for first 4 years
- overlapping tax and interest payments in 5th year
- acceleration of full estate tax balance if Sec. 6166 requirements not met

that relieves the executor from personal liability for the entire installment period. It may be elected if the executor, as well as all parties having any interest in the property to which the lien will attach, files a written agreement consenting to creation of the lien in favor of the federal government instead of a bond. This agreement must name a responsible individual to deal with the Internal Revenue Service on behalf of the beneficiaries and all other parties who consented to the lien. A bond may not be required by the IRS except to the extent that no adequate security exists for the unpaid principal plus interest.

IRC SEC. 303 REDEMPTION

Sec. 303 redemption

The purpose of Sec. 303 is to reduce the tax impact on the estates of decedents who owned incorporated businesses. An IRC *Sec. 303 redemption* allows a redemption of closely held stock for the purpose of paying funeral and administrative expenses and death taxes without the redemption being treated as a dividend. If the redemption qualifies, it is treated as a sale, and the gain is treated as capital gain if the stock was held as a capital asset in the hands of the decedent at the time of the sale.

Example:	At his death, Marvin owned 10,000 shares of Marvalus, his closely held business, which were included in his estate. Each share had an estate tax value of $90 at his death and an adjusted basis of $0. Marvin's estate is responsible for $400,000 in funeral costs, federal and state death taxes, and administration expenses. Several months after Marvin's death, when the value of the stock was $100 per share, the corporation redeemed 4,000 shares of Marvalus, Inc., for $100 per share. If this redemption qualifies for Sec. 303 treatment, the estate will have long-term gain of $40,000 due to the per-share gain of $10 from the date-of-death value. If the redemption does not qualify for Sec. 303 treatment (that is, capital-gain treatment), the estate will be treated as having received a dividend of $400,000 (4,000 shares x $100 a share). The $400,000 dividend will be taxed as ordinary income.

In order to qualify for capital-gain treatment under this section, the decedent's stock must represent more than 35 percent of the *adjusted gross estate*. Ownership of 20 percent or more of the stock of each of two or more corporations may be aggregated to satisfy this 35 percent test.

If any redemption is made more than 4 years after the decedent's death, capital-gains treatment is available only for the distribution that represents the lesser of (1) the amount of the qualifying death taxes and funeral and administration expenses unpaid immediately before the distribution and (2) the aggregate of these amounts paid within one year after the distribution.

This favorable tax treatment applies to the distribution by a corporation only to the extent that the interest of a shareholder is reduced directly or through a binding obligation to contribute to the payment of the estate's expenses or taxes. In other words, the party whose shares are redeemed must be the one who actually bears the burden of the estate and other death taxes, or funeral and administration expenses in an amount equal to the redeemed value of the stock. This rule can be illustrated by the following example. Assume a block of otherwise qualifying stock is left to a surviving spouse in a manner that qualifies for the marital deduction and that the decedent's will provides that the marital bequest will bear no portion of taxes or administrative costs (a common provision). In this case, the stock left to the surviving spouse could not be redeemed under Sec. 303 even though in all other respects it qualified, because there is no liability on the marital bequest to pay death taxes or administrative costs.

It should be noted that if a redemption qualifies for capital-gains treatment under Sec. 303 or under other Code sections, an estate recognizes less or no taxable gain because the stock receives a new stepped-up basis. However, should a redemption not qualify for capital-gains treatment, it is treated as a dividend distribution, and the estate will recognize ordinary income on the full value of the stock on the applicable valuation date.

Sec. 303 Stock Redemption

- *Without* its being treated as a dividend with capital gain, it allows the redemption of stock to the amount of
  - funeral costs
  - estate administration expenses
  - death taxes
- Redemption of stock is treated as an *exchange*.
- Decedent's stock has to represent more than 35% of the adjusted gross estate.

Planning point: With proper advance planning, a closely held business that otherwise does not meet the greater than 35 percent test can be made to qualify for Sec. 303. For instance, by making lifetime gifts of nonbusiness property, the business owner can reduce his or her adjusted gross estate and thereby increase the percentage of the business included in the estate. When a gifting program, however, is implemented to increase the percentage of a business included in an estate, planners must be aware that the 3-year rule under Sec. 2035 pulls the value of gifts made within 3 years of the donor's death solely for the purpose of calculating qualification of Secs. 303 and 6166.

Example:	Mae died with an adjusted gross estate of $10 million and a business valued at $3.6 million that was included in her estate.
	Based on these simple facts, Mae's estate meets the 35 percent test and qualifies for Sec. 303 (or 6166) treatment. Suppose, however, that a year and a half before her death Mae gave $500,000 to each of her two sons. Because Sec. 2035 requires the $1 million in gifts to be included in Mae's gross estate for purposes of Sec. 303 qualification, the business does not meet the 35 percent test (35 percent of $11 million adjusted gross estate requires that the business be valued in excess of $3.85 million).

MINI-CASES

Mini-Case 1

X is a successful businessman who owns a one-half interest in a profitable partnership that he and his brother, Y, organized to develop real estate. He has also engaged from time to time in other real estate ventures with his brother independently of the partnership. X and his wife are both 49 years old.

X holds personal assets in his own name as follows:

One-half of the partnership interest in the XY Company	$1,500,000
Common stock	120,000
Cash in bank	90,000
Household furnishings and personal effects	50,000
Municipal bonds—face amount	120,000

> *See the following pages for "Chart for Computing Federal Estate Tax," "Rate Schedule for Computing Estate and Gift Tax: 2002 and Beyond," and "Estate Tax Credit Schedule." Mini-Case 1 continues after these three pages.*

CHART FOR COMPUTING FEDERAL ESTATE TAX

STEP 1   (1)   Gross estate

minus

      (2)   Funeral and administration expenses
           (estimated as _____ % of _____) $_____

      (3)   Debts and taxes   _____

      (4)   Losses   _____   (−) _____

equals

STEP 2   (5)   Adjusted gross estate $_____

minus

      (6)   Marital deduction $_____

      (7)   Charitable deduction   _____

      (8)   State death tax deduction[1]   _____   (−) _____

equals

STEP 3   (9)   Taxable estate $_____

plus

      (10) Adjusted taxable gifts (taxable portion
           of post-1976 lifetime taxable transfers
           not included in gross estate)   + _____

equals

      (11) Tentative tax base (total of taxable estate
           and adjusted taxable gifts) $_____

compute

      (12) Tentative tax $_____

minus

      (13) Gift taxes payable on post-1976 gifts[2]   (−) _____

equals

STEP 4   (14) Estate tax payable before credits $_____

minus

      (15) Tax credits
          (a) Applicable credit amount $_____
          (b) Allowable state death tax credit[3]   _____
          (c) Credit for foreign death taxes[4]   _____
          (d) Credit for gift tax for pre-1977 gifts[5]   _____
          (e) Credit for tax on prior transfers   _____   (−) _____

equals

STEP 5   (16) Net federal estate tax payable $_____

---

1. 2005 through 2009 (replaces Step 4(15)(b)).
2. Once the tentative tax is determined, gift taxes generated by taxable gifts made after 1976 in excess of the applicable credit amount are subtracted from it.
3. Reduced by 25 percent in 2002, 50 percent in 2003, and 75 percent in 2004; repealed in 2005 and replaced with a deduction in 2005 through 2009 as shown in Step 2(8).
4. Irrelevant credit for purposes of this course.
5. Credit still exists for gift taxes paid by a deceased on taxable gifts made before 1977 if the property is included in the gross estate. Irrelevant credit for purposes of this course.

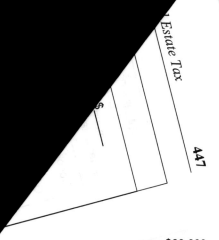

...PUTING ESTATE AND GIFT TAX: 2002 AND BEYOND

	The tentative tax is . . .
	18% of such amount
	$1,800, plus 20% of excess of such amount over $10,000
	$3,800, plus 22% of excess of such amount over $20,000
...ot over $60,000	$8,200, plus 24% of excess of such amount over $40,000
Over $60,000 but not over $80,000	$13,000, plus 26% of excess of such amount over $60,000
Over $80,000 but not over $100,000	$18,200, plus 28% of excess of such amount over $80,000
Over $100,000 but not over $150,000	$23,800, plus 30% of excess of such amount over $100,000
Over $150,000 but not over $250,000	$38,800, plus 32% of excess of such amount over $150,000
Over $250,000 but not over $500,000	$70,800, plus 34% of excess of such amount over $250,000
Over $500,000 but not over $750,000	$155,800, plus 37% of excess of such amount over $500,000
Over $750,000 but not over $1,000,000	$248,300, plus 39% of excess of such amount over $750,000
Over $1,000,000 but not over $1,250,000	$345,800, plus 41% of excess of such amount over $1,000,000
Over $1,250,000 but not over $1,500,000	$448,300, plus 43% of excess of such amount over $1,250,000
Over $1,500,000 but not over $2,000,000	$555,800, plus 45% of excess of such amount over $1,500,000
Over $2,000,000 but not over $2,500,000	$780,800, plus 49% of excess of such amount over $2,000,000
Over $2,500,000	$1,025,800, plus 50% (2002)
For 2003 to 2006: Eliminate the over $2,500,000 estate bracket; highest estate bracket becomes over $2,000,000	$780,800, plus (49% in 2003), (48% in 2004), (47% in 2005), (46% in 2006) of excess of such amount over $2,000,000
For 2007 to 2009: Eliminate the over $2,000,000 estate bracket; highest estate bracket becomes over $1,500,000	$555,800, plus 45% of excess of such amount over $1,500,000

ESTATE TAX CREDIT SCHEDULE

The applicable credit amount applies to both lifetime and after-death transfers. For gratuitous lifetime transfers (gifts), however, the exclusion amount remains at $1 million even though the estate tax exclusion increases to more than $1 million after 2003. The credit is first used to offset taxable gifts made during lifetime, with any remaining credit to be applied as a credit against federal estate taxes. The following chart shows the applicable credit amount per year as it is phased in for different time periods and the equivalent value of the gross estate exempted from taxation.

Year	Applicable Credit Amount	Applicable Exclusion Amount
1982	$ 62,800	$ 225,000
1983	79,300	275,000
1984	96,300	325,000
1985	121,800	400,000
1986	155,800	500,000
1987 to 1998	192,800	600,000
1998	202,050	625,000
1999	211,300	650,000
2000 and 2001	220,550	675,000
2002 and 2003	345,800	1,000,000
2004 and 2005	555,800	1,500,000
2006, 2007, and 2008	780,800	2,000,000
2009	1,455,800	3,500,000
2010	Repeal	Repeal

The requirement to file an estate tax return has been adjusted upward to reflect increases in the applicable credit amount. Executors of estates (including lifetime adjusted taxable gifts) having a gross value of less than the applicable exclusion amount shown in the right column above are not required to file federal estate tax returns.

Only estates having values exceeding the applicable exclusion amount are potentially subject to the federal estate tax.

X holds the following property in joint tenancy with Mrs. X (who has made no contribution to the cost of these assets):

Bank checking account	$ 12,000
Corporate bonds (purchased in 1990)	30,000
Automobile (purchased in 2001)	10,000

X and Mrs. X hold their residence, purchased in 1987 and valued at $350,000, as tenants by the entirety. Mrs. X paid 40 percent of the original purchase price from an inheritance that she received from her father. In addition, X and his brother own as tenants in common equal shares of undeveloped commercial real estate with a total value of $100,000.

X owns life insurance on his own life as follows:

Policy	Age at Issue	Face Amount	Beneficiary	How Payable
30-payment life	28	$ 10,000	X's estate	Lump sum
Ordinary life	34	120,000	Mrs. X	Lump sum
Ordinary life	38	150,000	Mrs. X and then her estate	Installments certain for 10 years
10-year term	48	50,000	Mrs. X	Lump sum

a. Assume that no change has been made in the manner in which X and Mrs. X hold title to their property, and that the values of their assets at X's death this year are those shown above. Prepare a list of assets, with their values, that would be included in X's gross estate for federal estate tax purposes if he predeceases Mrs. X.

b. X's will leaves the entire residue to his wife except his partnership interest, which he leaves to his two sons in equal shares. Assume X dies in 2005. Compute the federal estate tax payable. Assume that funeral and administration expenses are $130,000 and that the state death tax is $65,000.

c. How would your answer in b. differ if X made a gift of the $1.5 million partnership interest to his sons and a gift of $124,000 to his daughter 2 years before his death? X's wife did not join in the gifts. Assume X paid a gift tax of $250,950 when he made the gifts to his children. Assume also that state death taxes are now $12,000.

Mini-Case 2

Emily Smith, a widow, died this year at age 75. Prior to her retirement 10 years ago, Emily had been a corporate secretary. Emily is survived by a daughter, Eva, a son-in-law, and three grandchildren. Most of Emily's assets were left to her by her late husband, Henry Smith, who was an airline executive when he died 12 years ago.

After Henry's death, Emily became the sole owner of their personal residence. Eight months before her death, Emily deeded the property to her daughter Eva in exchange for a written agreement stating that she would be allowed to live in the house for as long as she wanted. Emily retained title to the furnishings.

Under Emily's will, she left $500,000 to State University. Her deductible funeral and administration expenses are $125,000, and her deductible debts are $75,000. The full amount of the applicable credit amount is available for her estate, and state death taxes are $60,000. Emily's date of death is the applicable date for federal estate tax valuation.

Emily's Situation on the Date of Her Death

Type of Asset	Fair Market Value	Owner(s)
Checking account	$ 20,000	Emily
Money market funds	340,000	Emily
Common stock	600,000	Emily and Eva, as joint tenants with right of survivorship. Emily and Eva equally contributed to the purchase of the stock.
Personal residence	$450,000	Eva
401(k) plan benefit	$600,000	Emily. At Emily's death the plan trustees are to pay the plan benefit to her husband, Henry, if living, otherwise to her estate in a lump sum.
Household furnishings	$ 30,000	Emily
Automobile	$ 15,000	Emily
QTIP trust	$750,000	Trustee, under the provisions of Henry Smith's testamentary trust. Emily receives the annual income, and at her death the trust corpus passes to Eva.

a. Prepare a list of assets, with their values, that would be included in Emily's gross estate for federal estate tax purposes.
b. Compute the federal estate tax payable for Emily's estate.

CHAPTER REVIEW

Answers to the mini-cases, the review questions, and the self-test questions start on page 717.

Key Terms

adjusted taxable gift
applicable credit amount
state death tax credit
adjusted taxable estate

credit for foreign death taxes
credit for tax on prior transfers
Sec. 303 redemption

Review Questions

18-1.   Given the taxable estate, explain how the tentative tax base is obtained.

18-2.   Mr. Bowden died this year with a gross estate valued at $2,300,000. His funeral and administration expenses are $100,000. At his death, Mr. Bowden owed $25,000 in accrued personal property and realty taxes. Mr. Bowden's estate left $625,000 to his wife outright and the remainder in trust for his two sons. At no time during his life did Mr. Bowden make any taxable gifts. Mr. Bowden's state has imposed $50,000 of state death taxes. Calculate the tentative tax (before credits) due on the transfer of Mr. Bowden's estate.

18-3.   What amount may be deducted from the tentative tax before credits are determined?

18-4.   What are the credits that may be deducted from the tentative tax, and what is the effect of a tax credit?

18-5.   Sam, a widower, died this year with a gross estate of $3,320,000; deductible administration expenses and debts totaled $140,000. Sam's three children, who are his sole beneficiaries, will receive equal shares of his estate. Their ages are 26, 23, and 21. Under his will, Sam donated $250,000 to his university. He also made post-1976 adjusted taxable gifts of $60,000, for which the gift tax liability was $13,000. Assuming the state death taxes are $70,000, calculate the net federal estate tax by using the applicable credit amount.

18-6.   What is the purpose of the applicable credit amount, and how does its use during lifetime affect its availability at death?

18-7.   What is the purpose of the credit for foreign death taxes paid, and to whom does it apply?

18-8.   Tom Grigson died this year with a taxable estate valued at $1,825,000. Will the following amounts paid be allowed as credits against his estate tax liability?
   a.   His estate paid $150,000 in state inheritance taxes.
   b.   Tom's sister, who died 3 years before Tom, had an estate valued at $500,000 after payment of debts and taxes. He was the sole heir of his sister's estate, which was settled shortly before Tom died. His gross estate included the $500,000 received from his sister. Federal estate taxes paid on her estate were $185,000.

18-9.   Explain the credit for gift tax paid on pre-1977 gifts and its relation to post-1976 gift taxes paid.

18-10.   Explain the credit for tax on prior transfers and its purpose.

18-11.   In which of the following situations is the executor required to file a federal estate tax return?
   a.   George Jessup died this year with a gross estate valued at $1,375,000.
   b.   Jim's gross estate is valued at $1,725,000, and the estate had $100,000 of deductions in debts and unpaid federal income taxes as well as funeral and administration expenses.

18-12.   Describe the duties of the personal representative of an estate with respect to the filing of federal tax returns.

18-13.   For what reasons might an extension of time to pay the federal estate tax usually be allowed?

18-14.   Describe the circumstances that must exist before the estate tax may be paid in installments.

18-15.   The following situations describe two sets of circumstances under which an extension of time for paying all or part of the estate tax liability may be obtained. Explain whether the extension in each case is granted at the discretion of the Internal Revenue Service or whether it may be elected by the executor as a matter of right.
   a.   Albert, a widower, died this year leaving a gross estate of $1,850,000 and an adjusted gross estate of $1,700,000. Albert's taxable estate is also $1,700,000. The executor has determined that a portion of the estate must be sold in order to pay the estate tax within the 9-month time limit. The only portion of the estate that can be sold is Albert's interest in a partnership in which he and his brother, Sam, were equal partners. Albert's partnership interest has an estate tax value of $450,000, and the executor has found a buyer at that price. However, the buyer will need several months to raise that amount of money.
   b.   Benjamin died recently leaving a gross estate of $1,800,000, an adjusted gross estate of $1,725,000, and a taxable estate of $1,650,000. Benjamin's executor has determined that the estate does not contain sufficient liquid assets with which to pay the estate tax. The only portion of the estate that could be converted to cash in time to pay the taxes is his interest in a closely held corporation engaged in the heating oil business. The estate owns 30 percent of the stock, which had a fair market value of $700,000 at the time Benjamin died. The two surviving stockholders are Benjamin's sons, who inherited the stock and are attempting to raise the money to pay the tax themselves so it will not be necessary to sell the stock to an outsider.

18-16.   Describe what circumstances will trigger an acceleration of the estate tax payable when installment payments are being made.

18-17.   Explain a Sec. 303 stock redemption and when it can be used.

Self-Test Questions

T F 18-1. Adjusted taxable gifts include only the value of taxable gifts made after 1976 that is not includible in the decedent's gross estate.

T F 18-2. A post-1976 gift not subject to tax as a result of the annual exclusion is not part of *adjusted taxable gifts*.

T F 18-3. Gift taxes actually paid within 3 years of death are includible in the gross estate.

T F 18-4. Once the tentative tax is found by applying the tax rate schedule to the tentative tax base, any gift tax payable (in excess of the applicable credit amount) on post-1976 gifts is subtracted before application of credits.

T F 18-5. A credit against the estate tax payable reduces the taxable estate before the tax rates are applied.

T F 18-6. A separate applicable credit amount is available against both lifetime and testamentary transfers so that a decedent's property valued at twice the applicable credit amount will avoid transfer tax.

T F 18-7. A deduction for the full amount of state death taxes paid by a decedent's estate may be taken from a decedent's adjusted gross estate.

T F 18-8. The personal representative is responsible for filing a federal estate tax return in all cases no later than 9 months after the date of the decedent's death for all U.S. citizens and residents.

T F 18-9. If it is impossible or impractical to complete a federal estate tax return within the 9 months following the decedent's death, a mandatory 6-month extension to file must be granted by the IRS unless the personal representative is abroad.

T F 18-10. A one-year extension of time to pay federal estate tax is available to executors who prove there has been reasonable cause for the extension, such as inability to locate assets or the existence of assets in foreign countries.

T F 18-11. There is no definition of *reasonable cause* in the Code and Regulations for extension of time for payment of federal estate taxes.

T F 18-12. If a closely held business or farm comprises more than 35 percent of the gross estate or 65 percent of the adjusted gross estate, the executor may elect to pay the tax in installments over not more than 10 years.

T F 18-13. The election to qualify the estate for deferred payments of tax attributable to a closely held business must be made by the decedent in his or her will.

T F 18-14. There is a special 2 percent interest rate for installment payments of estate tax attributable to the inclusion of the first $1,170,000 (2005 as indexed for inflation) of closely held business or farm property in the decedent's gross estate.

T   F   18-15.   The estate tax payable in installments, for which the 2 percent interest rate is available, will be reduced by the applicable credit amount.

T   F   18-16.   Withdrawal of 50 percent or more of the assets from a closely held business will trigger acceleration of all unpaid federal estate tax installments.

T   F   18-17.   Acceleration of federal estate tax installment payments will not occur if each subsequent transferee (of the business) is a family member of the transferor.

T   F   18-18.   The executor who elects installment payment of taxes may be relieved from personal liability by electing a special lien procedure and filing an agreement signed by all parties having any interest in the business.

T   F   18-19.   A Sec. 303 redemption for a decedent's closely held stock refers to redemption at ordinary income tax rates of the decedent's closely held stock when it comprises a large part of his or her estate.

T   F   18-20.   In order to qualify for capital-gains treatment under a Sec. 303 redemption, a decedent's stock must represent more than 35 percent of his or her adjusted gross estate.

19

The Basis Rules for Property Transferred during Lifetime or at Death

---

Learning Objectives

An understanding of the material in this chapter should enable the student to

19-1. Explain how basis is used to determine gain or loss when property changes hands in a taxable transaction.

19-2. Explain the rules for determining the basis of property transferred at death.

19-3. Explain the rules for determining the basis of property transferred during lifetime by gift or bargain sale.

Chapter Outline

COMPUTING GAIN OR LOSS

One cannot compute the amount of gain or loss on the sale of an asset without knowing its cost. In most cases, the basis of an asset is the original price paid to acquire the property increased by certain adjustments (such as expenditures for improvements) and decreased by certain tax benefits (such as depreciation taken during the term of ownership).

Before an asset is transferred, four factors must be established. The first is the basis in the hands of the transferor; second, whether the asset is characterized as a capital or noncapital asset; third, the holding period in the hands of the transferor; and fourth, the fair market value of the asset at a relevant point in time.

Function of Basis

The main function of basis is to measure gain or loss when property is sold, exchanged, or transferred in a taxable transaction. (A second function of basis—to serve as a departure point for depreciation—is not discussed here.) Basis becomes important when property changes hands. If the transaction is taxable, the transferor must establish the basis in order to calculate gain or loss on the transaction. The transferee's basis determines gain or loss on a later transfer. The basis assumed by the transferee varies, depending on the character of the transfer—that is, whether the transfer is a taxable sale or exchange, a nontaxable transfer by gift or inheritance, or a tax-free exchange. The transferee's basis is used to determine gain or loss when the asset is sold.

Basis

Used to determine gain or loss for income tax purposes when property is sold, exchanged, or transferred in a taxable transaction

Capital Assets

capital asset

The Internal Revenue Code defines a *capital asset* as "property held by the taxpayer with specified exceptions." A major exception under this definition is inventory or property held primarily for sale to customers in the ordinary course of business.

Unless such property falls within the ambit of certain depreciable real property used in a trade or business (which receives special tax treatment), this property is considered ordinary income property. All gain or loss on the sale of property other than capital assets is taxable as ordinary income. If the asset is treated as a capital asset, however, it receives capital-gain tax treatment and the seller is taxed only to the extent of gain.

Holding Period

holding period

The *holding period* is determined with regard to whether the taxpayer has long-term or short-term capital-gain or capital-loss treatment. Long-term capital gains or losses result in most cases from the sale of a capital asset held for more than 12 months. Property held at death and included in a decedent's estate is treated for income tax purposes as long-term capital gain property to the beneficiary, no matter what the decedent's holding period was.

Fair Market Value

The fourth element, the fair market value of an asset, may become important in determining basis for special situations involving gratuitous transfers at death. As previously discussed, fair market value can be defined as the price agreed upon by a willing buyer and a willing seller, neither being under compulsion either to buy or to sell.

BASIS OF PROPERTY TRANSFERRED AT DEATH

General Rule

The way property was acquired will influence its basis upon future disposition. There are special rules pertaining to the basis of property transferred at death. When property is acquired from a decedent, it acquires a new basis equal to the value of the property either on the date of death or on the alternate valuation date (6 months after death) if the estate is eligible to use the alternate valuation date and an election is made by the executor to use it. When an individual dies, the original basis becomes irrelevant. Property included in the decedent's gross estate acquires a new basis, which is either increased or decreased to the fair market value of the asset on the date of death. In the past two or three decades, the fair market value of property has steadily increased as a result of our inflationary economy. These upward trends have caused the basis of property inherited from a decedent to be adjusted in an upward direction more often than not. This increased basis is known as a *stepped-up basis*. The stepped-up basis can result in a windfall to

stepped-up basis

the transferee of the property. Property transferred by reason of death and included in a decedent's gross estate receives a step up in basis, regardless of whether or not a federal estate tax return is filed. The stepped-up-basis-at-death rule effectively eliminates the income tax on all potential gain accrued to the date of death. In those cases where property has greatly appreciated in

---

Basis for Property Held at Death

Basis is stepped up or down to fair market value at
the date of death or the alternate valuation date.

---

value, there is a substantial income tax advantage to the estate or beneficiaries. Actually the stepped-up-basis rule is a form of tax relief afforded to those people receiving property transferred at death.

Because the rule provides that basis becomes the fair market value on the date of death, it may also be *stepped down* if the asset has declined in value from the time it was acquired by the decedent. If the decedent possessed an asset that declined in value, he or she would have been wise to sell the asset while alive, thereby taking advantage of the loss on the sale. If a property that declined in value was not sold during the decedent's lifetime, the cost basis to the beneficiary becomes the fair market value at death. Any tax benefit from the unrealized loss is gone forever.

At the present time, inflation appears to be slowing down. This factor, if coupled with a recessionary economy, may reduce the benefit of this special basis rule in the future. More properties may be *stepped down* to their fair market value on the date of death than have been in recent decades. Lifetime estate planning judgments regarding the holding or disposition of assets should be made. Unquestionably, the basis rules should be factored into such decisions. The financial services professional has a responsibility to advise clients to take losses during lifetime if the property is not being held for sentimental value.

Under EGTRRA 2001, the basis rules are slated to change. EGTRRA 2001 provides that the step-up/step down basis rules of Code Sec. 1014 for property transferred as the result of a decedent's death will be replaced with a modified carryover-basis system for property passing from a decedent dying after 2009 under new Code Sec. 1022. Beginning in 2010, property that is acquired from a decedent dying after December 31, 2009 is to be treated for income tax purposes as though the property were transferred by gift (Sec. 1022(a)(1)). Generally, the basis of the person receiving the property will be the lesser of

- the decedent's adjusted basis or
- the fair market value of the property (at date of decedent's death)

However, a decedent's estate will be allowed a "modified step-up" of $1,300,000 and qualified spousal property may be increased by $3,000,000 (which is in addition to the $1,300,000 basis-increase rules for the decedent-spouse's property). This means that the basis of property transferred to a surviving spouse could be increased by as much as $4,300,000. Allocations of basis increases may be made on specific assets selected by the executor. Certain assets, such as items of income in respect of a decedent (IRD) and property acquired by the decedent gratuitously within 3 years of death, are excluded from the $1,300,000 and $3,000,000 basis increases (Sec. 1022(d)(1)(C)). With the anticipated changes in the basis rules, it is imperative that planners encourage clients to keep detailed and accurate records of their assets. Numerous planning practitioners are encouraging clients to do at least tentative-basis estate plan thinking now from a future-preparedness standpoint. Keep in mind that without congressional action, the basis step up would return with the estate and GST taxes in 2011 due to the sunset provision under EGTRRA 2001.

Property Subject to Power of Appointment

Also, if property passes to another because the decedent exercised a general power of appointment over the property under his or her will, that property is treated as property transferred by a decedent at death. Therefore, the value of the property is included in the decedent's gross estate. The property subject to the power receives a new basis stepped up to its fair market value on the date of the decedent's death.

Retained Powers

There are adjustments to basis for property included in the decedent's gross estate either as a retained lifetime interest or because the decedent possessed certain powers over the transferred property that were not released during the 3-year period prior to death. These powers include the right to revoke the transfer as well as the right to alter or control the beneficial enjoyment or the income from the property. The stepped-up-basis rules apply to these properties transferred during lifetime that were brought back into the gross estate for valuation purposes because of the retained powers.

Example:	If the decedent transferred real estate to a son, but retained the right to use the property for life or the right to income from the property for life, the property is included as a retained life income interest in the decedent's estate at its value on the day the decedent died. In that case the property then receives a new basis equal to the fair market value for federal estate tax purposes. Thus, if highly appreciated property is given away, the donee may benefit from the inclusion of that property in the decedent's gross estate since the donee receives a new stepped-up basis. When the property is subsequently sold, the new owner will have a smaller capital gains tax to pay.

Effect of Step Up in Basis on Jointly Held Property

Presently, the general rule that all property included in the gross estate receives a stepped-up basis at death also applies to property held jointly with right of survivorship. In the case of nonspousal joint tenancies or spousal joint tenancies created prior to January 1, 1977, (under the consideration-furnished rule), whatever value is attributed to the property that represents the decedent's joint interest receives a stepped-up basis to the date-of-death value in the hands of the surviving joint tenant or tenants. Should the entire value of jointly held property be included in the decedent's gross estate, the property will receive a fully stepped-up basis equal to the value on the date of death or alternate valuation date, if applicable. This value then becomes the new basis in the hands of the surviving joint tenant for later sale purposes.

This rule has a strange effect on joint tenancies between spouses. Because only one-half of the property can now be included in the gross estate of the decedent-spouse, the property receives a stepped-up basis for the value of one-half of the property only. The original basis of the other half of the property is retained by the surviving spouse. This affects the amount of gain realized should the property be sold during the surviving spouse's lifetime. If, however, the surviving spouse holds the property until death, the entire property will be included in the survivor's estate. The entire property will then acquire a fully stepped-up basis in the hands of the beneficiaries.

Example:	Mary Beth, and her husband, a decedent, acquired a principal residence 15 years ago for $250,000 and titled it in joint names with right of survivorship. The entire contribution was made by the decedent. At the decedent's death last year, the fair market value of the property was appraised at $800,000. Under current law, only one-half of the value of the property (the one-half that is included in the decedent's gross estate) receives a stepped-up basis. The new basis in the hands of the decedent's spouse is computed as follows: the one-half included in his estate receives a new basis of $400,000. The other half that is treated as contributed by the surviving spouse is valued at its original basis of $125,000. If the surviving spouse later sells the property for fair market value, the combined basis will be $525,000 ($400,000 plus $125,000), and a taxable gain will occur. Note that under current law, Mary Beth, as a single individual, is able to exclude $250,000 of taxable gain on the sale of a principal residence. If Mary Beth sells the house for $800,000, she

may have taxable gain on $25,000 ($800,000 less basis of $525,000 = $275,000, less $250,000 of capital gains exclusion). One way to avoid this additional gain is for the surviving spouse to hold the property until death.

To summarize, the current rule for estate tax inclusion with respect to jointly held property with right of survivorship is actually two separate rules depending on whether the property is held by the spouses alone or by the decedent and one or more persons. For all joint tenancies other than spousal joint tenancies, the consideration-furnished rule applies. The rule pertaining to spousal joint tenancies has been amended in the Code to define a *qualified joint interest* as any interest held by the decedent and the decedent's spouse as joint tenants with right of survivorship or as tenants by the entirety, if they are the only joint tenants. All former requirements pertaining to qualified joint interests have been eliminated, including filing a gift tax return on the creation of the joint tenancy as well as making elections under the gift tax provisions to treat the creation as a gift.

Exceptions to General Stepped-Up-Basis Rule

Basis of Income in Respect of a Decedent (IRD)

The stepped-up-basis rules do not apply to income that is included in the decedent's gross estate as *income in respect of a decedent* (*IRD*). Income in respect of a decedent is any income that the decedent was entitled to (but did not receive) while alive. The income is includible at full value for estate tax purposes. It is then also taxed to the beneficiary of the income as ordinary income for income tax purposes. However, the beneficiary is allowed an income tax deduction for the additional estate tax paid due to the IRD being included in the gross estate.

Receipt of Property in Kind

Also, if the beneficiary receives property in substitution for a cash bequest, the basis of the property in the beneficiary's hands equals the amount of cash bequest that the property transferred satisfies.

Example:	Suppose the decedent leaves $20,000 to a cousin. Instead of paying the cousin $20,000, the executor transfers property worth $20,000 to the cousin. The cousin acquires a basis of $20,000 for the property. If the fair market value of the property on the date of

death was $17,000, the basis to the estate is the date-of-death value, or $17,000. Because this property appreciated in value after the date of death and was distributed in lieu of $20,000 cash, the estate (being a separate tax-paying entity) realizes a gain of $3,000.

Basis of Community Property

A special rule pertains to community property held by the decedent and the surviving spouse under the laws of a majority of the community-property states. If at least one-half of the community property vesting in the surviving spouse was includible in the decedent's gross estate and received a basis equal to the value of that one-half share on the date of death, the property that represents the surviving spouse's one-half share of community property held with the decedent receives a new basis in the property adjusted to the fair market value of the property at the decedent's death.

Certain Property Acquired by Gift within One Year of Death

The stepped-up-basis-at-death rule is ignored under certain circumstances. The rule does not apply when appreciated property is acquired by the decedent by gift within one year before death if, upon death, the property then passes directly or indirectly back to the original donor or the original donor's spouse. This exception was carved out to eliminate schemes to obtain the stepped-up basis for certain property that, in actuality, did not belong to the decedent and was intended to return to the original owner at the decedent's death. This scheme involves a sham transfer made for the purpose of increasing the basis of the asset to the original owner. The nature of the bequest does not change the application of this exception to the basis rules.

The following situation illustrates the type of scheme this provision is designed to thwart.

Example: Sam Summers owns 500 shares of IBM stock that he acquired 20 years ago for one-tenth of its present value. Martin Summers, his brother, is terminally ill and expected to die shortly. Sam transfers stock that cost him $100,000 to Martin when the shares are worth $1,000,000. Martin subsequently dies and, under the terms of his will, there is a specific bequest of the IBM stock to his brother, Sam. At the time of Martin's death, the stock has a fair market value of $1,000,000. Sam sells the stock 2 months later for $1,100,000. If he had never transferred the stock to his dying brother,

Sam would have had long- term capital gains of $1,000,000. If Sam were allowed to obtain a stepped-up basis as a result of this sham transfer, he would avoid $900,000 of gain and would receive a stepped-up basis of $1,000,000 that would provide him with a long-term gain of only $100,000.

To prevent this type of windfall, Congress enacted a rule that any property transferred by gift to the decedent within one year of death that reverts to the original donor or the donor's spouse as a bequest from the decedent (either directly or indirectly) will not receive a stepped-up basis when the property is sold or exchanged. The property retains the same basis in the hands of the donor-heir that it had in the hands of the decedent immediately before death. This rule applies to property acquired after August 13, 1981 (the date the law was signed), by decedents dying after December 31, 1981. It also applies to gift transfers between spouses.

The stepped-up basis is denied only to the extent that the donor-heir is entitled to receive the appreciated value. Thus, if the heir inherits only a portion of the property that was transferred because it was used to satisfy debts or administrative expenses, the rule applies on a pro rata basis. It should be noted that if the decedent lives more than one year after the original transfer, the general stepped-up-basis rule is applicable. The general rule also applies to transfers made by the decedent to someone other than the original donor or the donor's spouse, although the property was transferred to the decedent within one year of death. If, in the preceding illustration, the decedent, Martin Summers, left the IBM stock to his brother's grandchildren rather than to his brother or his brother's wife, the stepped-up-basis rule would apply. This one-year rule was enacted to prevent a windfall to an heir who transfers appreciated property to a terminally ill relative shortly before the relative's death with the knowledge that the heir will get the property back through inheritance after the relative's death occurs, thus receiving a new basis equal to the fair market value of the property on the date of death.

For decedents dying prior to 2010, the stepped-up-basis provision offers excellent estate planning opportunities. Because there are relatively few ways to successfully avoid taxation of gain, the stepped-up-basis rules create an opportunity for elimination of potential gain when property has greatly appreciated in value. Any substantially appreciated property owned by the decedent at death is passed on to the heirs with a higher basis. That increment of gain (from the time the property was obtained until the decedent's death) is wiped out or eliminated when the property is subsequently sold. In effect, what exists is a loophole in the tax law because some gain escapes taxation entirely.

The estate owner can avoid potential tax by determining whether it would be more advantageous to hold the property for life or if a greater tax benefit would be derived if the property was disposed of during lifetime. Certainly the stepped-up-basis rule should be taken into consideration when a decision to hold or sell property is made by a mature estate owner. Again, the decision will vary depending on many factors, including the following: (1) whether property has substantially increased in value, (2) whether the basis is close to or greater than the fair market value when a transfer is contemplated, (3) whether there is the potential for future increase in value, and (4) the relative impact of the estate and gift taxes compared with the income tax, if the property is sold.

There is yet another tax consideration when property is transferred at death, which pertains to the holding-period rules for long-term capital-gains treatment. The length of time property was held by the decedent prior to death and the holding period by the estate or beneficiary afterward are not determinative for long-term capital-gains treatment on a later sale. The general rule is that any person acquiring property from a decedent that was included in the gross estate and to which the stepped-up-basis rules apply is considered to have held the property for more than 12 months. In other words, when an asset is transferred as a result of death, the transferee receives long-term capital-gains treatment, regardless of the holding periods before and after death.

PROPERTY TRANSFERRED DURING LIFETIME BY GIFT (SEC. 1015)

The stepped-up-basis rule for property passing at death does not apply to property transferred during lifetime by gift. A carryover- or substituted-basis rule applies to property transferred gratuitously during lifetime. For a gift made after December 31, 1976, the donee acquires the donor's basis increased by any gift tax paid on the net appreciation at the time of the gift. The net appreciation is the amount by which the fair market value at the time of the gift exceeds the donor's adjusted basis. The amount of gift tax paid that can be added to the donee's basis is computed by taking the ratio that the net appreciation bears to the fair market value of the gift and applying that ratio to the total gift tax paid (IRC Sec. 1015(d)(6)).

Any appreciation in the property that might result in capital gains if the property is sold is deferred until such later time as the donee disposes of the property. The increment of gain or appreciation in the value of the property between the date of the gift and the time it is transferred in a taxable exchange does not avoid taxation because the property was given away. It is merely deferred until the time of sale. This is called the carryover- or substituted-basis rule. When a gift is made, the basis of the property in the hands of the donor is carried over and becomes the basis in the hands of the donee.

The following situation illustrates the basis rule for property that is transferred by gift.

Example:	Early in the year, a father gifted $11,000 (annual gift tax exclusion amount after 2001) to his daughter. This gift was gift tax free because of the annual exclusion. Later that same year, the father made a gift to the daughter of property having a fair market value of $60,000. He originally acquired the property for $30,000. Because this transfer is a taxable gift, it is valued for gift tax purposes at $60,000. Assuming he did not make any other taxable gifts, his gift tax liability is $13,000. The gift tax attributable to the net appreciation in the property from the time he acquired it to the time of the gift is $6,500. Therefore, the daughter's basis is her father's basis of $30,000, plus that portion of the gift tax paid attributable to the net appreciation in the value of the gift (or $6,500). Thus, the daughter's basis is $36,500.

General Rule for Basis of Gifted Property

When property is acquired by gift, the basis to the donee remains the same basis that the donor had in the property increased (but not above fair market value) by the portion of the gift tax paid attributable to the net appreciation in the value of the gift. To determine the net appreciation, the fair market value of the property at the time of the gift is reduced by the donor's adjusted basis.

The rule is different when the donor gives away property whose fair market value is less than the adjusted basis. For purposes of loss, the donee's basis is the lesser of the donor's basis or the fair market value at the time of the gift. For purposes of gain, the donee's basis is the greater of the donor's basis or the fair market value at the time of the gift.

Example:	Suppose James gives away property worth $25,000, which had cost him $50,000, to Sally. If Sally then sells the property for any price between $50,000 and $25,000, she does not realize either a gain or a loss on the sale.

Bargain Sales to Individuals

A gift between individuals is not always entirely gratuitous. A bargain sale, rather than an arm's-length transaction, occurs when the purchaser (donee) pays less than fair market value for the property to the seller (donor). The transaction can be viewed as consisting of two components—part sale and part gift. In this circumstance, the seller cannot realize a loss on the sale if the proceeds received are less than the basis. However, a gain is realized if the proceeds received exceed the basis. The seller (donor) is deemed to make a gift of the excess of the fair market value over the amount received for the property.

Example:	Sam sells property with a current fair market value of $100,000 to his son for $60,000. Sam had a basis in the property of $75,000. Sam has made a gift to his son of $40,000 ($100,000 – $60,000). Sam realizes no loss on the sale despite receiving proceeds less than his basis.

The basis rules for the purchaser (donee) in the bargain sale situation require careful study. The purchaser (donee) acquires a basis equal to the greater of (1) the amount paid for the property increased by the gift tax paid by the seller (donor) attributed to the appreciated portion of the property while held by the seller and (2) the seller's (donor's) basis at the time of the transfer increased by the gift tax paid by the seller (donor) attributed to the appreciated portion of the property while held by the seller. However, the basis of the purchaser cannot exceed the fair market value of the property at the time of the original transfer for the purpose of determining loss on the part of the purchaser.

Example 1:	Sam transfers property with a fair market value of $100,000 to his son for $60,000. Sam had a basis of $75,000 in the property and paid gift tax on the transaction. The son gets a basis in the property of $75,000 plus the amount of gift tax paid that is attributable to the appreciation in the property.
Example 2:	Same facts as above except the son pays $80,000 for the property. The son now has a basis in the property of $80,000 plus the amount of the gift tax paid that is attributable to the appreciation in the property.
Example 3:	Sam transfers property with a fair market value of $75,000 to his son for $60,000. Sam had a basis of $100,000 in the property at the time of the transfer but paid no gift tax on the transfer. If the son later sells the property at a gain, the basis of the property in the hands of the son is $100,000 for the purpose of determining gain. However, if the son subsequently sells the property at a loss, the son's basis is limited

to $75,000 (fair market value at the time of the original transfer) for the purpose of determining the amount of the loss.

Bargain Sales to Charity

The transfer of property to a charity for less than fair market value has some advantages for planning purposes. However, the transaction creates some unique tax effects. For the purpose of determining the gain realized by the transferor, the transaction is fictionally divided into two components—part sale and part gift. The basis of the property sold must be allocated to the portion of the property deemed sold and to the portion deemed a gift to charity. The ratio of the basis of the property allocated to the sale portion of the transaction to the total basis is the same as the ratio of the amount realized on the sale to the fair market value of the property. The formula for determining the basis for the sale is as follows:

$$\frac{\text{Amount realized}}{\text{Fair market value}} \times \text{basis of property} = \text{basis for sale}$$

The portion of the basis deemed gifted to the charity is determined by subtracting the basis allocated to the sale from the total basis held by the transferor.

Example:	Bert makes a part sale/part gift of some of his valuable collection of watercolors by recognized artists to The American College for its lobby. Ignoring the annual gift tax exclusion, the collection sold and donated is valued at $1 million. Bert's basis in the watercolors is $200,000. The American College paid Bert $400,000. Bert's basis for the sale is $80,000:

$$\frac{\$400,000}{\$1,000,000} \times \$200,000 = \$80,000$$

CHAPTER REVIEW

Answers to the review questions and the self-test questions start on page 717.

Key Terms

capital asset   stepped-up basis
holding period

Review Questions

19-1.   What is the function of *basis* with respect to an asset?

19-2.   On the day he died, Mr. Jones owned 1,000 shares of IBM stock valued at $80 per share. When he had bought the stock 2 years earlier, he paid $65 per share. He also owned real estate at the time of his death in Atlantic City, New Jersey, valued at $200,000. He had purchased the property 4 years earlier for $60,000. His sole heir is his son, Richard. Assuming no alternate valuation date has been elected, what will be Richard's basis in each of these assets if he decides to sell them?

19-3.   Nine months before his death, Mr. Jones purchased gold coins for which he paid $120,000. At the time of his death the price of gold had dropped, and the coins were worth $75,000. His executor sold the coins at auction for $90,000.
     a.   What was the basis to the estate?
     b.   How much, if any, capital gain was realized?

19-4.   Define *income in respect of a decedent (IRD),* and explain the tax treatment for a beneficiary in receipt of such income.

19-5.   a.   After it had appreciated to $50 a share, Tom Taylor gave his Uncle Ed 1,000 shares of XYZ Corporation stock that he had purchased for $10 a share. He knew that Uncle Ed was dying of cancer. Uncle Ed died 6 months after the transfer and left the XYZ Corporation shares to Tom. What will be Tom's basis in the shares?
     b.   Use the same facts as above except that when Uncle Ed died, he left the shares to Tom's son instead of Tom. What basis will Tom's son have in the shares of XYZ Corporation?

19-6.   Suppose Joe gifts property to Sam that cost $80,000, but is now worth only $40,000. If Sam then sells the property for $60,000, how much gain does he realize on the transaction?

19-7.   Adam made a part sale/part gift to The American Cancer Society. The fair market value of the property is $1.6 million and the basis to Adam is $600,000. The American Cancer Society paid Adam $700,000. Ignoring the annual exclusion for gift tax purposes, what is the basis for the sale?

Self-Test Questions

T   F   19-1.   All gain or loss on the sale of property other than capital assets is taxable as ordinary income.

T   F   19-2.   If a decedent exercises a general power of appointment under her will and the property passes to another, the property subject to the power does not receive a stepped-up basis in the hands of the beneficiary.

T   F   19-3.   The stepped-up-basis rules apply to assets transferred during lifetime that were brought back into the decedent's gross estate for valuation purposes because of retained powers held by the decedent at death.

T   F   19-4.   When an asset is transferred to a beneficiary by reason of a decedent's death, the beneficiary must hold this asset for 6 months or longer before selling it to qualify for long-term capital-gains treatment.

T   F   19-5.   A donee of a gift obtains a new basis stepped up to the fair market value of the property at the time of the gift.

T   F   19-6.   In a bargain sale of property, the seller is deemed to make a gift of the excess of the fair market value over the amount received for the property.

20

Income Taxation of Estates and Trusts

Learning Objectives

An understanding of the material in this chapter should enable the student to

---

20-1. Briefly explain the tax status of estates.

20-2. Explain the similarities and differences between estates and trusts.

20-3. Explain how the income of estates is taxed.

20-4. Explain how the income of trusts is taxed.

Chapter Outline

Trusts and estates are separate tax-paying entities. As such, both trusts and estates may provide opportunities for tax savings through income allocation among taxpayers so that the most favorable tax treatment is achieved. While income tax saving is not the primary purpose of either trusts or estates, the financial services professional should not overlook potential tax savings. Knowledge of this area enables the financial services professional to make recommendations regarding the creation of trusts, which may be structured so that the trustee is given discretionary powers to either accumulate or distribute income earned by the trust.

A critical question is: To which tax-paying entity should the income be taxed and in what proportion? Should it be taxed to the taxpayers to whom income may be allocated or to the trust or estate, the beneficiaries, or the grantor? Sometimes, because of poor planning, the grantor is inadvertently the taxpayer. In addition, the rules pertaining to the unearned income of children under 14 years of age (kiddie tax) may have an impact on planning.

In order both to maximize tax savings and to avoid taxing the wrong taxpayer, an estate planner must understand the rules pertaining to income taxation of estates and trusts.

ESTATES AND TRUSTS

In chapter 5, the creation, elements, and purposes of trusts were described in detail. At this time, it is appropriate to briefly describe the decedent's estate.

Tax Status of Estates

A decedent's estate exists for a limited time—the estate appears when the decedent dies and then it ceases to exist when all its functions are ended. It exists for a finite time because its purposes are limited. One primary purpose is to effectuate the orderly, legal transfer of property. Until this task is accomplished, the personal representative must manage and safeguard the property within his or her control. The personal representative has a duty to keep the property both invested and income producing. Income earned from estate assets is taxable to the estate. As a separate taxpayer, the estate must file timely income tax returns. One of the first tasks of the personal representative is to obtain a special tax identification number for the estate.

The estate maintains its separate tax status until it is closed, which may take several months or years. An estate's duration varies with the complexity of estate assets. The estate may contain a business interest or assets in a foreign country as well as other complicated ownership interests or rights that require it to be held open for an extended time period. Technically, estates should not be closed before the federal estate tax return is filed and cleared, if one is required. The typical length of time that an estate remains open is one to 3 years. The state has an interest in the settlement and distribution of a decedent's estate to its beneficiaries. Furthermore, the personal representative may become liable to beneficiaries and creditors of the estate for negligence or fraud and the management of estate assets, and therefore the personal representative also has an interest in settling the estate. An estate should not be kept open without reason. Any tax benefits derived from the use of an additional taxpayer are not sufficient reasons by themselves to keep the estate open unduly, and an estate that unreasonably prolongs administration will lose its status as an estate for tax purposes. However, there may be income tax benefits to be derived from properly using the estate as a separate tax-paying entity. Income tax considerations should not be overlooked by the personal representative.

Similarities between Estates and Trusts

Estates and trusts have many similarities. The personal representative has duties and responsibilities similar to those of the trustee of a trust.

- Both administer property in a fiduciary capacity.
- Property is transferred from the decedent to the estate in a manner similar to the transfer of property by a grantor to a trust.
- Both decedents and grantors are responsible for the creation of the estate or trust.
- Beneficiaries of an estate have a relationship to the estate similar to that of the beneficiaries of a trust.

Estate and Trust Similarities

- fiduciary duties and responsibilities
- property transfers
- beneficiary relationships
- income taxation rate
  - different computational system from
    - individuals
    - corporations
    - partnerships

Differences between Estates and Trusts

There are, however, important differences. An estate comes into existence involuntarily by operation of law upon the decedent's death. A living trust is created intentionally and voluntarily by a specific action of the grantor. Estates exist for a limited time period. Trusts generally exist for many years and possibly span more than one generation.

The primary function of many trusts is to provide sound, professional asset management. Use of a trust can give the grantor a sense of security, peace of mind, and possibly some control over the management of one's property. The trustee's primary duty is to be a good manager. Whether an individual or institution, the trustee will be in charge of the management of the trust property for the duration of the trust. This period may extend over a long time.

On the other hand, an estate serves as a temporary receptacle for assets pending distribution to the new owners. The personal representative functions primarily as a liquidator who must marshal the decedent's assets, advertise the estate for the benefit of creditors, and pay its debts, expenses, and taxes. The personal representative must settle any claims against the estate and has a duty to keep the property income producing until its distribution.

Another significant difference between the two entities is their relationship to the court. An estate is created by operation of law and is supervised by the court until it is terminated. A trust, on the other hand, is generally a private arrangement. Unless a court accounting is requested by the beneficiaries or a court interpretation of trust terms is requested by the trustees or beneficiaries, in most cases the trust neither has direct contact with the court nor is guided by the court in its actions or investments.

Estate and Trust Differences

Estates	Trusts
• created involuntarily by operation of law	• created by grantor's voluntary action
• limited duration	• extended duration possible
• primary purpose: predistribution asset receptacle	• primary purpose: asset management
• court supervision	• private arrangement

INCOME TAXATION OF ESTATES AND TRUSTS

Trusts and estates are subject to the same rate of income taxation. However, they are subject to a slightly different computational system of taxation than are individuals, corporations, or partnerships, because they exist for the benefit of others. Not operating as mere conduits, they are taxable on income withheld but receive deductions for income distributed. If Congress had chosen to tax estates and trusts in a manner similar to corporations, double taxation would have resulted. If taxed like a corporation, the trust or estate would be taxed on income earned during its taxable year. Beneficiaries would then be treated as shareholders who would be taxed on the distribution when received, just as dividends are taxable to shareholders in the year received. The result would be double taxation. This tax burden undoubtedly would have detracted from the desirability of maintaining trusts.

Alternatively, if a trust or estate was taxed as a partnership, all income would be passed through to the individual beneficiaries in a manner similar to the way it is passed to partners. Using this method would be detrimental in cases where the grantor did not intend beneficiaries to be entitled to the income automatically. First of all, there would be a potential conflict with the law of trusts. Trustees normally derive their powers from the trust instrument. Taxation as a partnership would defeat the right of the grantor to give the trustee discretion to accumulate or distribute income. Also, a personal representative of an estate does not have a duty to distribute income before the estate makes final distribution to the beneficiaries. Under the theory of partnership taxation, a beneficiary would pay tax on amounts not yet received.

Having considered these various possibilities, Congress wisely adopted a hybrid method for income taxation of estates and trusts, which is known as the *sharing concept*. The general rule is that the trust or estate pays income tax on amounts of income retained, while the beneficiaries pay tax on trust or estate income distributed, or deemed distributed, to them. The result is that trust or estate income is generally taxed only once. To the extent it remains in the estate or trust, income is taxed to that entity. To the extent distributed, income is taxed to the beneficiaries (with certain limitations that are discussed later). With estates, the personal representative has discretion regarding retention or distribution of income. As for trusts, the trust instrument provides the standards and directions for taxation of trust income. Much depends on the type of trust and the trustee's exercise of any discretionary powers regarding distribution or accumulation of trust income.

Under the 2003 Jobs and Growth Tax Relief Reconciliation Act, the income tax rates for trusts and estates are shown in table 20-1.

TABLE 20-1
Income Tax Rates for Estates and Nongrantor Trusts (2004)

Taxable Income (TI)	Tax Payable
$0 to $1,950	15% of TI
Over $1,950 but not over $4,600	$292.50 plus 25% of excess over $1,950
Over $4,600 but not over $7,000	$955.00 plus 28% of excess over $4,600
Over $7,000 but not over $9,550	$1,627.00 plus 33% of excess over $7,000
Over $9,550	$2,468.50 plus 35% of excess over $9,550

So, for 2003 and until 2011, the income tax percentage rates are 25 percent, 28 percent, 33 percent, and 35 percent. After 2010, rates above 15 percent are slated to revert to the pre-2001 EGTRRA levels of 28 percent, 31 percent, 36 percent, and 39.6 percent.

Income Taxation of Estates

Decedent's Final Return

An executor or administrator has the duty to file two different types of income tax returns for a decedent—a decedent's last life return and an estate's income tax return.

Tax Return Filings

- decedent's final federal income tax return
- decedent's final state income tax return
- decedent's final local income tax return
- federal estate tax return
- state death tax return
- federal estate income tax return
- state estate income tax return
- local estate income tax return

A deceased taxpayer's tax year ends with the date of death. For example, if Greg dies on March 30, an income tax return must be filed for the short year of January 1 to March 30. The return must be filed by the regular due date, April 15, of the following year. The amounts of income and deductible expenses that must be reported depend on the deceased taxpayer's regular method of accounting.

For cash-basis taxpayers, only income actually or constructively received must be reported. Deductions can be taken only for expenses that were actually paid during the decedent's lifetime. If the decedent was on the accrual method, the return will show all income and deductions accrued through the date of death.

Even a decedent who did not live the entire year is still entitled to use the full standard deduction and personal exemption. If the taxpayer has a surviving spouse, the spouse can still file a joint return with the decedent for the year of the decedent's death.

Income in Respect of a Decedent (IRD)

Because this is the final income tax return for the individual, if he or she was a cash-basis taxpayer, income that was earned but that had not been received by the date of death would not be included in the decedent's final return, because the individual did not actually or constructively receive the item by the date of death. For example, an insurance agent's renewal commissions paid after death cannot be included in a last life return, assuming the deceased agent was a cash-basis taxpayer.

Income that the decedent would have included in gross income had he or she lived does not escape taxation. Instead, it is taxed to the recipient of that income. In other words, the estate or the beneficiary who receives the income is taxed on it in the same manner that the income would have been taxed to the decedent. If it would have been ordinary income to the decedent during lifetime, it will be ordinary income to the estate or beneficiary.

As mentioned in chapter 13, income in respect of a decedent is also subject to estate taxes. The estate or beneficiary that includes in income an

---

IRD (Income in Respect of a Decedent)

- earned by decedent but not received by death (would be included on decedent's final income tax return if received prior to death)
- taxable to beneficiary or entity (estate) receiving it
- subject to estate tax (with corresponding deduction to income recipient)
  - possible for IRD to be included on both the estate's income tax and estate tax returns

---

item of income in respect of a decedent is entitled to a deduction on the same income tax return for the amount of additional federal estate tax attributable to inclusion of that item in the decedent's gross estate.

Additional Considerations

As a taxable entity, an estate must pay tax on its income. If the income of the estate consists of dividends from stock and interest from bonds, these items constitute the gross income of the estate. Likewise, if there is rental income, royalty income, income from the sale or exchange of property, or income from a business carried on by the executor or administrator, then the income of the estate includes those items as well.

Because an estate is considered a separate tax entity, it has not only income but also deductions. Since an estate calculates income tax like other taxpayers, total miscellaneous itemized deductions must exceed 2 percent of adjusted gross income to be deductible by the estate.

However, expenses that are incurred solely by reason of estate or trust administration are deductible in full. An estate may deduct reasonable amounts paid for administration costs, including executor fees and legal fees in connection with the administration of the estate. (As mentioned in chapter 14, some of these expenses may be taken on either the income tax return of the estate or as deductions from the gross estate to obtain the adjusted gross estate for federal estate tax purposes.)

An estate is also entitled to a deduction for amounts of income distributed. It is not entitled to the standard deduction. An estate may take a $600 personal exemption. As previously mentioned, to the extent that the estate retains income, it is taxed; to the extent that the beneficiaries receive income, they are taxed. Furthermore, estates that are open for tax years ending 2 or more years after the decedent's death are subject to the estimated tax rules.

The only beneficiaries who do not pay income tax on distributions of income from estates are those who receive specific bequests under the will in three installments or less.

Example: Assume that the will of the decedent, Leslie Little, states: "I give $5,000 to my favorite nephew, Al, and all the rest, residue, and remainder to my cousin, Jeffrey Little." During the first year of the estate, assets held by the executor generate $16,000 of income. The executor distributes $5,000 to Al and $11,000 to Jeffrey. Because Al's $5,000 was a specific bequest, he is not taxed. This amount is considered a distribution of estate corpus for tax purposes. In this case, Jeffrey would be taxed on the $11,000 he received, and the estate would be taxed on the remaining $5,000 of income.

On the other hand, if Leslie's will stated that the $5,000 bequest to Al was to be paid in five equal annual installments and in the first year he received $1,000, he would be taxed on the $1,000 only if the payment is made out of income. Beneficiaries are taxed on any specific bequests that are required to be paid out of income.

income-first rule

Aside from the foregoing rule regarding specific bequests, there is an *income-first rule* requiring that all distributions are deemed to be paid out of income first, even if the executor, administrator, or trustee in fact distributes corpus in the form of cash or property. For example, assume in the previous example that the distribution to Jeffrey consisted solely of stock. Jeffrey would still be deemed to have received income.

Estate Income Taxation

- Estate income is taxed to either the beneficiaries or the estate.
- An income tax return must be filed.
- Estate administration expenses are deductible.
- Deductions are allowed for income distributed.
- The estate may take a $600 exemption (no standard deduction allowed).

Fiscal Year for Estate Income Taxation

Unlike with trusts, the personal representative of a decedent's estate is able to select the estate's income tax year. This means the representative can select the last day of any month for the estate's income tax year to end. All income tax years, however, must be 12 months in length except for the first and last years. If the personal representative chooses the end of any month other than December 31, the estate is reporting income tax for a *fiscal year*. If December 31 is selected as the end of the estate's income tax year, the estate is reporting its income as a calendar year taxpayer. The decedent's personal final tax year ends on the date of death, no matter how soon death occurs after January 1 of his or her calendar tax year. For example, if Marge dies on January 4 this year, the decedent's final tax year is January 1 through January 4.

Income tax savings can result for the estate if the fiscal year is carefully chosen. Savings are possible because income is treated for tax purposes as if it was distributed to beneficiaries on the last day of the estate's fiscal tax year even though the income may have been distributed much earlier in the tax year.

Example:	Derek's executor wants to make distributions of estate income to the beneficiary, Derek's son Darrell. The executor distributes the income to Darrell in early December of year 1 even though the estate earned the income in April of year 1. Because the estate's fiscal year ends on January 31, the income is treated as received on January 31 of year 2. Therefore, Darrell will not have to report the income on his income tax return until April 15 of year 3. The income avoids income taxation for 2 years from the time the estate actually received it.

Income Taxation of Trusts

nongrantor trust

A trust that is deemed irrevocable (a *nongrantor trust*—see below) is considered a separate taxpayer. These trusts may be testamentary (made irrevocable on the death of the testator) or inter vivos (living) trusts. Income from property in revocable trusts (grantor trusts) is taxed to the grantor rather than to the trust, because the power to revoke the instrument gives the grantor control over the trust assets. Trustees of irrevocable trusts may be given discretionary powers to distribute or accumulate income. To the extent a trustee exercises the right to distribute that income and sprinkle it among more than one taxpayer within the family group, the income may be shifted to a lower tax bracket and can be sheltered by multiple personal exemptions.

Trust Income—General Taxation

The essential concept of trust taxation is that trust income is taxed once, either (1) to the beneficiary(ies) or (2) to the trustee. If a trustee is required to distribute the entire income of the trust annually, that income is taxed to the recipient(s). However, some trusts authorize the accumulation of all or part of the income at the trustee's discretion. The tax law does not tax prospective beneficiaries on amounts they may never receive.

Trust Income Taxation

- irrevocable trusts—separate tax-paying entities
- revocable trusts—grantor trust rules

A system has been devised that taxes the trustee on income accumulated by the trust and the beneficiary on income receivable. To thwart tax avoidance, the beneficiary is taxed on the amount *distributable* to him or her rather than on the amount actually paid to him or her. This prevents the trustee from arbitrarily deferring payments in an attempt to keep trust income in lower brackets. Although the details of trust taxation are quite complex, in essence the taxation of trust income can be capsulized thus: Income that is accumulated by the trust is taxable to the trust; income that is payable to the beneficiary is taxable to the beneficiary; and income either accumulated or distributed by a grantor trust is taxable to the grantor.

Irrevocable Trust Income Taxation

- trust income taxed to either beneficiary or trust
  - beneficiary taxed on distributable net income (DNI) (whether or not distributed)
  - trust taxed on accumulated/retained income
- two types of trusts for income tax law:
  - simple trusts
  - complex trusts—may change from year to year

Simple Trusts

The income tax law classifies trusts into two types—simple and complex. A trust's designation as simple or complex may change from year to year; however, a trust will always be complex in its final year.

simple trust

A *simple trust* is one in which the trust agreement requires that all trust income be distributed currently to the beneficiaries. As long as the trust instrument provides for the trustee to distribute all of the trust's current year's income, the beneficiaries are treated as having received the income for taxation purposes, whether the income is distributed or not. If, on the other hand, the trust terms do not provide for trust income to be distributed each year, the trust is treated as a complex trust despite the fact that the trust actually did distribute all trust income for the year. In any year, a simple trust may not make distributions from amounts other than current income. Principal may not be distributed and no charitable gifts can be made by this type of trust; otherwise, it will be deemed to be a complex trust for that taxable year. The trustee may be given a power to distribute corpus, but as long as no distribution is actually made during the tax year, the trust is considered simple for that year.

A simple trust is treated as a separate tax entity subject to a $300 personal exemption. As such, it has—subject to certain exceptions—the same deductions as an individual. It also has a special deduction for income that is distributable to its beneficiaries. The net result is that a simple trust does not pay tax on income it pays out. The beneficiary of a simple trust in turn reports the income received—or receivable. In other words, a simple trust acts like a funnel—a conduit for passing the trust income from the grantor to the beneficiaries.

Most trusts operate as simple trusts. For example, a trust that provides income "to my wife for life with remainder to my children" or "income to be distributed to and among my spouse and children in such amounts and such proportions as my trustee may determine" is a simple trust until and unless a distribution of corpus is made. All trusts are complex trusts in the final year because in the year of termination, trusts must distribute all trust corpus.

Simple Trusts

- treated as conduits
- require distribution of all net income currently
- deduction for distributable income
- no distributions of corpus
- $300 exemption (no standard deduction)
- no charitable contributions/distributions
- beneficiaries taxed on distributable net income (DNI)

Complex Trusts

complex trust

The second type of trust is known as a complex trust. A *complex trust* is any trust that is not a simple trust; that is, a complex trust is one in which the trustee either must or may accumulate income. The trustee of a complex trust—unlike the trustee of a simple trust—can distribute corpus (principal). The trustee can also make gifts to charities. A complex trust—like a simple trust—is a separate tax-paying entity. It is allowed a special deduction for actual distributions of income but pays tax on any income it does not distribute. Generally, the same rules that govern complex trusts apply also to the income taxation of a decedent's estate.

It is impossible to understand the taxation of trusts unless the term *income* is defined. There is income in the trust sense and income in the tax sense. Most states have a Principal and Income Act that allocates receipts and payments between estate or trust income and principal. For example, if the trustee is required to pay out "all the income," then under the trust law definition of income the trustee would not be required to pay out capital gains or other items classified as corpus (as opposed to income). Capital gains are excluded from the trust law definition of income and treated as additions to corpus rather than income. But generally the grantor or decedent may override these rules. For example, gains from property can be designated by the grantor as trust income.

But note that a capital gain is every bit as much income in the tax sense as dividend income, rental income, or interest on a loan. Therefore, it is possible that even though a trustee of a simple trust is required to distribute all the income (and thus that amount is taxable to the beneficiaries rather than the trust), the difference between the total income in the tax sense and the total income in the trust sense is taxable to the trust.

Example:	Suppose a trust received $3,000 in capital gains from the sale of trust assets and $5,000 from dividends on stock it held. A trust that was required to pay out "all the income" to the beneficiaries would make a distribution of only $5,000 (the amount of dividends). The beneficiaries, rather than the trust, would be taxed on that $5,000. However, the remaining income in the tax sense, $3,000, would not be distributable by the trust because it is treated as an addition to corpus instead of income and therefore would be taxed to the trust. For this reason, a simple trust may be taxed even though it is required to distribute all of its income in the trust law sense.

A complex trust that is required to distribute all its income currently has an exemption of $300. For a complex trust (sometimes called an *accumulation trust*) that is not required to distribute income, the regular exemption is $100. No type of trust (or estate, for that matter) may deduct the standard deduction allowed to individual taxpayers.

Complex Trusts

- accumulation of income allowed
- distributions of corpus allowed
- charitable contributions allowed
- taxed on income retained
- deduction for actual distributions
- $100 exemption (no standard deduction)
- beneficiaries taxed on distributable net income (DNI)

  (Taxation of complex trusts is similar to income taxation of estates.)

Distributable Net Income

distributable net income (DNI)

The mechanical approach to the sharing concept (the trust pays income tax on the amount it retains, while the beneficiaries pay tax on the income of the trust distributable to them) occurs through the utilization of a concept known as *distributable net income (DNI)*. In general, distributable net income means taxable income before the deduction for distributions and before the $300 personal exemption for simple trusts ($100 for complex trusts) but after the exclusion of capital gains and losses. The concept of DNI is used to achieve three main results:

- First, it provides a limit on the deduction that a trust or estate may receive for amounts distributed to beneficiaries.
- Second, it limits the amount of distributions that may be taxable to the beneficiaries.
- Third, it establishes the character of the amounts taxable to the beneficiaries.

As a general rule, income retains the same character in the hands of the beneficiaries as it had in the hands of the trust. Therefore, tax-exempt income to the trust retains its tax-exempt status when distributed to the beneficiary.

The first purpose of DNI ensures that the trust or estate receives a deduction for amounts that it distributes and provides a limit for that deduction. For example, assume that a trust earns $10,000 in taxable income and distributes $6,000 of that income to its sole beneficiary. The DNI is $10,000. Accordingly, the estate or trust deducts $6,000. The trust will be taxed on the amount that it retains, $4,000.

The second purpose of DNI is to limit the portion of distributions that are taxable to beneficiaries. If the trust in the above example distributed $12,000 to the beneficiary, the trust would be allowed to deduct $10,000, the DNI. The trust, therefore, would have no tax liability. The beneficiary would be taxed on $10,000 of the $12,000 received. The first $10,000 would be considered to have come from income, while the remaining $2,000 would be considered an income-tax-free distribution of trust corpus. The DNI rule does not allow a trustee to determine whether income or corpus has been distributed. Instead, arbitrarily and automatically, all amounts distributed are first deemed to be income—to the extent of DNI.

The following examples illustrate trust income taxation with respect to DNI.

Example 1:	A simple trust has long-term capital gain allocable to corpus of $12,000, taxable income of $3,000, and dividends from a taxable U.S. corporation of $4,000. The trust's distributable net income is the $3,000 of income plus the $4,000 of dividends.

Example 2:   Under the terms of his will, Sam Snead left $24,000 a year to be paid to his surviving spouse and $18,000 to each of his two daughters out of the income his estate earned during its administration. For this year, the estate's DNI is $48,000. Because the amount taxable to the beneficiaries is limited to the estate's DNI, if distributions are greater than DNI, a proportional amount of DNI must be allocated to each beneficiary based on the total distributed to all beneficiaries. Mrs. Snead's proportional share is determined by dividing her portion by the total amount distributed to all beneficiaries: $24,000 ÷ $60,000 (the total amount of distributions is $24,000 + $18,000 + $18,000) = 2/5. Two-fifths of the estate's total DNI of $48,000 is $19,200. This is the amount that the surviving spouse must include in gross income. The balance of the estate's distribution to Mrs. Snead is treated as a distribution of corpus and is not included in income.

According to this arbitrary DNI rule, a beneficiary can be taxed even if the distribution received is actually from corpus. For example, assume a trust has interest income of $10,000 that the trustee decides to accumulate. If the trustee then decides in the same tax year to distribute $10,000 of corpus to one of its beneficiaries, the beneficiary will be deemed to have received $10,000 of income, even though the trustee is actually making a distribution from corpus.

The third function of DNI is to ensure that the character of the amounts in the hands of a beneficiary is the same as that in the hands of a trust or estate. Therefore, if dividends are received by a trust and distributed to a beneficiary, the dividends retain their character as dividends.

Likewise, if the trust receives tax-free income (such as from a municipal bond), the income remains tax free in the hands of the beneficiary. This result is achieved mechanically by limiting the trust's deduction to DNI determined without regard to tax-free income.

DNI

- limits trust/estate deductions for distributions
- limits taxable distributions to beneficiaries
- establishes character of distributions
- income in trust sense
- income in tax sense

Example: Assume a trust has $4,000 of tax-exempt interest and $6,000 of dividend income. Its distributable net income is $10,000, but the DNI for deduction purposes is $6,000. The $10,000 distributed would be the same in the hands of the beneficiary as it would be in the hands of the trustee—$4,000 of the interest would be tax exempt and $6,000 of the dividend income would be taxable, because the DNI received by the beneficiary will be $6,000.

Effect of Multiple Beneficiaries. When there is more than one beneficiary, each is taxed on his or her share of DNI. When special items are distributed (such as tax-exempt interest, dividends, and so forth), a beneficiary is considered to have received a proportionate share unless the trust agreement earmarks a particular type of income for a specified beneficiary. This makes it possible to pay out tax-exempt income to high-income-tax-bracket beneficiaries and to pay other income to lower-bracket beneficiaries as well as to pay other income to lower-bracket family members. (The distribution provisions cannot be arbitrary and must have some significance apart from their tax sense.) For example, it would be permissible to require that 40 percent of the trust corpus be invested in tax-exempt securities and that the grantor's spouse receive all such income.

grantor trust

Taxation of Grantor Trusts

A trust is typically created by a grantor with substantial assets, who contributes the trust property for the benefit of less wealthy family members. Quite often, one purpose for this transfer is to shift income, and the taxation thereof, from a higher-bracket grantor to lower-bracket beneficiaries, resulting in the availability of a greater amount of funds to the beneficiaries than if the grantor had received the income and paid the after-tax proceeds to the beneficiaries directly.

Trusts would be very popular indeed if the grantor could shift the taxation of trust income to lower-bracket beneficiaries while maintaining substantial control over the trust property and income. Congress recognized this possibility for abuse and devised the grantor-trust rules, which provide that the income from a trust is taxed to the grantor if the grantor retains certain proscribed powers and controls over the trust.

The grantor-trust rules also apply if the spouse of the grantor, living with the grantor at the time of creation of the interest, is given any of the proscribed powers that invoke the grantor-trust rules. In the case of a grantor trust, the trust is disregarded for income tax purposes and all income, deductions, and credits attributable to any portion of a trust declared a grantor trust are taken into account directly on the grantor's individual income tax return. The financial services professional should be aware of these rules to alert a client-grantor whose trust could be inadvertently designed as a grantor trust.

Trust Income Available for the Benefit of the Grantor. Grantor-trust taxation is applied to all or part of the income of a trust that is provided for the grantor or the grantor's spouse without the consent of an adverse party. Furthermore, the income will be taxed to the grantor for any portion of the trust if the income may be provided for the grantor or the grantor's spouse at the discretion of the grantor or nonadverse party. In the same manner, a trust is considered a grantor trust if it accumulates taxable or tax-exempt income for future distribution to the grantor or the grantor's spouse. The grantor will also be taxed on any portion of a trust in which the income may be applied to pay premiums for life insurance on the life of the grantor or the grantor's spouse.

Adverse Party (Grantor Trust Rules)

Party with beneficial interest in a trust who will have beneficial loss by grantor's exercise of trust powers and rights

---

The income from a trust that is applied to satisfy the legal support obligations of the grantor is paid to the benefit of the grantor and also causes grantor-trust tax treatment. However, the grantor is not taxed on this income if it is merely payable for a support obligation of the grantor at the discretion of the trustee unless the income is actually so applied.

Revocable Trusts. The revocable trust (as described in chapter 5) is an example of a trust in which the grantor has strings attached to the trust property and income. In this case, the grantor has not completed a transfer for tax purposes if the power is retained, at any time, to return the trust property to the grantor's possession. For this reason, the revocable trust is taxable as a grantor trust, and its creation does not alter the federal income tax picture of the grantor or the beneficiaries.

The grantor will also be treated as the owner of the trust if the power to revoke the trust is similarly held by either the grantor's spouse or a nonadverse party. For the purposes of the grantor-trust rules, a nonadverse party is any individual who does not possess a substantial beneficial interest in the trust that would be adversely affected by the exercise or nonexercise of any power held by the individual with respect to the trust. For example, a trust beneficiary who loses the benefit of the trust if the grantor revokes would be an adverse party.

Reversionary Interest. Grantor-trust tax treatment will occur for any portion of the trust in which the grantor retains a reversionary interest in either the trust corpus or the trust income if, at the creation of the portion of the trust in which the grantor holds the reversionary interest, the value of this reversionary interest exceeds 5 percent of the value of this portion of the trust. The IRS valuation rules are to be used to determine the value of any reversionary interest. Generally, the trust income interest would have to be gifted for a significant period of time (over 30 to 40 years, depending on the current AFMR) before the grantor-trust rules can be avoided. Thus, a temporary gift of an income interest followed by a reversionary interest in the grantor will rarely cause a shifting of income for tax purposes.

As an exception to the reversionary-interest rule, the grantor will not be treated as the owner of the income portion of a trust if the reversionary interest will take effect at the death of the beneficiary who (1) is a lineal descendant of the grantor and (2) has not attained age 21. These reversionary-interest provisions apply to transfers and trusts made after March 1, 1986.

Controls Retained by the Grantor. The grantor-trust rules contain a series of proscribed controls and powers that the grantor might desire to retain over a trust. These are included in the grantor-trust category to prevent the grantor from shifting taxation of the trust income while retaining enough control over the trust to possess substantial beneficial enjoyment of the trust income and property.

Power to Control Beneficial Enjoyment. Grantor-trust tax treatment occurs if the grantor retains (1) the beneficial enjoyment of the trust corpus and/or (2) the power to dispose of trust income without the approval or consent of an adverse party. The general rule provides that the grantor is taxed on the income when the grantor or nonadverse party holds the right to add or delete beneficiaries, to alter the shares of the beneficiaries in the income or principal, or to determine the timing of distributions. Fortunately this general rule is subject to several exceptions, which allow the grantor some flexibility in the design of the trust. Powers that may be held by the trustee, regardless of who the trustee is, that do not cause grantor-trust taxation include the following:

- the power to apply income toward the support of the grantor's dependents except to the extent that the income is actually applied to satisfy the grantor's legal support obligation
- the power to appoint the income or principal of the trust by will, other than income accumulated in the trust at the discretion of the grantor or nonadverse party

- the power to allocate income among charitable beneficiaries
- the power of the trustee to sprinkle or accumulate income, including
  - the power to invade corpus for the benefit of a beneficiary or beneficiaries provided that the trustee's power is limited by some definite standard (for example, the power to distribute corpus for the education, support, maintenance, or health of a beneficiary)
  - the power to withhold income temporarily from a current-income beneficiary
  - the power to withhold income during the legal incompetency or minority of a current-income beneficiary (this provision allows accumulation for the minor-beneficiary of a Sec. 2503(c) trust)
- the power, exercisable only by an independent trustee (an individual not subordinate to the grantor), to sprinkle income and principal among a class of beneficiaries
- the power to apportion income by a trustee (not the grantor or the grantor's spouse) among a class of beneficiaries guided by some reasonably definite standard in the trust instrument

Administrative Powers. Certain powers of administration over a trust held by the grantor or a nonadverse party create grantor-trust taxation. Basically, the powers included in the grantor-trust rules are ones that allow the trust to be operated substantially to the benefit of the grantor. These powers include those to dispose of trust property or income for less than adequate consideration or the power to obtain a loan from the trust without adequate interest or security.

**Grantor Trust Taxation
(Without Consent of Adverse Party)**

- power to revoke trust
- income for grantor's/spouse's benefit
  - income used for life insurance premiums on grantor's/ spouse's life
- reversionary interest
- power to control beneficial enjoyment
- retention of controls over trust

Taxation of Unearned Income of Children under 14: The "Kiddie-Tax" Problem

A popular income-tax-planning technique—shifting income from a high-bracket individual to the person's lower-bracket children—was curtailed severely by the Tax Reform Act of 1986 (TRA 1986). The new rules provide that a portion of the unearned income of a child under 14 years of age is taxed at the top rate of the parents. This provision applies to all net unearned income of a child under age 14, including income from a trust, and it applies regardless of when and from whom the child received the income-producing property. Therefore, as seen below, there is limited income tax savings if a parent transfers property to a trust that pays out income to a child-beneficiary under age 14. In fact, trusts in existence before these rules were established are also subject to this penalty.

kiddie tax

Calculating the Kiddie Tax. The procedure for calculating the *kiddie tax* is quite complex and is not described fully here. However, the law provides that the child pays the parent's tax rate on net unearned income. The net unearned income of the child is the child's unearned income less the sum of the $800 standard deduction (2005) as indexed for inflation, and an additional amount, which is the greater of (1) $800 (2005, as indexed for inflation) and (2) allowable deductions directly related to the production of the child's unearned income. The intent of this procedure is to apply no tax to the first $800 of unearned income due to the standard deduction. The next $800 of unearned income is taxed at the child's bracket, and income in excess of $1,600 is taxed to the child as if included in the parent's income for the year—at the parent's highest marginal bracket.

Example 1:	Sara Jones, aged 13, receives $900 of unearned trust income and no earned income in 2005. Sara's $800 standard deduction is allocated against this, leaving a net unearned income of $100, which will be taxed at Sara's tax rate.
Example 2:	Suppose instead that Sara had $1,800 of unearned trust income and no earned income. After applying Sara's $800 standard deduction, a net unearned income of $1,000 remains. The first $800 is to be taxed at Sara's rate, while the remaining $200 will be taxed at the parent's top federal income tax rate for the year.

Planning the Trust to Deal with the Kiddie-Tax Rules. It is obvious that the kiddie tax provides little or no income tax benefit to shifting income to children under 14 years of age. However, there are still some estate planning benefits to transferring income to children along with many personal nontax benefits for the creation of trusts for minor children. To minimize the impact of the kiddie tax when planning a transfer in trust for minor children, the client might consider the following:

- The trust can be designed to accumulate income until the child reaches age 14 or later. You will recall from the grantor-trust rules that while the child is a minor, a Sec. 2503(c) trust can be used to allow the trust to accumulate income that is taxable to the trust. Income paid out to the child from the Sec. 2503 (c) trust after the child attains age 14 is taxed at the child's, not the parent's, marginal tax rate. In general, the trust document may provide discretion for the trustee to temporarily withhold income from a trust beneficiary without the application of the grantor-trust rules.

- The trust property can be invested in assets in which income will be deferred—presumably until the child-beneficiary reaches age 14. Examples of investments that are suitable for this purpose include the following:

  - Series EE U.S. government bonds defer income until the bond is redeemed. For this purpose, the child must not already own Series EE bonds on which each year's income is being declared.

  - Growth stocks could be purchased with trust assets that pay little or no current dividends. The stock can be held until the child reaches age 14, at which time any gain would be taxed at the child's bracket.

  - Deep-discount tax-free municipal bonds can be purchased that mature after the child reaches age 14. The current interest will be tax free and any later gain will be taxed at the child's tax rate when the bond is redeemed.

  - Life insurance or annuity policies can be purchased on the life of the child-beneficiary without incurring either a grantor-trust or kiddie-tax problem. Any gain on a policy held until after the child reaches age 14 will be taxed at the child's rate. These policies are highly liquid since they may be surrendered at any time for the cash surrender value and, unlike stocks or bonds, are

---

How to Minimize the Kiddie Tax

- Design the trust to accumulate income until the child attains age 14.
  - Sec. 2503(c) trust
- Invest in income-deferred assets:
  - series EE U.S. government bonds
  - growth stocks
  - deep-discount tax-free municipal bonds
  - life insurance or annuity policies on child-beneficiary's life

not subject to market risk. However, it is important to remember that tax on the policy earnings is deferred only if the policy meets the statutory guidelines for the definition of life insurance.

Multiple Trusts

Prior to the enactment of the Revenue Reconciliation Act of 1993 (RRA 1993), a popular technique for saving income taxes was to use separate or multiple trusts. Rather than create a single trust in which each beneficiary was given a fractional interest, a grantor could create one trust for each beneficiary. In other words, instead of the grantor's providing that the residue of the decedent-grantor's estate was to be held in trust and that each of the decedent's four children was to receive one-fourth of the income each year and a one-fourth share of the principal on termination of the trust, the grantor could provide for separate trusts for each beneficiary. Therefore, if the same assets were divided into four equal shares and held in separate and distinct trusts (one trust for each child), each trust would have its own exemption, and each would have been subject to the lower trust income tax rates that prevailed before the 1993 Act. Because RRA 1993 imposes higher income tax rate brackets on trusts and estates at lower income thresholds, the use of separate or multiple trusts for the purpose of saving income taxes often results in only nominal savings.

It is possible to create several trusts for the same or different beneficiaries. If the tax law recognizes the existence of multiple trusts, then the income is taxed separately to each trust, which means that each trust receives a separate exemption, and each trust is treated as a separate tax entity for all income tax purposes. Conversely, if multiple trusts are considered by the IRS to be one trust, only one exemption is allowed. All of the trusts are treated as one entity for income tax purposes.

The grantor's intention is examined by studying the various trust instruments to determine whether or not more than one trust was established. The IRS will not question the separate tax status of multiple trusts if the following criteria are met:

- The trusts have substantially different grantors and/or substantially different beneficiaries.
- The trusts have substantially independent purposes or objectives, such as different dispositive goals for each beneficiary.
- The principal purpose for creating multiple trusts was not avoidance, deferral, or mitigation of the progressive income tax rates.

The trusts should also be separately maintained (that is, separate books and records should be kept for each trust, each trust should have its own bank account, and separate returns should be filed).

Accumulation of Income in Trusts

One frequently used technique of estate planning is to give a trustee the discretionary power either to pay income to beneficiaries or to accumulate it. If a beneficiary has sufficient other income, a trustee may decide to retain income from the trust and pay it out in some year when the beneficiary is in a lower tax bracket or more in need of the money. If the beneficiary has more than sufficient income, it is improper tax planning for the terms of the trust to require a distribution of income since the income, if distributable, is taxable to the beneficiary whether or not it is actually received.

The Revenue Reconciliation Act of 1993, however, has clearly diminished the advantages of income accumulation trusts. Because trusts and estates are taxed at the higher rates for taxable income of lower thresholds of income than individuals are taxed, it is likely that many beneficiaries will be in a lower tax bracket than the trusts benefiting them. Thus, there is pressure on trustees with the discretion to accumulate or distribute income to make income distributions before trust income reaches the higher tax brackets. In many instances, current distributions of income to beneficiaries (such as minors) defeat the very purpose for which the trust was originally established. A discretionary trustee is caught in a bind because if, in keeping with the trust purpose, the trustee does not distribute income currently and trust income is then taxed at tax rates higher than the beneficiary's rate, the trustee will overpay taxes.

Investing trust principal in securities having growth potential rather than current income may be one solution to the dilemma. Another is to make periodic income distributions to children over age 14 so that income is taxed at the children's lower individual rates.

The practical consequence of the new income tax rates is that planners and fiduciaries may have to weigh numerous factors concerning income distributions to beneficiaries who are subject to lower tax rates, especially where there are conflicting nontax considerations.

Purchase of Life Insurance by a Trustee

A trust instrument may authorize a trustee of a testamentary trust to purchase life insurance on the lives of the beneficiaries. State law must be examined to see if there is a prohibition against the use of income for this purpose. From a tax viewpoint, income used to purchase life insurance on the lives of beneficiaries is considered accumulated income; therefore, income used to purchase life insurance by the trustee of the testamentary trust is taxed to the trust. However, trust income used for premium payments for insurance on the life of the grantor of the trust (and/or on the life of the grantor's spouse) is taxed to the grantor.

Authorizing a trustee to purchase life insurance on the lives of the beneficiaries can yield some limited benefits under current income tax law.

For example, suppose one of the trust beneficiaries has a significant amount of taxable income this year and is already in a high marginal tax bracket. Suppose also that the trust has taxable income that will be taxed in one of the lower marginal tax brackets. If the trustee distributes the trust income to the beneficiary, it will be taxed at the beneficiary's higher rate, leaving less for the beneficiary to purchase life insurance and pay premiums. If, however, the trust itself purchases the life insurance and pays the premiums with the income, more income is available for the purchase and premium payments because of the trust's exemption and lower income tax bracket.

Sprinkle Provisions

One of the principles of proper tax planning is that income should be divided among family members whenever possible in order to lower the rate at which the income will be taxed as well as to take advantage of the multiple individual personal exemptions.

Example:	Assume a grantor's son, Jerry, is in the 35 percent income tax bracket. If the grantor left income-producing property in trust with the provision that the income was payable to Jerry, $10,000 of additional income would net the son approximately $6,500. But if the same $10,000 was spread among Jerry and his three children for tax purposes, the total intrafamily *net dollars* might be more than if all the income was paid to Jerry.

However, referring to the preceding example, because the kiddie tax is applicable to the unearned income of children under 14, the trust income distributed to children under age 14 will essentially be taxed as if included in Jerry's income for the year, resulting in no tax savings if the income is shifted to Jerry's children under age 14. Any income shifted to Jerry's children aged 14 and over may result in tax savings if the children are in the lowest bracket.

Assuming Jerry's children are all 14 and over, one way to accomplish the objective of shifting income to lower brackets is to require the trustee to pay the income to Jerry and his children in four equal shares. Yet the same tax savings may be accomplished with more flexibility if the trustee is authorized, rather than mandated, to pay income to Jerry or any one or more of his children at the trustee's discretion. The trustee can then allocate income among the family members in any manner that seems desirable from tax year to tax year. In exercising that discretion, the trustee would consider the individual needs of the various beneficiaries, the ultimate use to which the income would be put, and the collective as well as individual tax burdens.

There are also nontax advantages to clauses that *sprinkle* income according to needs. An example is a testator who wants to provide for the family of a deceased child but does not want to pay income for the lifetime of a deceased child's spouse. The testator may fear that if the surviving spouse remarries, income will go to the new spouse or the new spouse's children rather than to the testator's grandchildren. The *sprinkle provision* in a trust enables a trustee to pay income to the spouse only as long as the children are young or have varying needs and as long as the spouse does not remarry.

sprinkle provision

It should be noted that a possible tax consequence of using a sprinkle provision to provide financial protection to the family of a deceased child of the grantor is that if trust income is used to support a dependent, that income will be taxed to the person who is obligated to provide the support. In a trust with a sprinkle provision, to the extent that the trustee applies income for the support of a minor, the IRS may attempt to tax this income to the parent. *Obligation to support* means the duty imposed by law to support another person.

Trust income, though, is not generally considered to be used for the support of a dependent. There are a number of reasons that income will not be considered to be used for the discharge of the parent's obligation. First, if the beneficiary is over the age of majority, the obligation to support that child may be limited. However, some states hold that support obligations include college costs. A family court decree may create an obligation to support postmajority child costs. Second, a trustee would generally accumulate income when a minor is involved. Third, if the finances of a parent are limited, income used by the trustee for support may be over and above the parent's obligation.

Conservative planning suggests that a trust provision be included stating that income may be used only if the parent's funds are inadequate for the desired purpose. Alternatively, such funds can be used to provide nonsupport items such as toys, music lessons, travel, entertainment, cars, or other items that will not fall into the category of "legal obligation to support."

CONCLUSION

Trusts and estates, creatively structured, can provide some income tax advantages for the beneficiaries. Full utilization of tax planning opportunities for estates, trusts, and beneficiaries is generally overlooked by all but the most sophisticated tax planners. While the income taxation of estates and trusts is complicated to master, it may be worth the effort when considering potential tax savings.

Note to Students: See Appendix A for a summary of the advantages and disadvantages of different trusts covered in this chapter and throughout the text.

CHAPTER REVIEW

Answers to the review questions and the self-test questions start on page 717.

Key Terms

income-first rule

distributable net income (DNI)

nongrantor trust

grantor trust

simple trust

kiddie tax

complex trust

sprinkle provision

Review Questions

20-1.   When and for what purposes does an estate come into existence?

20-2.   Over what period of time is the estate held open?

20-3.   What are the similarities between estates and trusts?

20-4.   Explain the differences between estates and trusts with regard to purpose, mode of creation, and duration.

20-5.   How does the taxation of estates and trusts differ from the taxation of corporations or partnerships?

20-6.   Describe the income tax returns required to be filed by the personal representative of the estate with respect to filing dates, income, expenses, and accounting methods.

20-7.   Why may a deduction that involves income in respect of a decedent be allowable on the income tax return?

20-8.   What are the exemptions available to
a.   an estate
b.   a simple trust
c.   a complex trust

20-9.   How are specific bequests distributed by an estate in more than three installments treated for income tax purposes?

20-10.   An estate receives dividends of $15,000 during its second year of operation. The executor determines that $25,000 of corpus should be paid to a beneficiary and that the dividends should be retained and added to corpus. Explain how the $25,000 distribution will be treated for income tax purposes under the *income-first rule*.

20-11.   Briefly describe why an estate's personal representative would select a fiscal year for reporting the estate's income taxation.

20-12. How is trust income taxed to
    a. a beneficiary
    b. a trust

20-13. Larry Ladnor created a trust for the benefit of his mother, Laura. The trust provides that all income may be distributed annually to Laura for life. Any income not distributed is to be accumulated. The trust corpus generates $25,000 of taxable income annually, unless otherwise stated. Explain whether the trust is a simple trust or a complex trust in each of the following years:
    a. Five years ago, the trust distributed $25,000 to Laura.
    b. Four years ago, the trust distributed $22,000 to Laura and made a gift of $3,000 to Duke University, her alma mater.
    c. Three years ago, the trust distributed $20,000 to Laura and credited her trust account with $5,000 of income that was retained in the trust.
    d. Two years ago, the trust distributed $27,000 to Laura. The trust earned only $21,000 of income that year and $6,000 was a distribution from corpus.
    e. Last year, the trust earned $20,000 and distributed all of it to Laura.

20-14. a. Identify the three main results of distributable net income.
    b. How is DNI affected by multiple beneficiaries?

20-15. What is meant by the statement that items of income retain their character?

20-16. Assume that the sole income of the Madison family trust is $18,000 of tax-exempt interest from municipal bonds. Fifteen thousand dollars is distributed to the sole beneficiary. How much of this income will be taxable to the trust, and how much will be taxable to the beneficiary?

20-17. Explain who is liable for the tax resulting from income earned by a grantor trust.

20-18. X creates a trust for the benefit of his children. How will the taxation of the trust income be affected if Mrs. X holds the power to revoke the trust?

20-19. Paul creates an irrevocable trust providing that all income be distributed to Sheila, his 12-year-old daughter. If the trust distributes $1,700 of income to Sheila and she has no other income for the year, explain the tax consequences.
    Note: For 2005, the standard deduction for a person who *may* be claimed as the dependent of another (whether actually claimed or not) is $800 or the amount of the child's earned income. (For kiddie tax purposes, currently the net unearned income is generally equal to a child's unearned income less the greater of (1) $1,600 or (2) $800 (plus certain itemized deductions.)

20-20. Explain the use of multiple trusts.

20-21. Describe the income tax consequences of the accumulation of income in trusts.

20-22. What benefits may be derived from having the trustee purchase life insurance on a beneficiary's life rather than having the trustee distribute income to the beneficiary who then uses such income to make life insurance premium payments?

20-23. a. Explain how the existence of a sprinkle provision in a trust may enable the trust to save income.

   b. For what purposes, other than tax reasons, would a grantor use a sprinkle provision in a trust?

20-24. What is the tax effect when trust income is used to support a grantor's dependent?

20-25. Mr. Smith has a son, Harris, who has a sizable estate in his own right. Mr. Smith would like to give his son income from his property for life under a testamentary trust with the principal payable to Harris's children upon Harris's death. If the trustee of this trust is authorized in his sole discretion to use a portion of the trust income to purchase life insurance on Harris's life, how will the trust income used to pay such life insurance premiums be taxed for federal income tax purposes? Explain.

Self-Test Questions

T   F   20-1. An estate remains in existence until all the testator's assets have been transferred, debts and taxes have been paid, and distribution is made to beneficiaries.

T   F   20-2. All trusts come into existence and are funded when a person dies.

T   F   20-3. Trusts and estates file income tax returns for informational purposes only, as do partnerships.

T   F   20-4. Income in respect of a decedent is includible in the gross estate of the decedent and, therefore, is not taxable to the estate or beneficiary when received for income tax purposes.

T   F   20-5. With the exception of tax-exempt income, trusts and estates must pay income tax on income received but not distributed.

T   F   20-6. Trusts and estates each get a $600 income tax exemption.

T   F   20-7. An estate is entitled to take as a deduction any ordinary and necessary business expenses incurred in managing a decedent's business during the period of estate administration.

T   F   20-8. All living trusts are separate taxpaying entities whether they are revocable or irrevocable.

T   F   20-9. The general theory of trust income taxation is that trust income is taxed only once, either to the beneficiary or to the trust.

T   F   20-10. A distinguishing feature of a simple trust is that it can never make distributions of principal or have a charitable beneficiary.

T   F   20-11. A concept known as distributable net income (DNI) has been developed for the purpose of advising beneficiaries of the amount of income the trust has earned.

T   F   20-12. Revocable trusts provide opportunities for income tax savings by creating a separate taxpayer so income can be taxed in a potentially lower bracket.

T   F   20-13. For the purposes of the grantor-trust rules, the grantor can escape income taxation on the trust income by providing a reversionary interest, valued at 25 percent of the trust's total value, to the grantor's spouse.

T   F   20-14. For most purposes, transferring unearned income to a child under age 14 will provide little income tax savings to the parents.

T   F   20-15. When there is more than one beneficiary of a single trust, a separate trust should be established for each beneficiary or the beneficiary will be taxed on more income than received.

T   F   20-16. A trustee under a testamentary trust may be authorized to use trust income both to purchase life insurance on the lives of the beneficiaries and to pay the premiums.

T   F   20-17. A sprinkle provision may be used in a trust to provide flexibility to distribute income among beneficiaries as their needs arise and in proportion to those needs.

T   F   20-18. If a grantor establishes a trust to provide support for his minor children, the income will be taxed to either the trust or the minor beneficiary.

An Examination of the Generation-Skipping Transfer Tax

Ted Kurlowicz* and Constance J. Fontaine

Learning Objectives

An understanding of the material in this chapter should enable the student to

---

21-1. Describe the types of transfers that are subject to the generation-skipping transfer tax (GSTT).

21-2. Explain the importance of exemptions and exclusions from the GSTT and how a client should plan for allocation of the $1.5 million (2004/2005) exemption.

21-3. Describe in general the calculation of the GSTT and who has liability for the GSTT.

21-4. Identify the different aspects of planning for the GSTT.

Chapter Outline

---

* Ted Kurlowicz, JD, LLM, CLU, ChFC, AEP, is professor of taxation and holder of the Charles E. Drimal estate planning professorship at The American College. Constance J. Fontaine, JD, LLM, CLU, ChFC, is associate professor of taxation at The American College and holds the Larry R. Pike chair in Insurance and Investments.

INTRODUCTION TO GENERATION-SKIPPING TRANSFER TAX (GSTT)

The first generation-skipping transfer tax (GSTT) was enacted in 1976. However, when Congress made sweeping revisions to the federal tax code in 1986, it totally revamped the GSTT.

The Tax Reform Act of 1986 repealed the prior system of taxing generation-skipping transfers and replaced it with a completely different framework for the imposition of the tax. Rather than the rate of tax being equal to the estate tax bracket of the transferor (as under the old approach), the present approach imposes a flat rate on taxable transfers that is equal to the highest current federal estate and gift tax rate—50 percent in 2002, 49 percent in 2003, 48 percent in 2004, and 47 percent in 2005. Therefore, under EGTRRA 2001, the GSTT rate equals the highest estate tax rate in the relevant year. In 2004 and 2005, the GSTT exemption amount becomes the same as the federal estate tax applicable exclusion amount. The GSTT is repealed for the year 2010 (unless Congress takes further action). The objectives of the GSTT are to obtain at least one transfer tax per generation and to discourage the transfer of substantial assets to more distant family members in order to reduce transfer taxes.

GSTT

- 47% FLAT rate (2005)
- imposed on
  - gifts
  - bequests
  - transfers
  - distributions to skip beneficiaries
- *in addition* to gift and estate taxes on same property

As previously stated, EGTRRA 2001 reduces the top estate tax rate to 47 percent in 2005 and provides a schedule of reductions until repeal of the estate tax for the year 2010. The GSTT rate is determined with reference to the top estate tax rate, and therefore it will follow the same schedule, as shown in table 21-1.

TABLE 21-1
Generation-Skipping Transfer Tax Rate Schedule

Year	Rate
2001	55%
2002	50%
2003	49%
2004	48%
2005	47%
2006	46%
2007–2009	45%
2010	GSTT repealed
2011 and thereafter	55%

Beginning in 2004, the GSTT exemption amount under EGTRRA 2001 equals the estate tax applicable exclusion amount.

Table 21-2 shows the increase in the GSTT exemption under EGTRRA 2001.

TABLE 21-2
Increase in GSTT Exemption

Year	GSTT Exemption
2001–2003	$1,000,000 as indexed for inflation
2004–2005	$1,500,000
2006–2008	$2,000,000
2009	$3,500,000
2010	Repealed

TAXABLE TRANSFERS

The GSTT applies when a taxable transfer is made to a transferee more than one generation level below the transferor. For example, a generation-skipping transfer occurs when a grandparent transfers property to a grandchild. However, the GSTT applies only if the transfer avoids estate or gift tax one generation level above the transferee. That is, the GSTT applies only if a generation is "skipped" by the estate and gift tax system. Thus, a gift from a grandparent to a grandchild that causes estate and gift tax on such transfer at the parent's level will not invoke the generation-skipping tax. It is important to remember, however, that estate or gift tax in addition to GSTT may be applicable on such generation-skipping transfers, because a *grandparent* will probably be subject to the federal estate and gift tax system as well as the GSTT system when making gifts to a grandchild.

The GSTT is imposed on gifts, bequests, or other distributions to skip beneficiaries. A *skip beneficiary* is either (1) a person who is at least two generations below the level of the transferor or (2) a trust in which the beneficiaries are skip persons and from which no nonskip person (a person only one generation below the transferor) will benefit. In most instances, a skip person is a grandchild of the transferor and a nonskip person is a child of the transferor.

Example:	Grandfather Joe is survived by his wife, Jennie. Joe and Jennie had two children—Jack and Jake. Jack is married and has three children—James, Jason, and Julia. Jennie (the grandmother) and Jack and Jake (the children) are nonskip persons. James, Jason, and Julia are skip persons.
	Although most generation-skipping transfers are to family members, usually grandchildren, transfers may be made to nonrelatives and be subject to GST taxation. For purposes of nonrelated donees, a generation constitutes 37.5 years. Spouses are always treated as being of the same generation despite any age differences.

The taxes are imposed on three possible taxable events:

- direct skips
- taxable distributions
- taxable terminations

Direct Skips

direct-skip transfer

As defined in the generation-skipping transfer tax system, a *direct-skip transfer* is a taxable transfer to a skip person. A direct skip can be either an outright transfer or a transfer in trust for the benefit of an individual. A transfer in trust will be treated as a direct skip if

- the trust benefits only one individual,
- no portion of the income or corpus may be distributed to anyone else during the beneficiary's lifetime, and
- the corpus will be included in the beneficiary's estate if the beneficiary dies before the termination of the trust

Thus, a transfer to a life insurance trust will qualify as a direct skip if the trust meets the above requirements and provides current withdrawal powers, such as the Crummey withdrawal powers discussed in chapter 7. Under the predeceased ancestor rules, in most cases, direct skips, taxable distributions, and taxable terminations are not treated as taxable generation-skipping transfers if, at the time of the transfer, the parent of the skip person is already deceased. In this instance, the GSTT is eliminated because the grandchild is the natural recipient of the grandparent's wealth if the grandchild's parent is deceased.

Example:	James Dallop left a fully furnished condominium that he had owned for 14 years to his grandson, Scott, under the terms of his will. This transfer is *not* considered a direct skip triggering the GSTT if Scott's parent, who is the son or daughter of James, has predeceased James. If Scott's parent who is the son or daughter of James is alive at the time of James's death, the generation-skipping tax does apply to this direct-skip bequest. In either event, the regular federal estate tax applies to this transfer.

Skip Beneficiary

- a person two or more generations below transferor (*exception:* grandchild [skip person] of deceased parent) OR
- a trust with skip beneficiaries and no nonskip beneficiaries benefiting

Taxable Distributions

In addition to direct-skip situations, the GSTT may apply to what is known as a taxable distribution.

taxable distribution   A *taxable distribution* is any distribution of either income or principal from a trust to a person two or more generations junior to the trust settlor's generation. The recipients of a taxable distribution are called skip beneficiaries. To be taxable as a generation-skipping transfer, the distribution must otherwise escape federal estate and gift taxation at the first generation level below the original transferor.

The taxable amount in this scenario is the net value of the property received by the skip beneficiary reduced by any amount the beneficiary may have paid in order to receive the property. In addition, the taxable amount includes any GSTT paid by the *trustee* on such taxable distribution. The reason for this "gross-up" rule is that the GSTT liability falls on the skip beneficiary, not the trustee.

> ***Example:***   Ethel Bally created an irrevocable trust in early 1990 for the benefit of her son, Carlos, and her grandson, Julio. In December of this year, the trustee made a distribution of $20,000 of trust income to Carlos and $18,800 of trust income to Julio. The distribution to Julio is characterized as a taxable distribution that triggers GSTT. Note that the original transfer to the trust in 1990 could have been subject to taxation through the gift tax rules at that time.

Taxable Terminations

taxable termination

A *taxable termination* is defined as a situation in which there is a termination of a property interest held in trust, the termination occurring by death, lapse of time, release of a power, or otherwise, that results in skip beneficiaries holding the property interests in the trust. Four miscellaneous points must be noted:

- A taxable termination cannot take place if a skip beneficiary could not receive a distribution after the termination.
- A taxable termination cannot occur as long as at least one nonskip beneficiary has an interest in the property.
- There will be no taxable termination if an estate or gift tax is imposed on the trust property one generation level below the transferor at the time of the termination.
- A partial termination subject to GSTT is possible if a specified, separate portion of the trust is available only to skip persons after the termination.

GSTT Events

- direct skips
    - outright transfer or
    - trust with only one lifetime and at death beneficiary
- taxable distributions
    - trust distributions (income/principal) to skip beneficiaries (two or more generations below)
- taxable terminations
    - trust termination with property passing to skip beneficiaries

---

The taxable amount in the case of a taxable termination is the value of all property involved reduced by any amounts paid by the recipient for it and any expenses, debts, and income or property taxes triggered by that property.

Example:	Rosemary Campo's will directed that the income from her marketable securities was to pass to her daughter, Kim, for life, with the remainder interest to pass at Kim's death to Rosemary's granddaughter, Heather. When Kim died, her life interest in the trust property terminated and Heather received the underlying property. Heather is the skip beneficiary. A taxable termination occurred at Kim's death.

EXEMPTIONS AND EXCLUSIONS

Although the scope of the new GSTT is broad and could have a dramatic effect on a client's tax planning, it must be emphasized that there are several exemptions to, and exclusions from, this tax.

The GSTT Exemption

The most basic exemption is that every taxpayer is permitted to make aggregate transfers of up to $1 million (as indexed for inflation from 1999 through 2003—TRA '97; the indexed amount in 2003 was $1,120,000) either during lifetime or at death that will not attract the GSTT. According to EGTRRA 2001, in 2004 and 2005, when the estate tax applicable exclusion amount becomes $1.5 million, the GSTT exemption becomes the same as the applicable exclusion amount. Because the transferor's spouse also has a $1.5 million exemption against generation-skipping transfers, a total family basic exemption amount of $3 million is available.

Remember, the *gift tax* exclusion was capped at $1 million, starting January 1, 2002.

GSTT Exemptions

$1.5 million exemption (2004/2005)

- per donor *not* per donee
- lifetime/death
- $3 million for both spouses (amount is double the amount of individual single transferor) (2004/2005)

The Annual Exclusion Transfer

The $11,000 annual per-donee exclusion from gift tax was discussed in chapter 7. A similar exclusion from the GSTT is available for direct skips. A direct skip is either (1) an outright gift providing the donee with immediate possession or (2) certain gifts in trust providing a present interest to a skip person.

For GSTT purposes, the annual exclusion is more restrictive than the gift tax annual exclusion for gifts in trust. The gift in trust qualifies for the GSTT exclusion if it provides a present interest such as a current income interest or Crummey withdrawal power. In addition, the trust must limit distributions of income and corpus to a single beneficiary and must provide that the corpus will be included in the estate of the beneficiary if he or she dies prior to the termination of the trust. Thus, because only one beneficiary is permitted, the GSTT annual exclusion cannot be used on the typical inter vivos trust with sprinkle provisions. It is possible, however, to create a separate trust for each grandchild, such as a Sec. 2503(c) trust, that will qualify for both the gift tax and GSTT annual exclusions.

GSTT Exclusions

$11,000 (after 2001) annual exclusion
- outright gifts
- in trust
  - requires present interest (current income interest or Crummey power)
  - only one beneficiary with lifetime/death receipt of property

---

Exclusion for Transfers for Educational or Medical Expenses

Tuition or medical expense payments on behalf of a donee are also excluded from both gift tax and GSTT. Such gifts must be provided directly to the educational institution or medical provider for expenses incurred by the donee. The transfers excludible under this provision are not limited in amount, but the tuition payment exclusion is limited to transfers to educational institutions eligible for income-tax-deductible charitable contributions covering the direct tuition costs for the education or training of the donee. Direct tuition payments are an excellent gift for wealthy grandparents to consider, because

---

GSTT Exemptions and Exclusions

---

unlimited educational/medical expenses
- direct payments to provider
- $1.5 million GSTT exemption (2004/2005) unaffected

---

they (1) are not subject to gift or GSTT taxes, (2) do not reduce the annual exclusion gifts, and (3) do not reduce the GSTT exemption.

Medical expenses eligible for the exclusion are those expenses normally deductible by the donee under the income tax rules.

CALCULATION OF THE GSTT

The GSTT is calculated by a somewhat unusual process, which is discussed herein primarily to demonstrate the effect of the GSTT exemption. The GSTT is determined by multiplying the taxable amount by an applicable GSTT rate. The taxable amount is the value (less certain expenses) of any direct skip, taxable termination, or taxable distribution.

inclusion ratio

The applicable GSTT rate is the highest federal estate and gift tax rate (47 percent in 2005) multiplied by an *inclusion ratio*. The inclusion ratio is determined by the following formula:

$$\text{Inclusion ratio} = 1 - \frac{TE}{VT - (ET + CD)}$$

TE = transferor's exemption allocated to the transfer
VT = value of the transferred property
ET = amount of federal estate tax or state death tax recovered from the trust attributable to the transferred property
CD = charitable deduction attributable to the transferred property

Assuming no estate tax or charitable deduction, the inclusion ratio is one (and the applicable rate is 47 percent [2005]) if no exemption is allocated to the transfer. If the amount of the exemption is allocated equivalently to the value of the transferred property, the applicable rate is zero and the transfer is exempt from GSTT. It is possible, of course, to have an applicable rate somewhere between zero percent and 47 percent (2005) if the transfer is only partially exempt. However, a partially exempt trust should generally be avoided unless the transferor has insufficient remaining exemption to fully shelter the trust from GSTT. Partially exempt trusts will generally increase the complexity and fiduciary costs associated with the administration of the trust.

Example: Using the 2005 GSTT exemption amount and tax rate of 47 percent:

In 2005, a widower grandfather transfers outright (direct skip) $3,750,000 to his grandson. Ignore the annual exclusion for this example. His entire 2005 exemption of $1.5 million is allocated to the transfer.

The fraction is

$$\frac{\$1,500,000}{\$3,750,000} \text{ which is } 2/5$$

3/5 (1 minus 2/5) is the inclusion ratio
3/5 of 47% yields a tax rate of 28.2%
28.2% of $3,750,000 equals a GSTT of $1,057,500

Keep in mind that although not addressed in this example, gift tax will also apply to this transfer from grandfather to grandson.

LIABILITY FOR THE TAX

The liability for tax payment depends upon the type of generation-skipping transfer. Therefore, the transferor must consider the net amount to be received by the skip beneficiary in choosing the transfer mechanism.

- For direct skips, the tax is imposed on the transferor or the transferor's estate. Therefore, the direct-skip beneficiary receives the full amount of the transfer while the remainder of the transferor's estate is diminished by the transfer.
- In the case of a taxable distribution, the liability for the tax falls on the transferee. That is, the tax that is imposed reduces the amount of the transfer available to the beneficiary. Because the rate of tax is 47 percent (2005), the amount of the taxable distribution available to the skip beneficiary is substantially reduced after the GSTT liability.
- The tax is paid by the trustee in the event of a taxable termination. Thus, at the time of the termination, the skip person receives the proceeds reduced by the tax.

The GSTT is imposed by statute on the property transferred unless the transferor specifically allocates the tax elsewhere by the terms of a will or trust document. As with the federal estate and gift taxes, a lien is applicable against the transferred property for collection of the tax.

Liability for GSTT

Taxable GSTT Event	Liability
• direct skip	• transferor/ transferor's estate
• taxable distribution	• transferee (beneficiary)
• taxable termination	• trustee

PLANNING FOR THE GSTT

Because the GSTT is imposed at the highest marginal federal estate tax bracket, the tax will represent the highest percentage burden of any federal tax in the future. Because generation-skipping transfers are also potentially subject to estate or gift taxes, the combination of estate or gift tax and GSTT rates can be considerable. Obviously, this tax creates a substantial incentive to transfer property in a manner exempt from the tax.

Allocating the GSTT Exemption

Lifetime Transfers

One choice available to the taxpayer for allocating the $1.5 million GSTT exemption is to apply such exemption affirmatively to lifetime gifts. The allocation of such exemption to lifetime gifts is particularly appropriate because the exemption is leveraged. That is, the exemption need shelter only the value of the contribution at the time of the gift on a dollar-for-dollar basis. It is important to note that under Sec. 2632(b) the GSTT exemption is automatically allocated to lifetime direct skips unless the donor elects otherwise on a gift tax return (709) that is timely filed. EGTRRA 2001 added Sec. 2632(c) that provides that any unused GSTT exemption is automatically allocated to indirect skips made to a GST trust for the years 2001 to 2009. An *indirect skip* is any transfer of property, other than a direct skip, that is subject to the GSTT made to a GST trust. A transferor has the option to elect out of the automatic allocation rules by making the election on the appropriate return.

indirect skip

Gifts of appreciating property are good targets for lifetime gifts to take advantage of the GSTT exemption. The exemption will be applied to the value of the property at the time of the transfer, and any posttransfer appreciation will not be subject to the tax and need not be sheltered by part of the exemption. In addition, the exemption can be used to provide for skip persons through transfers in trust. The exemption must be allocated against current additions to the trust on a timely filed gift tax return. However, the appreciation on the corpus will avoid GSTT if all *additions* to the trust are sheltered by the exemption. Therefore, because the GSTT exemption is leveraged, wealthy clients can transfer appreciating property that will eventually expand into substantial wealth at a huge total transfer tax savings.

The irrevocable life insurance trust discussed earlier is an excellent device for using the GSTT exemption. Unless the trust has one beneficiary, the premium additions to a Crummey life insurance trust will not be eligible for a GSTT annual exclusion. However, the gift tax annual exclusion will be available, and the GSTT exemption will shelter the trust from GSTT unless aggregate premiums exceed $1.5 million (2004 and 2005). In this manner, substantial wealth may be transferred to the trust and avoid the gift tax or GSTT. The cash contributed to the trust can be used to purchase a life insurance policy on the life of the grantor. Therefore, the appreciation in the life insurance policy and subsequent proceeds at the death of the grantor are beyond the reach of the estate tax or GSTT. The life insurance received by the beneficiaries will prevent the diminution of the grantor's estate caused by the total transfer taxes imposed on any wealth *retained* by the grantor until death.

For example, suppose a $1.5 million policy is placed in the trust and will be paid up with 10 annual premium contributions of $25,000. The grandparent can then shelter such a transfer with $250,000 of his or her exemption instead of using the full exemption on a different type of $1.5 million gift.

Testamentary Transfers

Any exemption not used at the time of the taxpayer's death and not made by the taxpayer's executor is allocated according to the default rules. The unused portion of the decedent's GSTT exemption at the time of death is allocated under the following priorities:

- First, the GSTT exemption is applied to a direct skip of property (a specific outright bequest or devise of property) occurring at the individual's death.
- Second, the exemption is allocated to trusts in which the decedent is treated as the transferor and from which a taxable GSTT event might occur after the individual's death.

These rules provide that the exemption is allocated ratably to the priority list above based on the nonexempt portion of the properties included in such bequests or trusts. The nonexempt portion of such bequests is the amount of the property to which the $1.5 million (2004 and 2005) GSTT exemption has not been previously allocated.

Example:	Grandparent (GP) died last year. GP left separate $1.5 million parcels of real estate to each of his grandchildren, GC1 and GC2.
	GP had not used any of his $1.5 million GSTT exemption while he was alive and had not allocated any of the exemption affirmatively through the provisions of his will. The IRS allocation rules would apply the GSTT exemption ratably to the two pieces of property. Thus, $750,000 of each parcel of real estate left to the grandchildren will be exempt, and the remaining $750,000 of each parcel will become subject to GSTT.

These exemption allocation rules do not add complexity to a grandparent's estate if substantial direct-skip bequests are made to grandchildren. The exemption is simply allocated ratably among the bequests. If the grandparent leaves no such direct-skip bequest, however, the allocation rules add to the cost and complexity of administering testamentary trusts. The allocation of the exemption to such trusts is applied ratably against any trust that might result in a taxable distribution or termination subject to GSTT. In the usual marital-deduction will, the will divides the property between a marital trust and a credit-equivalent bypass trust. In either trust the property might later be subject to a GSTT, because grandchildren are almost certainly contingent or remainder beneficiaries. The allocation rules cause the exemption to be allocated ratably between the marital and the bypass trust. The result is that each trust would likely become partially exempt and partially nonexempt from GSTT. This adds to the administrative complexity for the trustee and, most likely, to the costs of administering the trust.

The mechanics of the GSTT calculation make it preferable to leave trusts either wholly exempt or wholly nonexempt. Of course, the taxpayer would prefer that the trust more likely to result in a GSTT liability receive the exemption and become wholly exempt. The taxpayer is incapable of controlling the allocation of such exemption unless he or she allocates the exemption affirmatively to lifetime gifts or directs the executor in the allocation of such gifts after the individual's death. The directions to the executor should be included in the decedent's will along with the normal directions with respect to estate tax elections. By giving the executor the appropriate discretion, the taxpayer is able to take a wait-and-see approach, and the executor will be able to make appropriate allocation of the exemption after the decedent's death.

Both spouses should make full use of their GSTT exemptions. The allocation of the exemption in the wills of both spouses should be carefully planned. The spouses should avoid wasting the exemption by allocating both exemptions to the same assets. A popular method is to provide the executors of the will with discretionary power in allocating the exemptions. After viewing the facts at the time of estate administration, the executor then allocates the exemption where it is most appropriate. The exemption should be allocated to a transfer, perhaps a credit-equivalent bypass trust, that is most likely to benefit skip persons. In addition, the executor should avoid allocating the exemption to a transfer if the surviving spouse's exemption will be available.

If one spouse does not have sufficient assets to use the exemption, an interspousal transfer may be indicated. By using the unlimited marital estate or gift tax deduction, the wealthy spouse can transfer assets to the other spouse without incurring transfer tax. These assets may enable the less wealthy spouse to use the GSTT exemption.

Note to Students: See Appendix A for a summary of the advantages and disadvantages of different trusts covered in this chapter and throughout the text.

CHAPTER REVIEW

Answers to the review questions and the self-test questions start on page 717.

Key Terms

direct-skip transfer   inclusion ratio
taxable distribution   indirect skip
taxable termination

Review Questions

21.1. What types of transfers will result in taxation under the GSTT rules?

21-2. What is the $1.5 million (2004 and 2005) exemption against the GSTT, and how should the exemption be allocated by the taxpayer?

21-3. How must a trust be designed for transfers to the trust to qualify for the annual gift tax exclusion from the GSTT?

21-4. How might a grandparent make gifts to a grandchild free of the GSTT without using either the annual exclusion or GSTT exemption?

21-5. How might an irrevocable life insurance trust be used in conjunction with the GSTT exemption ?

21-6. Describe the manner in which the IRS will allocate the GSTT exemption at a transferor's death if the exemption is not allocated by the decedent.

Self-Test Questions

T   F   21-1. The generation-skipping transfer tax (GSTT) is imposed on a progressive rate schedule similar to the estate or gift tax.

T   F   21-2. Either the GSTT or the regular estate or gift tax, but not both, will apply to a transfer to a grandchild.

T   F   21-3. The GSTT is imposed on lifetime or testamentary transfers that are direct skips, taxable distributions, or taxable terminations.

T   F   21-4. Substantial transfers are exempt from the GSTT since an applicable credit amount is available to shelter generation-skipping transfers from tax.

T   F   21-5.   Because the GSTT $1.5 million (2004 and 2005) exemption is available to both spouses (ignoring the annual, medical, and educational exclusions), a married couple can transfer a total of $3 million to skip persons free of GSTT.

T   F   21-6.   The annual per-donee gift tax exclusion is available for transfers to a generation-skipping trust if Crummey withdrawal powers are given to the beneficiaries in the same manner as for annual gift tax exclusion transfers.

T   F   21-7.   All benefits paid from an irrevocable life insurance trust will be exempt from GSTT if all annual premiums made to the trust were sheltered by the GSTT exemption or exclusion.

T   F   21-8.   The GSTT is calculated in the same way as the gift and estate tax except for the GSTT $1.5 million (2004 and 2005) exemption.

T   F   21-9.   For GSTT distributions, the liability falls on the transferee.

T   F   21-10.   If the GSTT exemption is not allocated by a decedent's executor, the IRS must allocate it in a manner that results in the lowest GSTT liability.

T   F   21-11.   A trust that is only partially exempt from the GSTT due to the incomplete allocation of the GSTT exemption will face increased administrative fees due to the added complexity of having an inclusion ratio other than zero or one.

22

Other Estate Planning Techniques

Ted Kurlowicz* and Constance J. Fontaine

Learning Objectives

An understanding of the material in this chapter should enable the student to

---

22-1. Describe the advantages, disadvantages, and tax treatment of installment sales.

22-2. Explain what private annuities are and their tax treatment.

22-3. Describe the gift and estate tax treatment of grantor-retained annuity trusts (GRATs) and grantor-retained unitrusts (GRUTs).

22-4. Describe the design considerations and transfer tax treatment of a qualified personal residence trust (QPRT).

22-5. Identify basic types of life insurance products.

22-6. Explain how an irrevocable life insurance trust can be designed to provide estate liquidity without adding to the estate tax burden.

Chapter Outline

---

* Ted Kurlowicz, JD, LLM, CLU, ChFC, AEP, is professor of taxation and holder of the Charles E. Drimal estate planning professorship at The American College.

Recent tax reforms have increased the significance of planning for federal transfer tax reduction. In many ways, the planning for estate and gift tax reduction can result in far greater gains to the taxpayer than planning for other taxes. This is particularly true for wealthy individuals with substantial estates. Reasons for the recent increase in the importance of estate planning include:

- The federal transfer tax rates have increased in relation to the marginal income tax rates. (Currently, marginal income tax rates peak at 35 percent. For 2005, the federal estate and gift tax rates have a 47 percent maximum.
- The generation-skipping tax is applicable to many transfers to skip beneficiaries at a flat rate equal to the highest current federal estate and gift tax rate.

- The combination of federal estate or gift taxes with generation-skipping transfer taxes can result in doubling high marginal rates for certain transfers to skip beneficiaries.
- The anti-freeze rules under Chapter 14 of the Internal Revenue Code present a new estate tax trap for the unwary, since they may cause additional unforeseen estate or gift taxes if property gifted during a donor's lifetime is returned to his or her gross estate.
- The population of the elderly in the United States has been increasing faster than the overall population.
- The unlimited marital deduction has delayed payment of estate taxes until the death of the surviving spouse, which occurs on the average about 10 years after the first spouse's death.

To prevent the Treasury from confiscating the wealth of those individuals who accumulate substantial assets, estate planning is particularly important. There are also several other estate planning considerations that a client and estate planner should discuss.

In conjunction with planning for transfer tax reduction, estate planners must also be cognizant of health care considerations. Health care and incapacity issues are not necessarily reserved until old age. To at least some extent, depending on the particular circumstances, these matters should be addressed in a comprehensive estate plan.

Last, the planner should be aware of the special circumstances that are often involved in estate planning for the elderly and incapacitated, issues that may arise when estate planning is undertaken for married couples, and considerations in estate planning for nonmarital partners.

INSTALLMENT SALES

An installment can be a useful technique for financial and estate planning purposes. It is a taxable sale of a property with the income tax reporting of gain accounted for under the installment accounting provisions of the Internal Revenue Code. An *installment sale* is any sale in which at least one principal payment is received in a year other than the year of the sale. The installment reporting provisions are the general rule when this definition for an installment sale is satisfied. However, the seller can elect to use normal accounting for an installment sale and recognize all gain in the year of sale.

installment sale

Advantages of Installment Sales

From the seller's standpoint, an installment sale of property can provide both income tax and estate tax benefits. If installment reporting is available, the gain of the sale of property in exchange for an installment note will be delayed and recognized gradually over the installment period. Thus, it is possible to sell highly appreciated property without immediate recognition of the full taxable gain. On the other hand, the ability to elect out of installment reporting provides the taxpayer with the possibility of recognizing all taxable gain immediately. For example, a taxpayer may elect to recognize all gain at the time of an installment sale in a year when the taxpayer either has little other income or shows a loss for income tax purposes. Under these circumstances, reporting the gain immediately on an installment sale could prevent the taxpayer from wasting other deductions and tax benefits. The flexibility of an installment sale's reporting rules permits a taxpayer to defer gain recognition and, to some degree, plan the timing of gain recognition on the sale of property.

The installment sale also provides estate tax saving possibilities for the seller. The installment sale, a particularly useful device for family estate planning, may be used when a senior family member wishes to pass property on to a successor in the family. Be aware that special related-party rules apply to installment sales between family members. For estate planning purposes, an installment sale is one method of "freezing" the seller's estate and shifting the appreciation potential to a junior family member. If performed properly and if the installment note is equal to the fair market value of the property at the time of the sale, the installment sale shifts the postsale appreciation to the junior family member without any transfer taxes being payable on the transferred property.

From the buyer's standpoint, the installment sale permits the buyer to defer some or all of the principal payments on the sale. This is particularly important for buyers without the funds for the entire purchase price. Quite often, the purchase and sale would be impossible without the payment deferral available in an installment sale.

Income Tax Treatment of Installment Sales

The sale of appreciated property in exchange for an installment note provides that some or all of the purchase price will be payable at some date in the future. From the seller's standpoint, the future payments can be broken down into three components for income tax purposes.

- One component of each annual payment on the installment note is treated as a return of the seller's original basis of the property. This return of basis is not taxable, because the seller is merely recovering his or her cost of the property.
- A second component of each payment received is treated as taxable gain.
- The third and final component of each payment is deemed interest. This interest is taxable to the seller as ordinary income.

Income Taxation of Installment Sales

- seller
  - three components of each installment payment
    - return of seller's basis: not taxable
    - taxable gain
    - interest: taxable as ordinary income
- buyer
  - interest paid may be deductible
  - principal payments constitute basis

Under the installment sales rules, the taxable gain component is recognized proportionally over the period in which the installment payments are made. The formula for recognizing gain from any particular installment payment is as follows:[*]

$$\text{Capital gain} = \text{payment received during the year} \times \frac{\text{gross profit}}{\text{total contract price}}$$

Example 1:	Ignoring the interest component in this case, assume that Tom Taxplanner, aged 52, would like to sell his vacation home to his daughter, Julia. The vacation home is valued at $200,000 and Tom's basis in the property is $50,000. Julia proposes an installment sale with a $50,000 down payment and the remaining principal payable in 10 annual installments of $15,000 beginning one year from settlement. Ten percent interest will be payable on any unpaid balance. Tom's gross profit is $150,000 and the contract price is $200,000. Thus, Tom will recognize 75 percent ($150,000 divided by $200,000) of each payment as gain.
Example 2:	Recently, Martin sold his collection of watercolors by recognized artists to his son, Roger, for $100,000. Roger made a down payment of $10,000 and will make principal payments in eight equal installments of $11,250 each year. Roger will also make monthly payments of interest. Because Martin's adjusted basis in the artwork is $40,000, Martin has a gross profit of $60,000. Each year he will recognize a

---

[*] This formula is simplified to demonstrate the gain recognition process without adding federal income tax complexity beyond the scope of this chapter.

capital gain of 60 percent ($60,000 ÷ $100,000) of the principal amount received. Therefore, in the year of the installment sale, Martin must report $6,000 of gain from the $10,000 received from Martin. For the next 8 years, he will have a gain of $6,750 (60% x $11,250).

Interest on Installment Sales

Interest paid by a buyer on an installment sale is potentially deductible for income tax purposes. Thus, it might be to the benefit of the buyer to recharacterize some of the purchase payment as interest if the interest on the transaction is deductible.

On the other hand, the buyer may wish to minimize the interest element of the installment sale if the interest is nondeductible. Under these circumstances, it may be more advantageous for the buyer to characterize the payments as principal. The additional amount of principal will provide the buyer with a higher basis, which may be available for depreciation deductions at a later date. Certainly the interest rate might be a consideration in the negotiation process for the installment sale.

Unfortunately, the tax rules provide for target rates of interest on installment obligations under either the imputed interest rules (Code Sec. 483) or original-issue-discount (OID) rules (Code Secs. 1271–1274). These rules minimize the flexibility by specifying a rate of interest that is deemed to apply for installment obligations falling within these rules. Although these rules are beyond the scope of this book, the estate planner should be aware that the appropriate tax advice should be sought for determining the rate of interest on an installment obligation.

Gift Tax Treatment of Installment Sales

There will be no gift tax ramifications for an installment sale if the transaction is a fair, arm's-length arrangement made for full and adequate consideration. When the parties to an installment sale are family members, the seller (usually the senior family member) may forgive an occasional future payment by the buyer (junior family member). Generally, the forgiven amount qualifies for the annual exclusion. Any amount forgiven in excess of the annual gift tax exclusion constitutes a taxable gift. Care, however, must be taken that the forgiveness of payments is not the result of a presale understanding between the parties to the sale. The appearance of a preunderstanding could result in an IRS challenge that the entire sale is a taxable gift to the purchaser.

Estate Tax Treatment of Installment Sales

An installment sale is a useful device in a family's financial and estate planning. The income tax advantages of installment reporting have been discussed above. In addition, the seller receives estate tax advantages. The transaction is particularly useful when a senior family member sells property to a junior family member. An installment sale for estate planning purposes is one of the methods of "freezing" the seller's estate and shifting the growth in family property to the next generation without the payment of transfer taxes on the growth element.

In our previous example, Tom Taxplanner sold a family vacation home to his daughter. To avoid any transfer tax consequences, the home was sold for an installment note equivalent to the fair market value of the home—$200,000. This transaction is one type of estate freeze. The maximum total value of the vacation home in Tom's estate will be $200,000. If Tom survives the 10-year installment period, no value of the home or the installment note will be included in his gross estate. Only the unconsumed amounts of the principal and interest payments received in the installment sale will remain in his estate. If Tom dies during the period of the installment term, the present value of the remaining installment payments will be included in his estate. In either event, none of the growth on the property following the sale to his daughter will be included in Tom's estate. The growth element has been transferred to his daughter free of transfer taxes. The transfer tax savings are substantial if rapidly appreciating property is transferred to the next generation in exchange for an installment note.

Installment Sales

- sale with one or more principal payments in year other than year of sale
- income tax treatment under installment accounting method
- seller's income tax gain recognized over each installment
- used to freeze gift/estate value and remove appreciation potential
- payments deferred for buyer
- estate inclusion of present value of remaining payments at seller's death

---

self-canceling installment note (SCIN)

Self-Canceling Installment Notes (SCINs)

One variation of an installment note is an installment note that includes a self-cancellation provision at the seller's death. The SCIN is designed like an installment note and is subject to normal installment-sale reporting rules but is automatically canceled by the terms of the sale contract if the seller dies before all the remaining principal payments are made. Because the mortality risk is borne by the seller, the buyer has to pay a higher than fair market price for the business, usually with a higher principal amount or greater interest rate. The seller's age is also a factor in the sale price. The older the seller is, the more the consideration is increased. The price is increased by the actuarial value of the contingency that not all installment payments will be made if the seller dies during the term period. It is particularly important in a family transaction that the IRC valuation rules under Sec. 7520 (discussed in chapter 10) be followed carefully. The SCIN should be equal in value to the property transferred or a gift is made to the buyer to the extent that full and adequate consideration is not received in the transaction. Because the note cancels automatically at the death of the seller, there is nothing left to be included in the seller's estate for estate tax purposes if he or she dies during the term. When, however, the seller dies prior to the installment sale period and remaining payments are canceled, the entire amount of the remaining gain on the deceased seller's note must be included on the decedent's fiduciary (estate) income tax return (Form 1041). Although the gain constitutes income in respect of a decedent (IRD), no corresponding income tax deduction is available for the proportionate amount of estate tax because the note is canceled at death and therefore not included in the decedent's gross estate. Through the use of the SCIN, there is the potential to pass property to the next generation, producing a windfall to the junior family member buyer and a substantial reduction in the net proceeds received from the sale by the senior family member.

Self-Canceling Installment Note (SCIN)

- The buyer's remaining principal payments are canceled at the seller's death prior to the installment term period.
- The buyer pays an increased price for the seller's bearing the mortality risk.
- The seller has no estate inclusion of (canceled) remaining payments.

PRIVATE ANNUITIES

private annuity

The private annuity is a variation of the installment sale with particular estate planning benefits. However, the rules and tax advantages are somewhat different. A *private annuity* is a sale of property, such as a family business, in exchange for the buyer's agreement to make periodic payments of a specified sum for the remainder of the seller's life. The amount of the payments is based on the actuarial factors determined under the rules of Sec. 7520.

Because the value of the property being transferred equals the present value of the expected and properly valued annuity, there are no gift tax consequences for the transaction. If the private annuity is not properly valued and a gift element exists, the annuitant will be treated as having a retained life interest at death under Sec. 2036, causing inclusion of the value of the transferred asset in the decedent-annuitant's gross estate. The U.S. Treasury's actuarial tables, the Alpha Tables, are used for the valuation of private annuities, unless at the time the private annuity is executed, the annuitant had a 50 percent or less probability of living one year.

A major advantage of the private annuity is its estate tax treatment. In a regular installment sale, some amount is included in the seller's estate if the seller dies holding the installment note. In this case, the remaining payments are an enforceable obligation held by the estate and, therefore, are a valuable asset to the estate. However, in a private annuity no further payments are due when the seller dies. Thus, there is nothing to include in the estate of a seller who dies holding a private annuity. For estate tax purposes the private annuity terminates at the seller-annuitant's death and no amount of the annuity is included in the seller's estate. (Of course, any annuity payments received by the seller that are not consumed before the seller's death are included in the seller's estate.) Any appreciation in the property after the exchange escapes gift or estate taxation. In other words, if the seller dies after one year, the property passes to the buyer (usually a family member) for only one annual payment. Keep in mind, however, that the buyer bears the risk of the seller's living beyond his or her life expectancy and the annual payments continuing until the seller's death.

Although the gift and estate taxation of private annuities is rather uncomplicated, income taxation is more complex. In a manner similar to the installment sale, the gain in the property sold in exchange for the private annuity is spread over the remaining portion of the seller's life expectancy. Each portion of the private annuity payments received over the life expectancy

---

Private Annuity

- seller's (senior family member) sale of property (family business) to buyer (junior family member)
  - appreciation out of estate
- buyer's unsecured agreement to pay seller periodic specified amounts for seller's life
  - no portion of payments deductible to buyer
  - termination of payments at seller's death
- risks
  - seller's premature death: estate inclusion of only unconsumed payments
  - seller's longevity: buyer pays more than property value

represents part gain and part return of the cost basis of the seller. The income taxation of a private annuity differs from the installment sale because private annuity payments fall under the Sec. 72 annuity rules. However, unlike the installment sale, no part of the purchase payments is deductible as interest by the buyer. Another distinguishing characteristic of the private annuity is the fact that the seller cannot take a security interest as collateral when receiving the private annuity. This lack of security can be disturbing to an annuitant who depends on the annuity payments for support. A private annuity is an un-secured promise to pay made by the buyer to the seller of the property. Of course, private annuity payments are generally limited to family situations where a senior family member is transferring property to the next generation.

ESTATE FREEZES THROUGH USE OF FAMILY TRUSTS

Irrevocable trusts provide an excellent opportunity for a wealthy individual to reduce total transfer tax. Property transferred to an irrevocable trust will be treated as a current gift for gift tax purposes. However, the gift tax annual exclusion, the GSTT annual exclusion, the applicable credit amount against estate or gift taxes, and the GSTT exemption may be used to reduce the actual current gift or GSTT liability to zero.

The estate tax treatment of the transfer to the irrevocable trust depends on the circumstances with respect to the terms and administration of the trust. Recalling the Sec. 2702 rules discussed previously, note that transfers with retained rights for the donor may cause serious estate or gift tax consequences for the donor. For example, the wrong retained rights could cause the entire property to be treated as a taxable gift. A retained right that does not end before the grantor's death will cause all, or a portion of, the trust property to be included in the donor's gross estate even if the transfers are treated as current gifts for gift tax purposes.

These estate tax rules are very important for designing a successful trust freeze. The grantor quite often would like to retain some use of the donated property. First, this gives the grantor the opportunity to draw on the trust income or principal to receive income payments during retirement, for instance. In addition, the retained rights held by the grantor may have value for gift tax purposes that can be used to offset the gift tax cost of transferring the property to the trust. As discussed in chapter 10, the subtraction method of valuation permits retained rights with "value" to reduce the gift tax cost of transfers subject to grantor-held retained rights.

Grantor-Retained Annuity Trust or Unitrust Freezes

grantor-retained annuity trust GRAT

Two examples of retained rights (qualified interests) that are treated as hav-ing value for gift tax purposes are the *grantor-retained annuity trust (GRAT)*

Grantor-Retained Annuity Trust (GRAT)

The grantor has the right for life or a term of years to receive at least annually a stated dollar amount or stated percentage of the initial value of property transferred to an irrevocable trust.

---

and grantor-retained unitrust (GRUT). A GRAT is an irrevocable trust in which the grantor retains the right to receive *fixed amounts* payable at least annually for life (or the joint lives of the grantor and others) or for a term of years. A GRAT is actuarially similar to a charitable remainder annuity trust (CRAT). The GRAT payments to the grantor are subject to income taxation. Thus, the grantor can gift property to a trust and retain a fixed annuity for life or for a period of years. A fixed annuity is a stated annual dollar amount or a stated percentage of the *initial* value of the trust property. At the end of the life interest or term, the remaining trust corpus is paid to the remainderperson(s). After the initial gift to the trust, no additions are permitted.

Example:	Maxwell contributes $1.3 million in securities to an irrevocable trust. He retains the right to receive $80,000 per year from the trust for the next 10 years. At the end of 10 years, the trust will terminate and the remainder will be paid in equal shares to his grandchildren. The retained interest is a qualified annuity interest and will be given full actuarial value under Sec. 7520 valuation rules. Thus, the value of the gift is equal to $1.3 million minus the value of a 10-year $80,000 annual annuity.

grantor-retained unitrust GRUT

A *grantor-retained unitrust (GRUT)* is an irrevocable trust in which the grantor retains the right to receive amounts payable, which are a *fixed percentage* of the trust's assets (as valued each year), at least annually for life (or the joint lives of the grantor and others) or for a term of years. A GRUT is actuarially similar to a charitable remainder unitrust (CRUT). Thus, the grantor retains a variable annuity and the annual payout is based on the value that the trust grows (or contracts) to each year. The trust payments to the grantor are subject to income taxation. The term of the trust may be based on the life of the annuitant or a specified term of years. At the end of the term of the trust, all remaining trust assets pass to the designated remainderpersons. The gift tax value of the GRUT may be subtracted from the value of the property transferred to the trust to determine the gift tax value of the remainder interest. In contrast to the rules for a GRAT, the grantor may make additional gifts to a GRUT.

Example:	Assume the same facts as the previous example. However, Maxwell instead retains the right to receive payments equal to 7 percent of the trust based on its current value each year. The retained interest is a qualified unitrust interest and will be given full actuarial value under Sec. 7520 valuation rules. Thus, the value of the gift is equal to $1.3 million minus the value of a 10-year unitrust interest.

Grantor-Retained Unitrust (GRUT)

The grantor has the right for life or a term of years to receive at least annually amounts that are a fixed percentage of an irrevocable trust's assets (as valued annually).

Gift Tax Treatment of the GRAT or GRUT

The irrevocable transfer of the remainder interest in the GRAT or GRUT is a current gift for gift tax purposes. Because the gift provides a future interest to the donees, the gift does not qualify for the annual exclusion. However, the gift is discounted from the full fair market value of the corpus by subtracting the value of the grantor's retained interest valued under the Sec. 7520 rules. This discounted gift can be sheltered by the grantor's applicable credit amount. Any retained trust interest other than a GRAT or a GRUT is generally valued at zero for gift tax purposes and the grantor will be treated as having gifted the entire remainder with no discounting for other retained rights.

Example:	Suppose Tom Taxplanner rents out the vacation home, valued at $200,000. If he transfers the home to a GRAT and retains a $12,000 (assume this is the actual net rental amount) annuity for 10 years, while gifting the remainder to Julia, he will be able to value the gift by subtracting the value of the annuity from the full value of the property. Assume the Sec. 7520 monthly rate is 7 percent, the value of the retained annuity is $81,031. Thus, the taxable value of the gift is $118,969 ($200,000 less $81,031).

Estate Tax Treatment of the GRAT or GRUT

If the grantor survives the retained interest term in a qualified GRAT or GRUT, Sec. 2036 does not apply and the corpus, including any posttransfer appreciation, is excluded from the gross estate of the grantor. In other words, a growing property interest can be transferred to family heirs for a significantly discounted transfer tax cost.

The estate tax benefits are reduced, however, if the grantor fails to survive the term. The amount included is the amount of principal of the trust that would be required under actuarial valuation principles to produce the annuity or unitrust payout. The upper limit on the inclusion is the actual amount of principal at the time of death. In many circumstances, the includible amount may be less than the entire trust principal. The amount includible is based on the annuity or unitrust amount and the Sec. 7520 discount rate at the time of the grantor's premature death. Presumably, the Sec. 7520 rate 6 months after the grantor's death can be used if the alternative valuation date is selected. In other words, the GRAT and GRUT could result in transfer tax savings even if the grantor does not survive the retained-interest term. Be aware, however, that the IRS has ruled privately that the full GRAT principal is includible in the gross estate of an annuitant who dies prior to the termination of a GRAT.

> *Planning point*: Because a major objective of a GRAT or GRUT is an estate freeze and the reduction of the grantor's estate, the more an asset is expected to appreciate after the transfer, the better it is as a trust investment. Securities and real estate are typically excellent assets to consider. Closely held corporate stock may be a less advisable investment because the GRAT or GRUT trustee would need to receive taxable dividends to make payments to the annuitant.

QUALIFIED PERSONAL RESIDENCE TRUSTS

qualified personal residence trust (QPRT)

A *qualified personal residence trust (QPRT)* is specifically excepted from the treatment of the anti-estate-freeze rules. By excepting the personal residence, Congress intended that a transfer of a personal residence to a trust can provide a retained interest to the grantor that is not limited to the GRAT or GRUT. The regulations on QPRTs make it clear that the Treasury intended to limit the corpus of these trusts to personal residences and other *de minimis* property.

For this purpose, a personal residence is either the principal residence of the term holder (within the meaning of Sec. 1034), one other residence of the term holder (within the meaning of Sec. 280A(d)(1)), or an undivided fractional interest in either.

In the typical QPRT, the grantor (usually a senior family member) retains the use of the home for a specified number of years. One or more remainder beneficiaries receive the personal residence at the termination of the trust. The longer the term of the grantor's retained interest in the QPRT, the lower the value of the gift to the remainderperson. To determine the value of the gift to the remainderperson, the value of the grantor's retained interest (as measured according to the Sec. 7520 valuation rules) is subtracted from the value of the residence placed in the trust. Thus, the gift tax value of the transfer is frozen at the present value of the remainder interest at the time of the transfer to the QPRT, since Sec. 2702 does not apply.

The personal residence is defined as the grantor's *principal* residence and a second home. The second home must be used for personal use by the grantor the greater of 14 days or 10 percent of the time the property is rented. Consequently, a vacation home that is both rented and used by the grantor can be used in the personal residence trust.

The QPRT may include a dwelling used as (1) the principal place of the taxpayer's business or (2) a place where the taxpayer sees customers, clients, and patients in the ordinary course of business. Thus, a personal residence trust could include a home with a qualified home office for income tax purposes as well as a vacation home rented part of the year.

A QPRT may also include appurtenant structures used for residential purposes and adjacent land not in excess of that which is reasonably appropriate for residential purposes (taking into account the residence's size and location). The personal residence subject to a mortgage can be contributed to a QPRT. However, the regulations will not permit corpus to include any personal property (for example, household furnishings). Therefore, the grantor continues to own household furnishings individually. To pay the essential expenses of the personal residence trust, the trustee may hold cash that is limited in the amounts and purposes for which it may be used. A taxpayer is limited to being a term holder in only two QPRTs at any point in time.

The regulations add some flexibility and permit the trustee to sell the residence held by the personal residence trust, but require that the trustee do one of the following or the gift tax advantages will be lost:

- Replace the residence with another qualifying residence within 2 years.
- Distribute the cash to the term holder.
- Convert the QPRT to a qualified grantor-retained annuity trust (GRAT).

The personal residence trust is a valuable transfer tax saving tool, but the trust must be drafted and administered with extreme care. The penalty for a drafting error is severe, because the full Sec. 7520 value of the grantor's retained interest will be treated as an additional gift at the time the IRS discovers the fact that the trust fails to qualify.

Gift Tax Consequences

The QPRT is irrevocable, and a completed gift of the remainder interest is made for tax purposes when the grantor establishes the trust. The value of the property for gift tax purposes is reduced by the present value of the retained-income interest. This is appropriate enough, although the grantor retains only the *use* of the corpus and not a right to cash payments. The taxable gift at the time of the establishment of the QPRT is merely the present value of the remainder interest. This taxable gift constitutes a future-interest gift that does not qualify for the gift tax annual exclusion. Frequently, the grantor will have his or her applicable credit amount available to shelter some or all of the transfer from gift tax.

The purpose of the QPRT is to reduce the overall transfer tax costs of passing the grantor's assets to his or her beneficiaries. Therefore, the key to the technique is establishing the highest value possible for the grantor's retained-income interest. This will result in a low present value for the remainder interest, and therefore the total amount subject to gift tax can be minimized.

Estate Tax Consequences

If the Grantor Survives the Retained-Interest Term

If the QPRT is properly designed, none of the property will be in the grantor's estate if the grantor survives the term period. If, however, the grantor survives the term of the retained interest and no trust property is included in the gross estate, the basis step up for the personal residence at the grantor's death is not available.

If the Grantor Dies during the Retained-Interest Term

The transfer tax savings available through the use of a QPRT are realized only if the grantor survives the term of the retained-income interest. You will recall that a transfer with a retained interest that does not end before the transferor's death is included in the gross estate under Sec. 2036(a). Therefore, the full value of the trust property, not just the value of the remaining term, will return to the grantor's estate if the grantor fails to survive the term. However, the applicable credit amount used on the original transfer, plus any gift tax actually paid, is allowed as a credit against the estate tax due. Furthermore, the benefit of the income tax basis step up is available because the assets are included in the gross estate.

Because the planning value of the QPRT is eliminated if the grantor does not survive the retained-interest term, it is advisable to select a term that the grantor is likely to survive. If the term of the QPRT must be kept short due to the health or age of the grantor, the value of the remainder interest increases, which in turn reduces the potential transfer tax savings of the technique.

However, from a federal tax viewpoint, the downside risk of attempting a QPRT is small, since it leaves the grantor's estate with no greater tax liability than it would have had if nothing had been done.

Income Tax Consequences

A QPRT is a grantor trust for income tax purposes during the retained-interest term. Therefore, the grantor bears all of the income tax consequences during the term of the trust. If there is income from the property (for example, if the home is rented during part of the year), the grantor is taxed on the income. If deductible expenses are incurred, the expenses are also passed through to the grantor.

Effect of a Mortgage

A mortgage on the property may create some complicated income and gift tax issues. For instance, the transfer of property with a mortgage greater than the transferor's adjusted basis usually triggers gain for income tax purposes. However, because the QPRT is a grantor trust, the gain is not recognized by the grantor until the retained-interest term ends. Furthermore, depending on who is responsible for the mortgage expenses under state law, if the grantor makes additions of cash to pay mortgage principal and interest, such additions could be treated as further gifts to the remainderpersons. This occurs when the remainderpersons-beneficiaries are responsible for the expenses but the grantor pays them. Tax counsel should be sought prior to gifting mortgaged property to a QPRT.

PLANNING WITH LIFE INSURANCE

Life insurance planning is an essential component of the estate planning process for wealthy individuals. For individuals of modest wealth, life insurance coverage may be the most significant asset they leave to their heirs.

Several unique aspects of life insurance make the product a vital asset in the estate planning process. For instance, some favorable tax rules apply only to life insurance; life insurance enjoys a significant appreciation in value upon the death of the insured; life insurance provides benefits when estate taxes and other settlement costs have to be paid and the income or other services of the insured must be replaced. Furthermore, life insurance products offer a substantial degree of flexibility in the estate planning process.

The goal of life insurance in the estate plan depends on many factors specific to the estate owner. Life insurance goals in general can be divided into two categories: estate enhancement and estate liquidity.

Clients generally have estate enhancement as the primary goal for their life insurance coverage because they are either too young or have otherwise failed to accumulate sufficient wealth to provide for their heirs. Life insurance is an excellent device to replace the financial loss created by premature death.

For older clients or clients with large estates, estate liquidity planning is the primary goal of life insurance coverage. If older estate owners have accumulated enough wealth and/or have an adequate retirement plan, the need for estate enhancement from life insurance is diminished in importance relative to their estate liquidity needs. For example, life insurance is appropriate for liquidity concerns when federal, state, and generation-skipping transfer taxes are significant and also when estates contain illiquid assets such as closely held businesses.

LIFE INSURANCE PRODUCTS

Today, there are many types of life insurance products. A general knowledge of the types of products is necessary to understand the uses of the products in the estate plan. Clearly, the services of a competent life underwriter are essential to the estate planning process because the selection of the most appropriate product in a particular estate planning case will maximize the efficiency of an entire financial plan. For the purposes of this course, the types of life insurance products are separated into single life policies and multiple life policies.

Single Life Coverage

Term Life

Term life insurance provides coverage for a finite period of time expressed as a number of years such as one, 5, or 10. The specified face amount of the policy will be paid to a designated beneficiary if the insured dies during that time period. If the insured survives the time period, the policy expires and the coverage terminates. If the coverage needs are longer than the specific term, a renewability provision may be considered. This provision allows the insured to renew without providing new evidence of insurability.

Conversion privileges that permit the insured to change a term policy for a permanent life policy without giving evidence of insurability are often included with term insurance policies. Term insurance is generally appropriate for estate planning uses only if the coverage need is temporary.

Permanent Life Insurance

Permanent insurance is coverage that is designed to exist for the entire life of an insured. A distinguishing characteristic of permanent insurance is the existence of a cash value or accumulation buildup within the policy. Permanent coverage can be designed either on a fixed-price premium or flexible-premium basis.

Simply stated, fixed-price premium life insurance, traditionally called whole life insurance, is life insurance coverage in which a constant guaranteed premium is paid for a specific face amount of coverage.

In flexible-premium life insurance policies (generally referred to as universal life policies), the insured pays a stipulated premium in the first year of coverage. Afterward, the policyowner may choose to pay whatever amount of annual premium he or she desires. Because flexible premiums provide for a cash-value accumulation similar to fixed-premium policies, the cash value will either grow or be expended to pay required annual policy charges after the first year. The policy's performance and the size of premiums the policyowner actually contributed after the first policy year will determine the growth (or shrinkage) of the cash value. The actual death benefit of a universal life policy is similarly flexible. The amount of the death benefit paid will depend on the actual premiums contributed by the insured and the policy options selected.

With variable life insurance, the policyowner has the ability to select the investment vehicle for the cash value of the policy. The investment risk for the cash value falls entirely on the policyowner. Both fixed-premium and flexible-premium variable life insurance products are available.

Multiple Life Policies

Survivorship Life Insurance

Survivorship life insurance (also called second-to-die or last-to-die insurance) is a permanent life insurance policy that provides coverage on the lives of two individuals. The death benefit under the survivorship policy is payable upon the death of the survivor of the two insureds. Survivorship life insurance is generally used to provide coverage for a married couple. It is popular because the estate tax rules allow an unlimited federal estate tax marital deduction at the first death of a married couple.

Survivorship life insurance coverage can be designed as fixed-premium or flexible-premium survivorship coverage.

Joint Life Insurance

Joint life insurance (also called first-to-die insurance) covers the joint lives of multiple insureds and provides its death benefit at the first death of the joint insureds. Joint life insurance is often used in buy-sell agreements in which the first death of two or more co-owners of the business will create the need to fund the purchase price required under the buy-sell agreement. The premium required for joint life coverage is attractive compared to the premiums for separate individual policies on each of the co-owners.

FEDERAL ESTATE TAXATION OF LIFE INSURANCE

Life insurance is often the single largest asset or group of assets in an individual's gross estate. The inclusion of life insurance can often mean the difference between a federal estate tax liability and no tax liability. There are three basic instances when life insurance is included in a decedent's gross estate:

- when it is payable to the insured's estate
- when the insured possessed incidents of ownership in the policy at the time of death
- when the insured transferred incidents of ownership by gift within 3 years of death

Proceeds Payable to Estate

Life insurance proceeds payable to the executor (that is, to or for the benefit of an insured's estate) are includible in the estate, regardless of who owned the contract or who paid the premiums. There are many reasons in addition to avoiding federal estate taxation why estate planners seldom recommend that life insurance be payable to a decedent's estate:

- Insurance payable to a decedent's estate subjects the proceeds to the claims of creditors.
- Insurance payable to a decedent's estate subjects the proceeds to costs of probate administration.
- Life insurance proceeds in many states, otherwise exempt from state death taxes (either fully or partially) if payable to a named beneficiary, become subject to such taxes if they are payable to the decedent-insured's estate.

In some instances, death benefits payable to named beneficiaries are included in an insured's gross estate if the proceeds can or must be used to pay settlement costs. The regulations under Sec. 2042 make it clear that proceeds payable to a named beneficiary (such as a trustee) are includible in the insured's gross estate if the beneficiary has a legal obligation to use the proceeds to pay the settlement costs for the estate. Failure to make an effective beneficiary designation could also cause the proceeds to be payable to the estate.

In addition to problems created by making life insurance payable to a decedent's estate, there are complications if life insurance is owned by a third party and made payable to a decedent's testamentary trust. Because a testamentary trust is created in a decedent's will and takes effect only at death, life insurance payable to a decedent's testamentary trust might be considered payable to his or her estate, depending on the trust law of the particular state. This could cause inclusion of the proceeds in the gross estate and might subject the proceeds to the expenses of probate and the claims of creditors. The result will vary from state to state.

Possession of Incidents of Ownership

A policy is also included in an insured's estate if he or she possessed an "incident of ownership" in the policy at the time of his or her death. When insurance proceeds are paid to a named beneficiary other than the insured's estate, incidents of ownership in the policy at the time of death are the key criteria for inclusion. An incident of ownership is broadly defined as any right to the economic benefits of the policy. The regulations provide that incidents of ownership include (but are not limited to) the power to

- change the beneficiary
- assign the policy
- borrow on the policy
- surrender the policy
- exercise any of the other essential contract rights or privileges

To remove life insurance proceeds from the reach of the federal estate tax, the insured must divest himself or herself of all significant rights and privileges under the contract.

Example:	Brenda, a widow, transferred ownership of three whole life insurance policies to her daughter, Sara, 6 years ago. However, it was clear at the time of the transfer that Brenda still had the right to borrow against the policies' cash values and the right to change the beneficiary by written notification to the insurance company. Although Brenda effectively transferred title in the policies to her daughter, the policies' proceeds will still be included in her gross estate for federal estate tax purposes because she retained the right to borrow against these policies and to change the beneficiary. To have successfully removed the proceeds from the gross estate, Brenda must not have reserved these rights.

It is clear that a directly held incident of ownership will cause inclusion, even if the incident is exercisable only with another's consent. However, planners must also be aware that inclusion may occur even if the insured is unaware that such incidents are held or is incapable of exercising the incidents. In other words, there have been instances when there are some hidden incidents of ownership that exist after it appears that the owner has effectively transferred all *traditional* ownership rights to a life insurance policy. For example, the Treasury regulations provide that incidents of ownership held by a corporation will, in some circumstances, be attributed to a majority shareholder.

Transfers within 3 Years of Death

In addition, under the unique rules of Sec. 2035, life insurance is included in the gross estate of an insured who transferred incidents of ownership in the policy by *gift* within 3 years of his or her death. Transfers made more than 3 years before the insured's death are not normally includible in the insured's estate, assuming the insured has retained no incidents of ownership.

Life Insurance and the Marital Deduction

Life insurance proceeds that are payable at the insured's death to the insured's surviving spouse can qualify for the federal estate tax marital deduction if the requirements for the deduction are met. Because the marital deduction is unlimited, the full value of life insurance proceeds payable in a qualifying manner to the surviving spouse is deductible from the insured's gross estate.

Qualification for the marital deduction, however, is more complicated if the surviving spouse does not receive the proceeds outright. For example, life insurance proceeds payable to a surviving spouse under available settlement options may or may not qualify for the marital deduction. Some settlement options terminate payment at the surviving spouse's death. If the remaining payments are not payable to the surviving spouse's estate or subject to the surviving spouse's control, the marital deduction will not be available unless the estate is eligible to make the QTIP election.

If the proceeds of a life insurance policy are payable to a trust that benefits the surviving spouse, the trust's remainder interest must be payable to the surviving spouse's estate or be subject to the surviving spouse's general power of appointment to qualify for the marital deduction. Without these provisions, the trust can qualify only if the decedent-spouse's executor makes the QTIP election.

Gross Estate Inclusion of Life Insurance

Policies on Life of Decedent

If a life insurance policy must be included in the decedent-insured's gross estate for federal estate tax purposes, the amount included is the *face amount* of the policy. The face amount is the death benefit adjusted by (1) deducting any policy loan or other encumbrance and (2) adding any accrued or terminal dividends. Such concepts as cash value, total premiums paid, or reserves in the policy are irrelevant in this context and have nothing to do with determining the amount included in the decedent-insured's gross estate.

Policies Owned by Decedent on Lives of Others

Under third-party ownership of life insurance, it is possible that a policyowner will die before the insured. In this case, the policy is included in the decedent's gross estate at its fair market value at the time of the decedent's death.

As stated in previous chapters, the fair market value of the unmatured life insurance policy at a given point in time depends on the type of coverage. If the policy is currently paid up, its value is equal to the sale price of the insurance company's comparable contracts, which is typically the single-premium cost of a similar policy on the life of a person at the insured's attained age. Sometimes a policy does not have a readily ascertainable value through the sale of a comparable contract. Generally, no ascertainable value is available when a contract has been in force for some time and still has future premium payments to be made. In this case, the value is equal to the policy's *interpolated terminal reserve* at the date of the decedent's death *plus* the proportionate part of the *unearned premium* (the amount of premium already paid covering the period after the policyowner's death).

Be aware, however, that if the alternate valuation date is used for purposes of valuing the policy in the decedent-policyowner's gross estate and if the insured dies within the 6-month alternate valuation period, there is inclusion of the full amount of the death proceeds in the decedent-policyowner's estate instead of just the fair market value of an unmatured life insurance policy.

Code Sec. 2206 stipulates that federal estate taxes attributable to life insurance proceeds included in the decedent's gross estate may be recovered by an executor from the beneficiary of the life insurance policy unless the decedent's will provides a contrary provision for tax apportionment.

Removal of Life Insurance from Insured's Gross Estate

There are two possible ways to remove life insurance from the insured's gross estate:

- *cross-ownership between spouses*—a criss-cross method wherein a husband owns the life insurance on his wife's life and the wife owns the life insurance on her husband's life
- *irrevocable life insurance trust*—a trust created for the express purpose of holding the life insurance policies involved

Cross-Ownership

Because of the incidents-of-ownership test, cross-ownership is a useful technique. If new life insurance is being acquired on one spouse's life, the other spouse should act as owner and applicant of the policy. If the spouse other than the insured spouse owns the policy from the outset, there is no transfer of life insurance and therefore no Sec. 2035 3-year-rule problem. If the insured already owns the policy, the ownership should be assigned to the spouse. This method also removes the death proceeds from the insured's gross estate, except that the transferor must live for more than 3 years after the assignment to avoid inclusion of the proceeds in his or her gross estate under Sec. 2035.

Although cross-ownership of life insurance is an effective way to defeat the incidents-of-ownership test, the arrangement is not without problems. First, if the spouses divorce, the life insurance arrangement will have to be restructured according to the specifics of the property settlement. If cross-ownership is not involved, the divorce settlement has one less element of complexity.

Another problem with cross-ownership is the unpredictability of the order of spouses' deaths. In the event that the spouse other than the insured predeceases the insured, the insurance will likely end up back in the insured's gross estate. Cross-ownership will have accomplished nothing.

In essence, even though cross ownership defeats the incidents-of-ownership situation, there are many potential problems with its use.

Irrevocable Life Insurance Trust

irrevocable life insurance trust (ILIT)

The *irrevocable life insurance trust (ILIT)* can be of particular benefit for estate planning purposes. The irrevocable life insurance trust can provide the following benefits:

- Gift taxes can be avoided for premiums contributed to the trust.
- Estate taxes can be avoided when the proceeds are received.
- Generation-skipping transfer taxes can be avoided if the insured's exemption is allocated to the trust.
- The insured's transferable wealth can be enhanced through leveraging.
- The expenses and publicity of probate can be avoided for transfers to the trust.

- Estate liquidity can be enhanced by the trust.
- The grantor-insured can control the disposition of the proceeds before the fact through the trust provisions.
- Income taxes can be avoided on the corpus buildup and receipt of proceeds.

Essentially, there are two rules that create problems for the purposes of the irrevocable life insurance trust. If these two problems are avoided, the life insurance trust will be able to provide for heirs or for the liquidity of the insured's estate without increasing the estate tax liability.

First, life insurance proceeds are included in the insured's gross estate if they are payable to the executor. Therefore, the grantor generally avoids directly naming his or her estate as beneficiary of the trust. The hidden trap is indirectly causing the trust to be deemed payable to the executor, which could occur if the trustee is directed to pay the expenses of the estate or merely given the discretion to pay the expenses of the estate. Because these trust provisions cause some, or all, of the proceeds to be included in the insured's gross estate, they should be avoided.

Trust provisions that can be used in the insurance trust to provide liquidity to the estate are discretionary powers to the trustee to lend trust funds to the insured's estate or to purchase assets from the estate. The loan or sale should follow normally acceptable commercial standards and be within the explicit powers of the fiduciaries involved. The purchase of assets should be for fair market value, and the loan should be secured and bear adequate interest. These provisions allow the cash proceeds held by the trustee to be transferred to the estate to increase estate liquidity without causing unnecessary additional estate taxes.

The second possibility for estate inclusion is the retention of any incidents of ownership by the insured with 3 years of death. Although this test sounds simple enough, it can be an additional trap for the unwary. First, the insured should possess no rights to the trust that would provide him or her with incidents of ownership in the corpus. The trust must be a truly irrevocable, no-strings-attached gift. Therefore, the insured is not able to change beneficiary designations on the policy or within the trust once the trust is executed, and he or she is not able to receive policy loan proceeds or use the trust as collateral for a loan.

Irrevocable Life Insurance Trust

- The trust must not have direct or indirect responsibility to pay the insured's estate expenses.
- The grantor must not have incidents of ownership within 3 years of death.

Assuming a trust is drafted to avoid attributed incidents of ownership to the insured, there are further concerns. First, the insured should avoid obtaining incidents of ownership in the policy prior to the gift to the trust. This may be unavoidable if an existing policy is used to fund the trust. In this case, the insured must live 3 years after the transfer of the policy to the trust, or Sec. 2035 brings the proceeds back into the estate. This transfer is often recommended regardless of the Sec. 2035 risk. Quite often, an older insured may use an existing policy to fund an irrevocable trust as estate tax concerns increase. The insured should do this when he or she is prepared to irrevocably name the beneficiaries of the trust and when it is economically impractical to purchase a new policy within the trust.

If a new policy is used to fund the trust, it would be a serious estate tax mistake for the insured to acquire incidents of ownership. In this case, the 3-year rule is a trap even if the intent is for the policy to be held in all events by an irrevocable trust. The insured should participate in the process only as trust grantor and insured. The insured should not sign as applicant or owner on the policy application. The trustee is the applicant and owner of the policy, and the trust should exist at the time of application.

If the trust is not in place and the application and underwriting process must be started, the child of the insured could be the applicant and owner. Then a transfer to an irrevocable trust can be made when the trust is drafted. If these steps are followed, current case law indicates that the insured does not hold incidents in the policy even if the insured actually makes all premium payments to the trust.

The ILIT can be designed to bypass both spouses' estates. The dispositive provisions should not give the surviving spouse any powers that will cause inclusion in his or her estate. For example, the surviving spouse should not have a general power over the corpus or have unlimited invasion powers. However, the surviving spouse could be given a life estate with limited invasion powers (that is, the 5-and-5 powers discussed in chapter 13). In addition, a discretionary invasion power in favor of the surviving spouse can be given to the trustee if the invasion is subject to ascertainable standards. A properly designed

---

Advanced Estate Planning Techniques

- installment sale
  - self-canceling installment note (SCIN)
- private annuity
- family trust
  - grantor-retained annuity trust (GRAT)
  - grantor-retained unitrust (GRUT)
- qualified personal residence trust (QPRT)
- irrevocable life insurance trust (ILIT)

trust can also be the owner of a second-to-die policy that covers the spouses, and the second-death benefits avoid inclusion in either spouse's estate.

As this discussion demonstrates, the ILIT might be the most advantageous estate preservation technique available under current tax law. However, the potential hazards discussed above indicate that the trust should be drafted and administered only with the advice of an attorney experienced in estate planning matters.

FEDERAL GIFT TAXATION OF LIFE INSURANCE

Gifts of life insurance are treated in the same way as gifts of any other asset as far as the $11,000 annual exclusion or the split-gift provisions are concerned. As stated in chapter 7, under the annual exclusion, $11,000 ($22,000 with gift splitting) of gifted value per year per donee may be excluded from the gift tax base when life insurance is gifted.

Often, a donor will continue to pay annual premiums even after an absolute transfer of the insurance has been made. Each premium paid subsequent to the policy transfer is considered a gift. As long as the transfer is outright to a donee, the gift of the policy is a present-interest gift and the $11,000 annual gift tax exclusion is applicable, not only to the gift of the policy itself but also to the gift of each premium payment as it is made. When gifts of life insurance policies are made in trust, however, the exclusion is forfeited unless the donee has an absolute and immediate power of withdrawal. With proper trust drafting, Crummey withdrawal powers are used to create a present interest for annual exclusion purposes.

Generation-Skipping Transfer Taxation of Life Insurance

Life insurance may also be subject to the federal generation-skipping transfer tax. If life insurance proceeds are payable directly to, or may someday benefit, skip persons, the proceeds might be subject to the GSTT.

Example: Grandmother makes a gift of a life insurance policy on her life to her grandson. The GSTT may apply to a gift of the policy to the grandchild.

The GSTT implications of life insurance trusts are more common and, in all probability, more difficult to avoid. The GSTT applies to trusts in two circumstances—taxable distributions and taxable terminations. A taxable distribution occurs if a distribution of trust income or principal is made to a skip (with respect to the grantor of the trust) beneficiary.

> *Example:*   Grandfather creates an irrevocable life insurance trust for the benefit of his children and grandchildren. At Grandfather's death, the trustee is directed to hold the proceeds and to distribute as much income and principal to the various beneficiaries as the trustee in its discretion determines. If the trustee makes a distribution to any of the grandchildren, a GST taxable distribution has occurred.

A taxable termination occurs when either (1) a trust terminates and all remainderpersons are skip persons or (2) all interests in the trust held by nonskip persons terminate.

> *Example:*   Suppose Grandfather in the above example had instead provided that the insurance proceeds would be held in trust for his children with all income payable annually to his children in equal shares. At the death of Grandfather's last child, when the trust terminates and the remainder is distributed to his surviving grandchildren in equal shares, a taxable termination occurs.

PRACTICAL USES FOR LIFE INSURANCE IN ESTATE PLANNING

There are many practical uses for life insurance in the estate planning context:

- estate enhancement (RLIT)
- estate liquidity (ILIT)
- grandparent-grandchild trusts
- equity of inheritance
- nonemployed spouse insurance

Revocable Life Insurance Trust

revocable life insurance trust (RLIT)

One useful estate planning device involves gifting a life insurance policy to a revocable trust. A *revocable life insurance trust (RLIT)* is advantageous because it can provide asset management and dispositive flexibility. Remember, however, that there are no tax benefits in using the revocable trust approach. For instance, the life insurance proceeds will be included in a decedent-grantor's gross estate for estate tax purposes because the grantor retained control over the policy within the trust until death. A revocable trust works extremely well in cases where estate tax planning is not the life insurance plan's primary concern. For example, a young couple with minor children might find a revocable trust to be helpful when the primary need for life insurance is estate enhancement. In this case, a revocable trust could be created to receive policy proceeds. At the death of the grantor-insured, the trust would become irrevocable and the trustee would then manage the proceeds for the surviving spouse, if necessary, and the minor children. If it is preferable for the surviving spouse to receive the proceeds outright, the revocable trust could be used as a secondary beneficiary to manage the proceeds for the minor children in the event of their parents' simultaneous death. In these circumstances, having the trust receive the proceeds avoids the need for a guardian of the minor's property to be appointed to manage the proceeds and the minor's other inherited property. The appointment of a guardian could cause delay and confusion. Moreover, the guardian might not have clear direction as to the disposition of the proceeds and other property for the minor's benefit.

Another common RLIT estate planning arrangement uses the RLIT in conjunction with the grantor's will that contains a pour-over provision. During lifetime the grantor creates a life insurance trust. The trust is named beneficiary of the policy(ies) on the grantor's life. At the grantor's death, the death proceeds are paid to the trust. In addition, the terms of the grantor's will require the residuary estate assets to be poured over into the life insurance trust (pour-over trust) when the grantor dies. Generally, the terms of the pour-over trust require it to be divided into two or three trusts: the marital trust (A trust), nonmarital trust (family, bypass, or B trust), and possibly, if the trust provides for three trusts, a QTIP trust (C or Q trust). In many instances, a funding formula in the pour-over trust for the marital and QTIP trusts results in the grantor's estate having no estate tax liability. The marital and QTIP trusts may receive assets from the pour-over trust in accordance with a funding formula that results in a zero estate tax for the grantor's estate. For some estate owners, the advantages of flexibility and control of an RLIT outweigh the disadvantage of inclusion of the life insurance in the gross estate.

Irrevocable Life Insurance Trust

As discussed earlier in this chapter, an irrevocable life insurance trust is often the best solution to an estate owner's liquidity problems. In fact, it is generally seen as the most beneficial and flexible estate planning technique currently available.

Grandparent-Grandchild Trust

One commonly used technique is for a grandparent to purchase insurance on the life of a child for the benefit of his or her grandchildren. When the grandchildren are minors, use of a trust rather than an outright gift is preferable. In a typical arrangement, the grandparent creates a funded irrevocable insurance trust with a trustee owning the policy on the child's life. The trustee also pays premiums and designates the trust as beneficiary. From a general estate planning perspective, this type of arrangement should

- provide some reduction of the grandparent's potential estate taxes
- reduce the amount of insurance the child must carry
- keep insurance proceeds out of the child's estate
- enhance the estate the grandchild will receive at his parent's death

Equity of Inheritance

There are many estate planning situations in which it is the estate owner's wish to equalize inheritances among children. A prime example is when an estate owner has brought some of his or her children into a family business and intends to give these children an ownership interest in the enterprise. The plan may be to pass the interest to these children either during his or her lifetime or after death. If there are other children in the family who have no contact with the business, however, the estate owner may wish to provide for them in some other way so that there is equality among the children. Life insurance in this context is appropriate.

Example:	Marcus is president and sole shareholder of Zipper-Do, Inc., a highly successful manufacturer of snag-proof zippers. He has three adult children—two sons and one daughter. The daughter and one of the sons would like to take over the business when Marcus retires. The other son, a musician, has no interest in this business
	Marcus arranges for the two employee-children to receive the business at his retirement or death and acquires life insurance on his life in an amount equal to the anticipated fair market value of Zipper-Do, Inc. Marcus pays the premiums, and the musician son is the designated beneficiary. Equity of inheritance has been achieved.

Nonemployed Spouse Insurance

There are many reasons why insuring a nonemployed spouse makes good estate planning sense. If the nonworking spouse is no longer living, someone must be paid for household and parenting services he or she previously rendered. Acquiring life insurance to offset those costs and losses could be an integral part of family estate planning. Another consideration is that if a nonworking spouse dies, a joint return for federal income tax purposes is no longer available to the survivor. The additional amount of income tax can be substantial over a period of years.

Gift taxes may also increase because the availability of the unlimited marital deduction and the ability to split a gift are lost.

For federal estate tax purposes, the death of the less wealthy non-employed spouse before the death of the working spouse can cause a considerable increase in the survivor's estate tax liability and a reduction in the net amount of property passing to children and other family members at the survivor's death as a result of the loss of the marital deduction. Although the marital deduction is available at the death of the first spouse, the deduction will not be significant if the deceased nonworking spouse has a relatively small estate.

Note: Regulation of insurance products and services varies from state to state. In Florida, for example, regulations prohibit doing business with an unauthorized insurance entity. An unauthorized entity is an insurance company that has not gained approval to place insurance in the jurisdiction where it or a producer wants to sell insurance. These carriers are unlicensed and prohibited from doing business in that state. In most cases where these carriers have operated, they have characterized themselves as one of several types that are exempt from state regulation. It is the financial planner's responsibility to exercise due diligence to make sure the carriers for whom they are selling are approved by the department of insurance in that state.

CHAPTER REVIEW

Answers to the review questions and the self-test questions start on page 717.

Key Terms

installment sale
self-canceling installment note
   (SCIN)
private annuity
grantor-retained annuity trust
   (GRAT)
grantor-retained unitrust (GRUT)

qualified personal residence trust
   (QPRT)
irrevocable life insurance trust
   (ILIT)
revocable life insurance
   trust (RLIT)

Review Questions

22-1.   Identify the advantages of an installment sale
   a.   from the standpoint of the seller
   b.   from the standpoint of the buyer

22-2.   Suppose a parent (P) would like to sell a rental property to a child (C) for $100,000 payable in five annual installments beginning one year after settlement. If P's basis in the property is $25,000, calculate how each installment will be treated for income tax purposes by P when paid.

22-3.   How can an installment sale be used as an estate-freezing technique?

22-4.   What is the gift tax treatment of an installment sale?

22-5.   Under what circumstances might a self-canceling installment note (SCIN) be useful for estate planning purposes?

22-6.   Explain why with a SCIN the buyer pays more than the fair market value for the property subject to the sale.

22-7.   What is a private annuity and how is it useful for estate planning purposes?

22-8.   What are the transfer tax implications if a private annuity is not properly valued?

22-9.   GRATs and GRUTs are retained trust interests having value that, in turn, reduces the gift tax cost of transferring a remainder interest in trust. What are the permissible payment forms for GRATs and GRUTs?

22-10.   In general, how are GRATs and GRUTs treated for gift and estate tax purposes?

22-11.   Explain the design and transfer tax considerations of a qualified personal residence trust.

22-12.   What type of property can be placed in a QPRT if a retained interest in such trust by the grantor will be valued at greater than zero for gift tax purposes?

22-13.   Explain the gift tax consequences when a grantor transfers a personal residence to an irrevocable trust and retains a term interest with the remainder to his or her children.

22-14.   Explain how gifts of life insurance made to a trust can qualify for the gift tax annual exclusion.

22-15.   What are two problems involving spousal cross-ownership of insurance?

22-16.   Identify the potential benefits of an irrevocable life insurance trust.

22-17.   How should an irrevocable life insurance trust be drafted to provide solutions to estate liquidity problems without the proceeds being deemed payable to the executor?

Self-Test Questions

T F 22-1. A sale of property will not qualify for installment-sale reporting unless the installments are paid over more than one taxable year and at least 30 percent of the purchase price is paid at the time of settlement.

T F 22-2. Once a sale of property qualifies for installment reporting for tax purposes, this installment reporting of the gain by the seller is mandatory.

T F 22-3. Generally speaking, the amount received by the seller annually in an installment sale will be treated as containing three separate components: return of basis, taxable gain, and taxable interest.

T F 22-4. The buyer and seller in an installment sale are generally free to negotiate the amount of interest payable for tax purposes on the amount of unpaid balance of sale proceeds.

T F 22-5. If installment-sale payments end before the seller's death, no value of the note is included in the seller's estate.

T F 22-6. A self-canceling installment note (SCIN) will be useful for estate planning purposes because the value of the note is not included in the seller's estate.

T F 22-7. A private annuity is a buyer's unsecured promise to pay a life annuity to a seller in exchange for property.

T F 22-8. GRATs or GRUTs are expressly revocable trusts to avoid current gift taxes.

T F 22-9. A GRAT will result in a successful estate freeze if the grantor survives the retained interest term.

T F 22-10. The annual gift tax exclusion will be useful in sheltering a portion of the transfers to a GRAT from gift taxes.

T F 22-11. The payments made by a GRAT or GRUT to a grantor during the grantor's retained-interest term are subject to income taxation to the grantor.

T F 22-12. A qualified personal residence trust (QPRT) generally should include all household furnishings if the trust is to provide favorable gift tax consequences.

T F 22-13. A qualified personal residence trust (QPRT) provides the grantor with substantial estate tax savings if the grantor fails to survive the retained-interest term.

T F 22-14. A grantor's transfer of property to a QPRT qualifies for the gift tax annual exclusion because the transfer constitutes a completed gift.

T F 22-15. A term life insurance policy with conversion privileges allows the insured to change the term policy into a permanent life policy.

T F 22-16. The irrevocable life insurance trust will provide a substantial estate tax savings if the trustee is directed to pay the estate tax liability of the insured.

T   F   22-17.   To avoid the 3-year rule of Sec. 2035, it is prudent to have the trust drafted and the trustee apply for the life insurance policy prior to any substantial involvement in the process by the insured.

T   F   22-18.   A revocable life insurance trust (RLIT) is often used to save estate taxes.

T   F   22-19.   Life insurance can be used by a business owner to equalize inheritances among heirs who are active and those who are inactive in the family business.

23

Postmortem, Health, and Special Groups Planning

Learning Objectives

An understanding of the material the previous chapters should enable the student to

---

23-1.　Describe the methods used for postmortem estate planning.

23-2.　Identify the documents used for health care planning.

23-3.　Explain how estate planning can be tailored to meet the special needs of certain people.

Chapter Outline

POSTMORTEM ESTATE PLANNING METHODS

While the term *estate planning* pertains to arrangements made during the estate owner's lifetime, planners must be aware that many of the methods and tax elections discussed previously are used for revising, adjusting, and fine-tuning an estate plan after the decedent's death. Some common postmortem practices are briefly discussed in the following summary.

Qualified Disclaimer

The disclaimer is a useful postmortem technique because it serves to rectify predeath planning mistakes and legal drafting errors. It allows a 9-month window of opportunity to redistribute a decedent's assets and influence tax consequences. When properly executed, the amount of property passing to one or more beneficiaries may be decreased in order to increase property passing to other beneficiaries. (See also chapters 6, 9, and 13.)

Although disclaimers are a part of the common law of most states, many states have specific statutes relating to their use. The purpose of the qualified disclaimer under Sec. 2518 is to provide uniform federal requirements aside from state law requirements. State statutes may impose other additional rules for disclaimers to be effective under state law.

Disclaimers may be used to refuse a power or interest in property that an individual receives by gift, will, or operation of law. The disclaimer is an excellent device for estate tax avoidance and estate planning because it can be used to rectify planning mistakes and legal drafting errors. The disclaimer provides a 9-month period to evaluate and correct uncertainties such as the sequence and time of deaths and estate valuation estimates. Because a disclaimed property interest passes to another person, the disclaimer can be used to redistribute property and readjust tax consequences. The amount of property passing to a named recipient can be decreased while property passing to another individual is correspondingly increased. Just because a disclaimant may not affirmatively direct to whom disclaimed property passes does not mean the disclaimant does not know or cannot determine the recipient of disclaimed property. In fact, disclaimers are usually used for the purpose of directing property to a specific recipient. For instance, a surviving spouse can disclaim unneeded marital-deduction property in order to use the full amount of the decedent-spouse's applicable credit amount.

Example 1:	Husband (H) died, leaving all of his assets, $2,800,000, to his wife (W). H's will states that if W predeceases him, the property is to pass equally to his three children. Although no estate tax is due at H's death (assuming that W survives H), due to the unlimited marital deduction, there is an overfunding of the marital-deduction transfer to W. W, who is in poor health, realizes that inflation and appreciation may increase the value of the property and cause un-necessary estate taxation at her death. W, there-fore, disclaims $1.5 million of property passing to her from H. The disclaimer results in a nontaxable transfer from H to the children because of H's available applicable credit amount (2004 and 2005). Ignoring expenses, appreciation, and depreciation, $555,800 of estate taxes on $1.5 million of property is saved as a result of W's disclaimer.
Example 2:	Jane and her two adult children are her Uncle Dan's sole surviving relatives. Jane knows that Uncle Dan is quite ill and that his will names her as beneficiary of his entire $1,200,000 estate and Jane's children as contingent beneficiaries. Jane has an estate of $1,325,000 in her own right. Jane plans to disclaim her inheritance after Uncle Dan dies and thereby make a nontaxable transfer to her children and avoid increasing the size of her own estate for estate tax purposes. In essence, Jane will be rewriting her uncle's will via the disclaimer

It is also possible for a life income beneficiary to disclaim property in order to accelerate the receipt of the property by the remainderperson.

Example: Several years ago, Kate's Uncle George executed a will in which he created a testamentary trust for the benefit of Kate and her sons, Ron and Don. At Uncle George's death, Kate was to become the life income beneficiary, and at Kate's death, the trust corpus was to pass to Kate's sons, Ron and Don. At the time of Uncle George's recent death, Kate made a qualified disclaimer of her life estate income interest. Kate's disclaimer accelerated the distribution of the remainder interests, causing the corpus to pass directly to Ron and Don.

Keep in mind that a disclaimer is not the same as a release. A release involves the relinquishment of a power or interest in property that has previously been accepted. A disclaimer, on the other hand, requires that the disclaimant must not expressly or by implication have accepted the disclaimed property interest or any benefits of the property interest. A disclaimant is not necessarily considered to have accepted property merely because title to the property vests in the disclaimant under state law at the time of the owner's death. However, if the disclaimant accepts rental income, interest income, or dividends from the property, the disclaimant is deemed to have accepted the property. Once the recipient of the property is deemed to have accepted the property, a transfer of the property to another constitutes a taxable gift.

One of the requirements of Sec. 2518 is that the disclaimer must be received by the transferor within 9 months after the date on which the transfer was made. For the disclaimant's protection it is advisable for the disclaimant to have some evidence of receipt and recognition of the disclaimer by the transferor or the executor of the transferor. Therefore, the disclaimer should include a form, signed and dated by the transferor, that the disclaimer was received.

Example: Receipt of disclaimer by (disclaimant's name) on (date)

(signature of transferor/executor)

The uses, benefits, and advantages of the disclaimer are quite numerous. The primary advantages are derived from the flexibility and freedom it provides clients. It is a relatively straightforward, uncomplicated estate planning and corrective device as long as legal requirements are properly met.

Current-Use/Special-Use Valuation for Real Estate of Closely Held Businesses and Farms

As discussed in chapter 10, if certain conditions are met, IRC Sec. 2032A allows the personal representative to elect that a farm and certain closely held business property included in a decedent's gross estate be valued for estate tax purposes at its current- or special-use value (limited to $850,000 in 2004, as indexed for inflation)* rather than at its highest and best-use value.

Extension of Time for Payment of Estate Tax on Closely Held Business Interests

Under IRC Sec. 6166 (see chapter 18), the personal representative may elect to defer the payment of estate tax attributable to the inclusion of a closely held business in a decedent's estate. If the closely held business comprises more than 35 percent of the decedent's adjusted gross estate and the estate otherwise qualifies, estate taxes may be paid over a 14-year period. This tax payment deferral allows the surviving business members to retain and continue operating the business instead of having to sell it to pay estate taxes.

IRC Section 303—Stock Redemption

This IRC section, discussed in chapter 18, allows an estate that contains stock to redeem a portion of or all of the stock for the purpose of paying funeral and administrative expenses and death taxes without the redemption's being treated as a dividend. This favorable tax treatment permits the estate to reduce its income tax liability.

Alternate Valuation Date

Another election available to the personal representative concerns the alternate valuation date. With this election, estate assets (with limited exceptions) can be valued 6 months after the decedent's date of death, providing the value of the assets on the later date is lower than the value on the date of death. By electing the alternate valuation date, the personal representative avoids paying higher estate taxes on estate assets that, overall, had a greater value at death than 6 months later.

The alternate valuation date is discussed earlier in this book (see chapters 9, 10, 12, and 13).

---

* This figure for 2005 had not yet been formally issued by the Treasury at the time of this writing. Consult our web site www.theamericancollege.edu for updated figures.

Marital Deduction Qualification of QTIP Trust Property

The QTIP election is also made by the personal representative on the decedent's federal estate tax return. This election allows certain terminable property interests to qualify for the marital deduction.

The property is placed in a special (QTIP) trust and, to the extent it is not consumed or given away during the surviving spouse's lifetime, it will be taxable in the estate of the surviving spouse. Although the property is included in the survivor spouse's gross estate, the property passes according to the terms of the trust. The QTIP election permits the deferral of estate taxes on certain otherwise nondeductible terminable property interests until the death of the surviving spouse.

Election by Surviving Spouse to Split Gifts

A postmortem election to split gifts made by the decedent spouse during his or her lifetime benefits the decedent's estate in three ways: a reduction in gift tax liability, a decrease in estate tax liability, and—because transfer taxes are lessened—a greater portion of estate assets (that is, the amount of gift and estate taxes saved) passed to the beneficiaries. (Gift splitting is discussed in chapter 7.)

Family Allowance

The family allowance, mentioned in chapter 8, is a small, limited sum of money set aside for the support of a surviving spouse and children during the time the estate is being administered. This property is not considered part of the distributable estate, is typically exempt from state death taxes, and may pass to the family whether or not it is needed.

Election against Decedent's Will by Surviving Spouse

According to state laws called *elective share statutes*, surviving spouses are entitled to receive a statutorily specified minimum percentage of their decedent spouse's estate. Generally, a surviving spouse with living children is entitled to about one-third of the decedent spouse's estate and, if there are no children, to one-half of the estate. If a decedent spouse's will leaves a surviving spouse less than the state's statutory amount, the survivor can file an election with the probate court to go against the will in order to receive the greater portion of the estate set out by statute. Making this election changes the decedent spouse's will because it results in a redistribution of his or her estate. The surviving spouse receives more than the will called for, and this in turn means other beneficiaries will receive less than under the will. (Chapter 8 discusses the spouse's right of election against the will.)

Deduction of Certain Administrative Expenses

As discussed in chapter 14, the expenses of administering certain property included in the decedent's gross estate are generally deductible from either the federal estate tax return, Form 706, or the estate's federal income tax return, Form 1041. The greater tax savings determines which form to use. Only certain administrative expenses may be deducted on each form, however. Administrative costs deductible on either Form 706 or Form 1041 include expenses incurred in the collection, distribution, and preservation of probate assets and in the payment of estate debts. Court costs, executor's commissions, attorney fees, accounting fees, the costs incurred on the sale of estate property, and the excise taxes included in these sales (if a sale was necessary for estate settlement) are deductible on either form.

Deduction of Medical Expenses

A decedent's personal administrator or surviving spouse may elect to deduct the decedent's unreimbursed medical expenses on the decedent's final income tax return (Form 1040) or on the federal estate tax return form (Form 706), depending on the greater overall tax savings. For instance, if the decedent's estate is less than the applicable exclusion amount (credit equivalent), the deduction would be lost, but if the expenses are taken on the income tax return, income taxes are saved. On the other hand, if the decedent's estate exceeds the exemption equivalent but there is no estate tax liability due to the applicable credit amount and marital deduction, deducting the medical expenses on the decedent's final income tax return again saves taxes. If there is federal estate tax liability, higher taxes may result from deducting medical expenses on Form 706.

Executor's Fees as Bequest or Income

An executor may find it tax-advantageous to waive the executor's fee. If an executor receives a fee for administering a decedent's estate, the fee is

Postmortem Devices

- disclaimer
- special-use valuation
- estate tax installment payments (Sec. 6166)
- Sec. 303 stock redemption
- alternate valuation date
- QTIP election
- gift splitting
- family allowance
- election against the will
- deductions on appropriate tax forms

deductible by the estate on the estate tax return (Form 706) or on the estate's income tax return (Form 1041); the fee, however, is taxable income to the executor. Executors who are also beneficiaries of the decedent's estate may wish to waive the fee. When the fee is waived, the estate is precluded from deducting that particular expense and the estate is thereby increased. More tax may be saved by the executor's receiving the fee income tax free as a bequest than by characterizing the executor's commission as a deductible expense of the estate. (See also chapter 14.)

POWERS OF ATTORNEY

Types of Powers of Attorney

There are three basic types of powers of attorney:

durable power of attorney

- A *durable power of attorney* can be a valuable estate planning tool. It enables a principal to grant powers that remain in effect throughout the principal's incapacity.

special (limited) power of attorney

- A *special (limited) power of attorney* enables the attorney-in-fact to act only with regard to one or more specific tasks or for a specified period of time.

springing durable power of attorney

- A *springing durable power of attorney* becomes operative only when a specified event occurs. The event is usually physical or mental incompetency or disappearance. A springing power of attorney is a solution for individuals reluctant to grant broad powers to another person while they are still capable of making decisions. It is important that the event triggering the power be carefully defined in the document. Most states recognize a springing power of attorney.

Of the three types, the durable power of attorney is the most useful for retirement and estate planning purposes. Therefore, the remainder of this section takes a closer look at some financial aspects of a durable power of attorney. (See Appendix B for a sample durable power of attorney.)

Advantages of a Durable Power of Attorney

There are many advantages to having a durable power of attorney. First, proper execution of this document can help to avoid the costs, delays, and emotional upsets of competency proceedings. Second, a court-appointed conservator or guardian may not be a person the principal would have chosen. Third, the activities transacted by an attorney-in-fact are private. In contrast, court supervision of a conservator's or guardian's actions on behalf of an incompetent involves records open to public scrutiny. A power of attorney can be advantageous in community-property states if one spouse becomes disabled and both spouses' signatures are necessary for community-property transactions.

Executing a power of attorney is relatively inexpensive and not time consuming due to the simplicity and availability of standard forms. Furthermore, a competent principal may revoke the instrument at any time. Assets do not have to be retitled or transferred. In most cases, it is not necessary to file or record a power of attorney with any governmental authority, although some states require recordation and other formalities for real estate transactions.

Estate Planning and Retirement Considerations. A durable power of attorney presents numerous retirement and estate planning possibilities. Retirement considerations include an agent's authority to exercise options under the principal's retirement plans (in this context the attorney-in-fact is referred to as an agent of the principal). Powers to be considered include powers to change beneficiary designations, elect payout options, satisfy spousal waiver requirements, and borrow from the plan.

Estate planning-type powers in a durable power of attorney can provide numerous transfer-tax benefits. For example, if there is authority to make gifts, an agent can use the federal annual gift tax exclusion (Sec. 2503(b)) to reduce the principal's gross estate by commencing or continuing a gifting program.

Example:	X, the father of five adult children, unexpectedly becomes incapacitated on December 18th. The doctors believe X's death is imminent. If X has executed a durable power of attorney specifically granting the authority to make gifts on X's behalf (and assuming no previous gifts from X to his children that year), X's agent could remove $55,000 of property from X's estate by the end of that year and another $55,000 at the beginning of the next calendar year, providing X survives until then. With gift splitting and additional gifts to the children's spouses, grandchildren, and other relatives, it is possible for the attorney-in-fact to remove a substantial amount of property from X's gross estate completely free of transfer taxes.

Making gifts of appreciating property will help to avoid additional estate taxes generated by appreciation. (Note, however, that gifts of appreciating property carry over the donor-principal's adjusted basis for income tax purposes as opposed to receiving a step up in basis if held until the donor's death and included in the donor's gross estate.) With gifting authority an agent can make tax-free gifts to the principal's spouse under the unlimited gift tax marital deduction to save gift and estate taxes. For example, an attorney-in-fact can transfer assets from a wealthy spouse to a less wealthy spouse to fully utilize the applicable credit amounts in both estates. In larger marital estates, tax savings may also be achieved if estates are equalized to take advantage of lower estate tax rates in each estate. In addition, by gifting the proper type of assets, it may be possible for an estate to meet the mathematical tests required for a Sec. 303 stock redemption, a Sec. 6166 installment payout of taxes, and Sec. 2032A special-use valuation for a farm and certain real property used in a closely held business.

Advantages of Power of Attorney

- principal's alter ego
- privacy
- flexibility
- inexpensiveness
- simplicity
- acceptance over living will
- viability despite disability
- avoidance of incompetency proceedings
- estate planning tool

Litigation concerning powers of attorney and gifting issues, however, emphasizes the importance of an express authorization of the agent's power to make gifts on behalf of the principal, including any limitations on the group of potential recipients and amounts to be gifted. The IRS will not infer the power to make gifts from a broad grant of authority to an agent. When the agent is both a relative *and* a potential gift beneficiary, it is advisable to include a provision permitting gifts to relatives, including the agent. For the agent's protection from a possible claim by the IRS that the agent holds a general power of appointment, the agent's power to make such gifts can be limited. For instance, the agent's ability to make self-gifts can be limited to an ascertainable standard, noncumulative lapsing amounts not to exceed the gift tax annual exclusion amount, or the greater of $5,000 or 5 percent of the principal's estate value. Another limitation could be the requirement of consent by an adverse party.

Another important estate planning consideration that a durable power of attorney may address is the agent's having authority to make disclaimers on behalf of a principal and having asset management powers that enable the agent to qualify a principal for Medicaid assistance.

HEALTH PLANNING

Advance Medical Directives

advance medical directive

It is always prudent for estate owners, prior to advanced age, to have arrangements in place for health care decision making. Fundamental to the decision-making system is a statement declaring the owner's intent for the medical treatment he or she wants should incapacity arise. Durable powers of attorney for health care and living wills are referred to as *advance medical directives*. Although a relatively small percentage of the American public currently have some type of advance medical directive, these documents are receiving more attention due to new legislation, court decisions, practical experience, and a growing recognition that *health* planning is as important as *wealth* planning. Advances in medical technology that prolong life have increased fears of lengthy artificial life support and family financial disaster. Modern medicine can keep a person alive by artificial mechanisms even though the individual is unconscious and essentially nonfunctional. Life-sustaining procedures are used in cases of accident or terminal illness where death is imminent and recovery highly improbable. Advance medical directives have evolved in response to these situations. By executing an advance medical directive such as a living will and/or a durable power of attorney for health care (medical power of attorney), individuals may make arrangements and give authority to others to carry out their health care instructions. (Samples of these documents are included in the appendixes.)

Living Wills

living will

A few decades ago living wills were virtually nonexistent, and by 1984 only a few states had enacted living will legislation. Practically all states now have statutes concerning the issues surrounding living wills. A *living will* addresses the inherent conflict of an individual's right to privacy and self-determination versus the medical oath to preserve life whenever possible. They apply to situations where the patient is terminally incapacitated or permanently unconscious and are limited to decisions concerning artificial life-support issues. Living wills have become the subject of public attention in recent years due to increased concerns about health and financial matters and the media coverage of certain right-to-die cases such as the *Cruzan v Director* case in Missouri and the physician-guided suicide cases in Michigan.

State statutes, while similar, contain variations. One common requirement is a statement by one or more physicians that the declarant's death is, indeed, imminent. Individuals who execute living wills make a decision not to prolong the dying process, which may involve pain, suffering, and financial disaster for them and their families if recovery or life as they know it is no longer possible.

An area in which state statutes vary concerns the definition of a terminal condition that will result in death.

There are many serious questions regarding the legal effect of living wills. It is important that state law be carefully examined. Actions taken by a state legislature could determine whether physicians and other health care personnel will follow living will directives. The potential civil or criminal liability of physicians and licensed health personnel who act in accordance with living will directives is an important legal issue involving the right to die. Most state statutes, however, grant immunity to medical providers acting in accordance with a patient's living will. Clearly, the law is still evolving in this area.

Advance medical directives also present moral considerations. Because the most fundamental mandate of a physician is to preserve life, a physician may consider that being party to a directive not to provide life support is contrary to medical training and principles. Also, persons executing or carrying out living wills may encounter personal obstacles of a religious or moral nature. In any event, concerns about the financial and emotional costs of artificially sustaining life are likely to result in an increasing number of individuals creating living wills in the future.

Living Wills versus Powers of Attorney

Living Wills	Powers of Attorney
• patient and physician only	• third-party agent necessary
• limited breadth and flexibility	• can cover broad spectrum of matters
• terminal condition necessary	• effective upon mere incompetency

Having Both Is Best

Medical Durable Powers of Attorney/Proxies

It is also advisable for estate owners to have a document appointing someone to act on their behalf with respect to personal medically related decisions—the idea being that the individual, while healthy and fully competent, expressed in writing (and ideally also verbally) his or her medical wishes and named someone to have the wishes carried out. This instrument is called a *health care proxy* or medical power of attorney. This document legally grants an agent, usually a close family member, the authority to act for the declarant and in the declarant's best interests in a medical context. The ideal situation is for the declarant to have expressed his or her wishes to numerous close family members at one or more times during the progression of family life.

health care proxy

At the present time, medical durable powers of attorney and health care proxies are statutorily authorized in all states. While the financial management advantages of a durable power of attorney have long been recognized, its use with respect to health and medical care is more recent. Because a durable power of attorney for health care covers a broad range of health care decisions, it may be an alternative or a supplement to a living will. A medical power of attorney, unlike a living will, may provide direction in nonterminal medical situations concerning such issues as access to and disclosure of medical records and personal information; anatomical gifts; psychiatric care; releases of medical personnel; hiring and discharging household, medical, and companion help; and life support provisions pertaining to mechanical respiration, cardiac resuscitation, organ transplants, blood transfusions, and withholding and withdrawing artificial nutrition and hydration. (Note, however, that the agent will be able to withhold or withdraw life support only when the principal's condition is terminal or death is imminent.)

If a patient has created an advance medical directive, such as a medical durable power of attorney, the individual acting on behalf of the patient is referred to as an agent, as mentioned above. If, however, the patient does not have an advance medical directive and has therefore not chosen an agent, the patient's family may choose a proxy to make medical treatment decisions for the patient. The proxy is someone who knows the patient well and knows what the patient's medical wishes are.

Today, there is federal legislation intended to encourage individuals to think about health care choices. As part of the Omnibus Budget Reconciliation Act of 1990, The Patient Self-Determination Act became effective in December 1991. The Act requires hospitals, nursing homes, health maintenance organizations, hospices, and home health care companies participating in Medicare or Medicaid to tell patients whether their state permits them to refuse life-prolonging treatment. Health service providers are required to note in the patient's medical file the patient's wishes to reject life support.

The Health Insurance Portability and Accountability Act (HIPAA) of 1996 and the regulations to this federal act became effective in April 2003. The regulations contain provisions on how health care information must be kept confidential and the circumstances under which individuals' health care information may be disclosed. Estate planners and estate attorneys drafting durable medical powers of attorney and advance medical directives must make certain the documents comply with the HIPAA privacy regulations to ensure the acceptance and effect of these documents. Previously existing powers of attorney and advance medical directives should also be reviewed for compliance and potential corresponding changes in state law with respect to HIPAA.

CPR/DNR

CPR/DNR Directives

Cardiopulmonary resuscitation (CPR) is an emergency procedure that occurs when an individual's heart stops beating or when an individual ceases to breathe. In attempts to restart the heart or respiration, CPR typically involves compressing the patient's chest and using mouth-to-mouth resuscitation. In this emergency process, it is possible the patient's ribs may be broken and/or a tube may need to be inserted into the patient's neck to locate an air passageway. CPR directives are documents permitting an individual to refuse cardiopulmonary resuscitation

A do-not-resuscitate (DNR) declaration is a type of CPR directive that exists in a hospital or nursing home setting. A DNR order is one in which either the patient or his or her agent limits resuscitative measures when and if the patient's heart and/or lungs no longer function. There are also statutes in some states that permit a CPR directive outside a hospital or nursing home setting. The purpose of this type of CPR directive is to limit paramedics or other rescue personnel in resuscitation efforts concerning the principal's heart or lungs in a home setting. Sometimes the subject of a nonhospital/nonnursing home CPR directive wears a necklace or bracelet stating, "No CPR." When an individual not in a hospital, nursing home, or hospice has a CPR directive, it is because the person is in a very advanced stage of illness. A DNR or CPR directive does not prevent other necessary medical procedures or limit pain control measures.

Five Wishes

Five Wishes

Another type of advance medical directive is called *Five Wishes*. This document is easy to understand and is often used to introduce conversations about the uncomfortable subject of terminal illness and dying. Five Wishes is a directive that has been recognized by the majority of states and a growing number of medical care providers and institutions. Physicians in states of acceptance will honor the Five Wishes form. It was created by known experts in the care of the terminally ill and the Commission on the Legal Problems of the Elderly of the American Bar Association. The intention of Five Wishes is to give seriously ill people a way to express their end-of-life wishes and to provide guidance for loved ones, care providers, friends, and clergy. Completion of the Five Wishes form helps to achieve emotional and psychological comfort to all concerned. The areas covered by the Five Wishes form are

- choice of health care agent
- medical treatment desired or not wanted
- care and comfort wishes
- personal treatment
- wishes for loved ones to know, including funeral and disposal of the body

Once this revocable, changeable form is signed and witnessed, it is a valid legal document in those states recognizing it. Executing Five Wishes revokes a previously executed advance medical directive or living will that the declarant may have had. Ideally, discussions on each of the five wishes have preceded its execution. Like any document of this nature, the form should be kept in a safe place in the person's home. Copies should be given to family members and other people who care about the declarant.

ESTATE PLANNING FOR THE ELDERLY AND INCAPACITATED

Another area of estate planning that deserves special attention is planning for elderly and incapacitated individuals. Although the proper emphasis of an estate plan might seem to be the distribution of property to the estate owner's heirs with the least tax liability, often the preservation of assets during lifetime is of far greater importance to the client than after-death issues. Preparing for the future financial and long-term care needs of the elderly, ill, and incapacitated presents some estate planning challenges. For instance, an estate plan that is oriented primarily toward passing property to the next generation becomes irrelevant if the estate is practically depleted by the cost of long-term care. On the other hand, retention of assets can prevent an estate owner from meeting Medicaid eligibility requirements. A comprehensive estate plan must address the implications of the client's potential need for long-term care.

One possible solution to achieving estate asset preservation goals and meeting long-term care needs is long-term care insurance (LTCI). For the owners of large estates, money expended to pay LTCI premiums escapes estate taxation. While it is established that long-term care costs may be deductible from the gross estate, there is no assurance that, without LTCI, lengthy long-term care will not exhaust or greatly diminish the assets in an estate.

Retaining Control with Trusts and Durable Powers of Attorney

Trust arrangements and durable powers of attorney are two devices that allow a client to have continued asset management despite incompetency. The trustee manages the trust property in accordance with the settlor's directions as established in the trust terms. For example, the settlor can grant the trustee the power to distribute income or principal at regular, preestablished intervals or at the trustee's discretion should the settlor later become incapacitated. Keep in mind, however, that trusts are used specifically for asset management; trustees cannot make personal health care decisions for an incompetent.

Durable powers of attorney can provide guidance for the personal care and financial decisions resulting from a client's incapacity.

**elder law durable
power of attorney**

Elder Law Durable Powers of Attorney

In many instances, financial advisers and estate planners recommend that individuals have a financial plan in place in the event of later incompetency. A durable power of attorney may be a valuable addition to an estate owner's financial plans, especially in later years of life. There are some unique qualities that may pertain to a durable power of attorney for an elderly person—qualities and requirements to which an elder law attorney must be especially sensitive. Powers of attorney that are specifically for elderly clients are called elder law durable powers of attorney. Many of the reasons for such specificity involve the capacity of the elder client. Perhaps what drives an elderly client to execute a durable power of attorney is that the principal is aware of the beginning or intermediate signs of one or more forms of impairment and therefore anticipates greater disability as time passes. Given the appropriate powers, the attorney-in-fact may expedite the principal's Medicaid eligibility, arrange for in-home or nursing home care, hire necessary health care personnel, employ companions, and so forth.

If the elderly client seeking the power of attorney displays signs of incompetency or the drafter has reservations about the client's mental capacity, the elder law attorney's choices are more limited. One solution may be to, with the client's consent, get a written opinion about the client's competency from the client's doctor(s), family, and/or other close acquaintances before proceeding to draft the document. If this fails, the attorney will have to work within the framework of prior instruments and arrangements. The choice of the most appropriate agent(s) for elderly individuals is crucial. Protection from financial and personal abuse is paramount. In many cases, it is recommended that more than one agent be appointed with the requirement that one must approve the other's decisions or that the agents must be in agreement before decisions are made. Because the elderly client's children and/or spouse are often the agents under the power, having more than one caring family member has obvious built-in safeguards. On the other hand, having multiple agents (co-agents/co-attorneys-in-fact) may be cumbersome and result in more difficulty in reaching an agreement. If a spouse or other close family member is not particularly financially minded, a workable solution may be to appoint an independent financial agent along with one or more close family members as co-agents to achieve financial acumen balanced with personal knowledge. Careful drafting is, of course, necessary because a document with multiple agents should contain provisions for dispute resolution, hierarchy in decision making, and so forth. The issues that may be addressed in elder law durable powers of attorney are practically infinite, depending on the principal's particular circumstances. As an example, an important and common issue to resolve before a durable power of attorney becomes effective is whether the elderly principal wishes to remain in his or her home with caregivers during the remaining years of life. Clearly, elder law durable powers of attorney must be drafted with extreme care.

Sometimes a client resists executing a durable power of attorney because of the perception that it is an admission of the inability to manage his or her own affairs. In such a situation, a springing power of attorney may be advisable. Because a springing power of attorney does not become operative until the time of the principal's incapacity, what constitutes incapacity for the particular principal should be carefully delineated in the document.

The combination of a trust and durable power of attorney allows the creator to indirectly maintain control of personal and financial matters when physical or mental limitations prevent one from managing matters directly. An elderly client can retain personal dignity. A trust and durable power of attorney drafted with incapacity provisions may serve to avoid conservatorship or guardianship proceedings. Compared to a trust or durable power of attorney, these two court-supervised alternatives are expensive and time consuming, and they may undermine a person's self-esteem. Executing a trust or durable power of attorney, however, does not guarantee that the client will be completely protected from the appointment of a conservator or guardian. No matter how carefully the instruments are drafted, it is possible for court proceedings to result from a challenge to the estate owner's trust or durable power of attorney. For example, a disgruntled heir may claim that the client lacked capacity or was unfairly influenced by another at the time the document was executed and may seek to have it set aside.

Guardianship and Conservatorship

Judicial guardianship and conservatorship are more complicated, time-consuming, costly, and restrictive solutions to incompetency compared to the relatively simple agency relationship created by a durable power of attorney. A power of attorney reflects a voluntary, consensual agreement in which an individual (the principal) arranges for an agent (the attorney-in-fact) or named guardian to attend to the principal's personal care and property if the principal becomes incapacitated. Although one agent may be named to care for the principal, usually a relative or trusted friend becomes responsible for the care of the person while a bank or other entity oversees the property. In the absence of a durable power of attorney, a court proceeding may be held to establish incompetency to manage one's affairs. After hearing evidence of incompetency, a court may appoint a guardian or conservator to act on behalf of the disabled party, called a *ward*. The process is generally an unpleasant one that, in the end, results in substantial loss of a ward's liberties. In some cases, the term *guardian* pertains specifically to care of the person and the term *conservator* to management of the property. Sometimes these terms are used interchangeably. The scope of the court-appointed guardian's powers to act for the ward may be broad or limited. Usually, however, the guardian has responsibility for the ward personally and the ward's property. It is the court supervision of the guardianship relationship that proves costly, time-consuming, and trying.

In addition to a durable power of attorney, other methods used to avoid judicial guardianship include joint ownership of property, advance medical directives, and trusts. When property is titled in more than one name, another party is already in place to manage the property, bank accounts, and so forth. As previously discussed, advance medical directives and living wills provide for health decision making prior to disability.

Guardianship may also be circumvented with trusts. A primary benefit of a revocable living trust is that the trustee manages the trust property according to trust terms stated by the grantor. The trustee continues to administer the assets during the grantor's incapacity. Another type of trust used in planning for incompetency is a *standby trust*. A standby trust often works in tandem with a durable or springing power of attorney. The trust is unfunded until such time as the grantor becomes incapacitated and an attorney-in-fact funds the trust with assets of the grantor for the trustee to manage.

The planner should take reasonable precautions to determine that the client is competent at the time documents are executed. To ascertain an elderly client's mental competency, the planner should establish that the client has knowledge of his or her property, recognizes the purposes of meeting with the planner with regard to the property, and understands the arrangements to be undertaken. Documentation supporting the client's apparent capacity can be placed in the client's file. Trusts and medical durable powers of attorney provide the estate planner and the estate owner with a broad scope of permissible powers and the necessary flexibility to fashion incapacity contingency plans.

Considerations Concerning Medical Assistance Programs

Another planning consideration is the possibility that the elderly client will inherit money or property from a family member's estate or receive death proceeds as the named beneficiary of a decedent's insurance policy. Since there is limited time to deal with the consequences of an unexpected increase in an elderly person's estate, such funds may cause greater estate tax liability than anticipated. In addition, if the recipient of the proceeds or inheritance is a Medicaid applicant, the property would be considered a Medicaid-available resource. Medicaid is a federal program that may help with payments for long-term care. States obtain financial assistance from the federal government by administering their medical assistance programs in accordance with federal Medicaid rules. Note that there are ethical issues related to planning for eligibility for Medicaid.

Medicaid has sometimes been described as a welfare health care program. If an applicant or the spouse of an applicant is determined to have sufficient wealth to pay for health care, Medicaid will not pay for it. To be eligible for

Medicaid benefits an applicant must be in relative poverty as determined under the Medicaid rules. Following changes in the Medicaid laws after the enactment of the Omnibus Budget Reconciliation Act of 1993 (OBRA '93), applicants may be denied Medicaid benefits if they or their spouses (1) have access to income in excess of a state's established maximum amounts, (2) have available assets in excess of permissible state-determined amounts, or (3) have made transfers of assets to other individuals within either 36 months or 60 months (depending on the nature of the particular transfer) prior to the date of application for benefits. (OBRA '93, 13611 and 13612, Pub. L.No. 103–66, 107 Stat. 312, 622–629 (August 10, 1993)).

Older persons who make lifetime gifts to reduce their taxable estates based on estate planning advice may delay eligibility for Medicaid assistance if the gifts occur within either a 36- or 60-month look-back period. If a client does not make gratuitous transfers within the appropriate time period before applying for Medicaid, transfers prior to that period will not cause disqualification. A properly drafted supplemental trust, also called a Craven trust, may be used, however, to provide supplemental maintenance for a nongrantor beneficiary without triggering the beneficiary's loss of governmental assistance benefits. Note also that an applicant's disclaimer of unexpected inheritance or insurance death proceeds to avoid being disqualified for Medicaid eligibility is likely to be unsuccessful because the particular state may consider the disclaimer to be a transfer for Medicaid eligibility purposes.

Due to the complexities and recent changes in the Medicaid laws, the prudent estate planner should be well versed in Medicaid eligibility planning and other considerations specific to elderly or incapacitated clients.

ESTATE PLANNING FOR MARRIED COUPLES

Estate planners may have to take special considerations into account when planning for married couples. In certain areas, U.S. law favors married status and treats a married couple as a single unit (for example, the unlimited marital gift and estate tax deduction and joint income tax returns), but a planner should be aware that the interests of a husband and wife may not be identical and may even be conflicting. Thus, one planner may not be able to fairly address the needs of both parties. In other words, just because a married couple seeks joint representation, the planner should not automatically conclude that the parties share identical objectives. Spousal estate planning and property disposition goals may be especially divergent and complicated when one or both have children from earlier marriages. Other areas of potential conflict may be the existence of one or both spouses' community property, the subjection of marital or separate property to the claims of one spouse's creditors, reciprocal wills, the tax consequences of gift splitting, and the control or lack of control a surviving spouse will have over property after the first spouse's death.

Clearly, an estate planner for a couple must ascertain whether the interests of both spouses are the same or adverse. If both spouses are in agreement and appear to be comfortable using the same planner, joint representation of both parties should not be an ethical or practical problem. However, if there seems to be marital conflict, the planner should recommend that each spouse seek separate estate planning advice. When a married couple with differing estate planning goals still want joint advice, all existing and potential conflicts should be disclosed, and the estate planner should obtain a written waiver or agreement from both parties concerning their joint representation for the planner's and the clients' protection. The agreement can establish some ground rules concerning the disclosure policy of each party's plan, documents, and joint and separate meetings. Addressing areas of potential conflict at the outset reduces the likelihood of problems for all parties. In keeping with current ethical concerns, some states require planners to send married couples a detailed joint representation letter outlining potential conflicts and to obtain the signatures of both parties before providing joint estate planning representation.

Separation and Divorce

Estate considerations also arise if spouses separate and divorce. In this situation, it is advisable, if possible, for each spouse to have an attorney or other professional adviser review the estate plans of both persons. This allows both individuals to plan more effectively for the benefit of any children from the union. Both former spouses should also execute new wills, even if their intentions upon death remain the same.

Frequently, an irrevocable life insurance trust is used in divorce situations to provide for a surviving spouse and children. Often a trust is set up and the trustee purchases a policy on the life of the wealthier spouse, naming the surviving former spouse or children as beneficiaries. This arrangement can provide for the surviving beneficiaries' financial needs and, as long as the decedent former spouse did not hold any incidents of ownership in the policy or name the estate as beneficiary, the life insurance proceeds avoid inclusion in the insured-decedent's estate.

For gift tax purposes, divorcing spouses who enter into a written agreement addressing their marital and property rights may transfer marital or property rights to each other pursuant to the agreement free of federal gift taxation. Transfers of property between divorcing spouses that are incident to the divorce are not subject to federal gift taxation because the transfers and giving up of marital rights are treated as being made for full and adequate consideration in money or money's worth. The divorce, however, must occur with a 3-year period (starting one year before the agreement is entered into) for the transfer to avoid gift tax.

ESTATE PLANNING FOR SINGLES

Eleven percent of adult women are widows. Widows, widowers, single parents, and confirmed singles over the age of 35 comprise almost 30 percent of the U.S. population, according to the Census Bureau. This group is reported to hold approximately the same percentage of the country's wealth. Estate planning for singles may present some unique, nonroutine planning situations that do not typically arise with married clients. There are often different psychological factors for single and married clients. For instance, some single clients, if they feel alone and vulnerable, may be less trusting. Therefore, more effort on the planner's part may be required to build rapport and establish trust. Single parents may be very dependent on child support payments to supplement income. Widows and widowers may be trying to live on monthly Social Security checks and small pension payments.

It is not uncommon for widows and widowers to need to know or feel that they can act independently. Many fear becoming dependent on their children and other family members. They want to be able to take care of themselves for as long as possible. Older singles may gain a sense of independence, security, and confidence by knowing they have any or all of the following: certain investments, a living trust to manage their affairs if they become disabled, a durable power of attorney, a living will, an emergency or funeral fund, disability insurance, and long-term care insurance. A consolidated written list of accounts and their values can also provide a source of comfort to singles.

The estate planner needs to recognize when planning for singles that their estate planning objectives and needs are likely to be somewhat different from the goals of married couples and two-parent family households. He or she must plan differently for single clients who are financially responsible for minor children than for those clients with adult children who are attempting to manage the parent's finances or whose family members are asking for loans. The individual who is left financially strapped as a result of becoming single has dissimilar concerns from the widow or widower who inherited substantial assets but is overwhelmed by the responsibility and complexity of the inheritance. Although planning for singles has some aspects in common (such as the loss of the marital deduction and gift splitting), the adviser must approach and analyze each situation individually and not according to a group stereotype.

ESTATE PLANNING INVOLVING NONTRADITIONAL LIVING ARRANGEMENTS

Modern society has become more receptive to nontraditional living arrangements. Prevailing attitudes today encourage the acceptance of living styles that once were socially impermissible. The failure of nearly half of all marriages and a weariness of litigating domestic issues have probably contributed to this tolerance.

When advising married couples, estate planners have ample state statutory and case law for guidance. However, with the exception of the 26 states (including Washington, D.C.) that recognize common-law marriages[*] and court decisions addressing palimony claims, there is no legal point of reference for individuals who live together outside of marriage. Simply living together is not sufficient to constitute a common-law marriage in those states that do recognize a common-law arrangement. A common-law couple must also publicly represent themselves as husband and wife and meet specific living requirements. Palimony lawsuits, on the other hand, are grounded on contractual claims for support after relationships have terminated. Discrimination law rather than marital law provides guidance for some other aspects of nontraditional living arrangements. Many of these cases arise from claims of different treatment due to sexual preference.

Just as the parties to a valid marriage can enter into agreements that delineate property ownership, rights, duties, expectations, obligations, and so forth in antenuptial or postnuptial contracts, unmarried persons who live together can also enter into cohabitation agreements. Such agreements can give structure to the living arrangements and may reduce the likelihood of palimony litigation if the relationship later dissolves.

Estate planners are sailing in relatively uncharted waters when planning for clients who are living together outside of marriage. As with married clients, a planner should at the very least suggest separate, independent planners for each of the partners to protect their rights and also to protect the planner from conflicts of interest and claims of malpractice. The planner has to factor into any estate plan for couples living together outside of marriage the fact that such relationships are more easily terminated by the parties than marriages that are recognized under state law.

The presence of children adds to the complexity of estate planning for clients living in nontraditional arrangements. One of the partners may be the biological, custodial parent of children from a previous marriage or relationship. A nonbiological partner, however, may have formed a personal attachment to one or more of the children and may seek custody or visitation rights or may otherwise want to provide for them. Grandparents and other senior generation members may also be relevant in estate plans. Adoptions, stepchildren, half-siblings, surrogate births, artificial insemination, and in vitro fertilization all make the planning process even more confusing and intricate. Typical methods that may be used to plan for children of a previous relationship include annual gift tax exclusion gifts, trusts for the children under the Uniform Transfers (or Gifts) to Minors Act, testamentary trusts, life insurance, and Social Security benefits.

---

[*] 2001 World Almanac, p. 745.

Negative family reactions and hostility add yet another layer of problems to estate planning for unmarried couples, especially same-gender couples. To deter anticipated will contests or other actions, some couples have resorted to adoption by one of the adult partners of the other as his or her legal child.

Nonmarried and same-sex couples may also have to contend with being denied visitation when a partner is in the hospital. Furthermore, a blood relative is more likely to be asked about a patient's medical wishes than a domestic partner is. The solution to both of these issues is a health care power of attorney (HCPOA) or a health care representative appointment (HCRA). If the patient-partner is unable to communicate his or her wishes, a living will used in conjunction with an HCPOA or HCRA that nominates the healthy partner as agent should protect the partner's wishes, including access to the patient-partner in the hospital.

Currently, few states are recognized as being progressive, proactive, and responsive to nontraditional living arrangement issues. Vermont provides for civil unions that are practically indistinguishable from marriage. Hawaii has a "reciprocal beneficiaries" law with limited rights. New Jersey offers limited domestic partnership benefits. California allows same-sex partners to register as domestic partners for the purpose of obtaining certain legal rights held by married couples, including the right to inherit a partner's property, adopt a partner's child (under California law, the rights and duties of marriage to persons registered as domestic partners are allowed starting in 2005), and participate in health care privileges. Massachusetts is, at the time of this writing, the only state to permit and grant full legal marital recognition to marriage between same-gender, Massachusetts-resident couples. Keep in mind, however, that despite the Full Faith and Credit Clause under the U.S. Constitution, which requires each state to give full effect to the laws of other states, there is an exception if giving effect to another state's law(s) violates a state's public policy.

A somewhat new document is also gaining acceptance and legal recognition in California, some municipalities, and places of private employment. This instrument may be referred to, for instance, as a cohabitation agreement, affidavit/contract of commitment, declaration of domestic partnership, domestic agreement, and similar terms. These documents, with relevant registration, may grant employees in nontraditional relationships benefits, like health care coverage and leave to care for an ailing partner, that typically were reserved for traditional married employees. Two additional considerations concerning these agreements are lack of confidentiality and the potential for joint financial responsibility.

Addressing Estate Planning Concerns of Nonmarital Partners

The unavailability of the unlimited marital gift and estate tax deduction is the greatest tax planning hurdle to overcome in estate planning issues involving couples who are not married. Other tax perspectives are necessary because tax matters cannot be postponed as readily without the marital deduction option. There are, however, several common estate planning methods used for nonmarital partners.

Joint Tenancy with Right of Survivorship

Titling property as joint tenants with right of survivorship is one way of providing for a partner. At death, the property passes directly to the surviving party to the relationship.

Although holding property in joint tenancy with right of survivorship provides a certain sense of security for same-gender or other unmarried parties, there are some considerations with respect to this form of ownership that the individuals should be aware of, as follows:

- It may be possible for one of the unmarried parties to sever a joint tenancy.
- With bank accounts and certain other assets, either partner may be able to make withdrawals or obtain the property irrespective of his or her percentage of contribution to the account.
- The creation of a joint tenancy may cause gift tax liability.
- The joint-tenancy property may be reachable by the creditors of both partners.

Gifting

Outright transfers of property utilizing the annual exclusion, or the donor's applicable credit amount if the transfer exceeds the annual exclusion amount, avoid gift tax liability. (Of course, gift splitting is not an option in nonmarital situations.)

Testamentary Bequests

Provisions may also be made under a client's will for a partner with whom the client lives. (Clearly, federal and state marital deductions cannot be used by unmarried couples.) Will provisions, however, do not become irrevocable until death and could then be vulnerable to will contests by the decedent's lineal heirs. Challenges to a will are especially likely from the decedent's children from a marriage. Therefore, partners who desire to provide for each other under a will need to be aware that family members, even those who appeared to accept their deceased relative's significant-other person prior to death, may contest the will after the death of their family member. In this case, a revocable trust may prove more dependable for making sure property passes according to the partners' wishes. If the survivor to the relationship receives less than what was promised or expected under his or her partner's will, an election against the will is not available. If the decedent dies without a valid will, the survivor will not receive anything, since state intestacy statutes are based solely on blood relationships. Also, if either of the life partners wishes the other partner to be executor, the will should specifically nominate the partner because a court will often, in the absence of a specific nomination, be more inclined to appoint a sibling, parent, or child rather than the unrelated partner. Figure 23–1 shows the intestate distribution scheme.

Revocable Trusts

An unmarried partner may use a living or a revocable trust arrangement to provide for the other party to the relationship by naming the partner as beneficiary. At the death of the grantor partner, the trust becomes irrevocable and the beneficiary partner receives the property or the income from the property according to the terms of the trust. The trust document may provide for alternates and may name a successor beneficiary in case the specific relationship is not sustained until the grantor's death.

FIGURE 23–1
Common Distribution Scheme of Intestate Succession

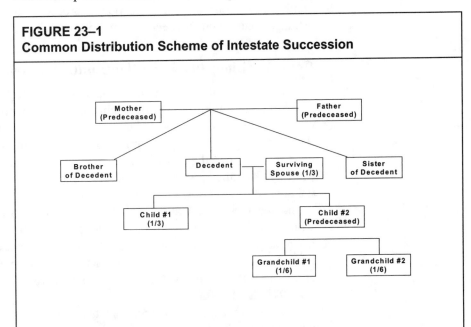

Surviving spouse takes 1/3; remaining 2/3 goes to children, or 1/3 to each. Child #2 predeceased decedent, so Child #2's share is divided equally, or 1/6 each, to each grandchild. If no children survived decedent, remaining 2/3 would pass to parents (1/3 each). If parents predeceased decedent, remaining 2/3 would go to their lineal descendants (brother and sister of decedent would receive 1/3 each). If no brothers or sisters of decedent survived, surviving spouse would get the rest. If there were no lineal descendants (including cousins), property would escheat to the state.

Life Insurance and Retirement Plans

Life insurance and retirement plans may name the partner as beneficiary, thereby providing the partner with a sense of security during lifetime and with funds at the insured's and/or plan participant's death. If the same- gender partners are concerned about listing their partner as the beneficiary of benefits their employer provides, naming a trust with the partner as trust beneficiary may be a possible solution. Also be aware that retirement benefits may not be made available to a surviving unmarried partner the way they are to a surviving spouse. Life insurance on the life of the pension participant may be considered to supplant the loss of retirement benefits when the retiree partner dies.

Because a domestic partner generally does not have an insurable interest in the insured partner's life, the purchase of a life insurance policy on the partner's life may prove difficult. An ILIT, however, may be used to overcome the insurability-requirement obstacle and achieve the partners' goals. With an ILIT, the trust is the policyowner and the partner is the trust beneficiary. For grantor-partners concerned about the irrevocability element of an ILIT and a potential for the relationship to fail in the future, the trust may be drafted to contain provisions directing the policy proceeds to someone other than an estranged partner under specified circumstances.

Court Decisions Involving Nontraditional Living Arrangements

A few notes of interest in this area include the following court decisions:

A judicial ruling in Ontario, Canada, recently recognized the legal status of same-gender marriages. Other provinces in Canada are likely to follow this Ontario ruling. Keep in mind, however, that the United States does not have to recognize the laws from other countries. Also, the 1996 Defense of Marriage Act allows states to disregard same-sex marriages recognized under the laws of other states.

In the U.S., one state's highest court recently ruled that an unmarried woman could make a claim for the loss of companionship that resulted from her male partner's car-accident-related injuries. Because the language used in rendering the decision was gender neutral, some practitioners believe the court may rule similarly for same-gender couples. (*Loyoza v. Sanchez*, 66 P.3d 948 (N.M.2003))

Last, in a recent U.S. state appellate court case, a former domestic partner was held liable for the financial support of children born during the relationship. (*L.S.K. v. H.A.N.*, 813 A.2d 872; 2002 Pa. Super. Lexis 3806)

The above mentioned issues and cases serve to highlight the increasing demand for the courts and legislatures to address the uncertainties and legal ramifications of nontraditional living arrangements.

Planning for individuals living in nontraditional circumstances can present an estate planning challenge. The planner must be diligent and thorough to obtain all the pertinent facts from the client(s). Finally, the planner must be alert to new laws and court decisions affecting parties living together outside of marriage.

Note to Students: See Appendix A for a summary of the advantages and disadvantages of different trusts covered in this chapter and throughout the text.

CHAPTER REVIEW

Answers to the review questions and the self-test questions start on page 717.

Key Terms

durable power of attorney	living will
special (limited) power of attorney	CPR/DNR
springing durable power of attorney	Five Wishes
advance medical directive	elder law durable power of attorney

Review Questions

23-1. Cornelia and Conrad had been happily married for 46 years at the time of Cornelia's death 3 months ago. Their two adult children are Steve, a struggling musician, and Susan, who works as a secretary while helping to pay for her husband's graduate school education. There are no grandchildren. Although Cornelia and Conrad were not wealthy in their own right, over the last 15 years of her life Cornelia inherited property from relatives. At her death, Cornelia had an estate valued at $2.1 million, which includes her portion of the couple's residence and bank accounts titled jointly with right of survivorship. She left her entire estate to Conrad and, due to the unlimited marital deduction, there will be no estate tax. Until his wife's death, Conrad's only property consisted of the jointly held home and bank accounts, currently valued at $600,000. He is not knowledgeable about financial matters and has always lived simply. Conrad told the attorney handling Cornelia's estate that he does not want the burden of so much money. Explain why a disclaimer could be recommended as a postmortem estate planning device for Conrad.

23-2. Explain the methods frequently used for postmortem planning.

23-3. Identify the different types of powers of attorney.

23-4. Explain what an advance medical directive is.

23-5. What are some of the special estate planning issues that may arise when planning for

      a.   the elderly
      b.   married couples

23-6. Identify steps that an individual may take to avoid the future possibility of judicial guardianship or conservatorship.

23-7. Explain what a stand-by trust is.

Self-Test Questions

T   F   23-1. Under a living will, an individual may request health care professionals to allow him or her to die naturally.

T   F   23-2. The agent under a durable power of attorney has to account to the local court only on an annual basis.

T   F   23-3. CPR and DNR directives are drafted for patients who wish to refuse all medical procedures, including cardiopulmonary resuscitation.

T   F   23-4. Five Wishes is a type of advance medical directive intended to give gravely ill individuals a way to express their end-of-life wishes.

T   F   23-5. Domestic partners in nontraditional living situations are unable to purchase life insurance on the life of a partner because of the insurable interest requirement.

Estate Planning Case

Learning Objective

An understanding of the material the previous chapters should enable the student to

---

Use financial data about a client's business and personal situation to develop an estate plan.

Chapter Outline

CASE NARRATIVE

Business Situation

Scott is vice president of marketing of the XYZ Corporation, a large automobile-and-truck-leasing company that is listed on a stock exchange.

The XYZ Corporation, a growth-oriented business, has established both a pension and a profit-sharing plan. Scott is a participant in both of these plans.

Currently, under XYZ Corporation's qualified noncontributory pension plan, Scott is entitled to a retirement income of $3,000 per month beginning at age 65 and to a preretirement death benefit of $450,000. The death benefit is payable in a lump sum to his estate. The current value of Scott's fully vested account in the company's qualified noncontributory profit-sharing plan is $46,000. It is payable to Sue, Scott's wife, in installments over a 5-year period.

Personal Situation

Family

Scott, aged 52, and his wife, Sue, aged 50, have two children—Ben, their son, aged 26 is a successful artist, and Cate, their daughter, aged 21, is in college. Ben is married and currently has three sons, aged 6, 3, and 1. Both Scott and Sue are in good health. They file a joint federal income tax return.

Sue has no experience or interest in business affairs or property management. Both of Sue's parents are deceased.

Scott's father is deceased. In his will, Scott's father established a trust that provides for income to be paid to Scott's mother during her lifetime. At her death, the trust property is to be paid to Scott, if living, otherwise to the person or persons designated by Scott's mother during her lifetime or in her will. If Scott does not survive her and if she does not appoint the property, it is to go equally to Scott's children or their descendants, per stirpes. The present value of the trust principal is $90,000. The present value of the life estate held by Scott's mother is one-sixth of the total value of the trust principal ($15,000). Scott's mother has not yet exercised her power of appointment by deed or in her will.

Scott contributes $500 per month toward the support of his mother, now aged 80.

Scott has recently been named a trustee of TU University, his alma mater, for which he has a great fondness. Scott has made gifts to TU University of $1,000 during each of the last 5 years and would like to aid the university financially in the future.

Scott and his friend, Dan, own a parcel of undeveloped land equally as tenants in common. The current value of the entire parcel of land is $580,000.

Property

Scott owns the following property in his own name:

Stock in XYZ Corporation (500 shares)	$240,000
Other listed common stock	340,000
Tax-free municipal bonds	80,000
Savings accounts	150,000
Household and other tangible personal property	30,000

Scott and Sue own the following property as joint tenants with right of survivorship:

Residence purchased in 1987 (net after mortgage)	$440,000
Vacation home (three-fourths of purchase price contributed by Scott and one-fourth by Sue; purchased in 1977—no gift tax return filed)	300,000
Checking account (all deposits contributed by Scott)	14,000

Scott and Dan own the following property equally as tenants in common:

Undeveloped real estate	$580,000

Sue owns the following property in her own name:

Savings account	$24,000
Other personal property	28,000

Employee Benefits

In addition to coverage under a group comprehensive major medical policy, Scott is entitled to the following pension and death benefits:

Plan	Beneficiary Designation	Settlement Arrangement	Death Benefit Amount
XYZ Corporation—pension (noncontributory)	Scott's estate	Lump sum	$450,000
XYZ Corporation—profit-sharing (noncontributory)	Sue	Lump sum	46,000

Life Insurance

Scott owns the following life insurance on his own life:

Plan	Age When Purchased	Beneficiary Designation	Settlement Arrangement	Face Amount
(1) Ordinary life	24	Sue	Lump sum	$ 30,000
(2) 20-payment life	26	Cate	Fixed-period option for 5 years with any remaining installments to TU University. Cate has the right to commute the payments during her lifetime.	70,000
(3) Ordinary life	37	Sue	Lump sum	200,000
(4) Term to 65	44	Scott's estate	Lump sum	300,000

Wills

Scott's will provides for a specific bequest of $10,000 to TU University. The remainder of his property passing under his will is to be divided as follows: an amount equal to $400,000 of his property will pass outright to Sue; the remainder will be divided equally between Ben and Cate, and it will be held in two separate trusts. Each trust provides for income to be paid annually to the trust beneficiary with principal distributed at age 35. All the debts, funeral expenses, and administration expenses are to be paid out of the remainder of the estate passing in trust to Ben and Cate. The will also contains a simultaneous death provision under which it will be presumed that Sue survives Scott in the event Scott and Sue die under circumstances that make it impossible to establish who died first. Sue has no will.

Income

Scott's income last year was $180,000 and came from the following sources:

Commissions from XYZ Corporation	$45,000
Dividends from XYZ Corporation stock	1,000
Dividends from other listed common stock	5,000
Interest on tax-free municipal bonds	3,000
Interest on savings accounts	1,000

Scott's salary in his position as vice president is $125,000 a year.
Sue's income last year was $1,000 from the interest on a savings account that she owns in her own name.

CASE QUESTIONS

Use the tax schedules and computation chart at the end of chapter 18 to assist in your calculations. Solutions to case questions are in the Answers section, which starts on page 717.

1. If Scott were to die this year, predeceasing Sue, and his executor elected his date of death as the valuation date, indicate those assets (and their values) that would be includible in Scott's gross estate for estate tax purposes. Also, explain your reasons for the inclusion or exclusion of each asset.

2. Based on Scott's current estate plan, indicate those assets and their values that would qualify for the marital deduction. Explain your reasons for the qualification or nonqualification of each asset for the marital deduction.

3. a. Calculate Scott's tentative tax base for federal estate tax purposes, and explain each step in your calculations. For purposes of this question, assume that the liabilities as well as funeral and administration expenses of Scott's estate amount to $40,000 and are to be paid out of the shares of Ben and Cate. Assume that Scott's state of domicile imposes a state estate tax equal to 2 percent of Scott's adjusted gross estate.

   b. Calculate Scott's federal and state estate tax liability, and explain each step in the calculations. Assume that Scott's state of domicile imposes a state estate tax equal to 2 percent of Scott's adjusted gross estate.

   c. Calculate Sue's tentative tax base for federal estate tax purposes, and explain each step in your calculations. Assume that funeral and administrative expenses at Sue's death amount to $72,000. Assume further that Sue lives 3 years after the death of Scott and that the proceeds from the $200,000 life insurance policy have been consumed. Also, for purposes of the problem, assume that all asset values from the time of Scott's death until Sue's death are exactly doubled and that state death taxes are 2 percent of a decedent's adjusted gross estate.

   d. Calculate Sue's federal as well as state estate tax liability, and explain each step in the calculations. Assume that Sue's state of domicile imposes a state estate tax of 2 percent of a decedent's adjusted gross estate. Assume further that Sue lives 3 years after the death of Scott and that the value of the assets is exactly double their value on the date of Scott's death.

4. Describe any weaknesses that currently exist in both Scott's and Sue's estate plans, and make recommendations that would correct these weaknesses. (Remember to evaluate proposals in terms of tax liabilities in both estates. For example, full utilization of the unlimited marital deduction may result in excessive and unnecessary estate tax liabilities at the death of the second spouse. This technique also wastes the applicable credit amount of the first spouse to die. Therefore, it is rarely the most advantageous estate plan.)

Appendix A

Fundamental Trusts

The following eight pages contain a brief summary, in table format, of the types of trusts covered in this textbook. The table gives a brief description of each trust, along with its advantages and disadvantages.

Fundamental Trusts

Trust	General Description
Revocable trust	Grantor can terminate/revoke
Grantor trust	Income taxation to grantor without consent of adverse party
Irrevocable trust	Completed, nonchangeable transfers to beneficiaries
Inter vivos/living trust	Created during grantor's life; revocable or irrevocable
Testamentary trust	Contained in grantor's will; revocable until death/incapacity
Simple trust	All trust income distributed to beneficiaries
Complex trust	Trust income may be accumulated
Reciprocal trust	Irrevocable trust arrangement for purpose of avoidance of trust property in life beneficiary/grantor's estate; grantor is in same economic circumstances as prior to trust arrangement
Totten trust (similar to pay-on-death (POD) and transfer-on-death (TOD) accounts)	Bank savings account where donor makes deposit for named donee; passes at death to donee; revocable
Pour-over trust	Estate residue "pours over" into preexisting trust; trust assets may pour over to estate (less common)
Sec. 2503(b) trust	Allows gifts to trusts for minor beneficiaries to qualify for gift tax annual exclusion

Advantages	Disadvantages
• Flexibility • Control • Management expertise	• No tax benefit
• Possible transfer tax benefits • Grantor's retention of controls/powers	• Income taxation to grantor • No income shifting • Possible estate inclusion
• Income/transfer tax benefits for grantor • Appreciation out of estate	• Grantor's loss of dominion and control
See revocable and irrevocable trusts	*See* revocable and irrevocable trusts
• Revocable/amendable until death/incapacity	• Trust property gross estate inclusion • Probate property
• Separate tax entity • No trust income taxation	• No accumulation of trust income • No charitable distributions • No corpus distributions
• Corpus/charitable distributions • Separate tax entity • Trustee flexibility	• Trust income taxation • More complexities (DNI)
• Variation in trust terms/purposes may accomplish exclusion of value from grantor's estate	• Legally unenforceable if same economic circumstances for grantors • Inclusion in grantors' estates
• Convenience • Flexibility • Control • Revocability • Nonprobate	• Donee accessibility
• Asset consolidation • Management expertise • Estate administration costs reduced • Amendable until death	• Existence of trust prior to death • Probate
• Annual exclusion for income value • Corpus may be kept in trust past age 21	• Mandatory annual income distribution

Fundamental Trusts (Continued)	
Trust	**General Description**
Sec. 2503(c) trust	Allows gifts to trusts for minor beneficiaries to qualify for gift tax annual exclusion
Power of appointment trust	Donee/powerholder has right to designate the disposition of the property subject to the power according to trust terms; may be general power or special power
Estate trust	Surviving spouse has life estate; remainder payable to surviving spouse's estate
Qualified terminable interest property (QTIP) trust	Allows qualifying terminable interest property to qualify for marital deduction
Qualified domestic trust (QDOT)	Marital-deduction-type trust for transfers to noncitizen spouse
Marital trust	Holds assets that qualify for marital deduction; often used in conjunction with credit-equivalent bypass trust for optimal planning for the marital deduction and applicable exclusion amount
Bypass trust	Holds assets covered by the applicable credit/exclusion amount

Advantages	Disadvantages
• Annual exclusion for income value • Income accumulation • Flexibility	• Mandatory distribution of income and principal at age 21 • Inclusion in minor beneficiary's estate
• Flexibility • Useful dispositive device • Allows delegation of dispositive decisions to another • Marital deduction device	• Possible tax consequences for donee • Annual or more frequent income distributions • Income-producing property required (generally)
• Income accumulation • Marital deduction device • Nonproductive property allowed	• Accumulated income in surviving spouse's estate • Reachable by creditors • Increased administrative costs possible
• Grantor spouse retains postmortem control • Marital deduction device • Provides for surviving spouse's life • Protection of heirs' interests	• Mandatory annual (at least) income distributions • Inclusion in surviving spouse's estate • Income-producing property required (generally)
• Alleviates harsh transfer tax ramifications associated with denial of marital deduction for transfers to resident-alien spouse • Income/hardship distributions transfer tax free	• Complex • Inflexible • Administratively expensive • Restrictive
• Provides for surviving spouse's life • Qualifies for marital deduction • Avoids stacking of assets in survivor's estate	• May provide inadequate support for surviving spouse if improper formula is used with credit-equivalent bypass trust due to increasing applicable credit/exclusion • Inclusion in surviving spouse's estate
• Provides optimal marital deduction/bypass tax savings	• Increasing applicable exclusion amount may undermine marital trust value

Fundamental Trusts (Continued)	
Trust	**General Description**
Grantor-retained annuity trust (GRAT)	Provides right to receive fixed payments at least annually for a life/lives or for a term of years followed by remainder to trust beneficiaries
Grantor-retained unitrust (GRUT)	Provides right to receive fixed percentage payments (as revalued annually) annually for life/lives or for a term of years followed by remainder to trust beneficiaries
Qualified personal residence trust (QPRT)	Allows grantor to retain control over/reside in home for term of years when home then passes to beneficiaries at reduced gift tax cost
Charitable remainder annuity trust (CRAT)	Provides noncharitable income beneficiary with a fixed annuity of at least 5 percent annually of initial fair market value for term or life/lives; remainder to charity
Charitable remainder unitrust (CRUT)	Provides noncharitable income beneficiary with fixed percentage of at least 5 percent of net fair market value (revalued annually) for term or life/lives; remainder to charity
Charitable lead annuity (CLAT)/ unitrust (CLUT) trust (guaranteed annuity/ unitrust interest trust)	Reverse of remainder trusts, CRAT/CRUT; income interest passes to charity at least annually for term or life/lives; remainder to noncharitable beneficiaries
Generation-skipping transfer tax trust	Created for benefit of individuals two or more generations below transferor (grandchildren/skip beneficiaries and no nonskip beneficiaries): taxable distributions/taxable terminations
Revocable life insurance trust (RLIT)	Created to hold life insurance during lifetime for estate enhancement often by young grantor or for pour over of estate assets at grantor's death

Advantages	Disadvantages
• Subtraction method of valuation (Sec. 7520) • Transfer tax savings • Appreciation out of grantor's estate	• Tax benefits diminished by grantor's death during term • Irrevocable
• Subtraction method of valuation (Sec. 7520) • Transfer tax savings • Appreciation out of grantor's estate	• Tax benefits diminished by grantor's death during term • Irrevocable
• Subtraction method of valuation (Sec. 7520) • Transfer tax savings • Grantor has home for term • Appreciation out of grantor's estate	• Irrevocable • No tax savings if grantor does not survive term • Remainderperson control after term
• Transfer tax benefit for partial interest charitable transfer • Estate tax charitable deduction • Allows provisions for noncharitable beneficiaries	• Irrevocable • Loss of dominion/control over remainder interest • Some complexities
• Transfer tax benefit for partial interest charitable transfer • Estate tax charitable deduction • Allows provisions for noncharitable beneficiaries • Additional contributions to trust allowed	• Irrevocable • Loss of dominion/control over remainder interest • Some complexities
• Remainder interest stays in family • Income/transfer tax benefits	• Irrevocable • Inclusion of remainder for noncharitable beneficiary
• Lifetime and at-death exclusion • Annual exclusion availability • Leveraging availability • Gift-splitting potential	• Flat, highest estate tax rate for year of transfer applies • Complex • Greater administrative expense
• Estate enhancement • Flexibility • Control • Revocable • Nonprobate	• No tax benefits • Insurance proceeds included in grantor's gross estate

Fundamental Trusts (Continued)	
Trust	**General Description**
Irrevocable life insurance trust (ILIT))	Trust owns life insurance policy(ies) on grantor-insured's life; at insured's death, proceeds pass according to trust terms
Grandparent-grandchild trust	Grandparent grantor creates trust to hold life insurance on life of grandchild's parent for benefit of grandchild

Advantages	Disadvantages
• No inclusion of proceeds in insured's gross estate • Transfer tax savings • Passes value to beneficiaries outside grantor's estate • Leverage of applicable credit/ exclusion • Estate liquidity	• Irrevocable • Loss of control • Careful avoidance of incidents of ownership
• Reduction of grandfather's estate • Enhances amount grandchild receives at parent's death • Reduces life insurance child carriers • Avoids transfer taxation • No incidents of ownership	• Irrevocable • Order of deaths uncertain • Loss of control

Credit for State Death Taxes

CREDIT* FOR STATE DEATH TAXES (Note: Repealed after 2004)	
If the **adjusted taxable estate**** is . . .	The maximum tax credit shall be . . .
Not over $90,000	.8 of 1% of amount by which taxable estate exceeds $40,000
Over $90,000 but not over $140,000	$400, plus 1.6% of excess over $90,000
Over $140,000 but not over $240,000	$1,200, plus 2.4% of excess over $140,000
Over $240,000 but not over $440,000	$3,600, plus 3.2% of excess over $240,000
Over $440,000 but not over $640,000	$10,000, plus 4% of excess over $440,000
Over $640,000 but not over $840,000	$18,000, plus 4.8% of excess over $640,000
Over $840,000 but not over $1,040,000	$27,600, plus 5.6% of excess over $840,000
Over $1,040,000 but not over $1,540,000	$38,800, plus 6.4% of excess over $1,040,000
Over $1,540,000 but not over $2,040,000	$70,800, plus 7.2% of excess over $1,540,000
Over $2,040,000 but not over $2,540,000	$106,800, plus 8% of excess over $2,040,000
Over $2,540,000 but not over $3,040,000	$146,800, plus 8.8% of excess over $2,540,000
Over $3,040,000 but not over $3,540,000	$190,800, plus 9.6% of excess over $3,040,000
Over $3,540,000 but not over $4,040,000	$238,800, plus 10.4% of excess over $3,540,000
Over $4,040,000 but not over $5,040,000	$290,800, plus 11.2% of excess over $4,040,000
Over $5,040,000 but not over $6,040,000	$402,800, plus 12% of excess over $5,040,000
Over $6,040,000 but not over $7,040,000	$522,800, plus 12.8% of excess over $6,040,000
Over $7,040,000 but not over $8,040,000	$650,800, plus 13.6% of excess over $7,040,000
Over $8,040,000 but not over $9,040,000	$786,800, plus 14.4% of excess over $8,040,000
Over $9,040,000 but not over $10,040,000	$930,800, plus 15.2% of excess over $9,040,000
Over $10,040,000	$1,082,800 plus 16% of excess over $10,040,000

*The credit is reduced by 25 percent in 2002; 50 percent in 2003; 75 percent in 2004; and in 2005 becomes a deduction until 2010 when the estate and GST taxes are repealed.
**For purposes of this chart, the term *adjusted taxable estate* means the taxable estate reduced by $60,000.

Appendix C

Example of a Durable Power of Attorney

KNOW ALL MEN BY THESE PRESENTS: That I, ___(name)___, a legal resident of____(street)____, __(city)__, ___(county)___, (state)__, have made, constituted, and appointed, and by these presents do make, constitute, and appoint John Doe of _____(street)_____, _____(city)____, ___(county)____, __(state)__, my true and lawful attorney to act in, manage, and conduct all my estate and all my affairs, and for that purpose for me and in my name, place, and stead, and for my use and benefit, and as my act and deed, to do and execute, or to concur with persons jointly interested with myself therein in the doing or executing of, all or any of the following acts, deeds, and things:

(1)   To buy, receive, lease, accept, or otherwise acquire; to sell, convey, mortgage, pledge, quitclaim, or otherwise encumber or dispose of; or to contract or agree for the acquisition, disposal, or encumbrance of any property whatsoever or any custody, possession, interest, or right therein, upon such terms as my said attorney shall think proper.

(2)   To satisfy, in whole or in part, any and all mortgages.

(3)   To make, do, and transact all and every kind of business of what nature or kind soever, including the receipt, recovery, collection, payment, compromise, settlement, and adjustment of all accounts, legacies, bequests, devises, interests, dividends, annuities, demands, debts, taxes, and obligations, which may now or hereafter be due, owing, or payable by me or to me.

(4)   To make, endorse, accept, receive, sign, seal, execute, acknowledge, and deliver deeds, assignments, agreements, certificates, notes, bonds, vouchers, receipts, and such other instruments in writing of whatever kind and nature as may be necessary, convenient, or proper in the premises.

(5)   To deposit and to withdraw for the purposes hereof, in either my said attorney's name or my name or jointly in both our names, in or

from any banking institution, any funds, negotiable paper, or moneys which may come into my said attorney's hands as such attorney, or which I now or hereafter may have on deposit or be entitled to, including full power to make deposits to and withdrawals from any checking account or savings account in my name in any financial institution.

(6)   To sign checks or otherwise make withdrawals from any checking or savings account in my name and to endorse checks payable to me and receive the proceeds thereof in cash or otherwise; to open and close checking or savings accounts in my name; purchase and redeem savings certificates, certificates of deposit, or similar instruments in my name; and to execute and deliver receipts for any funds withdrawn or certificates redeemed; and to do all acts regarding any checking account, savings account, savings certificate, certificate of deposit, or similar instrument which I now have or may hereafter acquire, the same as I could do if personally present.

(7)   To enter and examine the contents of any and all of my safe deposit boxes wheresoever located and to remove in whole or in part the contents thereof, to make deposits therein, to terminate the use of any such safe deposit box, or to open new safe deposit boxes, and to transfer contents among such safe deposit boxes.

(8)   To institute, prosecute, defend, compromise, arbitrate, and dispose of legal, equitable, or administrative hearings, actions, suits, attachments, arrests, or other proceedings, or otherwise engage in litigation in connection with the premises.

(9)   To act as my attorney or proxy in respect to any stocks, shares, bonds, or other investments, rights, or interests I may now or hereafter hold, including the power to vote in person or by proxy at any meeting, to join in any merger, reorganization, voting-trust plan, or other concerted action of security holders, to make payments in connection therewith, and in general to exercise all rights of a security holder.

(10)   To invest in all forms of real or personal property without any restriction whatsoever as to the kind of investment.

(11)   To hold property unregistered or in the name of a nominee.

(12)   To borrow money in such amounts for such periods and upon such terms as my attorney shall deem proper and to secure any loan by the mortgage or pledge of any property.

(13) To contract with and arrange for my entrance to any hospital, nursing home, health center, convalescent home, residential care facility, or similar institution; to authorize medical, therapeutic, and surgical procedures for me; and to pay all bills in connection therewith.

(14) To purchase on my behalf U.S. Treasury bonds redeemable at par in payment of federal estate tax in my estate, to borrow monies to acquire such bonds and to pledge property as collateral for such borrowing, and to deliver to the personal representative of my estate after my death all such bonds held at my death for use by my personal representative in payment of the federal estate tax in my estate.

(15) To make annual gifts to any one or more of the following persons or classes of persons listed below, each such gift to be not in excess of that amount which in the aggregate for that calendar year will qualify for the maximum amount allowable for the annual exclusion for federal gift tax purposes under the provisions of the Internal Revenue Code then in effect, provided that each such gift is made in a manner which will qualify for such annual exclusion; my attorney may make such gifts in unequal amounts and need not include all possible permissible donees as recipients of gifts in any one year:

(list names)

(16) To change the beneficiary designation on any and all of my life insurance policies, to effect loans on such policies either from the company issuing such policy or from other lending institutions by pledging such policies as security for such borrowing, and to transfer by absolute assignment any and all of my incidents of ownership to any and all of such policies.

(17) To create a trust for my benefit designating one or more persons (including my attorney-in-fact) as original or successor trustees and to transfer to the trust any or all property owned by me as the attorney-in-fact may decide, provided that the income and corpus of such trust shall either be distributable to me or to the guardian of my estate or be applied for my benefit or the benefit of my spouse and issue, and upon my death any remaining balance of corpus and unexpended income of the trust shall be distributed to my estate; the deed of trust may be amended or revoked at any time and from time to time, in whole or in part, by me or my attorney-in-fact, provided that any such amendment by my attorney-in-fact shall not include any provision which could not be included in the original deed.

(18) To transfer any or all of my assets of whatsoever nature as an addition to a certain inter vivos funded revocable trust which I as settlor created on _____, 20____, of which _____[name(s)]_____ is (are) the trustee(s), and to effect such transfer I authorize my attorney herein designated to execute any and all documents as may be required by any bank, financial institution, or securities transfer agent, or documentation of a similar nature.

(19) To withdraw and receive the income or corpus of a trust; to demand, withdraw, and receive the income or corpus of any trust over which I have the power to make withdrawals; to request and receive the income or corpus of any trust with respect to which the trustee thereof has the discretionary power to make distribution to me or on my behalf; and to execute a receipt and release or similar document for the property received.

(20) To claim the family exemption to the same extent as I personally could do under the provisions of Sections ____xxxx–xxxx____ of the Probate, Estates, and Fiduciaries Code, or any similar provisions then in effect.

(21) To claim an elective share of the estate of my deceased spouse to the same extent as I personally could do under the provisions of Chapter __xx__ of the Probate, Estates, and Fiduciaries Code or any similar provisions then in effect, including the power to disclaim any interest in property which I am required to disclaim as a result of such election; retain any property which I have the right to elect to retain; file petitions pertaining to the election, including petitions to extend the time for electing and petitions for orders, decrees, and judgments relating to determination of effect of election and enforcement; and take all other actions which the attorney-in-fact deems appropriate in order to effectuate such election; provided, however, that the election shall be made only upon the approval of a court of competent jurisdiction.

(22) To disclaim any interest in property to the same extent as I personally could do under the provisions of Section __xxxx__ or Chapter __xx__ of the Probate, Estates, and Fiduciaries Code or any similar provisions then in effect, provided that any disclaimer under Chapter __xx__ shall be in accordance with the provisions of Section __xxxx__.

(23) To renounce any fiduciary positions to which I have been appointed or in which I am then serving, and to either file an accounting with a court of competent jurisdiction or settle on receipt and release or other informal method as the attorney-in-fact deems advisable.

(24) To carry on any business interest owned by me for whatever period of time deemed proper, including the power to do any and all things deemed necessary or appropriate, including the power to incorporate any unincorporated business; to vote any and all shares of stock in any such business; to borrow and to pledge assets owned by me as security for such borrowing; to assent to, join in, or vote in favor of or against any merger, reorganization, voting trust plan, or similar action, and to delegate discretionary duties with respect thereto; to delegate all or any part of the supervision, management, and operation of the business to such person or persons as may be selected; and to close out, liquidate, or sell the business at such time and upon such terms as shall seem best. My attorney shall not be held to personal liability for shrinkage of income or loss of capital value that may be incurred in the course of the operation of the business, except loss that may result from willful misconduct.

(25) To engage and dismiss agents, counsel, and employees.

(26) To prepare, execute, and file income and other tax returns, and other governmental reports, applications, requests, and documents.

(27) To enter into, perform, modify, extend, cancel, compromise, enforce, or otherwise act with respect to any contract of any sort whatsoever.

(28) To acquire or dispose of real property or any interest therein; to partition and subdivide real property; to take, hold, possess, invest, lease or let, collect rent or mortgage payments, or otherwise manage any or all of my property or any interest therein; to eject, remove, or relieve tenants or other persons from, and recover possession of, such property by all lawful means; to maintain, protect, repair, alter, erect, or tear down any structure or part thereof; and to file such plans, applications, or other documents in connection therewith and do such other acts as may be requested by any government or other authority having or purporting to have jurisdiction.

(29) To procure, alter, extend, or cancel insurance against any and all risks affecting property and persons, and against liability, damage, or claim of any sort.

GIVING AND GRANTING unto my said attorney full power and authority to do and perform all and every act, deed, matter, and thing whatsoever in and about my estate, property, and affairs as fully and effectually to all intents and purposes as I might or could do in my own proper person if personally present, the above specially enumerated powers being in aid and exemplification of the full, complete, and general power herein granted, and not in limitation or definition thereof; and hereby ratifying all that my said attorney shall lawfully do or cause to be done by virtue of these presents.

AND I hereby declare that any act or thing lawfully done hereunder by my said attorney shall be binding on myself and my heirs, legal and personal representatives, and assigns.

This power of attorney shall continue in force and may be accepted and relied upon by anyone to whom it is presented despite my purported revocation of it or my death until actual written notice of such event is received by such person. In the event of my incompetency from whatever cause, this power of attorney shall not thereby be revoked but shall thereupon become irrevocable and may be accepted and relied upon by anyone to whom it is presented despite such incompetency, subject only to its becoming void and of no further effect only upon receipt by such person of either (1) written evidence of the appointment of a guardian (or similar fiduciary) of my estate following adjudication of incompetency or (2) written notice of my death. This power of attorney shall not be affected by my subsequent disability or incapacity.

The following is a specimen signature of the person to whom this power of attorney is given:

_____
John Doe

IN WITNESS WHEREOF, I have hereunto set my hand this day of _____, 20___.

_____

STATE OF

                                SS:

COUNTY OF

On the ___ day of _____, 20 __, before me, the subscriber, a Notary Public in and for the State of _____, residing in the County of _____, personally appeared the above named _____, and in due form of law acknowledged the foregoing Power of Attorney to be his act and deed and desired the same to be recorded as such.

Witness my hand and Notarial Seal the day and year aforesaid.

_____(SEAL)
Notary Public

Appendix D

Example of a Simple Will

I,_____(name)_____, of _____(address)_____,
revoke my prior wills and declare this to be my last will:

PROPERTY DISPOSITION

I. *Personal and Household Effects:* I give all my articles of personal or household use, including automobiles, and all insurance on that property

    A. *Husband*: To my husband, _____(name of husband)_____, if he survives me by 30 days. If he does not so survive me, I give all such property and insurance

    B. *Children*: To those of my children who so survive me, to be divided among them as they may agree.

    In the absence of agreement or if any child of mine is a minor, the division shall be made as my corporate executor may think appropriate. However, articles that my executor considers unsuitable for my children may be sold and the proceeds added to my residuary estate. My executor may, without further responsibility, distribute property passing to a minor under this article to the minor or to any person to hold for the minor.

II. *Residuary Estate:* I give the residue of my estate, real and personal,

    A. *Husband*: To my husband, _____(name of husband)_____, if he survives me by 30 days. If he does not so survive me, I give all such residue to my children in accordance with the following Part B of this Article.

    B. *Children*: In equal shares to such of my children who so survive me, provided that if a child does not so survive me but leaves descendants who so survive me, such descendants shall receive, per stirpes, the share such child would have received had he or she so survived me.

III.   *Powers of Appointment:* No provision of this will shall exercise any power of appointment I may have.

IV.   *Adopted Persons*: Adopted persons shall be considered as children of their adoptive parents, and they and their descendants shall be considered as descendants of their adoptive parents.

ADMINISTRATIVE PROVISIONS

V.   *Beneficiaries under 21:* Any property passing under this will to a person under 21 years of age shall be paid to_____ (name of custodian)_____ custodian for that beneficiary under the Uniform Gifts (Transfers) to Minors Act of ____(state)____. If (name of custodian) for any reason fails to qualify or ceases to act as custodian, I appoint ___(name of successor custodian)___ in his or her place.

VI.   *Protective Provision:* To the greatest extent permitted by law, before actual payment to a beneficiary no interest in income or principal shall be (i) assignable to a beneficiary or (ii) available to anyone having a claim against a beneficiary.

VII.   *Death Taxes:* All federal, state, and other death taxes payable on the property forming my gross estate for that purpose, whether or not it passes under this will, shall be paid out of the principal of my probate estate just as if they were my debts, and none of those taxes shall be charged against any beneficiary. This provision shall not apply to any property over which I have a general power of appointment for federal estate tax purposes.

VIII.   *Tax Provisions:* I authorize my executor

A. *Death Taxes*: To exercise any options available in determining and paying death taxes in my estate and to allocate my generation-skipping tax exemption;

B. *Income Taxes*: To join with my husband in filing a joint income tax return; and

C. *Gift Taxes*: To consent to any gifts made by my husband being treated as having been made one-half by me for the purpose of laws relating to gift tax.

In my executor's sole discretion, no compensating adjustments shall be required between income and principal, or between my trusts, or between my estate and my husband. All decisions under this article shall be made in my executor's sole discretion and shall be conclusive upon all persons concerned.

IX.   *Management Provisions:* I authorize my executor

A. *Retain/Invest*: To retain and to invest in all forms of real and personal property, including common trust funds, mutual funds, and money market deposit accounts operated or offered by my corporate executor or any affiliate of it, regardless of any limitations imposed by law on investments by executors, or any principle of law concerning investment diversification;

B. *Compromise*: To compromise claims and to abandon any property which, in my executor's opinion, is of little or no value;

C. *Borrow*: To borrow from and to sell property to my husband or others, and to pledge property as security for repayment of any funds borrowed;

D. *Sell/Lease*: To sell at public or private sale, to exchange, or to lease for any period of time, any real or personal property, and to give options for sales or leases;

E. *Capital Changes*: To join in any merger, reorganization, voting-trust plan, or other concerted action of security holders, and to delegate discretionary duties with respect thereto;

F. *Distribute*: To distribute in kind and to allocate specific assets among the beneficiaries (including any custodianship hereunder) in such proportions as my trustee may think best, so long as the total market value of any beneficiary's share is not affected by such allocation.

These authorities shall extend to all property at any time held by my executors or my trustee and shall continue in full force until the actual distribution of all such property. All powers, authorities, and discretion granted by this will shall be in addition to those granted by law and shall be exercisable without court authorization.

FIDUCIARY PROVISIONS

X.   *Executor:* I appoint my husband, _____(name of husband)_____, and (name of independent corporate executor) executors of my will. I direct that

A. *Resignation*: Any executor may resign at any time without court approval;

B. *Bond*: No executor shall be required to give bond;

C. *Singular/Plural*: The words "my executor" shall refer to those from time to time acting as such; and

D. *Compensation*: My corporate executor and custodian shall receive compensation in accordance with its standard schedule of fees in effect while its services are performed.

XI. *Guardian of the Person and Estate*: I direct that

A. *Guardians of the Person*: If my husband does not survive me, I appoint _____(guardian's name)_____ guardian of the persons of my children during their minorities; and

B. *Guardians of the Estate*: I appoint my husband and (name of bank) guardians of the estates of my minor children over any property that may pass to them other than under this will or a trust of mine. I direct that

1. The guardians shall manage the funds for each child as if the guardians were the custodian under the Uniform Gifts (Transfers) to Minors Act of _____(state)_____. However, each child shall have the unrestricted right to withdraw his or her share upon reaching majority; and

2. No guardian shall be required to give bond.

Executed (date)_____, 20____.

_____
(signature of testatrix)

In our presence the above-named testatrix signed this and declared it to be her will, and now at her request, in her presence, and in the presence of each other, we sign as witnesses:

(name)_____   (address)_____

(name)_____   (address)_____

(name)_____   (address)_____

STATE OF

:SS.

COUNTY

I, _____(name of testatrix)_____, having been duly qualified according to law, acknowledge that I signed the foregoing instrument as my will and that I signed it as my free and voluntary act for the purposes therein expressed.

(signature of testatrix) _____

We, having been duly qualified according to law, depose and say that we were present and saw _____(name of testatrix)_____ sign the foregoing instrument as her will; that she signed it as her free and voluntary act for the purposes therein expressed; that each of us in her sight and hearing and at her request signed the will as witnesses; and that to the best of our knowledge she was at that time 18 or more years of age, of sound mind, and under no constraint or undue influence.

_____

Witness

_____

Witness

Subscribed, sworn to or affirmed, and acknowledged before me by the above-named testatrix and by the witnesses whose names appear above on (date)_____, 20____.

_____

Notary Public

(SEAL)

Appendix E

Ohio's Health Care Power of Attorney

What You Should Know about a Health Care Power of Attorney

A Health Care Power of Attorney is a document that allows you to name a person to act on your behalf to make health care decisions for you if you become unable to make them for yourself. **This person becomes an attorney-in-fact for you.**

- A **Health Care Power of** Attorney is different from a financial power of attorney that you use to give someone authority over your financial matters.

- The person you appoint as your **attorney-in-fact** by completing the **Health Care Power of** Attorney form has the power to authorize and refuse medical treatment for you. This **authority is recognized in all medical situations <u>when you are unable to express your own wishes.</u>** Unlike a Living Will, it is not limited to situations in which you are terminally ill or permanently unconscious. For example, your physician or the hospital may consult with your attorney-in-fact should you be injured in a car accident and become temporarily unconscious.

- There are five <u>limitations</u> on the authority of your attorney-in-fact:

  1. **An attorney-in-fact has limited authority to order that life-sustaining treatment be withdrawn from you. Your attorney-in-fact may order that** life-sustaining treatment be refused or withdrawn only if you have a terminal condition or if you are in a permanently unconscious state. And even then, the attending physician and, if applicable, the consulting physician must confirm that diagnosis and your attending physician(s) must determine that you have no reasonable possibility of regaining decision-making ability.

2. **Your attorney-in-fact** does not have the authority to order the withdrawal of "comfort care." Comfort care is any type of medical or nursing care that would provide you with comfort or relief from pain.

3. **If you are pregnant, your attorney-in-fact cannot order the withdrawal** of life-sustaining treatment unless certain conditions are met. Life-sustaining treatment cannot be withdrawn if doing so would terminate the pregnancy unless there is substantial risk to your life or two physicians determine that the fetus would not be born alive.

4. **Your attorney-in-fact may order that nutrition and hydration be withdrawn only if** you are in a terminal condition or permanently unconscious state and two physicians agree that nutrition and hydration will no longer provide comfort or alleviate pain. If you want to give your attorney-in-fact the authority to withhold nutrition and hydration if you were to become permanently unconscious, you must indicate this in the appropriate section of the Health Care Power of Attorney form. If you also have a Living Will, it should be consistent with your Health Care Power of Attorney regarding the withholding of nutrition and hydration. In other words, if you indicate in your Health Care Power of Attorney that it is permissible for your attorney-in-fact to order that nutrition and hydration be withheld, then you also should indicate in your Living Will that it is permissible for your physician to withhold nutrition and hydration.

5. **If you previously have given consent for treatment** (before becoming unable to communicate), your attorney-in-fact cannot withdraw your consent unless certain conditions are met. Either your physical condition must have changed and/or the treatment you approved is no longer of benefit or the treatment has not been proven effective.

If you have a Health Care Power of Attorney and a **Living Will**, health care workers must go by the wishes you state in your Living Will, once the Living Will becomes effective. In other words, your Living Will takes precedence over your Health Care Power of Attorney.

You can change your mind and revoke your **Health Care Power of Attorney** at any time. You can do this simply by telling your attorney-in-fact, your physician and your family that you have changed your mind and wish to revoke your **Health Care Power of Attorney**. In this case, it is probably a good idea to ask for a copy of the document back from anyone to whom you have given it.

How to Fill Out the Health Care Power of Attorney Form

You should use this form to appoint someone to make health care decisions for you if you should become unable to make them for yourself.

NOTE:

1. **Read over all information carefully.** Definitions are included as part of the form.

2. **On the first two lines of this form**, print your full name and birth date.

3. **Under "Naming of My Agent,"** fill in the name of the person you are appointing as your attorney-in-fact, the agent's current address and telephone number. You may name alternative agents on the indicated spaces following but do not need to do so. If you choose not to name alternative agents, you may wish to cross out the unused lines. You may not name your attending physician or the administrator of any nursing home where you are receiving care as your attorney-in-fact.

4. **On the fifth page of the form**, written in bold face type under *Special Instructions* is the statement that will give your physician permission to withhold food and water in the event you are permanently unconscious. If you want to give your physician permission to withhold food and water in this situation, then you must place your initials on the line indicated in number 3.

5. **The form provides a section where you may write additional instructions** and impose additional limitations that you may consider appropriate to document. You may attach additional pages if needed. You should include all attached pages with any copy(ies) you make and you should note the attached pages on the form itself in the related area.

6. **Following "Additional Instructions or Limitations" is a section where you indicate** whether or not you have a Living Will. Immediately below this area is where you date and sign the form. Remember, the **Health Care Power of** Attorney is not considered valid or effective unless you do one of the following:

First Option—Date and sign **the Health Care Power of Attorney** in the presence of two witnesses, who also must sign and include their addresses and indicate the date of their signatures.

OR

Second Option—Date and sign the Health Care Power of Attorney in the presence of a notary public and have the Health Care Power of Attorney notarized on the appropriate space provided on the form.

The following people may not serve as a witness to your **Health Care Power of Attorney:**

- **The Agent and any successor agent named in this** document;

- Anyone related to you by blood, marriage, or adoption, including your spouse and your children;

- **Your attending physician or,** if you are in a nursing home, the administrator of the nursing home.

7. **NOTE:** The section titled NOTICE TO ADULT EXECUTING THIS DOCUMENT is required by law to be part of the document and must accompany it and its copies.

State of Ohio
Health Care Power of Attorney
of

_____

(Print Full Name)

_____

(Birth Date)

I state that this is my Health Care Power of Attorney and I revoke any prior Health Care Power of Attorney signed by me. I understand the nature and purpose of this document. If any provision is found to be invalid or unenforceable, it will not affect the rest of this document.

The Health Care Power of Attorney is in effect only when I cannot make health care decisions for myself. However, this does not require or imply that a court must declare me incompetent.

Definitions. Several legal and medical terms are used in this document. For convenience they are explained below.

Agent or attorney-in-fact means the adult I name in this Health Care Power of Attorney to make health care decisions for me.

Artificially or technologically supplied nutrition or hydration means the providing of food and fluids through intravenous or tube "feedings."

Cardiopulmonary resuscitation or CPR means treatment to try to restart breathing or heartbeat. CPR may be done by breathing into the mouth, pushing on the chest, putting a tube through the mouth or nose into the throat, administering medication, giving electric shock to the chest, or by other means.

Comfort care means any measure taken to diminish pain or discomfort, but not to postpone death.

Do Not Resuscitate or **DNR** Order means a medical order given by my physician and written in my medical records that cardiopulmonary resuscitation or CPR is not to be administered to me.

Health care means any medical (including dental, nursing, psychological, and surgical) procedure, treatment, intervention or other measure used to maintain, diagnose or treat any physical or mental condition.

Health Care Power of Attorney means this document that allows me to name an adult person to act as my agent to make health care decisions for me if I become unable to do so.

Life-sustaining treatment means any health care, including artificially or technologically supplied nutrition and hydration, that will serve mainly to prolong the process of dying.

Living Will Declaration or Living Will means another document that lets me specify the health care I want to receive if I become terminally ill or permanently unconscious and cannot make my wishes known.

Permanently unconscious state means an irreversible condition in which I am permanently unaware of myself and surroundings. My physician and one other physician must examine me and agree that the total loss of higher brain function has left me unable to feel pain or suffering.

Principal means the person signing this document.

Terminal condition or **terminal** illness means an irreversible, incurable and untreatable condition caused by disease, illness or injury. My physician and one other physician will have examined me and believe that I cannot recover and that death is likely to occur within a relatively short time if I do not receive life-sustaining treatment.

Naming of My Agent. The person named below is my agent who will make health care decisions for me as authorized in this document.

Agent's Name: _____

Agent's Current Address: _____

Agent's Current Telephone Number: _____

Naming of Alternate Agents. *[Note: You do not need to name alternate agents. You also may name just one alternate agent. If you do not name alternate agents or name just one alternate agent, you may wish to cross out the unused lines.]*

Should my agent named above not be immediately available or be unwilling or unable to make decisions for me, then I name, in the following order of priority, the following persons as my alternate agents:

First Alternate Agent   Second Alternate Agent

Name: _____   Name:_____

Address: _____   Address: _____

_____   _____

Telephone:_____   Telephone: _____

Any person can rely on a statement by any alternate agent named above that he or she is properly acting under this document and such person does not have to make any further investigation or inquiry.

Guidance to Agent. My agent will make health care decisions for me based on the instructions that I give in this document and on my wishes otherwise known to my agent. If my agent believes that my wishes as made known to my agent conflict with what is in this document, this document will control. If my wishes are unclear or unknown, my agent will make health care decisions in my best interests. My agent will determine my best interests after considering the benefits, the burdens, and the risks that might result from a given decision. If no agent is available, this document will guide decisions about my health care.

Authority of Agent. My agent has full and complete authority to make all health care decisions for me whenever I cannot make such decisions, unless I have otherwise indicated below. This authority includes, but is not limited to, the following: *[Note: Cross out any authority that you do not want your agent to have.]*

1. To consent to the administration of pain-relieving drugs or treatment or procedures (including surgery) that my agent, upon medical advice,

believes may provide comfort to me, even though such drugs, treatment or procedures may hasten my death. My comfort and freedom from pain are important to me and should be protected by my agent and physician.

2.   If I am in a terminal condition, to give, to withdraw or to refuse to give informed consent to life-sustaining treatment, including artificially or technologically supplied nutrition or hydration.

3.   To give, withdraw or refuse to give informed consent to any health care procedure, treatment, intervention, or other measure.

4.   To request, review, and receive any information, verbal or written, regarding my physical or mental health, including, but not limited to, all my medical and health care records.

5.   To consent to further disclosure of information, and to disclose medical and related information concerning my condition and treatment to other persons.

6.   To execute for me any releases or other documents that may be required in order to obtain medical and related information.

7.   To execute consents, waivers, and releases of liability for me and for my estate to all persons who comply with my agent's instructions and decisions. To indemnify and hold harmless, at my expense, any third party who acts under this Health Care Power of Attorney. I will be bound by such indemnity entered into by my agent.

8.   To select, employ, and discharge health care personnel and services providing home health care and the like.

9.   To select, contract for my admission to, transfer me to, or authorize my discharge from any medical or health care facility, including, but not limited to, hospitals, nursing homes, assisted living facilities, hospices, adult homes and the like.

10. To transport me or arrange for my transportation to a place where this Health Care Power of Attorney is honored, should I become unable to make health care decisions for myself in a place where this document is not enforced.

11. To complete and sign for me the following:

(a) Consents to health care treatment, or the issuance of Do Not Resuscitate (DNR) Orders or other similar orders; and

(b) Requests for my transfer to another facility, to be discharged against health care advice, or other similar requests; and

(c) Any other document desirable to implement health care decisions that my agent is authorized to make pursuant to this document.

Special Instructions. **By placing my initials at number 3 below, I want to specifically authorize my agent to refuse, or if treatment has commenced, to withdraw consent to, the provision of artificially or technologically supplied nutrition or hydration if:**

1. **I am in a permanently unconscious state; and**

2. **My physician and at least one other physician who has examined me have determined, to a reasonable degree of medical certainty, that artificially or technologically supplied nutrition and hydration will not provide comfort to me or relieve my pain; and**

3. **I have placed my initials on this line: _____**

Limitations of Agent's Authority. I understand that under Ohio law, there are five limitations to the authority of my agent:

1. My agent cannot order the withdrawal of life-sustaining treatment unless I am in a terminal condition or a permanently unconscious state, and two physicians have confirmed the diagnosis and have determined that I have no reasonable possibility of regaining the ability to make decisions; and

2. My agent cannot order the withdrawal of any treatment given to provide comfort care or to relieve pain; and

3. If I am pregnant, my agent cannot refuse or withdraw informed consent to health care if the refusal or withdrawal would end my pregnancy unless the pregnancy or health care would create a substantial risk to my life or two physicians determine that the fetus would not be born alive; and

4. My agent cannot order the withdrawal of artificially or technologically supplied nutrition or hydration unless I am terminally ill or perma-

nently unconscious and two physicians agree that nutrition or hydration will no longer provide comfort or relieve pain and, in the event that I am permanently unconscious, I have given a specific direction to withdraw nutrition or hydration elsewhere in this document; and

5. If I previously consented to any health care, my agent cannot withdraw that treatment unless my condition has significantly changed so that the health care is significantly less beneficial to me, or unless the health care is not achieving the purpose for which I chose the health care.

Additional Instructions or Limitations. I may give additional instructions or impose additional limitations on the authority of my agent. [*Note: On the lines below you may write in additional instructions or limitations. Here you may include any specific instructions or limitations you consider appropriate, such as instructions to refuse specific types of treatment that are inconsistent with your religious beliefs or unacceptable to you for any other reason. If the space below is not sufficient, you may attach additional pages. If you include additional instructions or limitations here and your wishes change, you should complete a new Health Care Power of Attorney and tell your agent about the changes. If you do not have any additional instructions or limitations, you may wish to write "None" below or cross out the unused lines.]*

_____

_____

_____

_____

_____

_____

_____

_____

_____

_____

_____

_____

_____

_____

_____

_____

No Expiration Date. This Health Care Power of Attorney will have no expiration date and will not be affected by my disability or by the passage of time.

Guardian. I intend that the authority given to my agent will eliminate the need for any court to appoint a guardian of my person. However, should such proceedings start, I nominate my agent to serve as the guardian of my person, without bond.

Enforcement by Agent. My agent may take for me, at my expense, any action my agent considers advisable to enforce my wishes under this document.

Release of Agent's Personal Liability. My agent will not incur any personal liability to me or my estate for making reasonable choices in good faith concerning my health care.

Copies the Same as Original. Any person may rely on a copy of this document.

Out of State Application. I intend that this document be honored in any jurisdiction to the extent allowed by law.

Living Will. I have completed a Living Will: ____Yes ____No

SIGNATURE
[See next page for witness or notary requirements.]

I understand the purpose and effect of this document and sign my name to this Health Care Power of Attorney on _____, 20___ at _____, Ohio.

_____
PRINCIPAL

[You are responsible for telling members of your family and your physician about this document and the name of your agent. You also may wish, but are not required to tell your religious advisor and your lawyer that you have signed a Health Care Power of Attorney. You may wish to give a copy to each person not filed.]

[You may choose to file a copy of this Health Care Power of Attorney with your County Recorder for safekeeping.]

WITNESSES OR NOTARY ACKNOWLEDGMENT
[Choose one.]

*[This Health Care Power of Attorney will not be valid unless it either is signed by two eligible witnesses who are present when you sign or are present when you acknowledge your signature, **or** it is acknowledged before a Notary Public]*

The following persons cannot serve as a witness to this Health Care Power of Attorney: *the agent; any successor agent named in this document; your spouse; your children; anyone else related to you by blood, marriage or adoption; your attending physician; or if you are in a nursing home, the administrator of the nursing home.*

Witnesses. I attest that the Principal signed or acknowledged this Health Care Power of Attorney in my presence, that the Principal appears to be of sound mind and not under or subject to duress, fraud or undue influence. I further attest that I am not an agent designated in this document, I am not the attending physician of the Principal, I am not the administrator of a nursing home in which the Principal is receiving care, and I am an adult not related to the Principal by blood, marriage or adoption.

_____ residing at _____
Signature

_____
Print Name

Dated: _____ 20 _____

_____ residing at _____
Signature

_____
Print Name

Dated: _____ 20 _____

OR

Notary Acknowledgment
State of Ohio

County of _____ss.

On _____ 20 _____ before me, the undersigned Notary Public, personally appeared _____, known to me or satisfactorily proven to be the person whose name is subscribed to the above Health Care Power of Attorney as the Principal, and who has acknowledged that (s)he executed the same for the purposes expressed therein. I attest that the Principal appears to be of sound mind and not under or subject to duress, fraud or undue influence.

_____
Notary Public
My Commission Expires:_____

[This notice is included in this printed form as required by Ohio Revised Code § 1337.17]

NOTICE TO ADULT EXECUTING THIS DOCUMENT

This is an important legal document. Before executing this document, you should know these facts:

This document gives the person you designate (the attorney-in-fact) the power to make MOST health care decisions for you if you lose the capacity to make informed health care decisions for yourself. This power is effective only when your attending physician determines that you have lost the capacity to make informed health care decisions for yourself and, notwithstanding this document, as long as you have the capacity to make informed health care decisions for yourself, you retain the right to make all medical and other health care decisions for yourself.

You may include specific limitations in this document on the authority of the attorney-in-fact to make health care decisions for you.

Subject to any specific limitations you include in this document, if your attending physician determines that you have lost the capacity to make an informed decision on a health care matter, the attorney-in-fact GENERALLY will be authorized by this document to make health care decisions for you to the same extent as you could make those decisions yourself, if you had the capacity to do so. The authority of the attorney-in-fact to make health care decisions for you GENERALLY will include the authority to give informed consent, to refuse to give informed consent, or to withdraw informed consent to any care, treatment, service, or procedure to maintain, diagnose, or treat a physical or mental condition.

HOWEVER, even if the attorney-in-fact has general authority to make health care decisions for you under this document, the attorney-in-fact NEVER will be authorized to do any of the following:

(1) Refuse or withdraw informed consent to life-sustaining treatment unless your attending physician and one other physician who examines you determine, to a reasonable degree of medical certainty and in accordance with reasonable medical standards, that either of the following applies:

   (a) You are suffering from an irreversible, incurable and untreatable condition caused by disease, illness, or injury from which (i) there can be no recovery and (ii) your death is likely to occur within a relatively short time if life-sustaining treatment is not administered, and your attending physician additionally determines, to a reasonable degree of medical certainty and in accordance with reasonable medical standards, that there is no reasonable possibility that you will regain the capacity to make informed health care decisions for yourself.

[This notice is included in this printed form as required by Ohio Revised Code § 1337.17]

   (b) You are in a state of permanent unconsciousness that is characterized by you being irreversibly unaware of yourself and your environment and by a total loss of cerebral cortical functioning, resulting in you having no capacity to experience pain or suffering, and your attending physician additionally determines, to a reasonable degree of medical certainty and in accordance with reasonable medical standards, that there is no reasonable possibility that you will regain the capacity to make informed health care decisions for yourself.

(2) Refuse or withdraw informed consent to health care necessary to provide you with comfort care (except that, if the attorney-in-fact is not prohibited from doing so under (4) below, the attorney-in-fact could refuse or withdraw informed consent to the provision of nutrition or hydration to you as described under (4) below. **(You should**

understand that comfort care is defined in Ohio law to mean artificially or technologically administered sustenance (nutrition) or fluids (hydration) when administered to diminish your pain or discomfort, not to postpone your death, and any other medical or nursing procedure, treatment, intervention, or other measure that would be taken to diminish your pain or discomfort, not to postpone your death. Consequently, if your attending physician were to determine that a previously described medical or nursing procedure, treatment, intervention, or other measure will not or no longer will serve to provide comfort to you or alleviate your pain, then, subject to (4) below, your attorney-in-fact would be authorized to refuse or withdraw informed consent to the procedure, treatment, intervention, or other measure.)

(3) Refuse or withdraw informed consent to health care for you if you are pregnant and if the refusal or withdrawal would terminate the pregnancy (unless the pregnancy or health care would pose a substantial risk to your life, or unless your attending physician and at least one other physician who examines you determine, to a reasonable degree of medical certainty and in accordance with reasonable medical standards, that the fetus would not be born alive).

(4) **Refuse or withdraw informed consent to the provision of artificially or technologically administered sustenance (nutrition) or fluids (hydration) to you, unless:**

   (a) **You are in a terminal condition or in a permanently unconscious state.**

[This notice is included in this printed form as required by Ohio Revised Code § 1337.17]

   (b) **Your attending physician and at least one other physician who has examined you determine, to a reasonable degree of medical certainty and in accordance with reasonable medical standards, that nutrition or hydration will not or no longer will serve to provide comfort to you or alleviate your pain.**

   (c) **If, but only if, you are in a permanently unconscious state, you authorize the attorney-in-fact to refuse or withdraw informed consent to the provision of nutrition or hydration to you by doing both of the following in this document:**

(i)   Including a statement in capital letters or other conspicuous type, including, but not limited to, a different font, bigger type, or boldface type, that the attorney-in-fact may refuse or withdraw informed consent to the provision of nutrition or hydration to you if are in a permanently unconscious state and if the determination that nutrition or hydration will not or no longer will serve to provide comfort to you or alleviate your pain is made, or checking or otherwise marking a box or line (if any) that is adjacent to a similar statement on this document.

(ii)   Placing your initials or signature underneath or adjacent to the statement, check, or other mark previously described.

(d)   Your attending physician determines, in good faith, that you authorized the attorney-in-fact to refuse or withdraw informed consent to the provision of nutrition or hydration to you if you are in a permanently unconscious state by complying with the above requirements of (4)(c)(i) and (ii) above.

5.   **Withdraw informed consent to any health care** to which you previously consented, unless a change in your physical condition has significantly decreased the benefit of that health care to you, or unless the health care is not, or is no longer, significantly effective in achieving the purposes for which you consented to its use.

Additionally, when exercising authority to make health care decisions for you, the attorney-in-fact will have to act consistently with your desires or, if your desires are unknown, to act in your best interest. You may express your desires to the attorney-in-fact by including them in this document or by making them known to the attorney-in-fact in another manner.

When acting pursuant to this document, the attorney-in-fact GENERALLY will have the same rights that you have to receive information about proposed health care, to review health care records, and to consent to the disclosure of health care records. You can limit that right in this document if you so choose.

[This notice is included in this printed form as required by Ohio Revised Code § 1337.17]

Generally, you may designate any competent adult as the attorney-in-fact under this document. However, you CANNOT designate your attending physician or the administrator of any nursing home in which you are receiving care as the attorney-in-fact under this document. Additionally, you CANNOT designate an employee or agent of your attending physician, or an employee or agent of a health care facility at which you are being treated, as the attorney-in-fact under this document, unless either type of employee or agent is a competent adult and related to you by blood, marriage, or adoption, or unless either type of employee or agent is a competent adult and you and the employee or agent are members of the same religious order.

This document has no expiration date under Ohio law, but you may choose to specify a date upon which your durable power of attorney for health care will expire. However, if you specify an expiration date and then lack the capacity to make informed health care decisions for yourself on that date, the document and the power it grants to your attorney-in-fact will continue in effect until you regain the capacity to make informed health care decisions for yourself.

You have the right to revoke the designation of the attorney-in-fact and the right to revoke this entire document at any time and in any manner. Any such revocation generally will be effective when you express your intention to make the revocation. However, if you made your attending physician aware of this document, any such revocation will be effective only when you communicate it to your attending physician, or when a witness to the revocation or other health care personnel to whom the revocation is communicated by such a witness communicates it to your attending physician.

If you execute this document and create a valid durable power of attorney for health care with it, it will revoke any prior, valid durable power of attorney for health care that you created, unless you indicate otherwise in this document.

This document is not valid as a durable power of attorney for health care unless it is acknowledged before a notary public or is signed by at least two adult witnesses who are present when you sign or acknowledge your signature. No person who is related to you by blood, marriage, or adoption may be a witness. The attorney-in-fact, your attending physician, and the administrator of any nursing home in which you are receiving care also are ineligible to be witnesses.

If there is anything in this document that you do not understand, you should ask your lawyer to explain it to you.

Appendix F

State of Ohio Living Will Declaration

I, _____, presently residing at _____, Ohio (the "Declarant"), being of sound mind and not under or subject to duress, fraud or undue influence, intending to create a Living Will Declaration under Chapter 2133 of the Ohio Revised Code, as amended from time to time, do voluntarily make known my desire that my dying shall not be artificially prolonged. If I am unable to give directions regarding the use of life-sustaining treatment when I am in a terminal condition or a permanently unconscious state, it is my intention that this Living Will Declaration shall be honored by my family and physicians as the final expression of my legal right to refuse medical or surgical treatment. I am a competent adult who understands and accepts the consequences of such refusal and the purpose and effect of this document.

In the event I am in a terminal condition, I do hereby declare and direct that my attending physician shall:

1. administer no life-sustaining treatment;

2. withdraw such treatment if such treatment has commenced; and

3. permit me to die naturally and provide me with only that care necessary to make me comfortable and to relieve my pain but not to postpone my death.

In the event I am in a permanently unconscious state, I do hereby declare and direct that my attending physician shall:

1. administer no life-sustaining treatment, except for the provision of artificially or technologically supplied nutrition or hydration unless, in the following paragraph, I have authorized its withholding or withdrawal;

2. withdraw such treatment if such treatment has commenced; and

3. permit me to die naturally and provide me with only that care necessary to make me comfortable and to relieve my pain but not to
postpone my death.

☐ ____IN ADDITION, IF I HAVE MARKED THE FOREGOING BOX
AND HAVE PLACED MY INITIALS ON THE LINE ADJACENT TO IT, I
AUTHORIZE MY ATTENDING PHYSICIAN TO WITHHOLD, OR IN
THE EVENT THAT TREATMENT HAS ALREADY COMMENCED, TO
WITHDRAW, THE PROVISION OF ARTIFICIALLY OR TECHNOLOGI-
CALLY SUPPLIED NUTRITION AND HYDRATION, IF I AM IN A
PERMANENTLY UNCONSCIOUS STATE AND IF MY ATTENDING
PHYSICIAN AND AT LEAST ONE OTHER PHYSICIAN WHO HAS
EXAMINED ME DETERMINE, TO A REASONABLE DEGREE OF
MEDICAL CERTAINTY AND IN ACCORDANCE WITH REASONABLE
MEDICAL STANDARDS, THAT SUCH NUTRITION OR HYDRATION
WILL NOT OR NO LONGER WILL SERVE TO PROVIDE COMFORT TO
ME OR ALLEVIATE MY PAIN.

In the event my attending physician determines that life-sustaining
treatment should be withheld or withdrawn, he or she shall make a good faith
effort and use reasonable diligence to notify one of the persons named below
in the following order of priority:

1. _____, _____
             (Name)   (Relationship)
presently residing at _____ Phone: _____

2. _____, _____
             (Name)   (Relationship)
presently residing at _____ Phone: _____

For purposes of this Living Will Declaration:

(A)   "Life-sustaining treatment" means any medical procedure, treatment,
intervention, or other measure including artificially or technologically supplied
nutrition and hydration that, when administered, will serve principally to
prolong the process of dying.

(B)   "TERMINAL CONDITION" MEANS AN IRREVERSIBLE, IN-
CURABLE, AND UNTREATABLE CONDITION CAUSED BY DISEASE,
ILLNESS, OR INJURY TO WHICH, TO A REASONABLE DEGREE OF
MEDICAL CERTAINTY AS DETERMINED IN ACCORDANCE WITH

REASONABLE MEDICAL STANDARDS BY MY ATTENDING PHYSICIAN AND ONE OTHER PHYSICIAN WHO HAS EXAMINED ME, BOTH OF THE FOLLOWING APPLY:

(1)   THERE CAN BE NO RECOVERY, AND

(2)   DEATH IS LIKELY TO OCCUR WITHIN A RELATIVELY SHORT TIME IF LIFE-SUSTAINING TREATMENT IS NOT ADMINISTERED.

(C)   "PERMANENTLY UNCONSCIOUS STATE" MEANS A STATE OF PERMANENT UNCONSCIOUSNESS THAT, TO A REASONABLE DEGREE OF MEDICAL CERTAINTY AS DETERMINED IN ACCORDANCE WITH REASONABLE MEDICAL STANDARDS BY MY ATTENDING PHYSICIAN AND ONE OTHER PHYSICIAN WHO HAS EXAMINED ME, IS CHARACTERIZED BY BOTH OF THE FOLLOWING:

(1)   I AM IRREVERSIBLY UNAWARE OF MYSELF AND MY ENVIRONMENT, AND

(2)   THERE IS A TOTAL LOSS OF CEREBRAL CORTICAL FUNCTIONING, RESULTING IN MY HAVING NO CAPACITY TO EXPERIENCE PAIN OR SUFFERING.

I understand the purpose and effect of this document and sign my name to this Living Will Declaration after careful deliberation on _____

                                                                            (Date)

at _____ , Ohio.
              (City)

_____

                                        DECLARANT

THIS LIVING WILL DECLARATION WILL NOT BE VALID UNLESS IT IS EITHER (1) SIGNED BY TWO ELIGIBLE WITNESSES AS DEFINED BELOW WHO ARE PRESENT WHEN YOU SIGN OR ACKNOWLEDGE YOUR SIGNATURE OR (2) ACKNOWLEDGED BEFORE A NOTARY PUBLIC.

I attest that the Declarant signed or acknowledged this Living Will Declaration in my presence, and that the Declarant appears to be of sound mind and not under or subject to duress, fraud or undue influence. I further attest that I am not the attending physician of the Declarant, I am not the administrator of a nursing home in which the Declarant is receiving care, and that I am an adult not related to the Declarant by blood, marriage or adoption.

Signature: _____   Residence Address: _____

Print Name: _____   _____

Date: _____   _____

Signature: _____   Residence Address: _____

Print Name: _____   _____

Date: _____   _____

OR

ACKNOWLEDGMENT

State of Ohio
County of _____ ss:

On this the _____ day of _____, 20 ____, before me, the undersigned Notary Public, personally appeared _____, known to me or satisfactorily proven to be the person whose name is subscribed to the above Living Will Declaration as the Declarant, and acknowledged that (s)he executed the same for the purposes expressed therein. I attest that the Declarant appears to be of sound mind and not under or subject to duress, fraud or undue influence.

My Commission
Expires: _____   _____
                                      Notary Public

NOTE: YOU MAY WISH TO GIVE EXECUTED COPIES OF THIS LIVING WILL DECLARATION TO YOUR AGENT UNDER ANY DURABLE POWER OF ATTORNEY FOR HEALTH CARE YOU HAVE EXECUTED, TO YOUR LAWYER, YOUR PERSONAL PHYSICIAN AND MEMBERS OF YOUR FAMILY.

NOTICE TO DECLARANT

This form of a Living Will Declaration is designed to serve as evidence of an individual's desire that life-sustaining medical treatment, including artificially or technologically supplied nutrition and hydration, be withheld or withdrawn if the individual is unable to make informed treatment decisions and is in a terminal condition or is in a permanently unconscious state.

If you would not choose to withhold or to withdraw any or all forms of life-sustaining treatment, you have the legal right to so choose and you might want to state your medical treatment preferences in writing in another form of Declaration.

Under Ohio law a Living Will Declaration is applicable only to individuals in a terminal condition, or a permanently unconscious state. If you wish to direct medical treatment in other circumstances, you should consider preparing a Durable Power of Attorney for Health Care.

As a public service, a special committee of the Ohio State Bar Association prepared this form, which has been approved by the Ohio State Medical Association.

© August 1991. Ohio State Bar Association and Ohio State Medical Association. May be reprinted and copied for use by attorneys, medical and osteopathic physicians, hospitals, bar associations, medical societies and associations, the public, and non-profit organizations. May not be reproduced or sold for profit.

Appendix G

Florida Designation of Health Care Surrogate

**Suggested Form of a Health Care Surrogate,
Florida Statutes Section 765.203**

Name: _____

In the event that I have been determined to be incapacitated to provide informed consent for medical treatment and surgical and diagnostic procedures, I wish to designate as my surrogate for health care decisions:

Name _____

Street Address _____

City _____State _____ Zip _____

Phone _____

If my surrogate is unwilling or unable to perform his or her duties, I wish to designate as my alternate surrogate:

Name _____

Street Address _____

City _____State _____ Zip _____

Phone _____

I fully understand that this designation will permit my designee to make health care decisions and to provide, withhold, or withdraw consent on my behalf; to apply for public benefits to defray the cost of health care; and to authorize my admission to or transfer from a health care facility.

Additional Instructions (optional): _____

_____

_____

_____

_____

I further affirm that this designation is not being made as a condition of treatment or admission to a health care facility. I will notify and send a copy of this document to the following persons other than my surrogate, so they may know who my surrogate is:

Name _____

Name _____

Signed _____

Witnesses   1. _____

                   2. _____

At least one witness must not be a husband or wife or a blood relative of the principal.

Appendix H

Five Wishes [*]

WISH 1
The Person I Want To Make Health Care Decisions For Me When I Can't Make Them For Myself.

If I am no longer able to make my own health care decisions, this form names the person I choose to make these choices for me. This person will be my Health Care Agent (or other term that may be used in my state, such as proxy, representative or surrogate). This person will make my health care choices if both of these things happen:

- My attending or treating doctor finds I am no longer able to make health care choices, AND

- Another health care professional agrees that this is true.

If my state has a different way of finding that I am not able to make health care choices, then my state's way should be followed.

The Person I Choose As My Health Care Agent Is:

_____   _____
First Choice Name   Phone

_____   _____
Address   City/State/Zip

If this person is not able or willing to make these choices for me, *OR* is divorced or legally separated from me, *OR* this person has died, then these people are my next choices:

Second Choice Name	Third Choice Name
Address	Address
City/State/Zip	City/State/Zip
Phone	Phone

Picking the Right Person To Be Your Health Care Agent

Choose someone who knows you very well, cares about you, and who can make difficult decisions. A spouse or family member may not be the best choice because they are too emotionally involved. Sometimes they **are** the best choice. You know best. Choose someone who is able to stand up for you so that your wishes are followed. Also, choose someone who is likely to be nearby so that they can help when you need them. Whether you choose a spouse, family member, or friend as your Health Care Agent, make sure you talk about these wishes and be sure that this person agrees to respect and follow your wishes. Your Health Care Agent should be **at least 18 years or older** (in Colorado, 21 years or older) and should **not** be:

- Your health care provider, including the owner or operator of a health or residential or community care facility serving you.

- An employee of your health care provider.

- Serving as an agent or proxy for 10 or more people unless he or she is your spouse or close relative.

I understand that my Health Care Agent can make health care decisions for me. I want my Agent to be able to do the following: **(Please cross out anything you don't want your Agent to do that is listed below.)**

- Make choices for me about my medical care or services, like tests, medicine, or surgery. This care or service could be to find out what my health problem is, or how to treat it. It can also include care to keep me alive. If the treatment or care has already started, my Health Care Agent can keep it going or have it stopped.

- Interpret any instructions I have given in this form or given in other discussions, according to my Health Care Agent's understanding of my wishes and values.

- Arrange for admission to a hospital, hospice, or nursing home for me. My Health Care Agent can hire any kind of health care worker I may need to help me or take care of me. My Agent may also fire a health care worker, if needed.

- Make the decision to request, take away or not give medical treatments, including artificially provided food and water, and any other treatments to keep me alive.

- See and approve release of my medical records and personal files. If I need to sign my name to get any of these files, my Health Care Agent can sign it for me.

- Move me to another state to get the care I need or to carry out my wishes.

- Authorize or refuse to authorize any medication or procedure needed to help with pain.

- Take any legal action needed to carry out my wishes.

- Donate useable organs or tissues of mine as allowed by law.

- Apply for Medicare, Medicaid, or other programs or insurance benefits for me. My Health Care Agent can see my personal files, like bank records, to find out what is needed to fill out these forms.

- Listed below are any changes, additions, or limitations on my Health Care Agent's powers.

_____

_____

_____

_____

_____

If I Change My Mind About Having A Health Care Agent, I Will

Destroy all copies of this part of the Five Wishes form. *OR*

- Tell someone, such as my doctor or family, that I want to cancel or change my Health Care Agent. *OR*

- Write the word "Revoked" in large letters across the name of each agent whose authority I want to cancel. Sign my name on that page.

WISH 2
My Wish For The Kind Of Medical Treatment
I Want Or Don't Want.

I believe that my life is precious and I deserve to be treated with dignity. When the time comes that I am very sick and am not able to speak for myself, I want the following wishes, and any other directions I have given to my Health Care Agent, to be respected and followed.

What You Should Keep In Mind As My Caregiver

- I do not want to be in pain. I want my doctor to give me enough medicine to relieve my pain, even if that means that I will be drowsy or sleep more than I would otherwise.

- I do not want anything done or omitted by my doctors or nurses with the intention of taking my life.

- I want to be offered food and fluids by mouth, and kept clean and warm.

What "Life-Support Treatment" Means To Me

Life-support treatment means any medical procedure, device or medication to keep me alive. Life-support treatment includes: medical devices put in me to help me breathe; food and water supplied by medical device (tube feeding); cardiopulmonary resuscitation (CPR); major surgery; blood transfusions; dialysis; antibiotics; and anything else meant to keep me alive. If I wish to limit the meaning of life-support treatment because of my religious or personal beliefs, I write this limitation in the space below. I do this to make very clear what I want and under what conditions.

_____

_____

_____

_____

In Case Of An Emergency

If you have a medical emergency and ambulance personnel arrive, they may look to see if you have a **Do Not Resuscitate** form or bracelet. Many states require a person to have a **Do Not Resuscitate** form filled out and signed by a doctor. This form lets ambulance personnel know that you don't want them to use life-support treatment when you are dying. Please check with your doctor to see if you need to have a **Do Not Resuscitate** form filled out.

Here is the kind of medical treatment that I want or don't want in the four situations listed below. I want my Health Care Agent, my family, my doctors and other health care providers, my friends and all others to know these directions.

Close to Death:

If my doctor and another health care professional both decide that I am likely to die within a short period of time, and life-support treatment would only delay the moment of my death (Choose *one* of the following):

☐ I want to have life-support treatment.

☐ I do not want life-support treatment. If it has been started, I want it stopped.

☐ I want to have life-support treatment if my doctor believes it could help. But I want my doctor to stop giving me life-support treatment if it is not helping my health condition or symptoms.

In A Coma and Not Expected to Wake Up or Recover:

If my doctor and another health care professional both decide that I am in a coma from which I am not expected to wake up or recover and I have brain damage, and life-support treatment would only delay the moment of my death (Choose *one* of the following):

☐ I want to have life-support treatment.

☐ I do not want life-support treatment. If it has been started, I want it stopped.

☐ I want to have life-support treatment if my doctor believes it could help. But I want my doctor to stop giving me life-support treatment if it is not helping my health condition or symptoms.

Permanent and Severe Brain Damage and Not Expected to Recover:

If my doctor and another health care professional both decide that I have permanent and severe brain damage (for example, I can open my eyes, but I cannot speak or understand) and I am not expected to get better, and life-support treatment would only delay the moment of my death (Choose *one* of the following):

☐ I want to have life-support treatment.

☐ I do not want life-support treatment. If it has been started, I want it stopped.

☐ I want to have life-support treatment if my doctor believes it could help. But I want my doctor to stop giving me life-support treatment if it is not helping my health condition or symptoms.

In Another Condition Under Which I Do Not Wish To Be Kept Alive:

If there is another condition under which I do not wish to have life-support treatment, I describe it below. In this condition, I believe that the costs and burdens of life-support treatment are too much and not worth the benefits to me. Therefore, in this condition, I do not want life-support treatment. (For example, you may write "end-stage condition." That means that your health has gotten worse. You are not able to take care of yourself in any way, mentally or physically. Life-support treatment will not help you recover. Please leave the space blank if you have no other condition to describe.)

_____

_____

_____

_____

_____

The next three wishes deal with my personal, spiritual and emotional wishes. They are important to me. I want to be treated with dignity near the end of my life, so I would like people to do the things written in Wishes 3, 4, and 5 when they can be done. I understand that my family, my doctors and other health care providers, my friends, and others may not be able to do these things or are not required by law to do these things. I do not expect the following wishes to place new or added legal duties on my doctors or other health care providers. I also do not expect these wishes to excuse my doctor or other health care providers from giving me the proper care asked for by law.

WISH 3

My Wish For How Comfortable I Want To Be.
(Please cross out anything that you don't agree with.)

- I do not want to be in pain. I want my doctor to give me enough medicine to relieve my pain, even if that means I will be drowsy or sleep more than I would otherwise.

- If I show signs of depression, nausea, shortness of breath or hallucinations, I want my caregivers to do whatever they can to help me.

- I wish to have a cool moist cloth put on head if I have a fever.

- I want my lips and mouth kept moist to stop dryness.

- I wish to have warm baths often. I wish to kept fresh and clean at all times.

- I wish to be massaged with warm oils as often as I can be.

- I wish to have my favorite music played when possible until the time of my death.

- I wish to have personal care like shaving, nail clipping, hair brushing, and teeth brushing, as long as they do not cause me pain or discomfort.

- I wish to have religious readings and well-loved poems read aloud when I am near death.

WISH 4

My Wish For How I Want People To Treat Me.
(Please cross out anything that you don't agree with.)

- I wish to have people with me when possible. I want someone to be with me when it seems that death may come at any time.

- I wish to have my hand held and to be talked to when possible, even if I don't seem to respond to the voice or touch of others.

- I wish to have the members of my faith community told that I am sick and asked to pray for me and visit me.

- I wish to be cared for with kindness and cheerfulness, and not sadness.

- I wish to have pictures of my loved ones in my room, near my bed.

- If I am not able to control my bowel or bladder functions, I wish for my clothes and bed linens to be kept clean, and for them to be changed as soon as they can be if they have been soiled.

- I want to die in my home, if that can be done.

WISH 5

My Wish For What I Want My Loved Ones to Know.
(Please cross out anything that you don't agree with.)

- I wish to have my family and friends know that I love them.

- I wish to be forgiven for the times I have hurt my family, friends, and others.

- I wish to have my family, friends, and others know that I forgive them for when they may have hurt me in my life.

- I wish for my family and friends to know that I do not fear death itself. I think it is not the end, but a new beginning for me.

- I wish for all my family members to make peace with each other before my death, if they can.

- I wish for my family and friends to think about what I was like before I became seriously ill. I want them to remember me in this way after my death.

- I wish for my family and friends and caregivers to respect my wishes even if they don't agree with them.

- I wish for my family and friends to look at my dying as a time of personal growth for everyone, including me. This will help me live a meaningful life in my final days.

- I wish for my family and friends to get counseling if they have trouble with my death. I want memories of my life to give them joy and not sorrow.

- After my death, I would like my body to be (circle one): buried or cremated.

- My body or remains should be put in the following location:

  _____

- The following person knows my funeral wishes:_____

  _____

If anyone asks how I want to be remembered, please say the following about me:

_____

_____

_____

If there is to be a memorial service for me, I wish for this service to include the following (list music, songs, readings or other specific requests that you have):

_____

_____

_____

_____

(Please use the space below for any other wishes. For example, you may want to donate any or all parts of your body when you die. Please attach a separate sheet of paper if you need more space.)

_____

_____

_____

_____

_____

_____

Signing The Five Wishes Form

Please make sure you sign your Five Wishes form in the presence of the two witnesses.

I, _____, ask that my family, my doctors, and other health care providers, my friends, and all others, follow my wishes as communicated by my Health Care Agent (if I have one and he or she is available), or as otherwise expressed in this form. This form becomes valid when I am unable to make decisions or speak for myself. If any part of this form cannot be legally followed, I ask that all other parts of this form be followed. I also revoke any health care advance directives I have made before.

Signature:_____ Social Security Number: _____

Address: _____

Phone: _____ Date: _____

Witness Statement • (2 witnesses needed)

I, the witness, declare that the person who signed or acknowledged this form (hereafter "person") is personally known to me, that he/she signed or acknowledged this [Health Care Agent and/or Living Will form(s)] in my presence, and that he/she appears to be of sound mind and under no duress, fraud, or undue influence.

I also declare that I am over 18 years of age and am NOT:

- The individual appointed as (agent/proxy/surrogate/patient advocate/ representative) by this document or his/her successor,

- The person's health care provider, including, owner or operator of a health, long-term care, or other residential or community care facility serving the person,

- An employee of the person's health care provider,

- Financially responsible for the person's health care,

- An employee of a life or health insurance provider for the person,

- Related to the person by blood, marriage, or adoption, and

- To the best of my knowledge, a creditor of the person or entitled to any part of his/her estate under a will or codicil, by operation of law.

(Some states may have fewer rules about who may be a witness. Unless you know your state's rules, please follow the above.)

_____   _____
Signature of Witness #1   Signature of Witness #2

_____   _____
Printed Name of Witness   Printed Name of Witness

_____   _____
Address   Address

_____   _____
                  Phone   Phone

Notarization. • Only required for residents of Missouri, North Carolina, Tennessee and West Virginia

- If you live in Missouri, only your signature should be notarized.

- If you live in North Carolina, Tennessee or West Virginia, you should have your signature, and the signatures of your witnesses, notarized.

STATE OF _____ COUNTY OF _____

On this _____ day of _____, 20 __, the said, _____,
and _____, known to me (or satisfactorily proven) to
be the person named in the foregoing instrument and witnesses, respectively,
personally appeared before me, a Notary Public, within and for the State
and County aforesaid, and acknowledged that they freely and voluntarily
executed the same for the purposes stated therein.

My Commission Expires: _____ Notary Public_____

What To Do After You Complete Five Wishes

- Make sure you sign and witness the form just the way it says in the directions. Then your Five Wishes will be legal and valid.

- Talk about your wishes with your health care agent, family members and others who care about you. Give them copies of your completed Five Wishes.

- Keep the original copy you signed in a special place in your home. Do NOT put it in a safe deposit box. Keep it nearby so that someone can find it when you need it.

- Fill out the wallet card below. Carry it with you. That way people will know where you keep your Five Wishes. [*Editor's Note: The wallet card is not reprinted here.*]

- Talk to your doctor during your next office visit. Give your doctor a copy of your Five Wishes. Make sure it is put in your medical record. Be sure your doctor understands your wishes and is willing to follow them. Ask him or her to tell other doctors who treat you to honor them.

- If you are admitted to a hospital or nursing home, take a copy of your Five Wishes with you. Ask that it be put in your medical record.

I have given the following people copies of my completed Five Wishes:

_____

_____

_____

Residents of Institutions In CALIFORNIA, CONNECTICUT, DELA-WARE, GEORGIA, NEW YORK, and NORTH DAKOTA Must Follow Special Witnessing Rules.

If you live in certain institutions (a nursing home, other licensed long-term care facility, a home for the mentally retarded or developmentally disabled, or a mental health institution) in one of the states listed above, you may have to follow special "witnessing requirements" for your Five Wishes to be valid. For further information, please contact a social worker or patient advocate at your institution.

Five Wishes is meant to help you plan for the future. It is not meant to give you legal advice. It does not try to answer all questions about anything that could come up. Every person is different, and every situation is different. Laws change from time to time. If you have a specific question or problem, talk to a medical or legal professional for advice.

Appendix I

Sample Tax Forms

Contents

Form **706**

(Rev. August 2004)

Department of the Treasury
Internal Revenue Service

United States Estate (and Generation-Skipping Transfer) Tax Return

Estate of a citizen or resident of the United States (see separate instructions).
To be filed for decedents dying after December 31, 2003, and before January 1, 2005.
For Paperwork Reduction Act Notice, see the separate instructions.

OMB No. 1545-0015

Part 1.—Decedent and Executor

1a Decedent's first name and middle initial (and maiden name, if any)	1b Decedent's last name		2 Decedent's Social Security No.

3a County, state, and ZIP code, or foreign country, of legal residence (domicile) at time of death	3b Year domicile established	4 Date of birth	5 Date of death

6a Name of executor (see page 3 of the instructions)	6b Executor's address (number and street including apartment or suite no. or rural route; city, town, or post office; state; and ZIP code) and phone no.

6c Executor's social security number (see page 3 of the instructions)

Phone no. ( )

7a Name and location of court where will was probated or estate administered | 7b Case number

8 If decedent died testate, check here ▶ ☐ and attach a certified copy of the will. | 9 If Form 4768 is attached, check here ▶ ☐

10 If Schedule R-1 is attached, check here ▶ ☐

Part 2.—Tax Computation

1	Total gross estate less exclusion (from Part 5, Recapitulation, page 3, item 12)	1
2	Total allowable deductions (from Part 5, Recapitulation, page 3, item 22)	2
3	Taxable estate (subtract line 2 from line 1)	3
4	Adjusted taxable gifts (total taxable gifts (within the meaning of section 2503) made by the decedent after December 31, 1976, other than gifts that are includible in decedent's gross estate (section 2001(b)))	4
5	Add lines 3 and 4	5
6	Tentative tax on the amount on line 5 from Table A on page 4 of the instructions	6
7	Total gift tax payable with respect to gifts made by the decedent after December 31, 1976. Include gift taxes by the decedent's spouse for such spouse's share of split gifts (section 2513) only if the decedent was the donor of these gifts and they are includible in the decedent's gross estate (see instructions)	7
8	Gross estate tax (subtract line 7 from line 6)	8
9	Maximum unified credit (applicable credit amount) against estate tax .	9	
10	Adjustment to unified credit (applicable credit amount). (This adjustment may not exceed $6,000. See page 5 of the instructions.)	10	
11	Allowable unified credit (applicable credit amount) (subtract line 10 from line 9)	11
12	Subtract line 11 from line 8 (but do not enter less than zero)	12
13	Credit for state death taxes (cannot exceed line 12). **Attach credit evidence** (see instructions). Figure the credit by using the amount on line 3 less $60,000. See Table B in the instructions. Enter the amount here from Table B ▶ .... x .25 . . . . ▶	13
14	Subtract line 13 from line 12	14
15	Credit for Federal gift taxes on pre-1977 gifts (section 2012) (attach computation)	15	
16	Credit for foreign death taxes (from Schedule(s) P). (Attach Form(s) 706-CE.)	16	
17	Credit for tax on prior transfers (from Schedule Q)	17	
18	Total (add lines 15, 16, and 17)	18
19	Net estate tax (subtract line 18 from line 14)	19
20	Generation-skipping transfer taxes (from Schedule R, Part 2, line 10)	20
21	Total transfer taxes (add lines 19 and 20)	21
22	Prior payments. Explain in an attached statement	22	
23	United States Treasury bonds redeemed in payment of estate tax . .	23	
24	Total (add lines 22 and 23)	24
25	Balance due (or overpayment) (subtract line 24 from line 21)	25

Under penalties of perjury, I declare that I have examined this return, including accompanying schedules and statements, and to the best of my knowledge and belief, it is true, correct, and complete. Declaration of preparer other than the executor is based on all information of which preparer has any knowledge.

Signature(s) of executor(s)   Date

Signature of preparer other than executor   Address (and ZIP code)   Date

Cat. No. 20548R

Form 706 (Rev. 8-2004)

Estate of:

Part 3—Elections by the Executor

Please check the "Yes" or "No" box for each question. (See instructions beginning on page 6.)

			Yes	No
1	Do you elect alternate valuation?	1		
2	Do you elect special use valuation? If "Yes," you must complete and attach Schedule A-1.	2		
3	Do you elect to pay the taxes in installments as described in section 6166? If "Yes," you must attach the additional information described on page 10 of the instructions.	3		
4	Do you elect to postpone the part of the taxes attributable to a reversionary or remainder interest as described in section 6163?	4		

Part 4—General Information (Note: *Please attach the necessary supplemental documents.* **You must attach the death certificate.**)
(See instructions on page 10.)

Authorization to receive confidential tax information under Regs. sec. 601.504(b)(2)(i); to act as the estate's representative before the IRS; and to make written or oral presentations on behalf of the estate if return prepared by an attorney, accountant, or enrolled agent for the executor:

Name of representative (print or type)	State	Address (number, street, and room or suite no., city, state, and ZIP code)

I declare that I am the ☐ attorney/ ☐ certified public accountant/ ☐ enrolled agent (you must check the applicable box) for the executor and prepared this return for the executor. I am not under suspension or disbarment from practice before the Internal Revenue Service and am qualified to practice in the state shown above.

Signature	CAF number	Date	Telephone number

1   Death certificate number and issuing authority (attach a copy of the death certificate to this return).

2   Decedent's business or occupation. If retired, check here ▶ ☐ and state decedent's former business or occupation.

3   Marital status of the decedent at time of death:
    ☐ Married
    ☐ Widow or widower—Name, SSN, and date of death of deceased spouse ▶ ....
    ☐ Single
    ☐ Legally separated
    ☐ Divorced—Date divorce decree became final ▶

4a Surviving spouse's name	4b Social security number	4c Amount received (see page 10 of the instructions)

5   Individuals (other than the surviving spouse), trusts, or other estates who receive benefits from the estate (do not include charitable beneficiaries shown in Schedule O) (see instructions). For Privacy Act Notice (applicable to individual beneficiaries only), see the Instructions for Form 1040.

Name of individual, trust, or estate receiving $5,000 or more	Identifying number	Relationship to decedent	Amount (see instructions)

All unascertainable beneficiaries and those who receive less than $5,000 . . . . ▶

Total . . . .

Please check the "Yes" or "No" box for each question.

		Yes	No
6	Does the gross estate contain any section 2044 property (qualified terminable interest property (QTIP) from a prior gift or estate) (see page 11 of the instructions)?		

(continued on next page)   **Page 2**

Form 706 (Rev. 8-2004)

Part 4—General Information *(continued)*

Please check the "Yes" or "No" box for each question.	Yes	No
7a Have Federal gift tax returns ever been filed? . . . . If "Yes," please attach copies of the returns, if available, and furnish the following information:		
7b Period(s) covered **7c** Internal Revenue office(s) where filed		

If you answer "Yes" to any of questions 8–16, you must attach additional information as described in the instructions.

	Yes	No
8a Was there any insurance on the decedent's life that is not included on the return as part of the gross estate?.		
b Did the decedent own any insurance on the life of another that is not included in the gross estate?.		
9 Did the decedent at the time of death own any property as a joint tenant with right of survivorship in which **(a)** one or more of the other joint tenants was someone other than the decedent's spouse, and **(b)** less than the full value of the property is included on the return as part of the gross estate? If "Yes," you must complete and attach Schedule E		
10 Did the decedent, at the time of death, own any interest in a partnership or unincorporated business or any stock in an inactive or closely held corporation?		
11 Did the decedent make any transfer described in section 2035, 2036, 2037, or 2038 (see the instructions for Schedule G beginning on page 13 of the separate instructions)? If "Yes," you must complete and attach Schedule G		
12 Were there in existence at the time of the decedent's death:		
a Any trusts created by the decedent during his or her lifetime?		
b Any trusts not created by the decedent under which the decedent possessed any power, beneficial interest, or trusteeship?		
13 Did the decedent ever possess, exercise, or release any general power of appointment? If "Yes," you must complete and attach Schedule H		
14 Was the marital deduction computed under the transitional rule of Public Law 97-34, section 403(e)(3) (Economic Recovery Tax Act of 1981)? If "Yes," attach a separate computation of the marital deduction, enter the amount on item 20 of the Recapitulation, and note on item 20 "computation attached."		
15 Was the decedent, immediately before death, receiving an annuity described in the "General" paragraph of the instructions for Schedule I? If "Yes," you must complete and attach Schedule I		
16 Was the decedent ever the beneficiary of a trust for which a deduction was claimed by the estate of a pre-deceased spouse under section 2056(b)(7) and which is not reported on this return? If "Yes," attach an explanation		

Part 5—Recapitulation

Item number	Gross estate		Alternate value	Value at date of death
1	Schedule A—Real Estate	1		
2	Schedule B—Stocks and Bonds	2		
3	Schedule C—Mortgages, Notes, and Cash	3		
4	Schedule D—Insurance on the Decedent's Life (attach Form(s) 712). . .	4		
5	Schedule E—Jointly Owned Property (attach Form(s) 712 for life insurance)	5		
6	Schedule F—Other Miscellaneous Property (attach Form(s) 712 for life insurance) .	6		
7	Schedule G—Transfers During Decedent's Life (att. Form(s) 712 for life insurance)	7		
8	Schedule H—Powers of Appointment	8		
9	Schedule I—Annuities	9		
10	Total gross estate (add items 1 through 9).	10		
11	Schedule U—Qualified Conservation Easement Exclusion	11		
12	Total gross estate less exclusion (subtract item 11 from item 10). Enter here and on line 1 of Part 2—Tax Computation	12		

Item number	Deductions		Amount	
13	Schedule J—Funeral Expenses and Expenses Incurred in Administering Property Subject to Claims . . .	13		
14	Schedule K—Debts of the Decedent	14		
15	Schedule K—Mortgages and Liens	15		
16	Total of items 13 through 15	16		
17	Allowable amount of deductions from item 16 (see the instructions for item 17 of the Recapitulation) .	17		
18	Schedule L—Net Losses During Administration	18		
19	Schedule L—Expenses Incurred in Administering Property Not Subject to Claims.	19		
20	Schedule M—Bequests, etc., to Surviving Spouse	20		
21	Schedule O—Charitable, Public, and Similar Gifts and Bequests.	21		
22	Total allowable deductions (add items 17 through 21). Enter here and on line 2 of the Tax Computation.	22		

Page 3

Form 706 (Rev. 8-2004)

Estate of:

SCHEDULE A—Real Estate

- *For jointly owned property that must be disclosed on Schedule E, see the instructions on the reverse side of Schedule E.*
- *Real estate that is part of a sole proprietorship should be shown on Schedule F.*
- *Real estate that is included in the gross estate under section 2035, 2036, 2037, or 2038 should be shown on Schedule G.*
- *Real estate that is included in the gross estate under section 2041 should be shown on Schedule H.*
- *If you elect section 2032A valuation, you must complete Schedule A and Schedule A-1.*

Item number	Description	Alternate valuation date	Alternate value	Value at date of death
1				

Total from continuation schedules or additional sheets attached to this schedule . . .			
TOTAL. (Also enter on Part 5, Recapitulation, page 3, at item 1.)			

(If more space is needed, attach the continuation schedule from the end of this package or additional sheets of the same size.)

(See the instructions on the reverse side.)

Schedule A—Page 4

Form 706 (Rev. 8-2004)

Instructions for Schedule A—Real Estate

If the total gross estate contains any real estate, you must complete Schedule A and file it with the return. On Schedule A, list real estate the decedent owned or had contracted to purchase. Number each parcel in the left-hand column.

Describe the real estate in enough detail so that the IRS can easily locate it for inspection and valuation. For each parcel of real estate, report the area and, if the parcel is improved, describe the improvements. For city or town property, report the street and number, ward, subdivision, block and lot, etc. For rural property, report the township, range, landmarks, etc.

If any item of real estate is subject to a mortgage for which the decedent's estate is liable; that is, if the indebtedness may be charged against other property of the estate that is not subject to that mortgage, or if the decedent was personally liable for that mortgage, you must report the full value of the property in the value column. Enter the amount of the mortgage under "Description" on this schedule. The unpaid amount of the mortgage may be deducted on Schedule K.

If the decedent's estate is NOT liable for the amount of the mortgage, report only the value of the equity of redemption (or value of the property less the indebtedness) in the value column as part of the gross estate. Do not enter any amount less than zero. Do not deduct the amount of indebtedness on Schedule K.

Also list on Schedule A real property the decedent contracted to purchase. Report the full value of the property and not the equity in the value column. Deduct the unpaid part of the purchase price on Schedule K.

Report the value of real estate without reducing it for homestead or other exemption, or the value of dower, curtesy, or a statutory estate created instead of dower or curtesy.

Explain how the reported values were determined and attach copies of any appraisals.

Schedule A Examples

In this example, alternate valuation is not adopted; the date of death is January 1, 2004.

Item number	Description	Alternate valuation date	Alternate value	Value at date of death
1	House and lot, 1921 William Street NW, Washington, DC (lot 6, square 481). Rent of $2,700 due at end of each quarter, February 1, May 1, August 1, and November 1. Value based on appraisal, copy of which is attached			$108,000
	Rent due on item 1 for quarter ending November 1, 2003, but not collected at date of death			2,700
	Rent accrued on item 1 for November and December 2003			1,800
2	House and lot, 304 Jefferson Street, Alexandria, VA (lot 18, square 40). Rent of $600 payable monthly. Value based on appraisal, copy of which is attached. . . .			96,000
	Rent due on item 2 for December 2003, but not collected at date of death . .			600

In this example, alternate valuation is adopted; the date of death is January 1, 2004.

Item number	Description	Alternate valuation date	Alternate value	Value at date of death
1	House and lot, 1921 William Street NW, Washington, DC (lot 6, square 481). Rent of $2,700 due at end of each quarter, February 1, May 1, August 1, and November 1. Value based on appraisal, copy of which is attached. Not disposed of within 6 months following death	7/1/04	90,000	$108,000
	Rent due on item 1 for quarter ending November 1, 2003, but not collected until February 1, 2004	2/1/04	2,700	2,700
	Rent accrued on item 1 for November and December 2003, collected on February 1, 2004	2/1/04	1,800	1,800
2	House and lot, 304 Jefferson Street, Alexandria, VA (lot 18, square 40). Rent of $600 payable monthly. Value based on appraisal, copy of which is attached. Property exchanged for farm on May 1, 2004	5/1/04	90,000	96,000
	Rent due on item 2 for December 2003, but not collected until February 1, 2004.	2/1/04	600	600

Schedule A—Page 5

Instructions for Schedule A-1. Section 2032A Valuation

The election to value certain farm and closely held business property at its special use value is made by checking "Yes" to line 2 of Part 3, Elections by the Executor, Form 706. Schedule A-1 is used to report the additional information that must be submitted to support this election. In order to make a valid election, you must complete Schedule A-1 and attach all of the required statements and appraisals.

For definitions and additional information concerning special use valuation, see section 2032A and the related regulations.

Part 1. Type of Election

Estate and GST Tax Elections. If you elect special use valuation for the estate tax, you must also elect special use valuation for the GST tax and vice versa.

You must value each specific property interest at the same value for GST tax purposes that you value it at for estate tax purposes.

Protective Election. To make the protective election described in the separate instructions for line 2 of Part 3, Elections by the Executor, you must check this box, enter the decedent's name and social security number in the spaces provided at the top of Schedule A-1, and complete line 1 and column A of lines 3 and 4 of Part 2. For purposes of the protective election, list on line 3 all of the real property that passes to the qualified heirs even though some of the property will be shown on line 2 when the additional notice of election is subsequently filed. You need not complete columns B–D of lines 3 and 4. You need not complete any other line entries on Schedule A-1. Completing Schedule A-1 as described above constitutes a Notice of Protective Election as described in Regulations section 20.2032A-8(b).

Part 2. Notice of Election

Line 10. Because the special use valuation election creates a potential tax liability for the recapture tax of section 2032A(c), you must list each person who receives an interest in the specially valued property on Schedule A-1. If there are more than eight persons who receive interests, use an additional sheet that follows the format of line 10. In the columns "Fair market value" and "Special use value," you should enter the total respective values of all the specially valued property interests received by each person.

GST Tax Savings

To compute the additional GST tax due upon disposition (or cessation of qualified use) of the property, each "skip person" (as defined in the instructions to Schedule R) who receives an interest in the specially valued property must know the total GST tax savings on all of the interests in specially valued property received. This GST tax savings is the difference between the total GST tax that was imposed on all of the interests in specially valued property received by the skip person valued at their special use value and the total GST tax that would have been imposed on the same interests received by the skip person had they been valued at their fair market value.

Because the GST tax depends on the executor's allocation of the GST exemption and the grandchild exclusion, the skip person who receives the interests is unable to compute this GST tax savings. Therefore, for each skip person who receives an interest in specially valued property, you must attach worksheets showing the total GST tax savings attributable to all of that person's interests in specially valued property.

How To Compute the GST Tax Savings. Before computing each skip person's GST tax savings, you must complete Schedules R and R-1 for the entire estate (using the special use values).

For each skip person, you must complete two Schedules R (Parts 2 and 3 only) as worksheets, one showing the interests in

specially valued property received by the skip person at their special use value and one showing the same interests at their fair market value.

If the skip person received interests in specially valued property that were shown on Schedule R-1, show these interests on the Schedule R, Parts 2 and 3 worksheets, as appropriate. Do not use Schedule R-1 as a worksheet.

Completing the Special Use Value Worksheets. On lines 2–4 and 6, enter -0-.

Completing the Fair Market Value Worksheets. *Lines 2 and 3, fixed taxes and other charges.* If valuing the interests at their fair market value (instead of special use value) causes any of these taxes and charges to increase, enter the increased amount (only) on these lines and attach an explanation of the increase. Otherwise, enter -0-.

Line 6—GST exemption. If you completed line 10 of Schedule R, Part 1, enter on line 6 the amount shown for the skip person on the *line 10 special use allocation schedule* you attached to Schedule R. If you did not complete line 10 of Schedule R, Part 1, enter -0- on line 6.

Total GST Tax Savings. For each skip person, subtract the tax amount on line 10, Part 2 of the special use value worksheet from the tax amount on line 10, Part 2 of the fair market value worksheet. This difference is the skip person's total GST tax savings.

Part 3. Agreement to Special Valuation Under Section 2032A

The agreement to special valuation by persons with an interest in property is required under section 2032A(a)(1)(B) and (d)(2) and must be signed by all parties who have any interest in the property being valued based on its qualified use as of the date of the decedent's death.

An interest in property is an interest that, as of the date of the decedent's death, can be asserted under applicable local law so as to affect the disposition of the specially valued property by the estate. Any person who at the decedent's death has any such interest in the property, whether present or future, or vested or contingent, must enter into the agreement. Included are owners of remainder and executory interests; the holders of general or special powers of appointment; beneficiaries of a gift over in default of exercise of any such power; joint tenants and holders of similar undivided interests when the decedent held only a joint or undivided interest in the property or when only an undivided interest is specially valued; and trustees of trusts and representatives of other entities holding title to, or holding any interests in the property. An heir who has the power under local law to caveat (challenge) a will and thereby affect disposition of the property is not, however, considered to be a person with an interest in property under section 2032A solely by reason of that right. Likewise, creditors of an estate are not such persons solely by reason of their status as creditors.

If any person required to enter into the agreement either desires that an agent act for him or her or cannot legally bind himself or herself due to infancy or other incompetency, or due to death before the election under section 2032A is timely exercised, a representative authorized by local law to bind the person in an agreement of this nature may sign the agreement on his or her behalf.

The Internal Revenue Service will contact the agent designated in the agreement on all matters relating to continued qualification under section 2032A of the specially valued real property and on all matters relating to the special lien arising under section 6324B. It is the duty of the agent as attorney-in-fact for the parties with interests in the specially valued property to furnish the IRS with any requested information and to notify the IRS of any disposition or cessation of qualified use of any part of the property.

Schedule A-1—Page 6

Checklist for Section 2032A Election. *If you are going to make the special use valuation election on Schedule A-1, please use this checklist to ensure that you are providing everything necessary to make a valid election.*

To have a valid special use valuation election under section 2032A, you must file, in addition to the Federal estate tax return, **(a)** a notice of election (Schedule A-1, Part 2), and **(b)** a fully executed agreement (Schedule A-1, Part 3). You must include certain information in the notice of election. To ensure that the notice of election includes all of the information required for a valid election, use the following checklist. The checklist is for your use only. Do not file it with the return.

1. Does the notice of election include the decedent's name and social security number as they appear on the estate tax return?

2. Does the notice of election include the relevant qualified use of the property to be specially valued?

3. Does the notice of election describe the items of real property shown on the estate tax return that are to be specially valued and identify the property by the Form 706 schedule and item number?

4. Does the notice of election include the fair market value of the real property to be specially valued and also include its value based on the qualified use (determined without the adjustments provided in section 2032A(b)(3)(B))?

5. Does the notice of election include the adjusted value (as defined in section 2032A(b)(3)(B)) of **(a)** all real property that both passes from the decedent and is used in a qualified use, without regard to whether it is to be specially valued, and **(b)** all real property to be specially valued?

6. Does the notice of election include **(a)** the items of personal property shown on the estate tax return that pass from the decedent to a qualified heir and that are used in qualified use and **(b)** the total value of such personal property adjusted under section 2032A(b)(3)(B)?

7. Does the notice of election include the adjusted value of the gross estate? (See section 2032A(b)(3)(A).)

8. Does the notice of election include the method used to determine the special use value?

9. Does the notice of election include copies of written appraisals of the fair market value of the real property?

10. Does the notice of election include a statement that the decedent and/or a member of his or her family has owned all of the specially valued property for at least 5 years of the 8 years immediately preceding the date of the decedent's death?

11. Does the notice of election include a statement as to whether there were any periods during the 8-year period preceding the decedent's date of death during which the decedent or a member of his or her family did not **(a)** own the property to be specially valued, **(b)** use it in a qualified use, or **(c)** materially participate in the operation of the farm or other business? (See section 2032A(e)(6).)

12. Does the notice of election include, for each item of specially valued property, the name of every person taking an interest in that item of specially valued property and the following information about each such person: **(a)** the person's address, **(b)** the person's taxpayer identification number, **(c)** the person's relationship to the decedent, and **(d)** the value of the property interest passing to that person based on both fair market value and qualified use?

13. Does the notice of election include affidavits describing the activities constituting material participation and the identity of the material participants?

14. Does the notice of election include a legal description of each item of specially valued property?

(In the case of an election made for qualified woodlands, the information included in the notice of election must include the reason for entitlement to the woodlands election.)

Any election made under section 2032A will not be valid unless a properly executed agreement (Schedule A-1, Part 3) is filed with the estate tax return. To ensure that the agreement satisfies the requirements for a valid election, use the following checklist.

1. Has the agreement been signed by each and every qualified heir having an interest in the property being specially valued?

2. Has every qualified heir expressed consent to personal liability under section 2032A(c) in the event of an early disposition or early cessation of qualified use?

3. Is the agreement that is actually signed by the qualified heirs in a form that is binding on all of the qualified heirs having an interest in the specially valued property?

4. Does the agreement designate an agent to act for the parties to the agreement in all dealings with the IRS on matters arising under section 2032A?

5. Has the agreement been signed by the designated agent and does it give the address of the agent?

Form 706 (Rev. 8-2004)

Estate of:	Decedent's Social Security Number

SCHEDULE A-1—Section 2032A Valuation

Part 1. Type of Election (Before making an election, see the checklist on page 7.):

☐ **Protective election (Regulations section 20.2032A-8(b)).** Complete Part 2, line 1, and column A of lines 3 and 4. (See instructions.)

☐ **Regular election.** Complete all of Part 2 (including line 11, if applicable) and Part 3. (See instructions.)

Before completing Schedule A-1, see the checklist on page 7 for the information and documents that must be included to make a valid election.

The election is not valid unless the agreement (i.e., Part 3—Agreement to Special Valuation Under Section 2032A)—
* Is signed by each and every qualified heir with an interest in the specially valued property, and
* Is attached to this return when it is filed.

Part 2. Notice of Election (Regulations section 20.2032A-8(a)(3))

Note: *All real property entered on lines 2 and 3 must also be entered on Schedules A, E, F, G, or H, as applicable.*

1   Qualified use—check one ▶ ☐ Farm used for farming, or

  ▶ ☐ Trade or business other than farming

2   Real property used in a qualified use, passing to qualified heirs, and to be specially valued on this Form 706.

A Schedule and item number from Form 706	B Full value (without section 2032A(b)(3)(B) adjustment)	C Adjusted value (with section 2032A(b)(3)(B) adjustment)	D Value based on qualified use (without section 2032A(b)(3)(B) adjustment)

Totals . . . .

Attach a legal description of all property listed on line 2.

Attach copies of appraisals showing the column B values for all property listed on line 2.

3   Real property used in a qualified use, passing to qualified heirs, but not specially valued on this Form 706.

A Schedule and item number from Form 706	B Full value (without section 2032A(b)(3)(B) adjustment)	C Adjusted value (with section 2032A(b)(3)(B) adjustment)	D Value based on qualified use (without section 2032A(b)(3)(B) adjustment)

Totals . . . .

If you checked "Regular election," you must attach copies of appraisals showing the column B values for all property listed on line 3.

(continued on next page)

Schedule A-1—Page 8

Form 706 (Rev. 8-2004)

4 Personal property used in a qualified use and passing to qualified heirs.

A Schedule and item number from Form 706	B Adjusted value (with section 2032A(b)(3)(B) adjustment)	A (continued) Schedule and item number from Form 706	B (continued) Adjusted value (with section 2032A(b)(3)(B) adjustment)
		Subtotal from Col. B, below left	----------------------------------

Subtotal. . . . . . .

Total adjusted value . . .

5 Enter the value of the total gross estate as adjusted under section 2032A(b)(3)(A). ▶ _____

6 **Attach a description of the method used to determine the special value based on qualified use.**

7 Did the decedent and/or a member of his or her family own all property listed on line 2 for at least 5 of the 8 years immediately preceding the date of the decedent's death? . . . . ☐ **Yes** ☐ **No**

8 Were there any periods during the 8-year period preceding the date of the decedent's death during which the decedent or his or her family:

	Yes	No
a Did not own the property listed on line 2 above?		
b Did not use the property listed on line 2 above in a qualified use?		
c Did not materially participate in the operation of the farm or other business within the meaning of section 2032A(e)(6)?		

If "Yes" to any of the above, you must attach a statement listing the periods. If applicable, describe whether the exceptions of sections 2032A(b)(4) or (5) are met.

9 **Attach affidavits describing the activities constituting material participation and the identity and relationship to the decedent of the material participants.**

10 Persons holding interests. Enter the requested information for each party who received any interest in the specially valued property. **(Each of the qualified heirs receiving an interest in the property must sign the agreement, and the agreement must be filed with this return.)**

	Name	Address
A		
B		
C		
D		
E		
F		
G		
H		

	Identifying number	Relationship to decedent	Fair market value	Special use value
A				
B				
C				
D				
E				
F				
G				
H				

You must attach a computation of the GST tax savings attributable to direct skips for each person listed above who is a skip person. (See instructions.)

11 **Woodlands election.** Check here ▶ ☐ if you wish to make a woodlands election as described in section 2032A(e)(13). Enter the Schedule and item numbers from Form 706 of the property for which you are making this election ▶ _____ You must attach a statement explaining why you are entitled to make this election. The IRS may issue regulations that require more information to substantiate this election. You will be notified by the IRS if you must supply further information.

Schedule A-1—Page 9

Form 706 (Rev. 8-2004)

Part 3. Agreement to Special Valuation Under Section 2032A

Estate of:	Date of Death	Decedent's Social Security Number

There cannot be a valid election unless:

- The agreement is executed by each and every one of the qualified heirs, and
- The agreement is included with the estate tax return when the estate tax return is filed.

We (list all qualified heirs and other persons having an interest in the property required to sign this agreement)

_____

_____ ,

being all the qualified heirs and _____

_____ ,

being all other parties having interests in the property which is qualified real property and which is valued under section 2032A of the Internal Revenue Code, do hereby approve of the election made by _____ ,
Executor/Administrator of the estate of _____ ,
pursuant to section 2032A to value said property on the basis of the qualified use to which the property is devoted and do hereby enter into this agreement pursuant to section 2032A(d).

The undersigned agree and consent to the application of subsection (c) of section 2032A of the Code with respect to all the property described on line 2 of Part 2 of Schedule A-1 of Form 706, attached to this agreement. More specifically, the undersigned heirs expressly agree and consent to personal liability under subsection (c) of 2032A for the additional estate and GST taxes imposed by that subsection with respect to their respective interests in the above-described property in the event of certain early dispositions of the property or early cessation of the qualified use of the property. It is understood that if a qualified heir disposes of any interest in qualified real property to any member of his or her family, such member may thereafter be treated as the qualified heir with respect to such interest upon filing a Form 706-A and a new agreement.

The undersigned interested parties who are not qualified heirs consent to the collection of any additional estate and GST taxes imposed under section 2032A(c) of the Code from the specially valued property.

If there is a disposition of any interest which passes, or has passed to him or her, or if there is a cessation of the qualified use of any specially valued property which passes or passed to him or her, each of the undersigned heirs agrees to file a **Form 706-A,** United States Additional Estate Tax Return, and pay any additional estate and GST taxes due within 6 months of the disposition or cessation.

It is understood by all interested parties that this agreement is a condition precedent to the election of special use valuation under section 2032A of the Code and must be executed by every interested party even though that person may not have received the estate (or GST) tax benefits or be in possession of such property.

Each of the undersigned understands that by making this election, a lien will be created and recorded pursuant to section 6324B of the Code on the property referred to in this agreement for the adjusted tax differences with respect to the estate as defined in section 2032A(c)(2)(C).

As the interested parties, the undersigned designate the following individual as their agent for all dealings with the Internal Revenue Service concerning the continued qualification of the specially valued property under section 2032A of the Code and on all issues regarding the special lien under section 6324B. The agent is authorized to act for the parties with respect to all dealings with the Service on matters affecting the qualified real property described earlier. This authority includes the following:

- To receive confidential information on all matters relating to continued qualification under section 2032A of the specially valued real property and on all matters relating to the special lien arising under section 6324B.

- To furnish the Internal Revenue Service with any requested information concerning the property.

- To notify the Internal Revenue Service of any disposition or cessation of qualified use of any part of the property.

- To receive, but not to endorse and collect, checks in payment of any refund of Internal Revenue taxes, penalties, or interest.

- To execute waivers (including offers of waivers) of restrictions on assessment or collection of deficiencies in tax and waivers of notice of disallowance of a claim for credit or refund.

- To execute closing agreements under section 7121.

(continued on next page)

Schedule A-1— Page 10

Form 706 (Rev. 8-2004)

Part 3. Agreement to Special Valuation Under Section 2032A *(Continued)*

Estate of:	Date of Death	Decedent's Social Security Number

- Other acts (specify) ▶ _____

By signing this agreement, the agent agrees to provide the Internal Revenue Service with any requested information concerning this property and to notify the Internal Revenue Service of any disposition or cessation of the qualified use of any part of this property.

Name of Agent	Signature	Address

The property to which this agreement relates is listed in Form 706, United States Estate (and Generation-Skipping Transfer) Tax Return, and in the Notice of Election, along with its fair market value according to section 2031 of the Code and its special use value according to section 2032A. The name, address, social security number, and interest (including the value) of each of the undersigned in this property are as set forth in the attached Notice of Election.

IN WITNESS WHEREOF, the undersigned have hereunto set their hands at _____ ,

this _____ day of _____ .

SIGNATURES OF EACH OF THE QUALIFIED HEIRS:

Signature of qualified heir	Signature of qualified heir
Signature of qualified heir	Signature of qualified heir
Signature of qualified heir	Signature of qualified heir
Signature of qualified heir	Signature of qualified heir
Signature of qualified heir	Signature of qualified heir
Signature of qualified heir	Signature of qualified heir

Signatures of other interested parties

Signatures of other interested parties

Schedule A-1—Page 11

Form 706 (Rev. 8-2004)

Estate of:

SCHEDULE B—Stocks and Bonds

(For jointly owned property that must be disclosed on Schedule E, see the instructions for Schedule E.)

Item number	Description including face amount of bonds or number of shares and par value where needed for identification. Give 9-digit CUSIP number.	Unit value	Alternate valuation date	Alternate value	Value at date of death
	CUSIP number				
1					
	Total from continuation schedules (or additional sheets) attached to this schedule				
	TOTAL. (Also enter on Part 5, Recapitulation, page 3, at item 2.)				

(If more space is needed, attach the continuation schedule from the end of this package or additional sheets of the same size.)
(The instructions to Schedule B are in the separate instructions.)

Schedule B—Page 12

Form 706 (Rev. 8-2004)

Estate of:

SCHEDULE C—Mortgages, Notes, and Cash

(For jointly owned property that must be disclosed on Schedule E, see the instructions for Schedule E.)

Item number	Description	Alternate valuation date	Alternate value	Value at date of death
1				

Total from continuation schedules (or additional sheets) attached to this schedule . .			
TOTAL. (Also enter on Part 5, Recapitulation, page 3, at item 3.)			

(If more space is needed, attach the continuation schedule from the end of this package or additional sheets of the same size.)
(See the instructions on the reverse side.)

Schedule C—Page 13

Form 706 (Rev. 8-2004)

Instructions for Schedule C—Mortgages, Notes, and Cash

Complete Schedule C and file it with your return if the total gross estate contains any:

- mortgages,
- notes, or
- cash.

List on Schedule C:

- Mortgages and notes payable **to the decedent** at the time of death.
- Cash the decedent had at the date of death.

Do not list on Schedule C:

- Mortgages and notes payable **by the decedent.** (If these are deductible, list them on Schedule K.)

List the items on Schedule C in the following order:

- mortgages,
- promissory notes,
- contracts by decedent to sell land,
- cash in possession, and
- cash in banks, savings and loan associations, and other types of financial organiations.

What to enter in the "Description" column:

For mortgages, list:

- face value,
- unpaid balance,
- date of mortgage,
- date of maturity,
- name of maker,
- property mortgaged,
- interest dates, and
- interest rate.

Example to enter in "Description" column:

Bond and mortgage of $0,000, unpaid balance: $4,000; dated: anuary 1, 1983; ohn Doe to Richard Roe; premises: 22 Clinton Street, Newark, N;J due: anuary 1, 2003; interest payable at 10% a year--anuary 1 and uly 1."

For promissory notes, list:

- in the same way as mortgages.

For contracts by the decedent to sell land, list:

- name of purchaser,
- contract date,
- property description,
- sale price,
- initial payment,
- amounts of installment payment,
- unpaid balance of principal, and
- interest rate.

For cash in possession, list:

- such cash separately from bank deposits.

For cash in banks, savings and loan associations, and other types of financial organiations, list:

- name and address of each financial organiation,
- amount in each account,
- serial or account number,
- nature of account--checking, savings, time deposit, etc., and
- unpaid interest accrued from date of last interest payment to the date of death.

Important: If you obtain statements from the financial organiations, keep them for IRS inspection.

Form 706 (Rev. 8-2004)

Estate of:

SCHEDULE D—Insurance on the Decedent's Life

You must list **all** policies on the life of the decedent and attach a Form 712 for each policy.

Item number	Description	Alternate valuation date	Alternate value	Value at date of death
1				

Total from continuation schedules (or additional sheets) attached to this schedule . .

TOTAL. (Also enter on Part 5, Recapitulation, page 3, at item 4.) . . . .

(If more space is needed, attach the continuation schedule from the end of this package or additional sheets of the same size.)

(See the instructions on the reverse side.)

Schedule D—Page 15

Form 706 (Rev. 8-2004)

Instructions for Schedule D—Insurance on the Decedent's Life

If you are required to file Form 706 and there was any insurance on the decedent's life, whether or not included in the gross estate, you must complete Schedule D and file it with the return.

Insurance you must include on Schedule D. Under section 2042 you must include in the gross estate:

- Insurance on the decedent's life receivable by or for the benefit of the estate; and
- Insurance on the decedent's life receivable by beneficiaries other than the estate, as described below.

The term "insurance" refers to life insurance of every description, including death benefits paid by fraternal beneficiary societies operating under the lodge system, and death benefits paid under no-fault automobile insurance policies if the no-fault insurer was unconditionally bound to pay the benefit in the event of the insured's death.

Insurance in favor of the estate. Include on Schedule D the full amount of the proceeds of insurance on the life of the decedent receivable by the executor or otherwise payable to or for the benefit of the estate. Insurance in favor of the estate includes insurance used to pay the estate tax, and any other taxes, debts, or charges that are enforceable against the estate. The manner in which the policy is drawn is immaterial as long as there is an obligation, legally binding on the beneficiary, to use the proceeds to pay taxes, debts, or charges. You must include the full amount even though the premiums or other consideration may have been paid by a person other than the decedent.

Insurance receivable by beneficiaries other than the estate. Include on Schedule D the proceeds of all insurance on the life of the decedent not receivable by or for the benefit of the decedent's estate if the decedent possessed at death any of the incidents of ownership, exercisable either alone or in conjunction with any person.

Incidents of ownership in a policy include:

- The right of the insured or estate to its economic benefits;
- The power to change the beneficiary;
- The power to surrender or cancel the policy;
- The power to assign the policy or to revoke an assignment;
- The power to pledge the policy for a loan;
- The power to obtain from the insurer a loan against the surrender value of the policy;
- A reversionary interest if the value of the reversionary interest was more than 5% of the value of the policy immediately before the decedent died. (An interest in an insurance policy is considered a reversionary interest if, for example, the proceeds become payable to the insured's estate or payable as the insured directs if the beneficiary dies before the insured.)

Life insurance not includible in the gross estate under section 2042 may be includible under some other section of the Code. For example, a life insurance policy could be transferred by the decedent in such a way that it would be includible in the gross estate under section 2036, 2037, or 2038. (See the instructions to Schedule G for a description of these sections.)

Completing the Schedule

You must list every policy of insurance on the life of the decedent, whether or not it is included in the gross estate.

Under "Description" list:

- Name of the insurance company and
- Number of the policy.

For every policy of life insurance listed on the schedule, you must request a statement on **Form 712,** Life Insurance Statement, from the company that issued the policy. Attach the Form 712 to the back of Schedule D.

If the policy proceeds are paid in one sum, enter the net proceeds received (from Form 712, line 24) in the value (and alternate value) columns of Schedule D. If the policy proceeds are not paid in one sum, enter the value of the proceeds as of the date of the decedent's death (from Form 712, line 25).

If part or all of the policy proceeds are not included in the gross estate, you must explain why they were not included.

Form 706 (Rev. 8-2004)

Estate of:

SCHEDULE E—Jointly Owned Property
(If you elect section 2032A valuation, you must complete Schedule E and Schedule A-1.)

PART 1.—Qualified Joint Interests—Interests Held by the Decedent and His or Her Spouse as the Only Joint Tenants (Section 2040(b)(2))

Item number	Description For securities, give CUSIP number.	Alternate valuation date	Alternate value	Value at date of death

Total from continuation schedules (or additional sheets) attached to this schedule . . . . . .

1a Totals	**1a**		
1b Amounts included in gross estate (one-half of line **1a**)	**1b**		

PART 2.—All Other Joint Interests

2a State the name and address of each surviving co-tenant. If there are more than three surviving co-tenants, list the additional co-tenants on an attached sheet.

Name	Address (number and street, city, state, and ZIP code)
A.	
B.	
C.	

Item number	Enter letter for co-tenant	Description (including alternate valuation date if any) For securities, give CUSIP number.	Percentage includible	Includible alternate value	Includible value at date of death

Total from continuation schedules (or additional sheets) attached to this schedule . . . . . .

2b Total other joint interests	**2b**		
3 **Total includible joint interests** (add lines 1b and 2b). Also enter on Part 5 Recapitulation, page 3, at item 5	**3**		

(If more space is needed, attach the continuation schedule from the end of this package or additional sheets of the same size.)
(See the instructions on the reverse side.)   **Schedule E—Page 17**

Form 706 (Rev. 8-2004)

Instructions for Schedule E—Jointly Owned Property

If you are required to file Form 706, you must complete Schedule E and file it with the return if the decedent owned any joint property at the time of death, whether or not the decedent's interest is includible in the gross estate.

Enter on this schedule all property of whatever kind or character, whether real estate, personal property, or bank accounts, in which the decedent held at the time of death an interest either as a joint tenant with right to survivorship or as a tenant by the entirety.

Do not list on this schedule property that the decedent held as a tenant in common, but report the value of the interest on Schedule A if real estate, or on the appropriate schedule if personal property. Similarly, community property held by the decedent and spouse should be reported on the appropriate Schedules A through I. The decedent's interest in a partnership should not be entered on this schedule unless the partnership interest itself is jointly owned. Solely owned partnership interests should be reported on Schedule F, "Other Miscellaneous Property."

Part 1—Qualified joint interests held by decedent and spouse. Under section 2040(b)(2), a joint interest is a qualified joint interest if the decedent and the surviving spouse held the interest as:

- Tenants by the entirety, or

- Joint tenants with right of survivorship if the decedent and the decedent's spouse are the only joint tenants.

Interests that meet either of the two requirements above should be entered in Part 1. Joint interests that do not meet either of the two requirements above should be entered in Part 2.

Under "Description," describe the property as required in the instructions for Schedules A, B, C, and F for the type of property involved. For example, jointly held stocks and bonds should be described using the rules given in the instructions to Schedule B.

Under "Alternate value" and "Value at date of death," enter the full value of the property.

Note: *You cannot claim the special treatment under section 2040(b) for property held jointly by a decedent and a surviving spouse who is not a U.S. citizen. You must report these joint interests on Part 2 of Schedule E, not Part 1.*

Part 2—Other joint interests. All joint interests that were not entered in Part 1 must be entered in Part 2.

For each item of property, enter the appropriate letter A, B, C, etc., from line 2a to indicate the name and address of the surviving co-tenant.

Under "Description," describe the property as required in the instructions for Schedules A, B, C, and F for the type of property involved.

In the "Percentage includible" column, enter the percentage of the total value of the property that you intend to include in the gross estate.

Generally, you must include the full value of the jointly owned property in the gross estate. However, the full value should not be included if you can show that a part of the property originally belonged to the other tenant or tenants and was never received or acquired by the other tenant or tenants from the decedent for less than adequate and full consideration in money or money's worth, or unless you can show that any part of the property was acquired with consideration originally belonging to the surviving joint tenant or tenants. In this case, you may exclude from the value of the property an amount proportionate to the consideration furnished by the other tenant or tenants. Relinquishing or promising to relinquish dower, curtesy, or statutory estate created instead of dower or curtesy, or other marital rights in the decedent's property or estate is not consideration in money or money's worth. See the Schedule A instructions for the value to show for real property that is subject to a mortgage.

If the property was acquired by the decedent and another person or persons by gift, bequest, devise, or inheritance as joint tenants, and their interests are not otherwise specified by law, include only that part of the value of the property that is figured by dividing the full value of the property by the number of joint tenants.

If you believe that less than the full value of the entire property is includible in the gross estate for tax purposes, you must establish the right to include the smaller value by attaching proof of the extent, origin, and nature of the decedent's interest and the interest(s) of the decedent's co-tenant or co-tenants.

In the "Includible alternate value" and "Includible value at date of death" columns, you should enter only the values that you believe are includible in the gross estate.

Schedule E—Page 18

Form 706 (Rev. 8-2004)

Estate of:

SCHEDULE F—Other Miscellaneous Property Not Reportable Under Any Other Schedule

(For jointly owned property that must be disclosed on Schedule E, see the instructions for Schedule E.)
(If you elect section 2032A valuation, you must complete Schedule F and Schedule A-1.)

		Yes	No
1	Did the decedent at the time of death own any articles of artistic or collectible value in excess of $3,000 or any collections whose artistic or collectible value combined at date of death exceeded $10,000? . . . . If "Yes," submit full details on this schedule and attach appraisals.		
2	Has the decedent's estate, spouse, or any other person, received (or will receive) any bonus or award as a result of the decedent's employment or death? . . . . If "Yes," submit full details on this schedule.		
3	Did the decedent at the time of death have, or have access to, a safe deposit box? . . . . If "Yes," state location, and if held in joint names of decedent and another, state name and relationship of joint depositor. If any of the contents of the safe deposit box are omitted from the schedules in this return, explain fully why omitted.		

Item number	Description For securities, give CUSIP number.	Alternate valuation date	Alternate value	Value at date of death
1				
	Total from continuation schedules (or additional sheets) attached to this schedule . .			
	TOTAL. (Also enter on Part 5, Recapitulation, page 3, at item 6.)			

(If more space is needed, attach the continuation schedule from the end of this package or additional sheets of the same size.)
(See the instructions on the reverse side.)

Schedule F—Page 19

Form 706 (Rev. 8-2004)

Instructions for Schedule F—Other Miscellaneous Property

You must complete Schedule F and file it with the return.

On Schedule F list all items that must be included in the gross estate that are not reported on any other schedule, including:

- Debts due the decedent (other than notes and mortgages included on Schedule C)
- Interests in business
- Any interest in an Archer medical savings account (MSA) or Health Savings Account (HSA), unless such interest passes to the surviving spouse
- Insurance on the life of another (obtain and attach **Form 712,** Life Insurance Statement, for each policy)

Note for single premium or paid-up policies: *In certain situations, for example where the surrender value of the policy exceeds its replacement cost, the true economic value of the policy will be greater than the amount shown on line 59 of Form 712. In these situations, you should report the full economic value of the policy on Schedule F. See Rev. Rul. 78-137, 1978-1 C.B. 280 for details.*

- Section 2044 property (see **Decedent Who Was a Surviving Spouse** below)
- Claims (including the value of the decedent's interest in a claim for refund of income taxes or the amount of the refund actually received)
- Rights
- Royalties
- Leaseholds
- Judgments
- Reversionary or remainder interests
- Shares in trust funds (attach a copy of the trust instrument)
- Household goods and personal effects, including wearing apparel
- Farm products and growing crops
- Livestock
- Farm machinery
- Automobiles

If the decedent owned any interest in a partnership or unincorporated business, attach a statement of assets and liabilities for the valuation date and for the 5 years before the valuation date. Also attach statements of the net earnings for the same 5 years. Be sure to include the EIN of the entity. You must

account for goodwill in the valuation. In general, furnish the same information and follow the methods used to value close corporations. See the instructions for Schedule B.

All partnership interests should be reported on Schedule F unless the partnership interest, itself, is jointly owned. Jointly owned partnership interests should be reported on Schedule E.

If real estate is owned by the sole proprietorship, it should be reported on Schedule F and not on Schedule A. Describe the real estate with the same detail required for Schedule A.

Line 1. If the decedent owned at the date of death articles with artistic or intrinsic value (e.g., jewelry, furs, silverware, books, statuary, vases, oriental rugs, coin or stamp collections), check the "Yes" box on line 1 and provide full details. If any one article is valued at more than $3,000, or any collection of similar articles is valued at more than $10,000, attach an appraisal by an expert under oath and the required statement regarding the appraiser's qualifications (see Regulations section 20.2031-6(b)).

Decedent Who Was a Surviving Spouse

If the decedent was a surviving spouse, he or she may have received qualified terminable interest property (QTIP) from the predeceased spouse for which the marital deduction was elected either on the predeceased spouse's estate tax return or on a gift tax return, Form 709. The election was available for gifts made and decedents dying after December 31, 1981. List such property on Schedule F.

If this election was made and the surviving spouse retained his or her interest in the QTIP property at death, the full value of the QTIP property is includible in his or her estate, even though the qualifying income interest terminated at death. It is valued as of the date of the surviving spouse's death, or alternate valuation date, if applicable. Do not reduce the value by any annual exclusion that may have applied to the transfer creating the interest.

The value of such property included in the surviving spouse's gross estate is treated as passing from the surviving spouse. It therefore qualifies for the charitable and marital deductions on the surviving spouse's estate tax return if it meets the other requirements for those deductions.

For additional details, see Regulations section 20.2044-1.

Form 706 (Rev. 8-2004)

Estate of:

SCHEDULE G—Transfers During Decedent's Life

(If you elect section 2032A valuation, you must complete Schedule G and Schedule A-1.)

Item number	Description For securities, give CUSIP number.	Alternate valuation date	Alternate value	Value at date of death
A.	Gift tax paid by the decedent or the estate for all gifts made by the decedent or his or her spouse within 3 years before the decedent's death (section 2035(b))	X X X X X		
B.	Transfers includible under section 2035(a), 2036, 2037, or 2038:			
1				
	Total from continuation schedules (or additional sheets) attached to this schedule . .			
	TOTAL. (Also enter on Part 5, Recapitulation, page 3, at item 7.)			

SCHEDULE H—Powers of Appointment

(Include 5 and 5 lapsing"powers (section 2041(b)(2)) held by the decedent.)
(If you elect section 2032A valuation, you must complete Schedule H and Schedule A-1.)

Item number	Description	Alternate valuation date	Alternate value	Value at date of death
1				
	Total from continuation schedules (or additional sheets) attached to this schedule . .			
	TOTAL. (Also enter on Part 5, Recapitulation, page 3, at item 8.)			

(If more space is needed, attach the continuation schedule from the end of this package or additional sheets of the same size.)
(The instructions to Schedules G and H are in the separate instructions.)   **Schedules G and H—Page 21**

Form 706 (Rev. 8-2004)

Estate of:

SCHEDULE I—Annuities

Note: *Generally, no exclusion is allowed for the estates of decedents dying after December 31, 1984 (see page 15 of the instructions).*

A Are you excluding from the decedent's gross estate the value of a lump-sum distribution described in section 2039(f)(2) (as in effect before its repeal by the Deficit Reduction Act of 1984)? . . . .
If "Yes," you must attach the information required by the instructions.

	Yes	No

Item number	Description Show the entire value of the annuity before any exclusions.	Alternate valuation date	Includible alternate value	Includible value at date of death
1				
	Total from continuation schedules (or additional sheets) attached to this schedule . .			
	TOTAL. (Also enter on Part 5, Recapitulation, page 3, at item 9.)			

(If more space is needed, attach the continuation schedule from the end of this package or additional sheets of the same size.)

Schedule I—Page 22   (The instructions to Schedule I are in the separate instructions.)

Form 706 (Rev. 8-2004)

Estate of:

SCHEDULE J—Funeral Expenses and Expenses Incurred in Administering Property Subject to Claims

Note: *Do not list on this schedule expenses of administering property not subject to claims. For those expenses, see the instructions for Schedule L.*

If executors' commissions, attorney fees, etc., are claimed and allowed as a deduction for estate tax purposes, they are not allowable as a deduction in computing the taxable income of the estate for federal income tax purposes. They are allowable as an income tax deduction on Form 1041 if a waiver is filed to waive the deduction on Form 706 (see the Form 1041 instructions).

Item number	Description	Expense amount	Total amount
1	**A. Funeral expenses:**		
	Total funeral expenses . . . . ▶		....
	B. Administration expenses:		
1	Executors' commissions—amount estimated/agreed upon/paid. (Strike out the words that do not apply.)		....
2	Attorney fees—amount estimated/agreed upon/paid. (Strike out the words that do not apply.) . .		....
3	Accountant fees—amount estimated/agreed upon/paid. (Strike out the words that do not apply.) .		....

Item number	Description	Expense amount
4	Miscellaneous expenses:	
	Total miscellaneous expenses from continuation schedules (or additional sheets) attached to this schedule	
	Total miscellaneous expenses . . . . ▶	

TOTAL. (Also enter on Part 5, Recapitulation, page 3, at item 13.) . . . . ▶

(If more space is needed, attach the continuation schedule from the end of this package or additional sheets of the same size.)
(See the instructions on the reverse side.)   **Schedule J—Page 23**

Form 706 (Rev. 8-2004)

Instructions for Schedule J—Funeral Expenses and Expenses Incurred in Administering Property Subject to Claims

General. You must complete and file Schedule J if you claim a deduction on item 13 of Part 5, Recapitulation.

On Schedule J, itemize funeral expenses and expenses incurred in administering property subject to claims. List the names and addresses of persons to whom the expenses are payable and describe the nature of the expense. **Do not list expenses incurred in administering property not subject to claims on this schedule. List them on Schedule L instead.**

The deduction is limited to the amount paid for these expenses that is allowable under local law but may not exceed:

1. The value of property subject to claims included in the gross estate, plus

2. The amount paid out of property included in the gross estate but not subject to claims. This amount must actually be paid by the due date of the estate tax return.

The applicable local law under which the estate is being administered determines which property is and is not subject to claims. If under local law a particular property interest included in the gross estate would bear the burden for the payment of the expenses, then the property is considered property subject to claims.

Unlike certain claims against the estate for debts of the decedent (see the instructions for Schedule K in the separate instructions), you cannot deduct expenses incurred in administering property subject to claims on both the estate tax return and the estate's income tax return. If you choose to deduct them on the estate tax return, you cannot deduct them on a Form 1041 filed for the estate. Funeral expenses are only deductible on the estate tax return.

Funeral Expenses. Itemize funeral expenses on line A. Deduct from the expenses any amounts that were reimbursed, such as death benefits payable by the Social Security Administration and the Veterans Administration.

Executors' Commissions. When you file the return, you may deduct commissions that have actually been paid to you or that you expect will be paid. You may not deduct commissions if none will be collected. If the amount of the commissions has not been fixed by decree of the proper court, the deduction will be allowed on the final examination of the return, provided that:

- The Estate and Gift Tax Territory Manager is reasonably satisfied that the commissions claimed will be paid;

- The amount entered as a deduction is within the amount allowable by the laws of the jurisdiction where the estate is being administered;

- It is in accordance with the usually accepted practice in that jurisdiction for estates of similar size and character.

If you have not been paid the commissions claimed at the time of the final examination of the return, you must support the amount you deducted with an affidavit or statement signed under the penalties of perjury that the amount has been agreed upon and will be paid.

You may not deduct a bequest or devise made to you instead of commissions. If, however, the decedent fixed by will the compensation payable to you for services to be rendered in the administration of the estate, you may deduct this amount to the extent it is not more than the compensation allowable by the local law or practice.

Do not deduct on this schedule amounts paid as trustees' commissions whether received by you acting in the capacity of a trustee or by a separate trustee. If such amounts were paid in administering property not subject to claims, deduct them on Schedule L.

Note: *Executors' commissions are taxable income to the executors. Therefore, be sure to include them as income on your individual income tax return.*

Attorney Fees. Enter the amount of attorney fees that have actually been paid or that you reasonably expect to be paid. If on the final examination of the return the fees claimed have not been awarded by the proper court and paid, the deduction will be allowed provided the Estate and Gift Tax Territory Manager is reasonably satisfied that the amount claimed will be paid and that it does not exceed a reasonable payment for the services performed, taking into account the size and character of the estate and the local law and practice. If the fees claimed have not been paid at the time of final examination of the return, the amount deducted must be supported by an affidavit, or statement signed under the penalties of perjury, by the executor or the attorney stating that the amount has been agreed upon and will be paid.

Do not deduct attorney fees incidental to litigation incurred by the beneficiaries. These expenses are charged against the beneficiaries personally and are not administration expenses authorized by the Code.

Interest Expense. Interest expenses incurred after the decedent's death are generally allowed as a deduction if they are reasonable, necessary to the administration of the estate, and allowable under local law.

Interest incurred as the result of a Federal estate tax deficiency is a deductible administrative expense. Penalties are not deductible even if they are allowable under local law.

Note: *If you elect to pay the tax in installments under section 6166, you may* **not** *deduct the interest payable on the installments.*

Miscellaneous Expenses. Miscellaneous administration expenses necessarily incurred in preserving and distributing the estate are deductible. These expenses include appraiser's and accountant's fees, certain court costs, and costs of storing or maintaining assets of the estate.

The expenses of selling assets are deductible only if the sale is necessary to pay the decedent's debts, the expenses of administration, or taxes, or to preserve the estate or carry out distribution.

Schedule J—Page 24

Form 706 (Rev. 8-2004)

Estate of:

SCHEDULE K—Debts of the Decedent, and Mortgages and Liens

Item number	Debts of the Decedent—Creditor and nature of claim, and allowable death taxes	Amount unpaid to date	Amount in contest	Amount claimed as a deduction
1				

Total from continuation schedules (or additional sheets) attached to this schedule . . . .

TOTAL. (Also enter on Part 5, Recapitulation, page 3, at item 14.) . . . .

Item number	Mortgages and Liens—Description	Amount
1		

Total from continuation schedules (or additional sheets) attached to this schedule . . . .

TOTAL. (Also enter on Part 5, Recapitulation, page 3, at item 15.) . . . .

(If more space is needed, attach the continuation schedule from the end of this package or additional sheets of the same size.)
(The instructions to Schedule K are in the separate instructions.)   **Schedule K—Page 25**

Form 706 (Rev. 8-2004)

Estate of:

SCHEDULE L—Net Losses During Administration and
Expenses Incurred in Administering Property Not Subject to Claims

Item number	Net losses during administration (**Note:** *Do not deduct losses claimed on a Federal income tax return.*)	Amount
1		
	Total from continuation schedules (or additional sheets) attached to this schedule	
	TOTAL. (Also enter on Part 5, Recapitulation, page 3, at item 18.)	

Item number	Expenses incurred in administering property not subject to claims (Indicate whether estimated, agreed upon, or paid.)	Amount
1		
	Total from continuation schedules (or additional sheets) attached to this schedule	
	TOTAL. (Also enter on Part 5, Recapitulation, page 3, at item 19.)	

(If more space is needed, attach the continuation schedule from the end of this package or additional sheets of the same size.)

Schedule L—Page 26   (The instructions to Schedule L are in the separate instructions.)

Form 706 (Rev. 8-2004)

Estate of:

SCHEDULE M—Bequests, etc., to Surviving Spouse

Election To Deduct Qualified Terminable Interest Property Under Section 2056(b)(7). If a trust (or other property) meets the requirements of qualified terminable interest property under section 2056(b)(7), and

  a. The trust or other property is listed on Schedule M, and

  b. The value of the trust (or other property) is entered in whole or in part as a deduction on Schedule M,

then unless the executor specifically identifies the trust (all or a fractional portion or percentage) or other property to be excluded from the election, the executor shall be deemed to have made an election to have such trust (or other property) treated as qualified terminable interest property under section 2056(b)(7).

  If less than the entire value of the trust (or other property) that the executor has included in the gross estate is entered as a deduction on Schedule M, the executor shall be considered to have made an election only as to a fraction of the trust (or other property). The numerator of this fraction is equal to the amount of the trust (or other property) deducted on Schedule M. The denominator is equal to the total value of the trust (or other property).

Election To Deduct Qualified Domestic Trust Property Under Section 2056A. If a trust meets the requirements of a qualified domestic trust under section 2056A(a) and this return is filed no later than 1 year after the time prescribed by law (including extensions) for filing the return, and

  a. The entire value of a trust or trust property is listed on Schedule M, and

  b. The entire value of the trust or trust property is entered as a deduction on Schedule M,

then unless the executor specifically identifies the trust to be excluded from the election, the executor shall be deemed to have made an election to have the entire trust treated as qualified domestic trust property.

		Yes	No
1	Did any property pass to the surviving spouse as a result of a qualified disclaimer? **1**		
	If "Yes," attach a copy of the written disclaimer required by section 2518(b).		
2a	In what country was the surviving spouse born? _____		
b	What is the surviving spouse's date of birth? _____		
c	Is the surviving spouse a U.S. citizen? **2c**		
d	If the surviving spouse is a naturalized citizen, when did the surviving spouse acquire citizenship? _____		
e	If the surviving spouse is not a U.S. citizen, of what country is the surviving spouse a citizen? _____		
3	**Election Out of QTIP Treatment of Annuities—**Do you elect under section 2056(b)(7)(C)(ii) **not** to treat as qualified terminable interest property any joint and survivor annuities that are included in the gross estate and would otherwise be treated as qualified terminable interest property under section 2056(b)(7)(C)? (see instructions) **3**		

Item number	Description of property interests passing to surviving spouse	Amount
1		

	Total from continuation schedules (or additional sheets) attached to this schedule		
4	**Total** amount of property interests listed on Schedule M	**4**	
5a	Federal estate taxes payable out of property interests listed on Schedule M . .	**5a**	
b	Other death taxes payable out of property interests listed on Schedule M . . .	**5b**	
c	Federal and state GST taxes payable out of property interests listed on Schedule M	**5c**	
d	Add items 5a, b, and c	**5d**	
6	Net amount of property interests listed on Schedule M (subtract 5d from 4). Also enter on Part 5, Recapitulation, page 3, at item 20	**6**	

(If more space is needed, attach the continuation schedule from the end of this package or additional sheets of the same size.)
(See the instructions on the reverse side.)

Schedule M—Page 27

Form 706 (Rev. 8-2004)

Examples of Listing of Property Interests on Schedule M

Item number	Description of property interests passing to surviving spouse	Amount
1	One-half the value of a house and lot, 256 South West Street, held by decedent and surviving spouse as joint tenants with right of survivorship under deed dated July 15, 1957 (Schedule E, Part I, item 1)	$132,500
2	Proceeds of Gibraltar Life Insurance Company policy No. 104729, payable in one sum to surviving spouse (Schedule D, item 3)	200,000
3	Cash bequest under Paragraph Six of will	100,000

Instructions for Schedule M—Bequests, etc., to Surviving Spouse (Marital Deduction)

General

You must complete Schedule M and file it with the return if you claim a deduction on item 20 of Part 5, Recapitulation.

The marital deduction is authorized by section 2056 for certain property interests that pass from the decedent to the surviving spouse. You may claim the deduction only for property interests that are included in the decedent's gross estate (Schedules A through I).

Note: *The marital deduction is generally not allowed if the surviving spouse is not a U.S. citizen. The marital deduction is allowed for property passing to such a surviving spouse in a "qualified domestic trust" or if such property is transferred or irrevocably assigned to such a trust before the estate tax return is filed. The executor must elect qualified domestic trust status on this return. See the instructions that follow, on pages 29–30, for details on the election.*

Property Interests That You May List on Schedule M

Generally, you may list on Schedule M all property interests that pass from the decedent to the surviving spouse and are included in the gross estate. However, you should not list any "Nondeductible terminable interests" (described below) on Schedule M unless you are making a QTIP election. The property for which you make this election must be included on Schedule M. See "Qualified terminable interest property" on the following page.

For the rules on common disaster and survival for a limited period, see section 2056(b)(3).

You may list on Schedule M only those interests that the surviving spouse takes:

1. As the decedent's legatee, devisee, heir, or donee;

2. As the decedent's surviving tenant by the entirety or joint tenant;

3. As an appointee under the decedent's exercise of a power or as a

taker in default at the decedent's nonexercise of a power;

4. As a beneficiary of insurance on the decedent's life;

5. As the surviving spouse taking under dower or curtesy (or similar statutory interest); and

6. As a transferee of a transfer made by the decedent at any time.

Property Interests That You May Not List on Schedule M

You should not list on Schedule M:

1. The value of any property that does not pass from the decedent to the surviving spouse;

2. Property interests that are not included in the decedent's gross estate;

3. The full value of a property interest for which a deduction was claimed on Schedules J through L. The value of the property interest should be reduced by the deductions claimed with respect to it;

4. The full value of a property interest that passes to the surviving spouse subject to a mortgage or other encumbrance or an obligation of the surviving spouse. Include on Schedule M only the net value of the interest after reducing it by the amount of the mortgage or other debt;

5. Nondeductible terminable interests (described below);

6. Any property interest disclaimed by the surviving spouse.

Terminable Interests

Certain interests in property passing from a decedent to a surviving spouse are referred to as *terminable interests.* These are interests that will terminate or fail after the passage of time, or on the occurrence or nonoccurrence of some contingency. Examples are: life estates, annuities, estates for terms of years, and patents.

The ownership of a bond, note, or other contractual obligation, which when discharged would not have the effect of an annuity for life or for a term, is not considered a terminable interest.

Nondeductible terminable interests. A terminable interest is *nondeductible,* and should not be entered on Schedule M (unless you are making a QTIP election) if:

1. Another interest in the same property passed from the decedent to some other person for less than adequate and full consideration in money or money's worth; and

2. By reason of its passing, the other person or that person's heirs may enjoy part of the property after the termination of the surviving spouse's interest.

This rule applies even though the interest that passes from the decedent to a person other than the surviving spouse is not included in the gross estate, and regardless of when the interest passes. The rule also applies regardless of whether the surviving spouse's interest and the other person's interest pass from the decedent at the same time.

Property interests that are considered to pass to a person other than the surviving spouse are any property interest that: **(a)** passes under a decedent's will or intestacy; **(b)** was transferred by a decedent during life; or **(c)** is held by or passed on to any person as a decedent's joint tenant, as appointee under a decedent's exercise of a power, as taker in default at a decedent's release or nonexercise of a power, or as a beneficiary of insurance on the decedent's life.

For example, a decedent devised real property to his wife for life, with remainder to his children. The life interest that passed to the wife does not qualify for the marital deduction because it will terminate at her death and the children will thereafter possess or enjoy the property.

However, if the decedent purchased a joint and survivor annuity for himself and his wife who survived him, the value of the survivor's annuity, to the extent that it is included in the gross estate, qualifies for the marital deduction because even though the interest will terminate on the wife's death, no one else will possess or enjoy any part of the property.

The marital deduction is not allowed for an interest that the decedent directed the executor or a trustee to convert, after death, into a terminable interest for the surviving spouse. The marital deduction is not allowed for such an interest even if there was no interest

Page 28

in the property passing to another person and even if the terminable interest would otherwise have been deductible under the exceptions described below for life estate and life insurance and annuity payments with powers of appointment. For more information, see Regulations sections 20.2056(b)-1(f) and 20.2056(b)-1(g), Example (7).

If any property interest passing from the decedent to the surviving spouse may be paid or otherwise satisfied out of any of a group of assets, the value of the property interest is, for the entry on Schedule M, reduced by the value of any asset or assets that, if passing from the decedent to the surviving spouse, would be nondeductible terminable interests. Examples of property interests that may be paid or otherwise satisfied out of any of a group of assets are a bequest of the residue of the decedent's estate, or of a share of the residue, and a cash legacy payable out of the general estate.

Example: A decedent bequeathed $100,000 to the surviving spouse. The general estate includes a term for years (valued at $10,000 in determining the value of the gross estate) in an office building, which interest was retained by the decedent under a deed of the building by gift to a son. Accordingly, the value of the specific bequest entered on Schedule M is $90,000.

Life Estate With Power of Appointment in the Surviving Spouse.
A property interest, whether or not in trust, will be treated as passing to the surviving spouse, and will not be treated as a nondeductible terminable interest if: **(a)** the surviving spouse is entitled for life to all of the income from the entire interest; **(b)** the income is payable annually or at more frequent intervals; **(c)** the surviving spouse has the power, exercisable in favor of the surviving spouse or the estate of the surviving spouse, to appoint the entire interest; **(d)** the power is exercisable by the surviving spouse alone and (whether exercisable by will or during life) is exercisable by the surviving spouse in all events; and **(e)** no part of the entire interest is subject to a power in any other person to appoint any part to any person other than the surviving spouse (or the surviving spouse's legal representative or relative if the surviving spouse is disabled. See Rev. Rul. 85-35, 1985-1 C.B. 328). If these five conditions are satisfied only for a specific portion of the entire interest, see the section 2056(b) regulations to determine the amount of the marital deduction.

Life Insurance, Endowment, or Annuity Payments, With Power of Appointment in Surviving Spouse. A property interest consisting of the entire proceeds under

a life insurance, endowment, or annuity contract is treated as passing from the decedent to the surviving spouse, and will not be treated as a nondeductible terminable interest if: **(a)** the surviving spouse is entitled to receive the proceeds in installments, or is entitled to interest on them, with all amounts payable during the life of the spouse, payable only to the surviving spouse; **(b)** the installment or interest payments are payable annually, or more frequently, beginning not later than 13 months after the decedent's death; **(c)** the surviving spouse has the power, exercisable in favor of the surviving spouse or of the estate of the surviving spouse, to appoint all amounts payable under the contract; **(d)** the power is exercisable by the surviving spouse alone and (whether exercisable by will or during life) is exercisable by the surviving spouse in all events; and **(e)** no part of the amount payable under the contract is subject to a power in any other person to appoint any part to any person other than the surviving spouse. If these five conditions are satisfied only for a specific portion of the proceeds, see the section 2056(b) regulations to determine the amount of the marital deduction.

Charitable Remainder Trusts. An interest in a charitable remainder trust will **not** be treated as a nondeductible terminable interest if:

1. The interest in the trust passes from the decedent to the surviving spouse; and

2. The surviving spouse is the only beneficiary of the trust other than charitable organizations described in section 170(c).

A "charitable remainder trust" is either a charitable remainder annuity trust or a charitable remainder unitrust. (See section 664 for descriptions of these trusts.)

Election To Deduct Qualified Terminable Interests (QTIP)

You may elect to claim a marital deduction for qualified terminable interest property or property interests. You make the QTIP election simply by listing the qualified terminable interest property on Schedule M and deducting its value. You are presumed to have made the QTIP election if you list the property and deduct its value on Schedule M. If you make this election, the surviving spouse's gross estate will include the value of the "qualified terminable interest property." See the instructions for line 6 of Part 4, General Information, for more details. **The election is irrevocable.**

If you file a Form 706 in which you do not make this election, you may not file an amended return to make the election

unless you file the amended return on or before the due date for filing the original Form 706.

The effect of the election is that the property (interest) will be treated as passing to the surviving spouse and will not be treated as a nondeductible terminable interest. All of the other marital deduction requirements must still be satisfied before you may make this election. For example, you may not make this election for property or property interests that are not included in the decedent's gross estate.

Qualified terminable interest property is property **(a)** that passes from the decedent, and **(b)** in which the surviving spouse has a qualifying income interest for life.

The surviving spouse has a *qualifying income interest for life* if the surviving spouse is entitled to all of the income from the property payable annually or at more frequent intervals, or has a usufruct interest for life in the property, and during the surviving spouse's lifetime no person has a power to appoint any part of the property to any person other than the surviving spouse. An annuity is treated as an income interest regardless of whether the property from which the annuity is payable can be separately identified.

Amendments to Regulations sections 20.2044-1, 20.2056(b)-7 and 20.2056(b)-10 clarify that an interest in property is eligible for QTIP treatment if the income interest is contingent upon the executor's election even if that portion of the property for which no election is made will pass to or for the benefit of beneficiaries other than the surviving spouse.

The QTIP election may be made for all or any part of qualified terminable interest property. A partial election must relate to a fractional or percentile share of the property so that the elective part will reflect its proportionate share of the increase or decline in the whole of the property when applying sections 2044 or 2519. Thus, if the interest of the surviving spouse in a trust (or other property in which the spouse has a qualified life estate) is qualified terminable interest property, you may make an election for a part of the trust (or other property) only if the election relates to a defined fraction or percentage of the entire trust (or other property). The fraction or percentage may be defined by means of a formula.

Qualified Domestic Trust Election (QDOT)

The marital deduction is allowed for transfers to a surviving spouse who is not a U.S. citizen only if the property passes to the surviving spouse in a "qualified domestic trust" (QDOT) or if

Form 706 (Rev. 8-2004)

such property is transferred or irrevocably assigned to a QDOT before the decedent's estate tax return is filed.

A QDOT is any trust:

1. That requires at least one trustee to be either an individual who is a citizen of the United States or a domestic corporation;

2. That requires that no distribution of corpus from the trust can be made unless such a trustee has the right to withhold from the distribution the tax imposed on the QDOT;

3. That meets the requirements of any applicable regulations; and

4. For which the executor has made an election on the estate tax return of the decedent.

Note: *For trusts created by an instrument executed before November 5, 1990, paragraphs 1 and 2 above will be treated as met if the trust instrument requires that all trustees be individuals who are citizens of the United States or domestic corporations.*

You make the QDOT election simply by listing the qualified domestic trust or the **entire value** of the trust property on Schedule M and deducting its value. You are presumed to have made the QDOT election if you list the trust or trust property and deduct its value on Schedule M. **Once made, the election is irrevocable.**

If an election is made to deduct qualified domestic trust property under section 2056A(d), provide the following information for each qualified domestic trust on an attachment to this schedule:

1. The name and address of every trustee;

2. A description of each transfer passing from the decedent that is the source of the property to be placed in trust; and

3. The employer identification number (EIN) for the trust.

The election must be made for an entire QDOT trust. In listing a trust for which you are making a QDOT election, unless you specifically identify the trust as not subject to the election, the election will be considered made for the entire trust.

The determination of whether a trust qualifies as a QDOT will be made as of the date the decedent's Form 706 is filed. If, however, judicial proceedings are brought before the Form 706's due date (including extensions) to have the trust revised to meet the QDOT requirements, then the determination will not be made until the court-ordered changes to the trust are made.

Line 1

If property passes to the surviving spouse as the result of a qualified disclaimer, check "Yes" and attach a copy of the written disclaimer required by section 2518(b).

Line 3

Section 2056(b)(7) creates an automatic QTIP election for certain joint and survivor annuities that are includible in the estate under section 2039. To qualify, only the surviving spouse can have the right to receive payments before the death of the surviving spouse.

The executor can elect out of QTIP treatment, however, by checking the "Yes" box on line 3. Once made, the election is irrevocable. If there is more than one such joint and survivor annuity, you are not required to make the election for all of them.

If you make the election out of QTIP treatment by checking "Yes" on line 3, you cannot deduct the amount of the annuity on Schedule M. If you do not make the election out, you must list the joint and survivor annuities on Schedule M.

Listing Property Interests on Schedule M

List each property interest included in the gross estate that passes from the decedent to the surviving spouse and for which a marital deduction is claimed. This includes otherwise nondeductible terminable interest property for which you are making a QTIP election. Number each item in sequence and describe each item in detail. Describe the instrument (including any clause or paragraph number) or provision of law under which each item passed to the surviving spouse. If possible, show where each item appears (number and schedule) on Schedules A through I.

In listing otherwise nondeductible property for which you are making a QTIP election, unless you specifically identify a fractional portion of the trust or other property as not subject to the election, the election will be considered made for all of the trust or other property.

Enter the value of each interest before taking into account the federal estate tax or any other death tax. The valuation dates used in determining the value of the gross estate apply also on Schedule M.

If Schedule M includes a bequest of the residue or a part of the residue of the decedent's estate, attach a copy of the computation showing how the value of the residue was determined. Include a statement showing:

• The value of all property that is included in the decedent's gross estate (Schedules A through I) but is not a part of the decedent's probate estate, such as lifetime transfers, jointly owned property that passed to the survivor on decedent's death, and the insurance payable to specific beneficiaries.

• The values of all specific and general legacies or devises, with reference to the applicable clause or paragraph of the decedent's will or codicil. (If legacies are made to each member of a class; for example, $1,000 to each of decedent's employees, only the number in each class and the total value of property received by them need be furnished.)

• The date of birth of all persons, the length of whose lives may affect the value of the residuary interest passing to the surviving spouse.

• Any other important information such as that relating to any claim to any part of the estate not arising under the will.

Lines 5a, b, and c. The total of the values listed on Schedule M must be reduced by the amount of the federal estate tax, the federal GST tax, and the amount of state or other death and GST taxes paid out of the property interest involved. If you enter an amount for state or other death or GST taxes on lines 5b or 5c, identify the taxes and attach your computation of them.

Attachments. If you list property interests passing by the decedent's will on Schedule M, attach a certified copy of the order admitting the will to probate. If, when you file the return, the court of probate jurisdiction has entered any decree interpreting the will or any of its provisions affecting any of the interests listed on Schedule M, or has entered any order of distribution, attach a copy of the decree or order. In addition, the IRS may request other evidence to support the marital deduction claimed.

Page 30

Form 706 (Rev. 8-2004)

Estate of:

SCHEDULE O—Charitable, Public, and Similar Gifts and Bequests

		Yes	No
1a If the transfer was made by will, has any action been instituted to have interpreted or to contest the will or any of its provisions affecting the charitable deductions claimed in this schedule? . . . . If "Yes," full details must be submitted with this schedule.			
b According to the information and belief of the person or persons filing this return, is any such action planned? If "Yes," full details must be submitted with this schedule.			
2 Did any property pass to charity as the result of a qualified disclaimer?. . . . . If "Yes," attach a copy of the written disclaimer required by section 2518(b).			

Item number	Name and address of beneficiary	Character of institution	Amount
1			

Total from continuation schedules (or additional sheets) attached to this schedule . . . .

3 Total		**3**	
4a Federal estate tax payable out of property interests listed above	**4a**		
b Other death taxes payable out of property interests listed above	**4b**		
c Federal and state GST taxes payable out of property interests listed above	**4c**		
d Add items 4a, b, and c		**4d**	
5 Net value of property interests listed above (subtract 4d from 3). Also enter on Part 5, Recapitulation, page 3, at item 21		**5**	

(If more space is needed, attach the continuation schedule from the end of this package or additional sheets of the same size.)
(The instructions to Schedule O are in the separate instructions.)

Schedule O—Page 31

Form 706 (Rev. 8-2004)

Estate of:

SCHEDULE P—Credit for Foreign Death Taxes

List all foreign countries to which death taxes have been paid and for which a credit is claimed on this return.

If a credit is claimed for death taxes paid to more than one foreign country, compute the credit for taxes paid to one country on this sheet and attach a separate copy of Schedule P for each of the other countries.

The credit computed on this sheet is for the ....

(Name of death tax or taxes)

.... imposed in ....

(Name of country)

Credit is computed under the ....

(Insert title of treaty or "statute")

Citizenship (nationality) of decedent at time of death

	(All amounts and values must be entered in United States money.)		
1	Total of estate, inheritance, legacy, and succession taxes imposed in the country named above attributable to property situated in that country, subjected to these taxes, and included in the gross estate (as defined by statute)	**1**	
2	Value of the gross estate (adjusted, if necessary, according to the instructions for item 2)	**2**	
3	Value of property situated in that country, subjected to death taxes imposed in that country, and included in the gross estate (adjusted, if necessary, according to the instructions for item 3)	**3**	
4	Tax imposed by section 2001 reduced by the total credits claimed under sections 2010, 2011, and 2012 (see instructions).	**4**	
5	Amount of Federal estate tax attributable to property specified at item 3. (Divide item 3 by item 2 and multiply the result by item 4.)	**5**	
6	Credit for death taxes imposed in the country named above (the smaller of item 1 or item 5). Also enter on line 16 of Part 2, Tax Computation	**6**	

SCHEDULE Q—Credit for Tax on Prior Transfers

Part 1—Transferor Information

	Name of transferor	Social security number	IRS office where estate tax return was filed	Date of death
A				
B				
C				

Check here ▶ ☐ if section 2013(f) (special valuation of farm, etc., real property) adjustments to the computation of the credit were made (see page 21 of the instructions).

Part 2—Computation of Credit (see instructions beginning on page 20)

Item	Transferor			Total A, B, & C
	A	B	C	
1 Transferee's tax as apportioned (from worksheet, (line 7 ÷ line 8) × line 35 for each column) . .				
2 Transferor's tax (from each column of worksheet, line 20)				
3 Maximum amount before percentage requirement (for each column, enter amount from line 1 or 2, whichever is smaller)				
4 Percentage allowed (each column) (see instructions)	%	%	%	
5 Credit allowable (line 3 × line 4 for each column)				
6 TOTAL credit allowable (add columns A, B, and C of line 5). Enter here and on line 17 of Part 2, Tax Computation				

Schedules P and Q—Page 32   (The instructions to Schedules P and Q are in the separate instructions.)

Form 706 (Rev. 8-2004)

SCHEDULE R—Generation-Skipping Transfer Tax

Note: *To avoid application of the deemed allocation rules, Form 706 and Schedule R should be filed to allocate the GST exemption to trusts that may later have taxable terminations or distributions under section 2612 even if the form is not required to be filed to report estate or GST tax.*

The GST tax is imposed on taxable transfers of interests in property located **outside the United States** *as well as property located inside the United States.*

See instructions beginning on page 21.

Part 1—GST Exemption Reconciliation (Section 2631) and Section 2652(a)(3) (Special QTIP) Election

You no longer need to check a box to make a section 2652(a)(3) (special QTIP) election. If you list qualifying property in Part 1, line 9, below, you will be considered to have made this election. See page 24 of the separate instructions for details.

1 Maximum allowable GST exemption	**1**
2 Total GST exemption allocated by the decedent against decedent's lifetime transfers	**2**
3 Total GST exemption allocated by the executor, using Form 709, against decedent's lifetime transfers	**3**
4 GST exemption allocated on line 6 of Schedule R, Part 2	**4**
5 GST exemption allocated on line 6 of Schedule R, Part 3	**5**
6 Total GST exemption allocated on line 4 of Schedule(s) R-1	**6**
7 Total GST exemption allocated to inter vivos transfers and direct skips (add lines 2–6)	**7**
8 GST exemption available to allocate to trusts and section 2032A interests (subtract line 7 from line 1)	**8**

9 Allocation of GST exemption to trusts (as defined for GST tax purposes):

A Name of trust	B Trust's EIN (if any)	C GST exemption allocated on lines 2–6, above (see instructions)	D Additional GST exemption allocated (see instructions)	E Trust's inclusion ratio (optional—see instructions)

9D Total. May not exceed line 8, above	**9D**	

10 GST exemption available to allocate to section 2032A interests received by individual beneficiaries (subtract line 9D from line 8). You must attach special use allocation schedule (see instructions) | **10** |

(The instructions to Schedule R are in the separate instructions.)

Schedule R—Page 33

Form 706 (Rev. 8-2004)

Estate of:

Part 2—Direct Skips Where the Property Interests Transferred Bear the GST Tax on the Direct Skips

Name of skip person	Description of property interest transferred	Estate tax value

1 Total estate tax values of all property interests listed above		1	
2 Estate taxes, state death taxes, and other charges borne by the property interests listed above.		2	
3 GST taxes borne by the property interests listed above but imposed on direct skips other than those shown on this Part 2 (see instructions)		3	
4 Total fixed taxes and other charges (add lines 2 and 3)		4	
5 Total tentative maximum direct skips (subtract line 4 from line 1)		5	
6 GST exemption allocated		6	
7 Subtract line 6 from line 5		7	
8 GST tax due (divide line 7 by 3.083333)		8	
9 Enter the amount from line 8 of Schedule R, Part 3		9	
10 **Total GST taxes payable by the estate** (add lines 8 and 9). Enter here and on line 20 of Part 2—Tax Computation, on page 1.		10	

Schedule R—Page 34

Form 706 (Rev. 8-2004)

Estate of:

Part 3—Direct Skips Where the Property Interests Transferred Do Not Bear the GST
Tax on the Direct Skips

Name of skip person	Description of property interest transferred	Estate tax value

1 Total estate tax values of all property interests listed above	1	
2 Estate taxes, state death taxes, and other charges borne by the property interests listed above	2	
3 GST taxes borne by the property interests listed above but imposed on direct skips other than those shown on this Part 3 (see instructions)	3	
4 Total fixed taxes and other charges (add lines 2 and 3).	4	
5 Total tentative maximum direct skips (subtract line 4 from line 1)	5	
6 GST exemption allocated	6	
7 Subtract line 6 from line 5	7	
8 GST tax due (multiply line 7 by .48). Enter here and on Schedule R, Part 2, line 9	8	

Schedule R—Page 35

SCHEDULE R-1
(Form 706)
(Rev. August 2004)
Department of the Treasury
Internal Revenue Service

Generation-Skipping Transfer Tax
Direct Skips From a Trust
Payment Voucher

OMB No. 1545-0015

Executor: File one copy with Form 706 and send two copies to the fiduciary. Do not pay the tax shown. See the separate instructions.
Fiduciary: See instructions on the following page. Pay the tax shown on line 6.

Name of trust	Trust's EIN
Name and title of fiduciary	Name of decedent
Address of fiduciary (number and street)	Decedent's SSN	Service Center where Form 706 was filed
City, state, and ZIP code	Name of executor
Address of executor (number and street)	City, state, and ZIP code
Date of decedent's death	Filing due date of Schedule R, Form 706 (with extensions)

Part 1—Computation of the GST Tax on the Direct Skip

Description of property interests subject to the direct skip	Estate tax value

1 Total estate tax value of all property interests listed above	**1**	
2 Estate taxes, state death taxes, and other charges borne by the property interests listed above	**2**	
3 Tentative maximum direct skip from trust (subtract line 2 from line 1)	**3**	
4 GST exemption allocated	**4**	
5 Subtract line 4 from line 3	**5**	
6 **GST tax due from fiduciary** (divide line 5 by 3.083333) **(See instructions if property will not bear the GST tax.)**	**6**	

Under penalties of perjury, I declare that I have examined this return, including accompanying schedules and statements, and to the best of my knowledge and belief, it is true, correct, and complete.

_____
Signature(s) of executor(s)   Date

_____
                                                                 Date

_____
Signature of fiduciary or officer representing fiduciary   Date

Schedule R-1 (Form 706)—Page 36

Form 706 (Rev. 8-2004)

Instructions for the Trustee

Introduction

Schedule R-1 (Form 706) serves as a payment voucher for the Generation-Skipping Transfer (GST) tax imposed on a direct skip from a trust, which you, the trustee of the trust, must pay. The executor completes the Schedule R-1 (Form 706) and gives you 2 copies. File one copy and keep one for your records.

How to pay

You can pay by check or money order.
- Make it payable to the "United States Treasury."
- Make the check or money order for the amount on line 6 of Schedule R-1.
- Write "GST Tax" and the trust's EIN on the check or money order.

Signature

You must sign the Schedule R-1 in the space provided.

What to mail

Mail your check or money order and the copy of Schedule R-1 that you signed.

Where to mail

Mail to the Service Center shown on Schedule R-1.

When to pay

The GST tax is due and payable 9 months after the decedent's date of death (shown on the Schedule R-1). You will owe interest on any GST tax not paid by that date.

Automatic extension

You have an automatic extension of time to file Schedule R-1 and pay the GST tax. The automatic extension allows you to file and pay by 2 months after the due date (with extensions) for filing the decedent's Schedule R (shown on the Schedule R-1).

If you pay the GST tax under the automatic extension, you will be charged interest (but no penalties).

Additional information

For more information, see Code section 2603(a)(2) and the instructions for Form 706, United States Estate (and Generation-Skipping Transfer) Tax Return.

Schedule R-1 (Form 706)—Page 37

Form 706 (Rev. 8-2004)

Estate of:

SCHEDULE U. Qualified Conservation Easement Exclusion

Part 1—Election

Note: *The executor is deemed to have made the election under section 2031(c)(6) if he or she files Schedule U and excludes any qualifying conservation easements from the gross estate.*

Part 2—General Qualifications

1 Describe the land subject to the qualified conservation easement (see separate instructions) _____

2 Did the decedent or a member of the decedent's family own the land described above during the 3-year period ending on the date of the decedent's death? . . . .   ☐ **Yes**   ☐ **No**

3 Describe the conservation easement with regard to which the exclusion is being claimed (see separate instructions).
_____

Part 3—Computation of Exclusion

4 Estate tax value of the land subject to the qualified conservation easement (see separate instructions).	**4**	
5 Date of death value of any easements granted prior to decedent's death and included on line 10 below (see instructions)	**5**	
6 Add lines 4 and 5.	**6**	
7 Value of retained development rights on the land (see instructions) .	**7**	
8 Subtract line 7 from line 6	**8**	
9 Multiply line 8 by 30% (.30)	**9**	
10 Value of qualified conservation easement for which the exclusion is being claimed (see instructions)	**10**	
Note: *If line 10 is less than line 9, continue with line 11. If line 10 is equal to or more than line 9, skip lines 11 through 13, enter ".40" on line 14, and complete the schedule.*		
11 Divide line 10 by line 8. Figure to 3 decimal places (e.g., .123) .	**11**	
If line 11 is equal to or less than .100, stop here; the estate does not qualify for the conservation easement exclusion.		
12 Subtract line 11 from .300. Enter the answer in hundredths by rounding any thousandths up to the next higher hundredth (i.e., .030 = .03; but .031 = .04)	**12**	
13 Multiply line 12 by 2	**13**	
14 Subtract line 13 from .40	**14**	
15 Deduction under section 2055(f) for the conservation easement (see separate instructions)	**15**	
16 Amount of indebtedness on the land (see separate instructions) .	**16**	
17 Total reductions in value (add lines 7, 15, and 16)	**17**	
18 Net value of land (subtract line 17 from line 4)	**18**	
19 Multiply line 18 by line 14	**19**	
20 Enter the smaller of line 19 or the exclusion limitation (see instructions). Also enter this amount on item 11, Part 5, Recapitulation, Page 3	**20**	

Schedule U—Page 38

Form 706 (Rev. 8-2004)   (Make copies of this schedule before completing it if you will need more than one schedule.)

Estate of:

CONTINUATION SCHEDULE

Continuation of Schedule _____
(Enter letter of schedule you are continuing.)

Item number	Description For securities, give CUSIP number.	Unit value (Sch. B, E, or G only)	Alternate valuation date	Alternate value	Value at date of death or amount deductible
TOTAL. (Carry forward to main schedule.)					

See the instructions on the reverse side.

Continuation Schedule—Page 39

Form 706 (Rev. 8-2004)

Instructions for Continuation Schedule

When you need to list more assets or deductions than you have room for on one of the main schedules, use the Continuation Schedule on page 39. It provides a uniform format for listing additional assets from Schedules A through I and additional deductions from Schedules J, K, L, M, and O.

Please keep the following points in mind:

● Use a separate Continuation Schedule for each main schedule you are continuing. Do not combine assets or deductions from different schedules on one Continuation Schedule.

● Make copies of the blank schedule before completing it if you expect to need more than one.

● Use as many Continuation Schedules as needed to list all the assets or deductions.

● Enter the letter of the schedule you are continuing in the space at the top of the Continuation Schedule.

● Use the *Unit value* column only if continuing Schedule B, E, or G. For all other schedules, use this space to continue the description.

● Carry the total from the Continuation Schedules forward to the appropriate line on the main schedule.

If continuing	Report	Where on Continuation Schedule
Schedule E, Pt. 2	*Percentage includible*	*Alternate valuation date*
Schedule K	*Amount unpaid to date*	*Alternate valuation date*
Schedule K	*Amount in contest*	*Alternate value*
Schedules J, L, M	*Description of deduction continuation*	*Alternate valuation date* **and** *Alternate value*
Schedule O	*Character of institution*	*Alternate valuation date* **and** *Alternate value*
Schedule O	*Amount of each deduction*	*Amount deductible*

Continuation Schedule—Page 40

Form **709**

Department of the Treasury
Internal Revenue Service

United States Gift (and Generation-Skipping Transfer) Tax Return

(For gifts made during calendar year 2003)

▶ See separate instructions.

OMB No. 1545-0020

2003

Part 1—General Information

1 Donor's first name and middle initial	2 Donor's last name	3 Donor's social security number

4 Address (number, street, and apartment number)	5 Legal residence (domicile) (county and state)

6 City, state, and ZIP code	7 Citizenship

		Yes	No
8	If the donor died during the year, check here ▶ ☐ and enter date of death.................., ...		
9	If you received an extension of time to file this Form 709, check here ▶ ☐ and attach the Form 4868, 2688, 2350, or extension letter .		
10	Enter the total number of donees listed on Schedule A—count each person only once. ▶		
11a	Have you (the donor) previously filed a Form 709 (or 709-A) for any other year? If "No," skip line 11b		
11b	If the answer to line 11a is "Yes," has your address changed since you last filed Form 709 (or 709-A)?		
12	Gifts by husband or wife to third parties.—Do you consent to have the gifts (including generation-skipping transfers) made by you and by your spouse to third parties during the calendar year considered as made one-half by each of you? (See instructions.) (If the answer is "Yes," the following information must be furnished and your spouse must sign the consent shown below. **If the answer is "No," skip lines 13–18 and go to Schedule A.)**		
13	Name of consenting spouse 14 SSN		
15	Were you married to one another during the entire calendar year? (see instructions)		
16	If the answer to 15 is "No," check whether ☐ married ☐ divorced or ☐ widowed, and give date (see instructions) ▶		
17	Will a gift tax return for this year be filed by your spouse? (If "Yes," mail both returns in the same envelope.)		
18	**Consent of Spouse**—I consent to have the gifts (and generation-skipping transfers) made by me and by my spouse to third parties during the calendar year considered as made one-half by each of us. We are both aware of the joint and several liability for tax created by the execution of this consent.		

Consenting spouse's signature ▶   Date ▶

Part 2—Tax Computation

1	Enter the amount from Schedule A, Part 4, line 11	1
2	Enter the amount from Schedule B, line 3	2
3	Total taxable gifts (add lines 1 and 2)	3
4	Tax computed on amount on line 3 (see Table for Computing Tax in separate instructions). . .	4
5	Tax computed on amount on line 2 (see Table for Computing Tax in separate instructions). . .	5
6	Balance (subtract line 5 from line 4)	6
7	Maximum unified credit (nonresident aliens, see instructions)	7 345,800 00
8	Enter the unified credit against tax allowable for all prior periods (from Sch. B, line 1, col. C) . .	8
9	Balance (subtract line 8 from line 7)	9
10	Enter 20% (.20) of the amount allowed as a specific exemption for gifts made after September 8, 1976, and before January 1, 1977 (see instructions)	10
11	Balance (subtract line 10 from line 9)	11
12	Unified credit (enter the smaller of line 6 or line 11)	12
13	Credit for foreign gift taxes (see instructions)	13
14	Total credits (add lines 12 and 13)	14
15	Balance (subtract line 14 from line 6) (do not enter less than zero)	15
16	Generation-skipping transfer taxes (from Schedule C, Part 3, col. H, Total)	16
17	Total tax (add lines 15 and 16)	17
18	Gift and generation-skipping transfer taxes prepaid with extension of time to file	18
19	If line 18 is less than line 17, enter **balance due** (see instructions)	19
20	If line 18 is greater than line 17, enter **amount to be refunded**	20

Attach check or money order here.

Sign Here

Under penalties of perjury, I declare that I have examined this return, including any accompanying schedules and statements, and to the best of my knowledge and belief, it is true, correct, and complete. Declaration of preparer (other than donor) is based on all information of which preparer has any knowledge.

▶ Signature of donor	Date

Paid Preparer's Use Only

Preparer's signature ▶	Date	Check if self-employed ▶ ☐
Firm's name (or yours if self-employed), address, and ZIP code ▶	Phone no. ▶ ( )	

For Disclosure, Privacy Act, and Paperwork Reduction Act Notice, see page 12 of the separate instructions for this form.   Cat. No. 16783M   Form **709** (2003)

Form 709 (2003)   Page **2**

SCHEDULE A	**Computation of Taxable Gifts** (Including transfers in trust) (see instructions)

A   Does the value of any item listed on Schedule A reflect any valuation discount? If "Yes," see instructions . . . . . .   Yes ☐   No ☐

B   ☐ ◀ Check here if you elect under section 529(c)(2)(B) to treat any transfers made this year to a qualified state tuition program as made ratably over a 5-year period beginning this year. See instructions. Attach explanation.

Part 1—Gifts Subject Only to Gift Tax. *Gifts less political organization, medical, and educational exclusions—see instructions*

A Item number	**B** • Donee's name and address • Relationship to donor (if any) • Description of gift • If the gift was of securities, give CUSIP no.	**C**	**D** Donor's adjusted basis of gift	**E** Date of gift	**F** Value at date of gift	**G** For split gifts, enter ½ of column F	**H** Net transfer (subtract col. G from col. F)
1							
*Gifts made by spouse—complete **only** if you are splitting gifts with your spouse and he/she also made gifts.*							

Total of Part 1 (add amounts from Part 1, column H) . . . . ▶

Part 2—Direct skips— gifts that are direct skips and are subject to both gift tax and generation-skipping transfer tax. You must list the gifts in chronological order.

A Item number	**B** • Donee's name and address • Relationship to donor (if any) • Description of gift • If the gift was of securities, give CUSIP no.	**C** 2632(b) election out	**D** Donor's adjusted basis of gift	**E** Date of gift	**F** Value at date of gift	**G** For split gifts, enter ½ of column F	**H** Net transfer (subtract col. G from col. F)
1							
*Gifts made by spouse—complete **only** if you are splitting gifts with your spouse and he/she also made gifts.*							

Total of Part 2 (add amounts from Part 2, column H) . . . . ▶

Part 3—Indirect skips— gifts to trusts that are currently subject to gift tax and may later be subject to generation-skipping transfer tax. You must list these gifts in chronological order.

A Item number	**B** • Donee's name and address • Relationship to donor (if any) • Description of gift • If the gift was of securities, give CUSIP no.	**C** 2632(c) election out	**D** Donor's adjusted basis of gift	**E** Date of gift	**F** Value at date of gift	**G** For split gifts, enter ½ of column F	**H** Net transfer (subtract col. G from col. F)
1							
*Gifts made by spouse—complete **only** if you are splitting gifts with your spouse and he/she also made gifts.*							

Total of Part 3 (add amounts from Part 3, column H) . . . . ▶

(If more space is needed, attach additional sheets of same size.)   Form **709** (2003)

Form 709 (2003)   Page **3**

Part 4—Taxable Gift Reconciliation

1	Total value of gifts of donor (add totals from column H of Parts 1, 2, and 3)	**1**
2	Total annual exclusions for gifts listed on line 1 (see instructions)	**2**
3	Total included amount of gifts (subtract line 2 from line 1)	**3**

Deductions (see instructions)

4	Gifts of interests to spouse for which a marital deduction will be claimed, based on items --------------------------------- of Schedule A	**4**	
5	Exclusions attributable to gifts on line 4	**5**	
6	Marital deduction—subtract line 5 from line 4	**6**	
7	Charitable deduction, based on items ....less exclusions . .	**7**	
8	Total deductions—add lines 6 and 7	**8**	
9	Subtract line 8 from line 3	**9**	
10	Generation-skipping transfer taxes payable with this Form 709 (from Schedule C, Part 3, col. H, Total) .	**10**	
11	Taxable gifts (add lines 9 and 10). Enter here and on line 1 of the Tax Computation on page 1. . . .	**11**	

SCHEDULE A **Computation of Taxable Gifts** *(continued)*

12 Terminable Interest (QTIP) Marital Deduction. (See instructions for line 4 of Schedule A.)

If a trust (or other property) meets the requirements of qualified terminable interest property under section 2523(f), and

    a. The trust (or other property) is listed on Schedule A, and

    b. The value of the trust (or other property) is entered in whole or in part as a deduction on line 4, Part 4 of Schedule A,

then the donor shall be deemed to have made an election to have such trust (or other property) treated as qualified terminable interest property under section 2523(f).

    If less than the entire value of the trust (or other property) that the donor has included in Parts 1 and 3 of Schedule A is entered as a deduction on line 4, the donor shall be considered to have made an election only as to a fraction of the trust (or other property). The numerator of this fraction is equal to the amount of the trust (or other property) deducted on line 6 of Part 4, Schedule A. The denominator is equal to the total value of the trust (or other property) listed in Parts 1 and 3 of Schedule A.

    If you make the QTIP election (see instructions for line 4 of Schedule A), the terminable interest property involved will be included in your spouse's gross estate upon his or her death (section 2044). If your spouse disposes (by gift or otherwise) of all or part of the qualifying life income interest, he or she will be considered to have made a transfer of the entire property that is subject to the gift tax (see Transfer of Certain Life Estates on page 4 of the instructions).

13 Election Out of QTIP Treatment of Annuities

☐ ◄ Check here if you elect under section 2523(f)(6) **NOT** to treat as qualified terminable interest property any joint and survivor annuities that are reported on Schedule A and would otherwise be treated as qualified terminable interest property under section 2523(f). (See instructions.) Enter the item numbers (from Schedule A) for the annuities for which you are making this election ►

SCHEDULE B **Gifts From Prior Periods**

If you answered "Yes" on line 11a of page 1, Part 1, see the instructions for completing Schedule B. If you answered "No," skip to the Tax Computation on page 1 (or Schedule C, if applicable).

A Calendar year or calendar quarter (see instructions)	B Internal Revenue office where prior return was filed	C Amount of unified credit against gift tax for periods after December 31, 1976	D Amount of specific exemption for prior periods ending before January 1, 1977	E Amount of taxable gifts

1	Totals for prior periods	**1**
2	Amount, if any, by which total specific exemption, line 1, column D, is more than $30,000	**2**
3	Total amount of taxable gifts for prior periods (add amount, column E, line 1, and amount, if any, on line 2). (Enter here and on line 2 of the Tax Computation on page 1.)	**3**

(If more space is needed, attach additional sheets of same size.)

Form **709** (2003)

Form 709 (2003)   Page **4**

| SCHEDULE C | Computation of Generation-Skipping Transfer Tax |

Note: *Inter vivos direct skips that are completely excluded by the GST exemption must still be fully reported (including value and exemptions claimed) on Schedule C.*

Part 1—Generation-Skipping Transfers

A Item No. (from Schedule A, Part 2, col. A)	B Value (from Schedule A, Part 2, col. H)	C Nontaxable portion of transfer	D Net Transfer (subtract col. C from col. B)
1			

Gifts made by spouse (for gift splitting only)

Part 2—GST Exemption Reconciliation (Section 2631) and Section 2652(a)(3) Election

Check box ▶ ☐ if you are making a section 2652(a)(3) (special QTIP) election (see instructions)

Enter the item numbers (from Schedule A) of the gifts for which you are making this election ▶ ....

1	Maximum allowable exemption (see instructions)	**1**
2	Total exemption used for periods before filing this return	**2**
3	Exemption available for this return (subtract line 2 from line 1)	**3**
4	Exemption claimed on this return (from Part 3, col. C total, below)	**4**
5	Allocation of exemption to transfers reported on Schedule A, Part 3	**5**
6	Exemption allocated to transfers not shown on line 4 or 5, above. **You must attach a Notice of Allocation.** (See instructions.)	**6**
7	Add lines 4, 5, and 6	**7**
8	Exemption available for future transfers (subtract line 7 from line 3)	**8**

Part 3—Tax Computation

A Item No. (from Schedule C, Part 1)	B Net transfer (from Schedule C, Part 1, col. D)	C GST Exemption Allocated	D Divide col. C by col. B	E Inclusion Ratio (subtract col. D from 1.000)	F Maximum Estate Tax Rate	G Applicable Rate (multiply col. E by col. F)	H Generation-Skipping Transfer Tax (multiply col. B by col. G)
1					49% (.49)		
2					49% (.49)		
3					49% (.49)		
4					49% (.49)		
5					49% (.49)		
6					49% (.49)		
					49% (.49)		
					49% (.49)		
					49% (.49)		
					49% (.49)		
					49% (.49)		
					49% (.49)		

| Total exemption claimed. Enter here and on line 4, Part 2, above. May not exceed line 3, Part 2, above . . . . . | | **Total generation-skipping transfer tax.** Enter here, on line 10 of Schedule A, Part 4, and on line 16 of the Tax Computation on page 1 . . . . | |

(If more space is needed, attach additional sheets of same size.)   ✱   Form **709** (2003)

ademption • disposition by testator of specific property (real or personal) bequeathed to a beneficiary in a will, so that at testator's death the property is no longer part of the estate. The beneficiary receives nothing unless the will substitutes another asset for the deemed property.

adjusted-book-value method • a valuation method in which the value of closely held corporation assets is adjusted to reflect the difference between true market value and book value

adjusted gross estate • an amount calculated for the purpose of determining the availability of certain tax benefits (such as installment payment of estate taxes) and arrived at by reducing the gross estate by allowable debts, funeral as well as medical costs, and administrative expenses

adjusted taxable estate • the phrase now used in computing the state death tax credit. It is the taxable estate reduced by $60,000.

adjusted taxable gift • total amount of gifts (less the charitable deduction, the marital deduction, and the annual gift tax exclusion) the decedent made after December 31, 1976—except for those gifts that were required for any reason to be included in the decedent's gross estate, such as gifts with retained interests or gifts of life insurance made within 3 years of death

administration • the management of a decedent's estate, including the marshaling of assets; the payment of expenses, debts, and charges; the payment or delivery of legacies; and the rendition of an account

administrator—executor/executrix • an administrator is appointed by the court to settle an estate. An executor is named by the estate owner in the will as the one to settle that estate. The administrator is always appointed by the court, and the executor is always named by the deceased in the will.

advance medical directive • durable power of attorney for health care and living wills

advancement • money or property given by a parent to a child, other descendant, or heir (depending upon the statute's wording), or expended by the former for the latter's benefit, in anticipation of the share that the child (for example) will inherit in the parent's estate and intended to be deducted from the child's eventual portion

adverse party • a beneficiary with an interest inconsistent with another beneficiary's interest in the same trust property

afterborn child • a child born after the execution of a parent's will or trust

alien spouse • a spouse who is not a citizen of the United States

alternate valuation date • the date 6 months after the decedent's death that may be used for estate tax valuation purposes

alternate value • for federal estate tax purposes, the value of the gross estate 6 months after the date of death, unless property is distributed, sold, exchanged, or otherwise disposed of within 6 months. In that case, the value of such property is determined as of the date of such disposition.

ancillary probate (ancillary administration) • a proceeding in a state other than the decedent's state of domicile and where a decedent owned property

annual exclusion • a gift tax exclusion of $11,000 that a donor is allowed each year for each donee, provided the gift is one of a present interest

annuity • a right to receive one or more payments for life or for a term of years

antenuptial (prenuptial) agreement • contract entered into by a couple prior to marriage and usually pertaining to issues of support and property distribution

applicable credit amount • a credit to which the estate of every individual is entitled, which can be directly applied against the gift or estate tax

applicable exclusion amount • equivalent value of an individual's property offset by the applicable credit amount (formerly called the credit equivalent)

appointee • person receiving the benefit under a power of appointment

appreciation • an increase in value, particularly the amount exceeding the basis of the property

arm's-length transaction • transaction between unrelated parties in which the parties act in their own self-interests

ascertainable standard • a power that allows an individual to consume or invade property for his or her own benefit, but the power is limited by a standard having a value that is ascertainable, such as the power to use or invade property for the individual's health, education, support, and/or maintenance

attestation clause • the paragraph appended to the will indicating that certain persons by their signatures thereto have heard the testator declare the instrument to be his or her will and have witnessed the signing of the will

attorney-in-fact • someone who is authorized by another to act in his or her place for a particular purpose or to transact general business

bad bargain • nongratuitous transfer for less than adequate money's worth

basis • an amount attributed to an asset for income tax purposes for determining gain or loss on sale or transfer and for determining the value of a gift in the hands of a donee

beneficiary • (1) one who inherits a share or part of a decedent's estate or (2) one who takes the beneficial interest under a trust (For income beneficiary, see *life tenant*.)

beneficiary (generation-skipping trust**)** • any person with a present or future interest or power in the trust

bequest • strictly, a gift by will of personal property as distinguished from a gift of real estate, although often used to cover a gift by will of either personal property or land, or both. "To bequeath" generally means to dispose of property of any kind by will. (See also *devise* and *legacy.*)

blockage discount • discount percentage attributed to the value of large blocks of corporate stock for estate and gift tax purposes, premised on the theory that a large block of stock is less marketable than smaller amounts of stock

book value • the worth of a business interest's assets minus the cost of its liabilities

buy-sell agreement • planning method used for the disposition and continuation of small business interests, the goals of which are the acquisition of a decedent business owner's interest by one or more business survivors or by the entity itself, and to peg the value of business interests or stock for transfer tax purposes

bypass trust • a testamentary trust designed to keep property transferred to it by the decedent- spouse out of the surviving spouse's gross estate

capital asset • asset of a permanent or fixed nature, or employed in carrying on a business or trade

capitalization-of-adjusted-earnings method • a valuation method in which the value of a closely held corporation is determined by multiplying the adjusted earnings of the business by a factor appropriate for the specific industry at the predetermined valuation date

carryover of donor's basis • basis of gifted property that is carried over from the donor to the donee

casualty loss • physical damage to a decedent's property during the administration of the estate, resulting from a sudden, unexpected, or unusual force

CEBT • See *bypass trust.*

charitable deduction • a deduction to a charitable organization (equal to the value of the gift) allowed against a reportable gift or as a deduction from the adjusted gross estate

charitable lead trust • tax planning device in which the donor transfers property inter vivos or by will to a trust whose earnings go to a charity for a certain period, after which the trust corpus reverts to the donor or some other party

charitable remainder annuity trust • charitable trust arrangement in which a fixed-income interest (worth at least 5 percent of the initial net fair market value of the property paid in trust) passes at least annually to one or more noncharitable beneficiaries, and at the death of the last income beneficiary or at the end of a term of years not greater than 20 years, the remainder interest passes to a qualified charity

charitable remainder trust • See *charitable remainder annuity trust, charitable remainder unitrust, and pooled-income fund.*

charitable remainder unitrust • charitable trust arrangement in which a fixed percentage (at least 5 percent of the net fair market value) of the trust assets as revalued annually is paid at least annually to one or more noncharitable income beneficiaries and at the death of the last income beneficiary or at the end of a term of years not greater than 20 years, the remainder interest passes to a qualified charity

charitable trust • a tax-exempt organization operated exclusively for charitable purposes as specified in Sec. 501(c)(3)

civil law system • legal system evolving from the Roman Empire based on codes enacted by a legislature rather than on a combination of many laws and judicial opinions

codicil • a supplement or addition to an existing will, to effect some revision, change, or modification of that will. A codicil must meet the same requirements regarding execution and validity as a will.

collateral relations • a phrase used primarily in the law of intestacy to designate uncles and aunts, cousins, and so forth (for example, those relatives not in a direct ascending or descending line, like grandparents or grandchildren, the latter of which are designated as lineal relations)

commingling • the mixing together of properties having different characters, such as the community and separate properties of either or both husband and wife in community-property jurisdictions

common law system • legal system, originating in England, that is based on statutory and case law according to changing customs and usages

common trust funds • commingled or collected investments

communication • a process of information exchange

community property • property acquired during marriage in which both husband and wife have an undivided one-half interest. Not more than one-half can be disposed of by either party individually by will. There are at present nine community-property states for federal tax law purposes: Arizona, California, Idaho, Louisiana, New Mexico, Nevada, Texas, Washington, and Wisconsin.

compensation • direct or indirect, monetary or nonmonetary payment for services completed or products delivered based on the value of the service or product

competence • the ability to do a certain thing

completed transfer • gift that is beyond the donor's recall

complex trust • any trust that is not a simple trust because the trustee may be required or given the discretion to accumulate or distribute trust income and principal and make gifts to charity

compliance • acting in conformity to the letter of the law, with or without concern for the spirit of the law

confidentiality • nondisclosure of private or secret information, such as a conversation between a financial planner and his or her client

conflicts of interest • situations in which the interests of two parties are in disagreement. Examples: a conflict between the interests of a financial planner and his or her client, or between two of a planner's clients (such as a husband and a wife).

conflicts of obligations • situations wherein a person has two clear ethical obligations which conflict with one another

contingent interest • a future interest in real or personal property that is dependent upon the fulfillment of a stated condition and may never come into existence

contingent remainder • a future interest in property dependent upon the fulfillment of a stated condition before the termination of a prior estate

controlled corporation • a corporation in which the decedent directly or indirectly owned or had the right, either alone or with any other person, to vote stock having at least 20 percent of the total combined voting power of all classes of stock

cooperation • a process of associating with another or others for mutual benefit

corpus • a term used to describe the principal or trustees as distinguished from the trust income

CPR/DNR • written directives permitting an individual to refuse resuscitative measures

CRAT • See *charitable remainder annuity trust.*

credit estate tax • prior to 2005, a tax imposed by a state to take full advantage of the amount allowed as a credit against the federal estate tax; also called a *gap* or *sponge* tax

credit-exclusion/equivalent bypass trust • See *bypass trust.*

credit for foreign death taxes • to prevent double taxation, a credit allowed against the federal estate tax for taxes actually paid by the decedent's estate to a foreign country for estate, inheritance, legacy, or succession taxes

credit for tax on prior transfers • to avoid double taxation on double transfers of property occurring within a reasonably short-time period, a credit allowed against the federal estate tax paid by the present decedent as a result of inherited property included in the decedent's gross estate

cross-purchase agreement • a contract binding closely held business interest owners to purchase an owner's business interest upon the occurrence of stipulated events, such as death

Crummey powers • rights granted to the beneficiaries of an irrevocable trust to demand all or a portion of a grantor's contribution to the trust, thereby creating a present interest in the grantor's gift

CRUT • See *charitable remainder unitrust.*

current-use valuation • See *special-use valuation.*

curtesy • a husband's right to a life estate in his deceased wife's real property

curtesy interest • under common law, the amount of his deceased wife's property to which a widower is entitled. This right has been abolished in many states and replaced with statutory rights of surviving spouses.

cy pres • a doctrine of law created to prevent the failure of trusts that cannot be applied to their original charitable purpose. When applying *cy pres,* the court attempts to find another charitable purpose similar to the settlor's initial charitable intention.

decoupling • action taken by many states to disassociate state death tax legislation from federal transfer tax legislation as provided under EGTRRA 2001

deed • a written instrument that conveys an interest in realty from the grantor to the grantee

de minimis rule • doctrine that the law does not concern itself with very small, unimportant matters

descent and distribution • Descent refers to the passing of real estate to the heirs of one who dies without a will. Distribution refers to the passing of personal property to the heirs of one who dies without a will. Technically, the laws of descent relate to real property; those of distribution relate to personal property. Modern usage has substituted *intestacy* to designate the legal effect of dying without a will.

devise • a gift of real property under a will, as distinguished from a gift of personal property. (See also *bequest* and *legacy.*)

direct-skip transfer • for generation-skipping transfer tax purposes, this is a taxable nontrust transfer to a skip person

disclaimer • a complete and unqualified refusal to accept property or an interest to which one is entitled. It must be made in a timely manner and without consideration or without directions as to what happens to such disclaimed property. The terms *disclaimer* and *renunciation* are synonymous.

distributable net income (DNI) • for fiduciary income tax purposes, the taxable income of the estate or trust for any taxable year, computed with certain modifications (See Code Sec. 643(a).)

domicile • an individual's permanent home—the place to which, whenever the individual is absent, he or she has the intention of returning

donee • the recipient of a gift. The term also refers to the recipient of a power of appointment.

donee of the power • the recipient of a power

donor • the person who makes a gift. The term also refers to the person who grants a power of appointment to another.

dower • a wife's right to a life estate in her deceased husband's real property

dower interest • under common law, the amount of her deceased husband's property to which a widow is entitled. This right has been abolished in many states and replaced with statutory rights of surviving spouses.

durable power of attorney • an estate planning tool with which a principal grants powers with respect to his or her property or health to an agent (attorney-in-fact)

elder law durable power of attorney • special durable power of attorney intended to address relevant issues of the elderly

entity (liquidation) agreement • a buy-sell agreement that provides that the entity will purchase and then liquidate the interest of a decedent-partner at death

entity-purchase agreement • a contract in which closely held business interest owners bind the business entity to purchase an owner's business interest upon the occurrence of specified events, such as death

equitable apportionment • the doctrine requiring that apportionment of taxes be made in the proportion that the value of the interest of each person interested in the estate bears to the total value of the interests of all persons interested in the estate

equitable ownership • the beneficial interest of a beneficiary under a trust, which may include the right to use, possess, and enjoy the property and/or have the income generated by the property

escheat • a reversion of property to the state in the absence of legal heirs

estate • an interest in real property as well as personal property that is or may become possessory or ownership measured in terms of duration

estate administration expenses • expenses incurred in the collection and preservation of probate assets, the payment of estate debts, and the distribution of probate assets to estate beneficiaries

estate and gift tax systems • tax systems in which a tax burden is imposed on transfers made during life and at death

estate for a term of years • a property interest established for a specific duration

estate freeze • a method to control future appreciation in the value of assets in order to reduce prospective estate taxes

estate in fee simple absolute • an interest that belongs absolutely to the estate owner, the heirs, and assigns forever without condition or limitation

estate planning • planning the accumulation, conservation, and distribution of an estate

estate tax • a tax imposed upon the right of a person to transfer property at death. This type of tax is imposed not only by the federal government, but also by a number of states.

estate trust • a type of trust commonly used to qualify property for the marital deduction. The surviving spouse is given an interest for life and the remainder is payable to the surviving spouse's estate.

ethical dilemma • situation in which there are good reasons for acting in a certain way and good reasons for not acting in that way

ethical temptation • situation in which there is a conflict between a person's interests and those of a client

executor/executrix • See *administrator.*

5-and-5 power • an individual's noncumulative right to withdraw annually the greater of $5,000 or 5 percent of the aggregate value of property from a trust

fair market value • the value at which estate assets are included in the gross estate for federal estate tax purposes; the price at which property would change hands between a willing buyer and a willing seller, neither being under a compulsion to buy or to sell and both having knowledge of the relevant facts

family allowance • the allowance of money from the estate to the family for support during administration

farm-method formula of valuation • a special (or limited) use valuation of land used for farming purposes, calculated by dividing the excess of the average annual gross cash rental for comparable farm property over the average annual state and local real estate taxes for such comparable property, by the average annual effective interest rate for all new Federal Land Bank loans

federal estate tax • an excise tax levied on the right to transfer property at death, imposed upon and measured by the value of the taxable estate left by the decedent

fee simple estate • an estate in which the owner is entitled to absolute ownership of property, with unconditional power to dispose of it during lifetime as well as the power to bequeath it to anyone at death

fiduciary • one occupying a legally defined position of trust (for example, an executor, an administrator, or a trustee)

fiduciary income tax return • the income tax return (Form 1041) filed by the fiduciary of an estate or a trust

Five Wishes • a type of advance medical directive that provides for seriously ill individuals to express their end-of-life wishes to loved ones and other concerned people

flower bonds • certain U.S. Treasury obligations that are purchased and traded at a discount. When owned by the decedent at death, they may be redeemed at par value plus accrued interest to pay federal estate taxes. The difference between par value and purchase price allows estate taxes to be paid at a "discount."

formula bequest • clause in wills, that can provide, by formula, an amount or share of the estate that effectively utilizes the estate owner's applicable credit amount and coordinates it with the unlimited marital deduction

formula clause • a clause that is aimed at achieving the appropriate marital deduction and shifting all property in excess of that amount so that it will not be taxed again in the surviving spouse's estate

fractional-share bequest • a provision in a will under which a spouse gives a fraction of his or her residuary estate that is sufficient to reduce the federal estate tax (after applicable credits) to the lowest possible amount

funded insurance trust • an insurance trust funded with cash, securities, or other assets whose income is used to pay premiums on the policies held in the trust

future interest • the postponed right of use or enjoyment of the property

future-interest gift • any interest or estate in which the donee's possession or enjoyment will not commence until some period of time after the gift is made

general power • a power of appointment that gives the donee a right at any time to designate the property to parties that include the donee or the donee's estate or creditors

general power of appointment • a power over the disposition of property exercisable in favor of any person the donee of the power may select, including the donee, the donee's estate, the donee's creditors, or the creditors of the donee's estate

generation-skipping transfer • outright transfer to a skip beneficiary and taxable distribution or taxable termination from a generation-skipping trust or its equivalent

generation-skipping trust • broadly defined in IRC Sec. 2611(b) as any trust that has younger-generation beneficiaries in more than one generation. Only a trust that has beneficiaries in at least two generations, both of which are below the grantor's generation, is a generation-skipping trust.

gift (for gift tax purposes) • property or property rights or interests gratuitously passed or transferred for less than an adequate and full consideration in money or money's worth (except for bona fide sales) to another, in trust or otherwise, directly or indirectly

gift *causa mortis* • a gift that is conditional upon the donor's dying

gift splitting • a provision allowing a married couple to treat a gift made by one of them to a third party as having been made one-half by each, provided the non-donor-spouse consents to the gift

gift tax • a tax imposed on transfers of property by gift during the donor's lifetime

gift tax charitable deduction • a gift tax deduction received for making a lifetime transfer of property to a qualified charity, the value of which is equal to the value of the gift to the extent not already covered by the annual exclusion

gift tax marital deduction • a deduction allowed for a gift made by one spouse to another, provided it qualifies. Outright gifts qualify; life estates qualify if the donee has the right to the income from the property for life and a general power of appointment over the principal.

goodwill • the economic advantage or benefit that is acquired by a business beyond the mere value of the capital invested in it because of the patronage it receives from constant or habitual customers, its local position, its reputation for skill or punctuality, other accidental circumstances or necessities, or public partialities or prejudices

grantor • a person who creates a trust; also called *settlor, creator,* or *trustor*

grantor (generation-skipping trust) • any person who contributes or adds property to a generation-skipping trust

grantor-retained annuity trust (GRAT) • an estate-freezing device in which a grantor's retained income right to a fixed annuity from property gifted to a trust is treated as having value for gift tax purposes

grantor-retained unitrust (GRUT) • an estate-freezing device in which a grantor's retained income right to a fixed percentage (as valued annually) of property gifted to a trust is treated as having value for gift tax purposes

grantor trust • a trust typically created for nontax advantages by a grantor with substantial assets who contributes the trust property for the benefit of less wealthy family members

GRAT • See *grantor-retained annuity trust.*

gross estate • an amount determined by totaling the value of all assets that the decedent had an interest in, which are required to be included in the estate by the Internal Revenue Code

gross-up rule • the rule whereby the decedent's gross estate is increased by the amount of any gift tax the decedent or the estate paid on a gift made by the decedent or the decedent's spouse after December 31, 1976, within the last 3 years of the decedent's life

GRUT • See *grantor-retained unitrust.*

guardian • a person named to represent the interests of minor children or disabled individuals

guardian ad litem • a guardian appointed by the court for a particular purpose such as defending a specific lawsuit or a legal proceeding involving a minor

guardian de son tort • an individual who assumes the guardianship of a minor or incompetent without obtaining court approval

health care proxy • medical directive appointing an agent to make medical treatment decisions for a patient

heir • technically, a person designated by law to succeed to the estate of an intestate (also designated as *next of kin*)

holding period • property acquired from a decedent that is sold within a year after the decedent's death, treated as having been held for more than a year if the following two conditions are met: (1) the person selling the property has a basis that is determined by reference to the property's fair market value on either the date of death or alternate valuation date, and (2) there is a disposition of the property within one year following the decedent's date of death

holographic will • a will entirely in the handwriting of the testator. In many states, such a will is not recognized unless it is published, declared, and witnessed as required by statute for other written wills.

homestead exemption • a statute exempting the homestead and, often, specified chattels from the debts of a deceased head of a household, notwithstanding provisions of a will or the intestate laws

ILIT • See *irrevocable life insurance trust.*

incidents of ownership • elements of ownership or degree of control over a life insurance policy

inclusion ratio • ratio used to determine the generation-skipping transfer tax rate

income in respect of a decedent (IRD) • income that was earned by a cash-basis taxpayer but not actually or constructively received by the taxpayer's date of death

income-first rule • the rule that requires that all distributions from the decedent's estate are deemed to be paid out of income first, even if the executor, administrator, or trustee actually distributes corpus in the form of cash or property

indefeasibly vested remainder • a vested absolute right to receive property at some future time after the present interest ceases

indirect skip • transfer of property other than a direct skip to a GST trust

inheritance tax • a tax levied on the right of the heirs to receive property; from a deceased person, measured by the share passing to each beneficiary, sometimes called a *succession tax*

installment sale • a sale in which at least one principal payment is received in a year other than the year of the sale

insurance trust • a trust composed partly or wholly of life insurance policy contracts

intangible personal property • property with no intrinsic value in and of itself, such as stock certificates, leases, mortgages, and bonds

intangible property • property that does not have physical substance (for example, a stock certificate or bond). The thing itself is only the evidence of value.

interest in property (for gift tax purposes) • present—an unrestricted right to the immediate use, possession, or enjoyment of property or income from the property; future—an interest other than a present interest

interpolated terminal reserve • the reserve on any life insurance policy between anniversary dates, regardless of whether further premium payments are due. It is determined by a pro rata adjustment upward (or downward in the case of certain term policies of long duration) between the previous terminal reserve and the next terminal reserve.

inter vivos trust • a trust created during the settlor's lifetime. It becomes operative during lifetime as opposed to a trust under will (testamentary trust), which does not become operative until the settlor dies.

intestacy laws • individual state laws providing for distribution of the property of a person who has died without leaving a valid will

intestate • the term for a person who dies without a valid will or for the condition of dying without a valid will

intestate-succession statutes • each state's statutory plan that clearly provides for the distribution of a decedent's probate property

irrevocable life insurance trust • trust arrangement in which the trust owns one or more life insurance policies on an insured's life within the trust

irrevocable trust • a trust created when the grantor permanently transfers property to the trustee and cannot alter, amend, revoke, or terminate the arrangement or reclaim the property

joint and survivor annuity • an annuity that is payable for two lives and does not expire with the death of the first annuitant (although the amount may vary after the first death)

joint tenancy with right of survivorship • the holding of property by two or more persons in such a manner that, upon the death of one, the survivor or survivors take the entire property by operation of law

joint will • the same instrument is made the will of two or more persons and is signed jointly by them. When it is joint and mutual, it contains reciprocal provisions. (See also *mutual wills.*)

kiddie tax • a provision in the Tax Reform Act of 1986 under which all net unearned income of a child who has not attained age 14 before the close of the taxable year and has at least one parent alive at the end of the taxable year will be taxed to the child

kiddie-tax rules • rules providing that a portion of the net unearned income of a child under 14 years of age is taxed at the top income tax rate of the parents

lapse • the failure of a testamentary bequest due to the death of the devisee or legatee during the life of the testator

last will and testament • the usual term referring to a will—an outgrowth of the old English law under which a *will* was a disposition of real estate and a *testament* was a disposition of personal property. The two terms originally meant different things, but the difference is no longer recognized.

legacy • a gift of personal property by will. It would perhaps be proper to use the term *bequest* to include any disposition by will, the term *devise* to cover gifts of real estate, and the term *legacy* to cover gifts of personal property. However, both at law and in common practice, these terms are not used with any great respect for this distinction and often appear more or less interchangeably.

legal-list state • a state having either a mandatory or permissive list of investments that fiduciaries must or may make unless the terms of the instrument or relationship permit otherwise

legatee • the person to whom a legacy is given

letters of administration • written documents granted by the judge of the court having jurisdiction over probate matters authorizing the person named therein to administer the personal estate of an intestate decedent

letters testamentary • written documents granted by the judge of an orphans, probate, or surrogates court having jurisdiction to an executor named in a will, authorizing that person or entity to act as such

life estate • the title of the interest owned by a life tenant (income beneficiary)

life interest or life estate • an interest that a person has in property that endures only during lifetime, with no possession of ownership rights that may be transferred during life or at death

life tenant • the person who receives the income from a legal life estate or from a trust fund during the person's own life or that of another person (income beneficiary)

limited power of appointment • a power granted to a donee that is limited in scope (special power)

liquid assets • cash or assets that can be readily converted into cash without any serious loss of principal (for example, CDs or life insurance paid in lump sum)

living trust • a trust that is created and operates before the death of the settlor

living will • written expression of an individual's wishes concerning life-sustaining procedures in terminal illness and imminent death situations

lump-sum distribution • distribution or payment from a qualified employee benefit plan (which takes place within one taxable year to the recipient) of the entire account balance of an employee, which becomes payable to the recipient because of death or separation from the service or after age 59 1/2

lump-sum payment • payment to the recipient of the entire amount due, which takes place within one taxable year

marital-deduction trust • a trust consisting of all property that qualifies for the marital deduction

Mortmain Acts • state laws to discourage persons near death from naming charitable or religious organizations as beneficiaries under their wills. If a bequest to a charitable or religious organization is made within a certain period of time prior to the decedent's death or if the bequest is over a specified limit, other potential heirs may contest the will and the gift to the charity can be voided.

mutual wills • the separate wills of two or more persons, with reciprocal provisions in favor of the other person contained in each will

needed marital deduction • also called a credit-maximizing formula or a marital deduction, but not the maximum allowable marital deduction, that is needed to reduce the taxable estate to an amount that is fully covered by the estate's exemption equivalent (that is, when the taxable estate produced a tentative estate tax that is fully covered by the estate's tax credit)

net gift • taxable gift requiring the donee to pay the gift tax on the transferred asset

nongrantor trust • a trust, either testamentary or inter vivos, that is deemed irrevocable and considered a separate taxpayer

nonliquid assets • assets that may not be readily convertible into cash without a serious loss (for example, real estate or business interests)

nonprobate property • property that passes outside the administration of the estate. It passes other than by will or the intestacy laws (for example, jointly held property, life insurance proceeds payable to a named beneficiary, or property in an inter vivos trust).

nonqualified joint interests • joint tenancy interests other than one held solely by a husband and wife

nonreversionary trust • a trust in which there is no possibility of the grantor's regaining the property, having it return to the estate, or having a power of appointment over it

nuncupative will • an oral will that is declared or dictated by the testator during his or her last illness before a sufficient number of witnesses and afterward reduced to writing

operation of law • the passage of property other than by will or contract

ordinary business transaction • a sale, exchange, or other transfer of property (a transaction that is bona fide, at arm's length, and free from donative intent) made in the ordinary course of business

overqualification • underutilization of an estate owner's applicable credit amount

pay-on-death (POD) account • a nonprobate arrangement in which a savings or bank account is controlled by the contributor (depositor) account during lifetime but any deposits remaining at death pass to a surviving party

pecuniary-amount bequest • a provision in a will under which one spouse gives the surviving spouse a dollar amount, taking into consideration not only property passing under the will but also all property qualifying for the marital deduction

per capita distribution • method of dividing a decedent's estate according to the number of individuals inheriting the decedent's property, each individual sharing equally

per stirpes • method of dividing a decedent's estate by representation or by family groups (as opposed to per capita distribution)

per stirpes distribution • division of a decedent's estate by representation or by family groups

percentage-of-contribution (consideration-furnished) rule • inclusion of property in a deceased joint tenant's (other than husband and wife joint tenants) estate to the extent of the decedent's interest (fractional share) in the jointly held property

personal property • property other than real property

personal representative • synonymous with administrator or executor. (See also *administrator.*)

personal residence trust • an estate-freezing device in which a trust provides the grantor with a retained interest in the residence(s) transferred to the trust and allows for favorable gift and estate tax treatment

pooled-income fund • fund maintained by a qualified charity that contains commingled donations from many sources and that allows a donor's estate an estate tax charitable deduction for the remainder interest

posthumous child • a child born after the death of the father

posting a bond • making some kind of security available to assure performance

pour over • a term referring to the transfer of property from an estate or trust to another estate or trust upon the occurrence of an event as provided in the instrument (for example, property disposed of by will *pours over* into an existing trust)

pour-over trust • a dispositive device into which property is transferred or poured over from an estate or trust

power • any authority to establish or to alter beneficial enjoyment of corpus or income of the trust

power of appointment • a property right created (or reserved) by the donor of the power enabling the donee of the power to designate, within such limits as the donor has prescribed, who will be the transferees of the property

power-of-appointment trust • a trust that provides for a power of appointment in a beneficiary

precatory language • language in a will that generally states the testator's wishes regarding the distribution of personal effects or other matters

present interest • a present right to use or enjoy property

present-interest gift • a gift to which the donee has an immediate, unfettered, and ascertainable right to use, possess, or enjoy the gift

prima facie duties • clear and unquestionable responsibilities

principal • the assets making up the estate or fund that has been set aside in trust, or from which income is expected to accrue (corpus). Trust principal is also known as the trust res.

principal • the person who gives authority to an agent to act for him or her

private annuity • a sale of property, such as a family business, in exchange for the buyer's agreement to make periodic payments of a specified sum for the remainder of the seller's life

probate • the process of proving a will's validity in court and executing its provisions under the guidance of the court. The process of probating the will involves recognition by the appropriate court of the executor named in the will (or appointment of an administrator if none has been named), and the determination of validity of the will if it is contested.

probate property • property that is passed under the terms of a will; if no will, it passes under the intestacy laws (for example, individually held property or one-half of community property)

proceeds payable to or for the benefit of an estate • phrase that is operative when life insurance is receivable by an estate, executor, or any other person who has the power to act on behalf of an estate

property • an interest or item capable of being owned, including actual outright ownership of material objects as well as a right to possess, enjoy, use, consume, or transfer something

prudent-person rule • a rule stating that a fiduciary, in acquiring, investing, reinvesting, exchanging, retaining, selling, and managing property for the benefit of another, shall exercise the judgment and care under the circumstances then prevailing, that persons of prudence, discretion, and intelligence exercise in the management of their own affairs

QPRT • See *qualified personal residence trust.*

qualified disclaimer • See *disclaimer.*

qualified domestic trust (QDOT) • a trust that meets the requirements for a marital deduction for property left to a surviving resident-alien-spouse by a decedent citizen-spouse

qualified joint interests • joint tenancy interests held solely by a husband and wife

qualified personal residence trust • an irrevocable trust to which the grantor transfers his or her home but retains the use of that home for a specified number of years, after which it is received by one or more remainder beneficiaries

qualified terminable interest property (QTIP) • a property that falls under an exception to the terminable interest rule of the gift and estate tax law by allowing a marital deduction to a transferor spouse (or a transferor spouse's estate) for the total value of a gift or bequest of property for the transferee spouse's life benefit, even if he or she receives only a qualifying income interest for life, with all other interests passing to third parties

real property • land and anything on the land that has been permanently attached or affixed to the land

recapture • for tax-benefit purposes, a provision that reclaims the tax benefits derived from certain favorable-tax-treatment Code sections if and when specific qualification requirements of the particular Code section are violated

reciprocal trust doctrine • doctrine that results in reciprocal trusts being "uncrossed" for tax purposes because the trusts are deemed to have no purpose other than tax avoidance and do not vary the economic positions of the trust creator

reciprocal trusts • trusts created by two individuals in which each party is a beneficiary of the trust established by the other party. The trusts are typically identical except that the creator and beneficiary are reversed on each document.

reduction in value by mere lapse of time • diminishing value over time of wasting assets, such as annuities, mortgages, and notes receivable

remainder interest • a future interest that comes into existence after the termination of a prior interest. For example, Alexis (the testator) created a testamentary trust under a will in which the corpus is to be retained with income paid to Bill (the lifetime beneficiary) until Bill's death, at which time the corpus (the remainder interest) will be given to Carl (the remainderperson).

remainderperson • the person who is entitled to receive the principal (corpus) of an estate upon the termination of the intervening life estate or estates

reserve (life insurance policy reserve) • the difference between the present value of future benefits (death claim and maturity value) and the present value of future net premiums for any life insurance policy. The term *reserve* is not synonymous with *cash surrender value,* although the cash surrender value ultimately equals the amount of the reserve after a policy (other than a term policy) has been in force for a number of years.

resident alien • a person who is not a U.S. citizen but does reside in the United States. Such an individual may receive transfers from a spouse qualifying for a marital deduction from estate or gift taxes only under specific circumstances.

residuary estate • the remaining part of a testator's estate after payment of debts and bequests. Wills usually contain a clause disposing of the residue of the estate that the testator has not otherwise bequeathed or devised.

residue • the property that remains after any specific bequests, devises, and legacies have been made and debts and expenses have been paid

reversionary interest • a right to future enjoyment by the transferor of property that is now in the possession or enjoyment of another party. For example, Anthony creates a trust under which a parent, Belinda, is to enjoy income for life, with the corpus of the trust to be paid over to Anthony at Belinda's death. Anthony's interest is a reversionary interest.

reversionary trust • a trust limited to a specified term of years or for the life of the beneficiary. At the termination of the trust, the trust property is then returned to the grantor.

revocable life insurance trust • an arrangement in which a trust owns one or more life insurance policies on one or more insureds but which can be revoked by the grantor

revocable living trust • a trust that can be revoked, amended, or terminated by the grantor and the property recovered by the grantor

RLIT • See *revocable life insurance trust.*

rule against accumulations • state law that restricts a trust from accumulating too much property for too long a period of time

rule against perpetuities • a limitation that restricts a person's power to alienate property in trust beyond the time of a life or lives in being plus 21 years

Sec. 303 redemption • redemption of stock for the purpose of paying funeral and administrative expenses and death taxes that is not treated as dividends

Sec. 2503(b) trust • a trust established for the benefit of a minor that qualifies the present value of trust income for the term of the trust for the annual exclusion. Trust income must be distributed to or for the minor's benefit at least annually. Trust corpus may be held after the age of majority or for the benefit of others.

Sec. 2503(c) trust • a trust established for the benefit of a minor in which transfers qualify as present-interest gifts as long as the gifted property and income from it are distributed to or for the benefit of the minor before the minor reaches age 21, and any amount not spent goes to the minor at age 21 (or his or her estate if the minor is deceased)

self-canceling installment note (SCIN) • variation of an installment note that provides that the note is canceled automatically if the seller dies before all remaining principal payments are made

self-proving provision • a notarized acknowledgment that witnesses saw the testator sign the will while the testator was of sound mind and competent to execute a will

separate property • property that can be demonstrated to be the property of one spouse or the other, especially for community-property-law states

sham gift • a transfer with no economic significance other than to shift the burden of income taxes from a high- to a relatively low-bracket taxpayer while keeping the income within the same family

shrinkage • a reduction in the amount of property that passes at death caused by loss of capital and income resulting from the sale of assets to pay death costs

simple trust • trust agreement that requires the distribution of all trust income to the beneficiaries, disallows the distribution of other than trust income, and disallows charitable gifts

situs • the physical location of property

skip person • a generation-skipping transfer tax term concerning either a person who is at least two generations below the level of the transferor or a trust in which the beneficiaries are skip persons and from which no nonskip person will benefit

sole ownership • the holding of property by one person in such a manner that upon death it passes either by the terms of the will or, if no will, according to the intestacy laws

special (limited) power • See *special (limited) power of appointment.*

special (limited) power of appointment • a power of appointment in which the donor of the power limits the donee's appointment of the property to other than the donee, the donee's estate, or the donee's creditors

special (limited) power of attorney • a power granted by the principal that enables the attorney-in-fact to act only with regard to one or more specific tasks or for a specified period of time

special-use valuation • election available to value certain real property by taking into consideration how the property currently is utilized instead of how it might be used if placed in its best and most profitable use

split-dollar insurance • insurance policy in which the premiums and benefits are shared by two parties, primarily an employer and employee

split-interest arrangement • arrangement in which interests in a charitable contribution are split between one or more noncharitable beneficiaries and a charity

spousal right of election against the will • surviving spouse's right to elect to receive a state-law-determined fractional or percentage amount of the decedent spouse's property

springing durable power of attorney • a power granted by the principal that becomes operative only when a specified event occurs, such as the principal's physical or mental incompetency or disappearance

sprinkle or spray trust • a trust under which the trustee is given discretionary power to distribute any part or all of the income or corpus among beneficiaries in equal or unequal shares

sprinkle provision • trust clause giving a trustee discretion to allocate income among beneficiaries in any manner that seems desirable from tax year to tax year

state death tax credit • credit against the federal estate tax for a portion or all estate, inheritance, legacy, or succession taxes actually paid to a state when attributable to property included in the gross estate

stepped-up basis • the new basis acquired by a decedent's gross estate in which the decedent's property is increased to fair market value of the asset on the date of death

stepped-up-basis property • property acquired from or passed from a decedent that is increased to the fair market value of the asset on the date of death

stock-redemption buy-sell agreement • a contract in which a closely held corporation is bound to purchase a shareholder's business interest upon the occurrence of certain specified events, such as death

super-annual exclusion • an increase in the gift tax annual exclusion to a basic amount of $100,000 (as indexed for inflation: $117,000 in 2005) for marital transfers to a noncitizen spouse

tangible personal property • property that has physical substance—that is, it may be touched, seen, or felt. The thing itself has value (such as a house, a car, or furniture).

taxable distribution • generation-skipping-transfer-tax term concerning any distribution of either income or principal from a trust to a person two or more generations junior to the trust settlor's generation

taxable estate • an amount determined by subtracting the allowable deductions from the gross estate

taxable termination • generation-skipping-transfer-tax term concerning a situation in which there is a termination of a property interest that is held in trust by death, lapse of time, release of a power, or otherwise, that results in skip beneficiaries holding the property interests in the trust

tax bracket creep • the subtle movement from a lower tax bracket to a higher one, especially as a result of inflation

tenancy by the entirety • the holding of property by a husband or wife in such a manner that, except with the consent of each, neither husband nor wife has a disposable interest in the property during the lifetime of the other. Upon the death of either, the property goes to the survivor.

tenancy in common • the holding of property by two or more persons in such a manner that each has an undivided interest, which can be sold or gifted at any time, and upon the death of one is passed to the person(s) designated in the deceased tenant's will (or by intestacy) and does not pass automatically to the surviving tenants in common

tentative tax base • the total of the taxable estate and adjusted taxable gifts

terminable interest rule • rule that allows the marital deduction to apply to a decedent spouse's property only when the nature of the property or the interest in property passing to the surviving spouse is such that, if retained until the surviving spouse's death, it will be taxed in the surviving spouse's estate

terminal reserve • the reserve on a life insurance policy at the end of any contract year and, for policies on which premiums are still due, the amount of the reserve prior to the payment of the next premium

testamentary • a document, gift, or power not to take effect irrevocably until the death of the maker

testamentary capacity • state law condition necessary for a valid will that requires the testator to be of age and have the mental competency to make a will

testamentary guardian • guardian named in a decedent's will

testamentary trust • a trust created by the terms of a will

testate • a term used when a person dies having left a will

testator • a person who leaves a will in force at death

theft loss • the loss of a decedent's property, resulting from its unlawful taking by another during the administration of the estate

Totten trust • a revocable transfer in which a donor makes a deposit in a bank savings account for a donee. The donor acts as trustee of the account and no gift occurs until the donee makes a withdrawal.

tracing • method of determining the character of property by identifying the source from which it evolved

transfer tax • gift, estate, or generation-skipping transfer tax on large transfers of property or money for less than adequate and full consideration in money or money's worth

transmutation • a voluntary change of the character of property by spouses for community-property law purposes

trust • a fiduciary arrangement whereby the legal title of property is held and the property is managed by someone for the benefit of another

trust terms • a set of powers, usually administrative, that may establish the scope of the responsibilities and duties of the respective parties

trustee • the holder of legal title to property for the use or benefit of another

underqualification • overutilization of an estate owner's applicable credit amount

unfunded insurance trust • an insurance trust that is not provided with cash and/or securities to pay the life insurance premium. Such premiums are paid by someone other than the trustee.

UTMA/UGMA (Uniform Transfers to Minors Act/Uniform Gifts to Minors Act) • state laws that authorize the transfer of property to a custodian who holds the transferred property for a minor and distributes all property and income to the minor when he or she reaches adulthood under local law

vested interest • an immediate fixed interest in real or personal property, although the right to possession and enjoyment may be postponed until some future date or until the occurrence of some event.

vested remainder • a fixed interest in property with the right of possession and enjoyment postponed until the termination of the prior estate

ward • a person placed by authority of law under the care of a guardian

widow's election • community-property election for the surviving spouse to defeat the decedent spouse's testamentary disposition of the entire community-property interest and thereby make claim to the one-half community-property interest to which the surviving spouse is entitled under community-property law

will • a legal instrument whereby a person makes disposition of his or her property to take effect after death

will contest • a legal dispute over entitlements under a decedent's will

willing buyer–willing seller rule • a standard for valuation of property— the price at which a willing buyer would buy and willing seller would sell, neither being under any compulsion to do so, and both being informed of the material facts surrounding the transaction

Answers to Review Questions and Cases

Chapter 1

Answers to Review Questions

1-1. Gift tax, estate tax, generation-skipping transfer tax (GSTT), and qualified domestic trust (QDOT) taxation are all types of transfer taxation.

1-2. In its broadest sense, estate planning is the accumulation, conservation, and distribution of an estate.

1-3. Throughout history, various cultures have recognized the need for postdeath transfers of property to meet family or individual needs. For example, the Code of Hammurabi indicates that the culture had a plan of intestate succession. Both the Greek and Roman civilizations allowed testamentary disposition of property. The Romans developed a system of forced heirship that is still in use today in Louisiana, the only civil-law state in the United States.

  The most widespread influence on modern statutes, however, is the English common law, which developed after 1066. In that feudal society—in which the only property that a person could transfer at death was his interest in the land—conflicts developed between tenants in possession of land, the presumptive heirs, and the overlord. Although conflicts were eventually resolved in favor of the tenants, it was not until 1540 that a testamentary right of disposition over property—the Statute of Wills—enabled property owners to dispose of most of their property via written instrument.

  The English common law became the foundation for American law in most legal areas, including estate planning. As the estate planning process evolved, various legislatures in the United States enacted state inheritance taxes in the late 19th century, and the federal government enacted laws taxing gratuitous transfers of property (property passing at death) in 1915 and lifetime gifts in 1932.

1-4. a. Intestacy statutes follow a standardized line of succession that controls who will succeed to ownership of a deceased person's property. The statutes are based on spousal and blood relationships to the decedent, rather than on the decedent's intentions or desires.

  b. Friends and charitable organizations typically cannot inherit any of the deceased's property through intestate succession.

1-5. A valid will largely—but not entirely— displaces the statutes of intestate succession. In order to avoid having the continued support of the deceased's spouse and minor children become a financial burden to the state, most states have either common-law rules or statutory provisions that protect a portion of the deceased's property for a surviving spouse, regardless of the provisions in the will. Although such laws vary from state to state, they are all a form of intestate succession.

1-6. A will should be revised periodically to ensure that it keeps pace with the estate owner's most recent intentions. For example, the birth of new children or grandchildren, a family member's illness or disability, shifts in the estate owner's objectives, or changes in tax laws are all reasons to review the will to make sure that it continues to meet the estate owner's goals.

1-7. The following provisions are often overlooked in an estate plan, will, or trust: guardianship, simultaneous death, the residuary estate, tax apportionment, and contingent beneficiaries.

1-8. Tax relief should not be the primary objective of estate planning, A plan that reduces the client's tax liability to zero but does not meet his or her objectives is a poor plan and a disservice to the client. The best estate plan reflects the client's wishes, needs, and objectives *and* reduces the potential tax liability to the lowest possible level.

1-9. The form of property ownership is an important consideration in estate planning because it often predetermines the estate tax liability and even the ultimate ownership of that asset upon the asset owner's death.

1-10. Medical expense insurance and disability income insurance are important concerns in estate planning because the costs of a protracted period of disability or a prolonged illness may erode an estate to the point that there will be nothing—except debt—to leave beneficiaries.

1-11.   The effects of inflation will have a direct impact on an estate. As the value of the dollar is eroded, the adequacy of the estate diminishes. Failure to take inflation into account when projecting the adequacy of an estate 10–30 years in the future will probably make it impossible to carry out the estate owner's intentions.

1-12.   The three factors that are important in assessing an estate's liquidity needs are (1) the amount and terms of the estate owner's debt, (2) the projected estate tax liability, and (3) the type of assets in the estate.

1-13.   When a closely held business is the primary asset and source of income to the decedent and family, the financial consequences to the family when the decedent's salary and bonuses cease can be enormous. With adequate planning, salary continuation plans, retirement plans, and life insurance proceeds can ease the financial burden and provide liquidity.

1-14.   Many people are afraid to confront the fact of their own death or are so overwhelmed by the magnitude of estate planning that they delay the process. Inability to confront their own mortality and procrastination are both impediments to proper estate planning.

1-15.   The stages in the estate planning process are as follows:
   - Data are obtained.
   - The existing estate plan is evaluated for potential impediments.
   - A plan is designed and reviewed and approved by the client.
   - The plan is implemented.
   - The plan is reviewed periodically to make sure it continues to meet the client's objectives as they evolve.

1-16.   The types of professionals who can be on an estate planning team are as follows: an attorney, an insurance specialist, a bank trust officer, an accountant, an investment specialist, and a financial planner. Their respective functions complement each other by enabling the client to achieve *total* financial planning. Combining the expertise of advisers in a variety of disciplines offers comprehensive solutions to the client's personal, business, and financial concerns.

1-17.   While there are activities that are universally recognized as the practice of law (drafting legal documents, for example) and, therefore, must be practiced only by lawyers, there are other areas that are not as clearly defined. An example is giving advice about taxation of a trust arrangement—is that advice solely within the province of an attorney, or can a trust officer give such advice?

As a guideline, if the advice is generally informational, giving it does not constitute the unauthorized practice of law. Even if the advice specifically relates to a client's situation, there is no unauthorized use if it is given on a settled area of the law that is common knowledge in estate planning. Nevertheless, because this issue is complex, it is wise to involve an attorney in the estate planning process as early as possible to avoid problems.

Answers to Self-Test Questions

1-1.   False. In addition to the conservation of existing assets, estate planning is also concerned with the accumulation and distribution of those assets.

1-2.   False. Since individuals began to accumulate property, different cultures have had various methods for the distribution of property at death.

1-3.   True.

1-4.   False. Intestate succession laws provide for the distribution of property in accordance with blood and marital relationships as specified in the statutes.

1-5.   True.

1-6.   True.

1-7.   False. While minimizing taxes is an important consideration in estate planning, the best estate plan is one that first addresses the client's wishes, needs, and objectives.

1-8.   True.

1-9.   True.

1-10.   True.

1-11.   True.

1-12.   True.

1-13.   True.

1-14.   False. Fact-finding is also concerned with obtaining information about factors such as family structure as well as the relationships and attitudes of family members toward each other.

1-15. True.
1-16. False. It is important for clients to be made aware of problem areas, and of options that are available to solve these problems, during the estate planning process.
1-17. True.
1-18. False. An attorney is an important member of the estate planning team and is needed to draft any legal document necessary for the estate plan.
1-19. True.
1-20. False. Giving information concerning tax laws is not the unauthorized practice of law as long as the advice is generally informational or on a settled area of law that is common knowledge in the estate planning field.

Chapter 2

Answers to Review Questions

2-1. It is inherent in professionalism for the estate planner to "ever keep the advantage of the client in mind." To insure an ethical world, there are times when a person must sacrifice his or her own needs rather than pursue a course that could be unjust or harmful to another or others.

2-2. Huebner cited four characteristics of the professional:
- The professional is involved in a "vocation useful and noble enough to inspire love and enthusiasm on the part of the practitioner."
- The professional's vocation in its practice requires an expert's knowledge.
- "In applying that knowledge, the practitioner should abandon the strictly selfish commercial view and ever keep in mind the advantage of the client."
- The practitioner should possess "a spirit of loyalty to fellow practitioners, of helpfulness to the common cause they all profess and should not allow any unprofessional acts to bring shame upon the entire profession."

2-3. "In this era of information-glut, it would take encyclopedic capabilities for one specialist to be fully informed, up-to-date and available to evaluate and respond to the myriad factors and nuances that come down from government and business to affect the financial future of each client."

2-4. An ethical temptation is a situation in which there is a conflict between the planner's interests and those of the client. In a dilemma, there is a conflict other than that between the planner and the client's interests—it is a situation in which there are good reasons for both acting and not acting in a certain way.

2-5. There are four questions to ask:
1. Is the proposed course of action fair?
2. Does the proposed course of action meet the agent's responsibilities?
3. Is the proposed course of action honest?
4. Does the proposed course of action harm any stakeholders?

2-6. In a conflict of duty, one is faced with two obligations that conflict with one another, such as conflicting loyalties or conflicting commitments. In a conflict of interest, the interests of one party are at odds with the interests of another. A person needing to adjudicate such a situation needs to at least recognize such conflicts exist, and to remove him or herself from the situation if it appears that such a conflict will not allow him or her to act independently.

2-7. A compensation structure can create a conflict between the professional's and a client's interests by rewarding the professional more for selling the client a product that fit the client's needs less.

2-8. The common areas where ethical issues arise are:
- Are the proposed solutions fair? (Does everyone get what is owed to them?)
- Do the practices meet the agent's responsibilities and obligations? (What does the agent owe, and to whom?)
- Are the practices honest? Lying to clients is not justified. According to the law of agency, the agent has a duty to act solely for the benefit of, and in accordance with, the directions of the client. The agent is a fiduciary of the client and, as such, occupies a special position of trust that imposes on the agent a duty of loyalty to the client.
- Do the actions harm any stakeholders? (Almost no practice is without some harm. The ethical resolution is to find the least harmful practices.)

    Compensation might tempt the planner to sell a product that may not be the best product for the client.

    Confidentiality is important because the planner needs to know all of the pertinent information about the client, but the right of the privacy means this should be kept confidential.

Conflicts of interest were discussed above. As a professional, the planner owes it to his client to be as *competent* as possible because the planner is the expert. The planner works in the delicate area of financial services where integrity and honesty are crucial for success and the mutual trust necessary to carry out complicated financial transactions. Hence, *compliance* with the law requiring that honesty is imperative. Planners must further *communicate* with, and *cooperate* with, clients and other planners to make sure the best job is being done.

Answers to Self-Test Questions

2-1. True.

2-2. True.

2-3. False. The major concern of business is to create a useful product for the consumer. Profit is the incentive, not the purpose, of business.

2-4. False. Estate planning is often too complex for one person to handle.

2-5. True.

2-6. False. A situation in which the client's interest conflicts with the planner's is a temptation not a dilemma.

2-7. False. In a dilemma, there are both reasons for and reasons against performing an action, hence, in those areas, the issue is not black and white, but gray.

2-8. False. Selfishness is self-interest at the expense of another.

2-9. True.

2-10. False. Packaged billing or referral fees can affect one's independent judgment and recommendations. Hence, they might create conflicts of interest.

2-11. False. One also needs to address whether the proposed action will cause harm to anyone.

2-12. False. There are times when the affairs are so specific that the client's name could be deduced from the circumstances. In that case, confidentiality is broken.

2-13. False. On the contrary, sometimes the necessity to keep things confidential (that a client's husband has a mistress) may jeopardize another (that the wife will be hurt by provisions the husband is making for the mistress).

2-14. True.

2-15. True.

2-16. False. Being a CPA alone does not give sufficient expertise to move into financial planning. Other training is needed.

2-17. False. Some legal actions are not ethical, for example, lying to one's spouse.

2-18. False. Even if the planner discloses it, simultaneous representation can cause problems, and the very disclosure might motivate confidentiality.

Chapter 3

Answers to Review Questions

3-1. The real value of intangibles is in excess of the value of the physical object that represents the property. The representation can be touched and felt, but it is not the thing itself. Some examples are stock certificates, leases, mortgages, bonds, and other such representations of property ownership.

3-2. The type of estate or real property that is created is as follows:

a. a fee simple estate

b. a life estate to Ben and a vested remainder interest to Chris

c. an interest for a term of years

3-3. John has a reversionary interest and Sally has a life estate.

3.4. Under some circumstances, the legal owner of property (the person who holds legal title to the property) and the equitable owner (the person with the right to beneficial enjoyment of that property) are different parties. An example of this division of ownership is property held in trust. Here, the trustee, who invests and manages trust property, is the party who holds legal title to the trust. The trust beneficiaries, however, hold equitable title to trust property since they are entitled to the income generated by the trustee's efforts.

3-5. Domicile is the place that individuals consider to be their permanent residence and to which they intend to return if they temporarily leave. Situs is the place where property is located.

Some examples that indicate an individual's intent to establish domicile are as follows: voter registration, automobile registration, driver's license, passport, location of a bank account or safe-deposit box, situs of a principal residence, reference to domicile in a will, address listed with the Social Security Administration, and payment of property and income taxes. In certain states there is a special form to file as a declaration of domicile to establish primary residence.

3-6.   Gloria's state of domicile, Alabama, would have a right to tax all her property except the real estate located in Florida. Since real estate is always taxed in the state where it is located, the state of Florida has the right to tax real estate located there. Her tangible personal property may be taxed by the state where taxable situs exists. This means New Hampshire may have jurisdiction to tax the personal property located there. The intangible personal property is subject to tax by the domiciliary state, Alabama. Texas may also tax her intangible personal property, unless Texas exempts the intangible personal property of a nonresident from taxation.

3-7.   A co-owner of property held as tenants in common has the following rights:

a.   Each co-owner is free to sell his or her interest to whomever the tenant wishes without the consent or knowledge of the other co-owners.

b.   Each co-owner can give away his or her interest to a third party without the other co-owner's consent or knowledge.

c.   Through the co-owner's will, each co-owner can freely dispose of his or her interest to beneficiaries at the co-owner's death.

3-8.   There are no survivorship rights. Each tenant's interest in the property can be left to the tenant's heirs, and the tenant's gross estate will include the fair market value of his or her proportionate interest at death.

3-9.   a.   Joint tenants can sell their interests during lifetime to third parties. This action generally severs the joint tenancy, causing partitioning of the property. Tenants by the entireties may transfer their interests only with the consent of the spouse-cotenant.

b.   See answer (a) above.

c.   Under both forms of ownership, the property transfers by right of survivorship to the survivor at the death of one of the tenants.

3-10.   a.   With a joint bank account, each joint owner owns a proportionate part of the account balance and is entitled to receive one-half of the interest income. There is no gift if a person uses personal funds to open a joint bank account. A gift is considered to have been made only when the other joint owner (the donee) makes withdrawals.

b.   When government bonds are held in joint ownership with right of survivorship, there is no gift when the savings bond is purchased because the joint owner who contributed the funds can cash the bond in at any time and get his or her money back. A gift occurs only when the other joint tenant (the donee) redeems the bond and retains a greater share of the proceeds than he or she contributed to the purchase price.

c.   If securities are registered in the names of the co-owners as tenants in common with right of survivorship, a gift occurs from the contributing joint tenant to the donee-joint tenant when the securities are transferred to or purchased for the account. The results are not the same, however, if the securities are registered in street name; no gift occurs when a joint street-name account is created even if one of the joint tenants furnishes more than one-half of the consideration. A gift occurs only when the other party withdraws more than his or her proportionate amount from the account.

3-11.   The advantages of owning property jointly with right of survivorship are as follows:

• Joint ownership is convenient for certain types of assets because either tenant has access to the account.

• Joint ownership may offer one or both of the tenants a feeling of security, especially if the owners are spouses and one of them has contributed most of the funds.

• When one tenant dies, property passes directly to the other tenant without probate delay and with little or no administrative or transfer cost.

• In many states, joint property ownership between spouses passes free of state death taxes.

• Since such property passes by operation of law and not under a will, it is not subject to public scrutiny.

Disadvantages are as follows:

• At the creation of some of these types of property ownership interests, there are potential gift taxes.

• There may be additional federal estate taxation.

• The survivor will gain full control of the property and can dispose of it in any way he or she desires. The decedent-tenant, therefore, loses all control of the property.

• Under most state laws, property owned as joint tenants with right of survivorship can be reached by creditors of an individual account.

Answers to Self-Test Questions

3-1.   True.

3-2.   True.

3-3.   False. The owner of a fee simple estate possesses all interests in the property and may pass the property to heirs at his or her death.

3-4.   True.

3-5.   True.

3-6.   True.

3-7.   False. It is possible for a future interest in property to be fixed and absolute when it is created, although it will not take effect until some future time.

3-8.   False. A reversionary interest is an interest in property that was retained at the time of disposition of the property because the owner conveyed less than total ownership.

3-9.   False. It is possible for the legal and equitable ownership of property to be split between different parties.

3-10.   False. The situs of property is the location of the property, which may be different from the domicile of the property owner.

3-11.   True.

3-12.   True.

3-13.   False. When a tenancy in common exists, cotenants can sell their particular interest in the property to whomever they wish.

3-14.   False. A joint tenancy with right of survivorship may be severed during lifetime. Each joint owner may sell his or her interest without the consent of the other.

3-15.   False. There is no gift upon the creation of a joint bank account. A gift is made only when the other joint tenant removes funds in excess of his or her own contributions.

3-16.   True.

3-17.   False. A tenancy by the entirety is an interest in property that can be held only by a husband and wife. The property automatically passes to the surviving cotenant when one of the tenants dies.

3-18.   True.

3-19.   True.

3-20.   False. Each state has developed its own variations, which makes it difficult to generalize.

Chapter 4

Answers to Review Questions

4-1.   There are nine community-property states. The eight traditional community-property states include Arizona, California, Idaho, Louisiana, Nevada, New Mexico, Texas, and Washington. Wisconsin is recognized as the ninth community-property state since its version of the Uniform Marital Property Act, incorporating many community-property concepts, became effective in 1986.

4-2.   Generally, property acquired by a husband and wife during their marriage belongs to them both in equal shares; it is community property. Property that can be proven to belong to a spouse separately is separate property. It may not be sufficient to rebut the community-property assumptions by simply having certain property titled in one spouse's name or acquired with one spouse's separate funds. The facts and circumstances concerning the property's use and the spouses' conduct toward the property may carry more evidentiary weight in determining ownership.

4-3.   The best way to overcome the general presumption favoring community property is for married partners who reside in or move in and out of community-property states to keep complete, organized, and accurate records of their personal financial matters.

4-4.   To determine and separate policy ownership interests in community-property states, three basic doctrines are used.

       First, the proration, or apportionment, concept views the separate and community components of policy proceeds proportionately to the separate and community funds applied to the premiums paid. In other words, this theory looks to the source of the payment of the policy proceeds.

       Second, the inception-of-the-title doctrine looks to the character of the funds used to purchase the policy, whether the purchase occurs before or after the marriage. The original funds used to purchase the policy establish its character. If community funds are used for other premium payments, the surviving spouse has a right to reimbursement for his or her share of community funds used for the payments but does not share in the growth in the policy's value.

    The third approach classifies life insurance ownership according to the nature of the funds used for the final or last premium payment. This approach views all but the final payment as voluntary installment payments and the final premium payment as completing the purchase of the policy. Whole life insurance cases follow a reimbursement theory.

    Simply stated, each of the three theories described above seeks to trace the source of the money applied to the premium payments to determine the character of the policy and the proceeds, and each approach may give rise to some inequities.

4-5. Property that was acquired during marriage by one spouse as a gift, by inheritance, as a result of a judgment award for personal injuries, or from purchase with a spouse's separate money or credit retains its separate identity.

4-6. The unlimited marital estate and gift tax deduction serves to equalize the transfer tax results between community- and non-community-property states when the surviving spouse is the beneficiary of the decedent spouse's estate. If someone other than the surviving spouse is the recipient of the decedent's property, transfer tax differences are more likely.

4-7. Because of the increasing mobility of today's families, estate planners need to understand the legalities in both common-law and community-property states even if their practice is in a common-law state. Changing domicile or moving from one jurisdiction to another can complicate clients' property ownership issues and pose estate planning problems. Planners need to be aware that legal agreements drafted in one jurisdiction may not be effective in the current jurisdiction.

Answers to Self-Test Questions

4-1. False. Community property is a form of ownership in certain states that can be held only by a husband and wife.

4-2. True.

4-3. True.

4-4. True.

4-5. False. None of the community-property states recognize the tenancy-by-the-entireties form of ownership.

4-6. True.

4-7. False. In such situations the widow may choose whether to take half the property outright under a widow's election or to take the benefits provided under her decedent husband's will. If she decides to abide by the terms of her husband's will, she may be deemed to have made a gift of her share of the community property received by the third party.

4-8. True.

4-9. False. Because of the marital deduction, there is no difference.

4-10. False. The separately owned property of one spouse is not available for claims by creditors of the other community spouse.

Chapter 5

Answers to Review Questions

5-1. A person or institution that holds or manages property for the benefit of another party is a fiduciary. The relationship between that individual or institution and the other party (the beneficiary) is a fiduciary relationship.

5-2. Executors, administrators, and guardians derive their power from state law and are appointed by a state court with competent jurisdiction. If an executor or guardian is named in a will, the court will often affirm that choice but is not bound to do so.

    Trusts are private agreements. The trustee derives his or her power from the trust document and is *not* court appointed.

5-3. Because a trust can be in existence for 20 or 30 years and sometimes even longer and a trustee's powers and duties do not end until the termination of the trust, a trustee's powers and duties can last for many years. The powers and duties of personal representatives of the estate, on the other hand, generally last for a relatively short period because the average estate exists for only one or 2 years. A guardian's powers and duties last until the ward's incompetency ends or the ward reaches the age of majority.

Personal representatives of the estate and guardians file an accounting with the court when their tasks are complete. They are discharged and the estate is then closed. A trustee, however, is not required to make an accounting to the court but is regularly accountable to beneficiaries.

5-4.   Common to all fiduciary relationships are the duties to
   - be loyal to the beneficiaries—to act for the beneficiaries in matters within the scope of the fiduciary relationship, not to delegate fiduciary responsibilities to others if they can be performed by the fiduciary, and to make full disclosure of all facts known to the fiduciary when entering into a personal transaction with the beneficiaries
   - not to self-deal or profit at the expense of the beneficiaries
   - to preserve and protect property to make it productive
   - to be impartial toward beneficiaries

5-5.   The trustee must try to act as objectively as possible regarding the various beneficiaries' interests—that is, not to invest or manage trust property so that it increases one beneficiary's share at the expense of another.

5-6.   Under the prudent-person rule, the trustee, in making investments of trust funds, is required to (1) make only investments that a prudent person would make of his or her own property, with the goal of preserving the estate and income derived from it, (2) to conform to all statutes governing investments by trustees, and (3) to conform to the terms of the trust.

Legal-list states dictate the investments that fiduciaries must make, unless the terms of the trust or the fiduciary relationship permit otherwise. A legal list state is mandatory if there is a prescribed list of investments in which the fiduciary must invest. Any investment made outside of the list is not legal. Permissive legal-list states print a list of investments (or classes of investments) in which fiduciaries must invest. There is no breach of duty if fiduciaries invest in property named on the list. They may also invest in property not stated on the list, however, and take the chance of having a beneficiary object to the investment.

5-7.   Two examples of a breach of fiduciary duties are (1) diverting money from the trust for the fiduciary's personal use or (2) letting trust funds remain idle. All fiduciaries are answerable to the beneficiaries for whom they act if a breach is committed.

5-8.   In selecting a trustee, the following must be considered:
   - the advisability of naming a beneficiary as a trustee
   - the possibility that the trustee will die or become incapacitated while the trust is still in existence
   - the wisdom of appointing a family as a trustee
   - the extent of auditing the trustee will undergo (individual trustees are not audited or consistently checked to the same degree as corporate trustees)
   - the complexity of the trustee's responsibilities

5-9.   An executor should have the following characteristics:
   - the business, financial, and administrative ability to assemble, conserve, and transfer estate assets
   - the time and effort required to fulfill the executor's duties
   - knowledge of the testator's business, personal affairs, and family relationships
   - no conflict of interest with any of the beneficiaries

5-10. There are several types of guardians, as follows:
   - guardian of the person, who cares for the ward
   - guardian of the property, who cares for and manages the ward's property
   - guardian ad litem, who is appointed by the court to perform a particular purpose on the ward's behalf and discharged when the issue is resolved
   - testamentary guardian, who is named in the testator's will as guardian of the minor children
   - guardian de son tort, who assumes guardianship without seeking or obtaining court approval

Unlike trustees, guardians do not have legal title to trust property. They are appointed by the court (except for the guardian de son tort) and must be discharged by the court when the term of guardianship ends. Thus, the guardian's authority derives from the statutory and judicial law of the state in which he or she serves. The trustee, on the other hand, derives authority from state law and from the trust instrument.

Guardians serve for the period of the ward's minority or incompetency. Trustees may serve succeeding generations of beneficiaries.

5-11.   These five elements are common to all trusts:
  - the creator
  - the trustee
  - the property
  - the beneficiaries
  - the terms of the trust

5-12.   a. The grantor may name himself as trustee of a trust that he creates for the benefit of someone else—in this case, his son. However, he must function in the role of trustee according to fiduciary principles solely for the benefit of the beneficiary. Depending on the kind of trust (revocable or irrevocable) and whether the trust income is used for the support of a minor son, there may be undesired tax consequences.

  b. A trust in which the grantor names himself as trustee and beneficiary is valid if there is another beneficiary. The son is a beneficiary with an adverse interest to the grantor. Here, the grantor would have to act impartially as trustee on behalf of both beneficiaries of the trust.

  c. This trust will be held invalid because the settlor is the sole trustee and also the sole beneficiary. He is actually dealing by and for himself as an individual. Legal and equitable title are said to merge and there is, in fact, no trust.

5-13.   There are two limitations on trust duration: the common-law rule against perpetuities and the common-law rule against accumulations.

    The traditional rule against perpetuities provides that no interest in property is valid unless the interest must vest no later than 21 years plus 9 months after some life or lives in being when the interest was created.

    The traditional rule against accumulations stipulates the period during which interest may accumulate. In most cases, the period during which the interest must vest is the same as under the rule against perpetuities.

5-14.   The more flexibility the trustee has, the better he or she will be able to meet the beneficiaries' needs as they arise, according to the grantor's intentions.

5-15.   Some nontax reasons to establish revocable trusts are as follows:
  - The grantor does not have the time or the ability to manage the property for the beneficiaries' maximum benefit.
  - The grantor can enjoy the psychological benefits of gifting the property in trust while still being able to reclaim the property.
  - The grantor can see how the trust operates under the current trustee and discern the trustee's dispositive intents before the trust becomes irrevocable.
  - At the grantor's death, the revocable trust will become irrevocable and pass to the beneficiaries without probate costs or publicity.
  - If the grantor's out-of-state intangible property is transferred to revocable trusts in the grantor's state of domicile, ancillary jurisdiction for out-of-state property can be avoided.
  - If the grantor is the sole proprietor of or partner in a business, he or she can transfer the business to a revocable trust to avoid the business's termination at the grantor's death.

5-16.   A living trust is created and becomes effective before the death of the settlor. A testamentary trust is created under a testator's will and becomes effective upon his or her death.

5-17.   The reasons why a grantor might transfer property to an irrevocable trust are as follows:
  - If the grantor wants to manage property for a needy dependent, he or she can establish an irrevocable trust, naming the dependent as beneficiary. The beneficiary will have to deal with the trustee for funds, instead of the grantor, which can prevent any potential conflict between the grantor and the dependent.
  - The trustee has investment and accumulation skills that the grantor does not have.
  - At the grantor's death, the trust will avoid probate.
  - Trust property is not subject to claims by the grantor's creditors.
  - The trust can shelter the grantor's assets from spousal election rights and thereby provide for the grantor's children from a former marriage at the grantor's death.

5-18.   A power of appointment is created when the owner of the property (the donor) creates the power in a donee to designate the donor's property that is subject to the power. The act of designating the property by the donee is the exercise of a power of appointment.

5-19.   The potential recipients of property under a general power of appointment are the donee, the donee's estate, or the donee's creditors.

5-20.   Mary has transferred property to the trust held by her husband, Tom, who is trustee. Mary may be concerned about her premature death and desires to delegate the dispositive control to Tom. Since Mary does not know which of her children will survive to college age, or actually go to college, she wants to delay the distribution decision. Mary could create a special power of appointment in Tom, exercisable when the children reach age 18, to appoint a portion of the property to any of her children then living. With this planning technique, Tom can provide the college funds at the time each child enters college.

Answers to Self-Test Questions

5-1.   True.

5-2.   False. A trustee receives his or her powers from the trust instrument and is not regulated by the court unless it is a testamentary trust created under a will. Of course, if the instrument is ambiguous or silent with regard to certain powers, the laws of the jurisdiction in which the trust is located will be looked to for guidance.

5-3.   False. Under the Uniform Prudent Investor Act, fiduciaries are encouraged to delegate to professionals when necessary.

5-4.   False. An executor steps into the shoes of a decedent at his or her death. While it is not essential that the executor have specialized knowledge in managing the testator's property or financial matters, the executor will be called upon to take responsibility for business, financial, and administrative decisions during the estate settlement period.

5-5.   True.

5-6.   False. The grantor or settlor of a trust may establish a trust for the benefit of any individual, including himself or herself or a charitable organization. The grantor may name certain individuals as income beneficiaries and other individuals as remainderpersons or second-generation beneficiaries.

5-7.   True.

5-8.   False. The rule against perpetuities is valid in most states today and prevents the creation of a trust that does not vest property within the period of some life that is in existence at the creation of the trust plus 21 years.

5-9.   True.

5-10.   False. One of the advantages of creating a trust is that one may choose the situs of the trust as well as the laws that will govern its administration. It need not be the domicile of the grantor or any state in which the grantor has a residence.

5-11.   True.

5-12.   False. A revocable trust may hold a sole proprietorship or partnership interest. This is a business-continuation technique that may be used to prevent the termination of an unincorporated business by operation of law at the death of an owner.

5-13.   True.

5-14.   False. An irrevocable inter vivos trust will avoid probate.

5-15.   False. To ensure the grantor's wishes as to the revocability or irrevocability of the trust, a statement specifying whether it is revocable or irrevocable should always be contained in the trust instrument. In the absence of such a statement, state law will prevail.

5-16.   False. A testamentary trust is revocable until the grantor's death. The testamentary trust is created by the testator's will and is revocable or amendable along with the other will provisions until the testator's death.

5-17.   True.

5-18.   False. The donor of a power is the person who gives another (the donee) the right to designate who will receive the property (the appointee) at some future date. The donor is not the individual who exercises the power over the property. He or she gives the donee the power to be exercised at some future time during lifetime or by will.

5-19.   True.

5-20.   True.

Chapter 6

Answers to Review Questions

6-1.   The nontax advantages of making lifetime gifts are as follows:

- Making a lifetime gift offers the donor privacy, which is impossible to obtain through a testamentary gift.
- Probate and administrative costs may be reduced by making a lifetime gift.
- A lifetime gift is protected from creditors' claims.

- The donor can enjoy seeing the donee use the gift.
- There is an opportunity for the donor to assess how well or how poorly the donee manages the gifted property.
- The gift can provide for the donee's education, support, and financial well-being.

6-2. The transfer of property must be completed. That is, a competent donor must transfer the property in a manner that divests the donor of dominion and control and places property within the control of the donee. A competent donee must accept the gift. The transfer must be for less than full and adequate consideration.

6-3. The transfer must be pursuant to a written agreement between Steven and Ellen in settlement of marital rights. The divorce must occur within a period beginning one year prior to and ending 2 years after the agreement.

6-4. In nonbusiness situations, forgiving a debt constitutes a gift. Thus, in this case, ignoring the annual exclusion, Mr. Powers will have made a gift of $15,000 to his son.

6-5. Because George's daughter is an adult, payment of the rent is not George's legal obligation. Consequently it constitutes a gift.

6-6. Ignoring the annual exclusion, Marty has given his daughter a direct gift of $4,000, which is the excess of $15,000 over the value of her car. Marty has also given his son an indirect gift of $11,000.

6-7. a. A gift has been made because Lara is performing no services for the partnership and has contributed no capital to its formation.
   b. If a new partner contributes capital or valuable services in exchange for a share of the business, there normally would not be a gift. However, a gift is likely to exist in this case since the bookkeeping service would have a value of less than $100,000. The gift value will be the $100,000 less the value of the services.

6-8. Alan and his wife may be considered by the IRS to have received a taxable dividend (equal to the value of the transferred real estate, less the price paid by the children). In addition, Alan and his wife would then be considered to have made a gift to their children (equal to the amount of the dividend).

6-9. When Jim dies, the IRS could argue that Joan has made a constructive gift to her children equal to the full amount of the life insurance policy's death proceeds—as if she received the proceeds and then gave the money to her children.

6-10. The rendering of services is not considered to be a gift.

6-11. The requirements for a qualified disclaimer of gifted property are as follows:

- The refusal must be in writing.
- The writing must be received by the transferor, the transferor's legal representative, or the holder of the legal title to the property no later than 9 months after the later of (1) the date on which the transfer is made or (2) the date the person who is disclaiming reaches age 21.
- The person disclaiming must not have accepted the interest or any of its benefits.
- Someone other than the disclaimant must receive the property, and the disclaimant cannot influence the selection of the recipient of the disclaimed property.

6-12. The factors to examine to determine whether property transferred is a gift or compensation are as follows:

- the length and value of the employee's services
- the way the employer determined the amount of the reputed gift
- how the employer treated the payment in the cooperate books and tax returns

6-13. a. The renewal commissions are treated as a gift from the general agent to his daughter.
   b. The general agent is subject to income tax on the commissions.

6-14. The following types of gifts are exempt from gift tax: qualified disclaimers, some transfers of property between spouses upon divorce, tuition paid to an educational institution, payment of medical care, and transfers of property or money to a political organization for that organization's use.

6-15. a. There is no completed gift until the son cashes the check.
   b. Neither the conveyance nor the return of the property is treated is a completed gift because the transfer of title was conditioned on Jim Johnson's death. A gift made in anticipation of death—a gift causa mortis—becomes complete only at the donor's death.
   c. There is no completed gift until one of the grandchildren surrenders the bond for cash.
   d. A completed gift was made when Stewart Hathaway withdrew funds from the joint account that Harry had established.

6-16. a. Gift tax liability is measured at the time the gift becomes complete. There is no completed gift until Gloria relinquishes the power to alter the trust beneficiaries' interests. If that happens when the stock has increased in value significantly, the gift tax that Gloria must pay will also substantially increase.

b. Once Gloria relinquishes the right to allocate income to Brian and Jamie, she has made a completed gift. Her tax liability is measured at that time.

6-17. a. Because the donor is not personally liable for the debt, the amount of the gift is the property's net value, or $40,000.

b. Under these circumstances, the amount of the gift is the value of the property unreduced by the debt, or $60,000.

c. In this situation, the amount of the gift is merely the amount of the donor's equity in the property, or $40,000. However, if Drew later decides to pay the mortgage debt, his daughter will have an additional gift of $20,000.

6-18. If a transfer consists of a block of stock large enough to depress the market value of each share if the entire block of stock is sold at once, a blockage discount may apply. This gives the taxpayer a discount below the stock's actual listed market value for determining the gift tax.

6-19. a. Since this policy is paid up at the time of the transfer, the value for gift tax purposes is the amount of premium the issuing insurer would charge for the same type of policy of equal face amount on Ben's life (based on his age at the time of transfer).

b. The value of this policy, which is in the premium-paying stage at the time Ben makes the transfer, is the interpolated terminal reserve plus the unearned premiums on the date of the gift.

c. The value the newly purchased policy on Ben's life for gift tax purposes is the gross premium paid to the insurer.

6-20. The value of the policy is the interpolated terminal reserve plus the unearned premium at the time of the gift. The interpolated terminal reserve was $26,500 on July 1, 2004 since this is the midpoint of the year during which the reserve increases $3,000. Half the premium ($1,250) is unearned at this time. Therefore, the policy value was $27,750 on July 1, 2004.

Answers to Self-Test Questions

6-1. True.

6-2. False. Before a gift is subject to tax, it must be accepted by the donee.

6-3. True.

6-4. True.

6-5. False. Forgiveness of a debt constitutes a gift to the borrower.

6-6. True.

6-7. False. Indirect gifts, like direct gifts, are subject to gift tax.

6-8. True.

6-9. False. Payment of life insurance premiums for another person constitutes an indirect gift.

6-10. True.

6-11. False. Gifts of services are not considered gifts that would fall within the scope of the gift tax. Only transfers of property or interests in property are treated as gifts potentially subject to the gift tax.

6-12. False. One of the requirements for a qualified disclaimer is that the refusal of the gift must be in writing. An oral refusal is not acceptable.

6-13. True.

6-14. False. The right to receive future income is a gift to the son. However, Mary will be subject to taxation on the income.

6-15. True.

6-16. False. When a personal check is the subject of a gift, the gift is considered to be completed on the date the check is cashed because the maker of the check has no legal obligation to honor it until that time.

6-17. False. A Totten trust or pay-on-death account is an incomplete gift because the contributor/depositor of the account retains dominion and control over the account during lifetime.

6-18. False. A gift to a trust is considered complete only when the donor relinquishes the right to revoke the gift or the donee receives the property from the trust.

6-19. True.

6-20. True.

6-21. False. Under the blockage rule, a block of stock is valued with consideration to the appropriate discount for a transfer of a large quantity of stock at one time.

6-22. True.

6-23. False. A net gift is one in which the donee, not the donor, is required to pay the gift tax on the gifted property.

Chapter 7

Answers to Review Questions

7-1. The gift tax is an excise tax. As such, it is not levied on the gift itself or the right to receive it but on an individual's right to transfer property to another for less than full consideration. The objective of the tax is to equalize the transfer tax treatment between taxpayers who make lifetime gifts and those who transfer their assets at death.

7-2. The nature of the estate and gift tax system reflects the fact that the tax is imposed on all property transferred in a taxable manner regardless of when the transfers occur. The tax is imposed at one set of rates, regardless of whether the transfer takes place during the donor's lifetime or is testamentary. Thus transfers should move the donor up the progressive rate structure as they occur. For this reason current gifts are added to prior gifts to determine the tax bracket applicable to such gifts. (As we will learn later, lifetime gifts made after 1976 are added to the taxable estate of a decedent to determine the estate tax bracket applicable to testamentary transfers.)

7-3. The tax advantages of making lifetime gifts are as follows:

- An individual can give tax free up to $11,000 (after 2001) per donee per year ($22,000 if he or she is married and uses gift splitting).
- If a gift is made more than 3 years before the donor's death, the amount of any gift tax paid is not brought back into the donor's estate and thus avoids the gross-up rule.
- Any appreciation in the gift escapes estate taxation.
- There may be income tax advantages if the amount of taxable income moves from a high-tax-bracket donor to a low-tax-bracket donee.
- Gifts of the right type of assets may enable the donor's estate to meet the tests for an IRC Sec. 303 redemption, a Sec. 6166 installment payout of taxes, or a Sec. 2032A special-use valuation.
- No gift taxes have to be paid until the donor makes cumulative taxable gifts in excess of the applicable (gift tax) exclusion amount of $1 million after 2001.

7-4. a. Louise can make the entire gift herself and still split the gift with Larry as long as he consents to gift splitting.

b. Each spouse is deemed to have given $7,500.

c. Gifts made while both Louise and Larry were alive, even if Larry dies before signing the consent, can still be split as long as Larry's executor makes that election.

7-5. The purpose of the annual gift tax exclusion is to eliminate the need for a taxpayer to report numerous small gifts and thus to lessen administrative record keeping.

7-6. Henry can give each child $22,000 and elect to treat it as a split gift with Cecelia. Therefore, he will file a gift tax return and make the election to have Cecelia split the gift with him. Although a gift tax return must be filed in order to make this election, no tax will be due. This is because when a person makes a gift and splits it with his spouse, it is treated as if $11,000 was given to the donee by each spouse, although, in fact, the gift was made by the donor-spouse. Therefore, Henry can give a total of $154,000 to his children without exceeding the annual exclusion.

7-7. a. Yes. An outright gift of $15,000 is a present-interest gift. Since an annual exclusion of $11,000 may be taken, Bill has made a taxable gift of $4,000 to his son, Bill, Jr.

b. Bill has made two gifts in this case. The gift of income to his daughter (which can be measured as the right to receive income for life based on her life expectancy) qualifies for the annual exclusion. The gift of the remainder interest to Bill's son is a future-interest gift and, although it can be valued actuarially at the time of the gift, no annual exclusion will be allowed since the son cannot enjoy and possess the property until his sister dies.

c. Since the trustee can accumulate income and is not required to distribute it, such income may be added to the principal to increase the remainderman's interest. Since this is the case, no annual exclusion will be allowed for either the gift to the income beneficiary or the gift to the remainderman.

d. This transfer will qualify for the annual exclusion as a transfer to Sec. 2503(c) trust. Although the trustee may accumulate trust income until the beneficiary reaches age 21, the entire principal must be distributed to him at that time. Sec. 2503(c) permits an exception to the general rule denying an annual exclusion when income is accumulated. However, the principal must become distributable when the beneficiary attains age 21.

7-8. In this situation, neither the gift of the trust income to Nancy nor the gift of the remainder or corpus to Nancy's children is eligible for the annual exclusion. A present-interest gift that qualifies for the annual exclusion generally transfers an immediate right to possession or enjoyment of the property or property interest to the donee. When a restriction or postponement is placed on the donee's right to the use, possession, or enjoyment of the property or interest therein, the gift is one of a future interest.

In this situation, the income is distributable only at the discretion of the trustee, which means that the income may be accumulated if the trustee so desires. Thus Nancy has no immediate right to the use and enjoyment of the income; therefore the income interest is a gift of a future interest. Likewise, the use and enjoyment of the remainder by Nancy's children is postponed until Nancy's death, making it a gift of a future interest.

7-9. Although minors can buy, sell, and deal with limited types of property (U.S. savings bonds, for example), outright gifts of other property can create problems. For example, in some states, minors cannot purchase, care for, sell, or transfer their own property. Some states do not allow securities to be registered in a minor's name. In many states, a minor can disaffirm a sale of stock sold at a low price that later rises in value. Similarly, a buyer receives no assurance of permanent title when a minor signs a real estate deed. And perhaps most important, a parent may not want to give a minor control over a large amount of cash or other property.

7-10. a. An outright gift of life insurance qualifies for the annual exclusion.

b. For the annual exclusion to apply, trust beneficiaries must receive a present interest. Simply transferring life insurance to the trust does not meet the present-interest requirement.

c. Premium payments on life insurance owned by a trust qualify for the annual exclusion if beneficiaries have Crummey demand powers. Crummy demand powers give beneficiaries a present interest.

d. Non-dividend-paying stock held in trust may not qualify for the annual exclusion. In many cases, the IRS has held that the exclusion does not apply because the stock does not represent a present interest.

7-11. a. A Sec. 2503(b) trust requires a current (annual) distribution of income. A Sec. 2503(c) trust does not require income to be distributed currently.

b. The trustee is given no discretion regarding income accumulation in a Sec. 2503(b) trust. In a Sec. 2503(c) trust, the trustee can be given broad discretion.

c. In a Sec. 2503(b) trust, principal can be distributed whenever the agreement specifies. It can be paid when the donee reaches 21, or corpus can be held for as long as the beneficiary lives or for a shorter period. Principal can also bypass the income beneficiary entirely and go to individuals the grantor or beneficiary selects.

A Sec. 2503(c) trust requires that principal be distributed when the donee reaches age 21 (or at a later age if the donor so stipulates, dependent on the donee's nonexercise of the right to immediate distribution at age 21).

d. A Sec. 2503(b) trust can control disposition of trust assets if the minor dies before receiving the trust corpus; assets do not have to be paid to minor's estate or appointees. With a Sec. 2503(c) trust, income and principal go to the beneficiary's estate or appointees if the minor dies before age 21.

7-12. a. Almost any type of property can be used in a Sec. 2503(c) trust. The type of property gifted under the UGMA must be permitted by statute.

b. With a Sec. 2503(c) trust, the donor can provide for disposition of trust assets. Disposition of trust assets must follow statutory guidelines under the UGMA.

c. The trustee can be given broad investment powers under a Sec. 2503(c) trust. Under the UGMA, investment powers are limited by statute.

d. A Sec. 2503(c) trust can continue even after the beneficiary is 21; furthermore, the trustee can distribute assets between the state law age of majority and age 21. Trust assets must be paid to the beneficiary when he or she reaches majority under the UGMA.

7-13. There is no gift tax. A person who transfers property to his or her spouse is allowed an unlimited gift tax marital deduction.

7-14. a. and b. The total taxable gifts made by Mr. Fisher and his wife this year would amount to $16,500, as shown below:

		Recipient	Mr. Fisher's Taxable Gifts	Mrs. Fisher's Taxable Gifts
Value of gift	$25,000	Son	$12,500	$12,500
Less annual exclusion			(11,000)	(11,000)
Taxable (net) gift			$ 1,500	$ 1,500

Value of gift	$52,000	Brother	$26,000	$26,000
Less annual exclusion			(11,000)	(11,000)
Taxable (net) gift			$15,000	$15,000
Value of gift	$23,000	XYZ Hospital	$11,500	$11,500
Less annual exclusion			(11,000)	(11,000)
Less charitable deduction			(500)	(500)
Taxable (net) gift			0	-0-
Value of gift	$50,000	Mrs. Fisher	$50,000	
Less annual exclusion			(11,000)	
Less marital deduction			(39,000)	
Taxable (net) gift			0	

First, for federal gift tax purposes, Mr. Fisher could split the $25,000 cash gift to his son in half, reducing it to $12,500. A gift made by one spouse to any person (other than the other spouse) can be treated as though one-half was made by the donor and one-half was made by the donor's spouse, provided the spouse consents to the gift. In this case, Mrs. Fisher did join in the gift.

In addition, each donor is entitled to an annual exclusion of $11,000 for gifts of a present interest to each donee. The cash gift is a gift of a present interest, and Mr. Fisher made no other gifts to his son this year.

Second, for federal gift tax purposes, the value of the gift of stock to Mr. Fisher's brother is its market value of $52,000. Again, Mr. Fisher could split the gift with his wife, reducing the amount given from each spouse to $26,000. Mr. Fisher could deduct the $11,000 annual exclusion, leaving a balance of $15,000.

Third, there would be no federal gift tax on the gift of stock to the XYZ Hospital. In computing his taxable gifts, a donor may take an annual exclusion and deduct in full the balance of all gifts to qualified charitable institutions.

Fourth, lifetime gifts between spouses are not taxable because there is an unlimited gift tax marital deduction. It is no longer necessary to file a gift tax return when one spouse makes an otherwise taxable gift to the other spouse.

Mrs. Fisher would have taxable gifts of $16,500 during this year.

Mrs. Fisher's share of the $25,000 cash gift to her son is $12,500. From this $12,500, Mrs. Fisher may deduct her $11,000 annual exclusion, leaving a net gift of $1,500.

Mrs. Fisher's share of the $52,000 gift of stock to Mr. Fisher's brother is $26,000. From this amount, Mrs. Fisher may deduct her $11,000 annual exclusion; $15,000 is her net gift.

Since all gifts to third parties must be split between the spouses if any one gift is to be so split, one-half of the gift to XYZ Hospital would be considered made by Mrs. Fisher. However, all gifts to qualified charities are fully deductible for gift tax purposes.

7-15.	a.	i.	Total gifts for year	$ 85,000
		ii.	Subtract annual exclusion(s)	(22,000)
		iii.	Gifts after subtracting exclusion(s)	63,000
		iv.	Subtract charitable deduction	(14,000)
			Taxable gifts	$ 49,000

Compute Gift Tax Payable

		v.	Gift tax on all taxable gifts	$ 10,360
		vi.	Gift tax credit	345,800
			Gift tax payable	-0-
	b.	i.	Gift tax on all taxable gifts regardless of when made	$38,500
		ii.	Gift tax on all taxable gifts made prior to present gifts	(23,800)
		iii.	Subtract b(ii) from b(i)	$ 14,700
		iv.	Enter remaining applicable credit amount ($345,800 – $23,800)	$322,000
		v.	Subtract b(iv) from b(iii) to obtain gift tax payable	-0-

7-16.   a.   No gift tax return is required because the gift is under the annual exclusion amount.

b.   No gift tax return is required because Jesse's gift qualifies for the marital deduction.

c.   A gift tax return is required because the $15,000 in trust is a future-interest gift.

7-17. $150,000 Gift value
        $\underline{-50,000}$ Donor's basis
        $100,000 Appreciation

$$\frac{\$100,000}{\$150,000} \times \$38,800 = \$25,866.70 \quad \begin{array}{l} \text{gift tax on net} \\ \text{appreciation} \end{array}$$

        $50,000.00 Donor's basis
        $\underline{+25,866.70}$ Gift tax on net appreciation
        $75,866.70 Basis of gift to Lee's son

7-18.   Some of the characteristics of an ideal gift are as follows:
   - The property is likely to appreciate in value
   - The donee is in a lower income tax bracket than the donor.
   - The property is not subject to indebtedness.
   - The donor is not likely to want or need the property in the future.
   - It is not necessary for the donor to keep the property in order for his or her estate to qualify for advantageous tax benefits under Secs. 303, 6166, or 2032A.
   - The property's basis is approximately the same as its fair market value.

Answers to Self-Test Questions

7-1.   True.
7-2.   True.
7-3.   False. A gift tax is imposed on transfers of property regardless of the fact that the property is exempt from income tax.
7-4.   True.
7-5.   True.
7-6.   False. Gift splitting means that a donor's spouse will join in a gift made by the donor so that the gift will be treated as if one-half was made by each spouse for gift tax purposes.
7-7.   True.
7-8.   False. A gift of life insurance is a present-interest gift if it is made outright. However, since it is not *income-producing property,* it is difficult or impossible to ascertain the value of the income interest. Therefore, a gift of life insurance is typically one of a future interest if it is transferred to a trust. Unless certain conditions are met, such a gift of life insurance to a trust will not qualify for the gift tax annual exclusion.
7-9.   False. When a gift is made in trust, each beneficiary is considered a donee. Thus, if an annual exclusion is allowed, an annual exclusion is permitted for each beneficiary.
7-10. True.
7-11. False. Under the Uniform Gifts to Minors Act, gifts in most states are limited to securities, cash, insurance policies, or annuities.
7-12. False. Either the Uniform Transfers to Minors Act or comparable legislation has been adopted in the majority of states.
7-13. True.
7-14. True.
7-15. True.
7-16. False. Each taxpayer has only one applicable credit amount for lifetime and at death transfers.
7-17. True.
7-18. True.
7-19. False. Although they complement each other, the gift tax and income tax systems are not always consistent.
7-20. False. For income tax purposes, the donee's basis is equal to the donor's adjusted basis with appropriate adjustments for the amount of gift tax paid by the donor.

Chapter 8

Answers to Review Questions

8-1.   Advantages of having a will include the following:

- An executor of choice can only be named by will.
- Under a will, a decedent can transfer real estate, stock, or business interests as he or she wishes (not as the state dictates).
- The decedent can ensure the maximum marital deduction for property passing to his or her spouse.
- A will can specify the estate's share of the tax burden.
- A will can designate a guardian.
- Trusts created under a will can control the management and timing of distribution and principal from the estate; trust provisions can give executors and trustees broad powers to invest and manage property and can protect beneficiaries' interests from creditors.

8-2.   The requirements for a valid will are as follows:
- The instrument must be signed at the end.
- The will must be dated.
- In many states, the will must be witnessed by competent witnesses at the time it is executed.
- Competent witnesses must be able to swear that the signature at the end of the will is the testator's when the will is admitted to probate.

8-3.   To meet the elements of testamentary capacity, the testator must
- be of legal age (which can vary by state) to make a will
- be mentally competent at the time the will is written
- recognize and know the property he or she intends to dispose of by will
- recognize family and friends who are the natural objects of his or her love and affection
- understand how and to whom his or her property is to be distributed

8-4.   Typically, a will includes
- a statement by the testator regarding his or her intention of domicile
- a direction for the executor to pay all debts, as well as the expenses of the testator's last illness and funeral, from the estate
- directions regarding burial or cremation
- bequests, written either in specific or precatory language
- directions regarding disposition of the testator's tangible personal property
- designation of executor, successor executor, or coexecutors, with clauses defining specific and general powers
- a clause stating that the testator either exercises or declines to exercise a power of appointment
- if there are minors or incompetents, a clause directing the executor to hold any assets for their benefit

8-5.   The most common way to revoke or amend a will is to make a more recent one that declares all prior wills are revoked. A codicil may also specifically invalidate a will. In addition, a will can be revoked if the maker of the will intentionally destroys or mutilates it.

   In some states, an act that causes invalidation under state law will revoke a will. A divorce may revoke an entire will, or it may revoke only the provisions that pertain to the former spouse. The will may also be revoked if the testator remarries, or if children are born or adopted after the will is drafted.

8-6.   a.   An election against the will does not question the validity of the will. It is simply an election by the surviving spouse to take her statutory elective share of the decedent's property in lieu of what was left to her in the will. The remainder passes according to the will.

   b.   The will contest by the wife is an attack on the actual validity of the will. For example, the survivor could claim that the will was a forgery, or that the testator was unduly influenced or legally incompetent when it was formed. If the will contest is successful, the will is invalid (or partially invalid) and the property will pass by the terms of a prior will or, if none, by the laws of intestacy of the relevant state.

8-7.   The grounds for contesting a will are
- improper execution
- legal incompetence of the testator
- duress or undue influence on the testator to make the will
- fraud
- forgery
- revocation

8-8.   A testamentary trust provides security and professional management of trust property after the testator is gone. It also gives the testator some control regarding both the immediate and final distribution of his or her property.

8-9.   Principal from a testamentary trust can be distributed at the discretion of the trust beneficiary, the trustee, or a designated third party. The testator may also specify when trust principal is to be distributed, and he or she generally has complete flexibility—that is, the method of distribution is subject only to the rule against accumulations.

8-10.   Life insurance proceeds are distributed under provisions of a will only if no designated beneficiary is named or the policy is made payable to the estate.

8-11.   A person is considered to have died intestate if he or she dies without a will or with a will that has been revoked or declared invalid in some other way.

Answers to Self-Test Questions

8-1.   True.

8-2.   True.

8-3.   False. The decedent or testator, who is the maker of the will, must have legal capacity to make a will at the time the will is written, not at the time of death.

8-4.   False. Per stirpes provides that members of a class take as members of a class or as representatives of deceased members of a class.

8-5.   True.

8-6.   False. If property subject to a specific bequest is disposed of prior to death, the legatee will receive nothing unless the will contains a provision to substitute other property.

8-7.   False. A holographic will is handwritten and does not need to be witnessed.

8-8.   True.

8-9.   False. A will can be revoked in one of several ways. It can be revoked by a later will declaring the prior will invalid, by making a codicil invalidating the will or parts of the will, or by physical destruction.

8-10.   True.

8-11.   True.

8-12.   False. A testamentary trust is created under a will and thus is part of the probate estate.

8-13.   False. To have legal effect, a pour-over trust must be executed prior to the will and must be in existence at the time the will is written.

8-14.   False. A will may be contested on several grounds: (a) it may have been executed improperly; (b) the testator may have been legally incompetent to write a will; (c) the testator may also have been under duress or undue influence when writing the will; (d) the testator may have been defrauded; (e) the will may be a forgery; and (f) the will may have been revoked by the testator before death.

8-15.   True.

8-16.   False. The intestate-succession laws of the states generally provide that if there is a surviving spouse and children, the decedent's estate will be divided among them in such proportions as the statute decrees.

8-17.   True.

Chapter 9

Answers to Review Questions

9-1.   All property that passes under and is subject to the terms of the will is admitted to probate. If there is no will, all property subject to the administration of the court due to intestacy is admitted to probate.

9-2.   The main advantages of probate are that it provides a process for the validation of a decedent's will and for the appointment of a personal representative of the estate. It permits court supervision of an executor's activities concerning the decedent's estate and grants a forum for the resolution of will contests and other matters concerning the estate. Probate oversees the inventorying, valuing, and distribution of estate property. It also establishes a time period prior to distribution of estate assets during which the decedent's creditors must come forward to present their claims to the estate.

    Disadvantages of probate typically concern the delays and inflexibilities concerning estate matters and distribution of estate property to the beneficiaries. The procedures necessitated by the probate process are according to statute and may be more time-consuming than is desired. Other negative aspects are lack of privacy and expenses. The will, creditors' claims, and other personal matters involving the decedent's estate are a matter of public record. There are costs for court supervision of the estate plus executor and attorney fees.

9-3.   The executor is responsible for managing the testator's estate—gathering all assets; collecting all amounts owed the decedent; paying debts, expenses, and taxes; and distributing assets to the beneficiaries.

9-4.   If the will is located in a safe-deposit box titled in the decedent's own name, the box is closed once that person dies. Immediate access to the will can therefore be a problem.

9-5.   The functions an executor must perform to manage an estate are as follows:
   - Establish an estate checking account and savings or money market account.
   - Locate, take possession of, and determine the value of estate assets as of the date of death; file an inventory of assets with the probate court.
   - Hire financial, business, tax, and estate specialists, as necessary.
   - File necessary tax returns, make sure elections and disclaimers are timely made, and pay taxes due.

9-6.   The order for payment of claims is typically as follows: (1) debts that have a special lien on property not exceeding the property's value, (2) funeral expenses, (3) taxes, (4) debts owed the United States government and the state, (5) court judgments, (6) wages due any servant or laborer for the year prior to the decedent's death, (7) medical expenses for the year preceding death, and (8) all other debts and claims.

9-7.   The executor must get records of prior gift tax returns (and must file a return for gifts in the year of death) and determine whether the taxable estate plus adjusted taxable gifts (post-1976 lifetime taxable transfers not included in the decedent's gross estate) exceeds the applicable exclusion amount.

   In addition, the executor should pay property taxes, state inheritance (or state) taxes, and relevant income tax returns. For example, the executor should file the decedent's final income tax return and an estate income tax return for each year the estate is open.

9-8.   A beneficiary might want to disclaim an inheritance because his or her own estate is substantial, and the beneficiary does not want the estate to incur additional estate taxes. The beneficiary might also disclaim in order to release the inheritance to other beneficiaries whose needs are greater.

Answers to Self-Test Questions

9-1.   False. The steps in the estate settlement process are basically the same whether a person dies intestate or with a will.

9-2.   True.

9-3.   False. Ancillary probate refers to administering the transfer of property located in a state other than where the decedent was domiciled.

9-4.   False. An administrator is a person named by the court when the decedent has failed to name an executor in the will, when the executor named in the will cannot or will not serve, or when the decedent dies intestate.

9-5.   True.

9-6.   True.

9-7.   True.

9-8.   False. If there is no tax clause in the will, taxes are allocated according to the state statutory tax allocation scheme.

9-9.   False. If any property is found after the estate is closed, it may be necessary to reopen the estate on a limited basis to have this property probated.

9-10   True.

Chapter 10

Answers to Review Questions

10-1.   There are a number of reasons why accurate asset valuation is important to the estate planning process. First, it is impossible to determine potential liquidity needs that an executor may experience unless proper values are placed on the owner's assets during life. Qualification for a Sec. 303 stock redemption or the installment payment of estate taxes under Sec. 6166 depend on the value of the decedent's stock relative to the value of the decedent's other assets. If the appropriate test(s) cannot be met, neither technique for paying estate taxes is available.

   Second, because of the income and estate tax advantages inherent in gifts, gratuitous transfers of property may be meaningful when they are subject to minimal gift tax costs. However, to properly consider the various ramifications and potential advantages involved in a lifetime transfer, a knowledge of valuation is essential. A third reason why valuing assets is important relates to the funding of buy-sell agreements. The first step in arranging such an agreement is to arrive at a fair market value for the business. Obviously, it is impossible to assure each costockholder (or partner) that beneficiaries will receive an equitable price on death or disability unless the current worth of each person's business interest is ascertained.

10-2.   A higher valuation of a business interest might be advantageous in the formula for a buy-sell agreement. From the point of view of the decedent's survivors, where alternative liquidity funding is impractical, it may be better to set a formula in a buy-sell agreement that puts a higher value on the business interest (and thereby provide more cash for the decedent's survivors) than to establish a formula that provides a lower estate tax value (yielding a lower price for the decedent's business interest). Moreover, when a business interest is valued high relative to other estate assets, the disadvantage of the additional tax payable due to the higher valuation may be more than offset by the advantages of qualifying for a Sec. 303 stock redemption or a Sec. 6166 election to pay federal estate taxes attributable to a business interest in installments.

10-3.   There is very little in the Internal Revenue Code about how to value items for federal estate tax purposes. Although the value of the gross estate is mentioned in the Code, the word *value* is not defined. The estate and gift tax regulations provide that value is meant to be *fair market value,* which is defined as follows: the price at which the property would change hands between a willing buyer and a willing seller, neither being under any compulsion to buy or to sell and both having reasonable knowledge of relevant facts

By this definition, the value that may be placed on property can vary substantially, depending on who is valuing the item and what factors are used. The regulations state that it is not necessary to have either an established market for an item or a willing buyer and seller as mentioned above. In the absence of an actual sale, the value of an asset is based on a hypothetical sale.

Generally, the following external factors are examined in deciding the extent to which sales price is indicative of value:

- the frequency of sales (Courts tend to disregard isolated or sporadic sales.)
- the relationship between the seller and the buyer (Sales that are between parents and children or employers and employees are seldom given great weight in light of their almost inherently unequal bargaining position.)
- options to purchase or sell (Offers, as opposed to options, present little evidence of value.)

Once all these value-affecting factors are considered, each factor must be given a relative weight.

10-4.   Some items present more difficult valuation problems when the following occurs:

- There are different markets for the same property.
- The appraisal of worth must be made on the basis of comparable property, which is a subjective standard.
- The property in question is unique.

In practice, valuation problems are frequently viewed by the IRS and the courts as problems of negotiation and compromise. An appraiser's objective is to derive a fair and sound value that, if litigated, would likely be sustained in court.

10-5.   Under the farm-method formula, the comparable net rental is capitalized at the federal land bank loan rate to determine the special-use valuation of farmland. For the Smith farm, the value is ($84,000 − $8,000) ÷ .08 = $950,000

10-6.   The tax benefit from special-use (current-use) valuation of real property may be recaptured under certain circumstances. If the property is disposed of to nonfamily members within 10 years after the death of the decedent, there is an additional estate tax or recaptured tax imposed on the qualified heir. If the heir or a member of the heir's family fails to participate materially in the business operation for 5 or more years during an 8-year period ending within 10 years after the decedent's death, it is treated as a cessation of the qualified use, causing recapture. There is a 2-year grace period following the decedent's death before the heir must commence the qualified use without risking recapture.

Recapture of the difference in tax between the current-use and highest-and-best-use methods of valuation occurs when the real estate is sold, disposed of, or no longer used for the same qualified use within the 10-year period. Also, the eligible qualified heir must be engaged in the active management of the farm or business during the recapture period. If during this period the heir is under age 21, disabled, a full-time student, or the surviving spouse, a fiduciary may qualify in providing active management for the heir.

10-7.   a.   The general rule for valuing household property and personal effects, such as watches, rings, and so forth, can be called the *willing buyer–willing seller rule.* In non-community-property states, household goods and the like personally acquired by and used by husband and wife during marriage are generally presumed to be the property of the husband. Therefore, in the absence of sufficient evidence to rebut this presumption, household goods and personal effects are includible in the husband's estate.

b. Where a stock has an established market and quotations are available to value the stock as of the date in question, the fair market value (FMV) per share on the applicable valuation date governs for both gift and estate tax purposes.

The FMV is based on selling prices when there is a market for the stock or bond. This is the mean between the highest and lowest quoted selling price on the valuation date. If there were no sales on the valuation date, but there were sales on dates within a reasonable period both before and after the valuation date, the FMV is determined by taking a weighted average of the means between the highest and lowest sales on the nearest date before and the nearest date after the valuation. The average is then weighted inversely by the respective number of trading days between the selling date and the valuation date.

When a large block of stock cannot be marketed in an orderly manner, the block might depress the market because it cannot be converted to cash as readily as a few shares could be. Therefore, selling prices and bid-and-asked prices may not reflect fair market value. Sometimes it may be necessary to value this type of stock as if it was closely held and not actively traded. If this can be established, a reasonable modification of the normal basis for determining FMV can be made. In some cases a blockage discount is determined by the effect that block would have had on the market if it was sold over a reasonable period of time and in a prudent manner. A similar situation occurs when sales at or near the date of death are either few or of a sporadic nature and may not indicate a fair market value.

The converse of the blockage situation above occurs when the block of stock to be valued represents a controlling interest (either actual or effective) in a going business. Here the price of normally traded shares may have little relation to the true value of the controlling lot. The large block can have the effect of increasing value because of its element of control.

c. Valuation of bonds is similar to valuation of listed common stock. The means of the selling prices on or near the applicable valuation date (or—if there were no sales—the means of bona fide asked prices weighted inversely to the number of trading days from the valuation date) determine the fair market value of the bonds.

In the absence of sales or bid-and-asked prices, the value must be determined by

- ascertaining the soundness of the security
- comparing the interest on the bond in question to yields on similar bonds
- examining the date of maturity
- comparing prices for listed bonds of corporations engaged in similar types of business
- checking the extent to which the bond is secured
- weighing all other relevant factors, including the opinion of experts, the goodwill of the business, the industry's economic outlook, and the company's position in the industry as well as its management

d. Series E (EE) bonds are valued at their redemption price (market value) as of the date of death, since they are neither negotiable nor transferable and the only definitely ascertainable value is the amount at which the Treasury will redeem them.

Certain U.S. Treasury bonds (so-called flower bonds) owned by a decedent at the date of death and forming part of the gross estate may be redeemed at par value if used to pay federal estate taxes. These bonds are valued at the higher of the market price and par value.

Even if such bonds are not used to pay estate taxes, the courts have often held that when the bonds could be used for the payment of estate taxes, they are valued at the higher of market and par value. When the bonds could not be applied to pay the estate tax, their value is market (the mean quoted selling price value).

e. Proceeds of life insurance on the life of the decedent receivable by or for the benefit of the decedent's estate are taxed in the decedent-insured's estate. In addition, when the decedent held incidents of ownership, such ownership invokes taxation. The amount includible is the amount receivable by the beneficiary. This includes dividends and premium refunds. In determining how much is includible, no distinction is made between an ordinary life policy, a term policy, group insurance, or an accidental death benefit.

If a settlement option is elected, the amount that is payable as a lump sum is the amount includible. If the policy did not provide for a lump-sum payment, the amount includible is the commuted amount used by the insurance company to compute the settlement option payments.

The value of an unmatured policy owned by a decedent on the life of another is included in the policyowner's gross estate (when the policyowner predeceases the insured) according to the following:

- If a new life insurance policy is involved, the gross premium paid is the value.
- If the policy is a paid-up or a single-premium policy, its value is its replacement cost—that is, the single premium that company would have charged for a comparable contract of equal face value on the life of a person who was the insured's age (at the time the decedent-policyholder died).
- If the policy is a premium-paying whole life policy, the value is found by adding any unearned portion of the last premium to the interpolated terminal reserve.
- If the policy is a term policy, the value is the unused premium.

10-8. The valuation of closely held corporate stock is often one of the most difficult and time-consuming problems faced by the executor of a decedent's estate. By definition, closely held stock is incapable of valuation solely by recourse to an established market (that is, closely held stock is seldom traded). In fact, the criteria used to define closely held stock include (1) a limited number of stockholders, (2) restrictions imposed upon a shareholder's ability to transfer the stock, (3) the absence of an exchange listing or regular quotation in the over-the-counter market, and (4) an irregular and limited history of sales or exchanges.

There is no formula provided by the Internal Revenue Code or the regulations that is applicable to every closely held stock valuation situation. However, there are guidelines that should be considered in every valuation case. The key IRS ruling on point, Rev. Rul. 59–60, suggests that the following factors be considered:

- the nature of the business and the entire history of the enterprise
- the economic outlook in general as well as the condition and outlook of the specific industry
- the book value of the stock and the financial condition of the business (The Tax Court considers this factor in almost every case.)
- the company's earning capacity (For many businesses—especially those that do depend heavily on capital to produce profits—this will be the most important valuation factor.)
- the company's dividend-paying capacity
- the existence of goodwill (Goodwill can be defined as the economic advantage or benefit that is acquired by a business *beyond* the mere value of the capital invested in it because of the patronage it receives from constant or habitual customers, its local position, its reputation for skill or punctuality, other accidental circumstances or necessities, or public partialities or prejudices. In short, goodwill is a broad term implying that a company has a purchase value exceeding the worth of its tangible assets. Note: A business may have goodwill value even if no amount for goodwill is shown on its accounting statements.)
- prior stock sales and size of the block of stock to be valued
- fair market value of stock of comparable corporations engaged in the same or similar type of business where the stock is actively traded in an established market

Rev. Rul. 59–60 reaffirms that no fixed formula of valuation can be devised that is applicable to all situations and that, ultimately, the fair market value of closely held stock must be determined on an individual basis.

10-9. Adjusted book value is particularly applicable in the following instances:

- when the business in question is primarily an asset-holding company, such as an investment company
- when the company is in the real estate development business and assets, rather than earnings, are the key to valuation
- when the company is a one-person corporation, which is generally worth only its liquidation value
- if the corporation is being liquidated at the valuation date or it is likely that it will be liquidated in the near future (It is important also to consider the impact of sacrifice sales and capital-gains taxation, since the true value of a liquidating corporation is the amount that is actually available to the shareholders after the liquidation.)
- when the industry is highly competitive but the business is only marginally profitable (Adjusted book value is particularly useful in these cases, because past earnings are probably an unreliable tool in the measurement of potential future profits.)

The adjusted-book-value method involves adjusting the asset components of a business to an approximate fair market value for each such component. An adjustment is necessary, since most accounting statements carry assets at some figure other than fair market value.

10-10.   The book value of business assets often differs from fair market value because for book purposes
- assets are valued at cost (Most accounting statements carry land, for example, on the balance sheet of a company at an amount far less than what it is worth on the open market. The result is a book value bearing little or no relationship to present worth.)
- assets have been depreciated at a rate in excess of their true decline in value (For instance, equipment may have been purchased for $500,000 and depreciated to $200,000. Although it is carried on the firm's books at $200,000, the asset may really be worth a lot more or a lot less than its cost, or the $200,000 used on the balance sheet.)
- mention of items such as potential future lawsuits or unfavorable long-term leases has been omitted or not clearly noted in the footnotes or body of the firm's balance sheets
- assets have been completely written off even though they possess substantial value, resulting in a book value far below reality
- assets such as franchises and goodwill are shown on accounting statements at nominal cost or not shown at all
- there are difficulties in collecting accounts receivable
- a firm's inventory includes items that have become obsolete or are not readily marketable

There are still other factors that indicate the need for adjustment of pure book value. For instance, a downward adjustment from pure book value is indicated when the business's liquidity position is poor (the business has low current assets relative to its current liabilities), the firm is experiencing a shortage of adequate working capital, or it is burdened with sizable long-term debt. If large selling expenses and capital-gains taxes are likely in the event of liquidation, downward adjustments from book value are indicated.

10-11.   A realistic appraisal of the earning power of a company can sometimes be obtained only through first adjusting earnings by
- adding back bonuses paid to stockholders or their families
- adding back salaries that were excessive, or reducing earnings when salaries paid were inordinately low
- adding back excessive rents paid to stockholders, or subtracting nominal and unrealistically low rents paid to stockholders
- eliminating nonrecurring income items
- adjusting for excess depreciation
- adjusting earnings to take into consideration nonrecurring expenses, a major change in accounting procedures, widely fluctuating or cyclical profits, abnormally inflated or deflated earnings, or strong upward to downward earning trends. (Sometimes the IRS averages earnings over a 3- to 5-year period and then weights the average so that an upward earnings trend is given greater weight.)

10-12.   When the shares being valued represent a minority interest in a business, a reduction in value is often allowed. This minority-interest discount arises because, by definition, minority shares have no power to force dividends, compel liquidation, or control corporate policy. This makes the stock less appealing and narrows the potential market to the remaining (and usually controlling) shareholders. It, therefore, reduces the price at which each share might be purchased. Discounts of from 10 to 30 percent are often allowed.

The opposite result occurs when the shares in question represent a controlling interest. In this case the IRS generally seeks to substantiate a higher value. In other words, the size of the block of stock itself is a relevant factor. Although it is true that a minority interest in an unlisted corporation's stock is more difficult to sell than a similar block of listed stock, by the same token the controlling interest of a corporation represents an added element of value. It, therefore, justifies a higher valuation for a specific block of stock. More than 50 percent of the voting shares constitutes a controlling interest, while less than 50 percent constitutes a minority interest.

Note that if a father leaves two shares to his son who already has 49 shares (assume that only 100 shares are outstanding), the two shares represent in value more than a mere 1/50 of the value of the outstanding stock. Together with the interest that the son already owns, those two shares represent control of the corporation.

10-13.   In the case of buy-sell agreements, a mandatory buy-sell (either a cross-purchase or a stock redemption) agreement will normally peg the value of a decedent's stock for federal estate tax purposes. Under this type of agreement, the estate of the deceased stockholder must sell and the corporation or other stockholders must buy at a predetermined price or according to a predetermined formula. The obligation to sell at the agreed-upon price, however, must be binding not only upon the decedent's executor at the decedent's death but also upon the stockholder himself or herself during lifetime. The price at death does not control if a shareholder is free during lifetime to realize a higher price. Likewise, restrictions that are binding only during the decedent's lifetime but not at death are equally ineffective. In a mandatory buy-sell agreement neither party controls the event.

A mere right of first refusal, which requires that any shares offered for sale must first be offered to the corporation (or other shareholders) at the proposed transfer price, does not conclusively peg the value of the stock. However, a first-offer commitment may have the effect of depressing the value of the stock.

10-14. The valuation of certain transfers with retained interests may be accomplished using the subtraction method of valuation. The subtraction method of valuation determines the value of the transferred interest as the difference between (a) the value of the entire property interest and (b) the value of all interests in the property that continue to be held by the donor and are *not* transferred.

Stated simply: *The value of the whole less the value of what is kept equals the gift tax value of what is given away.*

10-15. Congress wanted to be sure that at least some minimum value was assigned to an equity interest transferred to a family member in an estate freeze. Even if there are actual or deemed qualified payments (or other rights valued under traditional methods), the Code now specifies a minimum valuation for any *junior* equity interest transferred by gift or sale to a family member. Examples of junior equity interests include common stock or partnership interests with rights to capital and profits junior to other partnership interests.

Answers to Self-Test Questions

10-1. True.

10-2. False. For estate tax purposes it may now be better to establish a high value in a buy-sell agreement for at least one of the following reasons: If the property is stock in a closely held business or farm, the decedent's executor will want a higher value established to qualify the estate for installment payment of estate taxes. A lower value reached in an arm's-length agreement will cause fewer assets to pass to the decedent's heirs. Also, as the applicable credit amount increases, the floor at which the estate will incur federal estate taxes is being raised each year so that federal estate taxes may not be a consideration.

10-3. True.

10-4. False. In practice, valuation problems such as unique assets are resolved by the IRS and the courts through negotiation and compromise.

10-5. True.

10-6. False. Currently the maximum amount by which the gross estate can be reduced when special-use valuation is elected is $750,000 (as indexed for inflation after 1998).

10-7. True.

10-8. False. One of the requirements for special-use valuation is that the decedent must have been a U.S. citizen or resident.

10-9. False. One of the requirements of special-use valuation is that the qualified heir is a lineal descendant, family member.

10-10. True.

10-11. False. There will be an additional estate tax imposed if the property for which special-use valuation has been elected is sold to nonfamily members within the 10-year period after the decedent's death. Also, if the qualified heir fails to participate materially in the business for 5 or more years during the 8-year period ending within 10 years after the decedent's death, there will be a recapture (additional estate tax imposed). However, the qualified heir will be given a 2-year grace period following the decedent's death to actually participate in the business without risking recapture of the estate tax.

10-12. True.

10-13. True.

10-14. False. Series E bonds are valued at their redemption price (market value) as of the date of death.

10-15. False. The IRS emphatically does not automatically accept the executor's value of closely held stock. If dissatisfied, the IRS will place a value on the stock in accordance with a revenue ruling that lists eight factors that should be examined in arriving at a valuation for gift or estate tax purposes. In addition, other valuation factors have evolved through court cases.

10-16. True.

10-17. True.

Chapter 11

Answers to Review Questions

11-1. The advantages of a buy-sell agreement can be summarized as follows:
- It guarantees a market for the business interest.
- It provides liquidity for the payment of death taxes and other estate settlement needs.
- It makes the estate planning process more reliable for the owners because it helps to peg the estate tax value of the decedent's business interest.
- It provides for the continuation of the business in the hands of the surviving owners and/or employees.
- It makes the business more attractive to creditors since a plan to continue the business is in place.

11-2. Most properly drafted buy-sell agreements have several common provisions, regardless of the specific type of agreement. Common terms of a typical buy-sell agreement include the following:
- *parties involved.* All buy-sell agreements should have a provision clearly identifying the parties to the agreement.
- *purpose.* All agreements should have a statement indicating the agreement's purpose.
- *commitments.* The agreement should state the obligations of all parties to it (for example, that the decedent-business owner's estate will sell the decedent's interests to the surviving owners according to the terms of the agreement).
- *business interest description.* The document should contain a description of the business interests subject to the agreement.
- *transfer restrictions during lifetime.* Most buy-sell agreements should include a clause, which is referred to as a first-offer or right-of-first-refusal provision, that prevents the parties to the agreement from disposing of the business interest to outsiders while the parties are living.
- *purchase price.* The agreement should specify a fixed purchase price or a method for determining a price at which the business interest is to be bought and sold.
- *funding.* The document should specify how the purchase price is to be funded.
- *transfer details.* The agreement should describe the actual specifics of the business transfer.
- *modification/termination.* There should be provisions for modification or termination of the buy-sell agreement if the parties later determine that the form of the current agreement no longer achieves the parties' objectives.

11-3. Life insurance is uniquely suited for funding buy-sell agreements, since the very event that creates the need for cash provides the cash.

11-4. A sole proprietorship is a business that has only one individual owner. It is distinct from other forms of business ownership in many ways. Most important, this type of business is not treated as a business entity separate unto itself. There is no legal distinction between the business's and the owner's personal assets. This means that when the sole proprietor dies or loses legal capacity to operate the business, the sole proprietorship must terminate. Planning for this contingency is vital if the proprietor's family expects to get full value for the business.

Often a buy-sell agreement is used to ensure a definite sale and purchase when the time comes. The agreement binds the proprietor's estate to sell and the purchaser(s) to buy the business interest.

11-5. a. *Types of Partnership Buy-Sell Agreements*

Entity-Purchase Agreement. Under the entity approach, it is the partnership entity that becomes the purchaser in the buy-sell agreement. Technically, the partnership liquidates the interest held by the decedent-partner's estate. In other words, the partnership makes payments to the estate that liquidate the interest held by the estate. Under an entity buy-sell agreement both the partners and partnership are parties to the contract that provides for continuation of the partnership business by the surviving partners.

Cross-Purchase Agreement. With a cross-purchase buy-sell agreement the individual partners are the sellers and purchasers. The partners make mutual promises to be a buyer or seller depending on the circumstances. Each partner agrees to purchase a share of any decedent partner's interest and to bind his or her estate to sell its partnership interest to the surviving partners.

b. *Types of Corporate Buy-Sell Agreements*

Entity (Stock Redemption) Purchase Agreements. With a stock-redemption agreement, the corporation is the purchaser of the stock at the death of a shareholder. Each shareholder-party to the agreement binds his or her estate to transfer the stock to the corporation in exchange for the required purchase price. The corporation redeems a decedent-shareholder's stock in exchange for a redemption distribution. The corporation either retires the stock or holds it as treasury stock. From the surviving shareholders' standpoint, the practical effect of a stock redemption is that the percentage ownership held by each surviving shareholder increases proportionately when a decedent-shareholder's stock is redeemed.

Corporate Cross-Purchase Agreements. The corporate cross-purchase agreement is similar to the partnership agreement. Each shareholder agrees to purchase a specified percentage of the decedent-shareholder's stock at the time of death. Although the corporation is not a direct party to the agreement, the stock certificates it issues should be endorsed with a statement that the stock is subject to the terms of the buy-sell agreement.

11-6. There are essentially four methods that business individuals use as a price-setting mechanism in a buy-sell agreement. These price-setting mechanisms include

- fixed price
- formula-determined price
- appraisal-determined price
- combination of the above mechanisms

Fixed Price

Under this method, a final price is set and stated in the agreement. This method has the advantage of being simple and clear, although frequently the agreement provides for yearly reevaluations of the price to keep it up to date.

Formula Mechanism

The most common formula approach uses some type of capitalization-of-adjusted-earnings method. Often the parties take other value-affecting factors into consideration by the multiple used. For example, one business may be valued at 10 times average earnings for the past 5 years, while another might be valued at 3 times average earnings for the past 8 years. Obviously, the greater the risk and the lower the stability of a business, the lower the earnings multiple is. Adjustments for specific facts or abnormalities with regard to a particular business may have to be made. The multiple itself may vary from time to time as economic conditions change. In some cases, the formula gives more weight to the earnings of those years immediately preceding the decedent-business owner's death than to the earnings of prior years. If family members are parties, it is imperative that the formula chosen be consistent with similar arm's-length agreements.

Appraisal

Many authorities feel that the fairest means of ascertaining the value of a business is to state in the buy-sell agreement that two appraisers should be employed. One appraiser is hired by the surviving shareholders, while the other represents the decedent's interest. The two appraisers would come to an agreement on an appropriate valuation, or in the absence of agreement, a third appraiser would be appointed by the first two to make a final binding determination of value.

Combination Mechanism

A fixed-price mechanism coupled with a reappraisal and a formula method, which begins with a fixed price as a floor and enhances that amount if earnings or book values reach a certain level, are other ways to solve the difficult and perplexing problem of providing variable but realistic prices for a business owner's interest.

Answers to Self-Test Questions

11-1. False. A properly designed buy-sell agreement will enable the business purchasers, usually the surviving co-owners, to obtain the decedent's business interest according to the terms of the agreement and avoid the difficulties associated with probate.

11-2. True.

11-3. True.

11-4. False. In most instances life insurance is used for funding buy-sell agreements.

11-5. True.

11-6. False. Under a fully insured corporate cross-purchase agreement, each shareholder should purchase adequate life insurance on the life of the other shareholders.

11-7. True.

11-8. False. The main disadvantage of using a fixed price in a buy-sell agreement for a family corporation is that the agreement will likely fail the tests to peg the value of stock. Since a fixed price does not adequately reflect fluctuations in market value, it is likely that the IRS will find the agreement to be either (1) a device to pass the stock to family for less than full consideration or (2) inconsistent with the terms of an agreement reached at arm's length. Even if the parties are unrelated, the fixed-price provision generally provides an inaccurate result.

Chapter 12

Answers to Review Questions

12-1. The federal estate tax is based on the privilege to transfer property, recognizing that a tax limited to transfers at death would invite tax-avoidance schemes to transfer property during lifetime. Therefore, a cumulative estate and gift tax system was enacted for taxation of certain transfers of property during lifetime and at death at the same tax rates. Incomplete lifetime dispositions—transfers of property over which the donor retains control—are equivalent to testamentary transfers at death, which causes the property to be included in the decedent's gross estate for tax purposes.

12-2. The decedent's estate is primarily responsible for payment of estate taxes, but if the estate does not contain enough assets to pay the taxes, the estate beneficiaries may be liable to the extent of the value of the property they inherit.

12-3. The trust principal is includible in Mr. Jones's gross estate because it is a reversionary interest to which Mr. Jones or his estate has an absolute right.

12-4. a. This property is not included as it is a life estate conferred by another person that the decedent could not transfer at his death.

     b. The full fair market value of the bonds is includible. The value may be less than the par value of the bonds and will be determined either at the date of death or on the alternate valuation date as the executor elects.

     c. One-third of the value of the Arizona land is includible.

     d. The IBM stock is totally includible.

     e. No part of the wrongful death claim is includible in the decedent's gross estate because the decedent must be dead before a wrongful death action can be brought. The right to bring a wrongful death claim belongs to the decedent's personal representative or to his heirs, and not to the decedent.

     f. The $5,000 in dividends declared and of record at the time of the decedent's death is includible because he had an absolute right to receive the dividends in the future.

     g. The claim for damages is includible in the decedent's estate because he could have recovered them during his life. Valuation may be difficult as it is a contingent claim.

     h. The full amount of the commission income is includible as income in respect of a decedent because the decedent had an absolute right to receive it.

     i. The full fair market value of the Matisse painting is includible unless it can be proven that the property belongs to his spouse.

     j. No part of the trust property is includible in the decedent's estate as he held only bare legal title and had no beneficial interest in the trust.

12-5. a. The $94,000 in uncollected accounts and the $25,000 note are includible in Jennifer's gross estate because both are income in respect of a decedent—that is, income earned by the decedent but not yet received at the time of death. The rental income accrued up to the date of Jennifer's death is also includible in her gross estate.

     b. The recipient of the income—the estate or the beneficiaries—will be liable for the income tax but can deduct from the income tax the amount of the estate tax attributable to that income item.

12-6. a. The $128,000 in renewal commissions is includible in Richard Ricardo's estate because it is income in respect of a decedent.

     b. Without the special income tax deduction, there would be an overpayment of taxes without allowing the recipient of the property to deduct the amount of estate tax already paid.

12-7. Sarah's dower rights will have no effect on the inclusion of the farm in Sam's gross estate or the value of the farm for estate tax purposes.

12-8. a. No amount of the $100,000 certificate of deposit is includible in Sandra's gross estate because it is a completed gift.

     b. All the life insurance proceeds are includible because the transfer to the irrevocable trust was less than 3 years prior to her death.

     c. The entire balance of the custodial accounts ($100,000) is includible because as custodian she retained the power to distribute or withhold income and principal (that is, to affect the beneficial enjoyment of the property).

    d. The full value of the condominium is includible because she retained the right to use the property for her life.

    e. The value of the income interests will be includible as Sandra retained the right to affect beneficial enjoyment *of the income* by shifting the proportionate interests.

    f. Sandra has retained a contingent reversionary interest that will be includible in her gross estate if the value of the reversionary interest computed actuarially just prior to her death exceeds 5 percent of the transferred property (Sec. 2037).

    g. The full value of the trust property is includible in Sandra's estate since she retained the power to revoke the trust.

12-9.   Nothing is includible in Bobby Block's gross estate because he paid the gift tax 15 years ago and retained no interest in the policy. The $345,800 amount would have been includible in his estate if the gift tax had been paid within 3 years of his death.

12-10.   a. The $60,000 gift tax paid within 3 years of death is includible in Jamison's gross estate.

          b. Nothing is includible as the gift qualified for the gift tax marital deduction and no gift taxes were paid.

12-11.   Nothing is includible in Arthur's estate. Since he had retained no rights to the property, the fact that it appreciated in value is irrelevant. That amount is not brought back into Arthur's estate. Nor is the gift tax he paid includible because it was not within 3 years of his death.

12-12.   Because the donor retained the right to income from the property for life, the full amount of the property at the donor's death— $475,000—is includible in the donor's estate.

12-13.   If the trust was funded with income-producing property, one-fourth of which was used to satisfy the support obligation of the decedent, his gross estate will include the value of the property that generated the income used to satisfy his legal obligations. Therefore, one-fourth of the trust principal valued at the time of the decedent's death will be included in his estate.

12-14.   The value of the property at the time of Mitchell's death is includible in his gross estate. Even though the agreement that Mitchell could continue to live in the house was not in writing, the implied understanding is a retained interest in the property, which causes the townhouse to be included in Mitchell's estate.

12-15.   This is clearly a case of reciprocal trusts. Michael and Karen could just as easily have placed property in trust for the benefit of their own children, reserving a life income interest for themselves. Use of the reciprocal trust arrangement will be ignored by the IRS since each grantor was left in exactly the same position as if he had created a trust with income for life to himself and remainder to his children. Therefore, the entire value of the trust corpus that each created will be included in Michael's or Karen's gross estate.

12-16.   Since Watson retained the right to vote all his stock and he was a more-than-20-percent shareholder (indirectly) at the time of his death, the stock is includible in his gross estate as a transfer within 3 years of death. This is so despite the fact that he released all voting rights one year before his death. It does not matter that he created the trust and gave away the stock earlier in time.

12-17.   The amount of $700,000 is includible in Alan Anderson's gross estate. Retaining the right to determine what percentage of income would go to each daughter—even if it is in conjunction with an independent trustee—is enough to cause the value of the ranch at Alan's death to be included in his gross estate.

12-18.   The entire value of the property in the trust on the date of Mr. Allison's death is includible in his gross estate because he retained the power to invade corpus for the benefit of the remainderman during the life of the income beneficiary. This constitutes a power to alter the beneficial enjoyment of the property both of the income beneficiary and the remainderman. Therefore, the entire amount is includible in Mr. Allison's gross estate. If Mr. Allison had not retained the power to distribute principal but only to accumulate the income (that is, add it to the principal), the only interest that he could affect would have been that of Roger, the income beneficiary. In that case, the amount includible in his estate would be the value of Roger's income interest at the time of his death.

Answers to Self-Test Questions

12-1.   False. There are many reasons other than tax reasons to do estate planning. It is important to provide for liquidity needs and income for one's beneficiaries. Medium-sized estates require estate planning to prevent the estate from being eroded by inflation and other negative forces, such as improperly planned instruments. Furthermore, although the heir may not have a federal estate tax with which to contend, state death taxes may become a primary consideration. Also, a decedent may have specific lifetime goals and objectives with regard to beneficiaries and property. Lack of estate planning may defeat these objectives.

12-2. False. Only post-1976 adjusted taxable gifts are includible in the estate tax computation. Note that some taxable gifts may be brought back into the decedent's gross estate.

12-3. True.

12-4. True.

12-5. False. The federal estate tax is applied differently to residents or citizens of the United States than it is to those who are nonresidents and noncitizens at the time of their death. If the decedent is a U.S. resident or citizen, all the decedent's property at the time of death—regardless of the location—is includible in his or her gross estate. However, the only property owned by nonresidents and noncitizens that is subject to federal estate taxation is that located in the United States.

12-6. False. Foreign situs property held by U.S. residents is subject to the estate tax system at the time of their death.

12-7. True.

12-8. True.

12-9. True.

12-10. True.

12-11. True.

12-12. False. All gifts of life insurance made by the insured within 3 years of death are includible in the decedent's gross estate at the full value of the proceeds, regardless of whether the annual exclusion was applied and also regardless of whether a gift tax return was required to be filed.

12-13. False. The gross estate also includes the value of property in which a decedent retained an interest for life, property in which the decedent had a reversionary interest valued at more than 5 percent of the value of the property at the time of death, or property previously transferred but in which the decedent retained a right to revoke, amend, or terminate the transfer. Also includible in the decedent's estate are gifts of life insurance made within 3 years of death.

12-14. False. Any gift tax paid on transfers made within 3 years of death is included in the gross estate under the *gross-up* rule. This prevents a decedent from gifting substantial amounts of property in the period immediately prior to death in order to reduce the estate by the amount of the gift tax.

12-15. True.

12-16. True.

12-17. True.

12-18. False. The decedent has reserved a life estate in the property. It is not significant that the arrangement was informal. The test is whether the decedent had retained a substantial economic benefit in the property that he held until his death or that he did not relinquish within 3 years prior to his death.

12-19. True.

12-20. False. The decedent's gross estate includes all property transferred during lifetime in which the decedent retained the right to alter beneficial enjoyment, either alone or with the consent of any other party, including an adverse party.

12-21. False. Sec. 2037 provides that property transferred during a decedent's lifetime is included in the decedent's gross estate if the beneficiary can enjoy or possess the property only by surviving the decedent *and* the decedent's reversionary interest *exceeded* 5 percent of the value of the property at the time of death.

12-22. True.

Chapter 13

Answers to Mini-Case

The assets and their values that would be included in Mr. Smith's gross estate for federal estate tax purposes are as follows:

Property other than life insurance that Mr. Smith owns in his own name:

GBH Corporation stock	$2,250,000
Listed common stock	125,000
Marketable corporate bonds	90,000
Savings accounts	75,000
Household and other tangible personal property	70,000

These assets would be included in Mr. Smith's gross estate since they are owned solely by Mr. Smith. Property is included in a decedent's gross estate to the extent of his interest in the property at the time of his death (Sec. 2033).

Life insurance proceeds would be included in Mr. Smith's gross estate as follows:

Life paid up at age 65	$500,000
Ordinary life (purchased at age 35)	250,000
Ordinary life (purchased at age 35)	150,000
Group life	100,000

The proceeds of the foregoing would be included in Mr. Smith's gross estate since he was the owner of such policies at his death (that is, he possessed *incidents of ownership* in these policies at the time of death). In addition, the group life insurance is payable to Mr. Smith's estate. This would cause these proceeds to be included in his gross estate. In the absence of any problem concerning a gift within 3 years of death, the $200,000 proceeds payable under the 30-payment life policy that Mrs. Smith owns on Mr. Smith's life would not be included in his gross estate for federal estate tax purposes since Mr. Smith possessed no incidents of ownership in this policy.

Properties that Mr. Smith and Mrs. Smith own as joint tenants with right of survivorship that would be included in Mr. Smith's gross estate are as follows:

Principal residence (50 percent)	$225,000
Summer residence (50 percent)	110,000
Investment real estate (50 percent)	150,000

The general principle applicable to joint property with right of survivorship held solely by spouses is that 50 percent of the date-of-death value is included in the estate of the first spouse to die. Currently, the percentage-of-contribution rule is irrelevant and does not apply to spousal joint tenancies with right of survivorship.

Answers to Review Questions

13-1. The value of any annuity received by a beneficiary as a result of having survived the decedent is included in the decedent's gross estate. Payments that end at the decedent's death are not included in his or her estate.

13-2. Sec. 2039 of the Internal Revenue Code concerns the federal estate taxation of annuity products. With certain limited exceptions, a decedent's gross estate includes the present value of an annuity or other payment receivable by any beneficiary as a result of having survived the decedent. Included under this section are any agreements, commercial or private annuities, and employee retirement annuities (including all proceeds from qualified plans generally for decedents dying after December 31, 1984).

Specifically excluded from taxation under this Code section are all amounts paid "as insurance under policies on the life of the decedent." This is not to say that proceeds of life insurance will not be included in the decedent's gross estate. Proceeds of life insurance on the decedent's life are includible in the gross estate under another Code section (IRC Sec. 2042) if certain conditions exist. If a single contract contains or has contained both life insurance and annuity elements, the amount that is includible, if any, under this section is based on whether or not there was any insurance element in the contract at the moment of death.

13-3. Different types of annuities includible in a decedent's gross estate are

- an agreement under which the decedent was receiving or was entitled to receive payments before death and for the duration of his or her lifetime
- a joint and survivor annuity, under which the decedent was receiving payments before death with another person for their joint lives, with payments continuing to the survivor
- a contract between the decedent and his or her employer under which the decedent was receiving or entitled to receive an annuity after retirement for the duration of his or her life, with payments to designated beneficiaries upon the decedent's death
- a contract between the decedent and his or her employer that provided for an annuity to a designated surviving beneficiary if the decedent died before retirement
- an agreement under which the decedent was receiving or was entitled to receive annuity payments for a specified time period, with payments to continue to a named beneficiary if the decedent died before the time period expired

13-4. a. Since annuity payments cease with Mr. Leonard's death, the annuity will not be included in Mr. Leonard's gross estate and there will be no estate tax.

      b. Mrs. Leonard's life annuity will not be included in Mr. Leonard's gross estate because he has no right to any of the annuity payments.

      c. To the extent that the survivor furnishes part of the purchase price of a joint and survivor annuity, that portion will not be included in the decedent's gross estate. Therefore, two-thirds of the value of the Zelda's survivor annuity will be included in Mr. Leonard's gross estate.

13-5. Generally, an annuity is valued based on the cost of comparable contracts sold by the issuing company as of the date of the decedent's death.

13-6. The value of an annuity is determined on the primary annuitant's date of death.

13-7. Benefits under a qualified retirement plan are included in a decedent's gross estate unless one of the following exceptions applies:

- A nonemployee-spouse's interest in plan proceeds arising solely because of the application of community-property laws is completely excluded from his or her estate if the nonemployee-spouse predeceases the plan participant.
- If (1) plan proceeds were in pay status on December 31, 1984, and (2) prior to the enactment of the Deficit Reduction Act of 1984, the participant had irrevocably elected a beneficiary designation that would have qualified the plan proceeds for estate tax exclusion, the $100,000 exclusion amount is still available.

13-8. One-half of the value of jointly held property with right of survivorship held solely by husband and wife is included in the estate of the first spouse to die, regardless of which spouse furnished all or part of the consideration.

13-9. a. The entire value of the property ($200,000) will be includible in Harry's estate under the percentage-of-contribution (consideration-furnished) rule. Since the contribution furnished by Harry's son, Jimmy, was a gift from Harry, it is considered to have been furnished by Harry and not his son.

      b. Yes. In that case, only 75 percent of the value of the property ($150,000) would be included in Harry's estate.

      c. Only 75 percent of the value of the property ($150,000) would be included in Harry's estate in this event. Income generated by gifts of property made by the decedent can be applied as bona fide consideration by the recipient of the property to reduce the amount includible in the donor-decedent's estate.

13-10. a. One-half the value of the house ($155,000) will be included in Mary's gross estate for estate tax purposes. This results from the rule of 50 percent inclusion for the first tenant to die regardless of contribution for jointly held property with right of survivorship when only spouses are joint tenants.

      b. The amount of Tom's gain will vary according to the date the residence is sold. For home sales before May 7, 1997, Tom will have a capital gain of $90,000 determined as follows:

Original basis for half the property	$ 75,000
Plus stepped-up basis for half the property	155,000
Basis for property at time of sale	$230,000
Selling price	$320,000
Less basis	(230,000)
Capital gain	$ 90,000

      For home sales after May 6, 1997 (the enactment date of the Taxpayer Relief Act of 1997), Tom will have no taxable gain. Up to $250,000 of gain is tax free for the sale of a personal residence by an individual. The exclusion is $500,000 for married couples who file joint income tax returns. This section of the act essentially replaces the $125,000 exclusion for residence sellers age 55 and older.

13-11. Three advantages are as follows:

- Jointly held property with right of survivorship is generally nonprobate property, which means that it is not subject to estate administration.
- One-half of the property attributed to the decedent's interest and included in his or her estate is entitled to the full marital deduction. Thus, there is no estate tax liability because of the property's inclusion.
- Joint ownership often instills a feeling of comfort and harmony between spouses.

13-12. Two disadvantages are as follows:

- The surviving spouse gets full control of the disposition of the property, which may defeat a part of the estate plan of the first spouse to die.
- Only one-half of the property's value receives a step up in basis at the first joint tenant's death.

13-13.   All property over which the decedent had a general power of appointment at the time of his or her death will be included in the decedent's gross estate for federal tax purposes.

13-14.   Nothing will be includible in his gross estate. He exercised the power before his death and did not possess a general power of appointment or any rights over the property subject to it at his death. Property subject to a general power of appointment will be includible in a decedent's gross estate only if the decedent possessed the power at death.

13-15.   If the decedent's power to appoint property to himself is limited to an ascertainable standard (such as for health, education, support, or maintenance), the power is generally considered to be a special power and not a general one, and the property is not included in his or her gross estate.

13-16.   a.   If a general power of appointment can be exercised only with the consent of another person who is not an adverse party, a fractional part of the property (determined by dividing the value of the property by the number of people in whose favor the power could be exercised) is included in the donee's estate.

   b.   A power that can be exercised only with a person who has a substantial adverse interest in the property is not treated as a general power, and the property is not includible in the donee's estate.

   c.   An adverse interest is one that, if the power is exercised, would not be in favor of the party holding the interest.

   d.   If the decedent is given what is otherwise a general power of appointment, property is not included in his or her estate if the power is limited to the 5-and-5 rule. This rule restricts the decedent's noncumulative right to withdraw the greater of $5,000 or 5 percent of the aggregate value of the property each year. When the decedent dies, only the amount that the decedent could have appointed in his or her favor that year is includible in his or her estate.

13-17.   For federal estate tax purposes, if an individual accepts a general power and disclaims it 3 months later, the disclaimer is ineffective. The value of the property subject to the power will be treated as a lifetime gift made by this individual to another. Once accepted, the property subject to the general power of appointment is within her control. This gives her ownership rights. Any subsequent transfer will be considered a gift potentially subject to gift tax.

13-18.   In general, life insurance proceeds are included in the decedent's gross estate if one of the following occurs:

   •   The decedent possessed incidents of ownership in the policy.
   •   The proceeds are receivable by the estate.
   •   The proceeds are receivable by another for the benefit of the estate.

13-19.   a.   Yes. The policy is payable to the decedent's estate.

   b.   Yes. The decedent owned the policy.

   c.   Yes. The right to borrow the loan value of the policy without security is an incident of ownership sufficient to require inclusion of the proceeds.

   d.   No. The insurance was transferred to the trust more than 3 years before Edgar's death and the trustee is not legally obligated to pay estate taxes from the proceeds.

   e.   Yes. The decedent owned the policy.

13-20.   a.   Yes. The value of life insurance policies the decedent owns on the life of another is included in the decedent's estate as property owned at death.

   b.   If the policy is new, the gross premium paid is the value of the policy included in the decedent's estate. If the policy is paid up or a single-premium policy, the value is its replacement cost. If it is a premium-paying whole life policy, the value is determined by adding any unearned portion of the last premium to the interpolated terminal reserve. If it is a term life policy, the value is the unused premium.

13-21.   Life insurance proceeds payable to the spouse or the spouse's estate in a lump sum qualify for the marital deduction only if the spouse survives the decedent by up to 6 months. If proceeds are left at the interest option for the life of the surviving spouse, they qualify for the marital deduction if they are payable to the spouse's estate or to persons to whom he or she appoints the proceeds at death. If the spouse does not exercise this power of appointment, proceeds may still qualify if they are received by named contingent beneficiaries as a result of the spouse's failure to appoint them.

   If proceeds are to be paid in installments or if there is a refund feature, they qualify for the marital deduction if payments following the surviving spouse's death are to the beneficiaries the spouse designated to receive remaining payments. Proceeds also qualify if the spouse receives all the interest for life and the proceeds pass to a trust or named beneficiary at the spouse's death under the qualified terminable interest rules.

13-22.   a.   The full value of the proceeds will be includible in Mr. Grant's estate because the transfer was made within 3 years of his death.

     b.   As long as Mr. Grant retained no incidents of ownership in the policy, the proceeds will not be included in his estate because the transfer was not made within 3 years of his death.

Answers to Self-Test Questions

13-1.   True.

13-2.   True.

13-3.   False. If the employee dies after reaching retirement age, the death benefit from a nonqualified retirement plan will be treated under the general annuity rules and will be included in the decedent's gross estate.

13-4.   False. Since annuities diminish with the mere passage of time, annuities are always valued as of the date of death regardless of whether the alternate valuation date has been chosen by the executor.

13-5.   False. As a general rule, death benefits from qualified plans are fully includible in the gross estate.

13-6.   False. One-half of property held by spouses as tenants by the entirety is automatically includible in the estate of the first spouse to die regardless of the respective contributions.

13-7.   False. Fifty percent of all jointly held property with right of survivorship is includible in the estate of the first joint tenant to die only when the joint tenants are husband and wife. The percentage-of-contribution rule applies to all other joint tenancies.

13-8.   False. If the contribution to acquire an interest in a jointly held tenancy has been received by gift from the donor-joint tenant, it will be considered a contribution of the donor-joint tenant.

13-9.   True.

13-10. True.

13-11. False. Since only one-half of the spousal joint tenancy is includible in the decedent's estate, only one-half of the property receives a stepped-up basis. The surviving spouse's interest retains the original cost basis from the time the property was acquired.

13-12. True.

13-13. False. A general power of appointment is one in which the decedent can appoint property to himself, his estate, his creditors, or his estate's creditors. If he is limited in any way with regard to the persons to whom he can appoint the property, it will not be considered a general power of appointment that will cause the property to be includible in his gross estate.

13-14. True.

13-15. True.

13-16. True.

13-17. False. If a person possesses a general power of appointment at death, it is irrelevant that he or she was legally incompetent to exercise it. Mere possession of the power is sufficient to cause the inclusion of the value of the property subject to the power.

13-18. True.

13-19. False. While there are a few cases that have held that the value of policy proceeds will be includible in a decedent's gross estate, although he or she could have exercised any incidents of ownership only in the role of trustee, there have been other cases in which the proceeds were not taxable in his or her estate if the decedent was given certain discretionary powers that were merely administrative in his or her role as trustee.

13-20. True.

Chapter 14

Answers to Review Questions

14-1.   After the gross estate is determined, the next step in calculating the taxable estate is to determine the adjusted gross estate by deducting the following:

- funeral expenses
- administration expenses attributable to property subject to claims against the estate
- claims against the estate
- unpaid mortgages

- other administration expenses
- losses

14-2. Certain taxes are deductible on the estate tax return as claims against the estate. These include income taxes, unpaid gift taxes, and real property taxes accrued to the date of death. Federal income taxes owed to the date of death are deductible only on the federal estate tax return. However, state, local, or foreign income taxes, as well as property taxes, may be deducted on either the federal estate tax return or the federal estate income tax return. Real estate taxes not accrued before death, as well as local and foreign income taxes on estate income, are deductible on the income tax return of the estate. Any federal income taxes on estate income are not deductible either on the estate tax return or for income tax purposes.

14-3. A mortgage debt will be allowed as a deduction for federal estate tax purposes if the following two conditions are met: (1) the full value of the property unreduced by the mortgage amount or indebtedness must be included in the value of the gross estate; and (2) the decedent's estate must be liable for the amount of the indebtedness. Here the two foregoing conditions have been met. Therefore, a deduction of $300,000 is permitted for federal estate tax purposes.

14-4. a. The estate may deduct $25,000 as a *casualty loss* calculated as follows:

Cost of repair	$80,000
Less insurance	(55,000)
Loss	$25,000

   b. A casualty loss accruing during estate settlement may be deducted either from the federal estate tax return or the estate's income tax return, but not from the decedent's final income tax return.

14-5. Executors who are also named beneficiaries of the decedent may consider the desirability of waiving their executor fees, since they receive a bequest that is income tax free. If an executor's commission is deductible on the federal estate tax return, it is then received as taxable income whether or not the executor is a beneficiary of the estate. However, if the commission or devise is considered a bequest, it is not deductible by the estate for either estate or income tax purposes. Executors must act promptly to waive any commissions if they find that more tax is saved by receiving the bequest income tax free than is saved by characterizing the executor's commission as a deductible expense of the estate. The critical factor to evaluate is whether greater tax savings results from a deduction on the federal estate tax return when the additional income tax incurred by the executor is taken into consideration.

Answers to Self-Test Questions

14-1. False. Reasonable funeral expenses are deductible for estate tax purposes only.
14-2. True.
14-3. True.
14-4. True.
14-5. True.
14-6. True.

Chapter 15

Answers to Review Questions

15-1. Because of the community property law concept, only one-half of the community property is includible in the estate of whichever spouse dies first. This tax advantage has been reflected in the income and gift taxation of community-property residents as well as in the estate taxation. As a result of this disparity, Congress aimed for tax parity by making a federal estate tax marital deduction available to married residents of common-law states. Therefore, the Internal Revenue Code now allows a deduction for the value of any qualifying property interests includible in the decedent's gross estate that pass from the decedent to the surviving spouse.

15-2. Net value refers to the gross estate tax value of a property interest—that is, its date-of-death value or, if applicable, its value as of the alternate valuation date, minus any charges against that interest. Generally speaking, this means that the gross value of a property interest passing to the surviving spouse must be reduced by (1) taxes payable out of the interest, (2) mortgages or liens against the interest, and (3) administration expenses payable out of the interest.

15-3. A number of very strictly construed technical requirements must be met before property qualifies for the marital deduction, and there are certain qualifications and limitations that must be considered:
- the citizenship requirement for the surviving spouse
- the requirement that property be included
- the requirement that property must *pass or have passed*
- the marital-status requirement
- the *terminable-interest rule*

15-4. Transfers to a surviving resident-alien spouse are eligible for the marital deduction if (1) the surviving spouse becomes a U.S. citizen before the decedent spouse's estate tax return is filed and (2) the surviving spouse remains a U.S. resident after the death of the citizen spouse.

If the surviving resident-alien spouse does not obtain U.S. citizenship, a qualified domestic trust (QDOT, or QDT) can be used to transfer assets to a surviving resident-alien spouse while preserving the marital deduction for such transfer.

15-5. If a third party makes a timely disclaimer, the result is the same as if no interest had ever passed to the him or her. If the third party's refusal to accept the property causes all or a portion of it to pass to the surviving spouse, it qualifies as property passing from the decedent to a surviving spouse. In other words, if the effect of a disclaimer by a third party is to increase the amount of property passing from the decedent to the surviving spouse, the result may be to increase the marital deduction.

15-6. a. The regulations provide that when it is impossible to ascertain which spouse died first, any presumption— whether established by the decedent in a will, by state law, or otherwise—will be recognized. The importance of a presumption-of-survivorship clause in a decedent's will or life insurance settlement should not be underestimated. Having a presumption of survivorship clause can result in estate tax savings through utilization of the marital deduction and applicable credit amount.

b. To the extent the presumption results in the inclusion of a bequest in the gross estate of the spouse deemed to have survived, a marital deduction is allowed.

15-7. The marital deduction is not a tax-avoidance device; it merely defers taxation until the death of the second spouse. This is the general theory and goal of the terminable-interest rule—to allow the marital deduction only when the nature of the interest passing to the spouse is such that, if retained until death, it will be taxed in the surviving spouse's estate. Emphasis should be placed on the words *general, theory*, and *goal*. Generally speaking, the *intent* of the law is to deny a deduction for any interest acquired by a surviving spouse that would not be includible in the surviving spouse's estate for federal estate tax purposes if held until death.

15-8. a. Actually there are two terminable-interest rules. The first provides that property is considered a nondeductible terminable interest if the following conditions exist:
- It is a terminable interest, that is, if it is an interest in property that will terminate or fail upon the lapse of time or upon the occurrence or nonoccurrence of some contingency.
- Another interest in the same property passed from the decedent to some person other than the surviving spouse or the spouse's estate.
- The interest passes or has passed to the "other person" for less than adequate and full consideration in money or money's worth.
- Because of its passing, the "other person(s)" or his or her heirs could possess or enjoy any part of the property when the surviving spouse's interest terminated.

The second type of terminable interest that does not qualify for the marital deduction—even though no person other than the surviving spouse acquires an interest in the property—is a situation in which the decedent in his or her will has directed the executor (or a trustee) to take assets ostensibly available to the surviving spouse and purchase a terminable interest with them.

b. There are important exceptions to the terminable-interest rules.
- An interest will still qualify for the marital deduction (it will not be considered a nondeductible terminable interest solely because it will terminate or fail upon the surviving spouse's death) if the bequest to the surviving spouse was conditional upon his or her surviving for up to 6 months after the decedent's death—as long as the surviving spouse does, in fact, survive for the specified period. (For example, an interest is not disqualified for the marital deduction merely because it states "if my husband

fails to survive me by 6 months, this will and all its provisions shall be construed as if he predeceased me.") However, if the specified termination does occur, the marital deduction is lost.

- A bequest of a life estate can qualify for the marital deduction if it is coupled with a general power of appointment. An interest passing to a surviving spouse for life with the remainder payable to his or her estate may also qualify for the marital deduction.
- A life insurance policy payable to the surviving spouse for life can qualify if the spouse has a general power of appointment over the proceeds.
- A qualified terminable-interest property election can also qualify.

Normally, these transfers of property would violate the terminable-interest rules and, therefore, not qualify for the marital deduction. The exceptions to the terminable-interest rules, however, specifically permit these kinds of transfers to a surviving spouse to qualify for the deduction if the requirements of the exceptions are met. All of the exceptions other than the 6-month survival contingency exception involve trust arrangements that qualify for the marital deduction.

15-9.   The power-of-appointment trust exception to the terminable-interest rule is that the interest is not disqualified if it meets all of the following five conditions:

- The surviving spouse is entitled to all the income from the interest in question.
- The income is payable annually or more frequently to the surviving spouse.
- The surviving spouse has the power to appoint the interest to himself or herself or to his or her estate.
- The power must be exercisable by the surviving spouse alone and in all events. It can be a lifetime power or a power exercisable by the surviving spouse only at death (that is, by will) or a power exercisable in either event.
- No person other than the surviving spouse has a power to appoint any part of the interest to anyone other than the surviving spouse.

15-10.   An estate trust is a useful alternative to the power-of-appointment trust for a number of reasons. First, in contrast to the power-of-appointment trust, under which all income must be payable to the surviving spouse annually or more frequently, the trustee of an estate trust can accumulate income within the trust instead of paying it out. If the trust is in a lower income tax bracket than that of the surviving spouse, the power to accumulate can result in income tax savings. Second, because the spouse does not have to receive all the income annually, a trustee can either invest in nonproductive (non-income-producing) property or retain nonproductive assets, such as non-dividend-paying stock in a family-owned corporation.

15-11.   There are four conditions that must be met before QTIP treatment is allowed:

- The decedent-spouse (or donor, in the case of a lifetime gift) must make a transfer of property.
- The surviving spouse (donee, in the case of a lifetime transfer) must be given the right to all the income. The income must be payable at least annually, and the surviving spouse must be entitled to that income for life.
- No one can be given the right to direct that the property will go to anyone (other than the spouse) as long as that spouse is alive
- The first decedent-spouse's executor must make an irrevocable election on the decedent's federal estate tax return.

15-12.   The first decedent-spouse's executor must irrevocably elect QTIP tax treatment on the decedent's federal estate tax return. The election provides that, to the extent the QTIP property has not been consumed or given away during the lifetime of the surviving spouse, its date-of-death value (at the surviving spouse's death) will be included in the surviving spouse's estate.

15-13. a.   If all or most of a client's estate consists of unproductive real estate (and/or stock in a closely held corporation that has not paid, and probably never will pay, any significant dividends), the surviving spouse is unlikely to receive the statutorily required "all income at least annually."

The surviving spouse must be given an interest that realistically is expected to produce income (or will be usable by the spouse in a manner consistent with its value). Most closely held stock will never pay dividends or realistically be expected to produce an income consistent with its value. Therefore, without planning, the marital deduction could be lost.

b.   If there is no state law giving the surviving spouse the power to require that trust assets be sold and that trust property be made productive in a reasonable period of time, the attorney drafting the marital formula must insert a provision in the will or trust clearly giving the survivor that power. If the surviving spouse can demand that the trustee sell the stock (or other unproductive assets) and use the proceeds to purchase income-producing property, the marital deduction can be saved (even if the power itself is never actually exercised).

15-14. Overqualification occurs when there is an underutilization of the estate owner's applicable credit amount. The result is that more property than necessary to reduce the estate owner's federal estate tax to zero goes to the surviving spouse. Thus, at the surviving spouse's death, more property than necessary is exposed to tax. This is where the proper funding of a CEBT is important. It assures an efficient use of both spouses' applicable credit amounts and prevents unnecessary stacking of assets in the surviving spouse's estate.

15-15. a. The following property is included in the decedent's gross estate in whole or in part because he owned the property or had rights to the property at his death:

Gross Estate	
Cash	$ 75,000
Life insurance	250,000
Residence held as tenants by the entirety (50 percent of property held as tenants by the entirety by spouses is included in the estate of the first spouse to die)	160,000
Automobile	10,000
Sole proprietorship	1,600,000
Gross estate	$2,095,000

b. Debts and administrative expenses are $155,000. The adjusted gross estate before reduction by the marital deduction equals $2,040,000.

c. The marital deduction could potentially be $1,940,000 because the will provides that all property passes to the decedent's wife. Also, the life insurance that passes outside the will and is payable in a lump sum to his wife will qualify for the marital deduction as an interest in property that passes to the surviving spouse in a qualifying manner. The maximum marital deduction is an unlimited 100 percent marital deduction. Therefore, the deduction is the entire amount of the estate after reduction for debts and expenses, which leaves a taxable estate of zero.

d. Although there will be no federal estate taxes to pay when this decedent dies because all the property passing through his estate qualifies for the unlimited marital deduction, he has not taken advantage of the applicable credit amount that exists for the estate of every decedent. Therefore, upon the death of the surviving spouse, if she has not remarried, there will be no marital deduction to shelter all property included in her estate in excess of the applicable credit amount in the year of her death. An applicable credit amount effectively exempts from estate tax an amount equal to $600,000 from 1987 through 1997. (The credit exempts $625,000 in 1998; $650,000 in 1999; $675,000 in 2000 and 2001; $1 million in 2002 and 2003; $1.5 million in 2004 and 2005; $2 million in 2006, 2007, and 2008; $3.5 million in 2009 and will be repealed for the year 2010. The decedent could have given his surviving spouse an amount exactly sufficient (and no larger) to reduce the federal estate tax due, at his death, to the lowest possible figure, and he could have bequeathed the balance equal to a *credit-exclusion/equivalent bypass trust* (CEBT) to the children. In this way, he would have utilized the marital deduction as well as the applicable credit amount existing at the time of his death to obtain the maximum federal estate tax savings both at his death and when his spouse dies.

15-16. There are two types of formula bequests:
- the pecuniary (dollar) amount
- the fractional share

The *pecuniary-amount bequest* provides that the survivor will receive a fixed-dollar amount, and it takes into consideration not only property passing under the will but also all property that qualifies for the marital deduction. The *fractional-share bequest* is an attempt to accomplish the same goal by giving the surviving spouse a fractional share in the residue of the estate—that is, a fractional share of each asset after specific bequests have been made.

15-17. It is advisable to determine how much the surviving spouse should be given under the marital bequest. It may be that the surviving spouse should be given less than the amount necessary to reduce taxes in the decedent's estate to zero. Perhaps the surviving spouse should be given only one-half of the estate. Although the time-use (or psychological) value of tax money saved on the death of the first spouse may offset the cost, the (potential) increase in total taxes payable should be considered. Such decisions may depend on the use to which tax savings are put at the first death. If the money is used to assure or enhance the lifestyle of the surviving spouse, then it is likely to result in a long-run benefit.

Until the estate tax is repealed, if the excess of the amount necessary to *equalize the two estates* is invested by the surviving spouse, greater estate taxation may result when he or she dies. The net result will be fewer assets passing to the next generation. (Until 2010, there may be—mathematically, at least—a tax savings by equalizing spousal estates, especially if it is assumed that the second spouse is merely accumulating and not spending the equalization amount.) Equalization of spousal estates, however, is of decreasing importance as the amount of the applicable credit amount increases.

15-18.   There are many means of obtaining the marital deduction. One method is outright transfer of property to the surviving spouse by will or through life insurance death proceeds. There are advantages to an outright bequest, as follows:

- The spouse has the right to use and manage marital assets as he or she desires.
- No trustee fees or court accountings are required.
- Giving the spouse the marital share discourages him or her from electing against the testator's will.
- Assets the surviving spouse receives are available to his or her executor to meet estate liquidity needs.
- The surviving spouse can be given (and can safely retain) non-income-producing assets, such as the non-dividend-paying stock in a family-owned corporation.

But an outright bequest has a number of disadvantages.

- No protection is provided for a spendthrift spouse.
- There is no management with investment expertise.
- The surviving spouse's creditors can attach the bequest both during lifetime and at death.
- The surviving spouse can easily dispose of the bequest however he or she wishes during lifetime—even to the exclusion of his or her children and in favor of a second spouse and children.
- Assets the surviving spouse has not given away or consumed will be included in his or her probate estate.

15-19.   a.   One method of providing a marital bequest is to leave property in a power-of-appointment trust. Typically, the power-of-appointment trust gives the spouse a lifetime interest in the trust property, coupled with the right to specify the identity of the remainderperson during lifetime or in his or her will. It usually also provides that if the surviving spouse fails to name the beneficiaries of trust assets, the trust corpus will go to a *taker in default*, a beneficiary named by the grantor of the trust. The trustee (as well as sometimes the surviving spouse) is often given additional powers over trust assets. These might include the right to use trust principal for emergencies or to make gifts to children and grandchildren.

Another form of marital bequest under a will is known as an *estate trust*. This type of trust is not required to give the surviving spouse all the income during his or her lifetime, but pays all the accumulated income and the corpus to the surviving spouse's estate when he or she dies.

b.   The advantages of a power-of-appointment trust include the following:

- As in the case of an outright gift, the surviving spouse may be discouraged from electing against the decedent's will.
- Protection is afforded to some degree against the surviving spouse's possible spendthrift habits.
- Protection is provided against the surviving spouse's creditors and against the creditors of the spouse's estate.
- Principal distributions can be varied, depending on the surviving spouse's needs.
- The surviving spouse's right to dispose of the property during lifetime can be limited.
- Probate of the trust corpus can be avoided when the surviving spouse dies.
- Management and financial guidance are provided for the surviving spouse.

But there are disadvantages of a power-of-appointment trust.

- Certain trustee fees and accounting costs are involved.
- Assets in a power-of-appointment trust may not be available to the surviving spouse's executor for the payments of costs and taxes (unless the surviving spouse appoints the assets to his or her estate).
- Non-income-producing property, such as life insurance, cannot safely be obtained or retained in the trust.

Advantages of the estate trust include the following:

- Non-income-producing property can be purchased and safely retained by the trustee.
- Income tax savings can be realized by the accumulation of the income in the trust in years when the trust's income tax bracket is lower than the surviving spouse's bracket.
- Protection is provided against the surviving spouse's spendthrift habits, if any.
- Protection is afforded against the surviving spouse's creditors during lifetime.

- The surviving spouse is unable to make lifetime assignments of trust property.
- Assets are available to the surviving spouse's executor.

Disadvantages of the estate trust consist mainly of its inflexibility from the surviving spouse's viewpoint.

- The surviving spouse has no freedom to use and manage trust assets.
- The surviving spouse is restricted in disposing of any property in the trust during lifetime.
- Assets in the trust generate trustee fees and accounting costs.

Answers to Self-Test Questions

15-1. False. The maximum marital deduction is an unlimited deduction for the full value of property passing to a surviving spouse in a qualifying manner.

15-2. False. The estate tax marital deduction is allowed on the net value of the marital interest passing to the surviving spouse, which means the gross value of the property interest passing less taxes, mortgages, or administration expenses payable out of the marital interest.

15-3. True.

15-4. False. The marital-deduction rules require that the surviving spouse (not the decedent) be a United States citizen.

15-5. False. Probate property is only one type of property that can qualify for the marital deduction if left to the surviving spouse.

15-6. True.

15-7. False. If the decedent dies while legally married, all property left to a surviving spouse (in a qualified manner) will qualify for the marital deduction.

15-8. True.

15-9. True.

15-10. True.

15-11. True.

15-12. True.

15-13. False. A credit-equivalent bypass trust (CEBT) is a nonmarital (family) trust, providing the surviving spouse with income and only limited amounts of principal. A marital trust provides income plus a general power to appoint principal to the survivor's estate or creditors.

15-14. True.

15-15. True.

15-16. False. On the contrary, most authorities believe the investments in a QTIP trust should be income producing to qualify as a QTIP.

15-17. True.

15-18. False. It is true that if an individual leaves all property to a surviving spouse in a qualifying manner it will pass entirely free of estate tax because of the unlimited marital deduction. However, assuming the surviving spouse does not remarry, all property in his or her estate in excess of the amount equivalent to the applicable credit amount will be taxable in the survivor's estate. For tax and other reasons, it remains important to plan an estate if the decedent wishes to save estate taxes in the two combined estates as well as to make sure that the decedent's property passes to the intended beneficiaries.

Chapter 16

Answer to Mini-Case

The calculation of the gross estate, adjusted gross estate, and taxable estate of George Johnson is as follows:

a. *Gross estate*

   i.   Property owned by decedent alone

	Probate or Nonprobate	Value	
Cash	P	$ 125,000	
Real estate	P	810,000	
Municipal bonds	P	500,000	
		1,435,000	1,435,000

plus	ii.	One-half of jointly held spousal property	NP		185,000	185,000
plus	iii.	Life insurance proceeds (included because decedent was owner)				
		Policy A—beneficiary W	NP		50,000	
		Policy B—beneficiary W	NP		500,000	
		Policy C—beneficiary— charity	NP		130,000	
					680,000	680,000
plus	iv.	Qualified plan death benefit payable as annuity	NP			450,000
plus	v.	Gift tax on taxable gift of $40,000 ($51,000 – $11,000 [annual gift tax exclusion] = $40,000)			8,200	8,200
equals		Gross estate				2,758,200

b. *Adjusted gross estate*

minus	Debts and expenses		31,000	31,000
equals	Adjusted gross estate			2,727,200

c. *Taxable estate*

Probate estate		$ 125,000	
Cash		810,000	
Real estate		500,000	
Municipal bonds			1,435,000
Property qualifying for marital deduction			
One-half of probate estate		$717,500	
One-half of residence held as joint tenants with right of survivorship		185,000	
Life insurance passing to surviving spouse		550,000	
Qualified plan death benefit		450,000	
		1,902,500	1,902,500
Adjusted gross estate			2,727,200

minus	i.	Marital deduction	1,902,500	
minus	ii.	Charitable deduction ($130,000 life insurance proceeds)	130,000	
		State death taxes	0	
		Total deductions	2,032,500	2,032,500
equals		Taxable estate		$694,700

Answers to Review Questions

16-1. An estate tax charitable deduction is allowed for the full value of property transferred to a qualified charity, but only if the property is included in the donor's gross estate.

16-2. If property is transferred from a decedent's estate to a charitable organization because there has been a qualified disclaimer by a prior beneficiary, a charitable deduction is allowed for amounts actually transferred to the charity.

16-3. If, under the terms of the will or provisions of local law, payment of death taxes or other deductible expenses is to be made from the charitable bequest, the charitable deduction is reduced by those amounts used to pay debts or taxes. In other words, the deduction is limited to the actual amount that passes free and clear to the charity for its charitable purposes.

   If the will provides that taxes and administration expenses are payable from the residue and the charitable bequest is also payable out of the residue, the residuary bequest is diminished by the amount of expenses and taxes paid.

16-4. In addition to outright bequests of entire interests, charitable gifts can be in other forms, including
   - powers of appointment
   - partial interests
   - charitable remainder trusts
   - guaranteed annuity interests
   - split gifts

16-5. If the decedent transfers a remainder interest in property to a charity in trust, it must be made in the form of a charitable remainder unitrust, annuity trust, or pooled-income fund. Otherwise, no estate tax charitable deduction is allowed. These arrangements usually provide for an income interest to a noncharitable beneficiary with the remainder to the charitable organization.

16-6. For transfers made after 1981, a donor-decedent may create a charitable remainder trust and obtain deductions for both the charitable and noncharitable bequests. If a spouse is the only noncharitable income beneficiary for life, the estate obtains a marital deduction for the income interest to the surviving spouse as well as a charitable deduction for the gift of the remainder interest to the charity. The result is that no transfer tax is imposed on the creation of a charitable remainder annuity or unitrust for either the remainder or income portion, provided that the income interest to a spouse qualifies under the new qualifying terminable interest rules. Thus, a split gift to a spouse and charity in the form of a charitable remainder annuity or unitrust may pass entirely estate tax free by use of the combined marital and charitable deductions.

Answers to Self-Test Questions

16-1. False. A charitable deduction will be received for a gift of one's entire estate to a qualified charity at death only if the subject property is included in the donor's gross estate.

16-2. True.

16-3. True.

Chapter 17

Answers to Review Questions

17-1. *Inheritance Tax*

The inheritance tax is a tax imposed on an individual's right to inherit property from the estate of a decedent. The amount of inheritance tax is based on two factors: (1) the value of the property received by each beneficiary and (2) the rate of the tax (and the amount of exemption, if any exists), which depends on the beneficiary's degree of blood relationship to the deceased.

Estate Tax

A state estate tax is similar in nature to the federal estate tax. It differs from the inheritance tax in that the inheritance tax is imposed upon a beneficiary's right to inherit, while the estate tax is imposed on a decedent's right to transfer or pass property to beneficiaries.

17-2. In the majority of states, state law groups beneficiaries who are entitled to receive estate assets into classes. The closest blood relatives of the decedent have the lowest state death tax rate and the largest exemption. In a state that provides for two classes, class 1 (or class A) may include the deceased's surviving spouse, children, parents, and grandchildren. Class 2 (or class B) may include aunts, uncles, brothers, sisters, nephews, nieces, and all other beneficiaries. The class 2 individuals are subject to a higher tax rate than the members of class 1. If the particular state also provides exemptions, the beneficiaries in class 2 will have smaller exemptions than those in class 1. A state may also have different exemptions within a class according to how closely the beneficiary is related to the decedent.

17-3. a. Real property is real estate and property that is permanently attached to the land. Generally, real property is taxable only by the state in which the property is located (has situs).

b. Tangible personal property is property such as cars, furniture, jewelry, and artwork. In general, tangible personal property is taxable by the state in which the property is usually kept, whether or not the state is the decedent's state of domicile.

c. Intangible personal property includes stocks, bonds, insurance policies, mortgage liens, notes, debt instruments, and the like. These kinds of property may be taxable by more than one state if the states can establish a sufficient nexus or contact with the property.

17-4. Intangible property may be subject to multiple state death taxation under the following circumstances:

- The decedent owned residences in more than one state and it is unclear which of the states was the decedent's state of domicile.
- Intangibles held in trust may be taxable by the deceased grantor's state of domicile and the trustee's state of domicile.
- Securities transferred due to the shareholder's death may be taxable by the shareholder's state of domicile and by the issuing company's state of incorporation.

Answers to Self-Test Questions

17-1.   True.

17-2.   True.

17-3.   False. Decoupling is a relatively new term used to identify the legislation of states that no longer reference state death taxation to EGTRRA 2001 for purposes of the state death tax credit and/or the applicable exclusion amount increases.

17-4.   True.

17-5.   True.

17-6.   True.

17-7.   False. While the state of domicile has a claim against all the decedent's property for state death tax purposes, the state in which the decedent's real estate is situated will impose some form of transfer tax at death. The state of domicile will probably exempt from taxation real estate owned by the decedent located outside its borders.

17-8.   True.

17-9.   True.

17-10. False. A decedent-spouse's one-half interest in community property is subject to death taxation in most of the community-property states.

17-11. False. Many states have adopted the federal government's time frame of 9 months from the date of the decedent's death for filing and paying death taxes.

Chapter 18

Answers to Mini-Cases

1.   a.   The assets includible in X's gross estate for federal estate tax purposes if he predeceases Mrs. X are as follows:

Property in his own name

One-half of partnership interest in the XY Company	$1,500,000	
Common stock	120,000	
Cash in bank	90,000	
Household furnishings and personal effects	50,000	
Municipal bonds—face amount	120,000	
One-half of real estate held as tenants in common with brother, Y	50,000	
		$1,930,000

Life insurance owned by X

Policy	Face Amount	
30-payment life	$ 10,000	
Ordinary life	120,000	
Ordinary life	150,000	
10-year term	50,000	
		$ 330,000

One-half of all property held jointly or by the entirety with Mrs. X

Personal residence	$ 175,000	
Bank checking account	6,000	
Corporate bonds (purchased in 1990)	15,000	
Automobile (purchased in 2001)	5,000	
		$ 201,000
Total value of assets included in X's gross estate		$2,461,000

   b.   CHART FOR COMPUTING FEDERAL ESTATE TAX

	STEP 1	(1)	Gross estate		$2,461,000
minus		(2)	Funeral and administration expenses (estimated as ____% of _____)	($130,000)	
		(3)	Debts and taxes	—	
		(4)	Losses	—	
			Total deductions	($130,000)	

equals	STEP 2	(5)	Adjusted gross estate		2,331,000
minus		(6)	Marital deduction*	(766,000)	
		(7)	Charitable deduction	—	
		(8)	State death tax deduction **	(65,000)	
			Total deductions	(831,000)	
equals	STEP 3	(9)	Taxable estate		1,500,000
plus		(10)	Adjusted taxable gifts (post-1976 lifetime taxable transfers not included in gross estate)	—	
equal		(11)	Tentative tax base (total of taxable estate and adjusted taxable gifts)		1,500,000
compute		(12)	Tentative tax	555,800	
minus		(13)	Gift taxes payable on post-1976 gifts	—	
equals	STEP 4	(14)	Estate tax payable before credits		555,800
minus		(15)	Tax credits		
		(a)	Applicable credit amount (2005)	(555,800)	
		(b)	Credit for foreign death taxes	—	
		(c)	Credit for gift tax for pre-1977 gifts	—	
		(d)	Credit for tax on prior transfers	—	
			Total credits	(555,800)	
equals	STEP 5	(16)	Net federal estate tax payable		0

* This amount is determined after other deductions from the adjusted gross estate. (The marital deduction is equal to the amount of all assets passing to Mrs. X, which include the entire estate less the $1.5 million partnership interest passing to the sons. All the life insurance qualifies for the marital deduction as it is payable directly to Mrs. X or X's estate and passes to her under his will or paid to her in such a way that any payments left at her death will pass to her estate.)

** State death taxes are a deduction from the adjusted gross estate after 2004.

c. First, the gift taxes paid within 3 years of death ($250,950)* would be added into the computation of the gross estate.** In addition, the assets gifted prior to death are removed from the gross estate, but the value of the gift to the daughter ($113,000, or $124,000 − $11,000) and the gifts to the sons ($1,478,000, or $1,500,000 − $22,000) are added to the taxable estate as adjusted taxable gifts. The entire gross estate now qualifies for the marital deduction (with the exception of the $250,950 gift tax gross-up amount) since all assets are passed to the spouse (the partnership interest was gifted during the decedent's lifetime). The tentative tax base is now simply the adjusted taxable gifts plus the $250,950 gift tax paid within 3 years of death.

* Note that for gift tax purposes, although X made gifts totaling $1,624,000 to his sons and daughter, the gift tax payable is based on $1,591,000 because of three $11,000 annual exclusions.

** The gross estate is calculated as follows:

Gross estate	$ 2,461,000
Less gift to sons	(1,478,000)
Less gift to daughter	(113,000)
Less gift tax paid	(250,950)
Gross estate before Sec. 2035 gross-up rule	619,050
Plus gift taxes paid within 3 years of death (Sec. 2035)	250,950
Gross estate	$ 870,000

CHART FOR COMPUTING FEDERAL ESTATE TAX

	STEP 1	(1)	Gross estate		$870,000
minus		(2)	Funeral and administration expenses (estimated as ____% of _____)	(130,000)	
		(3)	Debts and taxes	—	
		(4)	Losses	—	
			Total deductions	($130,000)	

equals	STEP 2	(5)	Adjusted gross estate		740,000
minus		(6)	Marital deduction*	(477,050)	
		(7)	Charitable deduction	—	
		(8)	State death tax deduction**	(12,000)	
			Total deductions	($489,050)	

* The $250,950 of gift taxes paid does not qualify for the marital deduction.
** State death taxes are a deduction from the adjusted gross estate after 2004.

equals	STEP 3	(9)	Taxable estate		250,950
plus		(10)	Adjusted taxable gifts (post-1976 lifetime taxable transfers not included in gross estate)		1,591,000
equal		(11)	Tentative tax base (total of taxable estate and adjusted taxable gifts)		1,841,950
compute		(12)	Tentative tax	709,678	
minus		(13)	Gift taxes payable on post-1976 gifts	(250,950)	
equals	STEP 4	(14)	Estate tax payable before credits		458,728
minus		(15)	Tax credits		
			(a) Applicable credit amount (2005)	(555,800)	
			(b) Credit for foreign death taxes	—	
			(c) Credit for gift tax for pre-1977 gifts	—	
			(d) Credit for tax on prior transfers	—	
			Total credits	($555,800)	
equals	STEP 5	(16)	Net federal estate tax payable		$ 0

2. a. The assets includible in Emily's gross estate for federal estate tax purposes are the following:

Checking account	$ 20,000
Money market funds	340,000
Common stock (one-half)	300,000
Personal residence	450,000
401(k) plan benefit	600,000
Household furnishings	30,000
Automobile	15,000
QTIP trust	750,000
Total value of assets included in Emily's gross estate	$2,505,000

The personal residence is included in Emily's gross estate under Sec. 2036 since Emily retained a life interest in the property at death.

b. CHART FOR COMPUTING FEDERAL ESTATE TAX

	STEP 1	(1)	Gross estate		$2,505,000
minus		(2)	Funeral and administration expenses (estimated as ____% of _____)	(125,000)	
		(3)	Debts and taxes	(75,000)	
		(4)	Losses	—	
			Total deductions	(200,000)	
equals	STEP 2	(5)	Adjusted gross estate		$2,305,000
minus		(6)	Marital deduction	—	
		(7)	Charitable deduction	(500,000)	
		(8)	State death tax deduction (after 2004)	(60,000)	
			Total deductions	($560,000)	

equals	STEP 3	(9)	Taxable estate		1,745,000
plus		(10)	Adjusted taxable gifts (post-1976 lifetime taxable transfers not included in gross estate)	—	
equal		(11)	Tentative tax base (total of taxable estate and adjusted taxable gifts)		1,745,000
compute		(12)	Tentative tax	666,050	
minus		(13)	Gift taxes payable on post-1976 gifts	—	
equals	STEP 4	(14)	Estate tax payable before credits		666,050
minus		(15)	Tax credits		
			(a) Applicable credit amount (2005)	555,800	
			(b) Credit for foreign death taxes	—	
			(c) Credit for gift tax for pre-1977 gifts	—	
			(d) Credit for tax on prior transfers	—	
			Total credits	($555,800)	
equals	STEP 5	(16)	Net federal estate tax payable		$ 110,250

Answers to Review Questions

18-1. Once the taxable estate is determined, the amount of adjusted taxable gifts made after 1976 is added to the taxable estate. The result is the tentative tax base.

18-2. Federal estate tax is computed by subtracting certain allowable deductions from the gross estate to arrive at the adjusted gross estate; then other deductions may be taken to find the taxable estate. Any adjusted taxable gifts (post-1976 taxable gifts that are not included in the gross estate) are added to the taxable estate to form the tentative tax base. A tentative tax is derived by multiplying the tentative tax base rate by an applicable rate found in the gift and estate tax rate schedule. Any gift taxes payable (in excess of the applicable credit amount in the year of the decedent's death) after 1976 may then be subtracted from the tentative tax. The tentative tax may also be reduced by certain credits. The most notable credit is the federal estate tax applicable credit amount, which is $555,800 in 2005.

   In Mr. Bowden's case $100,000 of funeral and administration costs and $25,000 in accrued taxes may be subtracted from the gross estate of $2,300,000. The adjusted gross estate is $2,175,000, from which the estate of Mr. Bowden is entitled to subtract a marital deduction for property passing to a surviving spouse in a qualifying manner. In this case, the marital deduction is $625,000—the amount left outright to his surviving spouse. Mr. Bowden's estate may also deduct $50,000 of state death taxes (after 2004). The taxable estate is $1.5 million. Since Mr. Bowden made no taxable lifetime gifts, the tentative tax base consists solely of the taxable estate of $1.5 million. Applying the appropriate tax rate, the tentative tax is $555,800 (2005). The tentative tax may be reduced by any gift taxes payable after December 31, 1976 (there are none here), and, thus, the estate tax payable before credits is also $555,800.

18-3. After the tentative tax is determined, gift taxes generated by taxable gifts made after 1976 in excess of the applicable credit amount are subtracted from this figure. The determination of the amount of reduction allowable because of taxes attributable to post-1976 taxable gifts is made through the following steps:
   1. Total all post-1976 taxable gifts.
   2. Compute the gift tax payable by applying the tax rate schedule in effect at the decedent's death to the total taxable gifts. In other words, all the post-1976 taxable gifts are treated as if they were made at one time—the date of the decedent's death.
   3. Reduce the gift tax payable by the applicable credit amount for the year of the decedent's death (for example, $121,800 for 1985; $192,800 for 1987 through 1997; $202,500 for 1998; $211,300 for 1999; $220,550 for 2000 and 2001; $345,800 for 2002 and 2003; $555,800 for 2004 and 2005; $780,800 for 2006, 2007, and 2008; $1,455,800 for 2009; repealed for the year 2010).
   4. If the gift tax payable exceeds the applicable credit amount, subtract the excess from the tentative tax.
   The result is the estate tax payable before credits.

18-4. Once the estate tax is computed, there are four possible credits after 2004 that may be applied against the tax to arrive at the net federal estate tax payable. As with income tax credits, these credits are allowed as a dollar-for-dollar reduction of the estate tax. They are the

- applicable credit amount
- credit for foreign death taxes
- credit for gift tax paid on pre-1977 gifts
- credit for taxes paid on prior transfers

18-5. The net federal estate tax payable on Sam's estate is calculated as follows:

Gross estate	$3,320,000
Less administration expenses and debts	(140,000)
Adjusted gross estate	3,180,000
Less charitable deduction	(250,000)
Less state death taxes	(70,000)
Taxable estate	2,860,000
Plus adjusted taxable gifts	60,000
Tentative tax base	2,920,000
Tentative tax ($780,800 + 47% x $920,000)	1,213,200
Less gift taxes payable on post-1976 gifts	0
Estate tax payable before credits	1,213,200
Less applicable credit amount (in 2005)	(555,800)
Net federal estate tax payable	$ 657,400

18-6. The estate and gift tax credit came into existence for estates of decedents dying after December 31, 1976. The term *unified credit* was adopted under the 1976 Act because the credit may be used as an offset against gift taxes as well as estate taxes. Actually, the credit must first be used to offset gift taxes on lifetime transfers. Any remaining credit is applied as a credit against the federal estate tax.

After 1997, the unified credit became known as the *applicable credit amount*, and it increases incrementally until 2010. The credit for 2002 and 2003 is $345,800, and the applicable exclusion amount (credit equivalent) is $1 million. Under EGTRRA 2001, the applicable credit amount and applicable exclusion amount do not increase for gift tax purposes as they do for estate taxation—for gift taxation, the credit remains at $345,800 and the exclusion at $1 million.

18-7. There is a credit allowed against the federal estate tax for taxes actually paid by the decedent's estate to any foreign country for any estate, inheritance, legacy, or succession taxes. The purpose of the *credit for foreign death taxes* is to prevent double taxation. It is allowable only to the estate of a decedent who was either (1) a citizen of the United States or (2) a resident of the United States who was not a citizen at the time of death. Nonresident aliens are denied the foreign death tax credit. The credit exists for taxes actually paid by the decedent's estate to any foreign country, U.S. possession, or political subdivision of a foreign state.

18-8. a. No, state death taxes are not a credit after 2004. Tom Grigson's estate will be able to deduct the entire amount of $150,000 in state inheritance taxes from the adjusted gross estate.

   b. A credit for tax in prior transfers is permitted when the first decedent dies less than 10 years before the second decedent. In this case, the property was inherited 3 years before the death of the second decedent. Under these circumstances, the credit is limited to 80 percent of the taxes paid in the first decedent's estate.

18-9. Gift tax payable on post-1976 gifts becomes part of the computation for determining estate tax liability under the gift and estate tax system, as explained earlier. Therefore, no separate credit is allowed for taxes attributable to these gifts. However, a credit still exists for federal gift tax paid by a decedent on taxable gifts made before 1977 if the property is included in the gross estate.

18-10. Circumstances may arise in which a decedent has inherited property from someone who died less than 10 years before the decedent's death or within 2 years following the decedent's death and the property transferred to the decedent was already taxable in the estate of the transferor-decedent. To avoid double taxation on double transfers of property occurring within a reasonably short time period (that is, 10 years before or 2 years after the decedent's death), a credit is allowed against the federal estate tax paid by the present decedent as a result of this inherited property inclusion in the decedent's gross estate.

18-11. a. The applicable credit amount for estate tax purposes currently available (2005) is $555,800. However, the equivalent value of the estate credit amount in 2005 is $1.5 million. George Jessup's gross estate is $1,375,000, or $125,000 less than the equivalent value required to file an estate tax return. Therefore, the executor of the estate is not required to file an estate tax return.

b. Jim's gross estate is valued at $1,725,000, which is $225,000 more than the applicable exclusion amount in 2005. It means that Jim's executor must file a federal estate tax return. Since the requirement for filing is based on the gross estate (plus adjusted taxable gifts), the fact that Jim's estate has $100,000 of debt deductions is not pertinent for filing purposes. The $100,000 of deductions is, of course, important in that the $100,000 will be deducted from the gross estate of $1,725,000, which will reduce the estate value to $1,625,000. Even when no federal estate tax is payable, an estate tax return must still be filed as required under certain circumstances.

18-12. A primary duty of the personal representative is to file the federal estate tax return when due and to see that estate taxes are timely paid. The personal representative must also timely file any estate income tax returns when they are due. If the estate is sizable enough to warrant filing a federal estate tax return, the return is due and the tax is payable no later than 9 months after the decedent's death unless an extension is granted.

18-13. There are mitigating circumstances that the IRS will accept for granting an extension of time to pay the estate tax. An extension for up to 12 months to pay the estate tax will be granted if the Internal Revenue Service determines there is reasonable cause.

18-14. There is a special provision that allows the personal representative to elect a deferral for payment of estate tax attributable to the inclusion of a closely held business or farm business in the decedent's gross estate if certain conditions are met (IRC Sec. 6166). The law provides that an executor may be able to elect to defer payment of estate tax attributable to inclusion in the estate of a farm or other closely held business if that business consists of more than 35 percent of the adjusted gross estate. If the estate qualifies, such an election is made at the sole discretion of the estate's personal representative.

To determine whether more than 35 percent of the adjusted gross estate is made up of a closely held business or farm, the *adjusted gross estate* is defined as the gross estate reduced by deductible debts, expenses, claims, and losses, but before reduction by the marital or charitable deductions (IRC Sec. 6166(b)(6)).

For purposes of the 35 percent rule, an *interest in a closely held business* is defined as (1) an interest in a proprietorship, (2) an interest in a partnership carrying on a trade or business with no more than 45 partners or where 20 percent or more of its assets helped determine the decedent's gross estate, or (3) stock in a corporation with no more than 15 shareholders or where 20 percent of its voting stock is included in the decedent's gross estate. Property owned by a corporation, partnership, estate, or trust is regarded as owned proportionately by its shareholders, partners, or beneficiaries. In addition, for purposes of this election, interests in two or more closely held businesses are treated as a single closely held business if 20 percent or more of the total value of each business is included in the decedent's gross estate. Also, all stock and partnership interests belonging to a decedent and any family members will be aggregated in order to meet the requirements of stock ownership.

18-15. a. If requirements are met to qualify for installment payment of tax, the executor may elect to defer payment of tax as a matter of right. The estate tax value of the closely held business must comprise more than 35 percent of the adjusted gross estate. Albert's adjusted gross estate is $1,700,000 and the partnership interest is $450,000, which is less than 35 percent of the adjusted gross estate. Therefore, the executor cannot elect deferred payment of estate tax. However, there is a discretionary extension allowed by the IRS for one year and up to 10 years if the executor can show reasonable cause to extend time for the payment. Because of the liquidity problem, the estate could probably qualify for a delayed payment of tax under the Code if reasonable cause exists. Granting an extension for reasonable cause is at the discretion of the IRS.

b. Benjamin's adjusted gross estate was $1,725,000 and the stock in the closely held corporation was valued at $700,000, which is more than 35 percent of the adjusted gross estate. Therefore, the executor has a right to elect to extend tax payment attributable to the closely held stock over a 14-year deferral period. Interest at the rate of only 2 percent will be due for the first 4 years, with equal annual installments of interest and principal payable beginning in the fifth year and continuing over the following 10-year period, unless certain changes occur that would cause acceleration of the tax. (*Note:* Prior to the Taxpayer Relief Act of 1997, the special interest rate was 4 percent. The act, however, provided that for decedents dying after 1997, the special interest rate of 2 percent applies when a Sec. 6166 election is made and the estate qualifies for the installment payment of estate taxes.)

18-16. The events that cause acceleration are
- late payment or failure to pay any individual installment
- withdrawal of 50 percent or more of the assets (including cash and property) from the business

- distribution, sale, exchange, or disposition of 50 percent or more of the value of the business interest to anyone other than a beneficiary who is entitled to receive the interest under the decedent's will or trust or under state intestacy laws

18-17. Sec. 303 of the Code allows a redemption of stock for the purpose of paying funeral and administrative expenses and death taxes without the redemption being treated as a dividend. If the redemption qualifies, it is treated as a sale, and the gain is treated as capital gain if the stock was held as a capital asset in the hands of the decedent at the time of the exchange. In order to qualify for capital-gains treatment under this section, the decedent's stock must represent more than 35 percent of the adjusted gross estate. Ownership of 20 percent or more of the stock of each of two or more corporations may be aggregated to satisfy this 35 percent test.

Answers to Self-Test Questions

18-1. True.

18-2. True.

18-3. True.

18-4. True.

18-5. False. There are essentially four credits that may be taken against the tax. These credits reduce the federal estate tax on a dollar-for-dollar basis after the tax rates have been applied to the sum of the taxable estate plus adjusted taxable post-1976 gifts.

18-6. False. The applicable credit amount is applicable to lifetime and/or testamentary transfers and only one such credit is available.

18-7. True.

18-8. False. A federal estate tax return need not be filed for gross estates plus adjusted taxable gifts valued at less than an amount equal to the applicable exclusion amount in the year the decedent died. If the gross estate plus adjusted taxable gifts exceeds the applicable exclusion amount that would be exempt because of the applicable credit amount available in the year of death, the personal representative must file a federal estate tax return no later than 9 months after the date of the decedent's death.

18-9. False. An executor must file a Form 4768 for a 6-month extension of time to file the federal estate tax return. It is not necessarily a mandatory extension.

18-10. True.

18-11. True.

18-12. False. The law provides that an executor may elect to defer payment of federal estate tax attributable to the inclusion of a closely held business or farm in the decedent's gross estate for up to 14 years if the business or farm comprises more than 35 percent of the adjusted gross estate.

18-13. False. The election must be made with the estate tax return by the decedent's executor.

18-14. True.

18-15. True.

18-16. True.

18-17. True.

18-18. True.

18-19. False. Redemption of stock that was includible in the decedent's estate for the purpose of paying death taxes will be treated as a sale or exchange and taxed as a capital gain if the stock represents more than 35 percent of the decedent's adjusted gross estate.

18-20. True.

Chapter 19

Answers to Review Questions

19-1. The main function of basis is to measure gain or loss when property is sold, exchanged, or transferred in a taxable transaction.

19-2. The basis of property transferred at death in this case would be stepped up to the date-of-death basis as follows:

IBM shares $ 80,000 ($80 x 1,000)
Real estate   200,000

19-3.   a. Property transferred at death acquires a new basis increased or decreased to the fair market value of the asset on the date of death. Here the property's basis in the estate would be stepped down to $75,000, since the value declined from the time the asset was acquired from the decedent.

   b. | Auction price | $90,000 |
       |---|---|
       | Less basis | (75,000) |
       | Gain | $15,000 |

19-4.   *Income in respect of a decedent* is any income that the decedent was entitled to (but did not receive) while alive. The income is includible at full value for estate tax purposes. It is then also taxed to the beneficiary of the income as ordinary income for income tax purposes. However, the beneficiary is allowed an income tax deduction for the additional estate tax paid due to the IRD being included in the gross estate. The stepped-up-basis rules do not apply to income that is included in the decedent's gross estate as income in respect of a decedent (IRD).

19-5.   a. Tom's basis in the shares is $10 a share because of the one-year rule.

   The stepped-up-basis-at-death rule is ignored under certain circumstances. The rule does not apply when appreciated property is acquired by the decedent by gift within one year before death if, upon death, the property then passes directly or indirectly back to the original donor or the original donor's spouse.

   b. Tom's son's basis in the shares is $50 a share because the transfer was not to the original donor of the shares and, therefore, is outside of the one-year rule.

19-6.   Sam does not realize either a gain or a loss on the sale. The property could have been sold for any price between $40,000 and $80,000 without Sam realizing a gain or a loss.

19-7.   The basis for the sale is $262,500, computed as follows:
$700,000 (amount realized) ÷ $1,600,000 (fair market value) = .4375 x $600,000 (basis) = $262,500

Answers to Self-Test Questions

19-1.   True.

19-2.   False. If property passes to another because the decedent exercised a testamentary general power of appointment, the property subject to the power is included in the decedent's gross estate and thereby receives a step-up in basis to fair market value.

19-3.   True.

19-4.   False. When an asset is transferred at death, the asset will always be treated as if it was held more than 12 months when it is subsequently sold.

19-5.   False. When property is transferred by gift, the donee has a carryover basis, which is the same as the basis in the hands of the donor but increased by the amount of any gift taxes paid.

19-6.   True.

Chapter 20

Answers to Review Questions

20-1.   An estate is a tax-paying entity that comes into being when a taxpayer dies for the purpose of effectuating the orderly, legal transfer of the decedent's property.

20-2.   A decedent's estate exists for a limited period of time—typically 1 to 3 years.

20-3.   Estates and trusts have many similarities.
   - Both administer property in a fiduciary capacity.
   - Property is transferred from the decedent to the estate in a manner similar to the transfer of property by a grantor to a trust.
   - Both decedents and grantors are responsible for the creation of the estate or trust.
   - Beneficiaries of an estate have a relationship to the estate similar to that of the beneficiaries of a trust.

20-4.   Estates and trusts have some important differences. An estate comes into existence involuntarily by operation of law upon the decedent's death. A living trust is created intentionally and voluntarily by a specific action of the grantor. Estates exist for a limited time period. Trusts generally exist for many years and possibly span more than one generation.

   The primary function of many trusts is to provide sound, professional asset management. The trustee's primary duty is to be a good manager. Whether an individual or institution, the trustee will be in charge of the management of the trust property for the duration of the trust.

On the other hand, an estate serves as a temporary receptacle for assets pending distribution to the new owners. The personal representative functions primarily as a liquidator who must marshal the decedent's assets, advertise the estate for the benefit of creditors, and pay its debts, expenses, and taxes. The personal representative must settle any claims against the estate and has a duty to keep the property income producing until its distribution.

Another significant difference between the two entities is their relationship to the court. An estate is created by operation of law and is supervised by the court until it is terminated. A trust, on the other hand, is generally a private arrangement.

20-5. Trusts and estates are subject to the same rate of income taxation. However, they are subject to a slightly different computational system of taxation than are individuals, corporations, or partnerships, because they exist for the benefit of others. If Congress had chosen to tax estates and trusts in a manner similar to corporations, double taxation would have resulted. If taxed like a corporation, the trust or estate would be taxed on income earned during its taxable year. Beneficiaries would then be treated as shareholders who would be taxed on the distribution when received, just as dividends are taxable to shareholders in the year received.

Alternatively, if a trust or estate was taxed as a partnership, all income would be passed through to the individual beneficiaries in a manner similar to the way it is passed to partners. Using this method would be detrimental in cases where the grantor did not intend beneficiaries to be entitled to the income automatically. Taxation as a partnership would defeat the right of the grantor to give the trustee discretion to accumulate or distribute income. Also, a personal representative of an estate does not have a duty to distribute income before the estate makes final distribution to the beneficiaries. Under the theory of partnership taxation, a beneficiary would pay tax on amounts not yet received.

20-6. An executor or administrator has the duty to file two different types of income tax returns for a decedent—a decedent's last life return and an estate's income tax return.

A deceased taxpayer's tax year ends with the date of death. The return must be filed by the regular due date, April 15, of the following year. The amounts of income and deductible expenses that must be reported depend on the deceased taxpayer's regular method of accounting.

For cash-basis taxpayers, only income actually or constructively received must be reported. Deductions can be taken only for expenses that were actually paid during the decedent's lifetime. If the decedent was on the accrual method, the return will show all income and deductions accrued through the date of death.

20-7. If income in respect of a decedent is included in the decedent's gross estate for estate tax purposes, the estate tax attributable to the inclusion of those income items in the estate will be deductible by the recipient of the income as and when it is received.

20-8. Exemptions available to a trust are
   a. an estate—$600
   b. a simple trust—$300
   c. a complex trust—$100

20-9. The only beneficiaries who do not pay income tax on distributions of income from estates are those who receive specific bequests under the will in three installments or less. Therefore, beneficiaries are taxed on payments from income in four or more installments.

20-10. The income-first rule requires that all distributions be made first out of income. Since the estate received $15,000 of income and made a distribution of $25,000 to its beneficiary, the beneficiary would be taxed upon receipt of $15,000 of income and receive a nontaxable distribution of corpus in the amount of $10,000. The estate will receive a deduction for the $15,000 of income distribution. The distribution of corpus is neither deductible to the estate nor taxable to the beneficiary.

20-11. Estates are permitted to have a fiscal income tax year, rather than being restricted to a calendar year. By carefully selecting the estate's fiscal year for reporting the estate's income and giving consideration to the timing of distributions of estate income to estate beneficiaries, the beneficiary's payment of the tax on the income earned by the estate can be delayed by years.

20-12. a. The essential concept of trust taxation is that trust income is taxed once, either (1) to the beneficiary(ies) or (2) to the trustee. If a trustee is required to distribute the entire income of the trust annually, that income is taxed to the recipient(s). However, some trusts authorize the accumulation of all or part of the income at the trustee's discretion. The tax law does not tax prospective beneficiaries on amounts they may never receive.

b. The trustee is taxed on income accumulated by the trust. In essence the taxation of trust income can be capsulized thus: Income that is accumulated by the trust is taxable to the trust; income that is payable to the beneficiary is taxable to the beneficiary; and income either accumulated or distributed by a grantor trust is taxable to the grantor.

20-13. a. Five years ago the trust was a simple trust.

b. Four years ago the trust was a complex trust since it made a gift to a qualified charity that year.

c. Three years ago the trust was a complex trust since it accumulated $5,000 of income.

d. Two years ago the trust was a complex trust because it made a distribution from corpus in addition to distributing all the income earned that year.

e. Last year the trust was a simple trust because all the income earned was distributable to the beneficiary.

20-14. a. The concept of DNI is used to achieve three main results:

- First, it provides a limit on the deduction that a trust or estate may receive for amounts distributed to beneficiaries.

- Second, it limits the amount of distribution that may be taxable to the beneficiaries.

- Third, it establishes the character of the amounts taxable to the beneficiaries.

b. When there is more than one beneficiary, each is taxed on his or her share of DNI. When special items are distributed (such as tax-exempt interest, dividends, and so forth), a beneficiary is considered to have received a proportionate share unless the trust agreement earmarks a particular type of income for a specified beneficiary.

20-15. One function of DNI is to ensure that the character of the amounts in the hands of a beneficiary is the same as that in the hands of a trust or estate. Therefore, if dividends are received by a trust and distributed to a beneficiary, the dividends retain their character as dividends.

Likewise, if the trust receives tax-free income (such as from a municipal bond), the income remains tax free in the hands of the beneficiary.

20-16. Although the total tax-exempt interest is $18,000, with $15,000 distributable to the beneficiary and $3,000 left in the trust, neither the beneficiary nor the trust will be subject to tax on their respective sums since the interest is tax exempt.

20-17. In the case of a grantor trust, the trust is disregarded for income tax purposes and all income, deductions, and credits attributable to any portion of a trust declared a grantor trust are taken into account directly on the grantor's individual income tax return.

20-18. The grantor-trust rules also apply if the spouse of the grantor, living with the grantor at the time of creation of the interest, is given any of the proscribed powers that invoke the grantor-trust rules.

20-19. The trust income is treated as unearned income of minors under age 14. The net unearned income of the trust is determined as follows:

Sheila's unearned income	
Less the sum of (2005)	$1,700
a. the standard deduction, as indexed for inflation	(800)
b. $800, as indexed for inflation (taxed at child's rate)	(800)
Net unearned income to be taxed at the parents' highest marginal bracket	$ 100

20-20. Because the Revenue Reconciliation Act of 1993 imposes the higher tax rates on trusts and estates having taxable income at lower thresholds than individuals are subject to, the use of separate or multiple trusts for the purpose of saving income taxes often results in only nominal savings.

It is possible to create several trusts for the same or different beneficiaries. If the tax law recognizes the existence of multiple trusts, then the income is taxed separately to each trust, which means that each trust receives a separate exemption, and each trust is treated as a separate tax entity for all income tax purposes. Conversely, if multiple trusts are considered by the IRS to be one trust, only one exemption is allowed. All the trusts are treated as one entity for income tax purposes.

20-21. As stated above the Revenue Reconciliation Act of 1993 has clearly diminished the advantages of income accumulation trusts. Since trusts and estates are taxed at the higher rate brackets for taxable income at lower threshold amounts than individuals are taxed, it is likely that many beneficiaries will be in a lower tax bracket than the trusts benefiting them.

20-22. Authorizing a trustee to purchase life insurance on the lives of the beneficiaries can yield some limited benefits under current income tax law. Suppose one of the trust beneficiaries has a significant amount of taxable income this year and is already in a high marginal tax bracket. Suppose also that the trust has taxable income that will be taxed in one of the lower marginal tax brackets. If the trustee distributes the trust income to the beneficiary, it will be taxed at the beneficiary's higher rate, leaving less for the beneficiary to purchase life insurance and pay premiums. If, however, the trust itself purchases the life insurance and pays the premiums with the income, more income is available for the purchase and premium payments because of the trust's exemption and lower income tax bracket.

20-23. a. One of the principles of proper tax planning is that income should be divided among family members whenever possible in order to lower the rate at which the income will be taxed as well as to take advantage of the multiple individual personal exemptions. Tax savings may be accomplished with more flexibility if the trustee is authorized, rather than mandated, to pay income to trust beneficiaries at the trustee's discretion. The trustee can then allocate income among the family members in any manner that seems desirable from tax year to tax year. In exercising that discretion, the trustee would consider the individual needs of the various beneficiaries, the ultimate use to which the income would be put, and the collective as well as individual tax burdens.

b. There are also nontax advantages to clauses that sprinkle income according to needs. An example is a testator who wants to provide for the family of a deceased child but does not want to pay income for the lifetime of a deceased child's spouse. The testator may fear that if the surviving spouse remarries, income will go to the new spouse or the new spouse's children rather than to the testator's grandchildren. The sprinkle clause in a trust enables a trustee to pay income to the spouse only as long as the children are young or have varying needs and as long as the spouse does not remarry.

20-24. If trust income is used to support a dependent, that income will be taxed to the person who is obligated to provide the support. In a trust with a sprinkle clause, to the extent that the trustee applies income for the support of a minor, the IRS may attempt to tax this income to the parent. Obligation to support means the duty imposed by law to support another person.

20-25. If the trustee is authorized in his sole discretion to use a portion of the trust income to purchase life insurance on Harris's life, the trust income used to pay premiums will be taxed to the trust. It should be noted that Harris is a life income beneficiary of a trust created by his father and not the grantor of the trust. To the extent the income is used to pay premiums, it will not be distributed to Harris and, therefore, will not be included in Harris's gross income for income tax purposes. This result may be an advantage if Harris is already in a relatively high income tax bracket and has a sizable estate of his own.

Answers to Self-Test Questions

20-1.   True.

20-2.   False. While testamentary trusts are trusts created under a will and do not become funded until the creator dies, there are other kinds of trusts that are created during lifetime. (Also see chapter 6.)

20-3.   False. Trusts and estates are separate taxpaying entities and are not taxed under a conduit theory of taxation. To the extent income earned by the trust or estate is retained, it is taxed to the trust or estate. Any income distributed is deductible by the trust or estate and taxable to the recipient of the income.

20-4.   False. Income in respect of a decedent is an asset of the estate because the decedent was entitled to receive it had he or she lived. However, when the income is finally received, it is taxable for income tax purposes to the recipient of the income. There is, however, an income tax deduction allowed for any estate tax payable because the income in respect of a decedent was included in the gross estate.

20-5.   True.

20-6.   False. Estates get an income tax exemption of $600, but trusts receive an exemption of $100 if they are classified as complex trusts or $300 if they are classified as simple trusts.

20-7.   True.

20-8.   False. By definition, income from revocable trusts is taxable to the grantor since the grantor has the power to alter, amend, revoke, or terminate the trust. Irrevocable trusts may be separate taxpaying entities if trust income may be and is accumulated rather than distributed.

20-9.   True.

20-10. True.

20-11. False. Distributable net income is a concept that has been developed for the following purposes:

- It limits the deduction a trust may receive for amounts distributed to beneficiaries.
- It limits the amount of distribution that may be taxable to the beneficiaries.
- It establishes the character of the amounts taxable to the beneficiaries.

20-12. False. A revocable trust is treated as a grantor trust for tax purposes, and the trust's income continues to be taxed to the grantor.

20-13. False. The grantor is deemed to hold any interest held by a spouse living with the grantor when the interest is created. Thus, the reversionary interest causes the grantor-trust rules to apply, and the grantor is taxed on the trust's income.

20-14. True.

20-15. False. Although a trust has multiple beneficiaries, each beneficiary is taxed only on the amount of income received under the sharing concept.

20-16. True.

20-17. True.

20-18. False. If trust income is used to satisfy a grantor's legal support obligation, the trust income will be taxed to the grantor to the extent it is so used.

Chapter 21

Answers to Review Questions

21-1. Imposition of the GSTT results when a taxable transfer is made to a transferee who is more than one generation level below the generation level of the transferor. The GSTT applies only if a generation is "skipped" by the estate and gift tax system.

21-2. The $1.5 million GSTT exemption (2004 and 2005) is the most basic exemption that every taxpayer is entitled to make in the aggregate for transfers up to and including that amount without having to pay GSTT. Although the Code provides allocation rules of the GSTT exemption, by electing not to have the automatic rules apply, the allocation of the exemption is according to the transferor's wishes as it may be utilized partially or fully during lifetime and/or at death.

21-3. A gift in trust qualifies for the GSTT annual exclusion if it provides a present interest or Crummey withdrawal power. Also, the trust must limit distributions of income and corpus to a single beneficiary and must provide that the corpus be included in the beneficiary's estate should he or she die prior to the trust's termination.

21-4. Direct education tuition payments are an excellent gift for grandparents to make to a grandchild since they are not subject to gift tax, GSTT tax, and do not reduce either annual exclusion gifts or the GSTT exemption. The same rules apply for direct medical payments.

21-5. The irrevocable life insurance trust provides an opportunity for a grantor to affirmatively allocate the GSTT exemption to premium gifts to the trust. It should be used when beneficiaries are (or are likely to include) grandchildren. The exemption allocated in this way gives the grantor the opportunity to leverage the exemption since all proceeds will be exempt from GSTT if the premiums are sheltered by allocating the exemption to them on a timely filed gift tax return. Annual Crummey powers should shelter the premiums from gift tax if the annual gift tax exclusion is not exceeded.

21-6. Any exemption not used at the time of the taxpayer's death and not made by the taxpayer's executor is allocated according to the default rules. The unused portion of the decedent's GSTT exemption at the time of death is allocated under the following priorities:

- First, the exemption is applied to a direct skip of property (a specific outright bequest or devise of property) occurring at the individual's death.
- Second, the exemption is allocated to trusts in which the decedent is treated as the transferor and from which a taxable GSTT event might occur after the individual's death.

These rules provide that the exemption is allocated ratably to the priority list above based on the nonexempt portion of the properties included in such bequests or trusts. The nonexempt portion of such bequests is the amount of the property to which the $1.5 million (2004 and 2005) GSTT exemption has not been previously allocated.

Answers to Self-Test Questions

21-1. False. The GSTT is imposed at a flat rate equal to the highest marginal estate or gift tax rate rather than a progressive set of rates.

21-2. False. The GSTT is applicable to transfers that are also subject to estate or gift taxes. Thus, a gift to a grandchild could be subject to both GSTT and gift tax.

21-3. True.

21-4. False. The applicable credit amount provided for estate or gift tax is not available for generation-skipping transfers. However, there is a lifetime and testamentary cumulative GSTT exemption for such transfers.

21-5. True.

21-6. False. The annual exclusion for GSTT is more restrictive than the gift tax annual exclusion for generation-skipping gifts in trust. Such gifts will be permitted an annual exclusion for GSTT purposes only if the trust limits distribution of income and corpus to a single beneficiary and provides that the corpus will be included in the estate of the beneficiary if he or she dies prior to the termination of the trust.

21-7. True.

21-8. False. The GSTT is calculated by an unusual process that is very different from the gift and estate tax calculation. The applicable GSTT rate of 48 percent (in 2004) is multiplied by an inclusion ratio that is determined by a formula.

21-9. True.

21-10. False. The IRS allocates the exemption by mechanical default rules, and the actual tax results may be less than optimal.

21-11. True.

Chapter 22

Answers to Review Questions

22-1. a. For a seller, an installment sale of property can provide both income tax and estate tax benefits. If installment reporting is available, the gain on the sale of property in exchange for an installment note will be delayed and recognized gradually over the installment period. Thus, it is possible to sell highly appreciated property without immediate recognition of the full taxable gain. On the other hand, the ability to elect out of installment reporting provides the taxpayer with the possibility of recognizing all taxable gain immediately. For example, a seller may elect to recognize all gain at the time of an installment sale in a year when the taxpayer either has little other income or shows a loss for income tax purposes. Reporting the gain immediately on an installment sale could prevent the seller from wasting other deductions and tax benefits. The flexibility of an installment sale's reporting rules permits a seller to defer gain recognition and, to some degree, plan the timing of gain recognition on the sale of property.

The installment sale also provides estate tax saving possibilities for the seller. The installment sale, a particularly useful device for family estate planning, may be used when a senior family member wishes to pass property on to a successor in the family.

       b. From the buyer's standpoint, the installment sale permits the buyer to defer some or all of the principal payments on the sale. This is particularly important for buyers without the funds for the entire purchase price.

Interest paid by a buyer on an installment sale is potentially deductible for income tax purposes. Thus, it might be to the benefit of the buyer to recharacterize some of the purchase payment as interest if the interest on the transaction is deductible.

On the other hand, the buyer may wish to minimize the interest element of the installment sale if the interest is nondeductible. Under these circumstances, it may be more advantageous for the buyer to characterize the payments as principal. The additional amount of principal will provide the buyer with a higher basis, which may be available for depreciation deductions at a later date. Certainly the interest rate might be a consideration in the negotiation process for the installment sale.

22-2. The taxable amount of each installment is calculated as follows:

$$\text{amount of payment} \times \frac{\text{gross profit}}{\text{total contract price}}$$

Thus, 3/4 (75,000 ÷ 100,000) of each payment will be reported as gain in the year received.

year 1 3/4 x 20,000 = 15,000 gain reported
year 2 3/4 x 20,000 = 15,000 gain reported

year   3 3/4 x 20,000 = 15,000 gain reported
year   4 3/4 x 20,000 = 15,000 gain reported
year   5 3/4 x 20,000 = 15,000 gain reported

    There will also be an interest component attributed to the deferred installments, but these facts and the material in the text do not provide enough information to calculate the interest required.

22-3.   For estate planning purposes, an installment sale is one method of "freezing" the seller's estate and shifting the appreciation potential to a junior family member. If performed properly, and if the installment note is equal to the fair market value of the property at the time of the sale, the installment sale shifts the postsale appreciation to the junior family member without any transfer taxes being payable on the transferred property.

22-4.   If the arrangement is a fair, bona fide, arm's-length sale made for fair market value, there will be no gift tax consequences.

22-5.   Because a SCIN cancels automatically at the death of the seller, there is nothing left to be included in the seller's estate if he or she dies during the term. Through the use of the SCIN, a senior family member can transfer property to the next generation, which may result in a substantially discounted purchase price for the junior family–member purchaser and the receipt of significantly less in net proceeds for the senior family member–seller. This arrangement may remove appreciated property from the seller's estate and reduce the seller's transfer taxes.

22-6.   The buyer of a SCIN has to pay a price in excess of the fair market value for the sale property because the risk of a premature death and loss of remaining installment payments is born by the seller.

22-7.   A private annuity is a sale of property, such as a family business, in exchange for the buyer's agreement to make periodic payments of a specified sum for the remainder of the seller's life. In a private annuity, no further payments are due when the seller dies. Thus, there is nothing to include in the estate of a seller who dies holding a private annuity. For estate tax purposes, the private annuity terminates at the seller-annuitant's death and no amount of the annuity is included in the seller's estate. (Of course, any annuity payments received by the seller that are not consumed before the seller's death are included in the seller's estate.) Any appreciation in the property after the exchange escapes gift or estate taxation.

22-8.   If a private annuity is not properly valued and a gift is present, the seller-annuitant will have inclusion of the property in his or her gross estate under the retained life interest rules of Sec. 2036.

22-9.   A GRAT is an irrevocable trust in which the grantor retains the right to receive fixed amounts payable at least annually from the trust. Thus, the grantor can gift property to a trust and retain a fixed annuity for life or for a period of years. A fixed annuity is a stated annual dollar amount or a stated percentage of the initial value of the trust property.

    A GRUT is an irrevocable trust in which the grantor retains the right to receive amounts payable at least annually that are a fixed percentage of the trust's assets as valued annually. Thus, the grantor retains a variable annuity and the annual payout is based on the value that the trust grows (or contracts) to each year.

22-10.   The irrevocable transfer of the remainder interest in the GRAT or GRUT is a current gift for gift tax purposes. Since the gift provides a future interest to the donees, the gift does not qualify for the annual exclusion. However, the gift is discounted from the full fair market value of the corpus by subtracting the value of the grantor's retained interest valued under the Sec. 7520 rules.

    If the grantor survives the retained interest term in a qualified GRAT or GRUT, Sec. 2036 does not apply and the corpus, including any posttransfer appreciation, is excluded from the gross estate of the grantor.

    The estate tax benefits are reduced, however, if the grantor fails to survive the term. The amount included is the amount of principal of the trust that would be required under actuarial valuation principles to produce the annuity or unitrust payout. The upper limit on the inclusion is the actual amount of principal at the time of death. In many circumstances, the includible amount may be less than the entire trust principal. The amount includible is based on the annuity or unitrust amount and the Sec. 7520 discount rate at the time of the grantor's premature death.

22-11.   Congress intended that a transfer of a personal residence to a trust can provide a retained interest to the grantor that is not limited to the GRAT or GRUT. The regulations on QPRTs make it clear that the Treasury intended to limit the corpus of these trusts to personal residences and other *de minimis* property.

    In the typical QPRT, the grantor (usually a senior family member) retains the use of the home for a specified number of years. One or more remainder beneficiaries receive the personal residence at the termination of the trust. The longer the term of the grantor's retained interest in the QPRT, the lower the value of the gift to the remainderperson. To determine the value of the gift to the remainderperson, the value of the grantor's retained interest (as measured according to the Sec. 7520 valuation rules) is subtracted from the value of the residence placed in the trust. Thus, the gift tax value of the transfer is frozen at the present value of the remainder interest at the time of the transfer to the QPRT since Sec. 2702 does not apply.

22-12.   The QPRT may include a dwelling used as (1) the principal place of the taxpayer's business or (2) a place where the taxpayer sees customers, clients, and patients in the ordinary course of business. Thus, a personal residence trust could include a home with a qualified home office for income tax purposes as well as a vacation home rented part of the year.

A QPRT may also include appurtenant structures used for residential purposes and adjacent land not in excess of that which is reasonably appropriate for residential purposes. The personal residence subject to a mortgage can be contributed to a QPRT. However, the regulations will not permit corpus to include any personal property (for example, household furnishings). Therefore the grantor continues to own household furnishings individually. To pay the essential expenses of the personal residence trust, the trustee may hold cash that is limited in the amounts and purposes for which it may be used.

22-13.   The QPRT is irrevocable, and a completed gift of the remainder is made for tax purposes when the grantor establishes the trust. The value of the property for gift tax purposes is reduced by the present value of the retained-income interest. This is true even though the grantor retains only the use of the corpus. The taxable gift at the time of the establishment of the QPRT is merely the present value of the remainder interest. This taxable gift constitutes a future-interest gift that does not qualify for the federal gift tax annual exclusion.

22-14.   For gifts of life insurance to an ILIT to qualify for the annual gift tax exclusion, the donee must have an absolute and immediate power of withdrawal. If the trust document provides for a Crummey demand/withdrawal power, the transfer will generally qualify for the annual exclusion.

22-15.   The two problem areas often associated with the cross-ownership of life insurance by spouses are the possibility of a future divorce and the unpredictability of which spouse will die first. Cross-ownership, however, is an effective way to avoid the incidents-of-ownership rules.

22-16.   The irrevocable life insurance trust can provide the following benefits:

- Gift taxes can be avoided for premiums contributed to the trust.
- Estate taxes can be avoided when the proceeds are received.
- Generation-skipping transfer taxes can be avoided if the insured's exemption is allocated to the trust.
- The insured's transferable wealth can be enhanced through leveraging.
- The expenses and publicity of probate are avoided for transfers to the trust.
- Estate liquidity can be enhanced by the trust.
- The grantor-insured can control the disposition of the proceeds before the fact through the trust provisions.
- Income taxes are avoided on the corpus buildup and receipt of proceeds.

22-17.   Trust provisions that can be used in the insurance trust to provide liquidity to the estate are discretionary powers to the trustee to lend trust funds to the insured's estate or to purchase assets from the estate. The loan or sale should follow normally acceptable commercial standards and should be within the explicit powers of the fiduciaries involved. The purchase of assets should be for fair market value, and the loan should be secured and bear adequate interest. These provisions allow the cash proceeds held by the trustee to be transferred to the estate to increase estate liquidity without causing unnecessary additional estate taxes.

Answers to Self-Test Questions

22-1.   False. The only requirement for installment-sale reporting is that the entire purchase price not be paid in the year of the sale.

22-2.   False. Although the installment-reporting rules are the general rules for sales qualifying for such treatment, a taxpayer can affirmatively elect out of the installment accounting and treat all gain as recognized in the year of sale.

22-3.   True.

22-4.   False. The tax rules provide for required target rates of interest on installment obligations under either the imputed interest rules or original-issue-discount rules of the Code.

22-5.   True.

22-6.   True.

22-7.   True.

22-8.   False. GRATs or GRUTs are irrevocable trusts since a completed transfer is necessary if the transaction is to provide the grantor with any potential estate tax savings.

22-9. True.

22-10. False. The gift portion of the GRAT transfer is a future-interest gift to the remainderperson, and the annual exclusion is unavailable.

22-11. True.

22-12. False. IRS regulations limit the personal residence trust to a personal residence, necessary land, and *de minimis* cash.

22-13. False. Substantial estate tax savings are available to the grantor of a personal residence trust only if he or she survives the retained interest term.

22-14. False. Although the transfer of property to a QPRT is a completed gift for gift tax purposes, it is a future-interest gift that does not qualify for the annual exclusion.

22-15. True.

22-16. False. This trustee power should generally not be included in the irrevocable life insurance trust since the direction to pay the costs of the estate will cause the life insurance proceeds in the trust to be deemed payable to the executor and included in the insured's gross estate.

22-17. True.

22-18. False. Because RLITs are revocable trusts, they do not provide any tax benefits. RLITs are primarily used for estate enhancement.

22-19. True.

Chapter 23

Answers to Review Questions

23-1. Although there will be no estate taxes due at Cornelia's death (because of the unlimited marital deduction), Cornelia's applicable credit amount is being wasted. Without the benefit of Cornelia's applicable credit amount, there is likely to be an even greater estate tax liability at Conrad's death (assuming he does not remarry) than is necessary. If Conrad makes a qualified disclaimer of the applicable credit amount for the relevant year of Cornelia's property, that amount of property will pass to their son and daughter and avoid estate tax liability. Thus (ignoring inflation and appreciation), as long as the value of Conrad's property is less than or approximates his own applicable exclusion amount, little, if any, estate tax will have to be paid at his death.

23-2. Methods used for postmortem planning:
- Qualified disclaimers (Sec. 2518)
- Special-use valuation for real estate of closely held businesses or farms (Sec. 2032A)
- Installment payment of estate taxes under Sec. 6166
- Stock redemption under Sec. 303
- Alternate valuation date
- Marital deduction qualification of QTIP trust property (Sec. 2056)
- Gift splitting election by surviving spouse
- Family election
- Election against decedent's will by surviving spouse
- Certain administrative expenses deduction
- Medical expenses deduction
- Characterization of executor's fee

23-3. There are four basic types of powers of attorney. A general, nondurable power of attorney terminates at the incapacity of the principal and is, therefore, an ineffective estate planning document. A durable power of attorney, on the other hand, allows the attorney-in-fact to act for the principal despite the principal's incapacity and is an effective estate planning tool. A special or limited power of attorney is one in which the attorney-in-fact is granted the power to accomplish specific tasks or else is operative for only a certain period of time. A springing power of attorney is one that becomes effective only at the time of the principal's incapacity as expressly defined in the document.

23-4. Durable powers of attorney for health care and living wills are often referred to as advance medical directives.

23-5. a. Preparing for the future financial and long-term care needs of the elderly, ill, and incapacitated presents some estate planning challenges. For instance, an estate plan that is oriented primarily toward passing property to the next generation becomes irrelevant if the estate is practically depleted by the cost of long-term care. On the other hand, retention of assets can prevent an estate owner from meeting Medicaid eligibility requirements. A comprehensive estate plan must address the implications of the client's potential need for long-term care.

b. A planner should be aware that the interests of a husband and wife may not be identical and may even be conflicting. Thus, one planner may not be able to fairly address the needs of both parties. In other words, just because a married couple seeks joint representation, the planner should not automatically conclude that the parties share identical objectives. Spousal estate planning and property disposition goals may be especially divergent and complicated when one or both have children from earlier marriages. Other areas of potential conflict may be the existence of one or both spouses' community property, the subjection of marital or separate property to the claims of one spouse's creditors, reciprocal wills, the tax consequences of gift splitting, and the control or lack of control a surviving spouse will have over property after the first spouse's death.

23-6. In addition to a durable power of attorney, other methods used to avoid judicial guardianship include joint ownership of property, advance medical directives, and trusts. When property is titled in more than one name, another party is already in place to manage the property, bank accounts, and so forth. Advance medical directives and living wills provide for health decision making prior to disability.

Guardianship may also be circumvented with trusts. A primary benefit of a revocable living trust is that the trustee manages the trust property according to trust terms stated by the grantor. The trustee continues to administer the assets during the grantor's incapacity.

23-7. Another type of trust used in planning for incompetency is a standby trust. A standby trust often works in tandem with a durable or springing power of attorney. The trust is unfunded until such time as the grantor becomes incapacitated and an attorney-in-fact funds the trust with assets of the grantor for the trustee to manage.

Answers to Self-Test Questions

23-1. True.

23-2. False. The efforts of an agent/attorney-in-fact under a durable power of attorney are private and not subject to court supervision.

23-3. False. CPR and DNR directives are essentially limited to cardiopulmonary resuscitation and are not intended to prevent other necessary medical procedures.

23-4. True.

23-5. False. It may be possible for unmarried partners to meet the insurable interest requirement by establishing an irrevocable life insurance trust. The trust owns the policy for the benefit of the surviving partner–beneficiary.

Chapter 24

Answers to Estate Planning Case

1. The assets and their values that would be included in Scott's gross estate for federal estate tax purposes and the reasons for inclusion are as follows:

   • *Property that Scott owns in his own name*

Stock in XYZ Corporation (500 shares)	$240,000
Other listed common stock	340,000
Tax-free municipal bonds	80,000
Savings accounts	150,000
Household and other tangible personal property	30,000

   Property is included in a decedent's gross estate to the extent of his interest in the property at the time of his death. The full value of these assets would be included in Scott's gross estate since they are owned solely by Scott.

   • *Property that Scott and Sue own as joint tenants with right of survivorship*

Residence	$220,000
Vacation home	150,000
Checking account	7,000

   All property held by spouses as joint tenants with right of survivorship will be considered to be 50 percent owned by each spouse without taking into consideration who paid for the property. The percentage-of-contribution rule still applies to all joint tenancies other than those held solely by husband and wife.

- *Property that Scott owns as a tenant in common with Dan*

  Undeveloped real estate $290,000

When property is held as a tenancy in common, only the value of the deceased owner's fractional interest is included in his gross estate at his death. Since no fraction is specified and there are only two tenants involved, it is presumed that Scott's interest is one-half of the total value of $580,000.

- *Employee benefits*

Pension plan death benefit	$450,000
Profit-sharing plan proceeds	46,000

The full value of the pension plan's death benefit ($450,000) and the profit-sharing plan proceeds ($46,000) would be includible in his gross estate under Sec. 2039.

- *Life insurance proceeds*

(1) Ordinary life (purchased at age 24)	$ 30,000
(2) 20-payment life	70,000
(3) Ordinary life (purchased at age 37)	200,000
(4) Term to 65	300,000

The proceeds of a life insurance policy are includible in the insured's gross estate if he possessed any incidents of ownership in the policy at the time of his death. This remains true even though the proceeds are receivable by a beneficiary other than the estate of the insured. The fact that an insurance policy is payable to the insured's estate would, in itself, be sufficient to cause the proceeds to be includible in his gross estate. Policies (1), (2), (3), and (4) are all owned by Scott, and policy (4) is payable to Scott's estate. Therefore, the proceeds of all four policies would be includible in Scott's gross estate.

The aggregate of all property included in Scott's gross estate for federal estate tax purposes is $2,603,000.

2. The maximum marital deduction allowable in Scott's estate is the value of all qualifying property passing to Scott's spouse. In order for Scott's property to be eligible for the marital deduction, it must be includible in his gross estate for federal estate tax purposes and must pass either to Sue outright or in such fashion that it would be includible in her gross estate at her subsequent death, unless given away or consumed during her lifetime.

    Fifty percent (or one-half) of all property held jointly by Scott and Sue will be included in Scott's gross estate (that is, the residence, vacation home, and checking account, for a total of $377,000) and this amount will qualify for the marital deduction because Sue succeeds to this property as the sole and absolute owner by right of survivorship.

    To determine the value of the property passing under Scott's will that qualifies for the marital deduction, an initial determination of all amounts and items of property passing under Scott's will must first be made. These items and amounts are the following:

Term-to-65 policy	$300,000
XYZ Corporation pension benefit	450,000
XYZ Corporation stock	240,000
Listed common stock	340,000
Tax-free municipal bonds	80,000
Savings accounts	150,000
Household and other tangible personal property	30,000
Undeveloped real estate	290,000
Total	$1,880,000

Scott's will grants a specific bequest of $10,000 to TU University, leaving a remainder of $1,870,000. Of this remainder, Sue is bequeathed $400,000 outright. Her share is not diminished by Scott's debts, funeral expenses, and administration expenses because the will specifically provides that these items are to be paid out of the share of the estate passing to Ben and Cate. Thus, Sue's share of the property passing to her by will is $400,000, and it qualifies for the marital deduction because it passes to her outright.

With respect to the life insurance on Scott's life, the $30,000 ordinary life policy (purchased at age 24) and the $200,000 ordinary life policy (purchased at age 37) will qualify because they are payable to Sue in a lump sum. The 20-payment life policy does not qualify for the marital deduction because it is not payable to Sue.

The $46,000 death benefit payable under the XYZ profit-sharing plan, payable to Sue, does qualify for the marital deduction because it would be included in Scott's gross estate.

Thus, $230,000 of life insurance, $377,000 of joint property, $46,000 of proceeds from the profit-sharing plan, and $400,000 of property passing under Scott's will—for a total of $1,053,000—qualify for the marital deduction.

3. a.
Gross estate	$2,603,000
Less funeral and administrative expenses	(40,000)
Adjusted gross estate	2,563,000
Less charitable bequest	(10,000)
Less marital deduction	(1,053,000)
Less state death tax deduction*	(51,260)
Taxable estate	1,448,740
Plus adjusted taxable gifts	0
Tentative tax base	$ 1,448,740

b.
Gross estate	$2,603,000
Less funeral and administrative expenses	(40,000)
Adjusted gross estate	2,563,000
Less charitable bequest	(10,000)
Less marital deduction	(1,053,000)
Less state death tax deduction*	(51,260)
Taxable estate	1,448,740
Plus adjusted taxable gifts	0
Tentative tax base	$1,448,740
Tentative tax	533,758
Less applicable credit amount (2005)	(555,800)
Federal estate tax liability	0
State estate tax liability	$ 51,260

c.
Residence	$ 880,000
Vacation home	600,000
Checking account	28,000
Savings account	48,000
Personal property	56,000
Life insurance proceeds	60,000
Profit-sharing plan proceeds	92,000
Property under Scott's will	800,000
Gross estate	2,564,000
Less funeral and administrative expenses	(72,000)
Adjusted gross estate	2,492,000
Less marital deduction	0
Less charitable deduction	0
Less state death tax deduction*	(49,840)
Taxable estate	2,442,160
Plus adjusted taxable gifts	0
Tentative tax base	2,442,160

d.
Gross estate	$2,564,160
Less funeral and administrative expenses	(72,000)
Less debts and taxes	0
Less losses	0
Adjusted gross estate	2,492,000
Less marital deduction	0
Less charitable deduction	0
Less state death tax deduction*	(49,840)

Taxable estate	2,442,160
Adjusted taxable gifts	0
Tentative tax base	2,442,160
Tentative tax**	979,772
Less gift tax payable on post-76 gifts	0
Estate tax before credits	979,772
Less applicable credit amount (2008)	(780,800)
Less credit foreign death tax	0
Less credit for gift tax on pre-1977 gifts	0
Credit for tax on prior transfers	0
Net federal estate tax payable	$ 198,972

*   In 2005 and 2008 (3 years after Scott's death), state death taxes are a deduction, not a credit.

**   45% on excess over $1,500,000 is $423,972 plus base tax amount of tax on $1,500,000, which is $555,800 = $979,772. Please note that for 2008 the rate schedule for computing estate and gift tax eliminates the "over $2,000,000 but not over $2,500,000" category and the "over $2,500,000" category because the top tax rate in 2008 is 45 percent. This means that the highest (last) bracket is over $1,500,000 in 2008.

4. A number of weaknesses now exist in the estate plans of Scott and Sue:

  a. Scott's estate plan, particularly his will, is very rigid. No real thought has been given to marital-deduction planning. Some of Scott's applicable credit amount is wasted since too much property passes to Sue in a manner qualifying for the marital deduction. A formula marital bequest and a credit equivalent bypass family trust would optimize the marital deduction and applicable credit amount. If Scott is concerned about Sue's welfare, the CEBT could be drafted to provide her with income during her lifetime.

  b. Because of Sue's lack of financial experience and sophistication, a marital-deduction trust rather than outright marital-deduction bequests is a good plan.

  c. All the life insurance that Scott owns is included in his estate for federal estate tax purposes. Although these proceeds are currently protected from federal estate tax liability by the marital deduction and the applicable credit amount, they unnecessarily absorb the credit that may be needed to shelter other assets as Scott's estate grows. An irrevocable life insurance trust with a Crummey provision could be utilized to own and be the beneficiary of some of these insurance policies. The settlement options could be changed to lump-sum payments to the trust, allowing the trust provisions to control distributions. The trust instrument should provide that trust income and corpus can be used as necessary for the benefit of Sue, as well as Ben and Cate. In addition, the trustee can be empowered (but not required) to make loans to or buy assets from Scott's estate. This provides the estate with additional potential liquidity. A trust designed in this way provides maximum flexibility in meeting the changing needs of Scott's survivors. There could be a gift tax incurred on the value of the policies at the time of the gift to the trust. However, because of the Crummey provision, the gift will qualify as a present-interest gift and the federal gift tax annual exclusion is applicable. Future premium payments by Scott should not give rise to a gift tax liability for the same reason. Scott would have to live more than 3 years after the date of the gift to successfully exclude the insurance proceeds from his estate for estate tax purposes. Despite these limitations, the irrevocable insurance trust is a highly desirable and very effective estate planning tool.

  d. Scott has expressed a wish to further aid his alma mater, TU University, and has named the university in his will as the beneficiary of a $10,000 legacy. In lieu of this arrangement, Scott may wish to consider the purchase of life insurance on his life with TU University as owner and beneficiary of the policy.

       The advantages of such an arrangement are that the university could receive a larger gift than Scott's dollar expense, since the amount of death proceeds is apt to be larger than Scott's net premium outlay. At Scott's death, the university would immediately receive the full death proceeds of the policy in cash.

       In addition, during his lifetime Scott could utilize the premiums as a charitable deduction for federal income tax purposes. As owner of the policy, the university would be able to use the cash or loan values at any time during Scott's lifetime, if such a use became desirable.

  e. There appears to be only one major weakness in Sue's current estate plan: She does not have a will. She should certainly consider the execution of a will drawn to accomplish her personal objectives. The ability to transfer her property to the beneficiaries of her choice makes drawing a will a very important act. In addition, if she survives Scott, her estate would be substantial, making a will even more important.

f. Sue's estate passing under typical state intestacy laws would generally be divided between Scott and her children. Scott, of course, would receive all joint property by operation of law. This would leave less to be divided among her children, and much of her applicable credit amount would be wasted if she should predecease Scott. Because Scott would not need a share of Sue's estate, they should consider transferring assets to Sue to be held solely in her name and to be distributed under her will in some type of family bequest. The purpose of this transfer is to make effective use of Sue's applicable credit amount.

g. No consideration is given to Scott's mother in his estate plan. Because he currently provides her with substantial support, some provision should be made to guarantee her standard of living should Scott predecease her. Because it is a temporary need, perhaps a trust funded with term insurance could be used.

Index